The BEST of VIRGINIA FARMS
Cookbook & Tour Book

To two old Virginia farmers,
George Washington and Thomas Jefferson,
who wanted nothing more than to farm their land.

I hope, some day or another, we shall become a storehouse and granary for the world.
—George Washington

The greatest service that can be rendered any country is to add a useful plant to its culture. I know of no condition happier than that of a Virginia farmer might be.
—Thomas Jefferson

The BEST of VIRGINIA FARMS
Cookbook & Tour Book

CiCi Williamson
Illustrations by Garry Pound
Introduction by Willard Scott

MENASHA RIDGE PRESS

Library of Congress Cataloging-in-Publication Data:

Williamson, CiCi.
    The best of Virginia farms cookbook and tour book / by CiCi Williamson; illustrations by
    Garry Pound; introduction by Willard Scott.
        p. cm.
    Includes bibliographical references and index.
    ISBN 13: 978-0-89732-657-5
    ISBN 10: 0-89732-657-1
    1. Cookery, America—Southern style. 2. Cookery—Virginia. 3. Agriculture —Virginia.
    4. Virginia—Description and travel. I. Title.

TX715.2.S68 W547 2003
641.59755—dc21
                                                                    2002040977

Text illustrations by Garry Pound
Text design by Clare Minges
Cover design by Travis Bryant
First hardcover edition copyright © 2003 by Menasha Ridge Press

Menasha Ridge Press
P.O. Box 43673
Birmingham, AL 35243
www.menasharidge.com

The Best of Virginia Farms Cookbook and Tour Book publishing partners advocate and support agriculture education, the development of agriculture-related tourism, and the use of Virginia's farm products throughout the United States and internationally. They and the book's publishers believe that the story of agriculture is an integral part of the story of Virginia and America. A portion of proceeds from book sales is channeled through the publishing partners to develop and promote agriculture education, agriculture tourism, and state products.

The Virginia Tourism Corporation provides economic benefit to the Commonwealth through the support of Virginia's tourism and motion-picture industries.

The Virginia Department of Agriculture and Consumer Services promotes the economic growth and development of Virginia agriculture, encourages environmental stewardship, and provides consumer protection.

The Virginia Farm Bureau Federation advances the agricultural, economic, political, and social interests of county Farm Bureaus and their members primarily through education and communication.

WHRO serves the educational, informational and cultural needs of the people of Southeastern Virginia and Northeastern North Carolina through non-commercial broadcast and telecommunications technologies and services.

TABLE OF CONTENTS

INTRODUCTION

Willard Scott

Our earliest settlers didn't just sail into Hampton Roads; they sailed into what was to be the heart of the country for many years. When the Virginia Company first appeared in the Chesapeake Bay and went up the James River in 1607, it wasn't just by accident that, with the help of the Indians, they survived. They'd sailed into what H. L. Mencken called "the world's greatest protein factory." The crabs, oysters, and fish constituted the most abundant source of protein—and Virginia's blue crabs are my personal favorite.

The early colonists had known in England how to cure meats, so they later began to cure those inimitable Smithfield hams here. My favorite Virginia meal starts with a bowl of peanut soup, then thinly sliced Smithfield ham with lump crabmeat on top and a light cream sauce over it all, fresh asparagus, and home-grown corn. Sweet Virginia peaches would be my choice for dessert.

I grow peaches on my own farm outside Winchester, along with apples, pears, cherries, raspberries, and blueberries. Our Virginia climate lends itself to growing the world's greatest produce, and I enjoy gardening— cantaloupe and tomatoes, beans, corn, and potatoes.

To make that Virginia meal complete, two or three Virginia wines are necessary accompaniments. The state's wines have really come on strong in the last few years. Thomas Jefferson was our original vintner, and now a lot of others have followed in his footsteps.

And our Virginia maple syrup is some of the finest-grade syrup you can find. Everybody thinks you have to go to New England for maple syrup. That's not so, and every year Highland County has that wonderful Virginia Maple Festival when people can stock up.

Another misunderstood food, at least outside the South, is grits—has always been a favorite of mine. I'm a grits-lover from way back, preferring the yellow variety. The yellow can sometimes be hard to find, but you can always find them at The Cheese Shop in Stuart's Draft. My favorite way of enjoying grits is with Shrimp Creole, usually served over a bed of rice, but it's even better over grits. I've always said that two of the greatest foods in the world are grits and zucchini, because you can do so much with both of them. They each pick up the flavor of whatever you're cooking them with.

My grandfather and all of his family came from North Carolina and moved up to Abingdon about 1912 and then up towards Baltimore. I had the privilege of spending a lot of time on my grandfather's farm of about 75 acres when I was growing up. They cooked on a wood stove that ran 365 days a year, 24 hours a day. My grandmother made her own rolls every day with about 25 workers to feed. Everything, including the oats we ate at breakfast, was grown right there, on the farm.

We had only one or two lights in the whole house: a bare light bulb hung down from the ceiling over the kitchen table. We had one of the early Frigidaire refrigerators with the compressor on top, and we had a well; the pump was in the barn.

As the thrashing machines moved north every year, they came by and thrashed my grandfather's wheat. My grandmother used chicken manure on her strawberries—she had the most incredible strawberries!

As you can probably tell, I've been a food junkie all my life, and it all started with my grandparents. Because of that great spring house my grandparents had on their farm, where they put each day's fresh milk along with the buttermilk they separated, today I have spring houses on my farm in Rockbridge County, outside Lexington, as well as on the one outside Winchester.

My mother took up where my grandparents left off. She'd learned a lot from them but was also truly gifted. Her ice-box cookies at Christmas were a real specialty.

I still cook our beans with a ham bone in the tradition of my grandfather; and I smoke and cure local hams by my grandfather's recipe. At Thanksgiving, I cook the turkey with plain old bread stuffing and everybody brings something. Our two daughters come and humor me; but their heart just isn't into eating the way mine has always been. They're health-conscious—although my daughter, Sally, loves to make Toll House cookies.

My late wife, Mary, constantly reminded me that I'm a glutton—a foodaholic—saying I make too much fuss over food. She went more for the light cooking, but if you set her down in front of a platter of mashed potatoes and fried chicken once in a while, she'd tear into it almost as fast as I did. Mary made a great fruitcake— a much-maligned dessert that I love.

You don't have to go far west of Washington to hit beautiful farm country. Washington, of course, holds many memories for me. The first time I went to the White House was when Jack Kennedy was president. I was Bozo the Clown at a children's party that Ethel Kennedy coordinated, and Caroline was there.

Then, during the Reagan administration, I got to know the White House chef, who made the best ginger cookies for a party for the children of the diplomatic corps. We went over to a room in the West Wing and served lemonade and incredible trays of cookies. I told the chef he could have made a lot of soft money for the Republican Party by selling those terrific cookies.

I hope you enjoy *The Best of Virginia Farms* and that you'll keep a copy handy in the house for recipe reference as well as one in the car for touring. May it be a genuine source of great cooking and eating, coupled with many memories of traveling and experiencing the fine food products of this great Commonwealth of Virginia.

—Willard Scott

VIRGINIANS AND THEIR LAND

Preface

The Best of Virginia Farms celebrates the state's rich agricultural heritage. A quilt of writing formats drawn from a wealth of sources was patched together here to showcase the individuals and enterprises who, together, tell the story of 400 years of Virginians and their land.

From the "starving time" in Jamestown to the sideboards in Williamsburg or the hunt-country breakfast spreads; from a thoroughbred flying over steeplechase brush to the magic of a decorated Virginia-farmed Christmas tree; from jubilant apple blossoms dancing in the spring breeze to tranquil cows grazing in the Blue Ridge Mountains; from gristmills, gardens, and wineries to the fabulous James River plantations: in this book you can experience Virginia as you may never have before—from a farming perspective. And you will taste it in these recipes, learning how Virginians have expressed themselves via the state's favorite foods in the kitchens of yesterday and today.

You will find, in reading *The Best of Virginia Farms*, just as I did in writing it, that Virginia is just right for farming. Located about 1000 miles from the top of Maine and the same distance from the tip of Florida, America's first farm state is situated such that almost anything can be produced on its soil. The state's 47,000 farms cover 8.5 million acres, or one third of Virginia's total land area. It's the northernmost state where tobacco, cotton, and peanuts can grow and one of the southernmost states where apples can grow and maple syrup can be harvested. Virginia-grown poultry, beef, pork, seafood, tobacco, horses, and other farm products enjoy national and international renown.

Together agriculture and forestry are Virginia's number-one industry, generating nearly $50 billion annually. Farming is a diverse business that encompasses traditional crops and products such as milk, poultry, beef, and soybeans; uniquely southern crops like cotton, peanuts, and tobacco; and newer commodities such as farm-raised fish and nursery and landscaping products.

My only regret in preparing this feast of the state's farms is that the book is too short to showcase all the dedicated farmers who bring us our daily bread. My hope is that, in using this book—taking its tours and making its recipes—you will gain greater insight into the importance of farming in your life and your state.

A NOTE ABOUT THE RECIPES

This book contains an eclectic collection of recipes that were created and used at different times in Virginia's past. For example, a classic recipe for the colonial bread Sally Lunn follows a twenty-first-century recipe that can be prepared using a bread machine. A recipe from a James Beard Foundation Chef of the Year award recipient precedes one from a farmer's wife. There are recipes from Virginia's presidents, governors, congressmen; from proprietors of elegant hotels, cozy bed-and-breakfasts, historic homes, bakeries, restaurants, wineries, and plantations; and from food experts, and—of course—farmers. (Recipes that are not followed by information about a source are personal recipes of the author.)

A great effort was made to ensure that the recipes in *The Best of Virginia Farms* are representative not only of Virginia cooks and the state's farm products but also of the kinds of foods eaten at various times—appetizers, soups, salads, side dishes, breads, main dishes, desserts, beverages, preserves, and sauces. The recipes have all been carefully tested by the author.

—CiCi Williamson

ACKNOWLEDGMENTS

Without farmers this book would not have been possible, so my ultimate acknowledgment is to the hard-working Virginia agriculturists. To my husband, John A. Kelly, I say "thanks" for taste testing most of the recipes in the book and for his understanding while I spent numerous months at the computer. My mother, Carolyn Cheney, accompanied me for more than 1200 miles as I visited agricultural sites and interviewed farmers and farm experts around Virginia. She also helped me test some of the recipes. Thanks, Mom!

Countless Virginians contributed information for *The Best of Virginia Farms*. You can read about many of them in the book's interviews, essays, sidebars, and recipes. Other Virginians helped point my way to additional sources of information. At the top of this list is Elaine Lidholm, director of communications for the Virginia Department of Agriculture and Consumers Services (VDACS). As I was beginning research for this book, Terry Sharrer, curator of health sciences at the Smithsonian Museum, started me on my way with his valuable insight into the plight of farmers and their livestock during and after the Civil War.

Others who generously shared their advice and expertise are:

AMY BAILEY   Virginia Agriculture Statistics Service

AMANDA BARKER   Virginia's Explore Park

PRISCILLA BEVEL   Williamsburg Area Convention and Visitors Bureau

TRACY BLEVINS   Jamestown-Yorktown Foundation

CINDY BOGGS   Virginia Beef Industry Council

LORRAINE BROOKS   Colonial Williamsburg Foundation

JIM BRADLEY   Colonial Williamsburg Foundation

C.D. BRYANT, III   3rd generation tobacco grower, Danville

GARY CRIZER   Hotel Roanoke

SHIRLEY ESTES   Virginia Marine Products Board

BETTY JEAN EVERETT   Southampton Agriculture & Forestry Museum

KELLY FEARNOW   Monticello

CATHERINE FOX   Roanoke Valley Convention and Visitors Bureau

DR. G. FREDERICK FREGIN   Marion Scott DuPont Equine Medical Center

JAMES W. GARNER   Virginia Department of Forestry

GARY GRANT   local-history enthusiast

ANNE H. HALE   Shirley Plantation

ANDREA HEID   Virginia Horse Industry Board

CINDY HINES Shenandoah County Tourism

MARION HORSLEY   Virginia Department of Agriculture and Consumer Services

DIANE HOWARD   Isle of Wight Tourism Bureau

RHONDA HOWDYSHELL   Frontier Culture Museum, Staunton

NANCY ISRAEL   Virginia State Apple Board

PAMELA JEWELL   Virginia Department of Agriculture and Consumer Services

JUDY KEESEE   Pittsylvania County Chamber of Commerce

CATHERINE LARMORE   Marion Scott DuPont Equine Medical Center

JANE MENGENHAUSER   formerly of *The Journal Newspapers*

RODDY MOORE   Blue Ridge Institute & Museum

MARGARET MCMANN   Danville Area Chamber of Commerce

JANE OLMSTED   Sulgrave Club

BETSY PARKER   *Fauquier Times Democrat*

KATHLEEN W. THACKER   Isle of Wight Tourism Bureau

BETTY THOMAS   The Smithfield Inn

KEITH TIGNOR   Virginia Department of Agriculture and Consumer Services

LYNDA UPDIKE   Southampton County Historical Society

LU M. SADLER   Virginia's Explore Park

LARRY SANTURE   Joyner Smithfield Ham Company

JENNIE SAXON   Mount Vernon

JULIA SCOTT   Virginia Tourism Corporation

MARTHA STEGER   Virginia Tourism Corporation

KAY MONTGOMERY TYLER   Sherwood Forest Plantation

KATHERINE WRIGHT   Chippokes Plantation Farm Foundation

MELISSA YORK   Morven Park

I also wish to thank the following experts who worked so diligently to produce *The Best of Virginia Farms*: Molly Merkle and Gabriela Oates of Menasha Ridge Press; Carolyn Carroll, who edited the manuscript; Annie Long, who typeset the book; Steve Jones, who created the maps; and Ann Cassar, who made the indexes.

part one
POULTRY AND EGGS

Although poultry played second fiddle to meat in the United States until the last half of the twentieth century, Virginians have always loved to eat chicken and eggs. Colonial cooks used all the same methods for preparing chicken as we do today. However, the chicken of early Virginia was a scrawny little thing, about the size of the bantam hens still to be found in many English farmyards. And the colonial cook would marvel at the size of today's eggs. A cake recipe in 1771 calling for 30 eggs might need only eight or so today.

More than 1.3 billion pounds of chicken are produced in the Old Dominion annually, placing the state in the top ten among states. According to recent figures, Virginia exports about 200 million pounds of chicken and turkey. Most poultry-producing counties are in or near the Shenandoah Valley.

Turkeys were not domesticated until the early twentieth century, so for more than 300 years turkeys in Virginia were bagged wild or not at all. In fact, the father of the modern turkey industry was a Virginia farmer named Charles Wampler, Sr., who devised a way to brood turkey eggs for the first time in 1922. Since then, Virginia's poultry industry—including production and sales of eggs—has taken flight, and poultry continues to be one of the state's most valuable agricultural commodities. Virginia produces more than 530 million pounds of turkey a year; it ranks fourth among the states.

The domestication of the chicken is believed to have taken place about 3000 B.C. in India. In America, the chicken has been bred into a number of general classes: Rhode Island Reds, Wyandottes, Plymouth Rocks, Jersey Giants, and New Hampshires. Other common breeds originating across the world include Cornish, Leghorns, and Andalusians. Many breeds are becoming endangered as small farms become less common and the commercial poultry industry focuses on only a few breeds.

Today, the chicken population worldwide exceeds seven billion. Chickens continue to grow in popularity. Since 1960, consumption has increased 154% in America. Lower in calories and fat than most other meats, chicken provides important nutrients like protein, iron, and zinc. Almost half of chicken's fat is found in the skin; leave it on during roasting to prevent the meat from drying, but remove it after cooking to reduce calories and fat.

chapter one

CHICKENS

What's for dinner tonight? There's a good chance it's chicken, now the number-one species consumed by Americans. Virginia produces about 300 million broilers annually. That's enough for every Virginian to eat more than 30 chickens per year (of course, many chickens are exported). The state ranks in the top 10 in the United States in the number of broilers and in the number of pounds produced, and production is valued at more than $600 million. The average live weight of a Virginia broiler is about 5 pounds.

CHICKEN PICCATA MEANDER

This recipe is a favorite at the Inn at Meander Plantation.
Present this luscious main dish to special gathering of family and friends.

8 boneless chicken breast halves, divided

4 tablespoons unsalted butter, softened, divided

2 tablespoons all-purpose flour, plus additional flour for dredging

4 tablespoons olive oil, divided

⅔ cup vermouth or dry white wine

½ cup fresh lemon juice

½ cup chicken broth

½ cup capers, rinsed and drained

¼ cup chopped fresh parsley

Mix 2 tablespoons butter and 2 tablespoons flour in small bowl until smooth; set aside. Lightly pound chicken between 2 large sheets of plastic wrap to ½-inch thickness. Sprinkle with salt and pepper. Place additional flour in shallow baking dish. Dredge chicken in flour to coat; shake off excess.

Over medium-high heat, place 1 tablespoon of oil in heavy large skillet. Add 2 chicken breasts and cook until golden and cooked through, about 3 minutes per side. Transfer chicken to platter; tent with foil to keep warm. Cook remaining chicken breasts, two at a time, using the same method. Pour any oil out of skillet and bring wine, lemon juice, and broth to boil in same skillet over medium-high heat. Whisk in butter-flour mixture and boil until sauce thickens slightly, about 2 minutes. Stir in capers, parsley, and remaining butter. Season sauce to taste with salt and pepper. If sauce is too thick, add a small amount of chicken broth. Pour sauce over chicken and serve. Makes 8 servings.

Suzie Blanchard is chef/owner of the Inn at Meander Plantation majestically situated on 80 acres of rolling pastures and woods in Locust Dale. Thomas Jefferson and General Lafayette were frequent visitors to the estate, which dates back to 1766. The property has formal boxwood gardens, a hammock that faces the Blue Ridge Mountains, woods to explore, and fields where wildlife abounds. A full country, gourmet breakfast is included in the price of the stay, and full dinner service is available (phone (800) 385-4936).

Chicken skin color ranges from white to deep yellow, depending on the chicken's diet, but does not indicate a difference in nutritional value, flavor, tenderness, or fat content. When buying, check the label's "sell by" date. Refrigerate chicken immediately after purchase. Keep raw chicken refrigerated no longer than two days before cooking or freezing. Look for the safe-food-handling messages on fresh-chicken packages as a reminder for proper cooking, serving, and storing. Keep raw and cooked poultry separate, and after handling raw poultry, thoroughly wash knives, cutting surfaces, sponges, and hands with hot soapy water. Packaged fresh chicken may be refrigerated or frozen in its original wrappings. For long-term storage, enclose package in a plastic bag or wrap in foil. Parts can also be removed from store packages and wrapped separately in foil, freezer wrap, or freezer-weight plastic bags. Cooked chicken should be prepared for freezing the same way, unless topped with sauce or gravy. If sauce or gravy is included, pack chicken in a rigid container with a tight-fitting lid. Keep frozen until ready to use.

On Soups

"Always observe to lay your meat in the bottom of the pan with a lump of butter. Cut the herbs and vegetables very fine and lay over the meat. Cover it and set over a slow fire. This will draw the virtue out of the herb and roots and give the soup a different flavor from what it would have from putting the water in at first. When the gravy from the meat is almost dried up, fill your pan up with water. When your soup is done, take it up and when cool enough, skim off the grease quite clean. Put it on again to heat and then dish it up. When you make white soups, never put in the cream until you take it off the fire."
—Marie Kimball, author of *Thomas Jefferson's Cook Book*

Chicken Little, Chicken Small

Broiler-fryers, roasters, stewing/baking hens, capons, and Rock Cornish hens are all chickens. Broiler-fryers are about 7-weeks old and weigh 2.5 to 4.5 pounds. Rock Cornish game hen is a small broiler-fryer weighing between 1 and 2 pounds. A roaster is about 3- to 5-months old and weighs 5 to 7 pounds. Seldom seen in a store is capon—a male chicken about 16-weeks to 8-months old that is surgically unsexed. Capon weigh 4 to 7 pounds and have tender, light meat. Rarely seen in a store, stewing hens (mature egg-laying hens 10- to 18-months old) and roosters are used in the commercial soup and broth-making industry.

Popular in the Louisiana Purchase era of the 1800s, this recipe would have been made with bacon drippings or a mixture of lard and butter.

½ cup each flour and oil
2 cups chopped onion
½ cup chopped celery
½ cup green onions
½ cup parsley
6 cloves garlic, finely chopped
6 cups chicken broth
4 cups diced cooked chicken

3 cups chopped fresh tomatoes or 1 (20-ounce) can diced tomatoes
1 teaspoon cayenne or ground red pepper
2 cups cut fresh okra or 1 (10-ounce) package frozen cut okra
3 cups hot cooked rice
1 tablespoon filé powder

Place the oil in a black iron skillet over low heat. Sprinkle the flour in gradually while stirring. Stir constantly until roux turns dark brown, about 30 to 40 minutes. Do not burn. Immediately add onion and celery to halt further browning. Cook about 4 minutes, stirring a few times. Add green onions, parsley, and garlic. Cook about 3 minutes and transfer mixture to a 4-quart pot. Add broth, chicken, tomatoes, and cayenne. Cover with lid and bring to a boil; turn down the heat and simmer 20 minutes. Add okra and cook 10 minutes, or until okra is tender.

Microwave directions: Blend flour and oil in a 4-cup glass measure. Microwave on high 4 minutes; stir using a wooden spoon. Stirring after each minute, microwave on high 3 to 5 minutes, or until dark brown. Immediately stir in onion and celery. Microwave on high 4 minutes. Stir in green onions, parsley, and garlic. Microwave on high 3 minutes. Transfer mixture to a 4-quart pot or casserole. Add broth, chicken, tomatoes, and cayenne. Cover with lid and cook 20 minutes. Add okra and cook 10 minutes, or until okra is tender.

Serve over rice and sprinkle with filé. Makes 8 servings.

∽ *This recipe was adapted for modern use from* The Presidents' Cookbook. *Our fifth president was born in Westmoreland County in 1758 and was the third president to die on the Fourth of July; the others were Thomas Jefferson and John Adams. James Monroe served many years in France and negotiated with its government over the Louisiana Purchase. He liked Creole food such as this gumbo.* ∽

BRUNSWICK STEW CALLAHAN

Virginia House delegate Vince Callahan and his wife Dot were introduced to this tasty stew many years ago at a barn party in Farmville. The men prepared it in a huge cast-iron kettle over a high fire just outside the barn. It became a favorite of the Callahans.

1 whole chicken, cut up
1 onion, quartered
2 ribs celery, diced
1 teaspoon salt
¼ teaspoon pepper
3 cups fresh corn kernels or
   1 (16-ounce) bag frozen white
   shoepeg corn
2 cups shelled fresh lima beans or
   1 (10-ounce) package frozen small
   lima beans

2 cups chopped fresh tomatoes or
   1 (16-ounce) can tomatoes
2 small potatoes, cubed
⅓ cup ketchup
3 tablespoons cider or wine vinegar
1 tablespoon packed brown sugar
1 teaspoon Worcestershire sauce
½ teaspoon Tabasco or hot pepper
   sauce
¼ teaspoon dried marjoram
2 tablespoons butter

Place chicken in Dutch oven and add water to cover. Add onion, celery, salt, and pepper. Boil until chicken comes off bone easily. Remove chicken from pot to cool, and add corn, beans, tomatoes (including liquid), potatoes, ketchup, vinegar, and sugar. Cook two hours, or until vegetables are tender. Remove chicken from bones and add to vegetables along with Worcestershire sauce, Tabasco sauce, marjoram, and butter. Add more seasonings to taste. Makes 6 to 8 servings.

∽ *Vincent F. Callahan represented the 34th district in the Virginia House of Delegates for 39 years, from 1968–2007. As chair of the House Appropriations Committee, he was one of the most powerful elected officials in the state.* ∽

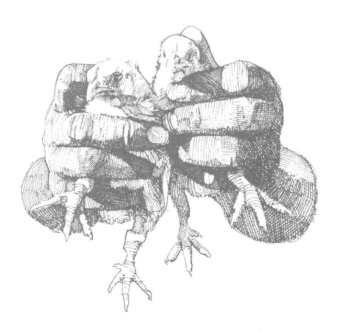

Sorry, sister states of the South who claim bragging rights, but Brunswick Stew originated in Virginia. It's well documented in many sources that Brunswick County, Virginia, was the birthplace, in 1828, of this hearty squirrel-meat-and-onion stew. According to the *Food Lover's Companion*, "Today it is generally made with rabbit or chicken and often contains a variety of vegetables, including okra, lima beans, tomatoes, and corn." Although made in all Southern states with a variety of ingredients, if the stew tastes like chicken, it probably is. Squirrel, while plentiful, scampering across suburban yards and occasionally flattened on roads, are not a USDA-inspected species, so you won't find any in supermarkets or restaurants. However, to hungry pioneers, its strong flavor tasted mighty good.

Ethlene Gates Hawkins Taylor (see Taylor Family interview on page 178) of Petersburg made her Brunswick Stew in a 60-gallon pot hung over an outdoor fire. Then she froze it in batches. Her recipe includes 15 pounds of chicken, 10 pounds of beef, 10 pounds of bacon, 25 pounds of potatoes, 3 gallons of butter beans, 3 gallons of white corn, 4 gallons of tomatoes, a pound of margarine, and salt, pepper, and sugar to taste.

Heidi Morf, chef at Four &
Twenty Blackbirds, takes full
advantage of local organic
produce, naturally raised
meats, and her own gardens
to update her dinner menu
every three weeks. The
restaurant is located in Flint
Hill, in the gorgeous Virginia
countryside, just an hour west
of Washington, D.C., and its
"eclectic new American cuisine" incorporates ethnic
accents that reflect America's
cultural diversity as well as
Chef Morf's travels abroad
and her culinary imagination
(call the restaurant at (540)
675-1111).

Colonial Williamsburg Taverns

More than four million people visit Colonial Williamsburg each year, which makes
it one of the top U.S. tourist
destinations. Many visitors
will dine in the historic taverns that re-create the
authentic ambiance, tastes,
and aromas of the eighteenth
century. The four taverns
(Chownings, Christiana
Campbell's, Shields, and
King's Arms) are operated by
the nonprofit Colonial
Williamsburg Foundation.
Foods are prepared in state-
of-the-art kitchens built
below ground to ensure they
don't ruin the colonial ambiance of the historic area.

FOUR & TWENTY BLACKBIRDS' INDIVIDUAL POT PIES OF NATURALLY RAISED CHICKEN AND WINTER ROOT VEGETABLES IN AN HERB CRUST

These homey pies derive multiple flavors from root vegetables and herbs.

FOR FILLING:

2 (3-pound) chickens
3 large yellow onions, divided
sprigs of fresh herbs (such as thyme,
    sage, rosemary)
salt and pepper to taste
2 cups each: peeled cubed butternut
    squash, sweet potatoes, carrots,
    Yukon Gold potatoes, and turnips
    or rutabagas

¼ cup olive oil
½ cup butter
½ cup flour
4 to 5 cups homemade chicken broth
1 teaspoon each dried thyme and
    sweet marjoram

FOR PIE CRUST:

2½ cups flour
¾ teaspoon salt
1 cup butter
1 cup cream cheese
1 tablespoon julienned fresh sage

1 teaspoon chopped fresh thyme
¼ cup cream
egg wash (one egg plus 1 tablespoon
    water)

Preheat oven to 425° F. Rinse birds and pat dry. Cut one onion in half and place a
half onion plus sprigs of fresh herbs in each chicken cavity. Salt and pepper the outside of the birds. Roast 1 hour or until internal temperature of thigh reads 180° F.
Cool, remove meat from bone, and cut into 2-inch pieces.

Toss vegetables in olive oil on a baking sheet. Sprinkle with salt and pepper and
roast until vegetables are tender and just starting to brown, about 30 to 40 minutes.

Prepare crusts by placing flour and salt in bowl of food processor or mixer. Cut
butter and cream cheese into ½-inch cubes. Add butter first and pulse briefly; then
add cream cheese, sage, and thyme. Pulse again and add enough cream to bring
dough together. Roll on a floured surface to approximately ⅛ to ¼ inch thick. Cut in
circles slightly larger than the circumference of the ramekins being used. Cut decorative slits or cutouts, brush with egg wash, and bake in 375° F oven until lightly
browned. (Crusts will brown more when placed on the filling.) Set aside.

Melt butter in a skillet. Chop remaining 2 onions and sauté over medium heat until
golden. Add flour; continue to cook for several minutes. Add broth and stir until
smooth. Add thyme, marjoram, and salt and pepper to taste; simmer sauce over low
heat for 10 minutes. Add chicken pieces and cooked vegetables to sauce; adjust seasoning. Put mixture into individual ramekins or heatproof bowls. Bake in 375° F oven
until edges start to bubble. Place crusts on top and press gently onto filling. Continue
to bake until crusts are golden. Makes 6 pies.

This recipe was created by Four & Twenty Blackbirds' chef / owner Heidi Morf.

CHOWNING'S TAVERN ROAST GAME HENS WITH WHITE WINE MUSHROOM SAUCE

Serve this lovely dish to guests for a special occasion.

4 Cornish game hens (20 ounces each)
10 tablespoons butter, divided
salt and pepper
½ pound small white button mushrooms, quartered

¼ cup flour
2 cups chicken broth
½ cup dry white wine, preferably from Burgundy
1 tablespoon chopped fresh parsley

Preheat oven to 450° F. Lightly oil a rack and set it in a large, shallow pan. Remove giblet packet from inside hens; save for another use. Rinse hens and pat dry with clean paper towels. Tuck wing tips "akimbo" (forward and under hens). Rub hens with 2 tablespoons butter. Season well with salt and pepper. Arrange, breast side up, on rack and sprinkle with pepper. Place in oven and turn heat down to 350° F. Roast the hens, basting often, about 45 to 60 minutes, or until they are golden brown and the juices run clear when thigh is pierced with a fork.

Meanwhile, make the mushroom sauce. In a large skillet over medium-high heat, melt 4 tablespoons butter. Add mushrooms and cook, stirring often, until well browned, about 10 minutes. Using a slotted spoon, transfer the mushrooms to drain on paper towels. Add remaining 4 tablespoons butter to same skillet. Using a whisk, stir in flour and cook until lemon colored, about 3 minutes. Whisk in chicken broth, increase heat to high, and bring to a boil, stirring often. Reduce the heat to medium and simmer until thick and creamy, about 5 minutes. Season with salt and pepper. Stir in wine and mushrooms; simmer 5 minutes longer. Stir in parsley and keep sauce warm.

When hens are done, remove from oven and let sit, covered loosely with foil, for about 10 minutes before serving. Place hens on individual plates and spoon over a small amount of the sauce. Serve the remaining sauce on the side. Makes 4 servings (one hen each) to 8 servings (½ hen each).

This recipe appears in The Colonial Williamsburg Tavern Cookbook. *Chowning's serves lunch and dinner daily (phone (800) 828-3767).*

Colonial Williamsburg Taverns (continued)

The kitchens are run by individual chefs under the direction of a single executive chef.

In 2001, Colonial Williamsburg celebrated its 75th year and the taverns' 50th year. John Gonzales, former executive chef of the four taverns, developed the recipes for The Colonial Williamsburg Tavern Cookbook. Gonzales grew up in the Robert Carter House on Palace Green in the historic area.

"All the recipes in the book have been served in the taverns. They were meticulously researched and are historical recipes," says Gonzales. "Each tavern has its own ambiance and class of clientele. King's Arms Tavern is the most exclusive tavern. It accommodated the landed gentry in colonial times. Meat and poultry on the King's Arms menu is served boneless," he explains.

In contrast, Chowning's (pronounced "CHEW-nings") is a peasant eatery near the market. "Shield's Tavern serves low-country cuisine. George Washington favored dining at Christiana Campbell's, across the street from the colonial capital building. Campbell's specializes in seafood, especially the oysters that were Washington's favorite," Gonzales says. For more information about Colonial Williamsburg and its taverns, visit www.colonial williamsburg.org.

Thawing and Cooking Chicken

Thaw frozen chicken in the refrigerator, in cold water, or in the microwave—never on a counter top. It takes about one to two days to thaw a four-pound chicken in the refrigerator. Cut chicken parts will thaw in about 24 hours. To thaw chicken in cold water, place it in the water in its original wrap or a water-tight plastic bag. Change water often. A whole chicken will thaw in two hours. Don't refreeze cooked or raw chicken once it has been thawed. After microwave-defrosting chicken, cook immediately, because some areas of the chicken can become warm or begin to cook.

Always cook chicken well, not medium or rare. For whole chicken parts or ground chicken, the internal temperature should reach a minimum of 165° F. To test for doneness, pierce chicken with a fork. It should insert easily and juices should run clear.

Never leave raw or cooked chicken out at room temperature for more than two hours. If not eaten immediately, cooked chicken should be kept either hot (above 140° F) or refrigerated. After cooking stuffed chicken, place stuffing in a separate container before refrigerating. When reheating cooked chicken or leftover chicken casseroles, heat to 165° F to ensure safety. Bring gravy to a boil before serving.

GRILLED CHICKEN WITH DIJON MUSTARD AND FRESH TARRAGON

This recipe is simple yet classic.

1 cup Dijon mustard
½ cup dry white wine
2 tablespoons chopped
   fresh tarragon

salt and pepper to taste
4 (2½-pound) chickens, halved

Whisk together mustard, wine, and tarragon in a stainless steel bowl. Season with salt and pepper. Coat chicken halves with marinade and enclose each half in plastic wrap. Refrigerate 24 hours before grilling.

Prepare barbecue grill. When coals are ready, preheat the oven to 350° F. Discard plastic wrap from chicken and season with salt and pepper. Grill over medium-hot fire 15 minutes, turning to grill both sides. Transfer to a baking sheet and finish cooking in oven for 10 minutes. Serve hot or let cool up to an hour. Makes 8 servings.

This recipe appears in Marcel Desaulniers's The Trellis Cookbook. *One of the country's best, The Trellis Restaurant in Williamsburg offers seasonal menus. Chef Desaulniers has won numerous awards and is renowned for his "Death by Chocolate" desserts and cookie books (phone the restaurant at (757) 229-8610).*

SOUTHERN INN RESTAURANT'S TARRAGON CHICKEN SALAD

This salad, a favorite of students at Washington and Lee University, tastes best when both white and dark meat are used, according to George Huger, Southern Inn chef/owner.

FOR POACHING LIQUID:

4 cups cold water
1 medium yellow onion, quartered
2 ribs celery, coarsely chopped
1 tablespoon dry tarragon

1 teaspoon kosher salt
2 pounds boneless, skinless chicken
   breast halves (or a combination of
   breast and thigh or leg meat)

FOR SALAD:

½ cup mayonnaise
2 tablespoons Dijon-style mustard
2 teaspoons fresh lemon juice
1 tablespoon coarsely chopped fresh
   tarragon or 1 teaspoon
   dried tarragon

2 tablespoons diced red onion
2 tablespoons diced celery

Combine poaching-liquid ingredients, bring to a boil, and then simmer for 15 minutes. Add raw chicken and cook until done, about 15 minutes. Drain chicken and cool 30 to 60 minutes. Mix mayonnaise, mustard, lemon juice, and tarragon in a large bowl. Dice chicken and toss with mayonnaise mixture, along with onion and celery. Season to taste with salt and pepper.

❧ *The contemporary, seasonal menu of the Southern Inn Restaurant, in historic Lexington, utilizes local produce and meats, as well as fresh seafood and in-house baked goods. In addition, the Southern Inn's cellar is home to the area's most extensive selection of wines. After college at Randolph-Macon and three years ski-bumming in Colorado, Southern Inn chef/owner George Huger, a Rockbridge County native, earned certificates from the Baltimore International Culinary College and was chef for ARAMARK at Oriole Park at Camden Yards. "I had always dreamed of having my own restaurant. One Christmas my mother said that the Southern Inn was for sale. So here we are." For more information, phone (540) 463-3612 or visit www.southerninn.com.* ❧

HOPE & GLORY PÂTÉ

If you like liver pâté but want to avoid the excessive cholesterol of livers, try this lighter version made with ground chicken.

1 pound ground chicken or turkey	½ teaspoon chopped fresh thyme
8 ounces Neufchatel (light) cream cheese, softened	½ teaspoon chopped fresh dill
2 tablespoons milk	¼ teaspoon pepper
1 teaspoon chopped fresh chives	1 cup finely chopped pistachio nuts or pecans
1 teaspoon salt	sliced French bread or crackers

In a non-stick skillet, brown chicken until cooked thoroughly. Measure cooked meat to make 3 cups. Place in a food processor or blender and pulse to chop fine; set aside.

Blend cream cheese and milk with chives, salt, thyme, dill, and pepper. Mix in chopped cooked chicken and nuts. Pack mixture in a ramekin or mold. Chill for several hours. Let stand at room temperature one hour before serving. Serve with French bread or crackers. Makes 4 cups.

❧ *Around 1890, a small school opened in Irvington on the property of the old Methodist church. It had two front doors: one for boys, one for girls. Today that small school has graduated into The Hope and Glory Inn, a beautifully decorated bed-and-breakfast; when dining at the inn, guests enjoy treats such as this pâté as well as sailing and fishing on the nearby Rappahannock River and Chesapeake Bay (phone (800) 497-8228; www.hopeandglory.com).* ❧

Gunston Hall's Dominiques

Among the historic animal breeds to be rediscovered at Gunston Hall Plantation in Mason Neck is the Dominique, a true American chicken descended from those introduced during the early settlement of New England. Dominiques, also called Domineckers, were the prevalent breed before the Civil War, according to Buck Jarusek, farm manager at the 550-acre plantation. The property once belonged to George Mason, a framer of the U.S. Constitution, and is located about 15 minutes south of Mount Vernon, on the Potomac River.

Dominiques, medium-sized birds with alternating rows of black and white feathers over the entire body, were at one time a "lost breed" but are undergoing a revival. These chickens produce brown eggs and meat; their heavy plumage, which protects them in cold weather, can be used to make pillows and featherbeds.

Also on the farm at Gunston Hall are silver-grey Dorkings; Narragansett, Spanish Black, and Norfolk Black turkeys; a Red Devon steer; and Hog Island sheep. The formal gardens at Gunston Hall are famous for their boxwoods, thought to be the oldest in the country, planted around 1755. Gunston Hall is open year-round (phone (703) 550-9220 or visit www.gunstonhall.org).

Turkey

Native to northern Mexico and the eastern United States, the turkey is the most recognizable symbol of Thanksgiving. The wild turkey is brown with buff-colored feathers on the tail and tips of the wings. The male turkey, known as a tom, is larger than the female or hen and has brighter plumage. He has a long wattle—a wrinkled, brightly colored fold of skin, hanging from the neck at the base—and a conspicuous tuft of bristles that looks like a beard extending downward from his chest. The female, called a hen, usually is smaller and more muted in color. First domesticated in Mexico, the turkey was brought into Europe in the early 1700s. Since then turkeys have been raised for the superb quality of their meat.

chapter two
TURKEYS

∾ *The Old Dominion is the original turkey-farming state. The industry began in the Shenandoah Valley in the 1920s. Today Virginia produces more than 500 million pounds of turkey—that's 21 million birds; only three other states produce more. Cash receipts for Virginia turkeys top a quarter of a billion dollars annually. Toms weigh more than hens, but both are sold and consumed when young and tender. The oldest turkeys on the market are only five-and-a-half months old.*

KATHERINE'S GRILLED TURKEY
WITH PEANUT SAUCE

"I think a brined turkey is better and keeps more moist during dry-heat grilling."

1 (3- to 5-pound) fresh turkey breast
   with skin on
water to cover
1 cup salt
½ cup packed fresh basil leaves
¼ onion cut into chunks
2 cloves garlic
1 tablespoon minced fresh ginger

1 small Thai chili pepper, seeded and
   deveined or 1 teaspoon hot
   chili oil
½ cup chunky peanut butter
½ cup teriyaki sauce
⅓ cup freshly squeezed lemon juice
⅓ cup peanut oil

Place turkey in a large pot. Cover with water into which 1 cup of salt has been dissolved. Let soak in the refrigerator for 8 hours. Remove from water; rinse, pat dry, and place in a large 2-gallon-size sealable bag.

Mince basil, onion, garlic, ginger, and chili pepper until fine, preferably in a food processor. Add peanut butter, teriyaki sauce, lemon juice, and peanut oil; process until smooth. Add ¾ to 1 cup of the sauce to turkey; seal bag and work the sauce to completely cover the turkey. Let the turkey marinate for 30 minutes to 1 hour. Reserve the remaining sauce for serving.

Meanwhile, light about 5 to 7 pounds hardwood lump charcoal and let burn down to form coals with a white ash. Scoot the coals away from the center of the grate and arrange a drip pan filled with 2 to 3 inches of water in the space beneath where the turkey will be placed on the grill rack. (The drip pan allows the turkey to cook by indirect heat so it doesn't burn.) You can do this on a gas grill, too. Place turkey, slathered with its marinade, on clean, oiled grill grate, breast side down. Cover the grill and let cook for about 20 minutes per pound until turkey reaches 170° F. Add more charcoal if necessary to keep the smoking temperature between 225° and 300° F.

Transfer turkey to a platter and cover with foil. Let sit for about 15 minutes. Slice and serve with some of the reserved sauce. (Note: The meat of smoked turkey may look slightly pink. This is not a safety problem if the turkey has reached 170° F.) Makes 10 to 14 servings.

---

* Katherine Newell Smith, president of KNS Promotion, Inc., a firm that promotes food products, is an avid gardener and passionate home cook who gets to talk about food, her favorite subject, all day as she promotes Virginia organic farms and other food and food-related companies nationwide. She is a past president of the Washington, D.C., chapter of Les Dames d'Escoffier, a women's professional culinary organization. *

TURKEY BREAST WITH WILD RICE

1 turkey breast half
1 (8.75-ounce) box instant long grain
   and wild rice mix

2 tablespoons slivered almonds
1 (10-ounce) box frozen chopped
   broccoli, thawed

Preheat oven to 325° F. Rinse turkey. Combine rice seasoning mix, almonds, and 1 cup water in a 3-quart casserole. Add turkey. Bake 1 hour. Stir in 1¼ cups hot water, rice, and broccoli. Bake 30 minutes more, or until turkey reaches an internal temperature of 170° F. Makes 4 servings.

---

* Recipe from Wampler Foods. *

When buying a whole turkey, calculate a pound of uncooked turkey for each person served. Most whole turkeys are frozen when purchased. The best way to thaw a turkey is to leave it in the original wrapping and place it in the refrigerator. Allow five hours per pound defrosting time. A 16-pound turkey, for example, will require about three or four days to defrost completely. If the turkey has not completely thawed when ready to cook, place it under cold tap water to hasten the thawing process. Check the "Buyer's Guide to Chicken," on page 3, for general poultry-handling tips.

Serve It Up Right

Katherine suggests that you accompany her Grilled Turkey with Peanut Sauce with a chilled salad of rice or noodles with sesame, paper-thin sliced cucumber, and julienned carrot, tossed with rice-wine vinegar and a bit of sugar syrup, cilantro, and chili powder.

that the bronze turkey you see in Thanksgiving pictures came from wild turkeys? "But when you plucked the feathers off a brown turkey, it would leave black dots all over the bird," says Charles Wampler, Jr. "A process of breeding made turkeys white so no color would be left when you plucked the feathers. That's what the consumers wanted."

First Thanksgiving

Some think that the first Thanksgiving dinner was served by the Pilgrims in 1621. Virginians disagree and stipulate that the first Thanksgiving actually took place in Virginia more than a year before the Mayflower set sail for Plymouth. At Berkeley Plantation, Captain John Woodlief, a veteran of Jamestown who had survived its starving time of 1608 and 1609, led his crew and passengers from their ship to a grassy slope along the James River for the New World's first Thanksgiving service on December 4, 1619. The English colonists dropped to their knees and prayed as the British company expedition sponsor had instructed. Today, on the site where Woodlief knelt, a brick gazebo bears the following inscription: "Wee ordaine that the day of our ships arrival at the place assigned for plantacon in the land of Virginia shall be yearly and perpetually kept holy as a day of Thanksgiving to Almighty God."

HOMEMADE TURKEY-AND-SAGE SAUSAGE

This sausage is easy to make yet so fragrant,
you'll think it contains much more fat than it actually does.

1 pound ground turkey	½ teaspoon each salt and pepper
2 cloves garlic, minced	½ teaspoon fennel seeds
1 tablespoon dried rubbed sage	¼ teaspoon cayenne or red pepper
1 tablespoon dried thyme	⅛ teaspoon ground allspice

In a mixing bowl, combine all ingredients. Mix until spices are well distributed. Shape the mixture into 16 patties about ½-inch thick. Brown patties in a non-stick skillet, about 2 minutes on each side. Makes 16 small patties. Note: Patties can be frozen uncooked or cooked. Refrigerate uncooked patties 1 or 2 days; cooked patties can be refrigerated up to 4 days.

DAVID'S WORLD-FAMOUS SECRET-RECIPE TURKEY CHILI

A crock pot makes it easy to simmer this chili and hold it until needed.
You can also make it on the stove.

1 tablespoon olive oil	1 teaspoon sea salt (or kosher salt)
1 medium onion, chopped	1 teaspoon black pepper
3 cloves garlic, minced	⅛ teaspoon ground red pepper
1 to 1½ pounds ground turkey	(or to taste)
1 (15-ounce) can tomato sauce	2 cups raw brown rice
2 tablespoons each	2 tablespoons masa flour
chili powder and ground cumin	1 (15-ounce) can dark red kidney
1 tablespoon each	beans, drained
paprika, cilantro, and oregano	shredded cheese or chopped green
1 teaspoon each	onions for garnish
basil, thyme, and sage	

Heat oil in a large skillet over medium-high heat. Sauté the onion until translucent. Add garlic and sauté for a minute or two. Crumble turkey into pan and brown, breaking it apart as it cooks.

Transfer the cooked mixture to a crock pot. Add the tomato sauce and all spices. Mix well. Cover and cook on low for 6 to 8 hours, or on high for 4 hours.

About 40 minutes before serving, begin cooking the rice according to package directions. Add flour and beans to the chili, allowing them to heat through as the rice cooks. Serve the chili over the rice in a bowl. Garnish with shredded cheese or chopped green onions as desired. Makes 6 servings.

Stove-top directions: If you don't have a crock pot, transfer cooked mixture to a large stock pot or dutch oven and add tomato sauce and all spices. In addition to the tomato sauce, add ½ can of water. Cover and simmer for about an hour, stirring frequently to prevent burning. Add the masa and beans about 15 minutes prior to serving. Serve as above.

Virginia-born David Kelley has won several chili cook-offs with this recipe.

CHARLES WAMPLER, JR.

Turkey Producer

The journey began in 1922 with some turkey eggs and an ingenious farmer, Charles Wampler, Sr. It ended in 2000, when the farmer's turkey- and chicken-processing company was sold for almost $300 million. The farmer's son describes what it was like along the way.

"In 1922, when I was seven years old, I helped take care of the first turkeys grown with a brooder stove," Wampler says. "As far as we know, they were the first artificially brooded turkeys grown in the United States."

"We had 12 to 15 turkey hens that ran loose on the farm. In the spring, when the hens would go into the woods and lay their eggs in a nest, my first job around the family farm was to find where they hid them, gather the eggs, and bring them to my dad."

"Dad," of course, was Charles W. Wampler, Sr., father of the modern turkey industry and the founder of the National Turkey Federation. He was also the first to contract with farmers to grow chickens. In those years, he was the county agent for Rockingham and Page Counties.

"Dad had a small shed, like a dog house, with a little oil stove in it to keep the eggs warm. It took four weeks to hatch a turkey egg. Then he would let the turkey hens out and they would lead the little birds around the farm just like a wild turkey would. There was no turkey feed in those days. My mom mixed hard-boiled eggs with cornmeal to feed them," Wampler explains.

"Dad wrote to all the extension agents he knew and asked them what they thought about growing turkeys in a house. All but one said it wouldn't work because turkeys were by nature wild creatures. The one man who thought it might work was Professor A. L. Dean of Virginia Tech. He encouraged my dad to try. So we gathered up 100 eggs, and out of that we hatched out 52 poults.

"My sister Ruth and I had the job of looking out after these turkeys. Raising turkeys was a new thing in those days. It attracted a lot of visitors. Ruth was a pretty little girl and when company would come, the journalists all talked to her. She did a good job. Ruth got all the credit and I did all the work."

In 1922, rural farms lacked the amenities of modern farms.

"We had a Johnny house, no inside bathroom. We didn't have electricity either. We used oil lamps and the kitchen stove was fired by coal. We had a stove to keep the downstairs warm but had no heat upstairs. Our house was half a mile from the road, and it took a long time before we got electricity."

The family got its first indoor plumbing when Wampler was a teenager. When he married Dot Liskey in 1938, he built a house near the road that cost $3000 to build.

"A Mennonite man and his four boys built our house. The man was paid 35 cents an hour, and the boys received 25 cents an hour each."

While the family continued to raise both chickens and turkeys on its Sunny Slope Farm, Charles Wampler, Sr., started, in 1927, Wampler Feed and Seed Company, a feed mill that produced 33 different kinds of feed for all sorts of livestock and pets. In 1937, Charlie finished college and took his first full-time job as "field man" for the young company. He earned $14 per week.

"Back in those days, you'd start growing turkeys in May and sell them at Thanksgiving and Christmas. During the late 1940s and early 1950s, there were dramatic changes in the poultry industry. Because of breeding, nutrition, and management breakthroughs, the feed conversion improved and the life cycle of birds was

Turkeys lived almost ten million years ago.

Benjamin Franklin proposed the turkey as the official United States bird.

Nearly 300 million turkeys are raised in the United States annually.

675 million pounds of turkey are eaten each Thanksgiving in the United States.

Turkey breeding has caused turkey breasts to grow so large that the turkeys can fall over. Today's larger birds must be artificially inseminated.

Wild turkeys can fly for short distances up to 55 miles per hour and can run 20 miles per hour. Commercially raised turkeys cannot fly.

Turkeys have heart attacks. United States Air Force test runs that break the sound barrier have caused nearby turkeys to drop dead with heart attacks.

In England, 200 years ago, turkeys were walked to market in herds. They wore booties to protect their feet.

Since 1947, the National Turkey Federation has presented a live turkey and two dressed turkeys to the President. The President does not eat the live turkey. He "pardons" it and allows it to live out its days on a historical farm.

shortened for the same weight gain. Right after World War II, Virginia became the top-producing turkey state," says Wampler.

"Most poultry in the beginning of the 1940s were free-range birds. Chickens were the first to be confined. It was not uncommon even into the 1950s that the processing plant called the farm family to ask them to keep the flock penned up for the pick-up crew. In 1969, Wampler hatchery, feed mill, and grow-out operation joined in with Virginia Valley Processing to form Wampler Foods, Inc."

In 1954, Wampler, Jr. was elected to the Virginia House of Delegates and represented Rockingham County and Harrisonburg for twelve years. During that time, he still kept an active hand in the family business. He began serving as chairman of the board of Wampler Foods when his father died, in 1976. In 2000, Wampler Foods was bought out by Pilgrim's Pride of Pittburg, Texas. Pilgrim's Pride thus became the second-largest chicken and fourth-largest turkey producer in the United States.

STEELES TAVERN MANOR COUNTRY INN'S LEMON-TURKEY CUTLETS

This wonderful dish can be held warm in the oven until time to serve.

6 turkey cutlets
1 cup half-and-half or milk
2 tablespoons each butter and
  olive oil
1 pound sliced fresh mushrooms
¼ cup dry white wine
2 cups chicken stock, divided

1½ tablespoons cornstarch
juice from 2 lemons (about 4 tablespoons); additional lemon slices
  for garnish
1 tablespoon chopped fresh parsley
lemon slices and parsley for garnish

Soak cutlets in half-and-half for 2 to 4 hours in the refrigerator. Heat butter and oil over medium-high heat in a large skillet or pan that is also ovenproof. Dredge cutlets in flour and sauté until lightly browned but not completely done.

Preheat oven to 350° F. Remove turkey; add more butter to the pan (if needed) to sauté mushrooms until they release some moisture. Add wine and deglaze pan. Mix ½ cup broth with cornstarch in a small bowl. Add remaining cups broth to pan; whisk in cornstarch mixture and lemon juice. Cook, stirring frequently, until liquid just thickens, about 5 minutes. Stir in 1 tablespoon chopped fresh parsley. Return cutlets to pan, cover, and bake in oven for 15 minutes, or until done. Garnish with fresh lemon and additional parsley. Makes 6 servings.

Steeles Tavern Manor Country Inn is a Georgian manor home on 55 acres in the Shenandoah Valley, built by the descendants of those who founded the town of Steeles Tavern, in 1916. Innkeepers Eileen and Bill Hoernlein conducted extensive restoration in 1994. Also available for lodging on the property is Alpine Hideaway Cottage. The inn is near the Cyrus McCormick Farm, featured on page 214. Contact the inn at (800) 743-8666 or (540) 377-9261.

VIRGINIA'S FARMING REGIONS

The Old Dominion—the Mother of Presidents and the Mother of States—includes the oldest mountain range in the world, the Atlantic Ocean, and the Chesapeake Bay, the world's largest estuary. Beginning in these waters, the land rises from sea level to mountain peaks a mile high. Within this elevation are five regions:

The Coastal Plain extends inland about 100 miles and covers the Tidewater area plus the two prolific grain- and soybean-producing counties on the Delmarva Peninsula. Also along this shore are three peninsulas cut out by the long, wide mouths of the Potomac, Rappahannock, York, and James Rivers, which are hospitable to many crops. The western shore of the Chesapeake Bay around Norfolk has the longest growing season in the state, some 250 days. It's in the coastal plain, where most of the state's peanuts and hogs are raised. The region produces small grains, wheat, barley, corn, double-crop soybeans, grain sorghum, asparagus, pumpkins, peas, and strawberries. The Coastal Plain is also where Virginia's seafood is landed.

The Piedmont Plateau lies west of the Coastal Plain. It is a region of low, rolling hills that reach from the Blue Ridge to the fall line—the place where rivers descend, often in rapids, from higher elevations. Much of the soil in the Tidewater and Piedmont regions was worn out by intensive tobacco growing, but it has been rebuilt, mainly by crop rotation. In the Northern Piedmont, farms grow pasture grasses, wheat, barley, double-crop soybeans, and corn. It's also a top area for beef and dairy-cattle production. Tobacco, peanuts, and cotton predominate in the Southern Piedmont.

The state's mountainous area encompasses three regions: the Blue Ridge, the Valley and Ridge, and the Appalachian Plateau. In this area, farms grow apples, peaches, pears, cool-season grasses (bluegrass, white clover, and orchard grass), Christmas trees, corn, alfalfa, soybeans, small grains, rye and wheat, and vegetables such as cabbage. It's also a huge producer of poultry, horses, beef, and dairy cattle.

The Blue Ridge stretches the length of the state in a northeast-to-southwest direction for about 300 miles. These highlands are widest near the North Carolina border. In the north the Potomac and Shenandoah Rivers join to cut a deep notch through the Blue Ridge Mountains at Harpers Ferry, West Virginia. To the southwest are the headwaters of the state's great Tidewater rivers—the Rappahannock (and its branch, the Rapidan), the York, and the James. Still farther south rises the Roanoke River, which crosses into North Carolina. On the border of Smyth and Grayson Counties is Mount Rogers. At 5729 feet, it is the highest point in the state.

The Valley and Ridge region covers most of western Virginia. Its outstanding feature is the Shenandoah Valley, a part of the Great Appalachian Valley. The Shenandoah hosts Virginia's number-one agricultural county, Rockingham. Its 1834 farms make it number 56 in the country. This region stretches for about 150 miles between the Alleghenies of West Virginia and the Blue Ridge. The limestone soils of the valley make it one of the most fertile parts of the state. The region has the highest farm cash receipts, mostly from livestock, dairy, hay, and corn for silage.

The Appalachian Plateau covers a small part of Virginia in Wise, Dickinson, and Buchanan Counties. The elevation here is from 2700 to 3000 feet. Streams have channeled the region into a maze of deep ravines and winding ridges. Livestock and hay are the main farm products in these mountainous areas.

The Virginia Century Farm Program

More than 1,000 Virginia farms have been named a Virginia Century Farm by the governor. This program honors the enduring spirit of agriculture and Virginia's early farm families. Today, descendants of the first farmers continue to produce food and fiber on the same land as their forefathers. The Virginia Century Farm Program recognizes and honors those farms that have been in operation for at least 100 consecutive years. It further recognizes the generations of Virginia farm families whose diligent and dedicated efforts have maintained these farms, provided nourishment to their fellow citizens, and contributed so greatly to the economy of the Commonwealth.

Virginia Century Farm families receive a certificate signed by the governor and the commissioner of VDACS, and a sign appropriate for outdoor display. The name of the farm and its owners are posted on the department's website.

The criteria a farm must meet to be certified as a Virginia Century Farm are:

1. It must have been owned by the same family for at least 100 consecutive years;

2. It must be lived on or actually farmed by a descendent of the original owner;

3. It must gross more than $2,500 annually from the sale of farm products.

chapter three

OTHER POULTRY

Virginia farmers are raising some really big birds, including ostrich, emu, and rhea, all of the ratite family. Such farms are mainly in the Shenandoah and Allegheny foothills. The lean meat, feathers, oil, and leather produced from these birds are all valuable farm products. Although ratites are poultry, the pH of their flesh is similar to beef. Therefore, they are classified as "red" meat. The raw meat is a very dark cherry red. After cooking, the meat looks like beef, and the flavor is similar but a little sweeter. The tenderness and texture of farmed ratite meat lends itself to light grilling, pan frying, or roasting. However, because ratite meat is so low in fat, care must be taken not to overcook it.

TERIYAKI OSTRICH

The secret to cooking ostrich is not to overcook it.

FOR OSTRICH:

- 8 ounces whole-muscle ostrich fillet
- 2 tablespoons oil, divided
- 1 medium onion, sliced
- 2 zucchini, julienned
- 1 cup sliced mushrooms

FOR SAUCE:

- ½ cup light soy sauce
- 2 tablespoons red-wine vinegar
- 1 tablespoon fresh lime juice
- 1 tablespoon sugar
- 1 teaspoon finely chopped jalapeño pepper
- ½ teaspoon finely chopped fresh garlic
- ½ teaspoon finely chopped fresh ginger root

Cook ostrich fillet in frying pan in 1 tablespoon oil. Turn. Continue cooking until medium rare to medium. Check often. Do not overcook. In a small saucepan, simmer all sauce ingredients for 5 minutes. In remaining oil, stir-fry onions 1 to 2 minutes; add zucchini and mushrooms and cook until crisp tender, about 1 to 2 more minutes. Add sauce. Thinly slice cooked ostrich meat and serve on top. Makes 2 servings.

This recipe was provided by Mike Thompson, owner and chef at Cuz's Uptown Barbecue in Pounding Mill. Mike serves delectable ostrich fillets, with meat from ostriches raised at Sandy Head Ostrich Farm. In addition, Mike and his wife Yvonne offer guest lodging in log cabins nestled at the base of the mountains (call (276) 964-9014).

CONICVILLE OSTRICH BURGERS

A delightful alternative to the fattier beef classic.

- 1 clove garlic, finely minced
- 2 tablespoons finely chopped onion
- 1 teaspoon olive oil
- 1 pound ground ostrich meat
- ½ teaspoon freshly ground black pepper
- 1 teaspoon salt

Sauté garlic and onion in oil. Gently mix into meat with salt and pepper. Form into patties. Heat a non-stick skillet over medium-high heat and cook for 2 minutes on each side. Or prepare a fire on the grill. Brush patties with oil to prevent sticking. Grill about 4 minutes on each side or to 160° F. Makes 4 patties. Serving suggestion: serve on hamburger buns with grilled onions, mushrooms, guacamole, sliced tomato, and lettuce.

Conicville Ostrich is a small farm in Mount Jackson, owned by Willard and Lorna Lutz. They raise ostrich, cattle, chickens, and organically grown berries. All the animals are raised primarily on alfalfa and corn. No commercial fertilizers, pesticides, or herbicides are used (phone (540) 477-3574 or visit www.conicvilleostrich.com).

Sandy Head Ostrich Farm

At the base of Buckhorn Mountain in Tazewell County, 30 acres of woodlands, pastures, springs, and streams—and a variety of wildlife, wildflowers, fish, and wild birds—comprise Sandy Head Ostrich Farm. "We maintain the different ecosystems and work with the land to produce healthful, excellent-tasting food," says Sue Carr, Sandy Head owner.

Carr says Sandy Head raises ostriches for their meat, hides, feathers, and eggs. She describes these birds as "curious and lively" and says that they "put on quite a show when they run, spin, and kick." The farm also has emus, turkeys, and "Easter Egg" chickens, a picnic area, gift shop, farm tours, and a pick-your-own produce section. Tours and some produce sites are handicap accessible.

All the farm's livestock are pasture raised, graze on fresh grass, and eat wholesome grains. No chemicals, antibiotics, growth hormones, or harmful animal by-products are used. The produce is grown without chemical fertilizers or insecticides, often in raised beds for easy accessibility. "Come visit!" Sue says (phone (276) 988-9090).

Emu

A bird that roamed the Australian outback for millions of years, the emu has provided sustenance to the aborigines since prehistoric times. In recent decades, limited commercial production of emus has taken place in America. Thousands of emu ranchers raise flocks of the bird, a cousin of the African ostrich. They believe the emu will play a larger role in the American diet as consumers seek healthier, leaner meats.

Emu ranching has many attractive qualities for those seeking a relatively low-maintenance agricultural business. The average ranch is fewer than 15 acres, and a breeder hen can produce about 20 chicks a year for 20 years or more.

Currently available in only a handful of restaurants or specialty markets across the United States, emu are 97% fat free. They are higher in protein, vitamin C, and iron than beef and lower in cholesterol than chicken.

EMU ON A STICK

These appetizers are bite sized and easy to prepare.

1 pound inside fillet of emu	2 teaspoons minced shallot or green
⅓ cup olive oil	onion
⅓ cup red-wine vinegar	1 clove garlic, minced
2 teaspoons dried rosemary	1 teaspoon dried thyme

Cut emu into 1-inch cubes. Place on short skewers. To make marinade, combine oil, vinegar, rosemary, shallot, garlic, and thyme. Marinate emu at least 2 hours. Drain marinade from emu and grill to medium rare. Makes 20 appetizers.

✎ Thunder Ridge Emu Farm is located a few minutes from Manassas on 30 acres in the foothills of the Shenandoah Mountains. Anne Geller's emu have roamed freely in large fenced pastures since 1993 (phone (703) 631-9074 or visit www.thunderridgeemu.com). ✎

HUNGARIAN-STYLE EMU GOULASH

This slow simmered stew is even better on the second day.
Make it with beef round steak if you don't have emu.

2½ pounds emu steak or	1 medium onion, finely chopped
beef round steak	2 tablespoons water
¼ cup flour	¼ teaspoon dried marjoram
2 tablespoons Hungarian paprika,	¼ teaspoon dried thyme
divided	1 cup burgundy wine
1 teaspoon salt	1 bay leaf
4 tablespoons oil	2 tablespoons sour cream

Cut steak into 1-inch cubes. On a piece of wax paper, combine flour, 1 tablespoon paprika and salt. Coat steak in flour mixture; set aside. In a large heavy Dutch oven, heat oil and brown onion for about 1 minute on high heat. Add steak mixture, stir and brown on all sides for about 7 minutes. Add water and deglaze bottom of pot. Add marjoram and thyme; stirring often, brown for another 12 minutes. Sprinkle with remaining 1 tablespoon paprika, reduce heat to very low, cover and simmer, for 40 minutes.

Stir in burgundy; add bay leaf. Cover and simmer for 1 hour or until fork tender. Remove bay leaf and stir in sour cream. Add more salt, if desired. Serving suggestion: Serve over cooked noodles or rice.

✎ This hearty recipe is from the kitchen of Anne Weber, Baranca Acres Emu Farm, Fork Union, Virginia (phone (434) 842-1111). ✎

chapter four
EGGS

∽ *Virginia's 4 million hens produce more than 800 million eggs annually—that's more than 200 apiece. Virginians today, however, consume more eggs than the state produces, importing extra eggs from neighboring states such as Pennsylvania and North Carolina. At about a dollar a dozen, eggs are a bargain for Virginia consumers. It takes close to four pounds of feed to produce one dozen eggs; Virginia's prime egg-producing area is the Shenandoah Valley. Most laying hens in Virginia are housed in wire cages with several other hens and produce white-shelled and large brown-shelled eggs; the value of production is more than $70 million.*

Egg packers evaluate egg quality using a process called candling, in which eggs pass over a light source that reveals defects. While some eggs in the carton may look slightly larger or smaller than the rest, it is the total weight of the dozen, not the individual dimensions of each egg, that determines whether the carton is labeled jumbo, extra large, large, medium, small, or peewee.

SIZE AND MINIMUM
NET WEIGHT PER DOZEN:
   Jumbo, 30 ounces
   Extra large, 27 ounces
   Large, 24 ounces
   Medium, 21 ounces
   Small, 18 ounces
   Peewee, 15 ounces

Many eggs reach stores only a few days after being laid by the hen. Egg cartons with the USDA grade shield on them must display the pack date, a three-digit code that represents the day of the year (starting with January 1 as 001 and ending with December 31 as 365) when they were packaged.

Choose Grade A or AA eggs with clean shells and no cracks. Do not purchase eggs that are beyond the "sell by" or "EXP" date printed on the carton. Make sure they've been refrigerated in the store; refrigeration is essential to maintain the safety and quality of eggs. Any bacteria present in an egg can multiply quickly at room temperature. Don't buy cartons with cracked, broken, or unclean eggs. Even unbroken fresh shell eggs may contain certain bacteria that can cause foodborne illness. The bacteria are Salmonella Enteritidis (SE). While the number of eggs affected is quite small, there have been some scattered outbreaks.

Store eggs in the grocery carton in the coldest part of the refrigerator and not in the door. If eggs crack on the way home from the store, break them into a clean container, cover them tightly, and keep refrigerated for use within two days.

Don't wash eggs. Use raw shell eggs within three to five weeks of purchase. Hard-cooked eggs will keep refrigerated for one week. Use leftover yolks and whites within four days. Eggs left out of the refrigerator more than two hours should be discarded.

Don't eat raw eggs. For recipes using eggs that won't be cooked, use in-shell pasteurized eggs or pasteurized

COLONIAL GARDENS' HERB-BAKED EGGS

Ramekins make it easy to cook individual eggs for a group.

12 eggs	8 teaspoons finely chopped fresh
4 tablespoons Dijon mustard	chives or other fresh herbs
1 cup plain yogurt	8 thin slices ham or Canadian bacon
2 cups shredded cheddar cheese	

Grease or spray with non-stick vegetable spray 8 (4- to 6-ounce) ramekins or large muffin tins. In a bowl, beat the eggs with the mustard and yogurt. Stir in half of the shredded cheddar cheese. Stir in the chives. Pour or spoon the egg mixture into the dishes. Sprinkle with the remaining cheese and herbs.

Place on baking sheet. Bake in oven at 375° F for 20 to 25 minutes or until firm and puffed. Remove from oven and let stand 5 minutes before removing from dish. Warm slices of ham or Canadian Bacon and place slices on plate. Run knife around inside of egg dishes; gently remove eggs and place on top of ham slices. Makes 8 servings.

✎ Colonial Gardens Bed & Breakfast is a colonial-style modern home located in Williamsburg's historic corridor. The quiet woodland setting with beautiful seasonal gardens invites you to relax and enjoy the inn's warmth and hospitality (phone (757) 220-8087 or (800) 886-9715 or visti www.colonial-gardens.com). ✎

VICTORIAN INN'S PUFFED PANCAKES

For a special brunch, try these eggy, baked pancakes with maple syrup, powdered sugar, whipped cream, and a long-stem cherry on top!

2 jumbo or 3 large eggs	1 tablespoon B&B liqueur
1 cup eggnog	1 golden delicious apple, sliced
1 cup flour	1 tablespoon butter
¼ teaspoon salt	1 teaspoon vanilla

Preheat oven to 450° F. Adjust rack to the top third of oven. Coat 2 (8- to 9-inch) round, ceramic or glass, baking dishes with butter and then dust with granulated sugar. Beat eggs; add eggnog and mix well. Add flour and salt and mix to a smooth and creamy texture. Mix in liqueur. Pour into prepared dishes and bake for 15 minutes. Reduce oven temperature to 400° F and bake about 5 more minutes, or until golden brown.

While pancakes are baking, slice apple and sauté in butter (do not let butter burn) a couple of minutes on high, constantly turning apple slices. Toss vanilla with apples. Put a bed of syrup on serving plate, place pancake on top and sprinkle with powdered sugar. Finish with apple slices topped with whipped cream and a long-stem cherry. Makes 2 servings.

✎ This is just one of many lavish breakfasts guests enjoy at the Victorian Inn and the other Woodruff Collection lodging options in Luray. The inns are situated near to the Shenandoah River, Luray Caverns, Skyline Drive, and golf courses (phone (540) 743-1494 or (866) 937-3466 or visit www.woodruffinns.com). ✎

FEDERAL CREST'S
INDIVIDUAL EGG CASSEROLES

Serve with baked apples and biscuits for a breakfast surprise.

8 to 9 slices of buttered bread
1 cup shredded cheddar cheese
½ to 1 cup crumbled cooked bacon,
    sausage, or ham
¼ teaspoon salt

¼ teaspoon pepper
6 eggs, lightly beaten
1½ to 2 cups milk
2 tablespoons chopped fresh parsley

Tear bread into small pieces and toss in a bowl with bacon, cheese, salt, and pepper. In another bowl, beat eggs and add 1½ cups milk. Pour over bread mixture and refrigerate overnight.

    Preheat oven to 350° F. Spray 5 (10-ounce) individual ramekins or custard cups with non-stick vegetable spray, or butter ramekins lightly. If bread mixture seems too thick, stir in remaining ½ cup milk. Fill each ramekin ¾ full with the egg mixture. Cook approximately 20 or more minutes. Garnish with parsley and serve immediately. Note: The casseroles rise, but will fall quickly. Makes 5 servings.

Federal Crest Inn Bed & Breakfast is a stately 8,000-square-foot Georgian Revival mansion built in 1909 by a wealthy Lynchburg lawyer on almost an acre of land at the crest of Federal and Eleventh Streets (phone (434) 845-6155 or (800) 818-6155 or visit www.federalcrest.com).

EXTRA-TART LEMON MERINGUE PIE

Using powdered sugar instead of granulated sugar to sweeten the meringue helps prevent "weeping," because powdered sugar contains corn starch that absorbs liquid.

1 (9-inch) pie crust
2 to 3 lemons
1½ cups sugar
½ cup cornstarch
⅛ teaspoon salt
1¾ cups water

4 large eggs, separated
2 tablespoons butter
½ teaspoon cream of tartar
½ cup confectioners sugar
½ teaspoon vanilla extract

Preheat oven to 400° F. Prick crust with a fork. Bake until light brown, about 12 minutes. Set aside. Grate the zest (yellow color on peel) off lemons to make 2 tablespoons; set aside. Squeeze juice to total ½ cup.

    Combine sugar, cornstarch, and salt in a heavy saucepan. Whisk in water, lemon juice, and egg yolks. Over medium-high heat, cook mixture, stirring constantly, until thickened and boiling, about 5 minutes. Stir in butter until melted. Stir in zest and pour into baked pie crust.

    Lower oven heat to 325° F. To make meringue, beat egg whites with cream of tartar until soft peaks form. Stir in powdered sugar and vanilla; beat until stiff peaks form. Spread meringue lightly over pie, making sure to seal meringue to edge of crust. Bake 15 to 20 minutes, or until meringue is brown. Cool at least 1 hour before serving. Makes 8 servings.

Buyer's Guide to
EGGS
(continued)

liquid eggs. Eggs must be cooked thoroughly until yolks are firm. Scrambled eggs should not be runny. Casseroles and other dishes containing eggs should be cooked to 160° F as measured with a food thermometer.

The most recent study done by the USDA's Agricultural Research Service showed cholesterol content of one large egg to be 213 milligrams. All of the cholesterol is in the yolk. The industry is testing various poultry-feeding and management practices to see if the cholesterol content can be reduced. Today's large egg contains 70 calories, 5 grams of fat, and 6 grams of protein. Eggs are good source of protein, vitamins A and B$_{12}$, riboflavin, folacin, iron, zinc, and phosphorus.

For more information about eggs and egg safety, call the USDA Meat and Poultry Hotline at (888) MP-HOTLINE (674-6854). Food-safety specialists will answer your questions Monday through Friday year-round from 10 a.m. to 4 p.m. eastern standard time.

that the breed of the hen determines the color of her eggs? Chickens with white feathers, such as the Leghorn, White Rock, and Cornish, lay white eggs. Red-feathered chickens, such as the Rhode Island Red, New Hampshire, and Plymouth Rock, lay brown eggs. Araucuna chickens in South America lay eggs that range in color from medium blue to medium green. There's no difference from a quality or nutrition standpoint between a white egg and a colored egg.

Which Came First?

The chicken or the egg? It's no contest. Eggs existed long before chickens, according to Harold McGee, who explains, in his book *On Food and Cooking: The Science and Lore of the Kitchen*, that these all-in-one reproductive cells evolved about a billion years ago in the ocean. As animal life emerged from the water, about 250 million years ago, eggs evolved a tough leathery skin to prevent dehydration of their contents on dry land. The chicken, on the other hand, evolved only about 5000 years ago from an Asian bird.

MILLER & RHOADS' CHOCOLATE-SILK PIE

Silk is definitely the word to describe this rich pie that's both easy to make and eye catching, with whipped cream and shaved chocolate on top.

2 cups sweetened whipped cream and shaved semisweet chocolate	1 ounce unsweetened baking chocolate, melted and cooled
1 graham-cracker pie crust, baked	pinch of salt
½ cup unsalted butter	1 teaspoon vanilla extract
¾ cup powdered sugar	3 in-shell pasteurized eggs

Bake and cool pie crust. Using an electric mixer, beat butter and sugar until light and fluffy. Add melted chocolate with salt and vanilla. Add eggs separately, beating for at least 5 minutes after each. (Don't try to take a shortcut with this recipe. Beating is the secret.) Pour filling into prepared shell and refrigerate 24 hours. Just before serving, decorate top with sweetened whipped cream and sprinkle with chocolate. Makes 8 servings.

Miller & Rhoads was an elegant locally owned Richmond department store that went out of business due to the influx of chain stores. But its recipes live on.

WILLIAMSBURG INN'S CRÈME BRÛLÉE

As decadent as the service at the historic inn, this relatively simple dessert soothes the psyche. Most preparation must be done the day before serving.

2½ cups heavy cream	⅔ cup sugar, divided, plus additional granulated sugar
½ vanilla bean, split	
5 egg yolks	

Preheat oven to 325° F. In the top of a double boiler, combine cream, vanilla bean, and ⅓ cup sugar. Bring to a simmer. Combine egg yolks with remaining ⅓ cup sugar. Gradually whisk in 1 cup of hot cream mixture. Add egg mixture to hot cream while stirring with a wooden spoon. Continue to stir until mixture is thick enough to coat the back of the spoon. Strain through a fine strainer.

Pour mixture into 6 crème brûlée dishes. Place dishes in a shallow baking dish covered ½-inch with water. Bake about 45 minutes, or until barely set. Remove from water bath when cool. Refrigerate desserts overnight.

Before serving, lightly cover each custard with sugar. Caramelize under a broiler or with a propane torch. Makes 6 servings.

Williamsburg Inn's Regency Dining Room is one of the best restaurants in North America. The inn's dining experience epitomizes what John D. Rockefeller, Jr. envisioned when he built it in 1937 during his extensive restoration of Virginia's colonial capital. The Williamsburg Inn is an enthusiastic supporter of local farmers. It uses Summerfield Farms for meats; Drinking Swamp Farm for cheese; Manikintowne for produce and custom lettuces; and East Field Farms for fruit and vegetables. This recipe was created by Calvin Belknap, formerly the executive chef of the inn (phone (804) 229-1000 or (800) HISTORY).

tour

MUSEUM OF
AMERICAN FRONTIER CULTURE

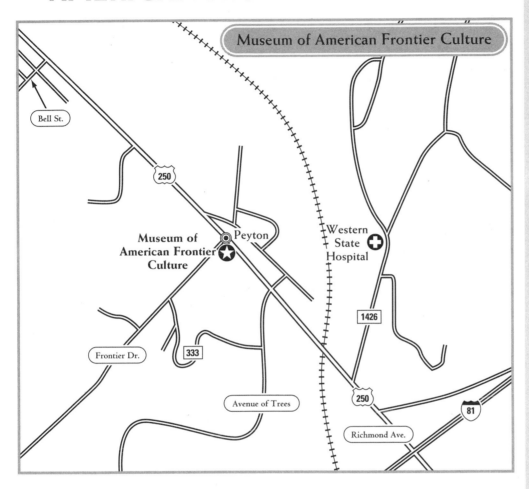

Museum of American Frontier Culture

Bell St.

250

Museum of
American Frontier
Culture

Peyton

Western
State
Hospital

1426

Frontier Dr.

333

Avenue of Trees

250

81

Richmond Ave.

Tour in a Nutshell

MUSEUM OF AMERICAN FRONTIER CULTURE

The outdoor museum offers an international farm-history experience as well as special programs and events.

DAYS/HOURS: The museum is open daily year-round except Thanksgiving Day, Christmas Day, certain days in January, and during severe weather.

FEES: General admission is charged.

DIRECTIONS: The museum is located near I-64 and I-81 in Staunton. From I-81, take Exit 222 and travel west on Route 250. Turn south at the museum's sign.

MORE INFORMATION: Call (540) 332-7850, extension 159 for reservations or extension 124 for information. Or visit www.frontiermuseum .org.

Immigrants from England were the overwhelming majority of settlers in Virginia and in the other East Coast colonies for more than 100 years after Jamestown was founded in 1607. But during the eighteenth century, German and Scotch-Irish farmers who wanted to escape religious oppression and unfavorable economic conditions in Europe began to pour into Virginia's western frontier. They fulfilled their dreams of becoming landowners, along with the English colonists who had preceded them.

Through the use of living-history interpreters and historic farm buildings, the Museum of American Frontier Culture illustrates the lives of members of these three primary ethnic groups before their immigration to America as well as after, revealing how the formerly distinct cultures evolved into a typical Virginia frontier farm of the early 1800s.

Begin your visit in the modern visitor-information center by viewing a short film about immigration and the settlement of Virginia's frontier; the center also houses changing exhibits and a museum store. Then set off to stroll through three authentic farms, which have been brought over from Europe. They include the German farm, circa 1700–1750; the Ulster (Scotch-Irish) farm, circa 1700–1830; and the English yeoman farm, circa 1675–1700. There is also the American farm

Older eggs make better can-
didates for hard cooking. The
fresher the egg, the more difficult it is to peel it after hard
cooking.

Dyeing eggs: Return dyed
eggs to the refrigerator within
two hours of cooking. If eggs
are to be eaten, use a food-
safe coloring. Use clean
hands before handling the
eggs. Do not eat dyed eggs
used as decoration for bread
or other food stored at room
temperature.

Blowing out eggshells: To
destroy bacteria that may be
present on the surface of the
egg, wash the egg in hot water
and then rinse in a solution of
one teaspoon chlorine bleach
per half cup of water. After
blowing out the egg, refrigerate the contents and use within two to four days; cook
thoroughly before eating.

Hunting eggs: Hide eggs in
places that are protected from
dirt, pets, and other sources
of bacteria. The total time for
hiding and hunting eggs
should not exceed two hours.
The "found" eggs must be re-
refrigerated until eaten.

from the Shenandoah Valley, which reflects daily life between 1840 and 1860.
Costumed blacksmiths demonstrate regularly in the eighteenth-century forge from
Northern Ireland.

Rare and minor-breed livestock, heirloom gardens, agricultural crops, and period furnishings help costumed interpreters showcase old-time ways of daily life and
living with the land. From mid-March through December, visitors can witness
work on the farms. In the winter, personally guided tours that focus on the history
of the farms, the buildings, the animals, the furnishings, and the people who lived
there are offered. Cooler weather and fall foliage combine with traditional crafts,
live bands, cultural performances, and historic foods for the museum's biggest
event, the Fall Family Heritage Festival, held in October. Summer-evening concerts, historic dining and dancing, and seasonal programs are also offered.

DOWN ON THE FARMS

German Heritage: The museum's German farm originally stood in the small farming village of Hordt located in the Rhineland-Palatinate region of Germany. The
peasant farmhouse was one of the oldest surviving houses in Hordt, dating back to
1688. The farm is interpreted during the first half of the eighteenth century, the
period of heaviest German emigration from this region.

Irish Heritage: The Irish (Ulster) farm buildings from Northern Ireland were in place
in the townland of Claraghmore, near the village of Drumquin, in County Tyrone.
These buildings show a traditional architectural form, the thatched one-story stone
farmhouse, which was dominant in the Ulster during the eighteenth and nineteenth
centuries. An eighteenth-century blacksmith's forge opened in May 1995.

English Heritage: The English exhibit reflects the time between 1675 and 1700
and includes buildings from two locations in England—a farm dating back to the
early sixteenth century in West Sussex, near Petworth, and a house from the West
Midlands region of England, in Worcestershire, from the Parish of Hartlebury.

American Heritage: On the American site are eleven buildings, all original to a
farm that once stood in Botetourt County. The farm was occupied from about
1835 until 1972. The museum interprets the farm by showing the lifestyle of the
Shenandoah Valley farmer circa 1840–1860.

The Museum's Irish Forge dates to the 1700s and originally stood in County Fer-
managh, Northern Ireland. Such forges and blacksmith shops provided important
services to farming communities in the 1700s.

The Bowman House originally stood in northern Rockingham County, Virginia.
The oldest section of the house dates to 1773 and was built either by or for a natu-
ralized German immigrant named Georg Baumann who purchased 260 acres of
land in what was then Augusta County in 1772. Baumann arrived in America in
1751, and lived in Berks County, Pennsylvania until the early 1770s when he relocated to Virginia with his son John. Early in Georg Baumann's time in Virginia his
name began to appear in official records as George Bowman.

tour

STRATFORD HALL PLANTATION

Birthplace of General Robert E. Lee

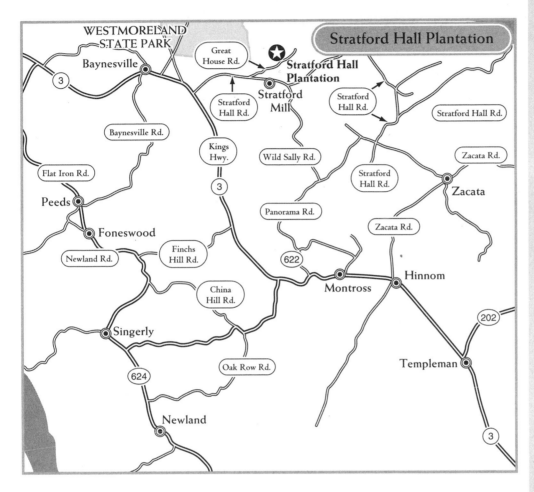

The working colonial plantation that was home to the family of Robert E. Lee includes the Great House, outbuildings, gardens, and walking trails. A plantation luncheon and à la carte items are served daily from 11:30 a.m. to 3 p.m. in a large log-cabin restaurant with an outdoor screened deck overlooking the woodlands.

DAYS/HOURS: Stratford Hall is open daily, except on Thanksgiving and during December and January. Special candlelight events are held in December. Call to learn about special events and to find out when the mill is operating.

FEES: Admission is charged.

DIRECTIONS: The Plantation is 38 miles east of Fredericksburg on Virginia's Northern Neck. Take SR 3 to SR 214, then follow signs 1 mile to 438 Great House Road.

MORE INFORMATION: Call (804) 493-8038 on weekdays, (extension zero on weekends), or visit www.stratfordhall.org.

Robert E. Lee, who became the commander of the Confederate Army, was born in the Great House of Stratford Hall Plantation, one of the country's finest examples of colonial architecture. The working plantation covers 1700 acres. Home to four generations of the Lee family, Stratford Hall contains Lee family memorabilia and period furnishings.

The Georgian-style buildings were constructed from brick made on the site and laid in Flemish bond. The roofs are supported with local yellow-poplar beams. Eight chimneys in two squares top the distinctive "H"-shaped brick home, which sits on high bluffs overlooking the Potomac. The home was built in the 1730s by Lee's great-great-uncle, Thomas Lee, president of the Council of Virginia and acting Colonial governor from 1749 to 1750. Two of Thomas Lee's sons, Richard Henry Lee and Francis Lightfoot Lee, were the only brothers to sign the Declaration of Independence. "Light Horse" Harry Lee, Robert E. Lee's father, was a Revolutionary War hero and a close friend of George Washington, who was born nearby.

Visitors approach the house from the south alongside an oval drive adorned with dogwood, hickory, and oak trees, and they can wander forested woods, meadows, and gardens. Some trees are labeled for easy identification. More than two

miles of wildflower-lined nature trails crisscross the plantation, some of which border the mill pond and overlook the river.

Buildings include a coach house, stables, kitchen, smokehouse, laundry, slave quarters, spring houses, and an operating, reconstructed gristmill that grinds wheat, corn, and barley. The coach-house bays are filled with a variety of nineteenth-century wheeled vehicles, including the Bremo Coach, which carried General Lafayette on his trip to Monticello in 1825, and a Landaulette, a fashionable conveyance much enjoyed by the ladies.

KITCHEN

When the Lees lived at Stratford Hall, the kitchen was one of the liveliest buildings on the plantation. The fireplace is large enough to roast a whole ox and to warm the huge copper and brass vessels gleaming on the hearth. Among the many utensils seldom seen today are a medicinal still and a spit jack that could be wound to turn the roasting spit automatically. Outside the kitchen, the well is only a few steps from the door, and kindling is conveniently stacked. Among the many kitchen-yard activities were candle dipping, soap making, and laundry chores.

MILL

The Stratford Mill was reconstructed in 1939 on the foundations of an older Lee mill. The huge waterwheel of the reconstructed mill turns wooden gears that power its millstones. Corn, wheat, and barley are ground, just as they have been for nearly 250 years, and are sold at the Plantation Store. The mill underwent an extensive restoration in 2002 to 2003.

GARDENS

In the early 1930s, The Garden Club of Virginia restored the formal East Garden in a typical eighteenth-century English style, enclosed by brick walls and made accessible by oyster-shell paths. The irregular parterres are outlined with English Box. The garden is planted with camellias, cornelian cherry trees, crepe myrtles, fringe trees, and goldenrain trees. To the north of the East Garden grows the small orchard. It offers a glimpse at a few of the varieties of fruits that would have been enjoyed by the residents of Stratford.

The West Garden is an example of an eighteenth-century flower garden and contains fragrant old-fashioned daffodils, heritage roses, sweet-faced johnny jumpups, and many other eighteenth-century-variety perennials, annuals, and bulbs. Enclosed within the borders of espalier-trained fruit trees are beds planted with eighteenth-century varieties of vegetables and herbs. Between the slave quarters is a small sampling of the varieties of herbs and vegetables grown and used by the African American population at Stratford. The Slave Garden is an added attraction for those interested in the heritage of plant culture brought to America by slaves.

part two
MEAT

Before the first English settlers landed in Jamestown, there were no cattle, hogs, or sheep in Virginia. But even after these animals became available, they were not necessarily dependable main courses. With no electricity or supermarkets, preservation in Virginia's humid Tidewater climate was a challenge. Virginian Landon Carter complained in 1775, "The weather is so hot, there is no killing anything that can't be immediately eaten up. I killed a mutton one day," he added, "and it was spoiled the next. So it was with the venison."

Beef and pork were preserved by salting, and so emerged the famous Smithfield Ham that remains a hallmark of Virginia specialties today. During the Revolutionary War, the scarcity of salt led some Virginians to attempt extracting it by boiling water from the Chesapeake Bay. And it is near the Bay—in southeastern Virginia—where most of Virginia's hogs are raised today. However, cattle and other livestock are raised predominately inland.

Cattle utilize pasture and forage from 3.5 million Virginia acres that are not suited for crop production and would otherwise have no market value. Virginia has a valued reputation nationally for having an outstanding purebred herd, but the state's animals are not raised to maturity. Most producers are in the business of breeding. Commercial cattlemen graze young animals until they weigh about 900 pounds, and then market them to operations in Pennsylvania, the Corn Belt, and the High Plain that feed the cattle high-grain diets for weight gain.

The top two lamb-producing counties are Augusta and Rockingham, in the Shenandoah Valley. This area is also home to the largest bison farm east of the Mississippi, as well as to venison farms and other livestock operations. Small farms raise specialty livestock, too, such as rabbits. Together, animals raised for meat make up more than 16% of the cash receipts earned by Virginia farm commodities.

When purchasing beef, refer to the package label that identifies the type of meat and the wholesale and retail cuts. Look for USDA choice or select grades; these are the lowest in fat and calories. The leanest cuts of beef are loin and round cuts. The "skinniest" six cuts of beef are round tip, top round, eye of round, top loin, tenderloin, and sirloin.

When selecting beef, consider color. Beef, including vacuum-packaged beef, is a dark, purplish-red color when first cut. The lean part should be a cherry-red color, unless it has been cured or smoked. Marbling, the small flecks of fat throughout the lean, improves the meat's flavor and juiciness. Look for a fat covering of one-eighth inch or less on steaks or roasts which keeps the beef from drying out and helps retain juices during cooking.

Fresh beef should be refrigerated as packaged and can be stored for one to four days. Beef can be frozen in the packaging for up to two weeks. The best way to defrost beef is in the refrigerator, but a microwave oven can also be used.

Tenderize lean cuts by cooking slowly with moist heat, cooking in liquid, or marinating. To prepare beef without adding fat, try roasting, broiling, pan broiling, grilling, and microwaving.

chapter one

BEEF AND VEAL

Cattle is second, only to chicken, as Virginia's most valuable agricultural product. Though none of the first cattle brought to the state in 1607 survived, by 1620—when the Mayflower landed at Plymouth Rock in Massachusetts—the state had 500 head, which swelled to 30,000 by 1639. Today the Old Dominion has nearly 2 million head of cattle including beef and dairy cows. Ninety percent of Virginia's cattle are in herds, which average 23,000 head, almost all grown on family farms that have been in the family for several generations. The sale of cattle and calves total more than $400 million annually in cash receipts. The top five cattle counties are Rockingham, Augusta, Fauquier, Washington, and Bedford.

BALSAMIC BRAISED BEEF

This dish has won beef cook-offs at state and national levels.

1 (3-pound) chuck roast
flour for dredging roast
2 tablespoons extra-virgin olive oil
¼ cup balsamic vinegar diluted in
    1½ cups water, divided
½ teaspoon salt

freshly ground pepper
2 onions, halved and thickly sliced
4 shallots, halved and thickly sliced
¼ cup pitted dates, chopped
1 teaspoon flour or cornstarch
1 tablespoon fresh chopped parsley

Preheat oven to 325° F. Dredge beef in flour. Heat olive oil in a Dutch oven over medium-high heat. Brown beef on all sides in olive oil. Remove beef and deglaze pan with 1 cup balsamic vinegar mixture. Add salt to liquid. Return beef to pan and sprinkle generously with pepper. Distribute onions, shallots, and dates around beef in liquid. Cover tightly with lid or foil. Bake 2 to 2½ hours, turning meat upside down every ½ hour. Pour remaining ¾ cup balsamic mixture over beef to replenish liquid as necessary. Beef should be tender when baking time is completed.

Remove beef from pan. Simmer remaining pan liquids and solids on stovetop. Sift in 1 teaspoon flour or cornstarch to thicken, stirring constantly. (Add additional water if sauce gets too thick.) Arrange beef slices on platter. Spoon sauce over sliced beef. Sprinkle with fresh chopped parsley. Makes 6 servings.

This recipe was created by Grace S. Fogg of Charlottesville.

BEEF AND EGGPLANT

Quick, easy, and delicious—this recipe delivers all three.

1 large eggplant
1½ pounds ground round
1 large onion, chopped
1 teaspoon salt

½ teaspoon black pepper
3 medium tomatoes
2 tablespoons vegetable oil
hot cooked rice

Peel eggplant and cut crosswise into ¼-inch slices. Place on cookie sheet and brush with oil. Broil for 5 minutes. Turn over, brush with oil, and broil for another 5 minutes. Meanwhile, brown ground round in skillet until no longer pink. Pour off drippings. Add chopped onions, salt, and pepper and cook for 5 minutes. Cut tomatoes into ¼-inch slices. Place half of sliced tomatoes in baking dish. Place eggplant on top of tomatoes. Sprinkle beef mixture on top and cover with remaining tomatoes. Cover with aluminum foil and bake for 15 minutes at 500° F. Serve over a bed of rice. Makes 4 servings.

This recipe by Ghada Shields of McLean was a finalist in the 1999 Virginia Beef Cook-Off.

Beef

Cattle have been domesticated in the Near East since at least 6500 B.C. Contemporary domestic breeds evolved from a single early ancestral breed, the aurochs. In addition to prehistoric cave paintings that help identify the breed, some aurochs actually survived until comparatively modern times. The last documented auroch was killed by a poacher in 1627 on a hunting reserve near Warsaw, Poland. Although there's no direct evidence to support the theory, some believe living aurochs could still remain in remote parts of Europe.

Early cattle served three purposes, providing meat, milk, and labor. Eventually, horses and machinery took over the labor function, and cattle were bred only for meat and milk. Some common breeds of beef cattle include Angus Charloise, Beefmaster, Brahma, Polled and Horned Hereford, and Limousin.

An all-American favorite, beef can be an important part of a healthy diet. A nutrient-rich food with high-quality protein, iron, zinc, and five B-complex vitamins, today's beef is 27% leaner than beef raised 25 years ago.

DID YOU KNOW . . .
that shanks are the front legs of beef, veal, lamb, or pork? Although very flavorful, this cut of meat is some of the toughest and therefore requires long, slow cooking at low temperatures.

PRESIDENT GEORGE W. BUSH'S OVEN-BARBECUED BRISKET

Don't worry about cold or rainy weather; this recipe for barbecue—which in Texas usually means brisket or beef ribs with red sauce—can be made in the oven.

1 (10-pound) whole brisket	3 tablespoons liquid smoke
2 cups ketchup	2 teaspoons chili powder
1 cup water	2 teaspoons celery seed
½ cup Worcestershire sauce	2 teaspoons salt
¼ cup lemon juice	

Preheat oven to 450° F. Don't worry about trimming the fat from brisket; it's much easier to trim after cooking and chilling. Place brisket in a large pan and brown in oven 30 minutes.

While beef is browning, combine the remaining ingredients in a saucepan and bring to a boil. Remove brisket from oven and reduce temperature to 325° F. Pour sauce over brisket and cover tightly, either with a lid or heavy foil. Roast 1 hour. Carefully turn brisket upside down and baste with sauce. Re-cover and continue to roast 1 to 1½ hours, or until meat is fork tender. Transfer brisket to a platter. Pour sauce into quart jars and let sit up to 2 hours; refrigerate overnight.

Slice brisket ¼-inch thick across the grain. Remove fat and overlap slices in rectangular baking dishes. Scoop fat off top of sauce and discard. Pour half the sauce over sliced meat. Cover and reheat in a 350° F oven. Heat extra sauce to pass. Serves 14 Virginians or 8 Texans.

Note: This recipe is best made a day in advance so it can be sliced uniformly.

President George W. Bush frequently dines at Virginia restaurants. His favorite foods are Mexican, and he especially enjoys sour-cream chicken enchiladas, barbecue, hamburgers, watermelon, and pralines-and-cream ice cream. Like his father, Dubya isn't overly fond of broccoli, but beets are his least favorite, according to the White House Press Office.

QUICK BEEF QUESADILLAS

Total preparation and cooking time is only 30 minutes.

8 (10-inch) flour tortillas	1 (12-ounce) package shredded
1 pound ground chuck (80% lean)	Mexican-style four cheeses
1 (10-ounce) can diced tomatoes	1 (8-ounce) carton sour cream
with green chilies	1 (8-ounce) jar pineapple salsa or
salt and pepper to taste	regular salsa

Wrap tortillas in foil to heat in oven at 300° F. Brown ground beef in a large skillet until the beef is no longer pink. Add canned tomatoes and heat through. Add salt and pepper to taste as desired. Add 10 ounces of cheese and stir until the cheese begins to melt. Spread the mixture on 4 tortillas. Top with remaining 4 tortillas. Next top with the remaining cheese. Place each serving on a plate and cut into wedges. Serve with sour cream and salsa. Makes 4 servings.

This recipe by Pauline Johnson of Farmville won the Ground Beef Category in the 1999 Virginia Beef Cook-Off.

VICE PRESIDENT AL GORE'S
MEMPHIS DRY RIBS

In Virginia, Al Gore's home state, Memphis is called "the rib capital of the world."
While ribs can be beef or pork, in Tennessee barbecue is most likely to be pork.

FOR RIBS:

- 6 pounds pork or beef spareribs
- 1 tablespoon salt
- 2 teaspoons coarsely ground black pepper
- ½ teaspoon crushed red pepper
- 4 to 6 handfuls hickory chips, soaked in water

FOR SAUCE:

- 1 cup tomato sauce
- 1 cup cider vinegar
- ⅓ cup Worcestershire sauce
- ⅓ cup water
- 1 tablespoon butter
- 1 small onion, chopped
- 1½ teaspoons salt
- dash of pepper

Place slab of ribs, bone side up, on table. Slide a knife under the membrane and against the end bone to separate the two. With a dry paper towel or rag, grasp the edge of the thin membrane and pull. The entire membrane should separate from rib. (This will result in a more tender rib and will allow your barbecue flavors to better penetrate the meat.)

Combine salt, pepper, and red pepper. Rub mixture over ribs and refrigerate 4 to 24 hours. Let stand 1 hour at room temperature before cooking.

Prepare a medium-hot fire in a covered charcoal or gas grill. Push the coals to the side. Just before placing ribs on grill, scatter about half the wood chips onto the hot coals or gas grill. Place ribs on grill, making sure they are not directly above coals. Cover grill. Turning ribs several times during cooking, grill about 1½ hours, or until meat is tender. Add remaining chips midway through cooking. Makes 6 servings.

Prepare Memphis rib sauce by combining all ingredients in a saucepan. After bringing to a boil, simmer on low for 10 minutes. Makes about 2 cups. Serve ribs with sauce.

Al Gore lives in Arlington, Virginia.

State Fair of Virginia

A petting zoo, livestock shows, contests, antique farm equipment, midway rides, and numerous other attractions have lured fairgoers for decades to The State Fair of Virginia at Strawberry Hill, near Richmond. In addition, Virginians from all over the state clamor for the coveted blue ribbons awarded to the winners of more than 5,000 fair contests each year. Contest fields include computer graphics, livestock, photography, baking, crops, plants, equine, and many, many more. Food competitions include categories in bread, cakes, candy, canned fruits, canned vegetables, cookies, dehydrated foods, home wine, honey cookery, peanut butter, pickles, relishes, catsups, pies, preserves, jellies, syrups, and vinegars.

The fair site will be changed in the future. The fair is held for ten days at the end of September; more information can be obtained by calling (800) 588-3247 or (804) 569-3232 or visiting www.statefairva.com.

Frenchman Gerard Pain—
former owner of Washington's
La Chaumière restaurant—is
quite comfortable in a black
tie, greeting diners. But he's
equally at home in a denim
shirt, working on his 350-acre
cattle ranch, Wolfcreek Farm.
Pain raises Black Angus cattle
and grows hay to feed them
on the farm, located in
Wolftown, in Madison
County, 25 miles north of
Charlottesville. That Pain
would be a restaurateur as
well as a cowboy makes
sense. His parents were in the
food business as are his three
brothers-in-law. Pain was
raised in the heart of Charolais cattle country in France.
His parents lived in the city,
but his uncles were in the
Charolais business. "I always
spent my time on the farm,"
he says. "That's where I wanted to be—with the cattle and
horses." On their Wolfcreek
Farm, the retired Pain and
his wife have established
soil-conservation and clean-
water management programs
that students come to study.
He works with the soil-
conservation service to control damage on the hilly
pastures. The farm is on
rolling hills with a stocked
pond and stream, and many
mature trees. A gorgeous view
of the Blue Ridge Mountains
lurks behind the buildings.

SENATOR GEORGE ALLEN'S LASAGNA

This is a favorite recipe from Virginia's former governor and his wife, Susan.

FOR SAUCE:

olive oil
1 large onion, finely chopped
2 large garlic cloves, minced
2 (28-ounce) cans tomatoes, coarsely
   chopped, including liquid
1 (12-ounce) can tomato paste
1 can of water

1 tablespoon oregano
1½ tablespoons basil
1 bay leaf
1 teaspoon garlic powder
2 teaspoons sugar
salt and pepper

FOR NOODLES AND FILLING:

1 large onion, chopped
1 garlic clove, minced
1½ pounds ground beef
1½ pounds Italian sausage
1 pound mushrooms, sliced (optional)
2 eggs, beaten
salt and pepper

8 ounces shredded mozzarella cheese
½ cup grated Parmesan cheese
½ cup grated Romano cheese
1 (16-ounce) box of lasagna noodles,
   cooked according to package
   directions

To prepare sauce, place a small amount of oil in a large stockpot over medium-high heat. Sauté onions and garlic until transparent. Add remaining ingredients and simmer several hours until smooth and thick.

   Sauté onions in a small amount of olive oil. Add garlic. Brown ground beef, sausage, and mushrooms. Cool mixture. Mix the 2 beaten eggs into the mixture. Add salt and pepper to taste. Toss cheeses together, set aside. Spread small amount of sauce in the bottom of a 9 × 13-inch pan. Line it with the noodles. Layer the meat mixture, sauce, and the cheese mixture. Repeat this step, ending with noodles on top. Spread the remaining sauce and top with the rest of the cheese. Bake at 350° F for 1 hour. Makes 8 to 10 servings.

Prior to being elected to the United States Senate in 2000, George Allen was Virginia's 67th governor, from 1994 to 1998. Senator Allen and his wife, Susan, reside in Chesterfield County with their three children.

STEAK GERALDINE

*Here's a fast and luxurious main dish for two
that's on the menu at La Chaumière restaurant.*

4 slices of beef tenderloin (about
   1-inch thick)
Dijon mustard
salt and pepper to taste
2 tablespoons finely chopped shallots

3 tablespoons brandy
¼ cup veal or beef broth
1 teaspoon Worcestershire sauce
2 teaspoons finely chopped parsley
1 tablespoon butter

Place the beef slices flat on a cutting board and pound lightly, using your fist. Then spread mustard on both sides of the meat. Add salt and pepper to taste. Place a nonstick skillet over medium-high heat. Add a few drops of oil to the pan, then quickly brown both sides of the meat. When meat is cooked, remove from heat and place on a warm serving platter.

Using the same pan, reduce heat to medium. Add shallots and stir with a wooden spoon. Shallots should get soft but not brown. Add brandy (it may flame up). Add broth, Worcestershire sauce, and parsley. Stir and cook until reduced, about 1 to 2 minutes. Remove pan from heat and stir in the butter. Spoon sauce over beef and serve immediately. Makes 2 servings.

This recipe was courtesy of Gerard Pain, longtime owner of La Chaumière ("the cottage") in Washington, D.C., which he opened in 1964, one year after emigrating from France. President Bush and movie stars such as Robert Redford have dined at the restaurant, which was managed by Pain's daughter, Geraldine.

essay

THREE YEARS TO A HAMBURGER

You're hungry for a burger, so what do you do? Go to the grocery store for supplies? Look in the refrigerator or freezer to see if you have some ground beef? Decide which fast food place or local restaurant you'll visit? When a cattle farmer starts thinking of a hamburger, his focus is more long term—a good three years longer.

First, the rancher makes sure his mother cows are healthy through the winter. In April, he takes the cows to grass pasture and in June, he takes the bulls to the pasture for the breeding season. Nine months later, usually in March or April, the baby calves are born. The calves, which weigh approximately 85 pounds at birth, will stay with their mothers in grass pastures all summer and into the early fall.

In November, the herd is taken out of the grass pasture, weaned, and placed in pens. The calves will be fed a growing ration of feeds—chopped corn silage, ground grains, protein supplements, and vitamins and minerals with a little salt.

All during the spring and summer, while the cow herd is in the grass pasture, the farmer/rancher has been growing feeds in preparation for feeding and finishing the calves: corn, milo, alfalfa, hay, and other forages. He spends several days during July getting his machines—silage chopper, trucks, and tractors—ready for silage harvest. When the corn for forage is ready, the "big push" is on. The plants need to be chopped at the right stage so that the leaves are green and the grain is formed but soft enough to be sweet. Chopped alfalfa is also harvested for forage for cattle.

In addition to feed, cattle need lots of water. Statistics from the Virginia Farm Bureau Federation show that the total amount needed to produce and process a pound of boneless beef from the farm to the plate averages 441 gallons. (Other meat animals need a lot of water, too. A pound of pork requires 385 gallons, and a pound of poultry requires 337 gallons.)

The cattle are fed in bunks in feedlots with other cattle of their size and weight. The cattle remain in the feedlots until all the cattle in that pen are ready for processing—usually when they have reached 1200 pounds. By this time, the cattle will be almost three years old.

When the cattle are "ready to ship," the rancher orders trucks and the cattle are loaded and sent to a packing plant designed especially for processing beef animals. One steer will make about 720 quarter-pound hamburger patties—enough for a family of four to enjoy hamburgers every day for almost six months—according to the Virginia Farm Bureau Federation.

Veal

Veal is the meat from a calf or young cow between 3 and 18 weeks of age. Male calves of dairy cows are used in the veal industry because they are of little or no value to the dairy farmer. (Only a small percentage are raised to maturity and used for breeding.) Dairy calves are breeds such as Holstein, Jersey, or Guernsey, while breeds used for beef include Angus, Charolais, Limousin, and Hereford, for example.

The majority of veal calves are "special fed" on diets of nutritionally balanced milk- or soy-based formulas until they weigh between 150 and 450 pounds. These diets contain iron and other essential nutrients, including amino acids, carbohydrates, fats, minerals, and vitamins. Veal calves are raised in specially designed facilities where they can be cared for and monitored. They are fed special diets rather than grass or hay to produce lean, fine-grained, velvety meat that is light pink in color. Meat from older calves and beef cattle is darker in color.

THE IVY INN'S OSSO BUCO

*Classic Italian osso buco is garnished with gremolada
(minced parsley, lemon peel, and garlic) and accompanied by risotto.
This recipe incorporates the parsley and lemon flavors in the roasting.*

2 to 2½ pounds veal shanks (cut crosswise about 1½ inches thick)	1 anchovy
flour	¼ cup dry Vermouth or dry white wine
⅓ cup Chippollini or pearl onions	2½ cups chicken broth
⅓ cup baby carrots	1 (16-ounce) can cubed tomatoes, drained
⅓ cup chopped fennel	1 teaspoon fleur de cel
1 clove garlic, minced	¼ teaspoon black pepper
1 sprig fresh thyme or ½ teaspoon dried thyme	2 teaspoons sherry vinegar or balsamic vinegar
1 teaspoon lemon zest	

Preheat oven to 325° F. Pat meat dry with a paper towel and dredge in flour. On the stove over high, heat a heavy pot with cover that can be used in an oven. Cover the bottom with a small amount of oil and brown the veal shanks on both sides. Remove the meat and sauté onions, carrots, fennel, and garlic. Add thyme, lemon zest, and the anchovy.

Add Vermouth and scrape bottom of pot to dislodge any brown bits. Add broth, tomatoes, fleur de cel, pepper, and vinegar. Return veal to pot. Cover and braise for 1 hour. Remove cover and continue to cook about 1 hour, or until veal is tender. Makes 4 servings.

Chef Angelo Vangelopoulos began helping in his father's restaurant business at the age of five. He graduated from the Culinary Institute of America in 1990 before returning home to become chef of The Ivy Inn Restaurant in Charlottesville (phone (434) 977-1222 or visit www.ivyinnrestaurant.com).

OVEN-ROASTED SMITHFRESH VEAL SAUSAGE AND POTATOES WITH ROSEMARY

2 (16-ounce) packages Smithfresh Veal Sausage (about 8 sausages)	1 teaspoon salt
¼ cup coarsely chopped onion	¼ teaspoon black pepper
2 tablespoons extra-virgin olive oil	½ teaspoon red pepper
8 medium-sized potatoes cut into large wedges	½ cup dry white wine (preferably Chardonnay)
	4 large sprigs fresh rosemary

Preheat oven to 350° F. Parboil sausages in water in a large skillet for about 5 minutes, or until firm. Remove from water and cut sausages into large pieces, about the same size as the potatoes. Set aside. In a medium-sized Dutch oven over medium heat, cook chopped onions in olive oil until they are transparent. Add the potatoes and cook for about 5 minutes on high heat, making sure that they don't stick. Add the sausage and season with salt, black pepper, and red pepper. Stir in wine. Add the sprigs of rosemary and cover pot. Bake until the potatoes are done, about 1 hour. Makes 6 servings.

Smithfresh Organic Meats, of Berryville, contributed this recipe (phone (877) 955-4389 or visit www. smithfieldfarm.com).

THE TOBACCO COMPANY RESTAURANT'S VEAL PICCATA

In this dish, Marsala wine is the defining flavor.

1 egg
2 tablespoons milk
⅓ cup dry bread crumbs
⅓ cup grated Romano cheese
2 tablespoons flour
4 (5- to 6-ounce) veal scaloppini, pounded flat
2 tablespoons butter

2 tablespoons fresh lemon juice
½ cup sliced fresh mushrooms
¼ cup red wine
½ cup Marsala wine
1½ tablespoons cornstarch
1 (10.5-ounce) can condensed beef consommé or broth

In a pie plate, beat together egg and milk. Mix crumbs and cheese on a piece of wax paper. Lightly flour veal and dip in egg mixture, then coat in crumb mixture. Melt butter in a large skillet over medium-high heat. Sauté coated veal in butter until each side has browned. Splash veal with lemon juice and remove from pan.

Add mushrooms to pan and sauté briefly. Add red wine to pan; scrape to dislodge any brown bits from bottom. In a measuring cup, combine Marsala with cornstarch. Stir into skillet along with consommé. Stirring frequently, cook until sauce thickens. Return veal to skillet and simmer to reheat veal and reduce sauce slightly. Makes 4 servings.

∽ Housed in an 1878 tobacco warehouse, this popular Richmond restaurant serves more than 5,000 diners weekly. The interior is decorated with furnishings from the Victorian era, when tobacco was Richmond's major industry. The antique brass elevator, made by Otis Elevator Company for the Con Edison building in New York, carries guests up the three-story atrium, from the first-floor cocktail lounge to the two dining floors above. The stairway was salvaged from the old St. Luke's Hospital in Richmond. The tall wooden Indian was carved by a craftsman in South Carolina. The brass chandelier came from the Federal Reserve Bank in Cincinnati. The hostess desk on the first floor was an old ticket booth purchased at an Atlanta auction. Phone (804) 782-9555 or visit www.thetobaccocompany.com. ∽

LOUDOUN COUNTY BEEF SALAD

Making good use of leftover roast beef is easy with this easy salad.

FOR SALAD:
1 head romaine lettuce
2 cups cooked roast beef, cubed
6 new potatoes, cooked, cooled, and sliced
20 cherry tomatoes, quartered

1 small onion, sliced in rings
¾ cup thinly sliced fresh mushrooms
1 tablespoon capers
2 tablespoons chopped fresh parsley

FOR DRESSING:
6 tablespoons olive oil
2 tablespoons wine vinegar
1 teaspoon horseradish

1 teaspoon dry mustard
⅛ teaspoon pepper
4 hard-cooked eggs, sliced

Break lettuce and combine with other salad ingredients in a large bowl and chill. In a jar with lid, combine and shake dressing ingredients, pour over salad, and garnish with eggs. Makes 6 servings.

∽ This recipe appeared in Cardinal Cuisine, *a collection of the Mount Vernon Hospital Auxiliary. ∽*

There are seven basic cuts into which veal is separated: leg (round), sirloin, loin, rib, shoulder, shank, and breast. From these are created the cuts available to shoppers in the market: rib chops, loin chops, cutlets, veal for stew, arm steak, blade steak, rib roast, breast, shanks, and round steak.

Use veal chops and roasts within five days of purchase, and ground veal or stew meat within two days. For best quality, use frozen veal chops and roasts within six months and frozen ground veal or stew meat within four months.

Veal is classified as a red meat, but typical lean meat on a veal carcass, which is up to 18 weeks old and weighs between 150 and 450 pounds, has a grayish-pink color. Typical calf carcasses—from older animals up to nine months old and weighing 750 pounds—have a grayish-red color of lean meat. A three-ounce portion of roasted veal cutlet from the leg, trimmed of visible fat, contains 130 calories, 3 grams fat (19% of total calories), 90 milligrams cholesterol, and 24 grams protein. Cook ground veal to 160° F and veal roast, chops, or steaks to 145° F for medium rare and 160° F for medium.

HISTORIC FARMSTEADS

CLAUDE MOORE COLO-
NIAL FARM is open April to
mid-December, Wednesday
through Sunday from 10 a.m.
to 4:30 p.m. and is located at
6310 Georgetown Pike in
McLean. To reach the farm
from the George Washington
Memorial Parkway, take the
exit for Route 123 and head
south towards McLean. At
the fourth light, turn right on
Georgetown Pike (Route 193
West). Turn immediately
right on Colonial Farm Road.
On your left, you will pass
one park entrance (Langley
Fork); take the next left at the
green sign that says "Pavilions
of Turkey Run." Park by the
picnic tables. Call (703) 442-
7557 or visit www.1771.org.
Admission is charged.

BUSHONG FARM is open
daily except Thanksgiving,
Christmas and New Year's
Eves, Christmas and New
Year's Day. The farm is located
in New Market. From I-81,
take Exit 264 to the New Market Battlefield State Historical
Park. The farm is on the park
grounds. For more information, call (540) 740-3101 or
visit (866) 515-1864 or visit
www.vmi.edu/newmarket.
Admission charge includes
New Market Battlefield and
The Hall of Valor.

The Old Dominion's most visited historic agricultural sites of interest include
Mount Vernon, Monticello, and the James River Plantations—all homes of wealthy
planters. But Virginia tourists can also visit farmsteads that portray the common
man's life of centuries past. Here are four not to be missed.

CLAUDE MOORE COLONIAL FARM

Just across a two-lane road from the high security fences and guarded barriers of
the Central Intelligence Agency is a pastoral site that portrays family life on a
small, low-income farm just prior to the Revolutionary War. Located in McLean,
the Claude Moore Colonial Farm is the only privately operated national park in
the United States and was established in 1972 under President Nixon's Legacy-in-
the-Parks program.

Nestled in the valley under tall trees, the farm transports guests back in time to
the year 1771. A walk around the farm is just under three quarters of a mile and
affords the opportunity to take in the barn and tobacco field, the hogs and turkeys
in pens nearby, the cattle and horse grazing in the meadow, and the family's home,
a one-room log building tucked between the apple orchard and the kitchen garden.

The Claude Moore Colonial Farm hosts several special events typical of those a
farm family of the period would have enjoyed. On the third full weekends of May,
July, and October, thousands of visitors join the farm family and period craftsmen,
entertainers, and merchants in an eighteenth-century market fair. On the third
Sunday in June, visitors help gather and bind the wheat, and in August, they help
cut tobacco and hang it in the barn to dry. After November harvests, visitors help
thresh and winnow wheat and make yeast cakes. The Christmas Wassail highlights
the farm's apple orchard, with dancing and caroling.

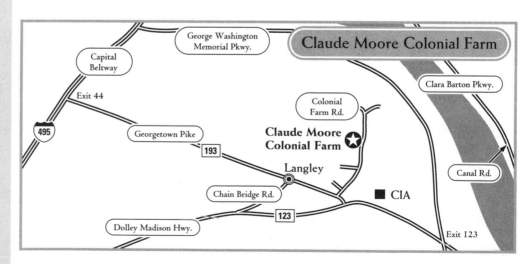

BUSHONG FARM

The Civil War Battle of New Market took place in May 1864 and was fought partially on the Bushong Farm, which Jacob and Sarah Bushong established in 1818. The current home was built in 1825 and faces south toward the town of New Market, one mile away. The family found shelter in the basement as the battle raged around them. Throughout the long Sunday they could hear cannon, muskets, and the shouts of the soldiers fighting around their home. Miraculously, the house received little damage. The orchard just behind the house is where the fiercest fighting occurred. After the battle, the house and barn served as a field hospital for a week, which left permanent blood stains in the parlor.

Today, visitors can explore nine structures interpreting mid-nineteenth-century Shenandoah Valley farm life, such as the bank barn, which takes its name from the dirt bank, or ramp, built on one side of the barn to allow wagons to be pulled directly into the upper level of the building. Other highlights include the complete blacksmith and wheelwright shops that would have provided additional income to the family. During the Civil War, commercially made cloth became scarce. Many southern families brought ancient looms out of storage and began to make homespun cloth. The Bushongs set up their loom in the front room of the Loom and Meat Storage House. The back room was used to store salt-cured meat.

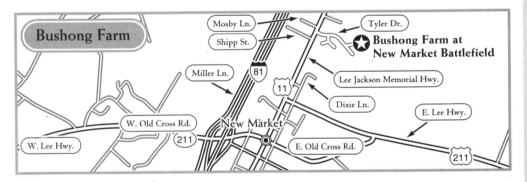

HISTORIC CRAB ORCHARD MUSEUM AND PIONEER PARK

The Historic Crab Orchard Museum and Pioneer Park focuses on the history of southwest Virginia from prehistoric times to about 150 years ago and helps to educate visitors about the difficulties of life in the remote Appalachian area.

The park and museum display Native American artifacts from the nearby Crab Orchard archeological site and also feature exhibits on the Revolutionary and Civil Wars and the agricultural and mining industries. Highway construction of US 19/460 unearthed the numerous Native American artifacts exhibited. The oldest points date back 11,000 years to the Paleo-Indians who hunted the woolly mammoth. (*Map on following page*)

Tour in a Nutshell

HISTORIC FARMSTEADS
(continued)

HISTORIC CRAB ORCHARD MUSEUM AND PIONEER PARK, in Tazewell, is open year-round. From I-81, take Exit 45 (Route 16) north to US Route 19. The site will be on the south side of Route 19. For more information, call (276) 988-6755 or visit www .craborchardmuseum.com. Admission is charged.

MEADOW FARM, in Glen Allen, is open Tuesday through Sunday from noon to 4 p.m. March through early December. From mid-January through early March, the farm is open only on weekends. From downtown Richmond, take I-95 12 miles north to Exit 84 (I-295 West). Take the Woodman Road South exit to 3400 Mountain Road and turn right. Follow the signs to the farm. Call (804) 501-5520 or visit www.co.henrico.va.us/ rec/current_programs/ meadow_farm.html for more information. Admission is free.

Virginia Farm Profile

The typical Virginia farmer is 56 years old.

The average farm is 180 acres and has assets worth about $385,000.

Farm debt is $40,000 per farm.

About 11% of Virginia farmers are female.

Farm production expenses average $79 a day, seven days a week.

The market value of an acre of the family farm averages $1920.

Today there are 49,000 farms in Virginia.

There were more than twice as many farms in Virginia in 1960 as there are today.

Virginia agriculture creates approximately 388,000 jobs in Virginia, or nearly 10% of the total jobs statewide. Of these, 235,800 jobs are directly related to agriculture, and 152,000 jobs are from agricultural effects.

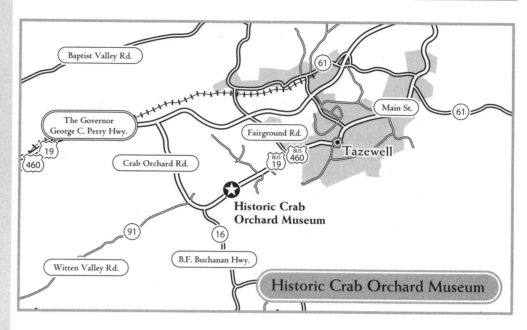

Historic Crab Orchard Museum

MEADOW FARM

High atop a grassy knoll in Henrico County stands the Meadow Farm living-history museum, where costumed guides tell stories of the lives of Dr. and Mrs. John Mosby Sheppard and their nine children, who lived in the middle-class farmhouse during the mid 1800s. Tours of the house, hearth cooking, a barnyard with animals, a smokehouse, the doctor's office, and a blacksmith forge are features of a farm visit.

The Sheppard family acquired the land in the 1700s as a 400-acre land grant. Cows, horses, sheep, pigs, and fowl breeds typical of the nineteenth century roam the 150 acres remaining today. The farm is listed on the National Register of Historic Places.

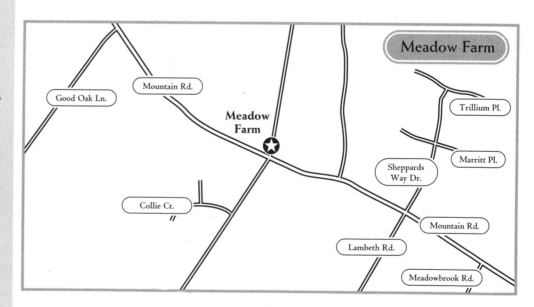

Meadow Farm

chapter two
PORK

〜 Pork was popular from the beginning of the Virginia Colony. In those days, all meat from the hog was called "bacon." But early hogs were not the short-snouted plump creatures we see today. The colonial hog had a long nose, large tusks, and a ridge of bristles down his back. Descendants of these hogs can still be found in rural parts of the South.

Most of Virginia's hogs are raised in the southeastern portion of the state, where the famous Smithfield hams—those which have been long cured and aged in the town of Smithfield—have been produced for more than 300 years. Cash receipts from hogs today generate $50 million annually for Virginia, making hogs Virginia's seventh most profitable edible farm product—more than tomatoes and apples. However, this is the value of the animals themselves. Once the meat is made into Smithfield hams and other retail pork products, the added value is much higher.

Pork

According to *The Hog Book* by William Hedgepeth, "pigs have been rooting about the globe's surface for at least 45 million years now, whereas men emerged and commenced to root around only about a million years ago, a mere gnat of time as such things are reckoned on the hogspan scale." One of the oldest livestock on earth, pigs were domesticated in China around 7000 B.C. Hernando de Soto introduced hogs to North America in Florida in 1539. Upon his death three years later, his original fifteen had bred to almost a thousand. Before becoming president, George Washington imported special hogs to establish breeding herds.

Compared to a decade ago, today's pork after cooking and trimming contains 31% less fat overall, 20% less saturated fat, 14% less calories, and 10% less cholesterol. Pork also provides a host of important nutrients, including protein, B vitamins, iron, and zinc.

When selecting pork, read the label to learn the kind of meat, the cut, and where on the animal the meat originated. Fresh pork comes mainly from the loin and shoulder areas and sometimes the leg and side. Cuts include chops, roasts, ribs, leg cutlets, and blade steaks. The leanest pork cuts are those with "leg" or "loin" in the names. Fresh pork will have a light-pink color. The lean part of the cut should be firm, fine grained, and free from excess moisture. The thin outside rim of fat should be white.

When buying, check the label's "sell by" date. After purchase, refrigerate pork right away. Keep refrigerated raw pork no longer than three to five days before cooking or freezing; uncooked ham, seven days; and ground pork or bulk sausage, two days. Packaged fresh pork may be refrigerated or frozen in its original wrappings. For long-time storage, enclose package in a plastic bag or wrap in foil.

Pork should be cooked to an internal temperature of 160° to 170° F, medium to well done. Pork cooked to 160° F will be slightly pink in the center. Well-done pork will have little or no pink color. Since pork is leaner than it used to be, overcooking will result in dry meat.

SMITHFRESH MAPLE-SMOKED HAM AND POTATO FRITTATA

The proprietors of the Smithfield Farm bed-and-breakfast make this recipe for guests, using the farm's maple-smoked organic ham and fresh free-range eggs.

3 cups diced peeled potatoes
1 each small red and green bell peppers, diced
2 cups shredded Monterey Jack, mozzarella, and cheddar cheese
2 cups shredded Smithfresh maple-smoked ham
¼ cup sliced green onion

8 Smithfresh free-range eggs, beaten
2 (12-ounce) cans evaporated milk or evaporated skim milk
¼ teaspoon pepper
⅛ teaspoon salt
¼ cup each chopped fresh thyme, rosemary, and chives

Grease a 3-quart square or rectangular baking dish. Arrange potatoes evenly in the bottom of the dish. Sprinkle with cheese, ham, and green onion. In a medium mixing bowl combine eggs, milk, pepper, salt, and herbs. Pour egg mixture over potato mixture in dish. (The dish may be covered and refrigerated at this point for several hours or overnight.) Bake, uncovered, in a 350° F oven for 40 to 45 minutes (or 55 to 60 minutes if made ahead and chilled), or until the center appears set and the edges are golden brown. Let stand 5 minutes before serving. Makes 10 servings.

Smithfield Farm is a seventh-generation working farm where the Pritchard family raises organic livestock in addition to operating the bed-and-breakfast. Set in the gentle hills of the Shenandoah Valley, in Berryville, the farm's nineteenth-century manor house is an example of traditional Federal period architecture. Smithfield Farm grounds, which include a gazebo and water garden, are particularly conducive to hammock dozing. A nature trail winds through the old orchard to entice wanderers. At the farm, visitors can buy all-natural beef, pork, and eggs, including the Smithfresh Organic Meat products (see the veal-and-potatoes recipe on page 34). Call (877) 955-4389 or visit www.smithfieldfarm.com for more information.

WILLARD SCOTT'S COUNTRY PORK SAUSAGE

If you want to have 96 people over for breakfast, this recipe is for you. Never fear: the sausage can be frozen. You can also cut the recipe in half.

24 pounds boneless pork (⅔ lean, ⅓ fat)
9 tablespoons salt
9 tablespoons rubbed sage

8 tablespoons black pepper
1 tablespoon cayenne pepper
1 tablespoon light brown sugar

Cut the pork into bite-size cubes and place them in a mixing bowl. Sprinkle in remaining ingredients. Mix with your hands the way you would toss a salad. Grind meat once or twice using a sausage grinder or in batches using a food processor. Divide sausage into 4-pound batches and place in plastic bags in the refrigerator for 24 hours for the flavors to blend. Divide sausage into 1-pound logs and freeze any you don't plan to cook within 2 days.

To cook, form into patties and brown in a medium-hot skillet until thoroughly cooked. Makes 24 pounds (96 servings).

For two decades, Alexandria-born Willard Scott was the nation's most beloved weatherman. He appeared on NBC's Today Show as weatherman and folklorist. Scott is now retired and lives on a farm in Middleburg where he cures hams and makes sausage. He also has a house in Alexandria.

VIRGINIA COUNTRY HAMS

Both "Virginia" and "Smithfield" are synonymous with "ham" in the minds of many. A Smithfield ham is a country ham cured—that is, made into the salty hams we all know and love—in the town of Smithfield, Virginia. However, country hams are made in many parts of the state.

Some Virginians call country ham "Redneck Prosciutto" and nothing could be closer to the truth. Prosciutto (from prosciugare, meaning "to lose water, to dry up") has been made in Italy since Roman times and was the protein of choice 1,000 years ago for Hannibal's army as it crossed the Alps with elephants.

Both prosciutto and country hams are dry cured and treated to destroy trichinae parasites. However in general, prosciutto manufacturers don't add smoke, pepper, or sugar to their ham cures as many country hams makers do. In fact, a few country ham manufacturers have prosciutto labels for their country hams.

In fact, Sam Edwards, President of S. Wallace Edwards & Sons, Inc., makes a Serrano-style ham, made in the Spanish custom, that mirrors Italian prosciutto.

Although it is safe to slice and eat raw Virginia country ham without soaking and cooking it first, most Virginians don't. Most Virginians and other lovers of country ham nearly always soak the hams to remove a lot of the salt before cooking.

MADE WITH MORE THAN A GRAIN OF SALT

Virginia hams have been made for about 400 years by a process of curing, smoking, and aging. Virginia Indians had a hand in the emergence of the state's famous country hams. The salt curing of pork dates back hundreds of years, but smoking meats was a new experience for the colonists. As early as 1608, Virginia Indians taught the Jamestown colonists the secret behind their methods of salting, smoking, and aging venison, and the Englishmen adapted this method to preserve the meat of the plentiful razorback hog.

Those early hogs were not the short-snouted, plump creatures we see today. The colonial hog had a long nose with large tusks and a ridge of bristles down his back. Descendants of these hogs can still be found in rural parts of the South. Today, the taste of the renown Virginia country ham is made by a traditional process developed by the early settlers.

We must thank our neighbors to the south for the pork to make Virginia hams. The majority of the two-million-plus hogs that become country hams every year are raised not in Virginia but in North Carolina. Even though we are forced to borrow North Carolina hogs to meet the huge demand for Virginia hams, a 1926 law passed by the Virginia General Assembly stated that a Smithfield country ham may be produced only in the town of Smithfield, Virginia.

It takes nine to twelve months to produce a genuine Smithfield long-cut country ham. The fresh hams are covered for 50 days in flaked salt and sodium nitrate of less than 1 ounce per ham. Then they are in the smokehouse for 30 days before being further aged for 100 more days.

Edwards' Virginia country hams are left in salt for considerably less time. "We rub the salt into the surface to keep it to a minimum," explains Edwards.

In the smokehouse, the hams are not wrapped. They are later placed in cotton bags for retail sale. But don't look for Virginia country hams in the refrigerated

Great Plate of Virginia

George Washington did sleep at the Smithfield Inn, but whether he ate the inn's famous ham biscuits is unknown. What is known is that those biscuits, winner of *USA Today*'s Great Plate award, are not to be missed. According to the paper, this simple country standard is "elegance personified" when prepared, as at the inn, with thin slices of smoky, salty Smithfield ham, whose "complex secondary flavors evoke the land and centuries of history."

But don't count on making these at home. Longtime Smithfield Inn cook Mozell Brown—a native of the town of Smithfield—doesn't share the recipe. And don't count on a crunch when biting into one of Brown's ham biscuits, because these soft, brown, butter-topped biscuits are more akin to yeast-risen dinner rolls than to the quick, firm bread Southerners typically associate with the term. Nevertheless, Brown's ham biscuits will make a trip to the inn worthwhile all by themselves.

The Cook's Guide to Country Ham

Uncooked country hams should be hung in a dry, cool place or stored in the refrigerator. It's normal to see mold on the outside of uncooked country hams. Scrub mold off with a stiff brush and hot water before soaking and cooking. Soak only uncooked (cloth-sack) hams. Change the water several times when soaking.

After washing and soaking your raw country ham 12 to 48 hours, consider one of these cooking methods:

STOVETOP BOILING: After ham has soaked, place skin-side down in a boiler on the stove. Add just enough water to cover ham. Bring water to a slight simmer. Cook about 25 minutes per pound, adding water as needed to keep ham covered. Some cooks add one or two cans of beer to the water. Ham is done when internal temperature reaches 160° F. Remove to carving board and let cool slightly before removing skin.

FIRST BAKING OPTION: Preheat the oven to 375° F. Place ham, skin-side up, in a roaster with 5 cups of water and cover with lid. Put roaster in the oven, and turn the oven to 500° F for 10 minutes only. Turn oven off and leave for 3 hours. Finally, turn the oven to 500° F for not more than 25 minutes. Turn the oven off and leave the ham in the oven for 6 to 8 hours. Do

case. They are shelf stable (stored at room temperature). Because they are dried, bacteria and other pathogens cannot grow on the meat.

For cooks with less time to spend soaking and boiling country hams, petite cooked country hams and cooked ham-biscuit slices are produced by S. Wallace Edwards & Sons, Inc. in Surry, Virginia. Edwards hams have been produced since 1926 by Sam Edwards' grandfather, who began the business by selling ham sandwiches on the ferry between Jamestown and Scotland, Virginia.

VIRGINIA COUNTRY HAM BASICS

After purchase, hang an uncooked country ham in a dry, cool place or store it in the refrigerator for up to a year. Although safe after that time, it may become extremely dry and moldy. After cooking, refrigerate the ham for up to a week or freeze for up to a month. If cured properly a raw country ham should not become rancid tasting.

It's normal to see mold on the outside of uncooked country hams. Simply scrub mold off with a stiff brush and hot water before soaking to remove some of the salt. Change the water several times and soak at least overnight and up to 48 hours. Follow the directions that accompany the ham or use one of the following cooking methods.

NOTE: Sam Edwards likes to pull his ham from the water at 155° F because the temperature will continue to rise to 160° F after taking it from the water. "A common mistake is overcooking country ham, which causes it to fall apart," says Edwards.

CARVING THE COUNTRY HAM

Carve your ham just prior to serving as follows:

1. Trim all excess fat off of ham if you desire. Turn ham lean side up, bone side down. Pick up knife with cutting hand. Grasp shank of ham with other hand so that the center of the ham is in front of you and not off to the side.

2. Going down about a third of the shank side of the ham, make a straight cross cut to give you a stopping point for the slices. Slice all the way down to the bone, rolling the knife forward and backward until ham is cut apart except for the bone.

3. Hold knife on a 45° angle and begin slicing from the center of ham to the cut you made in the ham earlier. Be sure to make slices even and very, very thin. Move the knife forward and backward around ham while slicing, and continue until most of the top of the ham is sliced. Turn ham on side, and continue slicing around the whole ham.

Support ham with cutting stand or towel while slicing. Save the bones and scraps for seasoning. Your cooked ham should be refrigerated and used within two weeks or sliced and frozen for later use. Each ham will provide up to 250–300 small party biscuits or rolls. Serving as a meal, up to 30 people can enjoy each ham.

TO MAKE A GLAZE FOR THE
SMITHFIELD OR COUNTRY HAM

1 cup brown sugar
½ teaspoon ground cloves or
   cinnamon

1 tablespoon dry mustard
2 tablespoons orange marmalade or
   fruit jams

Mix brown sugar, mustard, and ground cloves or cinnamon, adding just enough jam to make a stiff paste. Spread over hot, cooked ham. Put ham in 400° F oven for 15 to 20 minutes. Allow the glaze to caramelize and brown nicely. If desired, score and dot ham with cloves before glazing. This recipe can be doubled if you like a generous glaze or if your ham is larger than 13 pounds.

SMITHFIELD HAM BISCUITS
WITH ORANGE HONEY MUSTARD

*Have brunch or lunchtime guests assemble these hearty finger biscuits themselves,
or make them ahead of time to pack in the picnic basket for your next outing.*

⅓ cup Dijon mustard
3 tablespoons mayonnaise
¼ cup honey
2 tablespoons orange juice

16 slices thin-sliced cooked
   Smithfield Ham
16 biscuits or pan rolls, split

In a bowl, combine mustard, mayonnaise, honey, and juice. Spread biscuits with mixture and insert ham into biscuits. Makes 16 ham biscuits.

∽ *This recipe was contributed by V. W. Joyner & Co. of Smithfield, America's oldest continuously operating smokehouse, producing more than 50 dry-cured products. It is now owned by Smithfield and Co.* ∽

not open oven door at any point during this process. When done, insert thermometer to check if temperature has reached 160° F. Remove the skin while warm and trim away fat as desired.

SECOND BAKING OPTION: Preheat oven to 325° F. Shake 1 tablespoon of flour into a turkey-size oven bag inside a large roasting pan and add ham. Pour 4 cups of liquid into the bag (apple juice, wine, or any carbonated beverage) and close the bag with a nylon tie. Make 6 slits in the top of the bag, approximately ½ inch each. Puncture the thickest part of the ham with a knife and insert a meat thermometer. Cook 3½ to 4½ hours, or until the thermometer registers 160° F. Remove from the oven, discarding bag and drippings. Remove the skin and trim away fat as desired.

You've probably heard ads that pork is "the other white meat." This is a clever marketing ploy that attempts to capitalize on the consumer's increased use of "white" poultry and fish for perceived health benefits. Indeed, pork appears white after cooking; however, it certainly is not classified as a white meat biologically or nutritionally.

According to the U.S. Department of Agriculture, pork is classed as livestock, along with veal, lamb, and beef. All livestock are considered red meat. When fresh pork is cooked, it becomes lighter in color but it is still a red meat.

Oxygen is delivered to muscles by the red cells in the blood. One of the proteins in meat, myoglobin, holds the oxygen in the muscle. The amount of myoglobin in animal muscles determines the color of meat. Pork is a red meat because it contains more myoglobin than chicken or fish.

Pork is a nutrient-dense meat providing essential nutrients like vitamins B_1, B_2, B_6, and B_{12}, and is a good source of the minerals iron and zinc. A 3-ounce portion of cooked lean pork contains about 200 calories, 25 grams protein, 9 grams fat, and 70 milligrams cholesterol.

SAUSAGE WITH BUTTERMILK BISCUITS

This is an old Virginia breakfast favorite.

FOR BISCUITS:
  2 cups self-rising flour
  1 cup buttermilk
  ¼ cup oil

FOR GRAVY:
  1 pound bulk pork sausage
  ⅓ cup flour
  ½ teaspoon each salt and pepper
  3 cups milk

Preheat oven to 450° F. Place flour in a bowl. Add buttermilk and oil. Stir until no longer sticky. Form into a ball and turn out onto a floured board. Roll or pat dough ½-inch thick. Cut into biscuits and place on a greased baking sheet. Bake 12 to 15 minutes, or until light brown. Makes 12 biscuits.

Heat a large skillet over high heat. Crumble sausage and brown. Turn down the heat to medium and cook until sausage is no longer pink. Remove sausage using a slotted spoon, leaving 3 tablespoons drippings in skillet. Stir in flour, salt, and pepper. Brown flour for a few minutes, stirring often. Gradually stir in milk. Cook and stir until thick. Add sausage, reheat, and serve over biscuits. Makes 4 servings.

This recipe, provided courtesy of Rachel and Charlie Adkins of Ferrum, is from the pamphlet Blue Ridge Family Recipes, *distributed by the Blue Ridge Institute of Ferrum College.*

MAPLE MUSTARD GRILLED PORK TENDERLOIN

This simple marinade turns tenderloin into an impressive main dish.

2 pork tenderloins (about 1¼ pounds total)
2 tablespoons Dijon mustard
1 tablespoon pure maple syrup
2 teaspoons vegetable oil
1 teaspoon sambal oelek (Oriental chili-garlic sauce)

Place pork tenderloins in a plastic bag, non-metal bowl, or sealable container. Blend remaining ingredients; pour over pork; seal or cover and refrigerate for 3 hours or overnight.

Preheat barbecue on high; reduce temperature to medium. Remove pork from marinade and discard marinade. Place pork on grill. Close barbecue cover and grill 12 to 14 minutes, turning several times. Remove from grill; tent with foil and let stand 5 minutes before slicing. Serve with mushrooms, green beans, and a pasta salad. Makes 4 servings.

DOLORES'S WRAPPED PORK ROAST

Season this roast with salt and pepper or with favorite rubs or seasoning compounds, such as Szechuan or Thai seasoning.

3 to 5 pounds boneless or bone-in
   pork roast
2 tablespoons olive oil
½ cup all-purpose flour

1 teaspoon salt
1 teaspoon black pepper
1 bottle dry white table wine

With the rack in the lower third of the oven, preheat the oven to 450° F. Gloss a roasting pan with cooking spray. Score the fat on the roast. Massage the roast all over with olive oil. Combine the flour with the salt and black pepper. Roll the pork roast in the seasoned flour until coated on all sides.

Roast the meat for 30 minutes. (It should be golden brown. If not, roast several minutes longer.) Pour half the bottle of wine over the roast. Reduce the oven temperature to 400° F and roast for 30 more minutes. Pour the remaining wine over the roast. Reduce the oven temperature to 350° F and cook the pork, basting every 15 minutes, until it reaches 160° F. Remove the pork from the oven and wrap securely in heavy-duty aluminum foil. Keep the meat at room temperature for at least 30 minutes before serving. The wrapped meat will hold and stay warm for at least 1 hour and it will be uniformly cooked and tender throughout.

Lexington resident Dolores Kostelni is a restaurant reviewer for The Roanoke Times *and has contributed a weekly food column, "The Happy Cook," for the Lexington* News-Gazette *since 1979. She hosts a call-in radio program of the same name on WREL-AM in Rockbridge County.*

Recipe Tip

"I like my pork well done, but I also desire it tender and moist, a difficult state to achieve using today's leaner meat. The trick depends on roasting the pork to exactly medium (about 160° F), then wrapping it tightly in heavy-duty aluminum foil immediately after taking it out of the oven. This way the pork completes cooking in its wrap, does not dry out, and produces succulent meat with delicious flavor."

—Dolores Kostelni

The Smell of Bacon Frying

"Before anyone imagined how long the Civil War would last, Confederate Commissary General Lieutenant Colonel Frank Ruffin supposed the forces in Virginia could be supplied within the state. He built one packing plant at Richmond and another—the largest in the South—at Thoroughfare Gap (Prince William County), close to the two wealthiest livestock-raising counties, Fauquier and Loudoun. By the time General Joseph Johnston abandoned Manassas Junction in March 1862, Ruffin had stockpiled more than two million pounds of pork and beef at Thoroughfare Gap—perhaps the only time the Confederate Commissary got ahead of demand. When the packing house went up in flames, one retreating soldier wrote that the smell of bacon frying lingered in the air for 20 miles."

—G. Terry Sharrar,
A Kind of Fate, Agricultural Change in Virginia, 1861-1920

chapter three

LAMB

∾ *These sure-footed puff balls love wandering freely over grassy hills, grazing, and playing, which explains why most Virginia sheep are raised in the Shenandoah Mountains and Allegheny foothills. There are more than 1,500 farms in Virginia raising nearly 70,000 sheep and lambs. Cash receipts total more than $3 million annually. All 50 states raise these animals, and the Old Dominion ranks in the middle. Of the state's edible farm products, sheep and lambs are more profitable than watermelons and peaches but less so than cabbage and bell peppers.*

In many countries, lamb is the major source of meat eaten. But, according to the USDA's Economic Research Service, each American eats only 0.8 pounds of lamb each year—possibly because many Americans think of lamb as a springtime food. However, lamb can be enjoyed in a variety of dishes year-round. From sheep there's also wool. Virginia produces more than 250,000 pounds annually.

THE NEW AMERICAN LAMB BURGER

Serve your lamb burgers on toasted sourdough buns with spicy tomato and cilantro relish, cucumber, yogurt, mint, and dal (a spicy lentil dish).

1½ pounds ground lamb	2 teaspoons ground coriander
3 tablespoons plain yogurt	1 teaspoon salt
1 tablespoon minced fresh ginger root	½ teaspoon pepper
2 teaspoons ground cumin	1 pinch each ground cloves, nutmeg, cinnamon, and cayenne pepper

Crumble lamb into a mixing bowl. Add remaining ingredients and mix gently; mixing too long results in mushy burgers. Shape into 6 patties. Chill until ready to grill. Grill over hot coals to medium doneness, or until a food thermometer reads 160° F. Makes 6 servings.

⌒ The recipe for this sandwich, contributed by the U.S. Army Culinary Olympic Team, captured a gold medal in the 1992 world military culinary championship held in Frankfurt, Germany. The team again won the gold medal in 2000. The team is based in Fort Lee. ⌒

HAMPTON MANOR CURRIED LAMB

One of the best uses for a leftover leg of lamb or roast is in a curry dish.

3 tablespoons butter	2 tablespoons flour
½ medium-sized onion, diced	2 to 3 teaspoons curry powder
1 clove garlic, diced	2 cups chicken broth
½ apple, diced	2 cups cubed cooked lamb
2 ribs celery, diced	hot cooked rice

CONDIMENTS:

chopped hard-cooked eggs, chopped peanuts, coconut, chopped sweet pickles, bacon bits, diced banana, crushed pineapple, chopped fresh tomatoes, and mango chutney

Melt butter in a large skillet. Sauté onion, garlic, apple, and celery. Blend in flour and curry powder. Cook for 1 minute. Add broth and stir constantly until sauce boils. Add lamb and simmer 10 minutes. Serve over rice with assorted condiments. Makes 4 servings.

⌒ Hampton Manor is a lovely home in Caroline County built from Jeffersonian plans during the mid 1800s. In the late 1930s, the surrealist painter Salvador Dali lived in the house. This recipe is a favorite of the DeJarnette family that built the home, which is now privately owned and not open to the public. ⌒

Look for good marbling (white flecks of fat within the meat muscle) and meat that is finely textured and firm. The meat should be pink and the fat should be firm, white, and not too thick. The USDA quality grades are reliable guides.

There are five major cuts (shoulder, rack, shank/breast, loin, and leg) into which lamb is separated. The rack is the prime rib (sometimes called the hotel rack) of the carcass, which includes ribs 6 through 12. The rack is split to make two prime lamb rib roasts. A "lamb crown roast" is made by sewing two rib roasts together to form a circle or crown. Loin chops and rib chops are the most tender. Less expensive blade and arm chops (from the shoulder) and sirloin chops (from the leg) can be just as tender, but they are not as attractive, because the meat is separated by bands of connective tissue.

The fell is the thin, paper-like covering on the outer fat. It should not be removed from roasts and legs, because it helps these cuts retain their shape and juiciness during cooking. The fell has usually been removed at the market from smaller cuts, such as chops. If the phrase "spring lamb" is on a meat label, it means the lamb was produced between March and October.

"Despite his age and frail condition, [President William Henry] Harrison was a great walker. He arose early and trotted off to market, for doing his own shopping was one of his great domestic pleasures. Then he would go back to the White House, well satisfied that his choice of meat would be prepared by the cook to his satisfaction."
—Poppy Cannon,
The Presidents' Cookbook

Virginia Food and Beverage Directory

The Virginia Food and Beverage Directory contains a listing of producers and processors of a vast array of unique products including specialty fruits and vegetables, peanuts, hams, jams and jellies, cookies, cakes, candies, farm-raised fish, lamb and veal products, poultry products, herbs, spices, seasonings, cheeses, and much more. Listings include wholesale, retail, and foodservice companies and their complete product lines under all applicable categories. Also included are company mailing addresses, phone and fax numbers, and Internet e-mail addresses (if available). All producers and processors are located in Virginia. The Virginia Food & Beverage Directory is online at: www.vdacs.state.va.us.

PAN-BROILED LAMB CHOPS À LA HARRISON

President William Henry Harrison liked these lamb chops for breakfast.

2 lamb chops per person   fresh mint or parsley
salt and pepper

Sear the chops in a hot, non-stick skillet. Season with salt and pepper. Reduce the heat and allow chops to simmer. Pour off any fat as it builds up. Do not overcook. Lamb is at its most delicious slightly underdone and pink. Garnish with mint. Serve 2 lamb chops per person.

This recipe was adapted from The Presidents' Cookbook. *Our ninth president was born on a plantation in Charles City County in 1773. Harrison's father Benjamin signed the Declaration of Independence and served as governor of Virginia. Harrison became president in 1841, but, tragically, caught pneumonia and died one month after taking office.*

ROAST LAMB LEG ROSEMARY

Have the butcher de-bone your leg of lamb for ease of carving as you inhale the delightful roasted aroma.

1 boned leg of lamb (7 to 8 pounds)   1 large onion, sliced
3 cloves garlic, cut in half   2 bulbs fennel, sliced
2 tablespoons ground rosemary   3 carrots, diced
salt and pepper to taste   1 cup water

Preheat oven to 350° F. Insert garlic halves into bone pocket. Rub all sides of roast with rosemary and season with salt and pepper. Place onion, fennel, and carrots in the bottom of a shallow roasting pan and place roast on top. Pour water into pan and roast until lamb reaches 145° to 160° F as measured with a food thermometer.

Transfer lamb to a platter along with vegetables. Tent with aluminum foil. Strain juices and remove fat. Thicken, using 1 tablespoon cornstarch per cup of pan juices. Add vegetables to thickened juice. Carve roast and serve with sauce. Makes 8 to 10 servings.

JEFFERSON HOTEL'S ROASTED RACK OF SUMMERFIELD FARMS SPRING LAMB

with Byrd Mills Stone-Ground Grits, Mint-Cherry Chutney, and Lamb Jus

FOR GRITS (begin preparing 5 hours before serving):

1½ cups Byrd Mills stone-ground grits

2 cups chicken broth or water

3 cups whole milk

¾ cup butter

½ cup fresh Marscapone cheese

salt and white pepper to taste

FOR LAMB:

2 whole frenched racks of lamb (8 ribs each)

salt and white pepper to taste

⅓ cup whole-grain mustard

¼ cup Jack Daniels bourbon

1 cup fresh bread crumbs

FOR MINT-CHERRY CHUTNEY:

1 cup dried Bing cherries

5 ounces port wine

1 shallot, minced

1 tablespoon red wine vinegar

1 tablespoon sugar

2 tablespoon chiffonade of fresh mint leaves

Place grits, broth, milk, and butter in a large, heavy-bottomed pot. Place over low-to-medium heat. Bring to a simmer, cover and cook, stirring occasionally, about 5 hours, or until soft and creamy. Make sure they do not stick.

Preheat oven to 450° F. Season all sides of lamb with salt and pepper. Mix mustard with bourbon. Place a thin coating on front and back of lamb, coat with crumbs, and brown the front side of the lamb in a hot pan coated with 2 tablespoons butter.

Meanwhile, place cherries, wine, shallots, vinegar, and sugar for chutney in a small non-reactive saucepan over low heat. Cover and begin cooking. Stand racks of lamb in a shallow roasting pan and roast 18 to 20 minutes, or to desired doneness (for medium rare, cook to 145° F; for medium doneness, cook to 160° F); continue cooking covered chutney about 25 to 30 minutes, or until the cherries are rehydrated and flavorful.

Remove lamb from oven and allow it to rest 8 to 10 minutes. Fold mint into chutney and finish grits by folding in cheese, salt, and pepper. To serve, cut lamb between chops and arrange 4 on each plate. Accompany with lamb jus, grits, chutney, and seasonal green vegetables. Makes 4 servings.

∽ *This recipe was provided courtesy of Walter Bundy, executive chef at Lemaire, the five-diamond restaurant of The Jefferson Hotel built in Richmond in 1895 and recognized as one of the grandest in America. Lemaire features distinctive southern dishes and is named for Etienne Lemaire, who served as Maître d'Hôtel to Thomas Jefferson. Lemaire is widely credited for introducing to America the fine art of cooking with wines (phone (800) 424-8014).* ∽

Local Farmers Make the Difference

Fine cooking requires fine ingredients, and that is why executive chef Walter Bundy attributes part of the success of The Jefferson Hotel's fine-dining restaurant, Lemaire, to the work of local farmers. Those who run Summerfield Farms, which provides Lemaire with its lamb, are a perfect example. "At Summerfield," Bundy notes, "the animals are free to roam and graze and they receive plenty of their mother's milk, hay, and water. The end product is a rosy-colored meat with a wonderful, gentle flavor. It is this dedication to excellence that makes Summerfield Farms one of the best purveyors in the United States."

Byrd Mills, the Ashland company that produces the coarsely-ground grits used in the hotel's roasted lamb with grits, is another local farming operation from which the restaurant benefits. "It is essential to have such a great product for this tremendously Southern dish," says Bundy.

Contact Byrd Mills at (888) 897-3336 or visit www.byrd mills.com.

JAMESTOWN AND YORKTOWN:
The Beginning and Ending of Colonial America

• JAMESTOWN •
AND
YORKTOWN

Jamestown Settlement and Yorktown Victory Center living-history sites use films, museum collections, galleries, and outdoor participatory programs in full-scale re-created settings to educate visitors about the nation's first colonial settlement and first post-revolutionary settlement.

DAYS/HOURS: Jamestown Settlement is open daily, except Christmas and New Year's Days.

FEES: A combo ticket admits holders to both Jamestown and Yorktown or you can purchase separate tickets.

DIRECTIONS: Jamestown is 7 miles from Colonial Williamsburg, traveling southwest on the scenic Colonial Parkway. Yorktown is at the east end of the Parkway, 13 miles from Williamsburg.

MORE INFORMATION: The Jamestown–Yorktown Foundation can be reached at (888) 593-4682, (757) 253-4838, or via www.historyisfun.org. For information about Jamestown, the Original Site, contact the National Park Service at (888) 593-4682 or go to www.nps.gov/colo. The park is open from 9 a.m. to 5 p.m. daily. Admission is charged.

Jamestown, site of the first permanent English settlement in the New World, and Yorktown, where Lord Cornwallis surrendered to General Washington, are on a narrow peninsula of Virginia between the James and York Rivers, only 20 miles apart. Today they are living-history museums offering a myriad of activities and exhibits. Both are of interest not only to American-history enthusiasts but particularly to Virginia farm-history buffs, because they enlighten visitors as to the farming methods of three early groups of Virginians: Native Americans (at the Powhatan Indian Village in Jamestown), the first settlers (at the James Fort at Jamestown), and the first citizens of the United States (at the 1780s Farm at Yorktown).

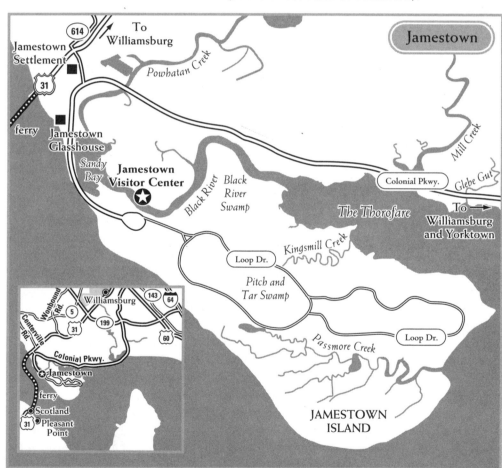

JAMESTOWN SETTLEMENT AND THE ORIGINAL SITE

On May 14, 1607, three merchant ships loaded with passengers and cargo—*Susan Constant, Godspeed,* and *Discovery*—reached an island in what the settlers would call the James River. Today the uninhabited island, called Jamestown, the Original Site, is joined to the mainland by an isthmus and is part of Colonial National Historical Park. The Archearium contains a display of seventeenth-century artifacts. Visitors drive along a five-mile nature route and stop to read information on signs.

On the mainland is another site where visitors can learn about the lives of Virginia's first settlers, Jamestown Settlement. Full-scale replicas of the three merchant ships convey the strenuous living conditions endured by the voyagers, while the re-created James Fort reveals how colonists endured the unfamiliar environment of coastal Virginia. The fort features replicas of Jamestown's earliest buildings, including homes, a church, a store-house, and an armory. Interpreters show activities typical of daily life, such as farming, animal care, blacksmithing, and cooking.

In the Powhatan Indian Village, visitors are introduced to the world of Pocahontas. The re-created village consists of several dwellings, a garden, and a ceremonial dance circle. The indoor Powhatan Indian Gallery traces the movement of people into Virginia beginning more than 10,000 years ago, as well as the evolution of their technology over the centuries.

YORKTOWN VICTORY CENTER

The majority of Virginians during the years immediately following the American Revolution lived and worked on small farms, usually less than 200 acres in size. At Yorktown's re-created 1780s farm, historical interpreters demonstrate the seasonal cycle of work. The site includes a home, a separate kitchen, a tobacco barn, fenced crop fields, and gardens planted with 1780s heirloom seeds.

The typical Virginia planter made his living by growing tobacco to sell and by cultivating corn for food and animal fodder. Farm families grew most of their own food in kitchen gardens tended by the women and children. The crops were grown in raised mounds because they were easier to hoe and didn't have to be plowed. Hogs, cattle, and poultry provided their meat, eggs, and dairy products. Hogs were salt cured, and often several farms shared a smokehouse.

Visitors are encouraged to participate in the seasonal farm activities: planting, hoeing, weeding, and watering crops; feeding the animals; scutching and combing flax; and making cornbread, soap, and candles.

The **Waterman's Museum** recounts the seafaring history of the area, where, along the waterfront, there were docks, ship-repair facilities, and a ferry that crossed the narrow river to Gloucester Point on the other side. A Revolutionary War army encampment and eyewitness accounts are also on site at Yorktown.

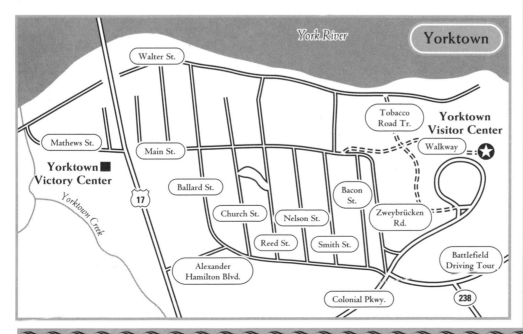

Rediscovering Jamestown

Central to Virginia's 400th anniversary commemoration in 2007 is Jamestown, the original site. The Jamestown Rediscovery Project was launched in 1994 by the Association for the Preservation of Virginia's Antiquities. In its first six years, the project has uncovered the remains of the 1607 Fort, long-believed lost to the James River, and more than 350,000 artifacts that reveal the early life of the settlement. Excavated seventeenth-century pottery indicates imports from many countries. Colonists didn't make pottery until about 1630. The Jamestown potter produced lead-glazed earthenware cooking pots, storage jars, pans, porringers, pipkins, pitchers, and mugs. The animal bones from food supplies reveal that the 104 men and boys who landed at Jamestown survived primarily on fish and turtles. The colonists also dined on rays, birds, oysters, raccoons, and other native Virginia animals, as well as provisions of beef and pork they brought from England. There is no indication the men relied on domesticated animals for food in the first years. For more information, visit www.jamestown 2007.org.

Bison

Bison (buffalo) are native to North America. Large herds once migrated through Virginia's Shenandoah Valley, making a path followed by Indians. Later, when pioneers migrated to Virginia from Pennsylvania and places farther north, that same path became known as "The Great Wagon Road." Once about 60 million in number, beginning in the 1600s bison were hunted for their furs and later for their tongues, bones, and meats; by 1893 there were only slightly more than 300 bison left. Currently there are more than 150,000 animals being raised across North America. Some wild bison run free in protected lands such as Yellowstone National Park.

The American buffalo belongs to the bovine family. The bison bull is the largest animal indigenous to North America. A bull can stand taller than six feet at the hump and weigh more than a ton. They are strong and aggressive and can jump as well as deer, outmaneuver horses, and break through fences that would imprison other livestock.

Bison are raised on the open range and eat hay or grass. During the last 90 to 120 days before slaughter they are given grain so their fat will be white as preferred by consumers. (The fat of grass-fed animals is yellow.) Some 20,000 buffalo are slaughtered each year, compared to approximately 125,000 cattle per day.

chapter four

FARM-RAISED GAME

⁓ *Consumer interest in nutrition and restaurant chefs who want unique meats on their menus have helped establish a market for Virginia's farm-raised game industry. Such diverse critters as bison, venison, and rabbits have rekindled an interest in meats that were once commonplace but today seem odd. No figures are available for this specialty niche, but the meats are meeting with approval from Virginians eager to try something new or those sticking to low-fat diets. Most farms that raise game animals are in the Shenandoah Valley and foothills. Missing, perhaps fortunately, from this group are the squirrels once integral to Virginia's famous Brunswick Stew recipe, which modern Virginians make with chicken.*

GEORGETOWN BISON FAJITAS

A nice change of pace for this Mexican classic.

1 pound Georgetown Farm pure
    bison fajita meat (or beef skirt
    steak)
½ teaspoon garlic salt

½ teaspoon pepper
¼ cup fresh lime juice (from about 2
    to 3 limes)
8 flour or corn tortillas, warmed

Sprinkle both sides of bison with lime juice, garlic salt, and pepper, and place slices in plastic bag. Tie bag securely and marinate in refrigerator 6 to 8 hours. Drain marinade and broil meat over medium-high mesquite coals 2 to 3 minutes on each side. Slice crosswise into thin strips. Serve in warmed flour or corn tortillas. Garnish with tomato, bell pepper, guacamole, onion, sour cream and/or picante sauce. Makes 4 servings.

∽ Recipe provided courtesy of Georgetown Farm. ∽

BUFF-A-LOAF UNDER ORANGE GLAZE

This fast-cooking meat loaf looks attractive baked in a ring pan and topped with glaze.

2 beaten eggs
¾ cup milk
½ cup fine, dry bread crumbs
¼ cup onion, finely chopped
1 tablespoon chopped fresh parsley
½ teaspoon ground sage
1 teaspoon salt

dash of pepper
1½ pounds ground bison or lean
    ground beef
3 tablespoons light corn syrup
2 teaspoons orange zest (finely grat-
    ed orange color from peel)

Thoroughly mix eggs and milk. Stir in bread crumbs, onion, parsley, sage, salt, and pepper. Add meat and mix well. Pat into a 6-cup ring mold.

Conventional-oven directions: Preheat oven to 350° F. Bake 40 minutes, or until mixture reaches 160° F as measured with a food thermometer. Remove meat loaf and place on a heatproof platter, drizzle with mixture of corn syrup and zest, and bake 5 minutes more.

Microwave-oven directions: Place the loaf on a 9 × 2-inch pie plate. Cover loosely with waxed paper. Cook in microwave on high power for 10 to 12 minutes, or until nearly done, rotating a quarter turn every 3 minutes. Combine syrup and orange zest. Spoon over meat. Cover with waxed paper and cook on high power for 2 to 3 minutes. Let stand, covered, for 5 minutes. Makes 6 servings.

∽ Recipe provided courtesy of Georgetown Farm. ∽

Basic Bison Cooking Tips

"There is no such thing as tough bison meat, only improperly instructed cooks," says Georgetown Farm's operations manager Charles Holley. Although bison meat is similar to beef and can be substituted for beef in recipes, it needs to be handled and cooked differently. The important things to remember are not to overcook it and not to allow the meat to dry out. Individual cuts of bison appear identical to beef, except for color. Raw bison meat is darker than beef—a dark, rich red with no marbling. The meat contains less fat and therefore less moisture than beef. Bison should be cooked to medium-rare or medium doneness. If you prefer meat well done, cook bison in a slow cooker. Cover the meat to retain moisture, whether grilling, roasting, or microwaving. Initially searing the meat on the outside will also help lock the moisture in. Stir-frying is also an excellent method of cooking bison.

Bison has a sweeter, richer flavor than beef and is leaner and lower in fat than beef, poultry, and other meats. A three-ounce portion of roasted buffalo contains about 145 calories, 22 grams of protein, 2 grams of fat, and 66 milligrams cholesterol. This is comparable to a lean cut of beef, such as the eye-of-round roast.

ROSEMARY-MARINATED BISON STEAK

Add a baked potato or rice for a lovely steak dinner.

1 bison steak (about 1½ to 2 pounds) or individual-size steaks
1 tablespoon dried rosemary

½ cup red wine
¼ cup olive oil

Combine ingredients and marinate steak for about 2 hours in the refrigerator. Let the meat warm to room temperature (about 30 to 60 minutes after removing from refrigerator). Grill over hot coals to medium-rare or medium doneness. Makes 6 servings.

✍ Recipe provided courtesy of Georgetown Farm and Buffalo Hill. ✍

Rabbit

Rabbits sold in the United States are not North American cottontails; rather, they are a cross between New Zealand and Belgian varieties, imported Chinese rabbits, or Scottish hares. No hormones are used in rabbit raising. The meat is finely grained and mild in flavor, and practically all of it is white. Like other lean white meats, rabbit meat is a good source of high-quality protein. A 100 gram (3.5-ounce) portion of cooked rabbit contains about 200 calories, 30 grams protein, 8 grams fat, and 80 milligrams cholesterol.

When cooking rabbit, first cut it into parts. To roast, set the oven temperature no lower than 325° F. Rabbit can be broiled about 15 minutes on each side. For safety, as well as doneness, the USDA recommends cooking rabbit to an internal temperature of 180° F. The use of a meat thermometer is recommended to make sure that the meat is neither under- nor overcooked.

RABBIT IN MUSTARD SAUCE

This is a classic French preparation in which the mustard perfectly complements the rabbit. You can substitute chicken thighs for the rabbit.

1 young rabbit (about 2½ pounds), cut into 8 serving pieces
salt and pepper to taste
½ cup Dijon mustard, divided
3 tablespoons oil
1 tablespoon unsalted butter
2½ cups dry white wine, divided

2 medium onions, chopped
1 tablespoon flour
1 teaspoon dried thyme
1 bay leaf
chopped fresh parsley
cooked noodles or rice

Salt and pepper rabbit. Brush one side of rabbit with ¼ cup mustard. Heat oil and butter in a large skillet over medium heat. Brown the mustard-coated side of rabbit about 10 minutes. Turn rabbit over and brush with remaining ¼ cup mustard. Cook until medium brown, about 10 minutes. Remove rabbit to a large platter. Deglaze pan using ½ cup wine. Add onions and cook, stirring frequently, until medium brown, about 5 minutes. Sprinkle flour over onions; stir to coat. Pour in remaining 2 cups wine, thyme, and bay leaf. Add rabbit pieces, adjust heat to medium, and cover slightly with lid. Simmer until rabbit is tender and sauce thickens, about 1 hour. Sprinkle with parsley and serve over cooked noodles or rice. Makes 6 servings.

SLOW-COOKED DORCHESTER VENISON STEW

Using a slow cooker tenderizes the venison in this no-watching-required stew.

6 carrots, peeled and sliced
6 small potatoes, peeled and
  quartered
4 ribs celery, sliced
1 medium onion
3 tablespoons oil, divided
2 to 3 pounds venison, cut into
  1-inch cubes
¾ cup flour, divided

4 cups hot water
1 (10½-ounce) can condensed beef
  broth
4 teaspoons Worcestershire sauce
1 bay leaf
2 teaspoons salt
1 teaspoon sugar
¼ teaspoon coarse black pepper

Turn slow cooker on high and add carrots, potatoes, celery, and onion. Dredge meat in flour. Heat 1 tablespoon oil in a large, heavy skillet. Brown meat 1 pound at a time before transferring to the slow cooker. Add water, broth, Worcestershire sauce, bay leaf, salt, sugar, and pepper. Cover and turn to low. Cook 10 to 12 hours, or until venison is tender. If desired, thicken gravy with a mixture of flour and water. Makes 6 to 8 servings.

Adapted from a recipe in Cardinal Cuisine, a Cookbook.

DEER STEAKS WITH CARAMELIZED ONIONS

Here's a simple way to prepare tender venison steaks.

3 tablespoons butter, divided
3 tablespoons oil, divided
2 onions, cut into ¼-inch slices

flour, salt, and pepper
4 venison steaks, about 1 to 1½
  inches thick

Heat 2 tablespoons butter and 2 tablespoons oil in a skillet over medium heat. Add onions; season with salt and pepper. Stirring often, cook onions about 20 minutes, or until they turn caramel color. Remove onions from skillet; keep warm.

Dredge steaks in flour seasoned with salt and pepper. Add remaining butter and oil to same skillet. Fry the steaks about 7 minutes on each side. Serve immediately, topped with the onions. Makes 4 servings.

Recipe inspired by dairy farmer and hunter Keith Dixon.

Venison

In culinary terms, venison can be meat from deer, elk, moose, caribou, antelope, or pronghorn, though the name of the animal from which the meat came must be specified on the package label.

Farm-raised game live in confined outdoor areas and are fed wheat, alfalfa, or corn. What the animal eats and how much exercise it gets can affect the taste of the meat. The tenderness of a particular cut of game is similar to the corresponding cut of domestically raised meat or poultry. All game animals are red meat.

Venison cuts include boneless tenderloin (the most tender); leg steaks; rump, neck, and shoulder roasts; and ground meat. Americans ate 2.5 million pounds of venison in 1996, and the market has been growing by 25% annually.

Deauville Fallow Deer Farm

At the 25-acre Deauville Fallow Deer Farm in Basye, owners Alex and Gail Rose raise an ancient breed of deer prized for its delectable and nutritious meat. Fallow venison graced the tables of Egyptian pharaohs and Mesopotamian kings. The Roses have a herd of 160 deer raised on chemical-free pastures. They also raise exotic chickens from 16 countries and sells fresh eggs in their natural colors—blue, green, brown, and white (phone (540) 856-2130).

CHIPPOKES PLANTATION STATE PARK
Chippokes Farm and Forestry Museum

• CHIPPOKES PLANTATION STATE PARK •

Chippokes Plantation State Park contains a farming museum, a furnished nineteenth-century mansion, a restored sawmill, a visitor center, campgrounds, a swimming complex, picnic facilities, and hiking and biking trails. In addition to permanent exhibits, special displays and demonstrations occur throughout the year.

DAYS/HOURS: The park is open Saturday from 10 a.m. to 4 p.m. and Sunday 1 to 4 p.m. between March and May and between September and November. Between June and August, hours are Wednesday through Sunday, 10 a.m. to 6 p.m. The park is closed from December through February. The Pork, Peanut, and Pine Festival is held the third weekend in July to celebrate the three main industries of Surry County. The Steam and Gas Engine Show, held the second weekend in June, features tractor pulls and working antique engines, trucks, cars, and tractors.

FEES: A combination pass for the mansion and museum or an annual family pass can be purchased. Parking/admission to the park is charged daily. Annual park admission per car can be purchased.

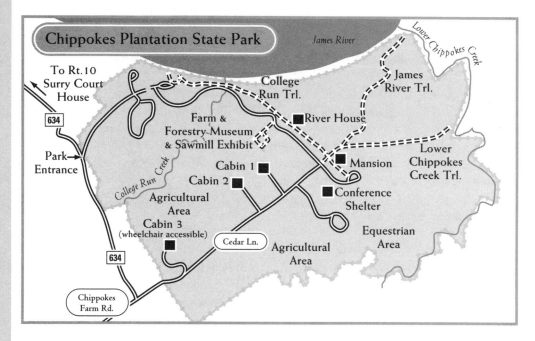

Chippokes Plantation State Park is one of the oldest working farms in the United States. Within the park is Chippokes Farm and Forestry Museum, housed in seven white buildings that represent various stages of farm life and contain 8000 farm artifacts that date from the 1600s through the early twentieth century.

The picturesque plantation has kept its original boundaries since the 1600s and has a variety of cultivated gardens and native woodland. Captain William Powell, a prominent colonial gentleman, received a grant for 550 acres of river frontage on Chippokes Creek in 1619. Under the ownership of Colonel Henry Bishop in 1646, the plantation was expanded to its present boundaries encompassing 1403 acres. The plantation and the bordering creek were named for an Indian chief who befriended the early English settlers.

To see the Farm and Forestry Museum, turn right off the main park-entry road onto Plantation Road. The exhibits in the self-guided tours are designed to educate visitors about farm life in the rural Virginia of 1850; topics include building a farm, preparing the soil, planting, cultivating, and harvesting. Additional exhibits feature tools used by craftsmen such as the blacksmith, wheelwright, cooper, and cobbler. Chippokes features many rare artifacts. One of the oldest is an oxen-drawn plow called a rooter or bull-tongue plow. It dates to the early 1600s. Another of the more valuable artifacts is the pre–Civil War wooden-tooth cultivator.

The museum is connected to an old restored sawmill by an 1800-foot forestry interpretive trail that offers a spectacular view of one of the plantation's ravines. If you wish, drive east on the same road to reach the sawmill, which is operated on special occasions, such as during the Chippokes Steam and Gas Engine Show and during the Pork, Peanut, and Pine Festival. After seeing the sawmill, continue walking or driving to the Chippokes Mansion, built in 1854. Tours of the Italianate home, furnished in period antiques, are available weekends April through October. The formal gardens surrounding the Chippokes Mansion are accented by azaleas, crepe myrtle, boxwood, and seasonal flowers.

In addition to the historic attractions, the park has a wide variety of traditional park offerings, including an Olympic-sized swimming pool, picnic facilities, and hiking and biking trails, portions of which are accessible to people with physical disabilities. The park also has picnic shelters, three furnished cabins (one, two, and three bedrooms), and 32 wooded sites, all with electricity and water.

Chippokes Plantation State Park is a non-profit site operated by the Virginia Department of Conservation and Recreation in cooperation with the Chippokes Plantation Farm Foundation.

Tour in a Nutshell

• CHIPPOKES PLANTATION STATE PARK •
(*continued*)

DIRECTIONS: From Williamsburg, take Jamestown Road to Jamestown and take the free Jamestown-Scotland Ferry across the James River. Follow the road to Route 10 and make a left. Turn left at Route 634 (Alliance Road) and look for the park entrance, 4 miles down, on the left.

MORE INFORMATION: Phone Chippokes Farm and Forestry Museum at (757) 294-3439. Phone Chippokes Plantation State Park at (757) 294-3625 or visit www .dcr.virginia.gov/state_parks/ chf.shtml. For reservations or information on availability of cabins, camping accommodations, or particular park amenities, call (800) 933-PARK (in Richmond, 225-3867). You can also reserve online. For information on other Surry County sites, visit www.tour surryva.com.

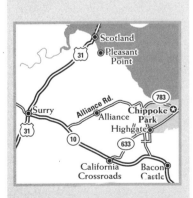

part three
SHELLFISH AND FISH

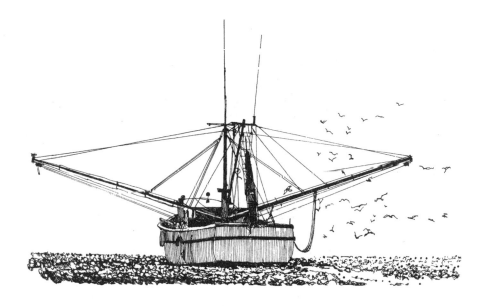

As the rising sun shimmers over the Chesapeake Bay, Virginia's watermen are already on the job, where they catch more than 700 million pounds of seafood a year. These hardy souls plying the bay, Virginia's great rivers, and the state's 112 miles of Atlantic Ocean shoreline have landed Virginia in the number-three slot nationally in revenues generated from commercial fishing, behind only Alaska and Louisiana, based on statistics from the National Marine Fisheries Service. The great Chesapeake Bay, which averages only 21 feet deep over its 195-mile length, dominates coastal Virginia. Its marshlands offer shelter for millions of migrating waterfowl; its tides nurse the state's network of creeks and rivers. Broad sloughs, coves, wetlands, and tidal ponds intermingle and embrace three lush, green "necks" (peninsulas) cut out by the long, wide mouths of the Potomac, Rappahannock, York, and James Rivers.

The Virginia seafood industry is America's oldest. In 1607, the Council in Virginia reported to the Mother Country that the James River was "so stored with sturgeon and other sweet fish as no man's fortune hath ever pos-

sessed the like," according to the Colonial Williamsburg Foundation. A few years later, Captain John Smith listed some of the varieties that made up this bounty: "Sturgeon, Grampus, Porpus, Plaice, Herrings, Conyfish, Rockfish, Eeles, Lampreyes, Catfish, Shades, Pearch of three sorts, Brabs, Shrimp, Crevises, Oysters, Cocles, and Muscles."

Nearly 400 years later, many of these species are still caught commercially in Virginia. In all, more than 295 species of fish swim in the Chesapeake Bay region, creating allure for the sports fishermen, exemplary offerings to the cook and diner, and bounty to the watermen at day's end, pointing their skipjacks (historic bay sailboats) toward the marshy shores to deposit their catch on land.

Unlike the industry that draws upon this vast fishing ground, the farmed-fish industry is in its infancy. Trout is the main fish farmed in Virginia, and commercial production is valued at a mere $2 million compared to the fish landed commercially from the bay and ocean, which are worth more than $450 million. However, fish farming is expanding. Trout farms operate in Virginia's mountain regions where an abundant supply of high-quality, cold-spring water provides excellent growing conditions.

Blue-Crab Facts

The Chesapeake Bay is the world's largest producer of blue crabs (*Callinectes sapidus*), recognized throughout the world as an epicurean treat. In his book, *Chesapeake*, James A. Michener touts the blue crab "the choicest morsel in the Bay."

For most of the year, the crabs are caught in the Bay and its tributaries using traditional "crab pots" (wire cages containing bait) hung from floats. In the winter, Virginia watermen harvest dormant crabs by dredging them from their sandy shelters in the deep mouth of the Bay, thus guaranteeing their year-round availability.

It's said that more calories are exerted picking the crab from its shell than gained by eating the meat obtained. Nonetheless, the blue crab is the most popular seafood landed in Virginia. The male, blue-clawed "jimmy" is prized by crab connoisseurs because it can grow larger than the female and does not contain bitter-tasting roe. When attempting to determine sex, remember that the female—called "she crab" or "sally"—paints her "fingernails" (has bright-red claw tips). The male prefers the unpainted look.

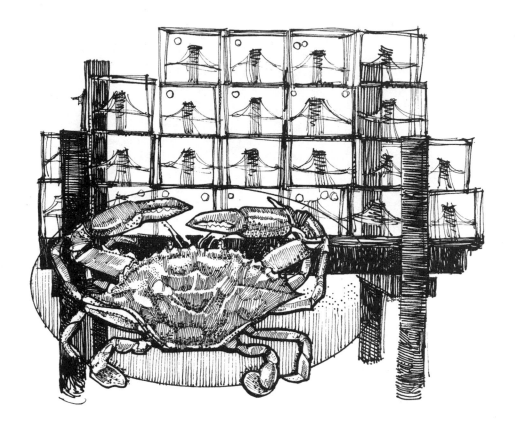

chapter one
SHELLFISH

∽ *As the name suggests, shellfish are aquatic animals with shells. The shells of crustaceans such as crabs, lobsters, and shrimp are visually obvious. Their "crusts," made of chitin, form the animal's armor or outer covering. Bi-valve mollusks such as the clam, oyster, and scallop are sandwiched between two shells that open to filter food from the waters. Though not apparent, squid and octopus are also shellfish. The shells or skeletons of these cephalopods are on the inside. A preferred method of preparation for many crustaceans and mollusks is steaming, which opens the shell to the good eatin' inside.*

CHESAPEAKE HOUSE CRAB CAKES

Crab-cake recipes are as plentiful as Virginia cooks.
This one is quintessential—brown on the outside, rich and creamy in the center.

2 slices bread
1 pound backfin crab meat
1 egg, lightly beaten
1 tablespoon mayonnaise
1 tablespoon Worcestershire sauce

1 teaspoon mustard
1 teaspoon Old Bay seafood
 seasoning
¼ teaspoon salt
vegetable oil for frying

Break bread into small pieces and place in a medium mixing bowl; moisten with a tablespoon or two of water. Stir in thoroughly cleaned crab and mix with remaining ingredients. Shape into 8 cakes.

Heat a large skillet over high heat. Add oil to cover the bottom. Fry crab cakes quickly until golden brown, about 4 minutes on each side. Makes 4 servings.

∽ *Hilda Crockett's Chesapeake House, located on Main Street in Tangier Island, serves family-style meals that include these crab cakes, as well as clam fritters, ham, potato salad, cole slaw, applesauce, corn custard, homemade bread, and pound cake. The late Hilda Crockett, a descendant of the early English family that settled the island, borrowed the money to purchase the white frame house in which the restaurant is located. Word of Hilda's excellent food spread quickly at the time, and today the food served is still made from her recipes. The restaurant is open from April 15 to October 15. Call (757) 891-2331 or visit http://tangierisland-va.com/cheshouse). ∽*

MARTHA WASHINGTON INN'S SHE-CRAB SOUP

This soup, a permanent fixture on the inn's menu, enjoys great renown.

⅓ cup butter
¼ cup diced red bell pepper
¼ cup diced yellow onion
½ cup flour
4 cups shrimp, fish, or chicken stock

1½ cups heavy cream
⅓ cup cream sherry
½ teaspoon salt
¼ teaspoon white pepper
½ pound crab meat

In a large saucepan, melt butter over medium-high heat. Stir in bell pepper and onion; sauté until tender. Stir in flour and cook 1 to 2 minutes. Using a whisk, stir in stock, heavy cream, sherry, salt, and pepper. Simmer 20 minutes, stirring often. Add cleaned crab meat and serve. Makes 6 servings.

Note: The amount of sherry used may be adjusted according to taste.

∽ *Steven Sweet, executive chef of the Martha Washington Inn, created this treasured dish. The inn, located in the historic district of Abingdon, was built in 1832; the mansion has served as a women's college and a Civil War hospital (phone (888) 999-8078 or (276) 628-3161 or visit www.marthawashingtoninn.com). ∽*

The Old Bay Seasoning Tradition

Cooks around the Chesapeake use Old Bay as their seafood seasoning of choice. According to McCormick & Company, Inc., "More than 100 million pounds of this distinctive spice mix are sold each year. The mix, which was once sold in a metal tin, was invented in 1938 by a German-Jewish sausage maker, Gustav Brunn, who arrived in Baltimore after fleeing Nazi Germany. He didn't bring much with him except his spice grinder and a knack for using it to create mixes to spice bland recipes. Brunn started a wholesale spice business above the Southern Sea Food Company on Market Place, across from the old fish market in Baltimore. He called the original mix Delicious Brand Seafood Seasoning."

McCormick bought the Old Bay brand in 1990. Although the recipe is proprietary, it's rumored to contain celery seed, black peppercorns, bay leaves, cardamom, mustard seed, cloves, sweet Hungarian paprika, and mace.

Yes, even the crab can be sub-
divided and named. Here are
the terms you may encounter:

LUMP are the largest (and
most expensive) pieces of
crab meat, located adjacent to
the backfin.

BACKFIN is the white body
meat, including lump and
large flakes, often used for
crab cakes and the dish
known as crab imperial.

SPECIAL are flakes of white
body meat other than lump
and are useful for crab cakes,
soups, casseroles, and dips.

CLAW, the brownish meat
from the claws, is best for
soups and dips.

The Root of Our Culture

"Agriculture is the root of our
culture in Virginia, virtually
defining how we view our-
selves," according to State
Senator Patsy Ticer, a member of the Senate Agriculture,
Conservation and Natural
Resources Committee. "Agricultural endeavors," she notes,
"built the solid economic
foundation of the Common-
wealth and still play a vital
role despite the move to an
information-technology
economy."

PRESIDENT ZACHARY TAYLOR'S CRABMEAT ON SHELLS (DEVILLED HARD CRABS)

This dish, with lemon wedges and parsley for garnish, makes a lovely presentation.

1 pound backfin crab meat	1 tablespoon mayonnaise
12 saltine crackers, crushed	1 teaspoon Worcestershire sauce
½ cup butter, melted (1 stick)	1 teaspoon fresh minced parsley
1 egg	¼ teaspoon dry mustard
3 tablespoons dry sherry wine	¼ teaspoon ground black pepper

Clean and butter 6 to 8 large crab-shell backs, shallow shells, or ramekins. Pick
through the meat and discard any shells or cartilage; set aside. Place crackers in a
medium mixing bowl and pour butter over them. Remove ¼ cup buttered crumbs; set
aside.

In a small bowl, beat egg with sherry, mayonnaise, Worcestershire, parsley, mustard, and pepper. Add to crumbs in mixing bowl. Using a fork, gently toss in crab
meat. Fill prepared shells with crab mixture, but do not pack down. Sprinkle with
reserved crumbs.

Place shells on a baking sheet in the center of the oven and bake about 30 minutes
at 350° F.

*President Taylor, America's twelfth president, had a reputation for gracious and bountiful hospitality. Official din-
ner parties were held in the state dining room of the White House twice a week during the congressional season. This
recipe was adapted from* The First Ladies' Cookbook. *

SENATOR PATSY TICER'S CRAB CASSEROLE

As an appetizer or main dish, this easy-to-assemble crab casserole is always a hit.

1 slice white bread	1 teaspoon dry mustard
1 (5-ounce) can evaporated milk or	1 teaspoon Worcestershire sauce
heavy cream	salt and pepper to taste
2 eggs	1 pound lump crab meat, picked over
4 tablespoons butter, melted	to remove shell and cartilage
1 tablespoon chopped parsley	

Butter a 1½-quart round casserole; set aside. Crumble bread in milk and let soak for a
few minutes. Add eggs; beat. Add remaining ingredients, fold in crab meat, and pour
into casserole. Bake 15 to 20 minutes at 425° F, or until top is light brown and casserole is bubbly. Do not overcook, because the crab is delicate. Makes 6 servings.

*State Senator Patsy Ticer is a former mayor of Alexandria was first elected in 1995 to represent Virginia's
30th District. *

OLD DOMINION CRAB STACK
WITH BLENDER HOLLANDAISE SAUCE

*In this dish, crab takes the place of eggs to create a daring twist
on the old Eggs Benedict standard.*

FOR SAUCE:

4 egg yolks	¼ teaspoon white pepper
3 tablespoons lemon juice	⅛ teaspoon cayenne or red pepper
¼ teaspoon salt	1 cup butter

FOR THE REST:

8 soft-shell crabs, cleaned	8 slices cooked ham, heated
3 tablespoons butter	4 English muffins, split, toasted, and
8 slices ripe tomato	buttered

Prick legs and claws of each crab with the tines of a fork to prevent popping. Sauté in butter about 4 minutes on each side over moderate heat.

For the sauce, place in blender the egg yolks, juice, salt, pepper, and cayenne. In a saucepan, melt butter until bubbling but not browned. Turn blender on medium speed. Very slowly, pour in the hot butter. Blend an additional 10 to 12 seconds, or until sauce is thickened and smooth. Makes about 1½ cups.

Place toasted muffin halves on plate. Top each with ham, then tomato and cooked crab. Spoon 3 tablespoons Hollandaise sauce over each. Serve immediately.

Recipe provided courtesy of Virginia Marine Products Board. Visit www.virginiaseafood.org.

LA PETITE AUBERGE'S SOFT-SHELL CRABS

A favorite dish from the favored Fredericksburg spot for fine dining.

8 small soft-shell crabs, cleaned	2 ounces toasted, sliced almonds
flour for dredging	2 shallots, chopped
4 tablespoons butter, divided	1 lemon
salt and pepper to taste	

Dredge crabs in flour. Using 2 ovenproof skillets, melt 2 tablespoons butter in each. Place 4 crabs in each skillet, back-side down, for 2 to 3 minutes; turn over for 1 to 2 minutes. Salt and pepper to taste. Sprinkle crabs with almonds and shallots; squeeze lemon over all. Place both skillets in 450° F oven for 4 to 5 minutes; serve immediately. Makes 4 servings.

La Petite Auberge owner/chef Christian Renault has been turning out local foods with a French accent in Fredericksburg for more than two decades (phone (540) 371-2727).

A Shell of His Former Self

As a child grows, he requires larger clothes to replace his smaller ones. Likewise with the crab and its shell. The crab sheds its hard shell in order to grow, and the seafood delicacy known to diners as "soft-shell crab" is simply blue crab that is harvested between the shedding of a hard shell and the donning of the next.

Crabs stay soft for only a couple of hours, so harvesting them at just the right time is essential. Out of water, they will not form another hard shell but will live only a couple of days and so are shipped or immediately cleaned and frozen.

When you bring a live soft-shell crab home, first clean it. Use scissors to snip off the eyes and mouth and the gills found under both sides of the soft shell. Because the "apron" (that little flap that looks like a "T" on the male or like a bell on the female) is chewy, you might want to remove it, too. Rinse and store dressed crab in the refrigerator for one to two days, or freeze it for future use. For one main-dish serving, buy two soft-shelled crabs per person.

Select scallops with firm meat and the characteristic creamy-white color. Both fresh and thawed scallops should have a sweet odor. Fresh scallops may be refrigerated one or two days before cooking or freezing. After frozen, scallops may be kept three to six months if wrapped in heavy, airtight packaging. Like most seafood, scallops cook quickly—and overcook quickly. When scallops barely turn opaque, they are done. Overcooked scallops will turn rubbery and develop cracks. When pan-frying or sautéing, heat the oiled or buttered pan first so the scallops will keep their natural juices as the outside browns lightly. To prevent splattering, always pat them dry before adding to the pan. Scallops can be threaded on skewers and grilled, or they can be microwaved on high for two to three minutes per pound. Always defrost frozen scallops before cooking by any method. To thaw scallops, place them in the refrigerator for a day or two, or submerge them—still in their airtight packaging—in cold tap water for about an hour. A 3.5-ounce serving has only 87 calories, contains less than 1% fat, and more than 16% protein.

ALEXANDER'S SEAFOOD MADAGASCAR

*Shrimp, scallops, and lobster are cooked in a
creamy peppercorn sauce and served over pasta.*

2 tablespoons clarified butter
½ pound sea scallops
½ pound shrimp
3 ounces lobster meat, cut into medallions (or lobster-flavored surimi seafood)
1½ tablespoons whole green peppercorns
1 tablespoon minced fresh garlic

2 ounces brandy
1 cup white sauce made with lobster broth or clam juice
½ cup heavy cream
1 tablespoon fresh basil
salt and pepper to taste
8 ounces pasta, cooked according to package directions

Heat clarified butter over medium heat. (Clarified butter is butter that has been melted and the milk solids discarded so the butter won't burn when used to sauté over high heat.) Sauté scallops on each side for 1 minute. Add shrimp, lobster, and peppercorns; sauté for 2 to 3 minutes. Add garlic; sauté for 1 minute.

Deglaze pan with brandy and flame. Add white sauce and cream; bring to a simmer. Add basil, salt, and pepper. Serve over pasta. Makes 4 servings.

⁓ The elegant Alexander's is a standout for its terrific view of the Bay and its fine dining. Main dishes range from seafood (including a mariner's platter loaded with five types of seafood) to steak and veal. Star desserts are the home-made cheesecakes. Be sure to ask for directions when you call, as Alexander's is off the beaten path near the Chesapeake Bay Bridge-Tunnel (phone (757) 464-4999 or visit www.alexandersonthebay.com). ⁓

BAKED CLAMS ON THE HALF SHELL

*Assemble this appetizer recipe ahead of time and refrigerate. Then pop it in the oven
just before guests are expected. For a larger crowd, make multiples of the recipe.*

12 clams, 2 inches or less in size
1 tablespoon olive oil
1 teaspoon minced garlic
1 cup fresh white bread crumbs (do not use dry crumbs)
2 tablespoons chopped fresh parsley

1 teaspoon lemon zest (grated yellow color from lemon rind)
¼ teaspoon salt
⅛ teaspoon ground red pepper
lemon wedges

Shuck the clams over a mixing bowl, reserving the liquor (shellfish juice) and shells. Coarsely chop the clams and add to the mixing bowl; set aside. Place 12 shells on a baking sheet; set aside.

Heat oil in a small skillet. Add garlic and cook until very light brown, about 1 minute. Add crumbs, parsley, zest, salt, and red pepper. Heat, stirring constantly, until bread turns brown.

Stir bread mixture into clams and their liquor, tossing well. If mixture is too dry, add some lemon juice. Stuff reserved shells with clam mixture.

Bake clams 10 to 15 minutes, or until lightly browned, in a 450° F oven. Serve three on each plate with lemon wedges. Makes 4 appetizer servings.

⁓ Recipe provided courtesy of Virginia Marine Products Board. ⁓

SEA-SCALLOP SALAD
WITH YELLOW RICE AND BLACK BEANS

*Going on a picnic? This is a great make-ahead main dish
with a sunburst of flavors and textures.*

⅓ cup plus 2 tablespoons olive oil
½ cup chopped onion
2 teaspoons minced jalapeño pepper
1 clove garlic, minced
2 cups water
½ teaspoon each ground turmeric,
   cumin, and salt
1 pound sea scallops, quartered, or
   whole bay scallops

1 cup long-grain white rice
1 (15-ounce) can black beans, rinsed
   and drained
1 cup chopped fresh tomatoes
¼ cup chopped fresh cilantro
   or parsley
3 tablespoons lime juice
lime wedges for garnish

Heat 2 tablespoons oil in a large saucepan over medium heat. Add onion, jalapeño, and garlic. Cook, stirring constantly, 3 to 4 minutes, or until onion is tender. Add water, turmeric, cumin, and salt. Bring mixture to a boil over high heat. Add rice. Cover, reduce heat to low, and simmer 15 to 20 minutes, or until most of the liquid is absorbed.

Stir in scallops; re-cover and simmer 2 to 3 minutes, or until scallops turn opaque and are cooked through. Set pan in a bowl of ice water to chill rice and prevent scallops from overcooking. Toss mixture every few minutes. When mixture is lukewarm, stir in beans, tomatoes, and cilantro.

Drizzle lime juice and remaining ⅓ cup olive oil over rice mixture. Salad can be served lukewarm or can be refrigerated up to four days. Makes 5 servings.

MICROWAVED CLAMS IN ITALIAN MOP SAUCE

*Use this recipe when in need of a simply-prepared appetizer
that can incorporate seafood.*

2 tablespoons olive oil
½ cup chopped fresh parsley
3 cloves garlic, chopped
1 cup crushed tomatoes, drained, or
   marinara sauce
¼ cup white wine

½ teaspoon dried oregano
¼ teaspoon black pepper
2 pounds small clams, scrubbed, or
   mussels, scrubbed and debearded
Italian bread for mopping sauce

Pour oil in a 10-inch glass pie plate or quiche dish and microwave on high 1 minute. Stir in parsley and garlic; microwave on high 2 minutes. Stir in tomatoes, wine, oregano, and pepper.

Arrange the clams in a circle on top of the tomato mixture, hinged end down. Cover with vented plastic wrap and microwave on high 5 minutes. Remove any clams that have opened. Re-cover and microwave on high 2 to 4 minutes, or until the remaining clams have opened. Discard any that do not open. Return all the clams to the plate; re-cover and let stand 2 minutes. Serve hot with bread for mopping up sauce. Makes 4 appetizers or 2 main-dish servings.

Sea Scallops

Opening and closing their hinged shells, scallops can swim across the bottom of the ocean. This unusual movement requires a strong abductor muscle. It's this white or cream-colored muscle that we eat in North America. In other countries, the orange-colored coral that surrounds the scallop is also eaten. All scallops landed in Virginia are sea scallops. Since unscrupulous vendors may take cheaper seafood such as skate or shark and cut imitation scallops from the meat, it's best to purchase scallops from a fish-monger you know. Also on the market are "calico scallops," a lower-valued seafood that are sometimes sold as bay scallops. These small calicos have a more pungent flavor and rubbery texture than true scallops.

☙ DID YOU KNOW . . .
that since 1607, when Captains John Smith and Christopher Newport landed in Jamestown and found an abundance of oysters "lying thick as stones," oysters have been a staple of the Virginian diet? In addition, a recipe called "tomato ketchup" that appeared in the 1824 edition of *The Virginia Housewife* cookbook is very nearly the same as the recipe for dipping sauce that accompanies the Tavern Oyster Fritters recipe on page 66.

Clams come in both hard and soft-shell varieties. Hard clams, also called quahogs, and soft clams, called steamers, live in sandy-bottomed bays and coves and along beaches. Soft-shell clams have shells that are so thin that they can be easily broken with the fingers and, as their nickname suggests, are best when steamed. Fishermen gather clams with rakes or hoes; at low tide, gatherers can locate them beneath their siphon holes. There is a minimum legal size—usually about two inches—for harvesting clams. The smallest hard shells are called "little necks," next are the "cherrystones," and the largest are called "chowders." The smaller the clam, the more tender and sweet it will be. Little necks are best for clams on the half shell (raw), because they are the most tender. Chowder clams need to be chopped and cooked to help tenderize them, and are therefore best for use in clam chowders or pasta sauces. Cherrystones are typically used for baked-clam appetizers.

Clams are sold live, so if there is no movement, discard them. Because they tend to be gritty, purge the clams in cold saltwater for at least two hours before using.

CHESAPEAKE CLAM PIE

*This is a classic way for preparing clams in the small fishing villages of the Bay.
Adding a salad makes a meal.*

1¼ cups potatoes, peeled and thinly sliced
¾ cup thinly sliced onion
½ cup diced celery
½ teaspoon salt
1 pint soft-shell clams, drained and chopped, with ⅓ cup liquor (clam juice) reserved

⅛ teaspoon pepper
2½ tablespoons flour
¼ teaspoon Old Bay seasoning
2 tablespoons butter or margarine
2½ tablespoons (about 2 slices) cooked, crumbled bacon
1 pie crust
paprika for garnish

Preheat oven to 350° F. Brush a pie pan lightly with oil. Create a layer of half the potatoes, half of the onion, and half of the celery in the pie pan. Sprinkle with half the salt and pepper. Place all the clams in a uniform layer over the vegetables and sprinkle with flour and seasoning. Dot with butter. Layer the remaining potatoes, onion, and celery over clams. Sprinkle with reserved clam juice and bacon. Roll out pie crust and place over top; flute edges and cut slits in the crust. Sprinkle with paprika. Bake for about 50 minutes, or until crust is brown and filling is bubbly. Let stand 5 minutes before serving. Makes 4 servings.

Recipe provided courtesy of the National Fisheries Institute, Arlington, Virginia.

CHRISTIANA CAMPBELL'S TAVERN OYSTER FRITTERS WITH DIPPING SAUCE

*The oysters in this dish are left whole in the batter to retain
their juice, shape, and creamy texture.*

FOR DIPPING SAUCE:
¾ cup ketchup
¾ cup mayonnaise

2 tablespoons drained, bottled horseradish or more to taste

FOR OYSTER FRITTERS:
6 tablespoons flour plus more for dredging
⅔ cup lukewarm water
2 tablespoons vegetable oil plus more for frying
1 tablespoon finely chopped fresh parsley

2 large egg whites, stiffly beaten
24 shucked medium-sized oysters, drained
salt and freshly ground black pepper to taste
lemon wedges for garnish

To prepare the sauce, in a small bowl combine ketchup, horseradish, and mayonnaise. Stir well; chill until ready to serve.

To make the fritter batter, in a large bowl combine flour, water, 2 tablespoons oil, and parsley. Whisk until smooth. Stir about ¼ of the beaten egg whites into the mixture to lighten. Gently fold in the remaining egg whites.

Fill an electric deep-fat fryer or large electric skillet with enough oil to measure 1 to 1½ inches deep. Heat to 375° F. Dredge the oysters in additional flour and drop into the batter. Transfer the batter-dipped oysters to the hot fat and fry, turning until golden brown, about 1 to 2 minutes. Sprinkle with salt and pepper. Drain well on paper towels and serve warm with the dipping sauce. Garnish with lemon wedges. Makes 4 servings.

Christiana Campbell's Tavern was George Washington's favorite tavern in Williamsburg, and it specializes today in seafood dishes just as it did in his time (phone (800) 828-3767 or (757) 229-2141). Situated across the grounds from the capitol, the tavern was run by Campbell to support herself and her two small children after her husband's death at an early age. This recipe was reprinted from The Colonial Williamsburg Tavern Cookbook. *

OYSTER CHOWDER

The simplicity of this traditional white chowder allows the oyster's delicate flavor to play the starring role.

3 tablespoons butter
¼ cup chopped onion
4 tablespoons flour
4 cups milk
4 cups peeled cubed potatoes, boiled

1 (12-ounce) can oysters, including liquid
1 cup corn kernels
salt and pepper to taste

Melt butter in a 3-quart saucepan. Cook onion in butter until very tender. Add flour and stir to blend. Gradually add milk, stirring constantly until milk thickens. Stir in oysters and their liquid, potatoes, corn, salt, and pepper. Heat until oysters and vegetables are steaming hot. Makes 4 servings.

MOUNT WHARTON SCALLOPED OYSTERS

For a Sunday supper or a buffet party, this simple, rich casserole is an Eastern Shore favorite.

1½ pints shucked oysters with their liquor
juice of ½ lemon (about 1 tablespoon)

6 tablespoons butter, melted
1 cup crushed saltine crackers
½ cup milk
pepper to taste

Preheat oven to 350° F. Drain oysters. Add lemon juice to melted butter. Butter a shallow baking dish and create a layer of oysters, half the crackers, and half the lemon butter. Repeat to form a second layer. Add sufficient milk and oyster liquor to moisten. Bake 30 minutes. Makes 4 to 6 servings.

*This recipe was provided by Mr. and Mrs. Fred Crebbin, III, owners of Mount Wharton, a colonial waterfront home on the Eastern Shore that belonged to John Wharton, a notorious merchant and smuggler of the early 1800s. *

Oysters

The oyster (*Crassostrea virginica*) was named after the state because biologists first identified it on Virginia's shores. Oysters grow best in estuaries, such as those of the Chesapeake Bay, that have moderate temperatures and salinity and abundant plankton for food. The Bay's oyster population began declining in the late 1950s primarily because of MSX disease, and aquaculture specialists and the fisheries of Virginia and Maryland have been working to supplement natural populations with disease-resistant strains. In the Bay, harvest is done by hand tonging or mechanized tonging and dredging. Although oysters are harvested year-round, catches are heaviest in October, November, and December, dispelling the myth that you should not eat oysters in months containing an "r." The upper shell of the oyster is flattish, and the lower shell is concave, providing a saucer for the soft body of the shellfish. The meat is cream, tan, or gray and can be eaten raw or prepared many different ways. The juices from shellfish are called "liquor" and should be used too. Oysters can be purchased in the shell and shucked. Keep them refrigerated and use within two days.

Squid

It's cheap, it's 70% edible, and it's 18% protein. Squid is the new star at the top of the restaurant menu. Fried for appetizers, sautéed for salads, and steamed in stews, "cala-mari," as it's called in Italy, is a fast-to-cook shellfish. Because its shell is a crystal quill inside the body, there's no hard shell to crack. Most squid sold are frozen, yet nei-ther the flavor nor texture is altered by freezing. The most reliable way to tell squid are desirable is to detect a deli-cate ocean smell. The squid should look shiny and firm and should not be sticky. Cleaned squid tubes are easy to use. The tubes can be stuffed, but most cooks slice them crosswise into quarter-inch rings. Overcooking makes them tough; once the rings are firm, cease cooking immediately.

How to Clean Squid

1. Cut off the tentacles just in front of the eyes.
2. Squeeze the cut edge of tentacles to coax the cartilage or beak out; discard.
3. Pull the head and viscera out of the body tube; discard.
4. Pull the long clear quill out of the body tube; discard.
5. Rinse the tube under cold running water and pull the skin (colored surface) off the tube; discard. Run water inside the tube and reach inside to pull out any viscera that remain. The tube should be empty. Slice or stuff.

SPANISH SQUID AND POTATO STEW

*The broth from this flavorful, light stew is so delicious,
you'll want to soak up the last drop with your bread.*

2 tablespoons olive oil
1 medium onion, chopped
2 green bell peppers, cored, seeded, and chopped
2 large cloves garlic, minced
1 bay leaf
1 (14.5-ounce) can chopped toma-toes, including liquid
1½ cups bottled clam juice or chicken broth
½ cup white wine
1½ pounds potatoes, peeled and cubed
¼ teaspoon turmeric
1½ pounds whole small squid, cleaned (see directions) or 12 ounces cleaned squid tubes
salt and pepper to taste
Italian bread

Heat oil in a large skillet. Add onion and bell peppers. Sauté until vegetables are soft, about 8 minutes. Add garlic; cook 1 minute. Add bay leaf, tomatoes, clam juice, and white wine. Bring to a boil and simmer about 3 minutes. Add potatoes and turmeric. Cook about 20 minutes, stirring occasionally, until potatoes are tender.

Cut the squid tubes crosswise into ¼-inch rings. Leave small tentacles whole and cut large tentacles in half. Add to skillet and simmer just until rings firm into "O" shapes, about 1 minute. Season to taste with salt and pepper. Serve in large bowls with Italian bread for dipping in stew liquid. Makes 4 servings.

SPICY SEAFOOD SOUP

*With a haunting fragrance of Southeast Asia, this soup is light
but filling enough for a main course. Pair it with soft vegetarian spring rolls,
a rice dish, and perhaps some shrimp crisps.*

8 cups chicken broth
2 stalks lemongrass, thinly sliced
1 (1-inch) piece galangal or fresh ginger root
2 cloves garlic, peeled and crushed
2 to 3 fresh chilies (or to taste), thinly sliced
1 tablespoon Thai fish sauce
¼ cup fresh lime juice
1½ pounds large raw shrimp, shelled and deveined
½ pound squid tubes, cut into thin rings
4 lime leaves, thinly sliced
6 scallions or green onions, thinly sliced
1 cup rinsed and chopped fresh cilantro leaves

Combine broth, lemongrass, galangal, garlic, chilies, fish sauce, and lime juice in a large saucepan and simmer for 10 minutes. Add shrimp, squid, and lime leaves; sim-mer 5 minutes and serve immediately, garnished with scallions and cilantro. Makes 6 servings.

Reston resident Alexandra Greeley has lived in the Far East and traveled throughout Asia. She has used her exten-sive knowledge of Asian food traditions and culture to author several cookbooks, including Asian Soups, Stews & Curries *and the 1993* Asian Grills, *in which this recipe appears. (Recipe reprinted with permission from the author.)*

SKIPJACK OYSTER DRESSING

This is a perfect dressing for stuffing the Chesapeake Bay's small, whole fish
or one of Virginia's many turkeys and chickens.

2 large stalks celery
1 medium onion
½ cup (1 stick) butter
1 teaspoon salt
½ teaspoon lemon-and-pepper
    seasoning

⅛ teaspoon each mace, tarragon, and
    poultry seasoning
½ teaspoon lemon juice
1 pint shucked oysters, with liquor
8 slices day-old bread, cubed

Finely chop celery and onion. Sauté in butter until tender. Mix in dry seasonings and lemon juice. Add oysters with liquor and simmer until edges of oysters just begin to curl. Remove from heat and gently mix in bread cubes. Adjust moistness with water as desired. Makes about 4 cups dressing (allow about ½ cup per pound for fish, 1 cup per pound for poultry). Note: For an extra-special tangy taste, core and finely chop 2 medium apples and add with celery and onions when cooking. Yield will increase about ½ cup.

Recipe provided courtesy of the National Fisheries Institute in Arlington.

ATLANTIC CALAMARI SALAD
WITH LEMON OLIVE-OIL DRESSING

Ready within 10 minutes, this main-dish salad can be kept for several days;
what's more, the flavor improves with each day that passes.

FOR SALAD:

1½ pounds whole squid, cleaned or
    12 ounces squid tubes
1 (16-ounce) can dark red kidney
    beans, rinsed and drained
2 medium tomatoes, coarsely
    chopped

1 cup each thinly sliced celery and
    green bell pepper
½ cup thinly sliced red onion
¼ cup chopped fresh parsley
¼ teaspoon each salt and freshly
    ground black pepper

FOR DRESSING:

5 tablespoons fruity olive oil
3 tablespoons fresh lemon juice
2 tablespoons tarragon vinegar or
    white wine vinegar

1 small clove garlic, minced
½ teaspoon each dried mint and
    dried basil or 2 teaspoons each of
    fresh herbs

Cut squid tubes crosswise into ¼-inch rings. If tentacles are large, cut in half lengthwise. Rinse; set aside. Place 1 cup water in a 2-quart saucepan. Cover with lid and bring to a boil. Using a fork, quickly stir in squid. Rings should begin to cook into slightly firm rings within 30 to 60 seconds. Immediately fill saucepan with cold water to stop the cooking; set aside.

In a large serving bowl, combine beans, tomatoes, celery, bell pepper, onion, and parsley. Place all dressing ingredients in a jar. Seal lid tightly and shake vigorously. Toss salad with dressing. When squid are cool, toss gently into salad along with salt and pepper. Cover and refrigerate up to 4 days. Makes 6 servings.

Conch Makes a Cameo Appearance

The number-nine seafood variety harvested by Virginia watermen is conch, a large marine snail in the heavy, spiral shell children press to their ears to hear the sound of the ocean. Despite how often it is caught in Virginia, it is seldom sold or consumed here. Almost all the conch harvested in Virginia is exported to China, though some is used in Italian restaurants in New York. The conch moves by digging its one claw into the sea bottom and pushing itself along in short, sudden spurts. The largest conch, called the queen conch (*Cassis cameo*), lives in the Atlantic Ocean in warm waters. Its shell can reach a foot or two in length and is carved into cameos. The queen conch and some other species of conch, such as the king conch and the trumpet conch, have ornamental value. The shells of some species are fashioned into trumpets for use in ceremonial music. Conch are also harvested for their edible meat, which is tough and must be pounded with a mallet, then cut into cubes for cooking. It is used extensively in the Bahamas and Caribbean islands to make conch chowder, salads, and stews.

UFO in the Chesapeake Bay?

Some 35 million years ago, an extraterrestrial body smashed into what is now the Chesapeake Bay, carving a crater twice the size of the state of Rhode Island and nearly as deep as the Grand Canyon. The collision of the body with the earth may have pre-determined the present-day location of Chesapeake Bay as well as the course of the York and James Rivers. The impact crater went unidentified until 1986, when it was discovered during groundwater-research drilling by the U.S. Geological Survey and the Virginia State Water Control Board; they drilled four cores while evaluating underwater sedimentary beds and their potential as sources of fresh groundwater. Texaco and Exxon provided another confirmation in 1993, during gas and oil drilling. Research revealed that the impact crater is buried beneath the Bay near the town of Cape Charles, on Virginia's eastern shore. The crater is 60 miles in diameter and almost a mile deep.

—U.S. Geological Survey

essay

TSCHISWAPEKI:

An Overiew of the Great Shellfish Bay

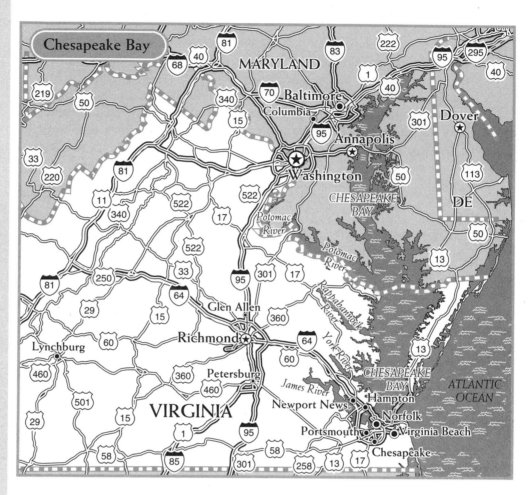

In the shallow waters of Chesapeake Bay, fine green ribbons of eelgrass sway like a hula dancer's skirt in the tidal current, spotlighted by filtered rays of the morning sun. Hiding from predators in the vegetation, a shedding blue crab waits perilously until his new shell has hardened. Widgeon grass, with its many fine branches and bristle-like leaves, makes a day-care center for a nursery of young spot and striped bass. An adult rockfish in its silvery pin-striped suit swishes by on his way to a power breakfast of other fish, crabs, mussels, and razor clams.

Above, the surface is abruptly punctuated by a Canvasback duck diving for a small clam appetizer. The duck returns to the surface and paddles off to join a Red-head duck in the neighborhood that is daintily nibbling on strands of pondweed.

Along the shore, a Great Blue Heron holds court in the tall reeds, bowing periodically to select a small fish or frog with its sharp bill, swallowing its choice head-first. The heron, as tall as a sixth grader, is startled by an approaching fishing boat, whose pilot rouses himself with a mug of hot coffee. The gray bird catapults into the air, powered by the six-foot span of its wings, and recovers its dignity perched high in a loblolly pine.

Overhead, a migrating flock of Canada geese flies by in a distinctive "V" pattern, honking at the morning rush hour below. "Kyew, kyew, kyew," answers an osprey nose diving toward an unsuspecting fish. Morning on the Chesapeake Bay has dawned.

HISTORY OF THE CHESAPEAKE BAY

Though it is the largest estuary in the United States and one of the most productive in the world, the Bay is very young, geologically speaking. The area was nothing but dry land 18,000 years ago, when the frozen sheet from the last great Ice Age was at its maximum over North America, and sea level was about 600 feet lower than at present. Approximately 10,000 years ago, however, the ice sheets began to melt rapidly, causing sea level to rise and flood the continental shelf and the coastal river valleys. The flooded valleys became estuaries like Delaware Bay and Chesapeake Bay.

An estuary is a semi-enclosed body of water that connects with the open sea and in which the salty ocean water is diluted with freshwater from rivers and creeks. The Bay we know today is nearly 200 miles long, fed by 48 major rivers and 100 small tributaries draining a 64,000-square-mile basin.

About half the fresh water flows in from the Susquehanna River, and northern Bay water is totally fresh. Near the Bay's mouth, the water is as salty as the Atlantic Ocean that tides into it. The ocean tides swell the Bay's waters upstream to the fall lines—waterfalls or rapids beyond which boats cannot navigate. The various types of water in the Bay support some 2700 species of plants and aquatic animals, both fresh- and salt-water life forms.

According to the Chesapeake Regional Information Service, "Historians disagree on who was the first European to travel into the Bay. Some accounts credit the Viking explorer Thorfinn Karlsfennias as early as the eleventh century. Others claim that the Italian Giovanni da Verrazano set foot on its shores when he sailed along the coast from the Carolinas to Maine in 1524. And yet a third group credits Pedro Menendez de Aviles, the Spaniard who founded St. Augustine in 1566. Regardless of who was first, the discovery was the start of big changes for the Bay as Europeans came in search of treasure, conquest, and resources to fuel expanding commercial ventures and burgeoning colonial empires."

Europeans found the Bay region inhabited. Native Americans living there since 8000 B.C. had already cleared fields, established large towns, and hunted in the woodlands. Indians also harvested the Bay and, according to archaeological finds, were quite fond of oysters. Every year, empty oyster shells were stacked on top of the past year's discarded shells to form piles known as "midden heaps." The largest midden heap found was between 18 and 20 feet deep and covered 30 acres near Popes Creek on the Potomac River, close to George Washington's birthplace.

Still, the bay the Europeans found seemed boundless and inexhaustible. The early colonists adopted some Native American ways (like eating oysters and smoking tobacco), and from the Indian word *Tschiswapeki*, which means "Great Shellfish Bay," derived the name "Chesapeake." The Europeans took over the ready-made fields and established their own towns on the old Indian sites but soon, like the Indians, revered the Bay as "Great Waters" and "Mother of Waters."

THE BAY TODAY

Virginia's more than 6,000 watermen bring in seafood valued at nearly half a billion annually, and more than 45 Virginia cities and counties are economically dependent

Chesapeake Bay Program

The Chesapeake Bay Program is a unique regional partnership—between Virginia, Maryland, Pennsylvania, the District of Columbia, the U.S. Environmental Protection Agency, and participating citizen advisory groups—that has worked to coordinate efforts to restore the Chesapeake Bay since 1983. The program coordinates and monitors efforts in such areas as water quality, public education, living resources, and population growth and development. For more information, contact the Chesapeake Bay Program Office in Annapolis at (800) YOUR-BAY or visit www.chesapeakebay.net.

Save the Bay

The Chesapeake Bay Foundation, formed in 1967, works throughout the Chesapeake's watershed to improve Bay conditions. The nonprofit organization is supported by more than 100,000 active members and has a staff of more than 200 full-time employees. Approximately 95% of CBF's $20 million annual budget is privately raised. For more information, call the Foundation's Virginia state office in Richmond at (804) 780-1392 or visit www.cbf.org.

EEEOHM!

"EEEOHM" isn't the sound a bungy jumper makes in midair. It stands for "Eastfields Environment Enhancing Oyster Holding Module." The square-sided oyster cage was developed for commercial use, but the system is extremely versatile and adaptable to smaller operations, such as the approximately 2000 oyster farms that operate between Reedville and Virginia Beach. "During the last 17 years, we at Eastfields Farms have tried many ways of growing oysters. We've found the EEEOHM to be one of the most efficient and cost-effective systems of off-bottom culture," said Peter Perina, the owner of Eastfields Farms. To use the EEEOHM, 200 oyster seeds—purchased from hatcheries for about $25—are placed in the cage, which floats partially in and partially out of the water. The cages can be floated under or alongside a dock, tied between posts, or deployed in rows strung together with crab-pot rope or clothes line run through the centers. It takes two years to grow the oysters. Peter and Diane Perina also have a spray-free blueberry farm and were instrumental in writing the requirements for the Virginia's Finest Program for blueberries. Contact Eastfield Farms at (804) 725-3948.

on the industry. However, the waterman's livelihood today is endangered by the decline in numbers of fish and shellfish in the increasingly threatened Bay.

Wadey Murphy, a third-generation skipjack captain who lives in Tilghman Island, owns what may be the oldest skipjack on the Chesapeake. The *Rebecca T. Ruark* was built in 1886. But he remarks, "If there are no oysters to harvest, what's the point of keeping an old boat going and beating her up to dredge for oysters that ain't there?"

The reasons for the decline of seafood in Chesapeake Bay are complex. The briefest answer is "people," according Earl White, whose nickname is "Admiral of the Bay." He says, "People don't realize what they're doing until it's too late."

The primary factors contributing to the Bay's poor health are pollution, fertilizer runoff, population growth, and shellfish diseases. According to the Chesapeake Bay Foundation (CBF), the estuary's health "bottomed out in 1983," when it received a rating of 23 on a 100-point scale (with 100 representing the water quality as Captain John Smith described it in the early 1600s).

"Population growth and its effect on the Bay is the most complex and politically sensitive issue facing Bay managers today," states the Chesapeake Bay Program, an organization whose mission, like the aforementioned CBF, is to improve the health of the Bay. It has predicted that another 2.6 million residents will live in the Bay's watershed by the year 2020, a 20% increase. If this growth is not rationally planned, the Bay will be subject to even more pollution. Many fear that sprawling or scattered development will undermine the progress made by Bay restoration efforts thus far.

"If the Bay is to be removed from the EPA's list of impaired waters by the year 2010, dramatic action must be taken to reduce the nutrients that pollute the Chesapeake," according to the CBF.

chapter two
FISH

Fish on Your Face

If you wear cosmetics, you might be wearing a fish. Too oily and bony for human consumption, Atlantic menhaden are netted in shallow bay water and processed into oil for cosmetics. They're also used as fish meal for animals and as bait for crab pots and to catch other fish. Indians of pre-colonial America called the fish "munnawhatteaug," which means "fertilizer." Menhaden are probably what the Indians urged the colonists to plant along with their corn seed. These silvery, herring-like fish with deeply forked tails are the "breadbasket" of the Bay, the favorite food for striped bass, bluefish, sea trout, tunas, and sharks. Menhaden are the 14th most profitable fish caught in Virginia. To see an exhibit about the menhaden fleet, visit the Reedville Fishermen's Museum (see page 84).

∽ *The most commonly landed fish in Virginia are the small golden croaker, followed by floun-der, striped bass, spot, black sea bass, monkfish, sea trout, dogfish, catfish, American eel, bluefish, Spanish mackerel, and Atlantic mackerel. Not in the top 15 but highly revered is the bone-riddled shad, a traditional harbinger of spring. Indian myth says the fish was once an unhap-py porcupine that was turned inside out by the Great Spirit. Most finned fish harvested in Vir-ginia are lean and white. Some, like the bluefish and mackerel, have darker flesh. One fish, the menhaden, is too oily to be eaten but has made a fortune for those who harvest its oil, which is used in the cosmetic industry. Fish are extremely important to Virginia's economy—and to its diners as well.*

When choosing fresh sea-
food, look for good color,
smooth skin, clear rather than
cloudy eyes, good odor without the smell of decay, clean
and intact gills, and resiliency
when pressed.

Look for frozen seafood that
is rock hard, free of ice crystals, has no signs of thawed
juices, and has no white spots
(indicators of freezer burn).
When defrosting frozen seafood, do so gradually to preserve its quality. The best way
to thaw it is overnight in the
refrigerator. Avoid thawing at
room temperature. If you
must thaw seafood quickly,
seal it in a plastic bag and
immerse in cold water for an
hour or microwave on the
defrost setting, stopping
when it is still icy but pliable.

Marinades or rubs enhance
flavor. Refrigerate seafood
when marinating. Dispose of
marinade after use, due to
potential for contamination.

Fish is best cooked quickly at
high heat. For every inch of
thickness, cook eight to ten
minutes. When microwaving
boneless fish, cook on the
high setting for three minutes
per pound. Determine doneness by the color and flaki-
ness of the flesh. Slip the
point of a sharp knife into
the flesh and pull aside; the
edges should be opaque and
the center slightly translucent, with the flakes just
beginning to separate.

PAN-SEARED ROCKFISH
WITH WHITE-BEAN MUSTARD SAUCE

*This was a favorite recipe of former Governor James Gilmore
when he lived in the Governor's Mansion in Richmond.*

FOR SAUCE:

2 tablespoons olive oil or clarified
  butter
2 applewood smoked bacon slices
2 teaspoons Smithfield ham, diced
2 tablespoons each diced carrot,
  Vidalia onion (or other sweet variety), and leeks (white part only)
1 teaspoon garlic, finely minced
1 serrano pepper, minced

¼ cup dry white beans; rinsed and
  soaked overnight
4 cups vegetable stock
½ teaspoon each sea salt and ground
  white pepper
1 bay leaf
2 tablespoons brandy
1 tablespoon Dijon mustard
2 teaspoons fresh thyme, chopped

Note: Soak beans overnight and start sauce 1½ hours before cooking fish.

FOR FISH:

10 to 12 (5- to 6-ounce portions)
  rockfish fillets, skin removed
1 ounce olive oil

sea salt and ground white pepper to
  taste

Heat oil in a saucepan over low heat. Add bacon and ham; cook for 1 minute. Add
carrots, onions, and leeks and continue cooking for about 10 minutes. Add garlic and
serrano pepper; cook an additional 3 to 4 minutes. Add the beans and vegetable
stock, stir in salt, pepper, and bay leaf. Bring to a boil. Reduce heat and cook for
approximately 45 minutes or until beans are soft.

Add brandy, mustard, and thyme; mix well. Turn off the heat and let sit for 10
minutes. Remove the bay leaf. Place mixture in a blender. Cover and blend until
smooth. Pour mixture into a clean saucepan. Bring to a simmer. Adjust consistency
and seasoning, if needed.

Season the fillets with salt and pepper. Using a sauté pan, heat the olive oil and
sear the fillets on both sides. Finish cooking in a 350° F oven until fillets are done.
Spoon sauce over cooked fillets. Makes 10 to 12 servings.

*Mark W. Herndon, executive chef to the governor, first discovered his culinary passion while working under
Master Chef Victor Gielisse at his Dallas restaurant, Actuelle. Herndon graduated with honors from the Culinary
Institute of America in 1993 and has since earned several awards, including gold and bronze medals in culinary
competitions. After a two-year stint at the five-star Williamsburg Inn, Mark arrived at the Executive Mansion in
1995. He served three of Virginia's first families, managing all culinary operations, from the family's daily meals to
official state functions.*

ALMOND-CRUSTED SEA TROUT
WITH CURRY SAUCE

*The crispness of the fish and the creamy texture of the sauce
work together for a pleasing result.*

FOR FISH:

4 (6-ounce) sea-trout fillets
2 teaspoons curry powder
salt and pepper to taste
¼ cup fresh bread crumbs

¼ cup almonds with skin on, finely
   chopped
½ teaspoon dried thyme

FOR SAUCE:

1 tablespoon butter
2 teaspoons curry powder
½ cup chicken broth
½ cup heavy cream

2 tablespoons chopped fresh parsley
   or cilantro
2 teaspoons lemon juice

Butter a shallow baking sheet. Rinse fish and pat dry with paper towels. Sprinkle the
best-looking side of each fillet with 2 teaspoons curry powder, salt, and pepper. Mix
the crumbs, almonds, and thyme on a piece of wax paper. Press the seasoned side of
the fish into the crumb mixture and place on prepared baking sheet. If desired, chill
up to 2 hours.

Preheat oven to 450° F. To make the sauce, heat butter with curry powder. Using a
whisk, stir in broth and boil about 5 minutes until volume reduces by half. Stir in the
cream and heat 2 to 3 minutes. Stir in parsley and lemon juice.

Bake fish until it flakes easily when tested with a fork, about 5 to 7 minutes. To serve,
divide the sauce over warmed plates and place fish in the center. Makes 4 servings.

PANFRIED VIRGINIA SPOTS

All you'll need to make this dish complete is a few wedges of lemon.

4 whole Virginia spots, cleaned
salt and freshly ground black pepper
1 cup cornmeal

½ cup butter or lard
4 lemon wedges

Score each fish three times on each side. Sprinkle the fish inside and out with salt
and pepper. Put the cornmeal on a plate, mix in 1 teaspoon salt and ½ teaspoon pepper, and roll the fish in it to coat both sides.

Heat the butter or lard in a frying pan large enough to hold all 4 fish at once.
When the fat is very hot, add the fish and cook briskly over high heat for about 10
minutes on both sides. Drain on paper towels and serve hot with lemon wedges.
Makes 4 servings.

∽ *Born in Freetown, Virginia, a farming community founded by her grandfather and his friends after emancipation,
Edna Lewis has become synonymous with honest American food, simply and lovingly prepared. She ran a restaurant
in New York, taught cooking classes, and worked as a caterer. Until her death in 2006 she lived in Decatur, Georgia. Recipe reprinted with permission from the book* In Pursuit of Flavor, *by Edna Lewis.* ∽

Buyer's Guide to
SEAFOOD
(continued)

Shrimp cook quickly, in two
to three minutes—just until
the meat loses its glossy
appearance, curls up, and
turns pink. To stop the cooking process, immediately rinse
shrimp in cool water.

Clams, mussels, and oysters
are done when they pop their
shells open, usually after
about five minutes. Discard
those that stay closed.

Keep raw and cooked seafood
and fish separate to prevent
bacterial cross-contamination.
After handling raw seafood
and fish, thoroughly wash
knives, cutting surfaces,
sponges, and hands with hot
soapy water.

Edna Lewis
on the
Virginia Spot

"Virginia spots are the sweet-
est scaled fish I know. They
are pale gray and lightly textured, and while they have
bones, they aren't as bony as
many fish. It's the bone that
gives them such good flavor.
I have found them in the
markets from early spring
until September and have
always felt the best way to
cook them is frying. They are
not sold in other parts of the
country, and I have not found
a fish that can be substituted
for them."

Striped Bass

Since colonial times, striped bass—also known as rockfish, rock, or striper—has proved an East Coast favorite. Nearly 90% of the Atlantic rockfish population, which roam from the St. Lawrence River (in Canada) to Florida, use the Chesapeake Bay for spawning and as a nursery. So to the delight of seafood lovers, Virginia rockfish is available year-round. It takes four or five years for this saltwater fish to become at least 18 inches long, the size that's legal to catch. If the fish evade hooks, it can grow to 54 inches in length and 50 to 60 pounds by the age of 15. An 18-inch striped bass will weigh 4 to 6 pounds when dressed (scaled and gutted), and can be baked whole or filleted. The white-fleshed fish is low in fat and mild in taste.

Croakers, Spots, and Sea Trout: The Talking Fish

These three prolific fish of the Chesapeake Bay are members of the drum family and make a drumming sound using their swim bladders when they stick their heads out of the water. Usually these fish are served whole and are ideal for stuffing. They have lean, tender meat with a sweet flavor and fine flake. The best cooking methods are panfrying, braising, and poaching; they can also be cut into chunks and cooked in soups or fish stews.

POTATO-CHIP ENCRUSTED STRIPED BASS WITH CRAB, PAPAYA, AND PINEAPPLE

This recipe's use of crust and fruits lend the finished fish a tropical appearance.

4 (6-ounce) skinless striped bass fillets
3 tablespoons flour
⅓ cup buttermilk
2 cups salted plain potato chips, crushed
4 tablespoons butter, clarified
½ pound fresh backfin crab meat
½ cup diced pineapple
½ cup diced papaya
2 tablespoons chopped fresh shallots
2 tablespoons each fresh orange juice and dry white wine
2 tablespoons chopped fresh cilantro
salt and white pepper to taste

Dredge the fish in flour, then buttermilk and crushed potato chips. In a large skillet, heat the butter and brown the fillets on both sides, being careful not to burn the potato chips. When brown, place on a baking pan and bake in a 350° F oven for 5 minutes.

To the remaining butter in skillet, add pineapple, papaya, and shallots. Cook for 1 minute on medium heat. Add orange juice and wine. Add cilantro and gently fold the crab into the sauce. Season with salt and pepper. Remove the fillets from the oven and pour the sauce over the fish. Makes 4 servings.

Chef Chuck Sass served this dish at Mahi Mah's Seafood Restaurant and Sushi Saloon in Virginia Beach, where diners can sit by the fireplace and enjoy a view of the ocean. In warm weather, diners enjoy meals outdoors (phone (757) 437-8030 or visit www.mahimahis.com).

BAKED CROAKER WITH POTATOES

Try this recipe on croaker or, in its absence, with any other whole-fish varieties.

2 (1-pound each) whole croaker, gutted and scaled
5 tablespoons virgin olive oil
2 (5-ounce) baking potatoes, scrubbed
1 teaspoon minced fresh garlic, divided
½ teaspoon dried thyme, divided
salt and pepper to taste
2 large fresh tomatoes, coarsely chopped
⅓ cup kalamata black olives, pitted and coarsely chopped

Preheat oven to 400° F. Rinse fish and pat dry with paper towels; set aside. Coat the bottom of a 1½-quart rectangular baking dish with 2 tablespoons oil. Thinly slice potatoes crosswise and layer one third of the slices in the baking dish. Sprinkle with one third of the garlic and thyme; sprinkle with salt and pepper. Repeat, making 2 more layers, drizzling 1 tablespoon oil over each layer. Bake 20 minutes.

Rub fish with remaining tablespoon oil and season with salt and pepper. Place the fish on top of the potatoes and surround with tomatoes and olives. Bake about 20 minutes, or until fish is opaque and flakes easily when tested with a fork. Serve immediately. Makes 2 servings. Recipe can be doubled, using a 3-quart rectangular dish.

FLOUNDER FILLET IN PARCHMENT

*Fish and chips are typically served—but not cooked—in a newspaper.
Here the flounder is cooked in parchment paper to keep the fish moist and
seal in the juices. Just don't try it with today's* Richmond Times-Dispatch!

4 (5- to 8-ounce) flounder fillets
4 tablespoons butter, softened
4 (12 × 16-inch) pieces of parchment
  baking paper
2 teaspoons Old Bay seasoning

¼ teaspoon each salt and pepper
8 lemon slices
2 carrots, peeled and cut into matchsticks (julienned)
2 ribs celery, cut into matchsticks

Preheat oven to 350° F. Rinse fish and pat dry. Spread butter in centers of baking papers. Sprinkle with seasoning, salt, and pepper. Place two lemon slices on top of butter and cover with carrot and celery. Place fillet skin-side up on top of vegetables. Fold paper together; flatten and crease tightly to close.

    Place packets on a cookie sheet. Bake 7 to 10 minutes. The paper should puff up slightly when fish is done. To serve, place packets on plates. Use a sharp knife to cut an "X" in top of parchment and peel back to expose fish. Makes 4 servings.

FLOUNDER WITH PORTOBELLO MUSHROOMS

*Portobellos are super-sized brown mushrooms that form a great
barrier reef between the delicate fish and the skillet during cooking.
After cooking, the mushrooms decorate the top of the fish.*

2 tablespoons olive oil
½ medium onion, coarsely chopped
2 teaspoons fresh lemon juice
1 tablespoon light soy sauce
1 (6-ounce) package sliced portobello
  mushroom caps

¼ teaspoon salt
4 flounder fillets (about 6 ounces
  each)
1 tablespoon chopped fresh dill or
  mint

Heat oil in a large skillet over medium heat. Sauté onion for about a minute. Add lemon juice and soy sauce. Add mushrooms and salt. Cook, stirring gently, until mushrooms become soft, about 10 to 12 minutes.

    Place fish on top of mushroom mixture and sprinkle with herbs. Cover skillet and cook 5 to 7 minutes, or until fish flakes when tested with a fork. Transfer fish to a plate and spoon the mushroom mixture over it. Makes 4 servings.

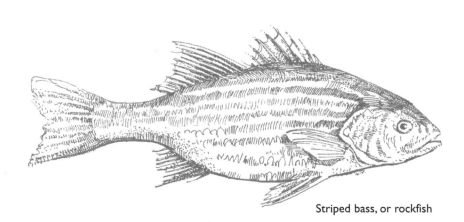

Striped bass, or rockfish

Flounder

Flounder is a flatfish renowned for its fine, tender-yet-firm texture. Its taste is delicate, sweet, and nutty. Both eyes of the winter flounder, sometimes called "lemon sole," are on the right side. Summer flounder, also called "fluke," sport both eyes on the left and sometimes grow to 26 pounds and 37 inches long. The winter flounder is much smaller, topping at 8 pounds and 25 inches long. Care must be taken not to overcook flounder, because it is a very low-fat fish. As soon as the flesh turns white, it is done. Never stir-fry or grill flounder. Thinner fillets are best rolled and baked or microwaved. Thicker fillets may be broiled or panfried.

Flounder Houses

No, they're not places to purchase seafood. Flounder houses are a style of eighteenth-century architecture in historic Alexandria, on the Potomac. These unusual buildings are set back from the street, with one side flat, featureless, and windowless and rising to the ridge of a steeply pitched roof. The blind side contrasts with the windows or "eyes" on the other; thus the houses resemble the flounder fish that have eyes only on one side. One explanation for the popularity of the design is that it served to avoid taxes levied on glass window panes. In addition, the houses conformed to narrow lot dimensions yet still provided space between homes.

—Alexandria Convention
and Visitors Bureau

Buyer's Guide to
• SHAD •

Because shad is riddled with bones—Native American myth says the fish was once an unhappy porcupine turned inside out by the Great Spirit—many cooks bake the fish with bones intact for a long period at a low temperature. When done, the shad bones will have disintegrated and can be eaten just as the bones in canned salmon are eaten. Shad steaks or fillets can be quickly sautéed or panfried.

Shad roe (eggs or caviar) are contained in sacks weighing three to ten ounces. The roe sacks are generally sold in pairs and fried in a small amount of fat or oil. Roe are an excellent source of protein but tend to be high in both fat and cholesterol.

Hush, Puppies, Hush; This Fish Is for Us

"According to legend, hush puppies were named during the War between the States. Dogs followed the camping soldiers, and when fresh fish was caught and cooked, bits of cornmeal were thrown into the fat and given to the dogs to keep them quiet. The cornbread was so good that it is now traditionally served with fried fish."

—Payne Bournight Tyler, *The James River Plantations' Cookbook*

OVEN-STEAMED SHAD

Sealed, slow steaming softens the bones for digestibility, adding calcium to this dish.

1 (3- to 4-pound) dressed shad
salt and lemon pepper to taste
1 cup white wine
3 to 4 cups water

2 ribs celery, broken into chunks
1 medium onion, coarsely chopped
2 bay leaves

Preheat oven to 300° F. Rinse and dry shad. Place on a rack in a roasting pan. Sprinkle fish inside and out with salt and lemon pepper. Add wine and water to a level just under the rack. Place celery, onion, and bay leaves in the water. Cover tightly with lid or aluminum foil. Steam in oven for 5 hours, basting frequently. Makes 6 servings.

SHAD ROE WITH BACON

Some consider the roe of this bony, relatively inexpensive fish the most decadent caviar.

4 strips bacon
1 medium onion
3 tablespoons flour
¼ teaspoon each salt and lemon
   pepper
⅛ teaspoon each garlic powder,
   onion powder, and fine herbs

2 pairs small shad roe (3 to 4 ounces
   per pair)
2 tablespoons lemon juice
chopped fresh parsley and lemon
   slices for garnish

In a large skillet, fry bacon and onion until almost done. Combine flour with dry seasonings. Dredge roe in flour mixture and place in skillet with bacon. Turn heat up to medium high, cover, and cook for 5 minutes. Roe is done when inside is no longer red. Drizzle with lemon juice, sprinkle with parsley, and serve with lemon, bacon, and onions. Makes 2 servings.

WESTOVER CHURCH HUSH PUPPIES

Don't even think about frying up some catfish without first making up a batch of these.

1 cup yellow cornmeal
2 tablespoons flour
1 teaspoon baking powder
½ teaspoon salt
¼ teaspoon baking soda

2 eggs
½ cup buttermilk
¼ cup milk
3 tablespoons minced onion

Sift together cornmeal, flour, baking powder, salt, and baking soda into a medium bowl. Add eggs, buttermilk, milk, and onion. Stir until well combined. Allow batter to stand 5 to 10 minutes before frying. Drop batter by dessert spoonsful into deep fat heated to 350° F. Cook until brown. Fry a few pieces at a time for about 2 minutes, or until golden brown. Makes about 16 hush puppies.

Westover Church was built in the early 1700s in Charles City, Virginia. The brick building with arched windows that extend to the roofline is testament to the early Episcopal heritage of Virginia. In addition to serving as a religious center, the building housed troops of two wars: British General Cornwallis and Union General McClellan. On Sundays, communicants take the same seats their families have had for generations.

CHESAPEAKE BAY BOUILLABAISSE

The numerous ingredients required to make this dish are deceiving—
it is a very easy, flavorful recipe. Serve it with warm sourdough to dip into its juices.

4 tablespoons olive oil
2 cups chopped onion
2 red bell peppers, cored and
    coarsely chopped
1 green bell pepper, cored and
    coarsely chopped
8 cloves garlic, minced
2 cups fish stock, clam juice, or
    chicken broth
2 cups vermouth or dry white wine
2 (16-ounce) cans chopped tomatoes,
    including liquid

1 tablespoon dried basil
1 teaspoon dried thyme
1 bay leaf
¼ teaspoon crushed red-pepper flakes
12 small cherrystone clams
¾ pound monkfish or other
    white fish
½ pound sea scallops
8 crab claws or crab-shaped surimi
    seafood
chopped fresh parsley

In a large pot, heat oil over medium-high heat. Add onion, bell peppers, and garlic.
Stirring occasionally, cover and cook over low heat about 25 minutes, or until tender.

Add stock, wine, tomatoes, basil, thyme, bay leaf, and red-pepper flakes. Partly
cover and simmer 30 minutes.

Note: This base can be prepared the day before or earlier in the day. Reheat before
completing recipe.

Scrub clams and place in a medium-large saucepan. Add an inch of water, cover,
and bring to a boil over high heat. Check every couple of minutes and remove those
clams that have opened; set aside. Discard any that don't open; they are dead and
shouldn't be eaten.

Add monkfish, scallops, and crab claws to the simmering tomato mixture. Cover
and remove from heat. Let stand until fish and scallops turn opaque. Serve immediately in large pasta or soup bowls garnished with parsley. Makes 4 generous servings.

DOGFISH AND CHIPS

Here is the classic British fish 'n' chips.

¾ cup flour
½ cup flat beer or nonalcoholic beer
1 tablespoon oil plus more for frying
4 medium russet potatoes, cut into
    wedges

salt to taste
1 egg, separated
1 pound dogfish shark or cod
malt vinegar, if desired

In a small bowl, blend flour, beer, and 1 tablespoon oil. Cover and refrigerate at least 1
hour. Pour about 1 inch of oil in a heavy skillet. Heat until oil reaches 365° F. Fry
about one third of the potato wedges at a time, frying 2 to 3 minutes on each side, or
until light brown. Drain on paper towels.

Meanwhile, stir egg yolk into flour mixture. Beat egg white with an electric mixer.
When soft peaks form, fold egg whites into flour mixture. Cut fish into 8 pieces. Dip
half the pieces into batter and fry about 3 minutes on each side, or until crispy and
brown. Place on paper towels and repeat with remaining fish. Serve immediately with
fried potato wedges. If desired, sprinkle fish with vinegar. Makes 4 servings.

Monkfish

The monkfish is one of the
ugliest fish in the ocean. Fishermen cut off its enormous
head and belly section at
sea—75% of the whole fish—
and bring in the meaty tail,
which is skinned and cut into
two cylinder-shaped fillets.
This meat is sweet, firm,
white, and similar to that of
lobster, so some call it "the
tenderloin of the sea;" it is
often eaten broiled and with
melted butter, like lobster.
Monkfish is also sautéed,
grilled on a skewer, baked, or
poached. Its texture is great
for soups or stews, and the
meat can be substituted in
recipes for scallops. Also
known as "lotte" and "angler-
fish," the monkfish is caught
as an incidental catch.

Catfish and Dogfish

Catfish and dogfish are as
different as, well, cats and
dogs. Revered by the British
for "fish and chips," dogfish
is a small, ocean-dwelling
shark also called "cape shark"
or "sand shark." Because dogfish is more fatty than a mako
shark or swordfish, it stays
moist even if accidentally
overcooked. It is a rich fish
and should not be paired
with buttery or fatty sauces.
Not unlike cats, catfish—recognizable by facial "barbels"
that look like cat whiskers—
wouldn't be caught dead in
an ocean. Of the 2000
species, the channel catfish is
the one most often eaten by
Americans.

Bluefish

Bluefish is a favorite of Chesapeake Bay sport fishermen. In fact, sport catches outweigh commercial landings. The fish travels in schools and is a voracious eater, consuming menhaden, herring, and mackerel. Named for its bluish-green color, the bluefish is flavorful due to its fat content, which is similar to that of tuna. The versatile meat can be baked, poached, broiled, grilled, or microwaved. However, the flesh is somewhat delicate and does not hold together well if fried.

Black Sea Bass

The black sea bass (*Centropristes striatus*) is known in the Chesapeake Bay area as black will or chub, or simply as sea bass. It is a year-round inhabitant of the mid-Atlantic region. Black sea bass are *protogynous hermaphrodites*, which means that initially they are females, but some larger fish (between 9 and 13 inches or 2- to 5-years old) reverse sex after spawning, to become males. These bluish-black fish are omnivorous bottom feeders and eat small fish, crustaceans, and shellfish. Their scales are pale blue with white centers. From a different family but also commonly caught in Virginia is the striped bass, or *Morone saxatilis* (also called rockfish, rock, and striper).

BLUEFISH GREEK STYLE

The acidic tomatoes are the perfect foil for this relatively fatty, flavorful fish.

2 tablespoons olive oil
1 medium onion, chopped
2 medium carrots, peeled and thinly sliced
2 cloves garlic, minced
½ cup dry white wine
1 (14.5-ounce) can chopped tomatoes, including liquid

2 tablespoons chopped fresh parsley
½ teaspoon salt
¼ teaspoon pepper
4 (6-ounce) skinless bluefish fillets, rinsed and patted dry
¼ cup kalamata or black Greek olives
¼ cup crumbled feta cheese

Preheat oven to 400° F. Heat oil in a medium skillet over medium-high heat. Add onion, carrots, and garlic. Cook, stirring frequently, until vegetables are tender. Add wine and scrape any brown bits from bottom of skillet. Add tomatoes to skillet along with parsley, salt, and pepper. Simmer on low heat 15 minutes.

Spread half of tomato mixture in bottom of a 2-quart rectangular baking dish. Place fish on top and spread remaining tomato mixture over top. Bake 10 to 15 minutes, or until fish flakes easily when tested with a fork. Top with olives and cheese; serve immediately. Makes 4 servings.

GRILLED BLUEFISH
WITH MANGO–RED ONION SALSA

Governor Mark Warner especially likes this recipe created by Mark Herndon, chef of the Executive Mansion in Richmond.

FOR SALSA:

2 mangoes, peeled and diced
½ cup finely chopped red onion
1 tablespoon rice wine vinegar or white wine vinegar

1½ teaspoons fresh lime juice
oil
2 teaspoons chopped cilantro
1½ teaspoons chopped fresh mint

FOR FISH:

1 teaspoon sugar
salt and white pepper to taste

4 bluefish, tuna, or salmon steaks (about 1½ pounds)

The day before serving or at least 4 to 6 hours in advance, place mangoes in a glass bowl. Add onion, vinegar, lime juice, 1½ teaspoons oil, cilantro, mint, sugar, and salt and pepper to taste. Cover bowl and store in the refrigerator.

Preheat a gas grill or ignite charcoal. When the fire is very hot, lightly oil the grill surface as well as the fish. Sprinkle fish with salt and white pepper as desired. Grill fish about 5 minutes on each side. Transfer to serving plates and top with Mango-Red Onion Salsa. Serve immediately. Makes 4 servings.

∽ *Mark Warner had never run for public office before being elected governor in 2001. Born in 1954, he worked his way through school and became the first in his family to graduate from college, earning a bachelor's degree from George Washington University in 1977 and a law degree from Harvard Law School in 1980. The governor went on to become a founding partner of Columbia Capital Corporation, a technology venture capital fund in Alexandria, and started more than 65 businesses that have grown to employ more than 15,000 workers.* ∽

PAN-SMOKED BLUEFISH

Smoking fish over fresh herbs imparts a marvelous flavor to one of Virginia's favorites—blue-fish. As bluefish season is limited, this indoor pan-smoking technique can also be used with any firm fish fillets. Use a large skillet with a tight-fitting cover and a rack.

1 bunch fresh thyme	1 tablespoon dried thyme
1 bunch fresh rosemary	½ teaspoon salt
¼ cup whole black peppercorns	⅛ teaspoon pepper
6 (6-ounce) bluefish fillets, skinned	peanut oil
¼ cup flour	

Soak fresh herbs and peppercorns in water for 15 minutes. Drain and set aside. Blend flour, thyme, salt, and pepper. Dredge fillets in flour mixture. Sauté in a large skillet coated with oil for 3 minutes. Wipe skillet with a paper towel.

Turn up heat under skillet until pan is almost smoking. Place fresh herbs and pep-percorns in skillet. Place fish on a rack over herbs. Cover and smoke for 15 minutes, or until fish are done. If desired, serve with a light cream sauce and lemon rind gar-nish. Makes 6 servings.

Note: According to John T. Maxwell, executive chef and owner of Chef Maxwell's Catering Company in Richmond, this smoking technique tends to fill the kitchen with aromas (which may be a bit too much for some bystanders), so you should move outside and use the side burner on a grill or a portable electric burner.

Recipe reprinted by permission from Culinary Secrets of Great Virginia, *by the Virginia Chefs Association and Martha Hollis Robinson.*

MACKEREL WITH DIJON MUSTARD BUTTER

Mustard is an excellent flavor with this rich fish.

4 (6-ounce) fresh mackerel fillets with skin on	2 teaspoons fresh lemon juice
salt and pepper to taste	⅛ teaspoon ground red pepper
3 tablespoons butter	¼ cup finely chopped fresh parsley
1 tablespoon Dijon mustard	lemon wedges

Rinse fish and pat dry with paper towels. Season with salt and pepper. Butter a heat-proof baking dish, using 1 tablespoon of the butter. In a small bowl, mix the remain-ing 2 tablespoons butter with mustard, lemon juice, red pepper, and parsley. Spread one side of the fish with the butter mixture and place fish in prepared dish.

Set oven rack about 4 inches from the broiler. Preheat the broiler and broil the fish about 5 minutes, or until fish flakes easily when tested with a fork. Serve immediately sprinkled with additional parsley and lemon wedges. Makes 4 servings.

Submarines in the Chesapeake?

The Atlantic croaker man-aged to fool the U.S. govern-ment and scientists during World War II. A hydrophone system set up in the Chesa-peake Bay to detect German submarines began to pick up incessant signals that set off an investigation. The signals turned out to be the croaking fish. Also known as hard head, King Billy, and grum-bler, the Atlantic croaker (*Micropogonias undulatus*), one of Virginia's most abundant fish, "talks"—vibrates its swim bladder with special muscles. It has a loud and distinctive voice, but no trace of a Ger-man accent.

Mackerel

A brilliant color pattern distin-guishes the mackerel from all other fish. The upper half of the fish is iridescent blue-green with a vertical black, wavy band, and the lower half and belly are silvery white. Atlantic mackerel average 14- to 18-inches long and 1 to 2.5 pounds. Like their relatives, tuna, mackerel travel in swift-moving schools of similarly-sized fish. The oily fish has a high percentage of heart-healthy omega-3 fatty acids. Mackerel can be baked or broiled, but grilling gives it a distinctive flavor. To broil, cut the mackerel into inch-thick steaks and marinate them in orange juice or other acidic liquid along with herbs such as basil.

Buyer's Guide to
• TROUT •

The freshest trout has a slippery skin. Scales are so small there's no need to scale the fish. Trout is sometimes sold boned but it maintains more flavor when cooked with bones intact. Cooking methods should be gentle—no grilling (the fish sticks to the grate), blackening, or deep frying. The best cooking methods are poaching, baking, steaming, and smoking. After cooking, the meat will be white to pale pink, with gray coloration along its lateral line. The texture will be soft to moderately firm. Store raw trout in the refrigerator up to two days after purchase. After cooking, refrigerate it up to four days.

FARM-RAISED TROUT WITH APPLES AND HAZELNUTS

The flavors of hazelnuts and apples work wonders for the rather bland farm-raised trout. Butterflying the fish makes this dish extremely attractive.

6 tablespoons butter, divided
2 medium Red Delicious apples, cored and cut into 16 wedges
4 (8-ounce) butterflied rainbow trout fillets
salt and pepper to taste

¼ cup flour
1 tablespoon fresh lemon juice
1 tablespoon dried chives
½ cup chopped, toasted hazelnuts or walnuts
lemon wedges

Melt 3 tablespoons butter in a large skillet over medium-high heat. Add apple and cook about 6 minutes, or until crisp tender. Remove apple with a slotted spoon; set aside.

Rinse trout and pat dry. Sprinkle with salt and pepper and dredge in flour. Place trout in skillet and cook about 2 minutes on each side. Transfer fish and apples to warm plates. Add remaining 3 tablespoons butter to skillet along with lemon juice, chives, and hazelnuts. Drizzle mixture over fish and apples. Serve immediately. Makes 4 servings.

Recipe provided courtesy of the Virginia Apple Growers Association.

CORNBREAD-STUFFED TROUT

It can be Thanksgiving any time of year when this country sage-and-cornbread stuffing spills from a lovely Virginia trout.

1 (3-pound) or 4 (1-pound) dressed trout
½ teaspoon each salt and pepper
1 cup coarsely crumbled cornbread
1 cup soft bread crumbs
½ cup chopped celery

¼ cup chopped onion
2 tablespoons chopped green pepper
¼ teaspoon rubbed sage
4 tablespoons melted butter
¼ cup water

Preheat oven to 350° F. Rinse fish and pat dry with paper towels. Sprinkle fish with salt and pepper. Butter a shallow pan and place fish on it.

In a medium mixing bowl, combine cornbread, bread crumbs, celery, onion, green pepper, and sage. Moisten with 3 tablespoons butter and stuff fish. Drizzle fish with remaining tablespoon butter and cover with foil. Bake 45 to 60 minutes for the large trout or 20 to 30 minutes for the small trout. Makes 4 servings.

Recipe reprinted from Audrey W. Mowson's book, Virginia Country Cooking.

tour

A MARINER'S TOUR OF THE LOWER CHESAPEAKE BAY

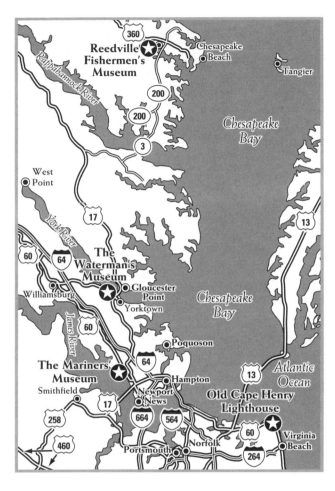

To experience the flavor of Virginia's maritime history, spend a couple of days on the shores of the Chesapeake Bay. To begin where the Bay is born, start at the Old Cape Henry Lighthouse in Virginia Beach.

OLD CAPE HENRY LIGHTHOUSE

Situated near the spot where Captain Norfolk set ashore and gave thanks for a safe crossing of the Atlantic, the 90-foot octagonal sandstone tower was the first authorized by the U.S. Congress. Completed in 1792, it is the third-oldest lighthouse in the United States and the oldest on the Chesapeake Bay. The first lightkeeper created the beacon with fish oil–burning lamps.

In 1870, Cape Henry Lighthouse began to crack; a replacement was built 357 feet to the southeast in 1881. It was thought that the old tower would collapse, but it is still standing today, and visitors can climb it. It was acquired by the Association for the Preservation of Virginia Antiquities in 1930; the lighthouse is a National Historic Landmark and serves as the official symbol of the City of Virginia Beach.

Nearby is Cape Henry Memorial, marking the location of the first landing of the settlers who eventually founded Jamestown. This small park also commemorates the Revolutionary War's Battle of the Capes, where our French allies prevented British ships from sailing to Yorktown to give reinforcements. Without more troops, the British were forced to surrender to General Washington. From the observation deck at night, visitors can see the flashing lights of the Cape Charles Lighthouse across the Bay on Virginia's Eastern Shore, and the somewhat unsightly modern Chesapeake lighthouse.

Also known as Chesapeake Light Station, this 120-foot metal tower marks the opening of the Chesapeake Bay. The actual light tower stands 37 feet above a helicopter deck. The tower is located halfway between the northern and southern channels leading into the bay, about 14.5 miles away from Cape Henry. Built in 1965, the 33 inch concrete-filled steel pilings were driven 180 feet into the ocean floor.

Tour in a Nutshell

• CHESAPEAKE • BAY

OLD CAPE HENRY LIGHT-HOUSE: The lighthouse is open daily from 10 a.m. to 4 p.m. between November 1 and March 14 and from 10 a.m. to 5 p.m. between March 15 and the end of October. The lighthouse is located at Fort Story Army Base on U.S. Highway 60 in Virginia Beach. For more information, contact the visitor center at (757) 422-9421 or visit www.apva.org/apva/light.html.

THE MARINERS' MUSEUM: The museum is open daily from and is located at Warwick and J. Clyde Morris Boulevards in Newport News. Call (757) 596-2222 or visit www.mariner.org. Admission is charged for ages 6 to adult.

THE WATERMAN'S MUSEUM: Between April 1 and November, the museum is open Tuesday through Saturday and weekends only December to March. It is located at 309 Water Street in Yorktown and can be reached by calling (757) 887-2641 or visit www.watermans.org. Admission is charged.

REEDVILLE FISHERMEN'S MUSEUM: Open weekends year-round, daily in summer, the museum is located at 504 Main Street in Reedville. Call (804) 453-6529 or visit www.rfmuseum.org for more information. Admission fee.

Trout in Virginia

Virginia's commercial trout production is valued at nearly $2 million, ranking it in the top ten nationally. (It is illegal to harvest wild trout for commercial sale. Therefore, wild trout are caught only by licensed sport fishermen. Commercially harvested trout are only farm raised.) Food-sized trout sold totals almost a million pounds and accounts for most of the state's trout sales. There are several varieties of trout in Virginia. Most live in lakes or streams, but some are "anadromous," migrating between fresh and salt water. Brook trout are indigenous to the eastern United States and are farmed in Virginia. Weighing about a pound, brook trout are dark-olive in color and have red-orange spots on their sides.

Production of rainbow trout raised via aquaculture is estimated at about 500,000 pounds annually. Trout farms operate in the Allegheny and Blue Ridge Mountain region, where an abundant supply of high-quality spring water provides excellent growing conditions.

The Virginia Trout Company has thousands of rainbow trout on view! Fish for your own dinner or purchase frozen trout to go. Open seven days a week. Route 220, five miles north of Monterey. Phone (540) 468-2280.

THE MARINERS' MUSEUM

In nearby Newport News, The Mariners' Museum is a large, most attractive institution begun in 1930 by the son of Collis P. Huntington, who founded the Union Pacific Railroad and Newport News Shipbuilding and Dry Dock Company. One of the largest international maritime museums in the world, the museum describes its mission as "illuminating mankind's experience with the sea and the events that shaped the course and progress of civilization." The museum is located in a beautiful, shaded park with a lake, walking trail, and picnic areas.

International in scope, the collection is composed of more than 35,000 maritime items, including ship models, scrimshaw, maritime paintings, decorative arts, intricately carved figureheads, working steam engines, and more. Permanent galleries and exhibitions include Defending the Seas, the Age of Exploration, the Chesapeake Bay Gallery, the August F. Crabtree Collection of Miniature Ships, the Great Hall of Steam, the Small Craft Collection, and the *U.S.S. Monitor* Center. The Museum's temporary exhibitions explore a variety of mari-time subjects.

The Museum's Research Library and Archives house some 78,000 volumes, 600,000 photographs and negatives, one million manuscript items, 5000 maps and charts, and 60,000 drawings. The library is also home to the boat-building archives of Chris-Craft Industries.

The Mariners' Museum and South Street Seaport Museum of New York City have formed an alliance to enable the two institutions to share collections, exhibitions, educational services, publications, and other related endeavors. In 1998, Congress designated the two museums America's National Maritime Museum.

THE WATERMAN'S MUSEUM AND THE REEDVILLE FISHERMEN'S MUSEUM

Learn more about the generations of men who have wrested a living from the Chesapeake Bay and nearby waters by visiting the privately supported, nonprofit Waterman's Museum, in a colonial revival manor house on Yorktown's waterfront. Interestingly, the house was floated across the York River on a barge in 1987. It was donated by its Gloucester owner to be used for the museum. Moving the house and preparing the museum site cost $150,000.

The five galleries inside house ship models, dioramas, and artifacts on themes including Chesapeake watermen, bay boats, harvesting fish, aquaculture, tools, and treasures. Outdoor exhibits include an original three-log canoe, dredges, engines,

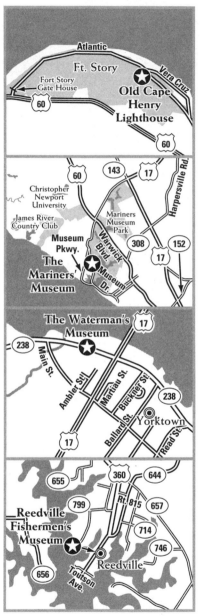

and other equipment used by working watermen past and present.

Cross the York River on U.S. Highway 17 to visit the Fishermen's Museum in Reedville. The historic town's golden age of prosperity from the menhaden fishing industry is reflected in the Victorian mansions that line Main Street. At the turn of the twentieth century, it was purported to be the richest town per capita in the United States. History is also preserved in the sturdy smaller homes, and particularly in the oldest house now standing in Reedville, which is part of the Fishermen's Museum.

The museum is located on the banks of Cockrell's Creek on land once owned by Captain Elijah Reed, who sailed down to the Chesapeake from Maine in 1867 and set up his first small fishery. Permanent exhibits take you through a series of displays featuring ship models, photographs, and artifacts that tell the story of the menhaden fishing industry and how it shaped Reedville, including such items as tools, compasses, old tackle, netting, and other pieces of ships from days gone by.

TANGIER ISLAND

From docks behind the KOA Kampground in Reedville, take a day cruise to Tangier Island, twelve miles from the mainland. The island, which is home to a small seventeenth-century fishing village, is located in the lower Chesapeake Bay and can be reached only by boat or small aircraft. Excursion boats leave Reedville for the island in the morning for a leisurely one-hour-and-fifteen-minute cruise and return in the late afternoon.

Flat and small, the island is ideal for bicycles; it has only three miles of roadway. By far the heaviest traffic at Tangier is on the water. Boats hold the same place in Tangier lives that automobiles do for mainlanders. You've just got to have one: skiffs for the little ones, outboards for the youths, and work craft for the breadwinners.

Tangier Island's population of 850 people, most of whom still speak with an Elizabethan or Cornish accent, is largely supported by the unpredictable waters of the Chesapeake Bay. Ninety percent of the men work on the water, while many women contribute to the growing tourism industry, providing trinkets, crafts, snacks, and take-home seafood.

No armchair traveler, the American shad may migrate more than 12,000 miles during its average life of five years at sea. The fish enter Chesapeake Bay from January to June between the ages of four and six but are only available as a fresh catch in Virginia between late February and April.

The running of shad has spawned a number of rituals; the most famous is known as "shad planking." This tradition consists of politicos, power brokers, or socializing Virginians gathering to share the venerable fish, which is secured on wooden boards and cooked facing a hot fire. The roe is deep fried and served with it.

From the mid 1800s to the early 1900s, the American shad fishery was the largest in the Chesapeake Bay, with annual catches that exceeded 22,000 metric tons. Sadly, the fishery has declined dramatically as a result of overfishing, the blockage of spawning rivers by dams and other impediments, and declining water quality. Even with a three-state Fisheries Management Plan now in place, it could take years for the shad population to rebuild.

part four
DAIRY PRODUCTS

Black dots litter the green grass along Interstate 81 and State Highway 11 around Harrisonburg and Staunton. As you drive closer, the dots become black patches on white, and a herd of Holstein cows comes into view. These cows have all the luck, roaming the picturesque Shenandoah Valley. When they break from their grazing, these bovine ladies doing lunch are treated to the sight of the gentle, ancient Blue Ridge Mountains.

Here, in Rockingham and Augusta Counties, live more than 25,000 dairy cows, the largest concentration in the state. Farther down the valley, in Franklin County—named for that Benjamin in Philadelphia—are about 10,000 more. Virginia is home to more than 100,000 milk cows living on nearly 1,000 commercial dairy farms. Each of these mamas churns out about 2,000 gallons of milk annually; that added up to about 222,000,000 gallons or 2 billion pounds.

Milk not used on the farm (to feed calves, for example) is trucked to one of the state's 15 fluid-milk processing plants, and most of what's produced in Virginia is used as fluid milk. However, in the state are a growing number of artisan or farmstead dairies—independent farmers who raise cows, goats, or sheep for producing handmade specialty cheeses, ice cream, full-fat yogurt, and nonhomogenized milk. Virginia is also home to commercial companies that make premium ice creams, butter, and other dairy products.

History of Milk

No one knows when people first used animal milk for food. Norwegian Vikings may have brought the first cattle to the Americas in the early 1000s. The people of ancient Babylon, Egypt, and India raised dairy cattle as early as 4000 B.C.

Historians are certain that Columbus brought cattle on his second voyage to America in 1493. English colonists brought dairy cows to Jamestown in 1611, helping to end terrible starvation. In the late 1600s, the colonists began feeding grain and hay to cattle during the winter, so that the cows could give milk all year rather than just during the warm months, when they fed in open pastures. The family cow was common during those times, and as pioneers moved west, almost every family traveled with a covered wagon and a cow—their mobile food source. When local laws prohibited cows within city limits, rural farmers increased their herds and established dairy businesses.

chapter one
MILK

∽ *Every U.S. state produces milk, and Virginia hovers around 20th—quite impressive for a relatively small state. Milk brings in about $300 million in cash receipts, and that makes it Virginia's third most valuable farm commodity, right after chickens and cattle. As of December 2001, the top five dairy counties based on milk production are Rockingham, Franklin, Augusta, Wythe, and Fauquier.*

Dairying is hard work; cows must be milked either two or three times a day, 365 days a year. The average cost of a dairy cow in Virginia is $1400. Each cow will deliver an average of six gallons of milk a day; the average value of a day's milk is about $24 per cow. To produce that much milk, each cow requires 35 gallons of water, 20 pounds of grain and concentrated feeds, and 35 pounds of hay and silage. In addition, to give milk, a cow must give birth. This happens about every 13 or 14 months, beginning a new lactation or milking cycle. Female calves are prized for their future milk giving, but the male calves of milk cows—because they can't give milk and are not of a breed that is developed into beef cattle—are raised for veal.

profile
J. CARLTON COURTER, III

Virginia Commissioner of Agriculture and Consumer Services
1994–2007

"I like to go back to my mother's farm to fix fences and get my hands dirty," says the handsome J. Carlton Courter, III. Unfortunately, this doesn't happen often enough to suit Virginia's genial Commissioner of Agriculture, who spends most of his time in meetings with producers and politicians.

J. Carlton Courter, III, the Old Dominion's high priest of farms, fowl, and fish, grew up on a Guernsey dairy farm in Amelia County, about 50 miles from Richmond. Courtland Farm, listed in the Virginia Century Farms program, has been in the family since 1737. The original 200 acres were used for growing dark tobacco and later for hay and forage, until Courter's grandfather, the first Carlton Courter, married and set up a small dairy.

Mr. J. C. Courter, Sr. was a pioneer in the early development of the Guernsey breed in Virginia. His first purchases were two registered cows, both old, one crippled, in 1914. When the cows arrived at the railroad station in Jetersville, he loaded the cripple on the wagon and tied the other behind the wagon for the ride home.

Dairying in those days was more affected by the weather than it is today. "My grandfather had to haul the milk by buckboard to meet the train at Maplewood, a whistle stop on the Norfolk & Western Railroad that no longer exists. Sometimes in the winter, the buckboard would get stuck in the stream at Frog Pond Hill," Courter explains. To remedy this problem, his grandfather eventually purchased 100 additional acres of land right by the railroad and moved the dairy there.

LANGWATER FOREMOST

Mr. Courter made many trips to shows and sales to buy Guernseys, and on one of these trips, in 1916, he bought a purebred Guernsey bull at the dispersal sale of the Lowell Goble Estate in New York for $4000. When he returned home and went to his local bank, the banker thought he had lost his mind, paying such a price for a bull, and refused to lend him the money. So Mr. Courter partnered with two other men, retaining half interest.

The bull's daughters averaged 10,677 pounds of milk and 555 pounds of butterfat per lactation. Word of the great bull's excellent daughters spread, and people from all over the United States began coming to Mr. Courter's farm to see this bull and buy some of his offspring. Courter eventually sold the famous bull, Langwater Foremost, in 1922, for the then-huge sum of $20,000 to J. C. Penney of the retail-store chain. "Just as the train pulled up, someone else offered $25,000, but Mr. Courter said the deal was done, and wouldn't take the higher offer," revealed Commissioner Courter. The bull's name "Foremost" became the name of a major dairy brand.

How Do You Like Your Milk?

Milk is available with varying levels of fat. Whole milk must contain at least 3.25% milk fat and at least 8.25% milk solids. Reduced-fat milk has a milk-fat content of 2%, while the fat content of low-fat milk is 0.5, 1, or 1.5%. Skim milk, also called nonfat or fat-free milk, has a fat content of less than 0.5%. All varieties with fat removed contain at least 8.25% milk solids. And because vitamin A is removed with milk fat, the vitamin is added back to the reduced-fat, low-fat, and skim varieties.

OTHER COMMON MILK PRODUCTS INCLUDE:

Chocolate milk—made by adding chocolate or cocoa and sweetener to whole or low-fat milk.

Cultured buttermilk—made by adding a bacterial culture to milk, most often skim milk. Salt is added for flavor.

Evaporated milk—made by evaporating enough water from whole milk to reduce the volume by half. It contains at least 7.25% milk fat and 25.5% milk solids.

Evaporated skim milk—concentrated skim milk, fortified with vitamins A and D, containing up to 0.5% milk fat and at least 20% milk solids.

Sweetened condensed milk—canned milk concentrate (whole or skim) with a sweetener added.

Eggnog—a mixture of milk, eggs, sugar, and cream that include flavorings like rum extract, vanilla, and nutmeg.

THE COMMISSIONER GOES TO COLLEGE

Courter II, Commissioner Courter's father, was one of eight children and the youngest of three boys. A childless couple who owned another dairy farm in the community offered to send Courter II to college. However, because his two older brothers went off to war, he had to man the dairy farm and couldn't accept their offer. For that reason, the Courter II wasn't eager for his son, Courter III, to learn dairy farming, a nonstop job that requires milking cows several times a day.

However, Courter III always loved agriculture, and at the age of ten he asked his dad to be put to work. "I think he was reluctant for me to become interested in making a living from dairy farming, because it had prevented him from going to college," says Commissioner Courter. "I was given the job of feeding the calves before leaving for school. I would get up at 6 a.m. and mix up the dry milk and put it in bottles. I'd feed older calves grain and hay."

The land along the railroad and the dairy herd were sold when Courter III was 13, and when Courter III was 16, his father died of a sudden heart attack. The rest of the farm machinery and a small beef-cattle herd were sold. Nonetheless, Courter III chose to earn his degree from Virginia Tech in Dairy Science, and his first job was a dairy fieldman for a regional milk-marketing cooperative. This entailed visiting the 100 or so member dairies.

Next, he joined the Virginia Agribusiness Council, where he worked as director of member relations and later as the executive director to defend and promote regulations and legislation affecting the agriculture industry.

During this time he married "the farmer's daughter," who first caught his eye at a Holstein Field Day held at her father's dairy farm. He spotted her again one day while shopping at a Ukrops supermarket in Richmond; he recognized her long, below-the-waist blonde hair. That's when he left a note on her car, asking to meet her. Scarlett Blalock phoned her dad to ask about Courter. The rest is history, a large part of which is J. Carlton Courter, IV, who has the blond hair and blue eyes of his mother.

FORESEEING THE FUTURE OF VIRGINIA AGRICULTURE

In 1994, Courter III was appointed commissioner of the Virginia Department of Agriculture and Consumer Services by Governor George Allen. He was re-appointed by Governor James Gilmore. What does the Commissioner see in the future of Virginia agriculture? "Farming here has followed the nationwide trend of fewer but larger farms. I'm working hard to preserve agriculture in Virginia. It's a continual challenge to identify what will be successful for farming and commercial fishing," he says.

"The burgeoning population encroaches on the farmland, eating up productive fields. On the other hand, Virginia is integrated with the huge population base on the East Coast so there's a ready market for farm products. Fortunately, technology is allowing us to produce more per acre as we lose farmland to housing developments.

"Watermen are increasingly challenged to make a living from the Chesapeake Bay. If they fish enough to make a living, it depletes the Bay's resources. You know the old saying, 'Don't eat your seed corn.' But aquaculture has the potential to mushroom. Seafood such as trout, tilapia, and hard clams are already being cultivated, with more to come," forecasts Courter.

Only a blip on the radar scope a few years back, the floriculture, turfgrass, and Christmas-tree industries are rapidly growing. Greenhouse and nursery products now account for 24.3% of all Virginia crops. "The turfgrass industry grows sod for homes as well as for diverse commercial properties such as the Washington Redskins' football stadium," Courter explains.

The apple industry faces ongoing challenges from Washington State, which is, in turn, being challenged by apples from China. "One way to bolster Virginia's apple industry is to grow more value-added specialty apples," Courter believes. The peach business suffers from the vagueries of the weather. "Virginia is far enough south to grow peaches, but far enough north that if we have a late-spring chill, it can freeze the blossoms," he notes. "On the other hand, our fresh-market tomato industry has zoomed to number four in the nation. Turkeys also came from a small business to number four in Virginia as well as in the nation. This took off when Mr. Charles Wampler, Sr. devised a way to incubate turkey eggs."

Courter explains that in Virginia there is a soybean consortium selling edible varieties directly to Japan, as well as a huge industry growing soybeans for animal feed. And fortunes were made on potatoes grown on the Eastern Shore.

"Agriculture is Virginia's oldest and largest industry," Courter concludes. "The continued success of Virginia agriculture is proof that farmers, agribusinesses, and consumers are willing to adapt to new markets and to the increasing changes in existing markets. Unlike Midwest agriculture, where corn, soybeans, wheat, cattle, and hogs dominate, the Commonwealth has a huge diversity of crops. We grow those important commodities as well, but also produce large amounts of poultry products, vegetables, potatoes, fruit, grapes, tobacco, cotton, peanuts, nursery, and seafood products. In fact, you only have to look at our Virginia's Finest program to see all the different raw and processed foods produced in the state."

LA VISTA PLANTATION'S
CREAMED VIRGINIA COUNTRY HAM

This comforting dish, served over English muffins, hot buttered toast,
or corn bread, is a La Vista breakfast favorite.

3 tablespoons butter	1 cup chopped Virginia country ham
3 tablespoons minced onion	1 tablespoon chopped parsley or
3 tablespoons green pepper, chopped	chives
3 tablespoons flour	⅛ teaspoon paprika
1½ cups milk (more, if needed)	2 tablespoons dry sherry

In a skillet melt the butter over medium heat, and sauté the onion and green pepper until light brown. Sprinkle in the flour and stir a few minutes. Add the milk slowly, stirring constantly. Add the ham and simmer, stirring until thickened. Remove the pan from the heat and season with the remaining ingredients. Makes 4 servings.

La Vista Plantation is located on ten acres with mature trees, flowering shrubs, pastures, woods, gardens, and a pond stocked with bass and sunfish. The home was constructed in 1838 and is located in the Spotsylvania County countryside just outside the historic city of Fredericksburg. Owner Ed Schiesser is chief of exhibits and design at the Hirshhorn Museum and Sculpture Garden at the Smithsonian Institution. Phone the bed-and-breakfast at (800) 529-2823 or (540) 898-8444 or visit www.lavistaplantation.com.

Buyer's Guide to MILK

When selecting milk, examine containers for leaks and other damage. Purchase only milk products that are in perfect condition. Check "sell by" dates on milk. If stored properly, milk will usually stay fresh for seven days past the "sell by" date. Pick up milk just before checking out of the supermarket so it stays as cold as possible. Take milk home after purchase and refrigerate immediately in the coldest part of the refrigerator.

Don't let milk remain at room temperature any longer than necessary. Pour only what milk is needed and return the rest to the refrigerator. Exposure to light destroys milk's flavor and riboflavin. Freezing affects the quality of milk and is not recommended.

Buttermilk and Sour Cream

With "butter" in its name, many people assume buttermilk is high in fat. However, the name came not from the butter content but from the origin of buttermilk as the watery product (whey) left from making butter. Today's buttermilk is made from low-fat or skim milk and has less than 2% fat and sometimes no fat at all. It's designated as cultured low-fat milk or cultured nonfat milk. To make cultured buttermilk, the milk is pasteurized at 180° to 190° F for 30 minutes, or at 195° F for two to three minutes. The heating process destroys all bacteria and minimizes the separating of liquid from solids. After cooling, a starter culture of desirable bacteria is added to develop the buttermilk's acidity and flavor. The ripening process takes about 12 to 14 hours. The buttermilk is gently stirred to break the curd and is cooled to 45° F to halt fermentation. It is then packaged and refrigerated. The same process is used to make sour cream, except that it is begun with light cream rather than with milk.

LONGWOOD HOUSE MILK PUNCH

This Southern alcoholic punch is attractively served in a punch bowl in which an "iceberg" of vanilla ice cream floats.

1 gallon milk
1 gallon and 1 quart vanilla ice cream
6½ cups bourbon

3¼ cups medium-dark rum
1 cup crème de cacao

The day prior to serving, mix milk, 1 gallon of ice cream, bourbon, rum, and crème de cacao; refrigerate. At serving time, place the remaining 1 quart ice cream in a punch bowl. Pour the milk mixture over the ice cream and garnish with nutmeg. (Nutmeg may also be sprinkled over individual servings, if desired.) Makes about 60 (6-ounce) servings.

Longwood House, built in 1815, serves as the president's home at the 3300-student, co-ed Longwood College in Farmville; the house is used for many social functions. Confederate General Joseph E. Johnston was born at this site. Farmville is located about halfway between Richmond and Lynchburg and is also home to Hampden-Sydney College. The source of this old Virginia recipe is attributed to Longwood College, but today's regents say alcohol is not served there.

JASMINE PLANTATION'S OLD-FASHIONED BUTTERMILK PIE

This airy, light pie is an old Vogt family recipe.

1 cup sugar
3 tablespoons flour
½ teaspoon salt
3 large eggs, separated
2 cups buttermilk

2 tablespoons butter, melted
¾ teaspoon lemon or vanilla extract
¼ teaspoon cream of tartar
1 (10-inch) deep pie crust, unbaked

Preheat oven to 375° F. In a large mixing bowl, blend sugar, flour, and salt; set aside. In a medium bowl, beat egg yolks slightly; add buttermilk and butter. Add gradually to dry ingredients and blend thoroughly; set aside.

Using an electric mixer, beat egg whites until fluffy; add cream of tartar and beat until stiff. Fold gently but thoroughly into the batter. Pour into pie shell and bake about 45 minutes, or until a knife inserted in the center comes out clean. Makes 8 servings.

Jasmine Plantation Bed & Breakfast is a restored eighteenth-century farmhouse situated on 47 acres in Providence Forge, between Richmond and Williamsburg. Joyce and Howard Vogt describe their inn as "country with an elegant flair." The Vogts serve a full country breakfast (phone (804) 966-9836 or visit www.jasmine plantation.com).

YODER DAIRY'S CRÈME CARAMEL

Crème caramel is the French version of the Spanish flan. This recipe calls for the use of only one dish rather than the individual ramekins used by some restaurants.

1 cup granulated sugar	4 egg yolks
1 cup water	1 teaspoon vanilla
2 cups milk	sweetened whipped cream and
1 cup whipping cream	berries for garnish
½ cup sugar	

Dissolve sugar in water. Bring to a boil. Boil until mixture turns a light caramel color. Remove from the heat and pour into a small flan or cake pan. Using oven mitts, tilt and turn pan so that the caramel covers bottom and as much of the sides of pan as possible. (Be careful; the caramel mixture will be very hot.)

Beat together milk, whipping cream, sugar, egg yolks, and vanilla. Pour into the caramel-lined pan. Bake at 325° F for 1 hour, or until custard is set. When cool, invert onto a rimmed serving plate. Serve with sweetened whipped cream and fresh berries. Makes 6 to 8 servings.

This recipe was provided by Yoder Dairies.

WHITE FENCE BED AND BREAKFAST'S CHOCOLATE BREAD PUDDING

A chocolate-bourbon sauce renders this version of the Victorian staple a true delight.

3 cups milk	3 eggs
4 (1-ounce) squares semisweet baking chocolate	3 tablespoons butter, melted
	1 teaspoon cinnamon
3 cups old bread cubes (about 6 to 8 slices bread, crusts removed)	1 cup chocolate syrup
	1 tablespoon bourbon
¼ cup sugar	sweetened whipped cream

Heat oven to 350° F. Butter a 1½-quart round casserole or soufflé dish; set aside. In a 2-quart saucepan, combine milk and chocolate. Cook over medium heat, stirring constantly, until chocolate is melted and blended. Do not boil. Stir in bread and set aside.

In a large bowl, combine sugar, eggs, butter, and cinnamon. Stir in milk mixture. Pour mixture into prepared casserole and set it in a baking pan containing warm water as high as possible up the sides of the casserole. Bake for 50 to 70 minutes, or until knife inserted in center comes out clean. Let stand until warm.

For the topping, combine syrup and bourbon; heat but do not boil. Serve pudding warm, topped with sauce and whipped cream. Makes 8 servings.

This recipe was provided by White Fence Bed and Breakfast in Stanley, in the heart of the Shenandoah Valley. The lovely Victorian home, built in 1890, is surrounded by mountains, tall oaks, and colorful flower beds (phone (540) 778-4680 or or (800) 211-9885 or visit www.whitefencebb.com).

Home Delivery

Yoder Dairies has been serving Norfolk, Virginia Beach, and Chesapeake since 1929, when Eli and Elmer Yoder, two Amish farmers from Kempsville, set up a small plant and began bottling milk from their dairy farms. In 1931, the health department required that they pasteurize the milk. The Yoders knew that this would be more than they could handle by themselves, so they formed a co-operative with all of the area Amish dairy farmers. The co-op built a large plant and purchased trucks to replace the horses and wagons. Today the dairy delivers milk and dairy products in old-fashioned returnable glass bottles to 5000 homes between 12:30 and 7 a.m. Yoder is one of only two home-delivery dairies remaining in the state; visit online at www.yoder dairies.com.

Border Collies

One of the most important members of a dairy-farm workforce is the border collie. These dogs run, walk, circle, nip—anything to herd livestock. Border collies have perfected their collecting skills over hundreds of years on the border between England and Scotland. Their herding instinct runs so deep that the dogs will attempt to herd most anything—cattle, sheep, chickens, children, and even bees. Two collies can do the equivalent of ten men when gathering up a pasture of cows or sheep to move them to another field, or into a truck or holding pen.

FROM COW TO CHEESE
Making Dairy Products at Shenville Creamery

In May 2001, the first on-farm dairy processing plant west of the Blue Ridge opened in Virginia. At Shenville Creamery and Garden Market in Timberville, visitors can watch milk being pasteurized and being made into dairy products, including butter, yogurt, soft cheese, ice cream, and creamy milk.

The 5000-square-foot, state-of-the-art facility processes raw milk from the lactating herd of cows just 200 yards away. The milking parlor is a special building for milking the herd. The dairy herd must be milked either two or three times daily, year-round. Shenville uses a herringbone milking parlor—a raised, zigzag-design milking stall which allows the group milking of several cows at one time in a pipeline milking system. Just minutes out of the cow, the milk is cooled by a falling film chiller and then placed in a tank truck. Milk received at the processing plant is tested before being unloaded. It is checked for odor, appearance, proper temperature, acidity, bacteria, and the presence of drug residues. These tests take no longer than 10 to 15 minutes. If the tank load passes the tests, the milk is pumped into the plant's refrigerated storage tanks. The milk is then stored for the shortest possible time.

Fresh, fluid milk requires the highest quality raw milk and is generally designated as Grade "A." This grade requires a higher level of sanitation and inspection on the farm than is necessary for milk of "manufacturing" grade. At Shenville, the HTST (high temperature—short time) pasteurizer is used to kill harmful bacteria. The milk is rapidly heated to 180° F for 22 seconds and then quickly cooled. This process preserves the taste of the milk. The HTST method is conducted in a series of stainless-steel plates and tubes, with the hot, pasteurized milk on one side of the plate being cooled by the incoming raw milk on the other side.

Pasteurized milk is not sterile and may contain small numbers of harmless bacteria. To prevent bacterial growth, the milk must be immediately cooled to 40° F or below and stored away from outside contamination. After pasteurization, the milk is held in insulated holding tanks before being bottled or turned into yogurt or cheese.

Most modern plants such as Shenville use a separator to control the fat content of various products. The separator is an airtight bowl with funnel-like, stainless-steel disks.

The homogenizer breaks up the large fat molecules into tiny particles, so that the cream remains in solution rather than floating to the top. Shenville's Cream Line products are purposely not homogenized, so the cream comes to the top of the glass bottles.

In addition to preventing cream separation, homogenizing milk renders a whiter look, a richer flavor, and a more digestible quality. Homogenization also lends body and texture to ice cream and products such as half-and-half, cream cheese, and evaporated milk.

Shenville packages milk in returnable glass bottles that require a deposit. The bottle-washing machine washes the returnable glass bottles in hot, soapy water, rinses them before they are filled, and then the automatic bottling machine fills the glass bottles again.

MAKING CHEESE

To make cheese, milk is mixed with live cultures in the cheese-curding tank. A major part of the water contained in fresh fluid milk is removed while most of the solids are retained. The dryer the cheese, the longer it can be stored; thus turning milk to cheese is also a way of preserving it.

The fermentation of milk into finished cheese requires several steps and only four basic ingredients: milk, microorganisms, rennet, and salt. First the prepared milk is innoculated with lactic-acid-producing bacteria. Next, the milk is curdled. Once the cheese has set, it is cut up by a screen. The curd is then gently heated, causing it to shrink. The degree of shrinkage determines the moisture content and the final consistency of the cheese. Whey is removed by draining or dipping.

Most cheese is ripened for varying amounts of time in order to bring about the chemical changes necessary for transforming fresh curd into a distinctive aged cheese. The cheeses at Shenville are soft and not aged. Cottage cheese is the most popular cheese. This familiar product is available in both cream and skim styles. It is in great demand with customers who remember the cottage cheese "mama used to make in a bag on the clothes line."

Shenville also makes Hallumi, an unusual cheese product that can be fried. The creamery's Farmer's Cheese and Queso Blanco are white, fresh cheeses made from the same ingredients but processed in different ways. Both are delicious when used as spreads or salad toppings. They can also be used in lasagnas and other pasta dishes.

The cheese trolley is where the whey is drained from the quark, which is then used to make dairy dips and spreads. Stirred and set yogurts are made in a variety of flavors. Stirred yogurts are those blended with fruit flavors; cultures are added and incubated, then yogurt is packaged in 6-ounce cups. Set yogurts are flavored and packaged, then incubated, which makes them firmer and thicker than the stirred varieties.

MAKING ICE CREAM

The batch pasteurizer is used to pasteurize the ice-cream mix before it is frozen into ice cream. The basic ingredients in ice cream are milk, cream, sugar, flavoring, and a stabilizer. Stabilizers and emulsifiers are added to prevent formation of ice crystals, especially during temperature fluctuations in storage. The ice-cream mix is pasteurized and the heated mix is usually homogenized to make a smoother texture. Milk and other ingredients are frozen in the ice-cream batch freezer.

Ice Cream in Early Virginia

Ices, sherbets, and milk ices enjoyed in the fashionable Italian and French royal courts were first served in Virginia by George Washington, Thomas Jefferson, and Dolley Madison. Dolley Madison served ice cream at her husband's second inaugural banquet at the White House in 1813. While George Washington's papers refer to an ice-cream maker, the first recipe for ice cream was handwritten by Jefferson, and he had a favorite 18-step recipe for a dessert resembling baked Alaska. Visitors frequently noted enjoying ice cream at meals with Thomas Jefferson. One commented, "Ice creams were produced in the form of balls of the frozen material inclosed in covers of warm pastry, exhibiting a curious contrast, as if the ice had just been taken from the oven." Jefferson enjoyed ice cream throughout the year because ice was "harvested" from the Rivanna River in winter and taken to the Monticello ice house, which held 62 wagon loads. The ice house was used primarily to preserve meat and butter, but also to chill wine and to make ice cream. Washington owned "two pewter ice cream pots" and spent $200 for ice cream in New York during the summer of 1790.

—Mrs. Mary Randolph, *The Virginia Housewife or Methodical Cook,* 1860

Milk is the official beverage of
the commonwealth. In fact,
there is a Milk Commission
that ensures a constant, available, and reasonably priced
supply of fresh and wholesome Grade "A" milk for its
citizens. Milk is regulated
because of its highly perishable nature requiring continual refrigeration. It must move
through marketing channels
within a few days of production. It is not possible for
dairy farmers to withhold production in the anticipation of
a more attractive price. Storage, transportation, and handling are problematic due to
the bulky nature of the product and its strict sanitary
handling requirements.

The Virginia Milk Commis-
sion was created in 1934 to
supervise the producer price,
supply, and sale of fluid milk
in Virginia. Since the Milk
Act was amended in 1974,
the commission is comprised
of four consumer members,
two milk producers, one milk
processor-distributor, and an
administrator, who is a non-
voting consumer member.

The Commission establishes
monthly producer prices at
competitive levels with adjacent markets and it preserves
market stability. On July 1,
2003, the Commission was
merged within the Virginia
Department of Agriculture and
Consumer Services. For more
information about The Virginia Milk Commission, see
www.vdacs.virginia.gov/smc.

essay

SHENVILLE CREAMERY
Milk Makes Dreams Materialize

Shenville Creamery and Garden Market in Timberville was the brainchild of owners Leon and Ida Heatwole, a Mennonite couple, who realized their dream of making their own dairy products and selling them directly to consumers.

In 1998, the local dairyman's co-op was sold to out-of-state owners, and Leon
and Ida decided it was a good time to consider changing the way they marketed
the milk from their dairy. Leon headed off to Penn State to take advantage of the
Dairy Science program. Next, he and Ida purchased Israeli manufactured Pladot
creamery equipment, and the whole family—including Andrea, 16; Amber, 14;
Weston, 11; and Trenton, 8—headed off to Israel to be trained in the technicalities
of turning the raw milk from their dairy into market-ready products.

But why would customers drive out to the farm in the country to buy dairy
products when all they have to do is grab a plastic jug of milk off the shelf in the
supermarket? Because they crave fresh, high-quality products that they can't find
elsewhere. And that's what Shenville Creamy delivers. Customers love Shenville's
Cream Line unhomogenized whole milk in glass bottles with a visible line of
cream at the top. Leon and Ida were determined that their products be unique and
delicious. As Leon says, "I don't want to sell just chocolate milk. I want to sell the
best chocolate milk people have ever tasted."

To achieve that goal, the family was involved in all aspects of the operation.
Leon was a farmer one minute and a businessman the next. It wasn't unusual for
him to be called from the office to tend to a new baby Holstein, to drive the milk
truck, or even to run the bottle washer in the creamery. He grew up on a dairy
farm in the Shenandoah Valley and has operated his own dairy at Shenville for
twelve years.

Ida has an eye for creative design and a green thumb that turns her yard into a
colorful flower garden and encourages fruits and vegetables to prosper in their rich
50 acres of bottom land along Virginia's historic Shenandoah River. The results
were sold in the creamery's Garden Market, housed in the new market building,
where customers can also purchase Ida's delectable baked goods and the farm's
many flavors of homemade ice cream. Everything sold in the market is grown on
the farm. It was always fresh, because it was harvested several times a day as needed. If it's not in season locally, it wasn't in the market.

Unfortunately, despite brisk sales and distribution from Williamsburg to
Washington, the Heatwoles got into a financial bind from borrowing hundreds of
thousands of dollars to put in a new well, two new 5,000-square-foot buildings for
production and retail, and other inspection-related alterations. The creamery was
sold piecemeal in 2003, and so far, no one has restarted the business despite the
popularity of the high-quality farm-made dairy products.

chapter two
BUTTER AND CREAM

∾ *Consumption of dairy products, many with a significant cream or butter-fat content, has been rising steadily in Virginia. For example, ice-cream consumption has been on the rise, and many of the most popular flavors are relatively high in cream content. Cream-cheese consumption doubled between 1984 and 1998, possibly due to the proliferation of bagel outlets in the state. Virginia is home to several large butter- and cream-producing dairies, including Bergey's Dairy Farm in Chesapeake, Flav-O-Rich Dairy in Bristol, Homestead Creamery in Wirtz, Marva Maid Dairy in Newport News, Richfood Dairy in Richmond, Morningstar Farms in Mt. Crawford, and Westover Dairy in Lynchburg.*

Butter

It takes ten quarts of milk to make a pound of butter. What's left is about nine quarts of skim milk and buttermilk, which at one time were disposed of as animal feed or waste, but with today's demand for low-fat dairy products, the skim portion has become more valuable. Commercial butter is 80 to 82% milk fat, 16 to 17% water, and 1 to 2% milk solids other than fat (sometimes called curd). Salt may be added to butter for flavoring and preservation purposes.

Virtually all butter in the United States today is sweet-cream butter made by agitating or churning non-homogenized milk. The churning process can take 40 to 60 minutes in a hand-operated churn, but in factories, butter is made in seconds by continuous "churns" that mix the milk with high-speed blades. USDA Grade "AA" is the highest grade of butter, based on aroma, flavor, and texture. Butter from cows that are eating dry, stored feed during the winter may not contain as much beta-carotene for proper coloring as butter from pasture-fed cows, so small amounts of a yellow vegetable coloring from the seed of the annatto tree may be added.

The largest number of cows in Virginia are those of the black-and-white **Holstein** breed that first came to the colony from Holland in 1621. Producing the most milk on average, Holsteins weigh 1500 pounds when mature. Dairy cows come in different sizes. **Jerseys,** at 900 pounds, are the smallest of the dairy breeds but produce milk with the highest protein and fat content. These fawn-colored cows with white markings came here from the Isle of Jersey in the English Channel. Also from a Channel island come the **Guernseys** with coloring similar to the Jerseys but slightly larger. Their milk is a distinctive golden color. **Ayrshires** came to the United States from the County of Ayr in Scotland in 1822. Their color varies from light to deep cherry red, mahogany, brown, or a combination of these colors with white. Some are all white. They top out at 1200 pounds. Lastly, we have the **Brown Swiss** of "how now, brown cow" fame. This solid light-to-dark brown breed arrived from Switzerland in 1869 and matches the Holstein in weight.

—Virginia
Tech Extension Service

SCONES FROM PORCHES ON THE JAMES

These feather-light scones are a treat for teatime or breakfast.

½ cup dried currants
6 tablespoons sugar, divided
¼ teaspoon ground cinnamon
2 cups all-purpose flour
2 teaspoons baking powder
¾ teaspoon salt
½ teaspoon baking soda

5 tablespoons unsalted butter or margarine
1 cup plain nonfat yogurt
1 large egg, separated
clotted cream, crème fraîche, or fruit butter

Soak currants in hot water to cover, let stand 5 minutes, then drain well and set aside. Combine 3 tablespoons sugar with cinnamon; set aside.

Preheat oven to 425° F. In large mixing bowl, combine flour, remaining 3 tablespoons sugar, baking powder, salt, and soda. Cut in butter with pastry blender until mixture resembles coarse crumbs. Stir in drained currants.

Blend yogurt and egg yolk; add to crumb mixture, stirring just until dough clings together. Turn out onto lightly floured surface and gently knead 10 to 12 strokes. Roll or pat dough to ½ inch thickness and cut with 2- to 2½-inch biscuit cutter or pat into 2 circles on an ungreased baking sheet and cut, pizza style, into wedges. Brush tops with lightly beaten egg white and sprinkle with cinnamon-sugar mixture. Bake in a 425° F oven 15 to 18 minutes or until light brown. Cool on wire rack 5 minutes, then serve warm with clotted cream. Makes 16 to 18 scones.

∽ *Porches on the James is a bed-and-breakfast located on a bluff 60 feet above the James River, about five miles north of Smithfield. The property includes a river beach (phone (866) 356-0602) or visit www.porchesonthejames.com).* ∽

PRESIDENT WILSON'S LEMON CAKE

This recipe is from the personal cookbook of Woodrow Wilson's mother.

1 cup butter
3 cups sugar
5 eggs, separated
1 teaspoon baking soda
1 cup milk

4 cups flour, sifted
grated zest (yellow color from peel) of 1 fresh lemon
juice of 1 lemon (about 2 tablespoons)

Grease well, then flour, 2 (9 × 5 × 4-inch) loaf pans; set aside. In a large bowl, cream butter with sugar. Set aside the egg whites in an electric-mixer bowl. In a separate bowl, beat egg yolks until frothy. Add yolks to butter mixture; mix well. In a small bowl or glass measure, dissolve the soda in milk. Add this to the butter mixture. Stir in lemon zest and juice. Slowly mix in the flour.

Preheat oven to 350° F. Beat whites until stiff peaks form. Gently fold into the butter mixture. Pour batter into prepared pans. Bake for about an hour, or until golden brown on top and a knife inserted in the center comes out clean. If the cake is browning too much on top, cover with aluminum foil until it finishes baking. Makes 2 loaves, about 20 servings.

∽ *Woodrow Wilson was America's 28th president and served two terms. Wilson's birthplace and museum, in Staunton, is restored to depict Wilson's family life in the Shenandoah Valley before the Civil War and features period furniture (phone (540) 885-0897 or (888) 496-6376).* ∽

INDIAN FIELDS TAVERN
RUM-CHOCOLATE CAKE WITH
CHOCOLATE-BUTTERCREAM FROSTING

Serve small wedges of this rich, frosted single-layer cake.

FOR CAKE:

1 cup cake flour (you can substitute bleached white all-purpose flour, but remove 1 tablespoon flour after measuring 1 cup)
⅔ cup sugar
1½ teaspoons baking powder
1½ teaspoons baking soda
pinch of salt

¼ cup cocoa powder
1½ cups milk
4 eggs
¾ cup (1½ sticks) sweet butter, melted
¼ cup rum
1 tablespoon rum extract (optional)

FOR CHOCOLATE-BUTTERCREAM FROSTING:

1¼ cups sugar
1 cup heavy cream
5 ounces unsweetened chocolate

½ cup butter (1 stick)
1 teaspoon vanilla

Preheat oven to 325° F. Grease and flour a 9-inch round cake pan; set aside. In the electric mixer's large bowl, sift flour, sugar, baking powder, baking soda, salt, and cocoa. In a separate bowl, combine milk and eggs; beat well. Add butter and half of the milk mixture to the flour mixture; beat with electric mixer until blended; then mix on a faster speed 5 to 7 minutes. Slow the mixer and add the rest of the milk mixture ⅓ cup at a time. Add rum and extract (if using).

Pour batter into prepared pan. Bake 25 minutes, or until a toothpick inserted in the center comes out clean. Let cake cool 5 to 10 minutes, then invert on a cake plate.

For frosting, combine sugar and cream in a saucepan. Simmer 5 minutes on low heat. Remove from heat and add chocolate, stirring to melt and blend. Stir in butter until melted, then stir in vanilla. Chill until mixture thickens, then beat until creamy. When cake is completely cool, spread top and sides with frosting. Makes 10 servings.

Indian Fields Tavern, in Charles City, opened in 1987 in what had been the falling-down farmhouse of an old 1880s Mennonite dairy farm. In its fine Southern cuisine, the eatery uses herbs from its garden. Diners can enjoy the good weather by having their meal on the porch (phone (804) 829-5004).

DIJON-MUSTARD BUTTER

This flavorful butter makes steamed vegetables or broiled fish or poultry a special treat.

3 tablespoons fresh parsley, chopped, or 3 teaspoons dried parsley
2 tablespoons green onion with some of green tops, finely chopped

½ cup (1 stick) butter, softened
1 tablespoon Dijon mustard
1 tablespoon lemon juice
1 clove garlic, crushed

Combine all ingredients and add salt and freshly ground pepper to taste. Shape butter into a log about 1½ inches in diameter. Wrap in plastic wrap. Keep in refrigerator up to 1 week or wrap in aluminum foil and freeze up to 1 month. Makes 8 servings.

This recipe was provided courtesy of Southeast United Dairy Industry Association.

Milking Machines and Barns

The first milking machines, used in the early 1880s, failed because they were not able to exert intermittent pressure. In 1905 the firm of Burrell-Lawrence-Kennedy introduced a pulsating machine with an arrangement of cylinders and valves that automatically increased and decreased the vacuum pressure. It simulated the mouth of a calf rather than a person's hand. Though hand milking was more thorough and kept the cows fresh longer, the pulsating machine reduced annual labor by about 28 man-hours per cow.

Perhaps the most important development in dairy equipment, however, was not a machine, but the sanitary dairy stable. Traditionally, barn builders aimed at tight construction with low ceilings that kept the stock warm in winter. Understanding of how tuberculosis and pleuropneumonia spread—on water droplets—spurred designers to think of ways to remove condensation and allow in as much light and fresh air as possible. They also eliminated various compartments and posts, and rounded over corners to prevent accumulation of dirt and germs.

—Terry Sharrer, *A Kind of Fate: Agricultural Change in Virginia, 1861–1920*

Cream

If freshly-drawn milk is left to settle, the high-fat portion rises to the top to form a thick layer of cream. The high fat content of cream gives it a rich, buttery flavor and velvety texture. Cream contributes body to a variety of sweet and savory puddings, custards, and mousses and is the basis for all ice creams. Cream also adds richness and texture to such confections as caramels, truffles, toffee, and pralines.

Cream holds a shape when whipped. Several varieties of cream are available:

- half-and-half, a mixture of milk and cream, containing 10.5–18% milk fat;
- light cream, coffee cream, or table cream, with a milk-fat content between 18 and 30%;
- light whipping cream or whipping cream, with a milk-fat content 30–36%;
- heavy whipping cream or heavy cream, which has milk-fat content of at least 36%.

Cream is highly perishable. Make it one of the last purchases at the supermarket and refrigerate it as soon as possible. Pasteurized cream stays fresh for at least one week. Ultrapasteurized cream keeps for six to eight weeks in an unopened container; after opening, use within one week. For maximum volume, chill beaters and bowl and keep cream as cold as possible before beating.

—Jane Horn,
Cooking A to Z

RAITA

*Fresh yogurt is made and eaten daily in Indian homes,
and this salad, or some variation of it, is a mealtime staple.*

2 cups plain yogurt
1 teaspoon salt
freshly ground black pepper
¼ teaspoon roasted and ground cumin seeds
1 cucumber, peeled and grated

½ cup slivered almonds
½ cup trimmed and washed fresh mint leaves
¼ to ½ cups raisins
2 whole potatoes, boiled and cubed (optional)

Place two paper coffee filters in a large strainer set over a mixing bowl. Place yogurt in the paper and let drain in the refrigerator 2 to 4 hours. Discard liquid and transfer yogurt to same mixing bowl. Beat yogurt with a wire whisk until smooth. Stir in salt, pepper, and cumin. Fold in potatoes, cucumber, almonds, mint, and raisins. Chill in refrigerator an hour or more. Makes 4 servings.

Recipe is reprinted by permission from the book Asian Grills *by Alexandra Greeley. Greeley, a resident of Reston, is a well-known food writer who lived in Hong Kong for four years and worked as the food editor/writer for the* South China Morning Post.

WARM ARBORIO RICE PUDDING WITH SUN-DRIED CHERRIES AND HAZELNUTS

*Arborio rice is a short grain used to make risotto.
Here the chef turns it into a creamy dessert.*

½ cup sugar
3½ cups half-and-half
1 vanilla bean, split
¼ cup plus 1 tablespoon sun-dried cherries

½ cup arborio or medium grain rice
2 ounces hazelnut liqueur
½ cup toasted hazelnuts, skins removed, lightly crushed

Preheat oven to 350° F. In an ovenproof saucepan, combine sugar, half-and-half, and vanilla bean. Bring to a boil, then add the rice. Cover with foil and bake, stirring every 30 minutes, for about 1 hour and 30 minutes.

In a small saucepan, warm the liqueur and ¼ cup cherries. When the rice pudding is done, add cherry mixture, and mix well. Garnish servings with remaining cherries and hazelnuts. Makes 4 to 6 servings.

This recipe is used courtesy of The Ashby Inn in Paris. The inn is a home built in 1829 near the foothills of the Blue Ridge Mountains and the site of the Ashby Tavern, which was frequented by George Washington when he was a young surveyor. Most of the inn's furnishings date to the early 1800s (phone (540) 592-3900 or visit www.ashbyinn.com).

PRESIDENT JOHN TYLER'S "TYLER PUDDING"

*This recipe for coconut pudding in a pie crust was a favorite at the Tyler table,
which at times might have included all of Tyler's 14 children. If your family
isn't as large, you may freeze one of the pies after baking.*

2 (9-inch) unbaked pie crusts	½ cup heavy cream
¼ cup butter	1 teaspoon vanilla
2½ cups sugar	½ fresh coconut, shredded, or 1½
3 eggs	cups flaked unsweetened coconut
¼ teaspoon salt	

Preheat oven to 400° F. Place pie weights or dried beans in pie crusts and partially
bake for 10 minutes. Turn oven down to 300° F.

Cream butter with half the sugar. Beat eggs well and add with the remaining sugar,
beating constantly. Add salt. Mix in cream well and add vanilla. Stir in coconut and
pour into the partially baked crusts. Bake for about 20 minutes, or until set. If the top
has not browned, place pies under the broiler for a few minutes. Makes 12 servings.

Note: If you like toasted coconut, reserve some and sprinkle it on the top of the
pies before baking.

---

*Our tenth president grew up on the family plantation, Greenway, in Charles City County on the James River.
The land has been in the family for almost 400 years. John Tyler renamed it Sherwood Forest (see tour on page 278),
because, like Robin Hood, he became known as a renegade during his presidency.*

SHIELDS TAVERN SYLLABUBS

*Popular in early Virginia, these fortified drinks lost favor
when ice cream became fashionable in the nineteenth century. Today, syllabubs are
typically served for dessert, garnished with berries and fresh mint.*

⅔ cup dry white wine	⅔ cup sugar
⅓ cup dry sherry	2 cups heavy cream
2 tablespoons grated lemon zest	sprigs of fresh mint and berries for
(yellow color from peel)	garnish
¼ cup lemon juice	

In a large bowl, combine the wine, sherry, lemon peel, and lemon juice. Add sugar
and stir until dissolved. Whip the cream in a large bowl until it forms slightly stiff
peaks. Fold into the wine mixture. Spoon into 8 wineglasses, cover with plastic wrap,
and refrigerate overnight. The mixture will separate and be ready to enjoy the next
day. Garnish just before serving. Makes 8 servings.

This recipe is reprinted from The Colonial Williamsburg Tavern Cookbook. *Shields Tavern, one of four
taverns operating in Williamsburg, is open for lunch and dinner daily (phone (800) 447-8679).*

Becoming
President

Becoming President

President John Tyler was
twice governor of Virginia, a
U.S. senator and representative, and chancellor of his
alma mater, the College of
William and Mary. He became
president when his neighbor,
President William Henry Harrison, died. Historians point
to him as the man who firmly
established the concept of
vice-presidential succession to
the presidency.

Bull of the Century

As incredible as it might
seem, one Virginia dairy bull
has sired at least 80,000
daughters and more than 2.3
million granddaughters. Elevation, a black-and-white Holstein calf born on August 30,
1965 at Round Oak Farm west
of Purcellville in Loudoun
County, is still siring progeny,
more than 20 years after his
death in 1979. The reason he
was such a star is that his
daughters gave significantly
more milk, had large, well-
formed udders, and beautiful
straight bodies. After a few
generations, Elevation's offspring spurred a massive
increase in milk productivity,
not only in the United States
but also in Europe and other
countries where the Virginia
bull's DNA traveled. About
15% of the DNA in today's
U.S. dairy cows came from
him. Voted "Bull of the Century" by dairy farmers, Elevation is the most influential
bull ever born.

President James Madison, oldest child in a family of twelve, grew up on his father's plantation, Montpelier, in Orange County. Madison had a 41-year political career. Over the years, he served in the Virginia House of Delegates, was elected to the Second Continental Congress, and served as a member of the United States House of Representatives. In the spring of 1787, he traveled to Philadelphia to attend the Constitutional Convention. Madison's dedication during the convention earned him the title of "Father of the Constitution" at the age of 36. He served two terms as president and died at Montpelier at the age of 85. He is buried in the family cemetery on the plantation. For information about touring Montpelier, call (540) 672-2728 or visit www.montpelier.org.

Dolley Madison, White House Hostess

Married to our fourth president, Dolley Madison initiated the Easter Egg Roll on the Capitol Lawn, was present when workers laid the cornerstone for the Washington Monument, and sent the first personal telegraph message. It was in her eulogy that the term "first lady" was coined. She was also the first to serve ice cream in the White House.

KING'S ARMS TAVERN GREENGAGE PLUM ICE CREAM

*If the greengage is not to be found,
substitute any variety of seasonal fresh or canned plums.*

5 large eggs, separated
1½ cups sugar, divided
2 cups milk
1½ pints half-and-half

⅓ cup lemon juice
3 cups fresh or canned (1 pound and 12 ounces) greengage plums or other plums, drained and pitted

In a large bowl, beat the egg yolks with 1 cup of the sugar. Warm the milk over medium-high heat until bubbles foam around the edges. Pour 1 cup of the hot milk over the beaten egg yolks, stirring until well blended. Return the mixture to the hot milk. Cook over medium heat until thick enough to coat the back of a metal spoon, about 5 minutes. Do not boil or the mixture will separate. Cool completely.

In another large bowl, beat the egg whites with the remaining ½ cup sugar until they form stiff peaks. Fold into the milk mixture. In a food processor or blender, puree the plums. Add the plums, half-and-half, and lemon juice gradually to the egg mixture. Freeze in an electric ice-cream maker, following the manufacturer's instructions.

Note: Allow the ice cream to ripen for at least 4 hours after freezing to bring out the delicate greengage plum flavor. If fresh plums are used, they should be blanched for 60 seconds in hot water so the skins can be removed.

This recipe was reprinted from The Colonial Williamsburg Tavern Cookbook. *King's Arms Tavern is the "highest class" of the taverns and can be reached at (800) 447-8679.*

DOLLEY MADISON'S PEPPERMINT ICE CREAM

What could be more refreshing?

1½ cups half-and-half
¾ cup sugar
¼ teaspoon salt
4 egg yolks

2 cups heavy cream
1½ tablespoons vanilla extract
½ pound peppermint-stripe candy, coarsely crushed to make 1¼ cups

Heat half-and-half in a heavy saucepan over low heat until film forms on surface. Do not boil. Stir in sugar and salt. In a medium bowl, beat egg yolks slightly. Gradually beat in small amounts of hot cream mixture until most of it is used. Return to saucepan, stirring constantly, until mixture thickens enough to coat the back of a metal spoon.

Cool thoroughly. Stir in heavy cream and vanilla. Cover and chill thoroughly in an electric ice-cream maker. Stir in peppermint candy and mellow at least 2 hours. Makes 1 quart.

This recipe was adapted for food safety and modern equipment from The Presidents' Cookbook *by Poppy Cannon. It's not actually Dolley's personal recipe; all of hers were burned when the British torched the White House in 1812.*

profile

PATSY WADDLE

Virginia Farm Bureau's Farm Woman of the Year 2001

A herd of almost 100 Holsteins grazes an Appalachian Mountains hillside on the Waddle's farm in Southwest Virginia. A spry Patsy Waddle, astride an ATV, leaves the barn to corral them homeward, followed closely by a barking Australian blue cattle dog. "I wouldn't be out without my dog, Ike. . . He's very helpful and very devoted. When he hears the four-wheeler, he's ready to go."

"My dad worked in a factory and he raised tobacco and cattle," Patsy Waddle recalls. "I've been involved with the farm my whole life." After she married John, Patsy followed suit. "I worked in a factory, but we wanted to farm." To realize their goal, the Waddles purchased land and 20 dairy cows. Today, their farm totals 2,000 acres, mostly devoted to cattle, including a herd raised for beef. They now grow all their own feed on 180 acres planted in corn and 150 in hay. Their milking capacity has increased, too. "When we first started, we milked four cows at a time; now we milk twelve cows at a time."

The Waddles struggled to establish their farm. "It takes a special kind of person to farm. It's hard work and dirty work." However, Patsy explains, "The biggest challenge is managing the money. With prices constantly changing you have to watch where you put your money."

Nevertheless, the benefits justify the work. "I feel like we've been very blessed. I'm my own boss. I've had the opportunity to be with my children." The Waddles' two grown sons still contribute to the family farm. Patsy feels strongly that farming offers valuable lessons for children, helping them to develop responsibility and an appreciation for nature.

"I've had the opportunity to be a community person by having my time available as I like to schedule it," continues Patsy, who still shuttles a group of children to 4-H and other activities. "Church is the center of my life," adds the Church Superintendent and Sunday School teacher.

Patsy Waddle's involvement with the community, and specifically the Smyth County Farm Bureau Women's Committee, led to her being named 2001 Farm Woman of the Year by the VFB. "The most rewarding thing I get to do is helping to educate people—and not just in the classroom, but in the community."

SPOON CUSTARD

A Waddle family recipe

½ cup sugar
1 tablespoon flour
pinch of salt
3 cups milk

4 eggs, separated
4 drops vanilla extract or 2 ounces
   lemon juice

Mix sugar, flour, and salt; set aside. Scald the milk. Mix a little milk with the egg yolks. Add the dry ingredients to the mixture. Combine that with the remaining milk on the stovetop. Heat to thicken, but do not boil. Let cool. Beat egg whites until stiff and fold them into the mixture. Flavor to taste with vanilla or lemon juice. Cover custard with plastic wrap to prevent a film on top, and refrigerate for an hour. Makes 4 to 6 servings.

Dolley Madison (continued)

Dolley Madison was born Dolley Payne in Guilford County, North Carolina, in 1768. She spent the first 15 years of her life in Virginia. Her Quaker parents moved to Philadelphia, where at 22 she married Quaker lawyer John Todd, Jr. Soon after that he, their infant son, and her in-laws perished in a yellow-fever epidemic. The young widow was introduced to Virginia Congressman James Madison, Jr.—17 years her senior—by the legendary Aaron Burr, and they were married in September 1794. The couple resided at the Madison family's Virginia plantation, Montpelier, until 1836, when James Madison died.

Dolley's social graces made her famous. Madison was secretary of state for Thomas Jefferson, and Dolley often served as Jefferson's hostess in the White House. In 1809, when Madison was elected president, Dolley refurbished the White House to make it more comfortable for guests. She was best known for her Wednesday evening receptions, where politicians, diplomats, and the general public gathered. These gatherings helped to soothe tensions between political parties.

How Cheese Came to Be

One legend has it that cheese originated by accident in the Middle East, when a Bedouin preparing for a journey across the desert filled his dried sheep-stomach pouch with ewe's milk for refreshment. After hours in the sun and the camel's jostling, the milk had turned into cheese. That Bedouin would be surprised to know there are today more than 400 different types of cheeses with more than 2,000 different names.

Soft and hard, cooked and not, ripened and unripe, cow's milk or goat's milk—there are many ways to classify the way cheeses are made. Fresh cheeses, such as cottage cheese, are the soft, moist curds that have been cut and drained of their whey but never cooked or ripened. Blue-veined cheeses—such as Roquefort, Stilton, and Gorgonzola—are ripened from within by molds; Brie and Camembert are ripened by molds rubbed on their surfaces.

chapter three
CHEESE

The Old Dominion doesn't have huge cheese factories like Wisconsin, but it does have many fabulous farmstead cheesemakers, who fashion cheese the European way. Some turn out velvety goat cheese from their own "billies" and sell it plain, flavored with herbs, or turning "bleu." Others make cow's-milk cheese from tranquil, grass-grazing cows raised via sustainable agricultural practices. There are crumbly fetas, dry Jacks, fresh mozzarellas, and soft farmer's cheeses. As the famed French cheesemonger Pierre Androuét once observed, "Cheese is the soul of the soil, the purest and most romantic link between humans and earth." Most of Virginia's cheesemakers live in the beautiful countryside where pure water, clean air, and natural pastureland make the perfect environment for farmsteads. Who would want to swap a Virginia farmstead cheese for an individually plastic-wrapped slice of, well, plastic?

MEADOW CREEK DAIRY'S CHEESE BREAD

Make this aromatic bread for a midwinter afternoon treat.

1 package active dry yeast
1 tablespoon sugar
1¾ cups warm water, divided
5 cups bread flour
1 tablespoon salt

¼ cup softened butter or olive oil
1 teaspoon hot sauce
1 cup grated Appalachian Jack cheese
   or cheddar

Dissolve the yeast with the sugar in ¼ cup of the warm water and allow to proof. In a large bowl, mix flour and salt. Make a well in the center and add the remaining warm water, the butter or oil, hot sauce, and yeast mixture. Stir with a wooden spoon until well mixed. Turn out on floured board and knead for 10 to 12 minutes, or until the dough is smooth and elastic, adding flour as needed. Place the dough in an oiled bowl and turn to coat on all sides. Cover with a towel and let rise in a warm, draft-free spot until doubled in bulk, 1½ to 2 hours.

Punch down the dough, turn it out on a lightly floured board and knead in the cheese. When blended, cut the dough in half and shape each piece into loaf. You can make any shape. Place in pans or baskets to rise until doubled, about 1 hour.

Bake in a preheated 375° F oven for approximately 30 minutes, or until loaves sound hollow when rapped on bottom with knuckles. Cool before slicing. Makes 2 loaves.

℞ *Meadow Creek Dairy, in Galax, allows its cows to graze on fresh pasture grass every day, which prevents over-grazing and gives the grass time to regrow. No herbicides or pesticides are used at the farm, and family members say they provide excellent nutrition for the herd while improving the health and fertility of their land. The dairy makes Appalachian Jack and Meadow Creek Feta. For information call (276) 236-2776 or visit www.meadowcreekdairy.com* ℞

GOAT CHEESE–STUFFED JALAPEÑO PEPPERS

*The crispy coating, spicy pepper, and soothing goat cheese create
a triple flavor sensation for these appetizers.*

12 medium-to-large green jalapeño
   peppers
12 ounces Applewood Smoked Goat
   Monterey Jack cheese or
   Smoked Goat Queso Fresco

2 eggs
½ cup Italian flavored bread crumbs
fresh salsa (optional)

Preheat oven to 375° F. Spray a baking sheet with nonstick vegetable oil; set aside. Slice a small pocket on one side of each jalapeño, carefully remove seeds, and place a thick slice of cheese inside. Beat eggs thoroughly and dip the jalapeños in them. Place bread crumbs on a piece of wax paper and roll the egg-dipped jalapeño to cover. Arrange on prepared sheet and bake 25 to 30 minutes, or until slightly browned. Accompany with salsa for dipping if desired. Makes 12 appetizers.

℞ *Drinking Swamp Farm makes more than 125 varieties of handcrafted cheeses from Nubian, Alpines, Toggen-burgs, and La Mancha goats' milk. The farm is situated on 50 waterfront acres in the Northern Neck. The name "Drinking Swamp Farm" originated in colonial days when the farmers took their cattle "down to the swamps" for water. One swamp had a sandy bottom and never fouled. So they would take their cattle to "the drinking swamp" for fresh water. The farm backs onto Drinking Swamp, which is still as pristine as it was back in the late 1600s and early 1700s (phone (804) 394-3508).* ℞

Buyer's Guide to CHEESE

Optimally, cheese should be cut fresh for your purchase. Cheese is best stored in the coldest part of the refrigerator, wrapped in aluminum foil, wax paper, or plastic wrap to enable it to breathe and further develop without drying out. Cheeses of various types need not be segregated. The harder the cheese, the longer it will stay fresh. Soft cheeses should stay fresh for a few weeks. Soft and fresh cheeses don't freeze well. However, shredded semihard cheese, such as cheddar, mozzarella, or Jack, can be frozen.

For best flavor, bring cheese to room temperature for about an hour before serving. Leave it wrapped or covered to stay moist. Serve with a crusty artisan-made or homemade bread.

℞ DID YOU KNOW . . . that the type of milk used to make a cheese may or may not remain constant? Feta, usually thought of as only a Greek goat's-milk cheese, can be made with cow or sheep's milk. It's the preservation process that gives feta a pleasantly sharp, salty zest. Mozzarella, traditionally made with water-buffalo milk, is now most often made with cow's milk. But chèvre (the French word for "goat") is always made with goat's milk.

Bent Tree Farm

Virginia Moyer, owner of Bent Tree Farm, explains how her family began making their award-winning Briar-Patch Cheese: "The does (females) were for our son's 4-H project. It did not take long for us to ask what we were going to do with the milk, because it was more than we could drink. I love to cook and preserve food, but how many sweets can a family handle? The cheese won out.

"The average day on the farm begins about 5 a.m. with the first milking," Virginia continues. "We have a Grade A dairy, and the goats are milked six at a time by machine. The milk is delivered to the cheese facility and the 'milkmaid' begins the process. We have a small pasteurizer that will process 15 gallons of goat milk with agitation at a time.

"After reaching proper temperature and being held for 30 minutes, the milk is cooled to whichever temperature is required for the type of cheese being made. We use a freeze-dried culture from France and vegetable rennet to help the milk coagulate and the curds and whey separate. We strain the curds and feed the whey to the animals. Nothing is wasted.

"Because we are a small family operation, we stick to two basic types of cheese, chèvre and feta. Ricotta is made on request."

BENT TREE FARM'S 17TH STREET SUMMER SKILLET

This dish functions well as a vegetarian main dish or as a side to grilled chicken or fish.

4 garlic cloves from Ms. Taylor (Butch's produce)
2 tablespoons olive oil
1 pound string beans from Sister Rose
3 large tomatoes from Ms. Amanda Atkins, peeled and chopped

1 yellow banana pepper from Sister Lucille, seeded and chopped
1 tablespoon fresh oregano from Charlie's Herb Barn
8 ounces crumbled Briar-Patch goat feta cheese from Bent Tree Farm

In an iron skillet, sauté the garlic in the olive oil. Add the beans, tomatoes, and freshly ground black pepper to taste. Cook only until tender. Stir in the banana pepper and oregano and cook for 1 minute. Remove from heat, toss with feta cheese, and serve hot. Serves 4 to 6 people.

Bent Tree Farm in Disputanta is home to some chickens, about 40 Nubian dairy goats, and the Moyer family, who make the Briar-Patch cheese used in this dish. Briar-Patch cheese has won various competitions at the Virginia State Fair (phone (804) 991-2121).

RUCKER FARM'S JORDAN RIVER CHÈVRE AND BROCCOLI FLAN

Serve this silky vegetarian dish with a tomato salad.

2 cups small broccoli flowerets
6 green onions, sliced
2 tablespoons butter
4 eggs

½ cup milk
pinch of salt and pepper
8 ounces Jordan River chèvre

Preheat oven to 350° F. Lightly butter a 5-inch flan mold or small soufflé dish; set aside. Rinse broccoli in cool water and lightly steam or microwave on high 2 minutes. In a small skillet, sauté onions in butter until soft. Do not brown. In a mixing bowl, beat eggs with milk, salt, and pepper. Stir in cheese, leaving little chunks that will remain whole. Gently stir in broccoli and pour into prepared mold. Set mold in a shallow pan of water and bake until a knife inserted in the center comes out clean, about 30 minutes. Loosen sides with a knife and remove onto a platter. Makes 4 servings.

Rucker Farm is a boutique creamery in Flint Hill, nestled in the foothills of the Blue Ridge Mountains. Owners Heidi and Lindsay Eastham keep only 30 goats, let them range freely, and use only the morning milk. This creates a rare, poetic purity that is savored in all the cheeses, including their Jordan River chèvre. Phone (540) 675-3444.

WAYSIDE INN WINE-AND-CHEESE SOUP

This silky but hearty soup is a warming winter pleasure.

½ cup dry orzo (rice-shaped pasta)
¼ cup butter
6 leeks, trimmed, rinsed, and thinly
   sliced (about 5½ cups)
1 cup dry white wine

5¼ cups chicken stock or 2 (10.5-
   ounce) cans condensed chicken
   broth plus 2 soup cans water
1 cup shredded Jarlsberg or Swiss
   cheese

Begin cooking orzo according to package directions. In a 4-quart saucepan over medium heat, cook leeks in hot butter until tender, about 20 minutes. Add broth and water. Heat to boiling and reduce heat to low.

Drain orzo and add to saucepan along with cheese and wine. Heat, stirring, until cheese melts. Garnish with additional cheese, if desired. Makes 8 servings (about 1 cup each).

✒ This recipe was provided by the Wayside Inn in Middletown. In 1797, the inn began welcoming guests who were pausing for bed and board as they journeyed across the Shenandoah Valley. During the Civil War, soldiers from both the North and South frequented the inn, and it was spared the ravages of the war only to be badly damaged by a fire in 1985. Diners at the lovingly restored inn bask in the inn's colonial ambience while enjoying dishes made with local ingredients (phone (877) 869-1797 or visit www.alongthewayside.com). ✒

CHEESY POTATO CASSEROLE

A great party dish, this casserole can be assembled early on the day needed.

2 pounds potatoes
1 (10.75-ounce) can cream of
   chicken soup
1 (8-ounce) carton sour cream
6 tablespoons margarine, melted
1 small onion, chopped

1 teaspoon salt
¼ teaspoon pepper
2 cups shredded cheddar cheese
   (8 ounces)
½ cup dry herb-seasoned stuffing mix

Cook potatoes in boiling water for 30 minutes, or until tender. Drain and cool. Peel and cut into ¼-inch slices; Set aside. Lightly butter a 13 × 9 × 2-inch baking dish; set aside.

In a large bowl, combine soup, sour cream, and 3 tablespoons melted margarine. Stir in onion, salt, and pepper. Gently stir in potatoes and cheese. Spoon into prepared dish. (If desired, casserole may be prepared to this point and held in the refrigerator until time to bake.) Preheat oven to 350° F. Combine remaining 3 tablespoons melted margarine with stuffing mix. Sprinkle over potato mixture. Bake, uncovered, for 25 to 30 minutes. Makes 8 servings.

✒ Recipe is from the Hill City Master Gardeners of Concord, Virginia. ✒

Virginia's Farmstead Cheesemakers

Here is a listing of the Old Dominion's farmstead cheesemakers as well as the kinds of cheeses they produce:

BENT TREE FARM: chèvre and feta from Nubian goats

BLUE RIDGE DAIRY: mozzarella and ricotta from cows

DRINKING SWAMP FARM: 114 styles of goat cheese, Montasio (aged hard cheese), and Gouda

EVERONA DAIRY: sheep-milk cheeses

GOURMET GOAT: aged blue goat cheese, chèvre, feta, and smoked hard cheese from Alpine goats

GREEN HAVEN FARM: mozzarella, feta, cheddar, and soft cheeses

LANDOVEL: chèvre plain and eleven other flavors

MEADOW CREEK DAIRY: Appalachian Jack, feta, Swiss (Appalachian Mountaineer), and Stilton

MONASTERY COUNTRY: Gouda from cows

MOUNTAIN HOBBY: chèvre, feta, Brie, and Camembert from Nubian and La Mancha goats

RUCKER FARM: soft chèvre flavored with lavender or herbs, and hard goat cheese

BLUE RIDGE INSTITUTE AND FARM MUSEUM

• BLUE RIDGE • INSTITUTE AND FARM MUSEUM

For more than two decades, Ferrum College's Blue Ridge Institute and Blue Ridge Farm Museum have documented, interpreted, and presented the traditional life and culture of the Blue Ridge and its people. Designated the "State Center for Blue Ridge Folklore" by the Virginia General Assembly in 1986, the Institute promotes an understanding of regional folklore past and present for all ages. The property consists of changing gallery exhibits in a modern building and a living-history farm museum.

DAYS/HOURS: The museum is open weekends between the middle of May and the middle of August. Group tours are available by reservation any day April through October. All tours and activities start at the Blue Ridge Institute Building. There is ample free parking.

FEES: Museum admission is charged. Admission is charged for the Blue Ridge Draft Horse and Mule Show in July and for the Blue Ridge Folklife Festival in October. Parking is free.

MORE INFORMATION: Blue Ridge Institute and Farm Museum of Ferrum College can be reached at (540) 365-4416. Or visit www.blueridge institute.org.

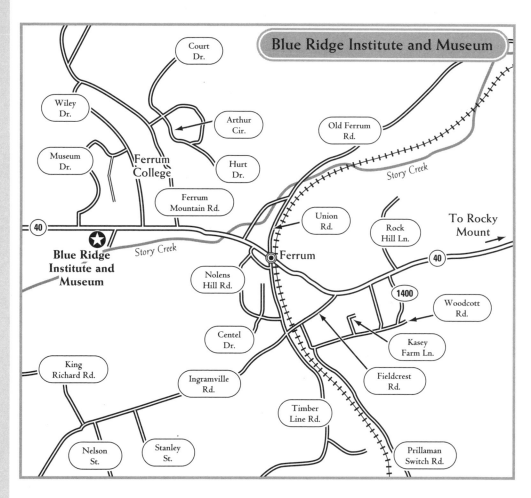

In a beautiful, unspoiled valley with green pastures and tall trees spiking through the sometimes low-hanging misty clouds, the folkways of the Blue Ridge spring to life on a re-created 1800 Virginia-German farmstead. First opened in 1979, the Blue Ridge Farm Museum—an educational arm of Ferrum College's Blue Ridge Institute—reflects the day-to-day lifestyle of prosperous German-American farmsteaders in this region.

The Blue Ridge Institute consists of a modern brick building that houses exhibits and a farm museum complex of historic houses, barns, and outbuildings moved piece by piece from their original locations. The buildings were reconstructed in an agricultural setting on the Ferrum College campus, which is up the hill from the Institute. The museum buildings are native to Franklin County—Virginia's number three milk-producing county—where the college and institute are located.

The 1800 farm reflects the lifestyles of the many families of German ancestry who began to settle in the Blue Ridge in the last quarter of the eighteenth century. The central-chimney "Flurkuchenhaus," a rare, three-room-house type with two rooms on the second floor, is the focal point of the site. The log construction categorizes it as German European and not British. The house has regional furnishings typical of the 1800s and ceramics that are copies of earthenware found locally. Two women who visited the home in the 1930s helped make up the inventory list of items that were in the Anglin-Bottom house moved 15 miles from its original site in Sontag, Virginia. Inside the house are a loom, corner cupboard, and dining room. The kitchen is a separate building from the house.

Also typical of the prosperous, well-managed German farmstead is the immense Swiss-German bank barn from Conestoga that belonged to the Calloway-Perlaman family in 1815. To supply the barn, the Blue Ridge Institute looked at other barns in the Shenandoah Valley and located agricultural equipment, tools, harnesses, hay, and fodder. There's a fully equipped blacksmith facility, a raised-bed garden, and additional outbuildings.

A 1900 farmstead illustrates the smaller homesteads established among later generations of farmers. In the gardens and around the farm buildings, heirloom vegetables and historic breeds of sheep, chicken, horses, pigs, and cattle illustrate the region's agricultural heritage. In a continuing effort to preserve our heritage breeds, the Blue Ridge Institute's exhibit includes various breeds of livestock from the nineteenth century.

Milking Shorthorn cows, often referred to as "Durhams," came to the United States in 1783. Suffolk Punch draft horses date back to 1880 and were used to till and harvest the land. Ossabaw Island Hogs, off the coast of Georgia, are descendants of Spanish pigs brought to the New World more than 400 years ago.

One of the oldest breeds indigenous to the United States, the Tunis sheep is a medium-sized meat-type sheep characterized by creamy wool, copper-red-colored faces and legs, and pendulous ears. Dominique chickens developed from the fowl introduced during the early settlement of New England and were widely distributed in the eastern half of the United States by the mid 1800s. In New England, they were known as "Plymouth Rock" and occasionally as "Pilgrim Fowls."

Through special participatory programs, visitors can don Institute costumes and take part in farm activities or try their hands at vintage crafts. Visitors may find costumed interpreters preparing meals over the open hearth, baking bread in an outdoor bake oven, blacksmithing, or carrying out other household and farm chores of the period.

Summer programming at the Blue Ridge Institute features the Blue Ridge Draft Horse and Mule Show, an annual showcase of draft horses and mules and the old-time skills used in handling those animals. Competitions include plowing, log skidding, and wagon driving. Most of the major draft horse breeds are on hand for this one-day, one-of-a-kind event. The show is held annually on the fourth Saturday in July from 10 a.m. to 5 p.m.

On the fourth Saturday in October, as many as 20,000 people converge upon Ferrum for the annual Blue Ridge Folklife Festival, "Virginia's largest celebration of regional traditions." The festival has celebrated regional folk traditions for 26 years. Its food is served by 25 local church or community vendors; in addition, crafts, music, and competitions help to make it unique among Virginia events.

Tour in a Nutshell

· ·
BLUE RIDGE INSTITUTE AND FARM MUSEUM
(*continued*)

DIRECTIONS: The Blue Ridge Institute and the Farm Museum are located on the west side of the Ferrum College campus, ten miles from Route 220 on Route 40 West. In travel time, Ferrum is about 45 minutes from both Roanoke and Martinsville.

From Rocky Mount, drive west on Route 40 past the Ferrum College chapel. Continue 0.1 mile further to the Blue Ridge Institute building, a brick building topped with a plow weather vane. Directions from out of town may also be obtained from the directions page of the Ferrum College website, at www.ferrum.edu.

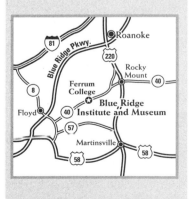

KEVIN RIDDLE

Crafting Farm Tools the Old-Fashioned Way

Early Virginia farmers settling the new land had to be self-sufficient. They built their homes and outbuildings, grew most of their food, made clothes from fabrics they wove, and crafted furniture and farm tools. Around the state today at historic living history sites, modern Virginians demonstrate many of these crafts. Others make crafts for a living. One such crafter who carries on "a dying trade" related to farming is Kevin Riddle of Eagle Rock. He makes wooden hay forks and rakes from white-oak logs, as well as slat-back chairs.

"I come from a long line of people who worked with their hands," says Riddle, a big friendly man with thick brunette hair. "I grew up in rural southwestern Virginia to the patterns of self-sufficient country life. Like many of my peers, I left for the money and glory of the big city. After a few years, I began to appreciate what I had left behind. On my visits home, I sought out the old-timers and soon realized there was more useful technology being lost than would ever be discovered. I saw the value in preserving the old ways, particularly the wood-craft skills."

"So I turned my back on high tech and returned home to the simple rural lifestyle I had left behind. The more I learned about the old how-to skills, the more committed I became to preserving them. A person properly trained in traditional woodworking would walk into a forest with a box of hand tools and an axe, and proceed to build a cabin and furnish it from the raw materials there. This scenario was repeated thousands of times in the early days of our country."

The hills and "hollers" of the Southern Appalachian Mountains have long been known as a source of quality handmade crafts. Riddle is one of these native craftsmen. He set up his own shop, "Mountain Woodshop," in 1990 in a farm building on the property owned by his grandfather in an unnamed hollow. He and his West Virginia–born wife live in the same home on the property built by his grandfather.

CRAFTING A HAY FORK

To begin, Riddle calls the local sawmill and asks if they have any green logs. Dry logs won't do because they can't be bent. He brings the log home in his truck and saws it into six-foot lengths to make hay forks. Using a hammer and wedges, he splits the wood into the right sizes and stores the logs in the creek near his workshop so they will stay green.

When it's time to make a hay fork, he fishes out the wood from the creek. In his workshop, he puts a piece of wood on his homemade shaving bench and begins shaping it. He'll need to make lengthwise cuts to make the fork tines and drill holes so he can later put in spacers.

When it's time to bend the wood, Riddle starts the heat in his steam box and puts in the wood. After 15 to 20 minutes, the wood will soften enough to become pliable. He then removes it from the box and inserts wedges to spraddle the tines. Into the holes, he puts wooden spacers and nails through the tines to secure them. Riveting the wrist area of the fork gives support to the tines.

Riddle built a wooden frame that bends the tines and handle of the fork. The fork remains in the frame until it's completely dry. The fork is finished after he smoothes the wood, stamps in his trademark, and oils the wood with boiled linseed oil.

"Today I live and work in the same 'holler' in which I was raised. I operate the woodshop between the regular chores required of country life. I am content, now, to create beautiful functional pieces while helping to preserve my mountain heritage."

To get in touch with Kevin Riddle, write to Mountain Woodshop, P.O. Box 40, Eagle Rock, VA 24085, or phone (540) 884-2197. On purpose, he doesn't own a fax or computer.

part five
FRUITS AND NUTS

Picture these contrasting landscapes: the cool hills of the Shenandoah Valley and the flat, sandy soil of Virginia's tidewater. Together they produce most of the state's fruits and nuts. Virginia's geography makes it conducive to growing fruits that like the cold, such as apples, as well as those that like the heat, such as goobers. Virginia ranks in the top ten in the nation in apple production and is one of the southernmost producing states. On the other hand, it's also among the top ten peanut-producing states, and the northernmost state where peanuts can grow.

In spring, trees in the western counties—stretching from Winchester in the north to the tier of counties along the North Carolina border—are adorned in pale-pink blossoms like ballet dancers in tutus. This is the time for festivals and hope that a late freeze doesn't ruin the blossoms and the fall harvest to come. The area's cool nights and warm days also make it perfect for growing peaches, nectarines, and pears.

Virginia peanuts are often referred to as "the peanut of gourmets." They are valued for their large size and beauty as well as their outstanding flavor and pleasing crunchy texture. More than 100 million pounds of peanuts are produced statewide, about half of them in the neighboring counties of Southampton and Isle of Wight. With the exception of peanuts, the harvesting of nuts is not an organized industry in Virginia. How-ever, there's plenty of gathering going on. Farmers sell pecans to stores and at roadside stands. There are more than 200 acres of trees growing these flavorful nutmeats that are essential to many Virginia recipes. Not as many walnut trees grace the state as pecan trees, though the Chesapeake region is noted for walnut trees, especially the black walnut.

chapter one

APPLES

⬿ *Warm days, cool nights, and a rich deep soil nurtured by consistent rainfall make the state's climate ideal for growing many apple varieties, so it's no wonder apples represent big business in Virginia. More than $35 million is added to the state's economy annually through the sale of fresh-market apples and products such as applesauce, processed apple slices, apple butter, apple juice, and apple cider, making Virginia the nation's seventh apple-growing state.*

There are more than 250 commercial apple growers producing 360 million pounds of apples on more than 15,000 acres of land. The majority of apple trees grow in the Shenandoah Valley, extending through the Roanoke Valley, the rich countryside of Albemarle and Rappahannock counties, and the southwest counties of Patrick and Carroll. The three leading varieties grown are Red Delicious, Golden Delicious, and York. The other major varieties grown are Rome, Stayman, Gala, Winesap, Granny Smith, Jonathan, Fuji, and Ginger Gold.

interview

JOHN BRUGUIERE
Appalachian Apple Farmer

Dickie Brothers Orchard is one of Virginia's select "century farms," so designated by the Virginia Department of Agriculture and Consumer Services for having been operated by the same family for at least 100 years. But "two-and-a-half-century farm" would be a more accurate description for this unique orchard, which is owned and operated by Thomas Bruguiere along with sons Tommy and John. Approximately 20,000 apple trees occupy 100 acres of the wooded 1000-acre property, on which the family also raises beef cattle. This interview was conducted with John Bruguiere.

John says the farm's location contributes to the high quality of the apples his family grows. "The orchard is nestled against the eastern edge of the Blue Ridge Mountains in the Appalachians, and our view is as beautiful as anywhere in the United States, especially when the fall foliage is in full color and the apples are fresh on the tree. Our orchard is at an altitude of between 1200 and 1500 feet at the base of the Little de Priest Mountain. The cool mountain air gives our apples great color and excellent flavor.

"We now grow eleven apple varieties, including McIntosh, Paula Red, Gala, Red Delicious, Golden Delicious, Stayman, Rome, Winesap, Fuji, Empire, and Granny Smith. We harvested 68,000 bushels last year, and a half-million bushels of apples are harvested in Nelson County, a county with no stoplights, one middle school, and one high school. We are 16 miles from the nearest grocery store."

The work of raising apples is a year-round, hands-on job. John explains the work, season by season. "Most people know that apple harvest is in the fall. Harvest of early-ripening varieties begins in late July and continues to the end of October. But the work of raising apples goes on all year; farmers also have to mow between the rows, prune, plant new trees, repair fencing, grow hay (if they also have livestock), feed the livestock, and spray to keep weeds down.

"Apple growing is all manual, and labor for picking and packing is our biggest expense. We pay migrant workers to pick the apples and try to get the same people every year. We provide their housing and pay them either by the piece or the hour. All our apples are picked by hand and placed in wooden bins. Packers are local people.

"We do a taste test to see if the apples are ready to harvest. From September 1 to end of October, we will be picking constantly. After the harvest is over, we store the apples in our cold storage, which maintains them at 35° F through March or whenever we sell them all. We pack to order, and work depends upon demand.

Visit Dickie Orchard

Dickie Brothers offers Pick-Your-Own apples, on-site retail sales, and mail orders. The orchard is located near Massies Mill, about 40 miles south of Charlottesville and 32 miles north of Lynchburg. If you come to the packing shed, you may select your own individual apples or purchase a pre-packed unit (phone (434) 277-5516 or visit www.dickiebros.com).

Apple Harvest

If you think you have to wait 'til fall to enjoy the crisp and crunchy, succulent and sweet taste of just-picked Virginia apples, think again. Paula Red apples—with their unique sweet-tart flavor—launch the apple harvest in late July. Then in early August come Virginia Ginger Gold apples, noted for their outstanding taste and crisp white flesh. Popular Galas debut in mid-August. Easy to spot with their distinctive red-orange color and yellow stripes, Virginia Gala apples are crunchy, juicy, and full of flavor. Fall apple harvest begins the last week in August and extends through early November, including favorites such as Red and Golden Delicious, Staymans, and Fujis.

Virginia's Finest Trademark Program

If you see the famliar Virginia's Finest red-and-blue checkmark on a food product, in an ad, or on a sign, you can be certain of top quality. Introduced in 1989, the Virginia's Finest Trademark Program was developed to identify, differentiate, and promote those Virginia-grown and processed agricultural products that meet industry-approved quality standards. Since it began, the program has grown to honor more than 500 food and beverage companies. Quality standards used in the program are established by agricultural groups and are approved by the Virginia Department of Agriculture and Consumer Services (VDACS).

Fresh produce, specialty foods, hams, peanuts, wine, potted plants, and Christmas trees are just a few examples of the diversity of products represented by the program. Virginia's Finest food and beverage products can be found in most gift, gourmet, and specialty shops and in grocery stores. Virginia's Finest produce and nursery products are available at selected nurseries, greenhouses, orchards, and farms. Many Virginia ABC stores carry Virginia's Finest wines and liquors.

Some weeks we pack five days a week. Most of our apples are sold fresh but some are made into juice by companies like Murray's in Roanoke and Zieglers in Pennsylvania.

"After we receive an order, the apples are washed, brushed, and waxed. Ultraviolet lamps dry the water-soluble wax and consumers can wash it off. It's not necessary to wax apples, but if your unwaxed apples are next to waxed apples in the store, no one will buy them, because natural apples aren't as shiny, so everybody has to do it. It costs $800 for 50 gallons of wax, and that coats approximately 20,000 bushels of apples. The final task is to take a hand-held gun and touch every apple with the variety sticker so the store clerk will know which type of apple to charge for.

"In winter, from December to March, it's time to plant new trees and prune all the trees while they're dormant because there's less stress on the tree. In springtime, the three weeks after bloom are most crucial. You have to thin the crop. At that time, the apples will be between eight and twelve millimeters—about as big as your thumb. You also have to thin in the summer. If you leave too many apples on the tree, they will be small and will not color well. Then the next year the tree won't produce as well. Mother Nature will go to biennial bearing (one crop every two years), and you don't want that."

The orchard's history is a long and rich one, but John harbors concerns about its future. "Our family has been farming this land since England's King George granted it to our family in 1752. The first Dickie was a seafaring officer, Captain James Dickie. I'm a seventh-generation farmer, and apples have been grown here—that we know of—since the mid 1800s.

"My grandfather William Lewis Dickie and my great-uncle Herbert, who was a country doctor, are the Dickie Brothers for whom the business was named, around 1900. When my father, Thomas Bruguiere, came to Nelson County, he met my mother, Emilie Dickie, and married the farmer's daughter. At that time, my grandfather was growing Albemarle Pippin and Winesap for juice and cider making. Grandfather had a cider mill. In those days, you didn't have cold storage and couldn't keep fresh apples very long. In the 1960s, my family planted other fresh-apple varieties.

"I remember picking apples when I was eleven years old. After school, I would get off the bus and help in the packing shed. In those days, you had to put the boxes together, so I helped make boxes. My dad paid me $2.25 an hour. One gentleman, Massie Kirby, had worked at the farm 54 years, since he was nine. We also grew corn, and I remember him saying he would walk behind the corn planter and push the spilled corn kernels in with his toe when he first worked here.

"Now I have two preschool children, Sallie and Michael. My wife is from this same county and her father is an apple farmer, so I also married a farmer's daughter. But I don't know if our children will be eighth-generation farmers on the family land. There's an oversupply of apples and stagnant consumption. The government tries to keep the food supply cheap for Americans and puts caps and ceilings on commodities. Right now, the farmer gets only about 25 cents per pound; the middlemen and retailers get the remainder of the price consumers pay.

"It's a double-edged sword being a farmer. You want to sell your product and you want retail customers nearby, but if more people move into the county, the land prices rise and so do the taxes. More schools are needed, and someone has to pay for them—that's the landowners. I believe that the family farmer will become a thing of the past. In 20 or 30 years, there will be only superfarms."

APPLE TREE B&B'S APPLE-RASPBERRY TEA

Sip this wonderful iced tea while rocking on a front porch
on a hot evening after hiking, biking, or antiquing. On cooler evenings,
add a little cinnamon and cloves and serve it hot.

4 quarts apple juice
1 quart water
32 raspberry herbal tea bags
16 regular tea bags

2 teaspoons lemon juice
½ cup of sugar or equivalent sugar
    substitute

Bring the apple juice and water to a boil in a large pot. Turn off the heat and add tea bags, lemon juice, and sugar. Stir until sugar dissolves. Let tea bags steep until mixture cools to room temperature. Remove tea bags. After rinsing out the apple-juice jars, pour the apple tea into the empty jars and a pitcher. Keep it cool and serve over ice or serve warm. Makes about 40 (½-cup) servings. (Tea can also be made in a 30-cup coffee maker. Or the recipe can be divided to make a smaller quantity of tea.)

Apple Tree Bed & Breakfast is located in Damascus, in the heart of the Virginia Highlands, close to Mount Rogers, the highest mountain in Virginia. The 1904 transitional Victorian house is on the Appalachian Trail and within a block of the Virginia Creeper Trail, a 34-mile-long biking, walking, and horse trail. Nearby whitewater streams offer some of the best trout fishing anywhere. Backpacking and cross-country skiing are available in the right seasons to challenge the true outdoor activist (phone (276) 475-5261 or visit www.appletreebnb.com).

THORNROSE HOUSE BIRCHER-MUESLI

Prepare this healthful breakfast blend the night before it is needed.
In the morning, add the fresh fruit, and breakfast is ready.

1 cup old-fashioned oats
⅓ cup golden raisins
1 cup milk
1 apple, peeled and coarsely grated
1 tablespoon fresh lemon juice (about
    ½ lemon)

1½ cups chopped fruit of the season
    such as peaches, pears, pineapple,
    or berries
¼ cup vanilla yogurt or whipped
    cream

Soak oats and raisins in milk; refrigerate overnight. Add apple, juice, and fruit. Fold in yogurt or cream. Makes 4 servings.

Thornrose House at Gypsy Hill was a bed-and-breakfast located in Staunton, in the heart of the Shenandoah Valley. The Georgian revival home of Suzanne and Otis Huston is set in front of an acre of gardens, with the 300-acre Gypsy Hill Park located across the street. The park offers tennis and golf, and two outdoor concerts are scheduled there each week during the summer. The downtown historic district is within walking distance, and the Statler Complex is just down the street. It is now a private home.

Buyer's Guide to APPLES

Look for apples that are firm and free of bruises. Sort apples often; one bad apple can spoil the rest. Buy apples in bulk to cut down on costs. Most will stay fresh for several months if stored at cool temperatures. To keep the flavor longer, store apples in vented plastic bags. If necessary, apples can be allowed to ripen for up to two weeks at room temperature. To enjoy apples year-round, try canning, freezing, or drying. Adding lemon juice to cut apples prevents discoloration.

Celebrate

Festivals and other events celebrating Virginia apples abound, and not only can participants revel in apples galore, they can often enjoy music, dancing, and other folklife activities. Find out when and where by visiting www.virginia.org/events.

Picking your own apples, peaches, nectarines, grapes, or pumpkins at Stribling Orchard in Markham is much more than a mere fruit gathering. A visit to this Virginia Century Farm is also educational, scenic, and an opportunity for extra fun for kids and shoppers. Lunch? That, too. A picnic is always a bright idea, and Stribling is just the spot. When not eating or oogling various fresh foods, hop on the ponies or hayride wagons, or investigate the possibility of a tour to learn more about Stribling's rich past.

It was in the late 1700s that the original deed to the orchard's land was issued, and the same family has owned the orchard for six generations. Dr. Robert Stribling purchased the farm's main house, Mountain View, and the surrounding 93 acres in 1819. In 1850 the railroad was constructed through nearby Farrowsville. During the Civil War, the railroad and parallel road were used by both the Union and Confederate Armies. Mountain View was repeatedly used as officer's quarters by both sides.

Visit www.striblingorchard .com for more information about Stribling's seasonal selections as well as details about other pick-your-own orchards, or call Stribling at (540) 364-3040. See Stribling's recipe for Apple Butter on page 119.

EVANS FARM INN APPLE CRISP

Serve this dessert warm with a scoop of ice cream or whipped cream.

8 medium apples, peeled, cored, and sliced
1¾ teaspoon ground cinnamon, divided
2 cups sugar, divided

1 cup plus 2 tablespoons flour, divided
2 tablespoons butter
1 teaspoon baking powder
¼ teaspoon salt
1 egg

Preheat oven to 350° F. Butter a 2-quart rectangular baking dish. In a large bowl, blend apples with ¾ teaspoon cinnamon, 1 cup sugar, and 2 tablespoons flour. Place in baking dish and dot with butter. In a medium bowl, place remaining sugar and flour, as well as baking powder, the remaining 1 teaspoon cinnamon, and salt. Stir in egg until mixture is crumbly. Sprinkle topping over apples and bake about 30 minutes, or until apple mixture is bubbly and topping is brown. Makes 6 servings.

✎ *For several decades, Evans Farm Inn served lunch and dinner in an idyllic farm setting with a pond and gristmill in suburban McLean. In 2000, the 40-acre family farm was sold to developers. The townspeople fought to purchase the land to keep as a park, but the contract could not be reversed. The restaurant was bulldozed. Today, hundreds of townhomes and single-family houses are being built on the property.* ✎

SUMMERFIELD INN'S
APPLE-CINNAMON QUICHE

This eggy breakfast or brunch main dish is reminiscent of a rich apple pie.

2 apples, peeled and sliced
2 tablespoons butter
1 tablespoon sugar
1 teaspoon cinnamon

1 unbaked (10-inch) pastry shell
8 ounces grated cheddar cheese
4 large eggs
1½ cups whipping cream

Preheat oven to 375° F. Sauté apples in butter for 5 minutes. Sprinkle sugar and cinnamon over apples. Layer apples in pastry shell. Sprinkle cheese over apple mixture. In medium-sized bowl, lightly whisk together the eggs and whipping cream. Pour over the apple-cheese mixture. Bake for 35 minutes or until set. Makes 6 servings.

✎ *The Summerfield Inn is nestled in the foothills of the Appalachians in Abingdon. The spacious 1920s-era home offers guests the feeling of a private-home setting with luxurious comfort and hospitality (phone (276) 628-5905 or (800) 668-5905, or visit www.summerfieldinn.com).* ✎

FRANK'S SUGAR-AND-SPICE MICRO-BAKED APPLES

Serve for breakfast with a sprinkle of honey wheat germ and drop of heavy cream or with a scoop of honey-vanilla ice cream for dessert.

½ pound light brown sugar
½ pound dark brown sugar
2 teaspoons cinnamon
½ to 1 cup coarsely chopped pecans

1 whole nutmeg, freshly grated (about 2 teaspoons)
medium-sized Golden Delicious apples (1 per person)

To make sugar-and-spice mixture, thoroughly combine the light- and dark-brown sugars, cinnamon, nutmeg, and nuts. Store in an airtight container in a cool, dark place. Makes about 2 cups or enough to fill about 32 apples.

Core and peel desired number of apples. Place each apple in an individual heat-proof glass or ceramic custard cup or ramekin. Lightly pack about one heaping table-spoon of sugar mixture in each apple's center and sprinkle some on the top and sides. Cover with heavy-duty plastic wrap, and microwave on high up to 4 apples at a time: 1 apple, 4 to 6 minutes; 2 apples, 7 minutes; 4 apples, 8 minutes. When springy to the touch, they are done. Let stand at least 5 minutes before serving. Assembled apples can also be baked in a 375° F oven for 40 to 60 minutes, or until tender but not mushy. They will also hold in a warm oven for 30 to 45 minutes.

The Sampson Eagon Inn was a bed-and-breakfast just steps away from Staunton's beautifully restored down-town historic district. For its extensive restoration, the inn was presented with Historic Staunton Foundation's Annu-al Preservation Award and is listed by the National Trust for Historic Preservation. It opened in 1991 and received special recognition for outstanding accommodations and value before being purchased in 2006 as a private home.

SHENANDOAH VALLEY APPLE CAKE

For U.S. Congressman Bob Goodlatte and his family, the aroma of this dense, fruity cake, when cooking, "signals the approach of fall."

3 teaspoons sugar for coating the tube or Bundt pan
1 cup oil
2 cups sugar
2 large eggs
½ teaspoon vanilla
3 cups flour

1 teaspoon baking soda
1 teaspoon salt
½ teaspoon cinnamon
½ teaspoon nutmeg
3 cups chopped Virginia tart apples (Rome, York, or McIntosh)
½ cup chopped nuts

Prepare the Bundt or tube pan in advance by greasing and then shaking sugar in it until the sides and bottom are well coated. Combine oil and sugar until well mixed. Add eggs, beating well after each addition. Mix in vanilla. In a separate bowl, com-bine flour, baking soda, salt, cinnamon, and nutmeg. Slowly add flour mixture to the sugar mixture. Add the apples and nuts. Pour batter into pan and bake at 325° F for 1¾ hours. (Yes, this is correct!) Makes 16 servings.

Long-term U.S. Congressman Bob Goodlatte of Roanoke has provided leadership on a number of high-tech issues. He serves on the U.S. House of Representatives Committee on Agriculture, and was first elected in 1993.

Regional Peaks of Color

Fall's brilliant colors delight the visitor from early Septem-ber through November. You'll see the red-orange of the maples, the maroon of the tupelos, the golden flowers of the witch hazels, and the red of the sumac and sassafras.

First, mountain areas in the Heart of Appalachia and Southwest Blue Ridge High-lands regions are splashed in vivid reds, yellows, and oranges. By mid-October, nature's paintbrush decorates the Shenandoah Valley, Cen-tral and Northern Virginia. Then, in late October and early November, the Tidewa-ter and Eastern Shore catch the season's final brush strokes.

Autumn in the Valley

"The Shenandoah Valley, Allegheny Highlands, Roanoke, and Lynchburg, which I am privileged to rep-resent in Congress, are beau-tiful any time of the year, but are especially vibrant when autumn colors our mountains. For generations, travelers have enjoyed the natural beauty, bounty, and hospitali-ty of our area. You are cor-dially invited to explore and enjoy this beautiful part of Virginia."

—U.S. Congressman Bob Goodlatte

CONGRESSMAN FRANK R. WOLF'S APPLESAUCE CAKE

FOR CAKE:

2½ cups flour
1½ cups sugar
¼ teaspoon baking powder
½ teaspoon baking soda
1½ teaspoons salt
¾ teaspoon cinnamon
½ teaspoon each ground cloves and allspice

½ cup butter or margarine, softened
½ cup water
2 cups sweetened applesauce (not chunky style)
2 eggs
1 cup chopped raisins
¾ cup chopped nuts

FOR FROSTING:

⅓ cup butter
1 cup brown sugar
½ cup cream or whole milk

2 cups powdered sugar (or more, depending on desired consistency)

Preheat oven to 350° F. Grease a 9 ¥ 13-inch sheet cake pan; set aside. In a large bowl, combine flour, sugar, baking powder, baking soda, salt, cinnamon, cloves, and allspice. Add butter, water, and applesauce. Beat 2 minutes at medium speed with mixer. Add eggs; beat 2 more minutes. Fold in raisins and nuts. Bake in prepared pan 45 to 50 minutes, or until cake tests done. Melt butter for frosting in saucepan; add sugar and bring to a boil. Add cream. Remove from heat and cool to lukewarm. Add enough confectioner's sugar for good spreading consistency. Frost when cool. Makes 12 servings.

This recipe was provided courtesy of U.S. Congressman Frank R. Wolf, who has represented Virginia's tenth district since 1980. He lives in Vienna.

DOLORES'S BEST APPLE CRUMB CAKE

*This marvelous creation suits breakfast, brunch, or dessert,
or makes a wonderful snack with tea during respites.*

FOR CRUST AND TOPPING:

2 sticks unsalted butter
1 cup sugar
3½ cups all-purpose flour

1 tablespoon baking powder
2 teaspoons vanilla (or almond) extract

FOR FILLING:

8 cups sliced apples
½ cup currants or raisins, optional
½ cup chopped pecans, optional

½ cup sugar
juice of ½ lemon
2 teaspoons ground cinnamon

Place a cookie sheet in the oven and preheat oven to 325° F. Melt the butter in a wide heavy skillet. Stir in the rest of the crust ingredients and blend well. Using your fingers, mold ⅔ of this into the bottom and up the sides of a 9-inch springform pan.

Combine the sliced apples with remaining ingredients. Pour the sliced apples into the crust, arranging them as evenly as possible with a slight mounding in the center. Crumble remaining pastry mixture over the entire top. Bake about 90 minutes, or until the top is brown and the apples bubble up around the rim. Remove the cookie sheet with the apple cake from the oven. Cool the cake in the pan on a wire rack. Transfer to a serving plate. Dust heavily with powdered sugar before serving. Makes 10 servings.

This recipe was provided courtesy of food writer Dolores Kostelni of Lexington.

STRIBLING'S CROCKPOT APPLE BUTTER

What could be easier than making preserves in a crockpot?

16 cups chopped apples
2 cups cider
2 cups sugar

1 teaspoon cinnamon
¼ teaspoon cloves

Core and chop apples. Do not peel. Combine apples and cider in the crockpot. Cover and cook on low for 10 to 12 hours. Purée and then return the mixture to the crockpot and add the sugar, cinnamon, and cloves. Cover and cook on low 1 hour. This will keep for several weeks in the refrigerator. If desired, pour into hot, sterilized jars and seal, or pour into freezer containers and freeze. Makes about 8 cups.

Recipe courtesy of Stribling Orchard in Markham.

Copper Apple-Butter Kettles

Coppersmithing came to America with the colonists who used copper to make buckets for carrying water and kettles for cooking. Today coppersmith Porter Caldwell crafts these and other pieces such as chocolate pots, tea kettles, and wash boilers based on styles of the eighteenth and nineteenth centuries. He fashions them from flat sheets of copper, using flat seams or dovetailing, hammering, and welding with silver. After cleaning, they are hand polished and numbered, beginning with number one each year. The large kettles that hold from 15 to 75 gallons are used to make apple butter over an open fire. Most of these kettles are purchased by museums and re-enactors at historic homes.

Caldwell first became interested in metalwork and how things were made as a small boy. He tinkered in his father's shop, entertaining himself for hours. One apple-butter making season, he told his mother: "One day I'm going to make a copper kettle." And he finally did, but his mother didn't live to see it. She died at age 96, and Caldwell didn't make his first large kettle until he was 50. Caldwell's shop is in the Appalachians, about an hour outside of Roanoke. Call (540) 473-2167 to make an appointment or place an order.

WINCHESTER
Virginia's Apple Capital

• WINCHESTER: • VIRGINIA'S APPLE CAPITAL

There are many historic sites and orchards to visit in Winchester as well as one of Virginia's largest festivals, the Shenandoah Apple Blossom Festival, held the first week of May.

FEES: Admission to individual historic sites in Winchester varies. Combination tickets are available at the visitor center.

DIRECTIONS: Winchester is 75 miles west of Washington, D.C., and 13 miles north of the intersection of I-66 and I-81 on U.S. Route 11.

MORE INFORMATION: Call the Winchester-Frederick County Visitor Center at (540) 542-1326 or (877) 871-1326, or visit www. visitwinchesterva.com. The Shenandoah Apple Blossom Festival phone is (540) 622-3863; www.the bloom.com.

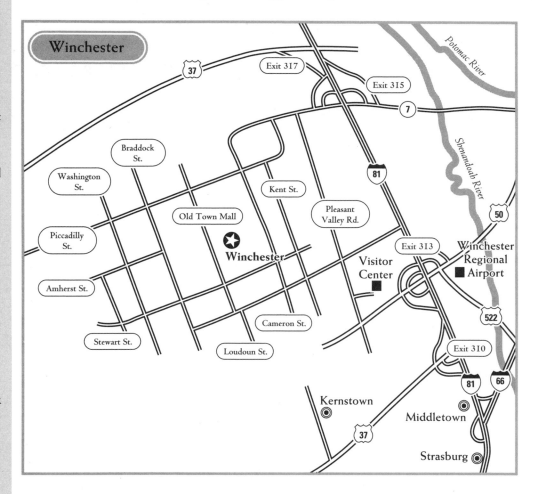

Trundling hills planted with battalions of fruit trees greet visitors to the Winchester area. Legend has it that a beautiful Indian maiden lived in the valley that begins here. Great wars are said to have been fought in her honor. The maiden's name was Shenandoah, which means "daughter of the stars." And the Shenandoah Valley, with Winchester at its northern tip, is certainly the guiding star of Virginia's apple industry.

Settled in about 1732, Winchester is named for Winchester, England. The writer Willa Cather, country-music legend Patsy Cline, and polar explorer and naval aviator Admiral Richard E. Byrd were born here. Much earlier, in 1748, George Washington began his surveying career in Winchester and maintained military headquarters here between 1755 and 1758, during the French–Indian War. An early landlord, Washington required each tenant to plant four acres of apples. This resulted in extensive orchards from the beginning of English settlement.

Because of its strategic location at the northern entrance of the Shenandoah Valley, the Winchester area was the scene of three important Civil War battles, in 1862, 1863, and 1864. The town changed hands more than 70 times during that period, including 13 times in one day. The Confederate and national cemeteries here contain the bodies of 7500 Civil War dead from both sides.

Today, the peaceful city, home to about 23,000, swells with more than 300,000 visitors during the Shenandoah Apple Blossom Festival, held the first week of May. It's a celebration of spring in the valley as evidenced by the blooming of the apple trees. The apple industry is one of the oldest and most important natural resources in the Winchester-Frederick County area. The city also serves as a commercial, transportation, and processing center for apples and other tree fruit, such as peaches and pears.

Festival week, a six-day extravaganza, provides a great excuse to visit Winchester. The festival is operated by more than 2500 volunteers and features dances, parades, band competitions, the Clyde Beatty–Cole Bros. Circus, a 10K run, the coronation of Queen Shenandoah, firefighters' events, live music, and celebrities.

But Winchester is a fine place to visit anytime. Stop first at the visitors bureau, housed in a restored gristmill half a mile off Interstate 81. It provides brochures and a free 18-minute video presentation about the area. The Visitor Center (1400 S. Pleasant Valley Road, (540) 542-1326) also houses a Civil War Information Center and exhibition galleries.

Points of interest include several historic sites. **George Washington's Headquarters,** the office from which he supervised the construction of Fort Loudoun between September 1755 and December 1756, is one such site. At **Confederate General Stonewall Jackson's Headquarters,** see where the general spent much of the winter of 1861–1862, planning for two campaigns, and view Jackson memorabilia and Civil War relics.

Abram's Delight Museum and Log Cabin is the oldest house in Winchester, built in 1754 by a Quaker. It's furnished in period style and contains an open-hearth kitchen. Located outside of the Old Town area, a manor house, **Glen Burnie,** was the home of Winchester's founder, Colonel James Wood. The home is a handsome Georgian red-brick house with sections dating as early as 1794. The interior contains examples of some of the finest early craftsmanship in the lower Shenandoah Valley. It is now a component of the Museum of the Shenandoah Valley history museum complex, which opened in 2005.

There are numerous orchards, farms, and a farm market near Winchester. See the Pick-Your-Own listings for Frederick County in the back of this book.

Don't Forget

When you decide to visit Winchester, be sure to leave time to see beautiful Belle Grove Plantation, located 13 miles south of Winchester near Middletown. Situated on 100 acres, this eighteenth-century grain-and-livestock farm encompassed about 7500 acres of land in its prime. The unique limestone house was completed in 1797 for Major Isaac Hite and his wife Nelly, sister of President James Madison. The house has remained virtually unchanged through the years, offering visitors an experience of the life and times of the people who lived there in the late eighteenth and early nineteenth centuries. During the Civil War, Belle Grove was at the center of the decisive Battle of Cedar Creek. Today, the plantation includes the main house and gardens, original outbuildings, a classic 1918 barn, an overseer's house, the slave cemetery, a heritage apple orchard, fields and meadows, and scenic mountain views. The site is open daily from April to October. Admission is charged. Phone (540) 869-2028 or visit www.bellegrove.org.

Peaches

First cultivated in ancient China, peaches went to Greece with Alexander the Great's soldiers around 322 B.C. A peach in Rome around 100 A.D. cost the equivalent of more than $4; in Victorian England it cost about $5. Spanish explorers traveling through Mexico and Florida brought the first peaches to North America, where they spread through missionary and Indian populations.

A refreshing taste for summer, peaches are a perfect blend of flavor and nutrition. They can be enjoyed as appetizers, desserts, and everything in between. And they contain important nutrients, like fiber, riboflavin, and beta carotene, which has been linked to a reduced cancer risk. Peaches are one of the lowest-calorie fruits.

chapter two

PEACHES, NECTARINES, AND PLUMS

✍ *Virginia's peaches have been called "The Queen of Fruits." Big, juicy, and sweet, they are the Commonwealth's number-one summer tree fruit, earning orchardists about $4 million. Production totals around 10 million pounds. Garnet Beauty and Laural are the first to appear in July, along with the white peaches, Morton and Raritan Rose. Coming along in August are Redhaven, Rich Lady, Topaz, Contender, Earnie's Choice, Loring, Harcrest, and White Lady. Fayette and Encore come in September. Peaches and nectarines are essentially the same, differing only in genes for surface fuzz. Flavorful nectarines are among Virginia agriculture's sweetest success stories. Grown in the mountains, nectarines thrive in the cool nights and warm days. Summer Beaut, Sunglo, Red Gold, and Flavor Top are the nectarine varieties grown here, ripening in July and August. Although Virginia also has thousands of tart-cherry trees and some plum trees, harvest of these is not a big business.*

PEACHES-AND-CREAM FRENCH TOAST

Assembled the night before, this all-in-one breakfast dish tastes as luscious as it sounds.

3 large eggs
⅓ cup plus 3 tablespoons peach
   preserves, divided
¾ cup half-and-half
¼ teaspoon vanilla
6 slices French or Italian bread
   (½ inch thick)

5 tablespoons butter or margarine,
   divided
2 fresh peaches, peeled and sliced
confectioner's sugar
¼ cup toasted almonds
pinch of salt

In bowl, blend the eggs and 3 tablespoons of peach preserves with fork or wire whisk. Beat in half-and-half, vanilla, and salt; add to egg mixture. Dip bread in liquid mixture and place in baking dish. Pour any leftover liquid over bread; cover and refrigerate overnight.

Using a wooden spoon, cream 4 tablespoons butter with ⅓ cup peach preserves; beat until light and fluffy. Refrigerate. Set out 30 minutes before using.

Heat a large griddle; melt remaining butter and add bread slices. Cook over medium-high heat until golden brown, turning once. Remove to servings plates and spread with peach butter. Top with peaches and sprinkle with sugar and almonds. Makes 6 slices.

Innkeepers Don and Mary Davis serve their special recipe to guests at Stone Manor Bed & Breakfast, located on beautiful Smith Mountain Lake, Virginia's largest with 500 miles of shoreline. The recreational opportunities just outside the door include boating, swimming, fishing, and golf. Guests enjoy 690 feet of waterfront with private docks and a lighted boardwalk. The inn is 25 minutes from Roanoke in Goodview (phone (540) 297-1414).

GRILLED GLAZED PEACHES AND PORK

A surprising combination of ingredients renders a scrumptious main dish.

1½ pounds pork shoulder steaks
⅓ cup frozen orange juice concentrate, thawed
¼ cup soy sauce
2 tablespoons dark molasses
¼ cup bourbon or rum

1 tablespoon vegetable oil
2 cloves garlic, minced
½ teaspoon finely chopped fresh
   ginger root
3 fresh peaches or nectarines

Place steaks in a sealable plastic bag. In a 2-cup glass measure, combine orange-juice concentrate, soy sauce, molasses, bourbon, oil, garlic, and ginger root. Reserve ⅓ cup of the mixture. Pour the remaining marinade over the pork. Seal the bag and refrigerate for 3 hours or overnight, turning bag occasionally.

One hour before cooking, halve peaches and remove pits, then slice each half into 3 wedges and place in another sealable plastic bag. Add reserved marinade and refrigerate 1 hour, turning bag occasionally.

Preheat gas grill on high or light a charcoal fire. Reduce gas grill to medium. Discard pork marinade. Pour marinade from peaches into a bowl. Place pork steaks on grill and grill covered for 8 to 10 minutes per side, basting several times with peach marinade. Add peaches to grill for last 5 minutes, turning as needed until they develop grill marks. Serve with rice pilaf and a vegetable salad. Makes 4 servings.

Recipe provided courtesy of the Virginia Pork Producers Board.

When selecting peaches, smell the fruit. A member of the rose family, peaches should have a pleasant, sweet fragrance. Look for a creamy gold or yellow under color. The red or "blush" of a peach indicates variety, not ripeness. Peaches should be soft to the touch but not mushy.

Look for a well-defined crease that runs from the stem to the point. Don't squeeze peaches, they bruise easily. Place firm peaches on the counter for a day or two to ripen. Promptly refrigerate ripe peaches and eat them within a week of purchase. To peel a peach, dip it into boiling water for 30 seconds, then into cold water. The peel should slide off easily. To keep sliced peaches from darkening, add lemon juice or ascorbic acid.

FIREHOOK BAKERY'S HAZELNUT CRUMB PEACH PIE

Hazelnuts and ripe, juicy peaches form a delectable duo in this delicious dessert.

FOR RICH PIE CRUST:

1¼ cups flour
½ teaspoon sugar
¼ teaspoon salt
2 to 3 tablespoons ice water
1 egg yolk

¼ cup each unsalted butter and vegetable shortening, blended and chilled
½ teaspoon vinegar

FOR PEACH FILLING:

6 large peaches
1 tablespoon lemon juice
⅛ teaspoon almond extract

½ to ¾ cup sugar
2½ to 3 tablespoons cornstarch
⅛ teaspoon ground nutmeg

FOR TOPPING:

½ cup packed light brown sugar
½ cup flour

6 tablespoons unsalted butter
1 cup chopped hazelnuts

Begin preparing this crust in plenty of time to freeze for at least an hour before baking; you can make it 2 to 3 days in advance and store in the refrigerator. Place flour, sugar, and salt in a medium-sized mixing bowl. Dice cold butter mixture into small pieces and cut into flour mixture until mixture resembles coarse meal.

Mix egg yolk and vinegar with 2 tablespoons ice water. Sprinkle liquid over flour and toss with a fork to moisten dough evenly. Add 1 additional tablespoon ice water if too dry, and gather into a ball. Flatten ball and wrap with plastic wrap; refrigerate at least 1 hour. Roll to fit a 9- or 10-inch pie plate. Flute or trim edge. Freeze shell for at least 1 hour before filling and baking.

To prepare filling, preheat oven to 425° F. Peel and slice peaches. You should have 6 cups sliced peaches. Toss with lemon juice and extract in a large bowl. Add the desired amount of sugar and cornstarch according to the sweetness and juiciness of the peaches; add nutmeg. Let stand 10 minutes.

To make hazelnut topping for pie, mix brown sugar with flour in a bowl. Cut in butter until crumbly; stir in hazelnuts. Pour peach filling into prepared pie crust and sprinkle with hazelnut topping. Bake 15 minutes. Reduce heat to 400° F and continue baking 35 to 40 minutes. Makes 8 servings.

Kate Jansen, a former pastry chef for Galileo restaurant, was the pastry chef and one of three founders of Firehook Bakery & Coffeehouse, established in 1992 in Alexandria. Many of Firehook's quality breads and pastries are prepared in the wood-burning oven, which was shipped from Spain and reassembled brick by brick by Emanuel de la Rosa of Barcelona. Firehook also features a lunch menu and has two locations in Alexandria and four locations in Washington, D.C. (phone (703) 549-0128 or (703) 519-8021 for the main bakery and the Old Town location, respectively, or visit www.firehook.com).

EASY PEACH FREEZER JAM

For busy people who don't want to pressure can preserves,
this microwave-prepared jam keeps in the refrigerator or freezer.

1 teaspoon Fruit Fresh (ascorbic acid
    powder)
2 tablespoons lemon juice
2 pounds peaches, quartered, peeled,
    and pitted

5 cups sugar
¾ cup water
1 (1¾-ounce) package powdered
    pectin (no substitutes)

In a 2-quart glass measure or round casserole, dissolve Fruit Fresh in lemon juice. Put half of peaches in a food processor with steel blades. Pulse to chop. Repeat with remaining peaches. Pulp should measure 2½ cups; add water if necessary. Add pulp to lemon mixture and stir in sugar; blend well.

In a 4-cup glass measure, combine water and pectin. Microwave on high 2 minutes or until mixture boils. Stir and microwave on high 1 minute (reduce power if mixture begins to boil over). Stir hot pectin into peach mixture and continue stirring for 3 minutes. Pour into sterilized jars, cover, and let stand 24 hours at room temperature to set. Freeze up to 12 months or refrigerate up to 3 weeks. Makes 7 (8-ounce) jars.

CHEZ FRANÇOIS'S PLUM PIE

"Tarte aux Quetsches" is the most famous dessert served
at this almost 50-year-old Alsatian restaurant.

2½ pounds small purple plums
    (Italian plums)
¼ teaspoon cinnamon
3 tablespoons graham cracker crumbs

1 (9-inch) pie crust, baked to light
    brown
4 to 7 tablespoons sugar, divided

Preheat oven to 400° F. Split plums lengthwise with a sharp knife and remove pits. Spread crumbs in bottom of baked pie crust. Place plums cut-side up in tight, concentric circles around the pie. Plums should be resting against each other at a slight angle. Bake 30 to 40 minutes, or until skins tear easily. Combine 1 tablespoon sugar with cinnamon. Sprinkle fruit with 4 to 6 tablespoons remaining sugar, depending on the tartness of the fruit. Dust with cinnamon sugar. Serve warm (if desired, with vanilla ice cream). Makes 6 to 8 servings.

∾ The Haeringer family's popular Alsatian-style restaurant, open since 1954, is one of Virginia's finest restaurants. The cooking is hearty and the portions generous. Chez François's specialties include choucroute garni—an enormous platter of sauerkraut garnished with pheasant, duck, sausages, smoked pork, and foie gras—and a winter-game platter of venison, antelope, and grilled quail. But this plum tart has always been diners' favorite dessert. The restaurant, located in Great Falls, is open Sunday for lunch and dinner and Tuesday through Saturday for dinner (332 Springdale Road; (703) 759-3800); www.laubergechezfrancois.com. ∾

Pears are delicate and must be picked by hand. They are deliberately picked before they are ripe, both to maintain quality during shipping and to promote a smoother texture. Even when pears are not ripe they are easily injured. Avoid buying bruised or too-soft fruit, and never count on being able to use them for a few days after purchase. When you bring them home from the store, don't refrigerate them. Place the pears in a bowl or a paper bag at room temperature for four to six days.

Pears come in many varieties and colors. For that reason, color change is not a good test of ripeness. To tell if pears are ripe, press the stem end gently with your thumb. If it gives, the fruit is ripe. Once they have reached desired ripeness, place them in the refrigerator to slow further ripening. Depending on their ripeness, pears can be stored in the refrigerator for almost a week.

To prevent sliced pears from darkening, toss them in equal parts lemon juice and water, or in orange juice, or sprinkle them with ascorbic-acid powder such as Fruit Fresh.

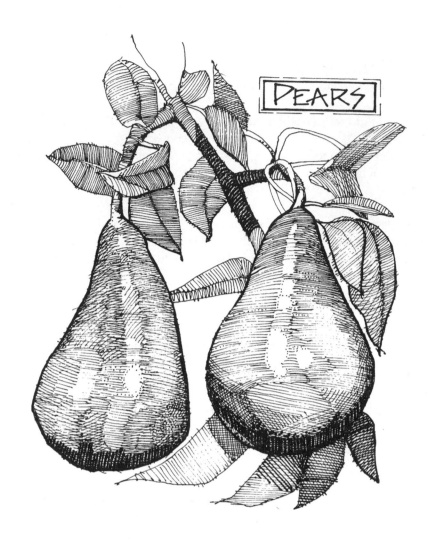

chapter three

PEARS

∽ *Bite into a ripe Bartlett pear and you may feel the succulent juice dripping down your chin. Nibble a crispy Asian pear and you're likely to feel the spray of a fine mist like the air around a waterfall. Pears grow on hundreds of Virginia farms. The trees produce wonderfully flavorful and ripe fruit less than a day away from the state's markets. The same climate that favors the Commonwealth's apple orchards—the Shenandoah and Alleghenies—is also home to this other fruit that loves cool nights.*

MESCLUN AND ASIAN-PEAR SALAD WITH RASPBERRY VINAIGRETTE DRESSING

Raspberry vinaigrette pairs well with Asian pears, and this fruity salad is especially good with baked chicken, roast pork, or hearty seafood such as salmon, swordfish, or halibut.

FOR SALAD:

- 8 cups mesclun (mixed baby lettuces) or leaf lettuce, rinsed and torn into bite-size pieces
- 2 medium, firm, ripe Asian pears, cored and thinly sliced
- ⅓ cup seedless raisins
- ¼ cup coarsely broken walnuts, toasted lightly and cooled
- salt and pepper to taste

FOR DRESSING:

- ⅓ cup extra-virgin olive oil
- ⅓ cup water
- ¼ cup white sugar
- ¼ cup raspberry vinegar
- 2 tablespoons sour cream
- 1 tablespoon Dijon mustard

Combine mesclun, pears, and raisins in a large bowl. Combine all dressing ingredients in a separate container and blend until smooth. Toss salad with dressing and season with salt and pepper. Garnish with walnuts. Makes 4 servings.

Paul and YoungSuk Estabrook, owners of Virginia Gold Orchard in Natural Bridge, suggest this as a way of merging the flavors of raspberries and pears—a combination they like. Their favorite way to eat Asian pears is raw, although they like to bake a tart by topping puff pastry with sliced pears. Even after cooking, Asian pears retain their crispy texture. Visit www.virginiagoldorchard.com.

ASHTON PEAR CRISP

This microwaved dessert is ready in less than 10 minutes.

- 4 firm pears, cored and cut into 12 wedges
- ¼ cup apple jelly (or honey)
- ½ cup chopped walnuts
- 2 tablespoons quick cooking oats
- 2 tablespoons brown sugar
- 2 tablespoons melted margarine or butter

Place pear slices in microwave-safe bowl. Spoon jelly on top. Sprinkle with nuts, oats, and sugar. Drizzle with margarine. Microwave on high 6 minutes, stir, and cook 3 or 4 minutes more until pears are fork tender. Makes 4 servings.

Ashton Country House Bed & Breakfast in Staunton is a Victorian mansion built in 1860 with lofty ceilings, solid brick interior walls, and magnificent heart-pine and maple floors. There are swings on the large porch, scenic mountain vistas, and flowered grounds (phone (540) 885-3001 or (877) 885-3001) or visit www.ashton housebnb.com.

Asian-Pear Farmers Paul and YoungSuk Estabrook

Virginia Gold Orchard was born in 1990 on 110 acres. Owners Paul and YoungSuk Estabrook had been living in New Hampshire, growing 500 Asian pear trees. YoungSuk is a Korean American, very talented at growing this fruit.

When Paul retired from his engineering career, the pair traveled around the country, looking for a place to start a larger orchard. They purchased land in Virginia's Shenandoah Valley and gradually have planted 4000 trees encompassing nine varieties.

The trees have come from various places in the United States, trucked to the orchard in "bare-root" form. Once planted, the trees are pruned to three feet. It's important for farmers to reach every part of the tree without having to use a ladder, because there's so much handwork involved in raising Asian pears. By shipping time, each pear will have been touched at least three times. There's no off-season in the orchard.

Most of the orchard's harvest is sold by mail order from September through February. To order Asian pears from Virginia Gold Orchard, call (540) 291-1481 or visit www.virginiagoldorchard. com. Tourists can visit the orchard between mid-August and December.

VIRGINIA HAM, ASIAN PEAR, AND DATE APPETIZERS WITH MINT

2 medium-sized Asian pears (about 1 pound total)
20 pitted dates
4 ounces Neufchâtel or reduced-fat cream cheese
40 small fresh mint leaves
3 ounces thinly sliced Smithfield ham

Quarter and core pears. Cut each quarter into five (¼-inch thick) slices. Halve each date lengthwise and fill indentation in each half with ½ teaspoon cream cheese. Place a mint leaf on each pear slice and top with a date half, cheese-side down. Fold a ham slice in half and wrap it around pear and date, tucking ends underneath. Repeat making remaining appetizers. Makes about 40 appetizers.

SPINACH, PEAR, AND BACON SALAD

The sweetness of the pears in this salad is nicely balanced by the salty, crisp bacon.

5 slices bacon, diced
¼ cup minced shallots
3 tablespoons sherry-wine vinegar
2 teaspoons Dijon mustard
2 teaspoons minced fresh thyme or 1 teaspoon dried
½ cup extra-virgin olive oil
1 pound baby spinach leaves
2 Asian or Bosc pears, halved, cored, and thinly sliced
1 medium-sized red onion, thinly sliced
1 head radicchio, separated into leaves

Brown bacon in a nonstick skillet over medium heat until crisp and drain grease. Pour bacon drippings into a bowl and add to it shallots, vinegar, mustard, and thyme; whisk to blend. Add oil; whisk to blend. Season with salt and pepper. (Dressing can be made one day ahead. Cover and chill along with reserved bacon. Bring to room temperature before continuing.)

Combine spinach, pears, red onion, and bacon in a large bowl. Toss with enough dressing to coat. Surround salad with radicchio leaves and serve. Makes 8 servings.

WATERMELON

chapter four
MELONS

∽ *More than 2,000 acres of cantaloupes and watermelon are planted in Virginia, bringing in about $4 million. Cantaloupes are the second largest crop in the Northern Neck. Virginia growers produce cantaloupes that are genetically developed for their sweetness and are sold throughout the eastern United States. The varieties grown are Athena, All Star, Cordele, Superstar, and Burpee Hybrid. The crop is raised on plastic with overhead or drip irrigation. Rows of rye are planted between the rows of melons to reduce the risk of wind damage. Most all harvested melons are placed in cold storage prior to shipment, to remove field heat and enhance shelf life. Virginia watermelons are sweet and hardy. They come to market just as the supply from more southern producers decline. Most Virginia watermelons average 22 to 28 pounds. Varieties grown include Fiesta, Royal Star, Mardi Gras, Starbright, Summer Flavor, Seedless, Tri X 313, and Millionaire. Once limited to southeastern Virginia, watermelons are now grown in several regions across the state.*

Watermelon

Famed explorer Dr. David Livingston found watermelons growing wild in the central part of Africa. Today, cultivated in the warm regions of every part of the world, watermelons are served differently by various cultures. Russians make a beer from the juice. Iraqis use the flesh as an animal feed and water source. Asians roast the seeds and eat them from the hand. Watermelons are low in calories, virtually fat free, and a good source of vitamins A and C. There are about 50 different varieties of watermelons in the United States.

When buying a whole watermelon, look for a firm, slightly dull rind and fully rounded sides. If buying a cut watermelon, look for firm, juicy, red flesh with no white strands. The lower side, where the watermelon came into contact with the soil, should be yellow in color. If a melon is hard, white, or very pale green on the underside, it's probably immature. Watermelons can be stored at room temperature until cut. Once cut, the watermelon should be refrigerated.

Cantaloupe

Probably the most popular melon, the cantaloupe is sweet and perfumey and, being 89% water, has succulent flesh. If you've ever overlooked one inside your car, the fragrance when you open the door announces a cantaloupe has been left behind.

The flesh varies from salmon color to bright orange, and the skin has a rough skin called "netting." Cantaloupes with tighter netting seem to have a firmer texture than those with a loose-looking one. They also slice better.

When choosing a cantaloupe, a common tactic is to push the stem end to see if it yields to pressure. This is not a valid test of ripeness, especially if others before you have tested the same melon in this manner. Fragrance and color are the most important determination. Look for a cantaloupe with a golden color and sweet odor.

A cantaloupe with a greenish cast will become riper if you leave it out at room temperature until the rind turns golden. After ripe, don't store it at room temperature, because it will mold rapidly.

Cantaloupes are an excellent source of vitamins A and C and have a barely measurable fat content.

CANTALOUPE AND AVOCADO SALAD WITH GINGER DRESSING

A pinwheel of tropical fruits, this salad is an attractive accompaniment to chicken, lamb, and pork dishes. If desired, substitute pears, oranges, and mangoes.

½ of a ripe cantaloupe
1 ruby-red grapefruit, sectioned
1 kiwifruit, peeled, halved, and sliced crosswise
¼ cup orange juice
¼ cup lime juice
⅓ cup olive oil
1 tablespoon grated fresh ginger root

1 teaspoon orange zest (grated orange color from rind)
1 teaspoon poppyseeds
¼ teaspoon salt
5 ounces mesclun or baby spinach leaves
1 ripe avocado

Cut cantaloupe lengthwise into 4 wedges. Using a knife, cut fruit from rind and slice crosswise into ¼-inch slices. Place in a bowl with grapefruit sections and kiwifruit. In a blender or food processor, place orange and lime juices, olive oil, ginger root, orange zest, poppyseeds, and salt. Purée until smooth.

Toss half the dressing with lettuces and distribute on four plates. Arrange the fruit slices in an attractive pinwheel design, alternating colors and textures. Cut avocado in half lengthwise. Twist halves in opposite directions to separate. Remove pit, peel, and cut into 16 lengthwise slices. Place avocado slices on top and drizzle remaining dressing over all fruits. Makes 4 servings.

GRILLED-PORK AND CANTALOUPE KEBABS

An array of tastes and colors recommends these festive finger foods.

1 pound boneless pork loin, cut into 1½-inch chunks
¼ cup frozen orange-juice concentrate, thawed
1 tablespoon vegetable oil
½ teaspoon dried basil

¼ teaspoon each salt and pepper
4 plums, halved and pitted
½ of a ripe cantaloupe, cut into 2-inch chunks
1 large ripe mango, peeled, cut into chunks

If using bamboo skewers, soak in water 1 hour to prevent burning. Preheat gas grill on high or light a charcoal fire. Reduce gas grill to medium. Thread pork on 4 skewers. Thread plums, cantaloupe, and mango alternately on 4 skewers. Combine orange juice concentrate, oil, basil, salt, and pepper; set aside.

Place pork kebabs on grill; baste with orange-juice mixture. Cover and grill 5 minutes; turn. Add fruit kebabs to the grill. Baste pork and fruit with orange-juice mixture. Close cover and grill 5 minutes, turning fruit kebabs and basting again after 2 minutes. Makes 4 servings.

Recipe courtesy of Virginia Pork Board.

LOBSTER-MELON SALAD

Prepare this salad with fresh melon for any summer gathering.

FOR SALAD:

- 2 pounds cooked lobster meat, cut into 1-inch pieces (or lobster-flavored surimi seafood)
- 3 cups cantaloupe balls
- 1 tablespoon freshly minced ginger
- 1 diced papaya (about 1¼ pounds), peeled, seeded, and cut into ½-inch dice
- 6 diced plum tomatoes (about 2 cups), seeded and cut into ¼-inch dice

FOR DRESSING:

- ¼ cup fresh orange juice
- 2 tablespoons red-wine vinegar
- 1 teaspoon Dijon mustard
- salt and black pepper
- ½ cup extra-virgin olive oil
- 1 teaspoon finely grated orange zest
- ¼ cup freshly snipped chives
- 2 heads radicchio, leaves washed and patted dry, for garnish

Place the lobster meat, cantaloupe, papaya, tomatoes, and ginger in a large bowl. Gently fold together with a rubber spatula. Set aside.

In a small bowl, combine the orange juice, vinegar, mustard, salt, and pepper. Whisking constantly, slowly drizzle in the olive oil. Continue whisking until the mixture has thickened slightly. Stir in orange zest. Shortly before serving, toss ½ cup of the dressing with the chives and lobster mixture. Serve on a decorative platter surrounded by radicchio leaves, or place serving portions inside the leaves. Serve remaining dressing on the side or reserve for future use. Makes 12 servings.

VIRGINIA WATERMELON PICKLES

When it's too hot to venture out, enjoy the red meat of the watermelon, then spend an afternoon preparing these pickles. You'll be glad you did.

- 10 pounds watermelon rind (from 2 large melons)
- ¼ ounce slaked lime
- 2 gallons plus 1 cup water, divided
- ¾ cup salt
- 10 pounds sugar
- 7 cups white vinegar
- 2 to 3 tablespoons whole cloves
- 2 to 3 tablespoons whole allspice
- 2 to 3 tablespoons cinnamon sticks, broken

Peel and cut rind into small pieces. Mix lime with 1 gallon water in a large crock. Add rind; cover with a heavy plate to keep the rind covered in liquid. Soak overnight; drain and wash 4 times in cool water. Squeeze all the rind by hand to remove most of the water.

Boil rind 20 minutes in 1 gallon water mixed with the salt. Drain and wash 3 times in cool water. Drain and squeeze water from rind. Make a syrup of remaining 1 cup water and other ingredients; cook until sugar dissolves. Add rind and cook 1 hour. Cool slightly. Pack jars with rind, cover with syrup, and seal. Store in refrigerator. To store in pantry, process in a pressure canner. Makes 12 pints.

As the twentieth century drew to a close, the oldest continuously-occupied governor's residence in the nation was beginning to show its age. Home to governors from James Barbour to the present, the magnificent 1813 Federalist-style brick mansion inside the cast-iron fence of Capitol Square hadn't been renovated in 50 years. Governor Gilmore and his family had to relocate during the six-month construction period. First Lady Roxanne Gilmore directed the $7.2 million renovation project and was frequently on site, wearing a hard hat. The most dramatic change is visible in the basement kitchen. Chef Mark Herndon designed the layout and selected the equipment for the now fully equipped commercial-grade kitchen. Thanks to the addition of a modern convection oven, food can now be cooked faster and more evenly. All the stainless-steel equipment is geared toward volume preparation, so the kitchen staff can adequately handle the numerous large gatherings that take place in the mansion. In the past, large parties had to be catered. Herndon and his one full-time assistant prepare seated dinners for 40 to 50 people and stand-up cocktail parties for 150, the maximum number the mansion can accommodate.

Strawberries

Strawberries have grown in the wild on coasts, in forests, and on mountains in the Northern and Southern hemispheres for thousands of years. Cato, a senator in ancient Rome, mentions strawberries in his writings. Literature from the first millennium describes the medicinal value of the strawberry plant, not the food value of its fruit. Twelfth-century Saint Hildegard von Binger pronounced strawberries unsuitable to eat; they grew too close to the ground, where snakes and toads could contaminate the fruit by touching them, the saint said. A few centuries later, famed botanist Charles Linnaeus helped debunk the myth by prescribing for himself a diet of only the fruit.

Explorers to the Americas found strawberry plants that surpassed all European varieties in appearance and taste. In the eighteenth century, agricultural experimenters on both sides of the Atlantic crossed various American varieties and improved the strawberry further.

Strawberries are not really fruit or berry, but rather the enlarged receptacles of flowers. This member of the rose family is grown in every state in the United States. Besides the pleasantly sweet flavor, strawberries offer plenty of nutrition. They are low in calories, fat free, and a good source of vitamin C, potassium, and antioxidants.

chapter five

BERRIES

∾ *Although Virginia's berry industry is relatively small, strawberries alone bring in more than $5 million in revenue from fewer than 1,000 acres planted. Strawberries are available throughout May and June; in July and August, blackberries, raspberries, and blueberries ripen. Berries are a consumer favorite fruit in the Virginia Department of Agriculture and Consumer Services Pick-Your-Own program. Although berries are grown throughout the entire state, there's a concentration of several berry varieties in the Northern Neck and of blackberries in Southside Virginia.*

OLD-FASHIONED STRAWBERRY SHORTCAKE

Nothing is better than this classic when made from scratch.

2 cups flour
6 tablespoons sugar, divided
3 teaspoons baking powder
½ teaspoon salt
6 tablespoons margarine
1 egg, beaten

⅔ cup milk
3 cups sliced or quartered fresh
   strawberries or other berries
sweetened whipped cream or
   whipped topping

Preheat oven to 350° F. In a bowl, sift together flour, 2 tablespoons sugar, baking powder, and salt. Cut in margarine until mixture is crumbly. Combine egg with milk, then add to flour mixture, stirring just until moistened.

Roll dough and cut into 6 (3-inch) shortcakes or spread in a 9-inch layer cake pan. Bake for 12 minutes. Sprinkle 1 tablespoon sugar over the top and bake for 18 minutes. Do not overbake. Combine strawberries and remaining 3 tablespoons sugar. Split shortcakes in half. Serve warm with sweetened crushed berries in the center and on top of shortcake halves; garnish with whipped cream. Makes 6 servings.

This is a Mennonite recipe of Esther H. Shank contributed by Shenville Creamery in Timberville. More information about the creamery can be found on pages 94–96.

HARMONY FARM STRAWBERRY MUFFINS

These brown (it's the cinnamon!) muffins are a pleasure, bite after bite.

1½ cups flour
1 cup sugar
2 teaspoons cinnamon
¾ teaspoon baking soda
½ teaspoon baking powder
½ teaspoon salt
2 eggs

½ cup vegetable oil
1 teaspoon almond flavoring
1 (10-ounce) package frozen strawberries, chopped into chunks,
   including juice
½ cup chopped almonds

Preheat to 350° F. Grease a 12-cup muffin pan. In a mixing bowl, combine dry ingredients. In a separate bowl, pour in oil and beat in eggs and flavoring; add to dry ingredients. Add strawberries (including juice) and almonds to the mix and fold in gently. (Almonds can be placed on top of each muffin before baking.) Spoon batter into prepared pan and bake 22 to 25 minutes. Makes 12 muffins.

Harmony Farm Bed & Breakfast is located in beautiful Floyd on the eastern flank of the Blue Ridge Mountains. It is within half mile of the scenic parkway and within one mile of Chateau Morrisette Winery. The farm consists of 90 acres of forests, open fields, wildflower beds, and a pond that provide habitat for wildlife. Guests can enjoy a marked trail system, picnic tables, viewing areas, and a hammock under the trees (phone (540) 593-2185 or visit www.harmony-farm.com).

Buyer's Guide to STRAWBERRIES

Select fruit that is firm but not hard, smells pleasant, and has deep red color and green caps attached. Avoid or remove badly bruised or moldy strawberries. Place strawberries in a single layer in a clean container covered with wax paper in the refrigerator. Just before using, remove caps and wash thoroughly in a colander.

Virginia: Cradle of the Banjo

The notes of the banjo could serve as the soundtrack for Virginia's history. More than three centuries, banjo has been played by African Americans, minstrels, Civil War soldiers, and bluegrass pickers. America's musical instrument descended from the African xalam or bandore. A gourd instrument called a strum-strum was played in the West Indies. Thomas Jefferson wrote in 1781, "The instrument proper to [blacks] is the Banjar, which they brought hither from Africa." The earliest references to blacks playing banjos in the colonies date from the 1750s and are concentrated in Virginia. In the 1880s, a regional mountain banjo was produced by folk artisans in southwest Virginia. The banjo has become a symbol of rural southern folklife.

Native to the Northern hemisphere, blueberries were an important food for many North American Indians, particularly in the winter, when they relied on dried berries in their diets. American settlers gave many names to the fruit, calling them hurtleberries, buckleberries, bilberries, and blaeberries. Although small, blueberries pack a lot of taste and vitamins. The blue-black fruit, which varies in size from one-eighth of an inch to more than an inch in diameter, matures several months after flowering and is a good source of vitamin C, iron, fiber, and potassium.

Beautiful One Day, Perfect the Next

Thistle Cove Farm, located in Tazewell on a beautiful stretch in the Appalachians, is a new name for an old farm, according to owner Sandra Bennett. "After the Civil War," Bennett says, "a two-story brick farmhouse, all barns, stables, granaries, and 800 acres were sold to an Ohio man for $300." During Christmas of 1899, the farmhouse burned to the ground and was rebuilt the following year.

Bennett and her husband have been working steadily to coax the historic structure back to its 1900 grandeur since they purchased the farm in 1995.

FRESH STRAWBERRY PIE

The glaze for this simple but luscious pie can be made in the microwave or on the stove.

¾ cup sugar
2 tablespoons cornstarch
¾ cup water
2 tablespoons light corn syrup
2 tablespoons strawberry or cherry-flavored gelatin

2 drops red food coloring (optional)
3 cups quartered fresh strawberries, rinsed and patted dry
1 (9-inch) pie crust, baked
sweetened whipped cream or whipped topping

Microwave method: Combine sugar and cornstarch in a 4-cup glass measure. Blend in water and corn syrup. Stirring with whisk midway through cooking, microwave on high 2½ to 3 minutes, or until thickened. Whisk until smooth; stir in gelatin and food coloring (if using). Cool to room temperature.

Stove method: Combine sugar and cornstarch in a heavy-bottomed saucepan. Blend in water and corn syrup. Place over medium heat. Stirring constantly with a whisk, cook until thickened. Whisk until smooth; stir in gelatin and food coloring (if using). Cool to room temperature.

Place strawberries in cooled pie shell and pour glaze over top. Refrigerate until set. To serve, top with whipped cream. Makes 6 servings.

∽ *Midlothian-born Virginia Shufflebarger was a food writer for many newspapers in the Northern Virginia area. She used to gather strawberries at Westmoreland Berry Farm. Wearing her straw hat and carrying a basket, Virginia was always the first to arrive at the Alexandria Farmers Market on Saturday.* ∽

BLUEBERRY DAMSON CONSERVE

"It's almost the best thing you'll ever taste."

1¼ pounds damson plums, pitted and halved
¼ teaspoon almond extract
2 cups blueberries, washed
1½ cups sugar

1 cup brown sugar
¼ teaspoon nutmeg
¼ teaspoon ground ginger
¼ cup orange juice
¼ cup excellent quality sherry

Mix plums with almond extract and let rest 30 minutes. Combine plums, blueberries, both sugars, spices, and orange juice in medium-sized pan. Bring to a boil; reduce heat and simmer, stirring frequently. It will take about 1 hour for mixture to thicken. At about the 50 minute mark, add sherry and simmer 10 to 15 minutes more. Pour into hot sterilized jars and seal. Store in cool place. Makes about 6 half-pints.

∽ *Sandra Bennett, owner of Thistle Cove Farm, says of her conserve: "Mother and Daddy (Gladys and Jim Bennett) own a homestead produce farm in Amelia. I pick fresh damson plums from Daddy's orchard, pick fresh blueberries from a neighbor, and make this conserve." For information on Thistle Cove, call (276) 988-4141 or visit www.thistlecovefarm.com.* ∽

NANCY'S BLUEBERRY-BUCKLE COFFEE CAKES

You'll know this coffee cake isn't store-bought, so go ahead and
make both cakes and freeze the second one if you can't use two at once.

FOR CAKES:

½ cup butter or margarine (1 stick)	4 teaspoons baking powder
1½ cups sugar	1 teaspoon salt
2 eggs	1 cup milk
3 cups plus 1 tablespoon flour, divided	2 cups blueberries, divided

FOR TOPPING:

¼ cup butter or margarine (½ stick)	⅓ cup flour
½ cup sugar	1 teaspoon cinnamon

Preheat oven to 350° F. Grease 2 (9-inch) cake pans; set aside. Cream butter and sugar; add eggs. Sift together 3 cups flour, baking powder, and salt. Add dry ingredients to butter mixture, alternating with milk. Reserve 30 blueberries. Toss remaining blueberries with 1 tablespoon flour and fold into batter. Divide batter into cake pans. Combine topping ingredients and crumble over batter; decorate with reserved berries. Bake 30 minutes, or until a toothpick inserted in center comes out clean.

∽ Farmer Nancy Cogsdale raises blueberries on her Sedley farm. She served in the Navy during World War II. ∽

WILLIE'S BLACKBERRY CRISP

FOR TOPPING:

1 cup flour	1 teaspoon baking powder
1 cup sugar	1 egg, beaten

FOR FILLING:

2 tablespoons flour	4 to 5 cups fresh or frozen
¾ cup sugar	blackberries
1 stick unsalted butter, melted	

Preheat oven to 375° F. In a medium bowl, combine flour, sugar, and baking powder. Make a well in the center of the dry ingredients and blend in the egg, mixing until crumbly. Set aside.

To prepare the filling, mix the flour and sugar, add the blackberries, and toss gently to evenly coat the blackberries. Transfer berry mixture to a well-buttered (8 ¥ 8-inch) glass baking dish and crumble topping over berries. Drizzle melted butter evenly over the topping. Place baking dish on a baking sheet to prevent spillovers. Bake for 45 minutes.

∽ This recipe was provided by Westmoreland Berry Farm in Virginia's Northern Neck, where visitors can pick their own strawberries, red raspberries, blueberries, black raspberries, blackberries, and peaches; watch goats walk the tight ropes; and enjoy any number of special events with the family. For information, call (800) 997-BERRY OR (804) 224-9171 or visit www.westmorelandberryfarm.com. ∽

Beautiful One Day, Perfect the Next (*continued*)

It's a project of the heart, which the pair began only two days after being married on the lawn in front of the house.

As if restoring the house, barns, fences, and other farm buildings isn't enough, the Bennetts also work the farm. For them this includes breeding American Curly Horses and raising Romney and Shetland sheep. "All the animals are rare-breed livestock and contribute fiber for spinning, weaving, knitting, and felting," Bennett says. In addition, the couple conducts educational tours for school children and other guests.

Thistle Cove hosts a sheep-shearing day in the spring and the Appalachian Heritage Festival, held the fourth Saturday in September. Festival crafters demonstrate spinning, weaving, basket making, ironwork, woodwork, making hand-tooled saddles, and more—everything an Appalachian homestead farm would need to survive 150 years ago.

"There's always something happening down on the farm, where it's beautiful one day and perfect the next!" Bennett says of her lovely home. For information, call (540) 988-4121 or visit www.thistlecovefarm.com.

Look for plump, firm, fresh blueberries that are powdery blue-gray in color. Overripe blueberries are dull and lifeless in appearance. If covered properly and refrigerated, fresh blueberries will keep up to three weeks. Wash just before using.

Frozen blueberries can last up to two years, if stored properly. Use hard frozen blueberries when baking with the fruit, to reduce color streaking. When preparing fresh fruit salads, add blueberries last to avoid coloring other fruit.

LIME MOUSSE WITH FRESH BLUEBERRIES

This White House recipe is said to have been one of Barbara Bush's favorites.

FOR LIME CREAM (similar to lemon curd):

8 limes
8 eggs
5 tablespoons fresh lemon juice

2½ cups sugar
1 pound butter, cut into chunks

FOR LIME MOUSSE:

1 cup lime cream, chilled
1 cup heavy cream and additional cream for garnish

1 pint fresh blueberries, sorted and washed

Over a very large saucepan, grate the zest off limes. Squeeze juice from limes into saucepan along with eggs, lemon juice, sugar, and butter. Whisk over low heat until butter is melted. Turn heat to high and, whisking constantly, bring mixture to a full boil. Strain into a clean pan to cool. For the mousse, whip the heavy cream on medium-high speed. This helps it attain greater volume. Gently fold the lime cream into the whipped cream (it does not have to be perfectly blended; a few streaks will make it interesting).

Spoon alternating layers of mousse and blueberries into a pretty china bowl, ending with mousse. Level the top with a spatula. Pipe rosettes of whipped cream around the border and decorate with blueberries. Makes 6 servings.

∽ *For almost two decades, Alexandria resident Franette McCullough was assistant pastry chef in the White House. She first trained as a dress designer, then spent 20 years traveling with her husband, who worked for the Navy. She attended the Cordon Bleu school in London and L'Academie de Cuisine in Bethesda. Franette has also owned a catering business and was a consultant to the Time Life Series* Healthy Home Cooking. ∽

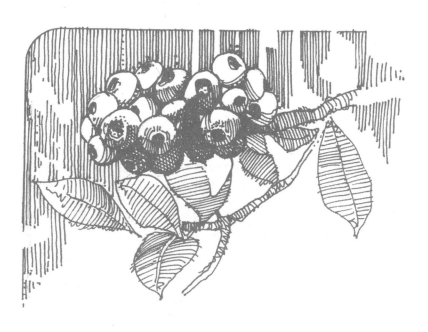

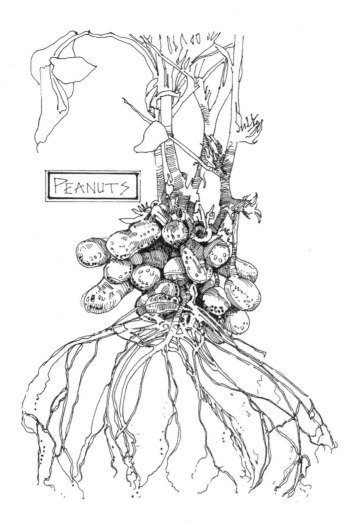

PEANUTS

chapter six
PEANUTS

Believed to have originated in Peru or Brazil about 750 B.C., peanuts filled jars placed in the graves of ancient Incas to provide food in the afterlife. Spanish explorers introduced the peanut to Europe, Asia, and Africa. Slaves then brought the nut back to America, where they planted them throughout the South. Although a staple for both Blue and Gray soldiers in the Civil War, peanuts were not grown much in the 1800s. But the groundbreaking work of George Washington Carver, an Alabama plant scientist who developed more than 300 uses of peanuts, and the decline in the value of cotton due to the boll-weevil epidemic helped increase the importance of peanuts as a cash crop for southern farmers in the early 1900s. Called "ground nuts," "ground peas," "goobers," and "goober peas," peanuts, unlike other nuts, flower above ground but the fruit develops below it. The nut is an excellent source of protein, B vitamins, vitamin E, zinc, magnesium, potassium, and phosphorus.

Virginia is the northernmost peanut-producing state and ranks among the top ten states in U.S. production. More than 60 million pounds of peanuts are produced throughout the state each year], about half that amount in the neighboring counties of Southampton and Isle of Wight. The climate and sandy soil in the southeastern corner of Virginia make it the only place in the state where peanuts can grow.

The Virginia peanut, the primary variety grown by Old Dominion farmers, is also the largest, having an oval shape and reddish-brown skin. Valued for its large size, beauty, outstanding flavor, and pleasing, crunchy texture, it's often referred to as "the peanut of gourmets." Other types of peanuts grown in the United States are the runner, the Spanish, and the Valencia.

Peanut production in Virginia brings in more than $10 million annually. However, this represents less than 20% of the $60 million earned from the 220 million pounds of peanuts

To maintain quality, store peanuts in a cool, dry place. Peanuts stay fresh indefinitely when stored in a tightly closed container in the freezer. When a recipe calls for raw peanuts, it should indicate the type required: in shell, shelled redskins, or shelled blanched (redskins removed). When roasted peanuts are called for, home roasted (without redskins), cocktail, or dry-roasted peanuts may be used interchangeably. To chop peanuts, drop them in a blender or food processor a few at a time or use an inexpensive nut chopper.

The History of Peanut Soup

Sorry, Virginia, you did not invent peanut soup. Sorry, Alabama, your George Washington Carver didn't either. Entwined with the memories of dining at the Hotel Roanoke and the King's Arms Tavern in Williamsburg (who challenge each other for being the first to serve it), this rich, smooth bisque originated an ocean away in Africa. For a hundred or more years before the United States was colonized, black cooks used peanuts in their cooking. One of the characteristic dishes on both sides of the Atlantic is chicken served with a peanut sauce. A soup made of "ground nuts" was brewed in Colonial American kitchens soon after the first slaves arrived.

produced nationally in 2002. That same year, the U.S. Congress passed the Farm Bill, removing the peanut quota system and allowing the American market to be flooded with cheap product from Vietnam and other countries in Southeast Asia. With lower yields and higher costs, Virginia can't compete, and acreage continues to decline.

WALDORF SALAD WITH PEANUT DRESSING

Make this delicious salad sweeter by using a sweeter variety of apple.

2 cups diced semitart apples, not peeled (about 2 medium apples)
⅓ cup raisins
½ cup diced celery
½ cup chopped salted peanuts

¼ cup creamy peanut butter
¼ cup honey
¼ cup mayonnaise
1 to 2 teaspoons lemon juice, optional (add if using sweeter apples)

In a bowl, toss together apple, raisins, celery, and peanuts; set aside. In a small bowl, blend peanut butter, honey, mayonnaise, and lemon juice if using. Toss with apple mixture and serve on a bed of lettuce. Makes 4 servings.

This recipe was provided courtesy of Lynda Updike, president of the Southampton County Historical Society. The society owns the Southampton Agriculture and Forestry Museum (see tour, pages 141–142), along with the Rochelle-Prince House.

HOTEL ROANOKE PEANUT SOUP

Peanuts and peanut butter in soup? Who could have known just how good it could be?

½ cup butter
1 small onion, diced
2 ribs celery, diced
3 tablespoons flour
2 quarts hot chicken broth

1 pint peanut butter
⅓ teaspoon celery salt
1 teaspoon salt
1 tablespoon lemon juice
½ cup ground peanuts

Melt butter in a large saucepan. Add onion and celery; cook, stirring often, for 5 minutes. Do not brown. Stir in flour, then broth. Cook, stirring occasionally, for 30 minutes.

Remove from stove and strain mixture. Return to saucepan and stir in peanut butter, celery salt, salt, and lemon juice. Sprinkle peanuts on soup just before serving. Makes 10 servings.

Nestled in the heart of the spectacular Blue Ridge Mountains, The Hotel Roanoke and Conference Center surrounds guests with the warmth of traditional southern hospitality. From the Florentine marble floors to the vaulted ceilings, the 1882 hotel has been lovingly restored to its rich nineteenth-century elegance and is listed in the National Register of Historic Places. The Market Square Bridge connects the hotel to downtown Roanoke's eclectic mix of museums, theaters, galleries, shops, restaurants, and the famous farmer's market. Call the hotel at (800) 222-1REE or (540) 985-5900, or visit www.hotelroanoke.com.

SMITHFIELD INN'S
ROASTED-PEANUT PORK CHOPS

Smithfield Inn Sous-Chef David Walker uses Smithfield Foods "Lean Generation" pork for this recipe, and because it is lower in fat than pork once was, it should not be overcooked.

4 (½-inch thick) boneless pork chops cut from loin (about 3½ ounces each)	2 tablespoons butter
	½ cup sliced mushrooms
	2 teaspoons sugar
salt and pepper	2 ounces bourbon
½ cup chopped roasted peanuts	½ cup cream

Preheat oven to 400° F. Spray a shallow baking sheet with nonstick spray. Salt and pepper the meat and press peanuts into one side of pork chops. Place, peanut side up, on baking sheet and roast 6 to 8 minutes.

To make the sauce, melt butter in a skillet. Sauté mushrooms until almost cooked. Sprinkle with sugar and toss to caramelize for 15 seconds. Deglaze pan with bourbon, scraping up any brown bits. Add cream and simmer until reduced by half. Pour sauce over cooked chops. Makes 4 small or 2 large servings.

George Washington did sleep at the Smithfield Inn. This 1752 house built by Henry Woodley served as an inn when the main stagecoach route from Norfolk to Richmond passed through Smithfield. A second owner, William Rand, applied for a license to operate a tavern on the premises in 1759. Today, the inn offers five luxurious suites with reproduction period furniture and an excellent restaurant. The menu's Southern slant reflects a culinary heritage of using the community's indigenous foods (phone (757) 357-1752 or visit www.smithfieldinn.com).

FROZEN PEANUT-BUTTER PIE

A peanut-butter classic straight from the kitchen of a peanut-farmer mom who knows well what a hit this pie makes—every time!

1 (3-ounce) package cream cheese, softened	½ cup milk
	1 (9-ounce) carton nondairy topping
1 cup powdered sugar	1 (9-inch) pie crust, baked
⅓ cup creamy peanut butter	¼ cup chopped salted peanuts

Whip cream cheese until soft and fluffy. Beat in sugar and peanut butter, then add milk. Fold in topping and pour into baked pie shell. Sprinkle with chopped nuts. Freeze. Thaw 30 minutes in refrigerator before serving. Makes 8 servings.

This recipe was provided courtesy of Lynda Updike of Courtland. Lynda grew up on Myrtle Acres Farm, as did her father and grandfather, so she says: "Farming's always been in my blood." Lynda is a home economist who says she tills the soil "by choice," explaining that she and her husband grow peanuts, corn, cotton, wheat, soybeans, sheep, and cattle. "We've also raised a son and two daughters," she adds.

DID YOU KNOW...
that if you're snacking on roasted peanuts, most likely they are Virginias? Virginia, the primary peanut variety grown in the Commonwealth and the largest one, accounts for most of those roasted and processed in the shell. The Runner, Spanish, and Valencia are the other predominant market varieties. The majority of Runners are used for peanut butter. Spanish-type peanuts, with smaller kernels covered with a reddish-brown skin, have a higher oil content and are used in peanut candies and for snack nuts and peanut butter. Valencias have three or more small kernels to a pod and are covered in a bright-red skin. They are very sweet and are usually roasted and sold in the shell; they are also excellent for fresh use as boiled peanuts.

Don't Eat That!

The shells, skins, and kernels of peanuts may be used to make a vast variety of nonedible products. For example, the shells may be used in wallboard, fireplace logs, fiber roughage for livestock feed, and kitty litter; and the skins may be used to make paper. Peanuts are often used as an ingredient in products such as detergent, salves, metal polish, bleach, ink, axle grease, shaving cream, face creams, soap, linoleum, rubber, cosmetics, paint, explosives, shampoo, and medicine.

No. Peanuts do not grow on trees, and guests of The First Peanut Museum can learn this and other truths about peanuts through rare collections, exhibits, and old photographs at one of America's smallest museums devoted to one of America's biggest agricultural crops. In fact, this museum is the only one devoted exclusively to the history of the peanut. The First Peanut Museum is located in Waverly (about one hour southeast of Richmond) and stands on peanut farmland. Shirley Yancey, one of the museum directors, who grew up on a peanut farm here, conducts tours. The small building is decorated with various peanut artifacts, including curtains made of burlap peanut sacks. A display on George Washington Carver highlights the accomplishments of this peanut pioneer. All the items were donated by citizens of this area; it was here that the first commercial peanut crop was grown in 1842. Guests get a glimpse of old-fashioned peanut roasters, peanut shellers, a peanut-planting machine, and a peanut digger plow, just to name a few highlights. The museum is open Thursday through Monday from 2 to 5 p.m. Admission is free (call (804) 834-3327 or (804) 834-2151)

SURREY HOUSE PEANUT-RAISIN PIE

Surrey House says this pie is "world famous."

3 eggs
1 cup dark corn syrup
½ cup sugar
6 tablespoons margarine, melted
1 teaspoon vanilla
1 teaspoon vinegar

1 cup chopped roasted Virginia
    peanuts
½ cup seedless raisins
1 (9-inch) unbaked deep-dish pie
    crust

Preheat oven to 350° F. Beat eggs; add corn syrup, sugar, margarine, vanilla, and vinegar. Stir in peanuts and raisins. Pour mixture into pie crust and bake 35 to 40 minutes, or until firm. Makes 8 servings.

The Surrey House was established in 1954 and is just across the river from Williamsburg via the Jamestown-Scotland free ferry. The restaurant sits in a pretty little town and offers some fine Southern cookin' for breakfast, lunch, and dinner daily, brought by servers in long country dresses. Mainstays are fried chicken, country ham, fritters, and turnip greens "like Grandma used to make." In Surry; call (757) 294-3389 or visit www.surreyhouse restaurant.com.

CLASSIC PEANUT-BUTTER COOKIES

The kids'll love 'em.

1½ cups flour
1 teaspoon baking soda
½ cup sugar
½ cup packed brown sugar

½ cup peanut butter
½ cup butter or margarine, melted
1 egg
dash of salt

Preheat oven to 375° F. Sift flour and soda together into a large mixing bowl. Stir in sugar and brown sugar. Stir in peanut butter, butter, egg, and salt. Make balls the size of English walnuts. Place on greased cookie sheets 3 inches apart. Press down with a fork. Bake until cookies are light brown, about 8 to 9 minutes. Makes 3 dozen.

This recipe was contributed by Teresa Jernigan of Sedley, a very active member of the Sedley Woman's Club who knows about peanut-butter cookies—she provides day care in her home. These cookies are favorites with her little tykes.

TRIUMPH OF A COMMUNITY

Southampton Agriculture and Forestry Museum

In Southside Virginia, on the flat, sandy soil of peanut-growing land, a core group of about 30 volunteers conceived a museum that now contains more than 5000 historic items and several structures related to agriculture, forestry, and farm life. Items on display—some include potato dotters, a goat wagon, a wooden plow from 1800, a corn sheller, a seed drill, a sulfur duster, a peanut picker, and a locomotive used to haul juniper logs out of the Dismal Swamp—were made in Virginia during the past two centuries. The museum encompasses 23 buildings, among them a blacksmith shop, country store and gas station, one-room schoolhouse from 1865, saw mill, fire tower, smoke house, dairy, ice house, medical building, 1920s four-seater outhouse, and shelter full of peanut farm equipment—as well as the Johnson Gristmill from near Sedley, the last in Southampton County powered by water.

The story of how the museum got up and running is one of community and dedication. It started with an idea—to take the old farm machinery that farmers in the Courtland area had piles of and make a permanent exhibit of them. So in June of 1989, after collecting and storing the equipment, a committee of individuals involved in agriculture and interested in preserving the old implements arranged to purchase a building in Courtland, with the help of the Southampton County Historical Society.

The museum had no money, so Elliott Parker loaned the money for the option and William Simmons loaned the down payment, interest free. Simmons, Elliott Parker, and Glynn K. Parker were nominated as trustees of the Southampton County Historical Society and along with its president, Lynda Updike, were authorized to purchase the property for $78,900. Dominion Bank, through Bobby Worrell, loaned the money, and 37 people signed individual guarantees for $1000 each.

In the meantime, the Sebrell Elm, the largest American elm tree in the United States at the time, died of Dutch Elm disease in 1988 and was donated to the Historical Society by J. P. and Paul Simmons. It was pulled down by Union Camp in 1990. From that wood many items were made and sold to help the museum make its

To Grow a Peanut Plant

1. Purchase raw peanuts in most grocery stores, at health food stores, or by mail order (see the peanut marketplace at www.aboutpeanuts.com).

2. Soak peanuts in water overnight.

3. Fill pot with soil to 1 inch below rim. Plant three peanuts 1 to 1½ inches deep; cover firmly with soil but do not pack.

4. Keep soil moist (not wet). Maintain a temperature of 65° F or above (80° F is ideal). Peanuts should sprout within five to eight days. Keep plant in a warm location exposed to direct sunlight as much as possible. Blooms will appear approximately 45 days after the plant has emerged. (Production of peanuts on potted plant is unlikely, but may occur after three months.)
—Source for peanut sidebars:
Virginia-Carolina Peanut Promotions

Southampton Agriculture and Forestry Museum/Heritage Village

Medical Building
Ice House
Dairy
Smoke House
Pig Pen
Log Corn Crib
Hen House
Blacksmith Shop
Out House
Forestry Shelter/ Grist Mill
4-Seat Out House
Country Dwelling
Equipment Shed
1-room School House
Exhibition Building Registration/Rest Room
Pavilion
Saw Mill
Country Store
Diesel Engine
Fire Tower
Peanut Shelter Food Court/ Rest Rooms

Nottoway River
Southampton Agriculture F.M./H.V.
Courtland
Boykins
Franklin and Suffolk

payments. Raymond Cobb carved 294 ducks, six different breeds, which sold for $100 each. Others made items that continue to sell at the museum.

The committee had to raise money not only for the annual payments, but also for the building's many repairs. In October 1990, a committee of about 15 people, chaired by Minnie Thomas Beaton and Kathryn Pittman, created a cookbook of about 850 favorite recipes, many donated by Southampton County Historical Society members, including some from generations back. About 3000 of these cookbooks have already been sold, and they continue to sell. The first barbecue dinner was held in 1990 and has become an annual event. The committee also sponsored some yard sales

Volunteers worked to fix up the building, sometimes warmed by a pot-bellied stove, and nourished by a pot of navy beans and franks. The committee held clean-up days Wednesdays and Saturdays for months. Before long, more than 600 pieces of antique farm equipment and small tools were cleaned up.

"The Country Acres Garden Club did our landscaping," said Updike. "Proceeds from the lunch sold the day of the Garden Club Tour helped tremendously. The Boy Scouts helped clean up roots and debris from the lot. Many, many people helped get the museum off the ground and many more continue to help."

When the dirt road to the museum was hard surfaced, they named it Heritage Lane. The third week in September, the museum volunteers put on a Fall Heritage Day where they demonstrate many historic farm activities and operate the sawmill. The museum is open Wednesday, Saturday, and Sunday during March through November from 1 to 5 p.m. Admission is minimal. For more information, call (757) 653-9554 or visit www.rootsweb.com/~vaschs/.

Pickled Watermelon Rind

Cut watermelon rind into thin strips,
removing the green outer skin.
This hard, mostly white mass disguises the
soft, syrupy condiment that is to come.
   Work done well now will later cause the
   salivary glands to relish, succor
   the melon's skin from the field's dark earth.
Soak in limewater — from a pharmacy —
overnight, then wash the rind four times,
followed by soaking in brine
and boiling till the water rolls in lines.
   Add cinnamon sticks and cider vinegar,
   three pounds of sugar, pickling spice.
   Pour rind and syrup into sterile jars.
   Screw the lids on right.
When turkey is passed on Thanksgiving Day
and the pickles follow not far behind,
all of the guests will look around and say,
"Where's the pickled watermelon rind?"
   It will pucker their lips.
   But only the cook will remember the
   sweet-sour smell of cider vinegar
   saturating the house this July day.
               —Martha Steger

part six
VEGETABLES

Heavy, lush tomatoes, cardinal red as the state bird, weigh down their vines in Hanover County; bowling-ball-sized cabbages grow in the mountains of southwest Virginia; and Eastern Shore summer potatoes hide beneath the soil, gaining girth. Green cucumbers, colorful bell peppers, and spicy jalapeños brighten the fields, while the Northern Neck's asparagus points at the sky. Southside pumpkin vines crawl their way toward Halloween, while sweet corn across the state is more than "knee high by the Fourth of July."

The Old Dominion's cornucopia of brightly colored vegetables includes almost any kind you can name, but tomatoes, potatoes, snap beans, bell peppers, cucumbers, cabbage, and corn are the state's major fresh-market vegetables. Soybeans are Virginia's top green crop; however, most are used as forage and for their oil.

The vegetable industry is a dynamic segment of the state's vigorous agricultural economy. Vegetables ranging from asparagus to zucchini are available mostly from the eastern part of the state, especially the Eastern Shore. The state's favorable location, within 750 miles of 60% of the U.S. population, makes its locally grown produce only a few hours away from the country's primary markets.

The state's population is growing exponentially, and Northern Virginia's technology corridor has brought an influx of upscale diners demanding the freshest and the best, making a ready local market for produce. The Virginia Department of Agriculture and Consumer Services (VDACS) is very supportive of vegetable farmers. VDACS promotes the state's produce through the Virginia's Finest, Virginia Grown, Pick-Your-Own, Shop Virginia's Finest, and Virginia Shippers' Directory programs.

Virginians love to harvest produce directly from the sunny fields of about 70 Pick-Your-Own farms, such as Culpeper Farms Produce in Chesapeake, Potomac Vegetable Farms in Vienna, King's Fruit and Vegetables in James City County, and Great Country Farms in Bluemont. The state supports more than 100 major farmers markets where farmers and consumers can meet to do retail business. And hundreds of roadside stands bloom seasonally along Virginia's scenic byways.

Tomatoes

Native to the Andes Mountains in South America, tomatoes were introduced to Central and North America by prehistoric Indian trade and migrations. European explorers returned to the Old World with tomatoes. Those of a yellow variety were known in the sixteenth century as "apples of gold." In England, tomatoes weren't eaten but given as tokens of affection; legend has it that Sir Walter Raleigh presented one to Queen Elizabeth. Few early American settlers ventured to eat the tomato, which many thought poisonous. By the 1830s, however, tomatoes were widely recognized as edible.

One of the most popular foods today, the tomato nonetheless still suffers from one perception problem: Is it a fruit or a vegetable? Technically, it is a fruit, more specifically, one of only four true berries. (The others are bananas, cranberries, and grapes.) However, tomatoes are generally consumed like vegetables in savory dishes. In any case, they are low in fat and calories and good sources of vitamins C and A.

chapter one

TOMATOES

∾ *Tomatoes are Virginia's most valuable vegetable crop. Virginia ranks fourth in the nation— after tropical Florida, mammoth California, and Georgia—for fresh-market tomato production, a remarkable feat considering the state's size and location. Fresh-market tomatoes earn farmers about $150 million annually in cash receipts, which makes tomatoes the ninth most valuable farm product—below apples, meat, and poultry but above wheat and other crops.*

Although vine-ripened tomato production is on the rise, mature green tomatoes that have been ripened under controlled conditions using ethylene gas are those most commonly shipped from Virginia to cities throughout the eastern United States and Canada. Virginia growers are also producing mouth-watering, vine-ripe, cherry, plum, and greenhouse/hydroponic tomatoes. The major varieties grown (most in Hanover County and on the Eastern Shore) are Solar Set, Sun Pride, Mountain Spring, Mountain Pride, and Sunbrite.

WOODLAWN PLANTATION'S GAZPACHO

Gazpacho, a dish of Spanish origin, has long been a Virginia favorite.

FOR GAZPACHO:

6 ripe tomatoes, peeled and seeded	½ teaspoon white pepper
1 medium onion	¼ teaspoon Tabasco sauce
1 green bell pepper, seeded	2 teaspoons Worcestershire sauce
1 cucumber, peeled	4 teaspoons olive oil
1 clove garlic	4 teaspoons lemon juice
2 teaspoons salt	1 cup tomato juice or V-8 juice

FOR CROUTONS:

2 tablespoons olive oil	3 slices firm white bread,
1 clove garlic, mashed	cut into ½-inch cubes

There are two ways to make gazpacho with the same ingredients. Place all ingredients in a blender or food processor and pulse to chop finely. Or first finely dice or chop the tomatoes, onion, green pepper, and cucumber before mincing or pressing the garlic and mixing it with the other ingredients. Chill the finished product thoroughly. A few minutes before ready to serve, heat oil for croutons in a skillet with the garlic. Add bread cubes and fry until golden brown. Discard garlic and drain croutons on a paper towel.

⁓ Woodlawn Plantation, completed in 1805, is located in Mount Vernon and was originally part of the Mount Vernon estate. The house, made wholly of native materials, was built for Washington's step-granddaughter and was designed by William Thornton, who drew up the original plans for the U.S. Capitol. The property is owned by the National Trust for Historic Preservation and was in fact the trust's very first historic site (phone (703) 780-4000 or visit www.woodlawnplantation.org). ⁓

PANZANELLA

*This tomato-and-bread salad is a delightful way
to enjoy a bumper crop of vine-ripe tomatoes.*

3 tablespoons fresh basil leaves cut in chiffonade	salt and pepper to taste
4 tablespoons virgin olive oil	8 large ripe tomatoes cut into 1-inch chunks (8 cups)
2 tablespoons balsamic vinegar	2 cups cubed day-old Italian bread
1 clove garlic, minced	lettuce leaves

In a large salad bowl, mix basil, olive oil, vinegar, garlic, salt, and pepper. Add tomatoes and toss gently. Add bread and toss again. Let stand 10 minutes. Serve on lettuce leaves. Makes 6 servings.

⁓ This recipe appears in Tomato Recipes and Tidbits, *a cookbook of the Hill City Master Gardeners of Lynchburg, a group of volunteers trained by the Virginia Cooperative Extension Service to provide free gardening advice to interested citizens. It is in Lynchburg where Thomas Jefferson's Tomato Faire has been held each year since 1986 on the first Saturday in August. Jefferson is said to have proven that the so-called "love apple," long believed to be poisonous, was perfectly safe. ⁓*

Buyer's Guide to TOMATOES

Look for well-formed tomatoes that are smooth, ripe, and free of blemishes. Fully ripe tomatoes will have a consistent, rich, red color and will be slightly soft. For tomatoes not quite ripe, look for firm texture and color, ranging from pink to light red. Tomatoes with stems attached retain moisture and stay fresh longer. Avoid over-ripe and bruised tomatoes, which are soft and watery, as well as those with green or yellow areas or cracks near the stem scar. Storing tomatoes in the refrigerator retards ripening.

In Praise of the Farmer

"Cultivators of the earth are the most valuable citizens. They are the most vigorous, the most independent, the most virtuous, and they are tied to their country and wedded to its liberty and interests by the most lasting bands."

—Thomas Jefferson

The Virginia
Department
of Agriculture
and Consumer
Services
(VDACS)

Virginia vegetable growers,
like the producers of so many
other agricultural products
across the state, often find an
ally in VDACS, which exists
to encourage the continued
development and expansion
of the state's $35 billion agri-
culture industry. The department's multifaceted functions
include helping to market Virginia's crops both nationally
and internationally and helping to improve the
quality of those crops. In
addition, the department
monitors water quality, pesticide application, and pest
control; inspects food stores,
warehouses, milking operations, and food-processing
plants to ensure safe, sanitary
conditions; and administers
the state's consumer laws.
Access the department's website at www.vdacs.virginia.gov.

L'ESPRIT DE CAMPAGNE'S
SUN-DRIED TOMATO CARBONARA

*Dinner couldn't be easier to prepare than assembling this pasta dish,
which uses dried tomatoes and Canadian bacon.*

12 ounces dry spaghetti
2 eggs, lightly beaten
2 tablespoons L'Esprit julienne dried
    tomatoes in oil
olive oil
¼ cup pine nuts

2 slices Canadian bacon, diced
    (about ¼ cup)
¼ cup white wine
¼ cup chopped fresh parsley
¼ cup grated Parmesan cheese
salt and black pepper to taste

Begin cooking spaghetti as package directs. Beat eggs in a small bowl; set aside.
Reserve oil from tomatoes, adding olive oil, if necessary, to make 2 teaspoons; set
tomatoes aside. In a small skillet, heat 1 teaspoon of the oil you just combined and
sauté nuts until lightly browned and fragrant. Remove from pan; set aside. In same
pan, place remaining oil and sauté bacon until lightly browned. Add reserved tomatoes and wine; cover and turn off heat. Let stand 3 minutes.

    When spaghetti tests done, drain and transfer to a warm serving bowl. Quickly
toss with eggs to coat (the heat of the pasta will cook them). Add tomatoes, bacon,
parsley, and cheese; toss well. Add salt and pepper to taste. Makes 4 servings.

---

*✎ This a favorite recipe of Joy and Carey Lokey of Winchester, who, in 1986, began L'Esprit de Campagne. The
company plants, grows, processes, packages, and distributes more than 50,000 pounds of Virginia sun-ripened, dried
Roma tomatoes and fruits annually. The tomatoes are washed, cut in half, and dried without preservatives in low-heat
wind tunnel dehydrators. It takes 17 pounds of tomatoes to make one pound of dried tomatoes. ✎*

SUMMER VEGETABLE CASSEROLE

*If you don't have time to prepare your garden vegetables individually,
use them together in this simple yet scrumptious casserole.*

3 eggs, beaten
⅓ cup milk
4 ripe medium tomatoes, peeled,
    seeded, and chopped
1¾ cups fresh corn kernels
¾ cup American cheese

1 cup soft bread crumbs (2 slices
    bread, crumbled)
2 tablespoons each chopped onion
    and diced green bell pepper
salt and pepper to taste

Preheat oven to 350° F. Butter a 1½-quart round casserole. Beat eggs and milk in
casserole. Stir in remaining ingredients. Bake 1 hour. Makes 4 servings.

✎ This recipe—from Rosie Hall of Stuarts Draft—appeared in Virginia Cooks: From the Mountains to
the Sea, *published in 1999 in conjunction with Virginia's public television stations. ✎*

interview
THOMAS JEFFERSON
The Gardener

Thomas Jefferson's brilliance, along with his accomplishments in many fields, render him in the minds of many our most intellectual president. In 1962, President John F. Kennedy addressed a White House dinner honoring Nobel Prize winners. He commented, "I think this is the most extraordinary collection of talent, of human knowledge, that has ever been gathered together at the White House, with the possible exception of when Thomas Jefferson dined alone."

Our third President was at heart a farmer, gardener, and early soil conservationist. His Virginia farm holdings were extensive. By 1794 he had acquired through his father's estate, through marriage, and through purchase more than 10,800 acres of farmland in four different counties. To manage his vast estate, he used a plantation system that originated in Virginia's Tidewater region, whereby the land was divided into separate "farms." The area surrounding the planter's dwelling constituted the "home farm"; for Jefferson, this was Monticello Mountain. Outlying lands were divided into manageable parcels known as "quarter farms" and were run by resident overseers. Jefferson sought to further organize his farms by dividing them into fields of 40 acres each. Jefferson tried various ways of producing crops; dividing the farms provided a way for him to compare yields.

Perhaps it was the intellectual in Jefferson that spurred him to continually expand his horizons as a farmer and a gardener and to document his efforts. While others were growing tobacco or maize and moving west when the soil was depleted, Jefferson was experimenting with different crops, with the growth of legumes to restore nutrients to the soil, and the use of fertilizers and "plastering" (liming). He recorded what he grew, his methods, and the results of his farm and garden experiments in his farm and garden notebooks, which he kept from 1774 until a few weeks before his death in 1826.

Jefferson also wrote thousands of letters to friends, family members, and colleagues. Here, excerpts from a variety of these letters have been compiled to create the "answers" Jefferson may have given in response to the questions of an interviewer intent upon learning more about his love of the land and of his home state. The letters from which Jefferson's "answers" are drawn are preserved by The Thomas Jefferson Foundation (see the tour following this interview or the Resources section for more information).

Mr. Jefferson, how do you like being a farmer?
"I know of no condition happier than that of a Virginia farmer might be. His estate supplies a good table, clothes him and his family with their ordinary apparel, furnishes a small surplus to buy salt, sugar, coffee, and a little finery for his wife

A Basket of Tomatoes Later

The tomato plant wasn't always such a garden favorite. In the early 1800s people of southern Europe and France were enjoying the "apple of love," as it was known, but England and the young United States considered it an ornamental plant. Physicians warned against eating it. "One dose and you're dead."

Finally, to put the rumors to rest, Colonel Robert Johnson, an eccentric gentleman from Salem, New Jersey, announced he was going to eat a whole basket of the "wolf peaches." On September 26, 1820, he lifted a tomato before a crowd of 2000 gathered in front of the Salem courthouse steps and declared: "The time will come when this luscious, golden apple, a delight to the eye, a joy to the palate, will be recognized as an edible food. To help speed that enlightened day, to dispel the tall tales you have been hearing about the thing, and show you that it is not poisonous, I am going to eat one right now!"

A basket of tomatoes later, the band struck up the victory march and the crowd began to cheer. It was one small bite for Colonel Johnson, one large juicy bite for mankind.

Do It the Old-Fashioned Way

and daughter, enables him to receive and to visit friends, and furnishes him pleasing and healthy occupation. My habits are formed to those of my own country. I am past the time of changing them and am therefore less happy anywhere else than [at Monticello]."

Mr. Jefferson, what do you think of Virginia's climate?
"On the whole, I find nothing anywhere else in point of climate which Virginia need envy to any part of the world. Spring and autumn make a paradise of our countryside. When we consider how much climate contributes to the happiness of our condition, by the fine sensations it excites, and the productions it is the parent of, we have reason to value highly the accident of birth in such an one as that of Virginia."

Mr. Jefferson, what do you learn from your garden?
"The garden serves as both a source of food for my family and a kind of laboratory where I experiment. I have 250 varieties of more than 70 species of vegetables from around the world. My plants include squash and broccoli imported from Italy; beans and salsify collected by the Lewis and Clark expedition; figs from France; and peppers from Mexico. I have 20 varieties of bean and 15 types of English peas. I note successes and failures in my Garden Book, for instance the dates when seeds were planted, when leaves appeared, and when their fruits came to table. I am curious to select one or two of the best species or variety of every garden vegetable and to reject all others to avoid the dangers of mixing or degeneracy."

Mr. Jefferson, tell me how you begin your day.
"Whether I retire to bed early or late, I rise with the sun. For 50 years, the sun has never caught me in bed. I rise as soon as I can read the hands of the clock opposite my bed. First I measure and record the temperature—the dawn of the day is the coldest. I also note the direction and speed of the wind and the amount of precipitation. After my record-keeping, I start my fire and soak my feet in cold water. I've done this for 60 years and attribute my good health in part to this habit."

Mr. Jefferson, what's your advice on eating properly?
"I have lived temperately, eating little animal food, and that as a condiment for the vegetables, which constitute my principal diet. The English pea is my favorite vegetable, but I also favor figs, asparagus, French artichokes, and my new vegetables—tomatoes, eggplant, broccoli, and cauliflower. Salads are an important part of my diet. I plant lettuce and radishes every two weeks through the growing season, grow interesting greens such as ochra, corn salad, endive, and nasturtiums, and yearly plant sesame in order to manufacture a palatable salad oil."

Mr. Jefferson, what is the most important farm implement?
"If the plough be in truth the most useful of the instruments known to man, its perfection cannot be an idle speculation. Ploughing deep for killing weeds is also the recipe for almost every good thing in farming. The plough is to the farmer what the wand is to the sorcerer. Its effect is really like sorcery. We now plough horizontally, following the curvatures of the hills and hollows, on the dead level, however crooked the lines may be. Every furrow thus acts as a reservoir to receive and retain the waters, all of which go to the benefit of the growing plant, instead

of running off into streams. In point of beauty nothing can exceed that of the waving lines and rows winding along the face of the hills and vallies."

Mr. Jefferson, can you advise me how to rid the garden of bothersome insects?

"We will try this winter to cover our garden with a heavy coating of manure. When earth is rich it bids defiance to droughts, yields in abundance, and of the best quality. I suspect that the insects which have harassed you have been encouraged by the feebleness of your plants; and that has been produced by the lean state of the soil. We will attack them another year with joint efforts."

Mr. Jefferson, is agriculture an art or a science?

"Agriculture is a science of the very first order. It counts among it handmaids of the most respectable sciences, such as chemistry, natural philosophy, mechanics, mathematics generally, natural history, botany. In every college and university, a professorship of agriculture, and the class of its students, might be honored as the first. The charitable schools, instead of storing their pupils with a lore which the present state of society does not call for, converted into schools of agriculture, might restore them to that branch qualified to enrich and honor themselves, and to increase the productions of the nation instead of consuming them."

Mr. Jefferson, now that your second term as president is at an end, is there anything I can give you to take home?

"If you should have any excellent pears, peaches, or grapes, I shall be able to carry and plant them myself at Monticello, where I shall then begin to occupy myself according to my own natural inclinations, so long kept down by the history of our times. I have been planning what I would show you if you come to visit me: a flower here, a tree there; yonder a grove, near it a fountain; on this side a hill, on that a river. Indeed, madam, I know nothing so charming as our own country. The learned say it is a new creation; and I believe them; not for their reasons, but because it is made on an improved plan. The greatest service that can be rendered any country is to add a useful plant to its culture."

by the same recipe, except that you cut it in two pieces instead of four."

—Mrs. Roane, Lynchburg, *Housekeeping in Old Virginia,* 1879

SPINACH
"Pick and soak several hours in cold water. Drain and shake each bunch. Throw in boiling water and boil till tender. Take up with a perforated skimmer. Put in a saucepan with a heaping tablespoonful butter; pepper and salt to taste. Stir in three hard-boiled eggs, chopped up. Let it simmer, stirring frequently. Put in a deep dish and cover with nicely poached eggs, buttered, peppered, and salted. Sea-kale may be prepared by the same recipe."

—Mrs. Samuel Tyree, Lynchburg, *Housekeeping in Old Virginia,* 1879

GREEN PEAS
"Early in the morning, either buy the peas from market or have them gathered in your garden, while the dew is on them. Shell and lay in cold water till half an hour before dinner. Then put in boiling water and boil steadily a half hour. Add a little salt, just before taking from the fire. Drain, add a heaping tablespoonful fresh butter and put in a covered dish."

—Mrs. Samuel Tyree, Lynchburg, *Housekeeping in Old Virginia,* 1879

Tour in a Nutshell
• MONTICELLO •

The home of our third president is a masterpiece in architecture that reflects Thomas Jefferson's passion for innovation. The grounds are also stunning and have been largely restored to appear as they would when Jefferson resided here.

DAYS/HOURS: The mansion is open daily 8 a.m. to 5 p.m. March through October and 9 a.m. to 4:30 p.m. November through February. Visitors Center hours are 9 a.m. to 5:30 p.m. March through October and 9 a.m. to 5 p.m. November through February.

FEES: Admission is charged. (Charlottesville and Albemarle County residents receive a discount.) Tickets entitle the visitor to a 25 to 30-minute guided tour of the home, access to the museum shop, and self-directed tours of the grounds and plantation. From April 1 through October 31, guided walking tours of the garden, slave sites, and the grounds are also offered.

A presidents-pass discount ticket is available for visitors ages 12 and above. This ticket affords admission to Monticello, President James Monroe's Ash Lawn-Highland, and Michie Tavern. Parking is free.

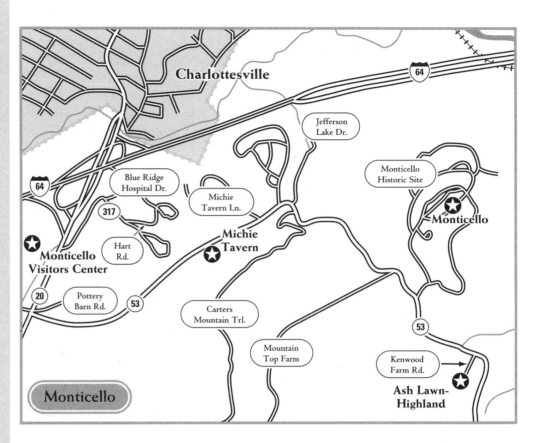

Monticello is the essence of Thomas Jefferson. You can feel his intellect and personality everywhere in the mansion and on the farm. He designed, redesigned, built, and rebuilt his home for more than 40 years. Jefferson described the house as his "essay in architecture," but today it is recognized as an international treasure. Monticello is the only house in America on the United Nations' prestigious World Heritage List of sites that must be protected at all costs.

The author of the Declaration of Independence and third president of the United States studied the buildings of ancient Rome and began building his house in 1768 atop the "Little Mountain" where he had played as a boy on his father's farm. However, after returning from France in 1789 with new ideas about architecture, he completely redesigned the house. As a result, this architectural masterpiece shows the remarkable integration of Jefferson's love of classical architecture and passion for modern innovation.

A good place to begin your tour is the **Monticello Visitors Center,** which is in the town of Charlottesville, not on the mansion grounds. You can view the free award-winning film and see more than 400 Jefferson objects in a permanent display there as well as buy tickets to tour Jefferson's home. Then drive to Monticello and park in the free lot. Buses leave the parking lot every 3 to 5 minutes and provide transportation to and from the house, or you can walk the half mile to the home.

If you plan to tour the house, be sure to obtain a line-release card at the East Walk if the wait is more than 45 minutes. This system allows visitors to walk around the gardens and grounds while waiting to see the house. Simply return to the line at the time indicated on the card.

There are a total of 43 rooms in the domed mansion, construction of which began in 1769 and was completed in 1784. Jefferson redesigned the mansion and enlarged it beginning in 1796. That work was completed in 1809. Amazingly, about one third of the window glass is original. Many of the furnishings and decorative items belonged to Jefferson; others are reproductions of the original. Throughout the beautiful home, you'll see Jefferson's clever inventions. For example, it wasn't possible for him to get out "on the wrong side of the bed." He built his bed into an alcove between two rooms so he could rise in either direction. There are eight fireplaces and two openings for stoves on the main floor of the house, which was heated primarily by wood (at the rate of about ten cords per month).

In addition to the mansion, be sure to tour Jefferson's flower and vegetable gardens and his orchards and vineyards, which have been restored to their original appearance. Many of the tree, vegetable, and flower species that Jefferson cultivated are here today. A few of the trees Jefferson planted himself are still alive. These include a red cedar; a sugar maple, the lone survivor of his efforts to create sugar plantations in central Virginia; a European larch; and an impressive tulip poplar adjacent to the mansion.

Near Monticello, tour **Michie Tavern** (circa 1784), where founding fathers and travelers alike have dined for more than 200 years. A costumed hostess welcomes you into the past as "stranger," an early eighteenth-century term for a traveler. You may partake of a hearty lunch much like the eighteenth-century visitor. Enjoy a buffet of homemade Southern fare based on recipes from the period—Colonial fried chicken, hickory-smoked pork barbecue, black-eyed peas, stewed tomatoes, mashed potatoes and gravy, hot green beans, whole baby beets, cole slaw, homemade biscuits, cornbread, and fruit cobbler.

The colonial tavern served not only as a place to eat, drink, and sleep but also as the center of the community. On the second floor is the Assembly Room, which once served as a ballroom, a makeshift school room, a place for worship, and extra sleeping accommodations. The other rooms on tour include the elaborately decorated Ladies' Parlor.

Near Monticello is **Ash Lawn–Highland,** home of Jefferson's good friend and the fifth president of the United States, James Monroe. Owned and operated by the College of William and Mary in Williamsburg, Monroe's alma mater, the complex comprises a historic house and museum, a 535-acre working farm, and a performing-arts site. Monroe and his wife, Elizabeth Kortright Monroe of New York, owned the estate from 1793 to 1826 and made it their official residence from 1799 to 1823. After the Monroes died, the name of their farm was changed from Highland to Ash Lawn, after the 100-some ash trees that shade and line the road to the home.

In nearby Orange, Virginia, don't miss seeing James and Dolley Madison's elegant home, **Montpelier.** Madison was the fourth U.S. president and a good friend of both Jefferson and Monroe. Over the years, the eighteenth-century home was updated many times. In 1901, the 2,650-acre Virginia estate became the property of William duPont and eventually was enlarged from 22 rooms to 55, including 12 bathrooms. A project costing $23 million and concluding in 2009 will return Montpelier to its original size.

All three presidential estates are open to the public.

If you are a Civil War history buff, be sure to take a tour of the **Wilderness Civil War Battlefield** in Orange County.

Tour in a Nutshell
· MONTICELLO ·
(continued)

DIRECTIONS: Monticello is located on Route 53, approximately two miles southeast of Charlottesville near the intersection of Route 20 South and I-64.

MORE INFORMATION: Call (434) 984-9822 or visit www .monticello.org.

THE MONTICELLO VEGETABLE GARDEN

When Thomas Jefferson referred to his garden during his lifetime at Monticello, he, like most early Americans, was speaking of his vegetable or kitchen garden, which functioned as both a source of food for his family table and as a kind of laboratory, where he experimented with 250 varieties of more than 70 different species of vegetables. Today, visitors to the Monticello Vegetable Garden, adjacent to the mansion (see preceding tour), can explore the garden as it existed between 1807 and 1814 and learn more about Jefferson's horticultural and landscaping experiments and nineteenth-century vegetable varieties.

For nearly 60 years Jefferson kept both a garden book and a farm book, in which he recorded his thoughts and the details of his lifetime of horticultural efforts at Monticello. His books have been edited and published in various forms. This wealth of documentary material unveils much about the character of early American gardens as well as the scientific and creative sensibility of Jefferson himself. In addition, it contributed immensely to the re-creation of the garden that Monticello visitors enjoy today.

The effort to re-create the Monticello vegetable garden began in 1979 with two years of archaeological excavations that attempted to confirm details of the documentary evidence. The vegetable garden evolved over many years, beginning in 1770 when crops were first cultivated along the contours of the slope. Terracing was introduced in 1806, and by 1812, gardening

activity was at its peak. The 1000-foot-long terrace, or garden plateau, was literally hewed from the side of the mountain with slave labor, and it was supported by a massive stone wall that stood more than twelve feet in its highest section. Archaeologists uncovered the remnants of the stone wall, stolen in the twentieth century and covered by eroding soil; they also exposed the foundation of the garden pavilion and searched for the garden walkways.

The pavilion, which was used by Jefferson as a quiet retreat where he could read in the evening and which was reputedly blown down in a violent wind storm in the late 1820s and reconstructed in 1984, is perched atop the stone wall, at the halfway point of the garden. It overlooks a separate eight-acre orchard of 300 trees, a vineyard, and plots of figs, currants, gooseberries, and raspberries.

The main part of the two-acre garden is divided into 24 "squares," or growing plots. Jefferson used the northwest border to plant peas very early in the season, and this should have provided a clear advantage in the annual neighborhood contests to bring the first English pea to table. The site and situation of the garden enabled Jefferson to extend the growing season into the winter months and provided amenable microclimate for tender vegetables such as the French artichoke.

There are a number of differences between the appearance of the original Jefferson garden and the re-created one. In 1811, the most intensive planting year for Jefferson, there were 85 plantings of vegetables throughout the year. Today, the garden is planted much more intensively, and the rows of vegetables are farther apart than those Jefferson planted.

It has been possible, however, to replant many of the perennials in the precise locations that Jefferson had specified. The figs along the submural beds, the cherry trees along the long grass walk, and the asparagus and artichoke squares conform precisely to their locations in the original garden. Many of the varieties Jefferson especially treasured, from the Marseilles fig to the Chile strawberry to the tennis-ball lettuce, have been replanted in today's garden.

POTATOES

chapter two
POTATOES

∾ *The second most money-making vegetable grown in the state is the potato, earning more than $10 million for farmers. Virginia ranks in the top ten in the United States for sweet-potato production and for the production of summer potatoes, all-purpose, round whites used for frying, baking, and boiling. Virginia's large or "chef" potato is widely distributed, and producers also supply top-quality potatoes for potato-chip processing. Round, red, and the newer yellow-fleshed varieties are also grown. The two main varieties of sweet potatoes are Beauregard and Hayman.*

More than 80% of the state's white potatoes are grown on the Eastern Shore, where cool ocean breezes coupled with modern irrigation systems provide the controlled moisture supply on which potatoes thrive. Whereas Virginia's white potatoes are harvested in June through August, the state's sweet potatoes are available almost year-round—from August to April.

Virginia's "Hip" Chip

Tour buses heading to Winchester often make a detour along Virginia Route 11 to a potato-chip factory named after the road. Route 11's combination factory and retail store is something of a tourist draw. Visitors watch the potato-chip making through an oversized viewing window and can purchase chips, dips, and even a T-shirt.

The company founders ran a chip company in Waldorf, Maryland until 1992, when they moved the company to a run-down Middletown feed mill. In the beginning, the founders were "young, clueless, broke, and full of dreams," according to Route 11's official brochure. However, people loved their house-made, thick-cut chips, prepared without additives or preservatives. "Lightly Salted" is Route 11's flagship seller, but chips cut from taro roots, sweet potatoes, parsnips, yuccas, beets, carrots, and purple potatoes and with seasonings—including barbecue, salt and vinegar, sour cream and chive, dill pickle, and Chesapeake crab—can also be enjoyed.

The company pumps out about 1000 pounds of chips per day and is open to the public Monday through Saturday from 9 a.m. to 5 p.m. (phone (800) 294-SPUD or visit www.rt11.com).

PLEASING POTATO PIE

A versatile dish that can be served for breakfast, lunch, or dinner, this recipe is a cross between hash browns and quiche.

2 cups shredded peeled potatoes
1¼ cup shredded cheddar cheese, divided
¾ cup shredded Monterey Jack cheese

1 teaspoon salt, divided
5 eggs
½ cup milk
½ teaspoon pepper

Combine potatoes, ½ cup cheddar cheese, and ½ teaspoon salt. Press into the bottom and up the sides of a greased 9-inch pie plate. In a bowl, beat eggs and milk. Add remaining cheeses and salt; pour over potato crust. Bake at 350° F for 45 to 50 minutes, or until a knife inserted near the center comes out clean. Let stand 5 minutes before cutting. Makes 4 to 6 servings.

⌇ *This pie is a mainstay at Chesapeake Charm Bed & Breakfast, located in the small town of Cape Charles, which is one of Virginia's largest historic districts and formerly was the southernmost terminus for the New York, Philadelphia, and Norfolk Railroad. Call Chesapeake Charm at (757) 331-2676 or visit the inn's Web site at www .chesapeakecharmbnb.com, where you'll find other treasured recipes.* ⌇

THALHIMERS' POTATO SALAD

This lively version of the old standard is sure to please diners every time.

8 small new potatoes
1 medium onion, minced
½ cucumber, peeled and diced
¼ cup diced celery
2 tablespoons minced green pepper

1 tablespoon minced fresh parsley
¼ cup French dressing
1 teaspoon lemon juice
¼ cup mayonnaise
salt and pepper to taste

Scrub potatoes and cook in boiling salted water until tender, about 20 minutes. Drain, cool slightly, peel, and slice thinly into salad bowl. Add onion, cucumber, celery, green pepper, and parsley and mix lightly. In a small bowl, combine French dressing, lemon juice, and mayonnaise and pour over vegetables while potatoes still are warm. Correct seasoning with salt and pepper. Mix well. Chill until ready to serve. Makes 4 servings.

⌇ *Richmond shoppers mourned the demise a few years ago of their locally owned department store, Thalhimers. However, recipes such as this one, from the store's restaurant, live on.* ⌇

DON'S TOMAHAWK MILL POTATOES

*This dish is reminiscent of potatoes Lyonnaise
but can be prepared solely with Virginia ingredients.*

2 pounds redskin potatoes, peeled
   and sliced
1 large onion, sliced
2 tablespoons oil or bacon drippings
¾ cup Tomahawk Mill Chardonnay
   wine, divided

1 teaspoon seasoned salt
½ teaspoon garlic salt
paprika
chopped fresh basil or parsley

Soak potatoes in water for a few minutes while sautéing the onion in oil. Add potatoes, sauté, and stir for about 5 to 7 minutes. Reduce heat and stir in ½ cup wine. Sprinkle with seasoned salt and garlic salt. Cover and cook on low heat 5 to 6 minutes. Add a dash of paprika and cook uncovered 4 to 6 minutes more. If dry, add remaining ¼ cup wine. Garnish with basil. Makes 6 servings.

Tomahawk Mill Winery, located 30 minutes north of Danville, in Chatham, is housed in an 1860 water-powered gristmill on Tomahawk Creek. It was operated continuously as a water-powered flour and saw mill from 1888 to 1988 by members of the Anderson family. James Anderson was a Confederate soldier in Pickett's Division. The winery produces five varieties of wine (phone (434) 432-1063 or visit www.tomahawkmill.com).

NEW-POTATO AND GREEN-BEAN SALAD
WITH FETA CHEESE

*New potatoes are great for this and other salads,
because they maintain their shape after cooking.*

2 pounds small red new potatoes,
   scrubbed and quartered
½ pound fresh green beans, cut into
   1-inch lengths
1 cup water
1 small red bell pepper, cut into thin
   strips

2 green onions, sliced
1 cup plain yogurt
2 teaspoons Dijon mustard
2 tablespoons chopped fresh dill or
   2 teaspoons dried dill
¼ teaspoon pepper
4 ounces feta cheese, crumbled

Place potatoes in a saucepan with ½ inch of water. Cover, bring to a boil, and cook over medium heat until fork-tender, about 20 minutes. Steam green beans separately until crisp tender, about 10 minutes.

Microwave directions: In a 2-quart glass measure or casserole, combine potatoes, beans, and water. Cover with vented plastic wrap or lid and microwave on high 8 minutes. Stir, re-cover, and microwave on high 10 minutes, or until tender.

Drain vegetables; stir in bell pepper and onion; set aside. In a bowl, combine yogurt, mustard, dill, and pepper. Stir into potato mixture. Gently toss in cheese. Serve at room temperature within 2 hours or refrigerate and serve chilled. Makes 8 servings.

SWEET POTATOES

When buying sweet potatoes, look for a firm, smooth potato, uniform in shape and color. Select thick, chunky, medium-sized vegetables that taper at both ends. Handle sweet potatoes gently to avoid bruising. Avoid buying sweet potatoes that show signs of decay or that contain blemishes. Store sweet potatoes in a cool, dark, well-ventilated place.

Hayman Sweets

An heirloom treasured for its luscious, sweet flesh and smooth, creamy texture, Haymans were introduced in the early 1800s by a ship's captain of the same name. However, production was so limited that nearly the entire crop was consumed by the 50 or so farmers who raised them for their families. A true Hayman potato fits in the palm of your hand. The flesh is white but turns to a sage-like green when cooked. They are very delicate to grow, have to be picked by hand, and cannot be refrigerated or their flesh will deteriorate. Once harvested, Haymans need to "cure" for two weeks to a month to develop their full, luscious flavor. Once cured, they are shipped to grocery stores that stock locally-grown vegetables. They are available seasonally and are sometimes made into specialty potato chips.

HAYMAN POTATO PECAN PIE

These potatoes are sweeter than the major varieties of sweet potatoes.

2 cups baked, mashed Hayman sweet potatoes (about 4 to 5 potatoes)
½ cup firmly packed dark brown sugar
2 eggs, lightly beaten
⅓ cup cream (heavy or light)

2 tablespoons butter, melted
¼ teaspoon vanilla extract
⅛ teaspoon each cinnamon, allspice, nutmeg, and salt
1 (9-inch) pie crust, partially baked
1 cup pecans

Preheat oven to 325° F. Combine mashed potatoes with remaining ingredients (except pecans). Pour into pie crust and arrange the pecans around the edge. Bake 35 to 45 minutes, or until a knife inserted in the center comes out clean. Makes 8 servings.

Recipe provided by Eastern Shore Select™ brand of Hayman potatoes.

PICKETT'S HARBOR B&B
SWEET-POTATO BISCUITS

These dense, pale-orange biscuits are delicious split and buttered or filled with turkey, Smithfield ham, or another meat.

3 cups sifted flour
¾ cup sugar
7 teaspoons baking powder
1 teaspoon salt

2 cups or 2 (15-ounce) cans sweet potatoes, mashed, hot
½ cup shortening

Preheat oven to 475° F. Sift together flour, sugar, baking powder, and salt. Add shortening to hot potatoes, combine with flour mixture, and roll out on floured board ¾-inch thick. Cut with a biscuit cutter. Place on an ungreased cookie sheet and brush tops slightly with butter. Bake 10 to 12 minutes or until very light brown. Makes about 16 biscuits.

"Pickett's Harbor Bed and Breakfast is part of a farm that was an early grant in the 1600s to my Nottingham family," says innkeeper Sara Goffigon. "It was a treat to grow up on this working vegetable farm, which was quite self-sufficent, with cows, pigs, turkeys, chickens, and ducks. The farm borders acres of private beach on the Chesapeake Bay, where I could walk, swim, fish, and crab in season. It is a special place to live and though I love to travel, my own back porch with its Bay view is my favorite spot. The farm has remained in the family for more than three centuries." The inn is four miles north of the Chesapeake Bay Bridge Tunnel and two miles west of Route 13 (phone (757) 331-2212; or visit www.pickettsharbor.com).

Snap Beans

Sparked by an interest in beans with stringless pods, Americans began planting snap beans, which don't split when ripe like most shell and dry beans, in 1890. Also known as string beans or green beans, they can play an important part in a healthy, well-balanced diet. Served steamed or boiled, they lend flavor, color, and texture to meals and are good sources of fiber, with no fat, sodium, or cholesterol. Most snap beans grow east of the Mississippi River. They thrive in warm climates with bright sunshine.

chapter three

SNAP BEANS

✍ *Produce departments "snap" to life with Virginia beans during the spring and fall. The state ranks seventh in U.S. fresh-market snap-bean production, and snap beans earn farmers about $10 million annually. Round, green types are in the majority, but producers also offer wax and flat green beans. Bean production is a staple in the Old Dominion, especially in the eastern part of the state, and acreage varies little from year to year. Green varieties grown are Round Green, Hialeah, Gator Green, Bronco; wax varieties are Nugget and Goldenrod.*

JAPANESE STIR-FRY VEGETABLES

These colorful and quickly cooked vegetables look attractive and retain their vitamins.

2 tablespoons cornstarch
2 tablespoons soy sauce
1 cup chicken broth
1 tablespoon each sesame oil and peanut oil
1 teaspoon hot-flavored oil
1½ cups snap beans, cut into 1-inch lengths

1½ cups broccoli flowerets
1½ cups mixed green and red bell pepper strips
1½ cups sliced white mushrooms
1½ cups sweet onion strips (such as Vidalia)
1 tablespoon sesame seeds (optional)

In a small mixing bowl, blend cornstarch and soy sauce. Stir in broth; set side. Heat sesame, peanut, and hot oils in a wok or large skillet. Add beans, broccoli, bell peppers, mushrooms, and onions. Stir quickly to coat vegetables in oil. Continue to stir-fry about 2 minutes. Reduce heat, cover, and let vegetables steam about 2 minutes, or until crisp tender. Stir in cornstarch mixture; stir constantly until mixture thickens. If desired, sprinkle with sesame seeds. Serve immediately. Makes 6 servings.

DiAnne H. Bryant uses snap beans and other vegetables she and her husband grow on their farm in the Sunbeam area of Southampton County to prepare this fresh family favorite.

SNAP BEANS WITH SMITHFIELD HAM AND PEANUTS

Three Virginia farm products go into this savory side dish.

2 pounds green snap beans
6 tablespoons butter, divided
¼ cup lemon juice
2 tablespoons Dijon mustard

salt and pepper to taste
1 cup julienned cooked Smithfield ham
¾ cup coarsely chopped peanuts

Leave beans whole but snap off the stem end. Place beans in a pot. Add 1 inch of water, cover, and bring to boiling over high heat. Turn heat to low and simmer beans 5 to 8 minutes, or just until crisp tender. Drain water to stop cooking. Melt 4 tablespoons butter; blend in lemon juice and mustard; toss with the beans and add salt and pepper to taste. Toss with ham; set aside.

Sauté peanuts in the remaining 2 tablespoons butter. Arrange beans on a serving platter and garnish with peanuts. Makes 8 servings.

This recipe was inspired by a similar dish in Chesapeake Bay Cooking *by John Shields.*

SUMMER VEGETABLE SOUP WITH PISTOU

This soup's name is taken from the French "pistou,"
for "pesto" sauce, which is served with the soup.

2 leeks
¼ cup olive oil
1 medium onion, chopped
4 cloves garlic, sliced lengthwise
8 cups broth plus 2 cups water
3 medium potatoes, peeled and
    cubed
4 medium carrots, halved lengthwise
    and sliced
2 bay leaves
1 teaspoon dried thyme or 1 table-
    spoon fresh thyme leaves
½ cup elbow macaroni

1 (14.5-ounce) can stewed tomatoes,
    including liquid
8 ounces fresh green beans, cut cross-
    wise into thin rounds
8 ounces zucchini, halved lengthwise
    and sliced
2 (15-ounce) cans navy beans or
    Great Northern beans, including
    liquid
freshly ground black pepper
homemade or purchased pistou
    (pesto sauce)

Cut off all but white and tender green parts of leeks. Cut off roots. To clean leeks, split lengthwise and rinse well to rid them of dirt. Slice leeks crosswise. Place olive oil in a large pot over medium heat. Add leeks, onion, and garlic. Cook about 2 minutes without browning. Add broth, water, potatoes, carrots, bay leaves, and thyme. Bring to a boil over high heat; then simmer 10 minutes. Add macaroni and cook until *al dente* and potatoes are tender.

Add tomatoes, green beans, and zucchini. Simmer 5 minutes, or until vegetables are tender. Add beans. Bring back to a simmer and add pepper to taste. Serve pistou alongside soup. Guests should stir about 1 teaspoon pistou into serving. Makes 5 quarts or 10 (2-cup) servings.

GREEN BEANS OREGANO

An attractive way to serve green beans is to toss them with red bell pepper.

1 pound fresh snap beans
½ cup water
½ red bell pepper, chopped
½ cup chopped onion

½ tablespoon olive oil
½ teaspoon dried oregano or 1½ tea-
    spoons chopped fresh oregano
salt and pepper, if desired

Place beans and water in a saucepan and cover. Bring to a boil, reduce heat to low, and steam 8 to 10 minutes, or until crisp tender. Combine bell pepper, onion, oil, and oregano in a 2-cup glass measure. Cover with plastic wrap and microwave on high 3 to 4 minutes. Drain beans and stir onion mixture into them. Add salt and pepper if desired. Makes 6 servings.

Pocahontas: The New World's First Celebrity

Just as celebrities today sell products, Pocahontas sold the English "resort property" in the New World for the Virginia Colony. Like some modern-day movie stars, the Indian princess had several names. She was born Matoaka ("Little Snow Feather") in 1595, but her father, Chief Powhatan, called her Pocahontas, meaning "Little Wanton" (or plaything). Later she took the Christian name Rebecca.

In 1610 she married an Indian named Kocoum. Then she was taken prisoner by the colonists and fell in love with John Rolfe, a prominent plantation owner who had introduced Caribbean tobacco into the colony; they were married on April 5, 1614.

In 1616, with her husband and son Thomas, Pocahontas traveled to England to great fanfare as the "Indian Princess" and received an audience with King James I and Queen Charlotte. The Rolfe family toured England for seven months. Aboard a ship returning to Virginia, Pocahontas became gravely ill. She was taken ashore and died on March 21, 1617, at Gravesend, England.

Pocahontas was an invaluable friend to the colonists; she empathized with their desperate conditions and attempted to provide aid in the forms of corn and fish.

Peppers

Columbus found Indians in the Caribbean growing peppers. His find was described on his return as "pepper more pungent than that of the Caucasus," a reference to the dried, ground seeds and berries of black pepper commonly used in Europe but in no way related to the New World pepper. Nonetheless, Europeans immediately adopted the new vegetable. Within 100 years, bell and chili peppers grew from England to Austria.

The common bell peppers are perhaps the most familiar peppers to Americans. Most varieties have a mild, sweet flavor, in sharp contrast to the hot—and usually more tapered—smaller chili peppers.

All bell peppers are good sources of vitamins C and A. Whether green, yellow, or red, bell peppers add color, flavor, and nutrients to many dishes. Green peppers are harvested before they reach maturity and will turn bright red if left on the vine.

chapter four

BELL PEPPERS

Multicolored bell peppers are so plentiful in the growing regions around Virginia that their sales contribute about $2 million to the state's economy each year. Remarkably, all six regions of the state grow peppers. Virginia's bell-type peppers—mostly the Camelot and Camelot XR3 varie-ties—are characteristically large, firm, and bell shaped, with thick walls. Most peppers are grown "on plastic" with drip irrigation to lengthen the marketing season, which extends from July into November. Virginia also grows jalapeños and Cubanelle hot peppers.

BARBARA TAYLOR'S STUFFED PEPPERS

Liven up what's left in the fridge with this easy recipe.

4 green bell peppers
1½ cups chopped leftover cooked
    meat or 12 ounces lean ground
    beef
½ cup uncooked rice

1 small onion, chopped
¼ teaspoon each salt and pepper
2 (8-ounce) cans tomato sauce
4 teaspoons ketchup
2 slices bacon, cut in half crosswise

Cut tops off peppers, scoop out seeds and ribs without cutting through shell of peppers. Stand in a baking dish large enough to hold peppers with at least an inch of space between. In a mixing bowl, combine meat, rice, onion, salt, and pepper. Stir in sauce and stuff peppers with mixture. Top peppers with 1 teaspoon ketchup each and put a half strip of bacon over top. Bake about 40 minutes, or until peppers are tender. Makes 4 servings.

Barbara Taylor runs her family's produce stand in Petersburg.

RATATOUILLE-STUFFED PEPPER HALVES

The three pepper colors render a beautiful presentation on dinner plates or a buffet.

1 large red, 1 yellow, and 1 green
    bell pepper
¼ cup olive oil
1 small eggplant
1 small onion, thinly sliced
1 clove garlic, minced
1 large tomato, coarsely chopped

1 cup sliced fresh mushrooms
½ teaspoon each dried basil, oregano
    leaves, and salt
dash of black and red pepper
1 zucchini, sliced lengthwise and cut
    into ½-inch chunks

Cut peppers in half lengthwise. Remove seeds and membranes without cutting through shell. Place pepper halves in a 2-quart rectangular glass dish, cover with vented plastic wrap, and microwave on high 4 to 5 minutes, or until peppers are crisp tender. Cover with cold water to stop the cooking; drain and set aside with cut sides up.

Heat oil in a large skillet over medium heat. Sauté eggplant and onion until soft, stirring occasionally, about 10 minutes. Add garlic, tomato, mushrooms, basil, oregano, salt, black and red pepper. Bring to a boil over medium-high heat; reduce heat to medium-low and simmer about 5 minutes. Add zucchini; simmer 5 minutes longer, stirring occasionally. Spoon ratatouille mixture into prepared pepper halves. Heat 15 minutes in a 350° F oven until mixture is steaming. Makes 6 servings.

The Inn at Little Washington

The refined American cuisine of The Inn at Little Washington capitalizes on the bounty of products from the Virginia countryside. Some farmers even grow food specifically to The Inn's order. The restaurant actually began on a farm. Cooking only with a wood-burning stove and an electric frying pan in their farmhouse kitchen, Patrick O'Connell and his partner Reinhardt Lynch began a catering business, which was so well received that they were encouraged to open a restaurant. In 1978, they opened The Inn, in an old garage in "Little" Washington, Virginia (population 185). The town was laid out in 1749 by an apprentice surveyor named George Washington. Together, The Inn's restaurant and hotel have won almost every prestigious culinary and hospitality award possible; some food critics have described the restaurant's food as "so good it makes you cry."

THE INN AT LITTLE WASHINGTON'S SWEET RED BELL PEPPER SOUP WITH SAMBUCA CREAM

Chef Patrick O'Connell says that "the complex, subtle heat of this simple, full-flavored soup manages to titillate everybody's palate."

FOR SOUP:

- ½ cup olive oil
- 1 cup chopped onion
- 1 tablespoon dried fennel seed
- ¼ teaspoon dried thyme
- ½ bay leaf, crumbled
- ½ teaspoon minced fresh garlic
- 1 tablespoon chopped fresh basil or ½ teaspoon dried basil
- 2 tablespoons minced jalapeño pepper
- ¼ cup flour
- 5 cups chicken broth, preferably homemade
- ½ cup peeled, seeded, and chopped tomatoes
- 1 teaspoon tomato paste
- 6 large red bell peppers, halved, seeded, and cut into 2-inch chunks
- ½ to 1 cup heavy cream
- pinch of sugar
- salt and freshly ground pepper to taste
- generous splash of sambuca (anise-flavored Italian liqueur)

FOR SAMBUCA CREAM:

- 1 cup heavy cream
- ½ teaspoon fresh lemon juice
- ¼ teaspoon lemon zest
- 3 tablespoons sambuca
- pinch of sugar

In a 4-quart heavy-bottomed saucepan, heat the oil over medium heat. Add onion, fennel seed, thyme, bay leaf, garlic, basil, and jalapeño pepper. Reduce heat to low and cook until onion is translucent, about 10 to 15 minutes. Add the flour and cook, stirring constantly, for 10 minutes.

In a separate pot, bring the stock to a boil. Carefully pour the stock over the vegetables, stirring well to incorporate. Add tomato and tomato paste.

Meanwhile, place a large skillet coated with olive oil over high heat. Sauté bell pepper chunks until the skins are blistered and lightly charred. Add the peppers to the soup and simmer, stirring occasionally to make sure nothing sticks to the bottom of the pot, for about 20 minutes. Remove the soup from the heat and purée in small batches in a blender or food processor fitted with a steel blade; strain. Return the soup to the saucepan, bring to a simmer, and add ½ cup of the cream and the sugar. Season with salt and pepper. If the soup is too spicy, add more cream. Add the sambuca.

Whip the cream for the sambuca cream in the bowl of an electric mixer until soft peaks form. Add the lemon juice and zest, sambuca, and sugar. Continue whipping until the cream is almost stiff. The soup can be made up to 2 days in advance and slowly reheated, but don't add the sambuca to the soup until serving time, and keep the sambuca cream refrigerated until serving time. When ready to serve, heat the soup, add sambuca, and top each serving with a dollop of cream.

Patrick O'Connell, who was voted America's best chef of 2001 by the James Beard Foundation, says this sweet red-pepper soup is consistently the "hands-down favorite" of guests at The Inn at Little Washington, which is located in Washington, Virginia (phone (540) 675-3800; or visit www.theinnatlittlewashington.com).

PASTA WITH PEPPERS AND LEEKS

For a filling vegetarian main dish,
try this bell-pepper recipe with your favorite pasta shape.

4 cups pasta (about 11 ounces)
1 pound leeks (about 3 or 4)
4 tablespoons olive oil
2 teaspoons minced fresh garlic
1 teaspoon each dried basil, thyme, oregano

1 each red, green, and yellow bell peppers, thinly sliced
1½ ounces dry-packed sun dried tomatoes, soaked in hot water
¼ teaspoon each freshly ground black pepper and salt

Begin cooking pasta according to directions on package. Discard tough green tops of leeks. Wash and slice remainder. Put leeks and oil into a 2-quart glass measure. Cover with vented plastic wrap and microwave on high 4 to 5 minutes.

Stir in garlic, basil, thyme, and oregano. Place bell peppers on top; re-cover. Stirring midway through cooking, microwave on high 4 to 6 minutes. When pasta tests done, drain. Toss in leek mixture. Drain and chop tomatoes; add to pasta along with pepper and salt. Serve warm. Makes 6 servings.

PEPPERY GREEN-TOMATO-AND-APPLE CHUTNEY

A condiment pairing three of Virginia's major produce items
is a great way to use green tomatoes left at the end of the growing season.

4 cups chopped green tomatoes (about 8)
2 tablespoons plus 2 teaspoons salt, divided
3 cups cider vinegar
1 cup lemon juice
2½ cups sugar
2½ cups packed dark-brown sugar (about 1 pound)

8 cups chopped peeled tart apples (about 10 apples)
½ cup chopped fresh ginger root
1 pound raisins
1 teaspoon cayenne pepper
2 onions, chopped
1 each green and red bell pepper, chopped

Place tomatoes in a colander and sprinkle with 2 tablespoons salt. Let stand overnight. Combine vinegar, lemon juice, sugar, and brown sugar in a large, heavy enameled or stainless-steel pot and bring to a boil. Add tomatoes, 2 teaspoons salt, apples, ginger root, raisins, cayenne, onions, and green and red bell peppers. Bring to a boil, reduce the heat, and simmer until thick, about 1½ hours. Place into hot, sterilized jars; seal and refrigerate. (For pantry storage, pressure-can the chutney.) Makes 6 pint jars.

Boiling-Water Bath Canning

Boiling-water bath canning is recommended for processing high-acid foods so they can be stored in the pantry. The temperature of the boiling-water bath canner is 212° F (100° C) and will kill bacteria in high-acid foods. The boiling-water bath-canning method is used for processing fruits, pickles, relishes, acidified tomatoes, fruit jellies, jams, butters, marmalades, and preserves. A pressure canner is necessary for low-acid foods such as green beans. Always check up-to-date canning information for correct processing times.

Use only standard canning jars for boiling-water bath canning. Peanut butter or mayonnaise jars are not acceptable for canning. Use new canning lids for each jar. Prepare lids according to manufacturer's directions. The hot boiling water should cover the tops of the jars during the entire processing time. Cover the canner during processing. For pints of chutney, process for 10 minutes.

After processing time is completed, remove hot jars and place on a towel or rack to cool. Keep jars out of drafts. Do not turn jars upside down. When jars have cooled, check for sealing. Contact your local Virginia Cooperative Extension office for the most recent information on canning for your area.

Cucumbers

Related to pumpkins, squashes, gourds, and melons, cucumbers probably originated in India and spread over much of the civilized world thousands of years ago. Cucumbers are one of the few vegetables mentioned in the Bible. Royalty loves the cucumber. Emperor Tiberius ate cucumbers at every meal. Charlemagne ordered that cucumbers be grown on his estate. The English tried to make cucumbers grow straight by placing them in glass cylinders. In 1535 the French found Indians growing cucumbers near what is now Canada; in 1539 the Spanish recorded seeing cucumbers cultivated in what became Florida.

Many Americans today enjoy cucumbers, because they are easy to prepare and complement side dishes and salads. Made up of 95% water, they add no fat or sodium and very few calories. There are two main varieties in America. Slicing cucumbers, also known as table cucumbers, feature white spines, grow fairly large, and retain their color for a long time. Picking cucumbers are smaller and don't keep their color as long.

CUCUMBERS

chapter five

CUCUMBERS

Large commercial growers on the Eastern Shore and in the Northern Neck keep produce markets in the eastern United States supplied with cucumbers throughout the summer and into fall. More than 3500 acres of the Old Dominion are planted in cucumbers, and the harvest is valued at almost $4.7 million. The state ranks in the top ten in U.S. fresh-market cucumber production. Most are grown in the counties of Accomack, Northampton, Chesapeake, and Virginia Beach.

Virginia cucumbers are characteristically tender, firm, straight, and are known for their outstanding green color. Virginia growers produce cucumbers from the more productive hybrid varieties and rely on modern scientific technology such as leaf-tissue testing to monitor crop growth. Varieties grown in spring and fall are Dasher II, Thunder, Speedway, and Lighting. Additionally, Indy and Daytona are grown in the fall.

CHERKASKY'S CHILLED CURRIED CUCUMBER SOUP

*This cooling, soothing, pale-green soup makes a delightful luncheon
or first course for a light spring or summer meal.*

2 tablespoons canola oil
½ small onion, finely chopped
½ red bell pepper, finely chopped
½ cup grated fresh coconut
2 teaspoons high-quality curry powder
2 medium cucumbers, peeled, seeded,
   and sliced into ½ inch crescents

1 cup chicken broth
1 quart buttermilk
salt to taste
1 teaspoon mustard seeds

In a medium saucepan, warm the oil over medium heat. Add onion and red pepper; sauté until tender, about 4 minutes. Stir in coconut and curry; sauté until the curry darkens slightly. Stir in cucumber and broth. Bring to a simmer, lower the heat, cover, and cook until cucumbers are tender, about 10 minutes. Chill mixture completely.

Stir buttermilk into cucumber mixture and season to taste with salt. Just before serving, coat a small frying pan with cooking spray. Add mustard seeds, cover, and set over high heat until the seeds pop. Ladle soup into bowls and top each with mustard seeds. Makes 4 servings.

Arlington resident Lisa Cherkasky is a renowned food stylist, writer, recipe developer, gardener, and enthusiastic cook. Cherkasky, now a regular contributor to The Washington Post, National Geographic Traveler, *and* Washingtonian *magazine, worked for eight summers at the Smithsonian's Festival of American Folklife, where her passion for traditional foods and historic food was sparked first.*

CUCUMBER CRESCENTS

Prepare this easy appetizer up to a day in advance.

1 cucumber
1 (3-ounce) package cream cheese,
   softened
1 (4-ounce) package crumbled bleu
   cheese

¼ cup chopped green onions
¼ teaspoon garlic powder
pimientos for garnish

To decorate cucumber, score lines lengthwise along peeling using a zester or fork tines. Cut cucumber in half lengthwise; remove seeds. Combine cream cheese, bleu cheese, onions, and garlic powder. Stuff cucumbers halves with cheese mixture; chill. Before serving, slice cucumbers crosswise into ¾-inch wide crescents. Makes 20 appetizers.

Cucumbers should be a true green color and firm all over, although they may have some white or greenish-white color and still be of high quality.

Look for well-shaped, well-developed cucumbers that are not too large in diameter. Even the best cucumbers could have small lumps on their surfaces. Avoid overgrown versions, large in diameter and dull yellow in color. Withered or shriveled ends are signs of toughness and signal bitter flavor.

COOL CUCUMBERS IN SOUR CREAM

A cool, refreshing side dish for spicy main dishes.

2 cups cider vinegar
4 cups water
1½ cups sugar
¼ cup salt

4 cucumbers, sliced paper thin
1 sweet onion, thinly sliced
½ cup sour cream
freshly ground pepper to taste

In a nonreactive saucepan, combine vinegar, water, sugar, and salt. Add cucumbers and onion; cover and refrigerate overnight. When ready to serve, drain marinade. Toss in sour cream and pepper. Makes 10 servings.

WILMA'S CUCUMBER PICKLES

Serve these pickles on a tray with other condiments such as Peppery Green-Tomato-and-Apple Chutney on page 163 and Virginia Watermelon Pickles on page 142.

8 pounds cucumbers, sliced
2 cups pickling lime
cold water
2 quarts vinegar

5 pounds sugar
½ box pickling spice, tied in a bag
2 tablespoons salt

Cover cucumber slices in lime and cold water and soak overnight. Remove from lime water. Wash 3 to 4 times in clear water to remove all trace of lime. Drain well.

Make a syrup of vinegar, sugar, spices, and salt, and boil several minutes. Add sliced cucumbers and boil rapidly for 30 minutes. Pack in sterilized jars and fill with syrup. Seal and store in refrigerator. To store in pantry, process in a pressure canner. Makes 5 quarts.

Wilma Nurney Bryant, a home economist from the Blackhead area of Southampton County, was well known locally as an "old-time homemaker" who made wonderful cucumber pickles.

chapter six
CABBAGE

∽ *Most Virginia cabbage is grown in the mountains of southwest Virginia, where the cool nights and warm days are ideal for producing some of the best cabbage available anywhere. Cabbage varieties grown in this area include Questo, Rio Verde, Green Boy, Gourmet, and Market Prize. The moderating influences of the Chesapeake Bay and the Atlantic Ocean also create optimum growing conditions for cabbage on the Eastern Shore, where the Blue Bayou, Green Cup, Blue Vantage, Gourmet, and Bravo varieties are grown. Virginia cabbage is available May through December; it is generally sweeter than cabbage grown elsewhere and is preferred for slaws and salads. Revenues from cabbage total about $3 million from 1500 acres harvested.*

Cabbage has been grown in the eastern Mediterranean and Asia Minor for thousands of years. Jacques Carter introduced cabbage, one of the first crops grown by colonists, to North America on his third voyage to the continent, in 1541. The vegetable belongs to the large cruciferous family, which also includes Brussels sprouts, kale, collards, rutabagas, turnips, and cauliflower. Hundreds of cabbage varieties grow in the United States.

Cabbage is packed with nutrients. Ounce for ounce it provides as much vitamin C as orange juice and may reduce the risk of some forms of cancer. One of the most versatile vegetables, cabbage can be cooked or served raw.

CHRIST CHURCH CARAWAY CABBAGE

Here's a fast and easy way to prepare a hot cabbage side dish.

1 tablespoon butter
1 pound cabbage, shredded
1½ teaspoons caraway seeds

1 teaspoon vinegar
1 teaspoon sugar
¼ teaspoon salt

Melt butter in a large skillet with a lid. Add cabbage and caraway seeds. Cover and simmer over low heat, stirring occasionally, for about 20 minutes. If cabbage begins to stick to the pan, add a teaspoon water. When cabbage is tender, remove from heat and stir in vinegar, sugar, and salt. Makes 4 servings.

Both George Washington and Robert E. Lee held pews in Alexandria's historic Christ Church, which was built in 1773 and remains in nearly original condition. Christ Church is a fine example of an English, Georgian, country-style church and is located in downtown Alexandria (phone (703) 549-1450; or visit www.historic christchurch.org).

ORIENTAL CABBAGE SALAD

Toasted noodles and raw cabbage make this salad a crispy delight.

1 head cabbage (about 2 pounds), chopped as for cole slaw
1 bell pepper, diced
8 green onions, sliced
¾ cup sliced almonds
⅓ cup sesame seeds
¼ cup rice vinegar

¼ cup soy sauce
2 cups cooked shrimp, tuna, or diced chicken breast
½ cup plus 2 tablespoons peanut oil, divided
2 (3-ounce) packages Ramen soup noodles

Combine cabbage, bell pepper, onions, and shrimp, tuna, or chicken in a salad bowl; chill. Heat 2 tablespoons oil in a skillet. Discard seasoning packet from soup mix. Toast noodles and almonds in a nonstick skillet until lightly browned. Add sesame seeds and brown quickly; set aside. Thirty minutes before serving, combine vinegar, soy sauce, and remaining oil. Toss cabbage with noodle mixture and dressing. Makes 8 servings.

Recipe courtesy of the Mount Vernon Hospital Auxiliary of Alexandria, publishers of Cardinal Cuisine.

GERMAN RED CABBAGE WITH APPLES

Quintessential to a traditional German dinner is rot kraut. *This version with apples pairs especially well with* sauerbraten, *or roast pork.*

2 tablespoons bacon drippings
   or butter
1 medium onion, thinly sliced
1 head red cabbage, thinly sliced
   (about 2 pounds)
2 tart cooking apples, cored and
   chopped
½ cup sugar
½ teaspoon salt

¼ teaspoon pepper
1 bay leaf
⅛ teaspoon ground cloves
4 cups water
½ cup red wine vinegar or cider
   vinegar
1 tablespoon lemon juice
2 tablespoons flour

Heat bacon drippings in a large, heavy pot with lid. Add onion and sauté until tender, about 4 minutes. Add water, vinegar, and lemon juice. Cover and bring to a boil, about 5 minutes. Stir in cabbage, apples, sugar, salt, pepper, bay leaf, and cloves. Cover and let simmer about 45 minutes, or until cabbage is tender. Add flour; stir to absorb liquid and thicken. Makes 8 servings.

NAPA CABBAGE VINAIGRETTE

This healthy side dish with an Asian flair is a nice accompaniment to fish and poultry.

1 head Napa or Chinese cabbage
2 tablespoons white wine vinegar
2 tablespoons sugar

1 tablespoon soy sauce
1 tablespoon oil
¼ teaspoon ground red pepper

Cut cabbage into 2-inch squares and pile into a 3-quart casserole. Don't worry if they appear to overflow the dish because they cook down considerably. Cover casserole and microwave on high 3 minutes. Stir, re-cover, and microwave on high 2 to 3 minutes; set aside.

In a 1-cup glass measure, combine vinegar, sugar, soy sauce, oil, and red pepper. Microwave on high 30 seconds, or until sugar dissolves. Drain cabbage and mix with hot vinaigrette mixture. Serve warm. Makes 4 servings.

Warm Slaw

Cut the cabbage very fine and sprinkle over it a tablespoonful flour. Put a piece of butter, the size of an egg, in the oven to melt. Salt and pepper the cabbage and put it in the oven with the butter. Mix half a teacup of cream with the same quantity of vinegar, pour it over the cabbage and heat thoroughly.
—Mrs. Susan Goggin,
Bedford County,
Housekeeping in Old Virginia,
1879

∽ DID YOU KNOW . . .
that the typical farm in Virginia is about 180 acres large and owned by a 56-year-old farmer? There are more than 45,000 farms in Virginia, less than half the number the state had in 1960.

Hominy

"As American as apple pie" is not an accurate phrase. Apples and the idea of baking fruit in a crust came from Europe. Better to say, "as American as hominy." Unknown anywhere else in the world, hominy seems to have come from the Algonquin Indians. A Virginia Algonquin Indian tribe, the Chickahominy, and a river were named for this nonfat product. Hominy is made from kernels of hulled, dried corn from which the germ has been removed. Captain John Smith wrote in his 1629 history of Virginia about hominy, which, he said, is "bruized Indian corne pounded, and boiled thick, and milke for sauce."

Ground hominy is called "grits." Dry hominy, known in the Southwest as "posole," must be soaked overnight before cooking in water or milk. Canned hominy, which has already been cooked, is the form most often used today. Hominy has a very mild taste, so it benefits from the addition of herbs, spices, or other savory ingredients. This vegetable contains no fat or cholesterol and two grams of dietary fiber per half cup.

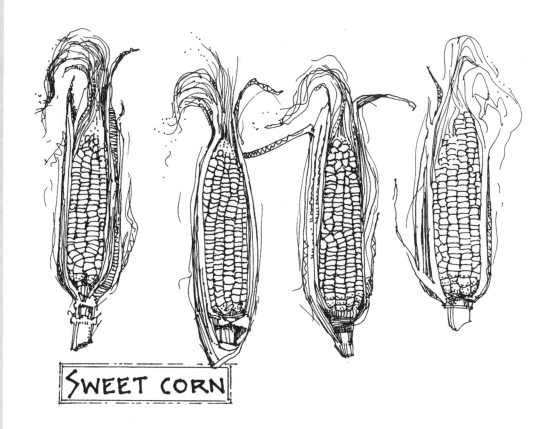

SWEET CORN

chapter seven

SWEET CORN

Virginians have been growing corn since the first settlers arrived in the New World, and long before that, Native Americans in the area grew the crop, which today is grown from special hybrids developed for their sweetness. The Old Dominion's sweet-corn season is short—only July and August—and the vegetable is grown mainly in the counties of Northampton, Hanover, Chesapeake, and Virginia Beach. Varieties grown are the yellow Summer Sweet 7100 and the white Sweet Magic and Ice Queen. Bicolor corn is also grown. Almost 20 times more corn is grown for grain than for consumption, but acreage of edible sweet corn has increased somewhat over the past few years. More than 3,000 acres of sweet corn are harvested annually for a revenue of more than $5 million.

RED FOX TAVERN'S CORN CHOWDER

This creamy, chunky soup is especially satisfying on a cold, winter day.

2 slices bacon, diced
1 large onion, chopped
1 rib celery, chopped
1½ cups diced, peeled potatoes
2 cups chicken broth
1½ cups water

2 cups corn kernels, fresh, canned,
　or frozen
¼ cup diced, cooked chicken
1½ cups heavy cream
4 tablespoons butter
salt and pepper to taste

Fry bacon in a heavy 3-quart pot until brown; remove. Add onion and celery to drippings; cook over medium heat for 10 minutes, stirring often. Add potatoes, broth, and water. Cook until potatoes are fork tender. Add corn and chicken; heat 5 minutes. Add heavy cream, butter, salt, and pepper. Reheat but do not allow to boil. Makes 8 servings.

The Red Fox Inn and Tavern stands at the center crossroads of Middleburg, a historic village in horse-farm country. Built in 1728, the original fieldstone structure is listed on the National Register of Historic Places. The Inn has inviting hotel rooms carefully furnished in the eighteenth-century manner and an excellent restaurant open every day of the year (phone (540) 687-6301 or (800) 223-1728; or visit www.redfox.com).

MANNING'S SOUTHWESTERN HOMINY SALAD

If it's healthful fiber you seek in your diet, try this most appealing salad,
which has a whopping 7.5 grams of fiber per serving.

1 (20-ounce) can Manning's pearl
　hominy
1 (15-ounce) can black beans, rinsed
　and drained
1 (4.5-ounce) can chopped mild
　green chilies
1 cup mild or medium salsa

½ cup each chopped red onion and
　green bell pepper
2 tablespoons fresh lime juice
1 teaspoon ground coriander
¼ cup chopped fresh cilantro
　(optional)

Place hominy in a large bowl and break it apart. Add beans and chilies. If you don't like raw onion and bell pepper, cook them before adding them to mixture, along with salsa, lime juice, and coriander. Gently stir in cilantro, if using. Refrigerate up to 4 days. Makes 8 servings.

Manning's Hominy operates in Lottsburg, where it cans hominy made from steam-peeled, white-corn kernels. It is sold in most Virginia grocery stores. Visit www.manningshominy.com

Buyer's Guide to CORN

Select corn with bright green, snug husks. Kernels should be fresh, tender, plump, and just firm enough to offer slight resistence to pressure. To store, cut away the base of the ear to the bottom kernels. Ears of corn will keep for several days in the refrigerator if wrapped tightly in plastic wrap or stored in airtight containers.

Corn-on-the-Cob Etiquette

"Corn may be eaten from the cob. Etiquette permits this method, but does not allow one to butter the entire length of an ear of corn and then gnaw it from end to end. To hold an ear of corn, if it be a short one, by the end, with the right and bite from the ear is good form. A little doily, or very small napkin, is sometimes served with corn to fold about the end of a cob that is to be grasped by the hand, but this arrangement is as inconvenient as it is unnecessary."

—*Good Form: Dinners Cermonious and Unceremonious,* 1890

The Amazing Vegetable

After Christopher Columbus landed in Cuba in 1492, two of his men returned from exploring the island to tell him about a "sort of grain called maize." This was the white man's first experience with the North American plant we call corn. But corn was a staple in the diets of the ancient Inca, Mayan, and Aztec civilizations. Fossilized pollen grains from corn plants have been found in Mexico that probably are more than 60,000 years old. The earliest written record of corn dates back to eighth-century Guatemala. Native Americans held elaborate ceremonies when planting and harvesting corn and used corn patterns to decorate pottery, sculpture, and other art. An Indian named Squanto taught the Pilgrims how to grow corn.

During colonial and antebellum times, acreage in corn exceeded that of any other crop. Southerners ate every possible variation, then found hundreds of other uses for corn, including a way to distill and drink it.

Corn is still a major bread grain in the South, cooked in a skillet, pan, or mold. Some popular corn foods are roasted ears, popcorn, hominy, grits, cornbread, dodgers, hoecake, johnny cake, pone, mush, fritters, spoon bread, pudding, porridge, parched corn, fish-frying batter, Hoppin' John, succotash, and cornstarch.

CUSTARD-FILLED CORNBREAD

As this amazing bread bakes, a creamy, barely set custard makes a layer of filling in the middle—no crumbling allowed!

2 eggs
3 tablespoons butter, melted
3 tablespoons sugar
½ teaspoon salt
2 cups milk
1½ tablespoons white vinegar

1 cup flour
¾ cup yellow cornmeal
1 teaspoon baking powder
½ teaspoon baking soda
1 cup heavy cream or whipping cream

Butter an 8-inch square baking dish and place it in the oven. Preheat oven to 350° F and let dish get hot while mixing batter. Beat eggs with butter until well blended. Add sugar, salt, milk, and vinegar; beat well. Sift together the flour, cornmeal, baking powder, and baking soda. Add to egg mixture. Mix just until batter is smooth. Pour into heated dish, then pour cream into center of batter. Do not stir. Place in oven and bake 45 to 55 minutes, or until lightly browned. Serve warm. Makes 9 servings.

Farm owner Jessie Cobb, from the Black Creek area of Southampton County, raises butterflies and grows beautiful flowers and herbs in her yard for them to feed on.

CORNOLOGY QUIZ

How much do you know about corn?
Answer TRUE or FALSE to these statements. Then look for the answers on the next page.

1. An acre of forestry is more beneficial to the environment than an acre of corn.

2. Grain corn can be harvested approximately 60 days after planting.

3. The corn plant has both male and female parts.

4. Corn is part of the grass family.

5. Grain corn by-products can be found in more than 2000 items.

6. Sweet corn and grain corn are the same.

7. Popcorn is grown only in the central part of the United States.

8. Typically, you can get six ears of corn or more per stalk of corn.

9. Corn develops from a small seed to a plant that is typically 6 to 11 feet tall.

10. The word "corn" can refer to maize, wheat, oats, and grain sorghum.

11. Each kernel of corn, when planted, will produce 300 to 1000 or more kernels.

ANSWERS TO THE CORNOLOGY QUIZ

1. FALSE. Both have environmental benefits. Both have large leaf areas that absorb lots of carbon dioxide and release oxygen during the entire summer period. The plant residue left after grain-corn harvest is returned to the soil as organic matter.

2. FALSE. This is true of sweet corn. However, grain corn is left standing in the field to fully mature and dry. Grain corn is usually harvested in October or November.

3. TRUE. The silk is the female part while the tassel is the male part.

4. TRUE. Theory has it that kernels of corn once had individual floral parts like oats, and cobs that broke apart easily, unlike the ears and husks which we know as corn today.

5. TRUE. In a typical 10,000-item grocery store, corn can be found in at least 2500 products.

6. FALSE. Sweet corn has a higher sugar and water content and is used for corn-on-the-cob, frozen, and niblet corn. Grain corn has many uses for both edible and non-edible products.

7. FALSE. Popcorn is grown in Ontario, Canada—more so in the southern part of the province.

8. FALSE. In ideal growing conditions you may get two fully matured ears of corn. Normally, one fully matured ear is harvested and a second ear can be seen, but is not well developed.

9. TRUE.

10. TRUE. However, in Canada and the United States "corn" usually refers to maize. The scientific name is *Zea mays*. Other names are "mais" (French) and "maiz" (Spanish).

11. TRUE. An ear of corn, when matured, will normally have 10 to 18 rows of kernels with up to 50 kernels per row. Good growing conditions will mean many ears with 600 to 800 kernels of corn each.

Virginia Department of Agriculture and Consumer Services' Office of Communication and Media Relations.

The Amazing Vegetable (continued)

Traditional nonedible corn products include pipes, torches, corn shelters, tool handles, jug stoppers, fishing corks, back scratchers, litter, hair curlers, salt-and-pepper shakers, knothole plugs, kindling, ornaments, Christmas-tree strings, and corn-husk dolls. Among the multitude of corn by-products are paint, insecticides, baby foods, chewing gum, soft drinks, hot dogs, cough drops, toothpaste, lipstick, shaving cream, shoe polish, detergents, tobacco, rayon, rubber tires, urethane foam, explosives, and embalming fluid.

Corn is the most valuable crop grown in the country and one of the most important vegetables in Virginia.

Maize Quest

Between August and November, after the corn stalks have matured, a life-size maze is mowed into five acres of fields near Shenandoah Caverns and the Meems Bottom Covered Bridge near Mt. Jackson, on Bridgemont Farms. Children and adults can step into this two-mile maze. In addition to being fun, the maze educates participants about the figures mowed into the cornfield. Bridges, tunnels, and dead ends all hold clues to the theme of this cornfield puzzle. For information, call Maize Quest at (540) 477-4200 or visit www.cornmaze.com.

Soybeans

Though the Chinese first cultivated this bean 5000 years ago, it was not brought to the United States until 1804. They were used primarily as a forage crop until George Washington Carver discovered, in 1904, that soybeans are a valuable source of protein and oil.

One acre of soybeans can provide 584 pounds of edible protein, enough to feed one person for 2224 days, and many claim that soy protein is more valuable in lowering cholestoral levels than more traditional sources. As more and more consumers recognize the environmental and nutritional benefits of the versatile bean, new soy-based food items are being marketed all the time. Producers use it to create everything from soymilk and other dairy and meat alternatives to roasted soy nuts and even soy-cheese pizza. Despite this, Virginia soybeans are still primarily used for animal feed, specifically for the state's huge poultry industry, or for export to other countries.

The versatile beans in dried form can be sprouted, ground into flour, or made into soybean oil, milk, or a curd called "tofu." To cook them, cover with water and boil for about two minutes, allow them to stand one hour covered with water, then cook until tender. In the green state, when the pods are easily shelled, plunge them into boiled water and cook for 15 minutes.

chapter eight

SOYBEANS

∾ *Soybeans are Virginia's top income-producing crop, with cash receipts of more than $100 million. More than half a million acres of the state are planted in soybeans, mostly on the Eastern Shore and in southeast Virginia. Glycine max is the scientific name for soybeans, "summer-annual" plants that complete their life cycle within one year. Each plant has 60 to 80 pods, and each pod typically has three beans. About 20% of the crop is used for human consumption in the form of soybean oil.*

"NEW" THREE-BEAN SALAD

*High-protein edamame (fresh soy beans)
make this salad nutrient-complete for a main dish.*

½ cup olive oil
¼ cup each balsamic and white wine
    vinegars
½ teaspoon dried oregano
2 cloves fresh garlic, diced
1 (14-ounce) can artichoke hearts,
    diced
½ cup edamame beans removed from
    pods, par boiled

1 (14.5-ounce) can garbanzo beans,
    drained
1 (14.5-ounce) can dark-red kidney
    beans, drained
½ cup feta cheese, cut into cubes
20 kalamata olives, sliced
20 marinated sun-dried tomatoes
salt and pepper to taste
red-leaf lettuce

In a medium mixing bowl, whisk together oil, balsamic vinegar, wine vinegar, oregano, and garlic. Add artichoke hearts, edamame, garbanzo beans, kidney beans, cheese, olives, and tomatoes. Add salt and pepper to taste. Marinate at least 1 hour in refrigerator. Serve on lettuce. Makes 4 servings.

⁓ Recipe from the Virginia Soybean Board. ⁓

ROASTED SOY NUTS

Snacking has never been better for you than with these crunchers.

1 cup soybeans, soaked in water 8 hours or more

Preheat oven to 350° F. Use up to 2 cups of beans per baking sheet. Drain the beans and spread in a single layer. Bake 15 minutes; stir. Bake 5 to 10 minutes longer, stirring every 5 minutes, until golden brown and crunchy. The total time will vary depending on the moisture of the beans, but should take about 25 minutes. Watch carefully when the beans are close to being done.

Microwave directions: Drain soybeans and spread in a single layer in a 9- or 10-inch glass pie plate. Microwave on high for 3 minutes. Stir, then cook 3 minutes more. Continue to cook for 1 minute at a time, stirring after each minute to ensure even browning. The total time will vary, depending on the moisture of the bean and the wattage of the oven, but will probably take about 9 to 12 minutes. When the beans are beginning to get hard and golden, you may want to cook for 30-second intervals, checking in between to avoid burning them. They are done when golden brown and crunchy.

⁓ Recipe courtesy of the Virginia Soybean Board. ⁓

The Roanoke Farmers Market is the oldest such market in continuous use in Virginia. The Alexandria Farmers Market claims the same. But farmers have exhibited at the market in Roanoke, which is held on First Street between Salem and Church Streets, since 1882, when licenses were issued to 25 hucksters. Today, 60 full-time farmers exhibit in 40 permanent stalls with brightly-colored canvas canopies, according to the market's president, Chris Hancock. Farmers can back their trucks up to the display tables on the adjacent sidewalks. Buyers know that if the produce is displayed on the tables, it is home grown by farmers who farm within a 60-mile radius. The Roanoke area is best known for its tomatoes, apples, peaches, cucumbers, and corn, but the farmers grow a wide variety of other vegetables and fruits. Three permanent stores facing the stalls—Wertz's Country Store, Thomas Family Farm Market, and Sumdat Farm ("some of this, some of that")—also sell produce and other food products, most of which originate in Virginia. The market is open Monday through Saturday from 8 a.m. to 5 p.m. and 10 a.m. to 4 p.m. on Sunday (phone (540) 342-2028 or visit www.roanokefarmers market.com).

EASY SOY TACOS

*Give these tacos a try when attempting to find ways
to utilize meatless products in your diet.*

1 package frozen or refrigerated pre-cooked soy crumbles (some brands include Morningstar Ground Meatless, Green Giant Harvest Burgers, and Lightlife Gimme Lean)

1 envelope taco-seasoning mix
¾ cup water
flour tortillas or taco shells
vegetable cheddar-flavor cheese or dairy cheese

Brown soy crumbles. Drain. Stir in taco seasoning and water and mix well. Continue heating until thoroughly hot. Serve ¼ cup meat in tortilla or taco shell. Garnish with cheese, olives, onions, and salsa. Makes 12 tacos.

Recipe from the Virginia Soybean Board.

NON-DAIRY RANCH SALAD DRESSING

This protein-packed dressing makes a salad a nutritionally complete meal!

1¼ cups soymilk
1 (12-ounce) package silken tofu

1 (1-ounce) package ranch salad-dressing mix

Put the soymilk, tofu, and dressing mix in a blender. Whirl until well blended, scraping down sides if necessary. Transfer dressing to a jar and store in the refrigerator.

Recipe from the Virginia Soybean Board.

chapter nine
OTHER VEGETABLES

∽ *Vegetables contribute eye appeal, vitamins, minerals, and fiber to our health. The value of Virginia's major fresh-market vegetable crop totals around $140 million from more than 17,000 acres harvested. The value of major vegetables grown for processing in Virginia totaled more than a million dollars, up from previous years. Although almost every vegetable imaginable is grown in the state, statistics are not kept on the small production of individual vegetables. But all a person has to do is visit one of the state's myriad farmers markets to see the array available. In addition, backyard gardens are extremely popular in the Old Dominion, whether for relaxation, for the appreciation of just-picked produce, or for the desire to revisit the land.*

Alexandria Farmers Market

Market Square is thought to be the site of the nation's oldest continually operating farmer's market, and George Washington sent wagons of produce from Mount Vernon to be sold here. The town of Alexandria was planned in 1749, adjacent to an existing tobacco warehouse. Scottish merchants led the town's evolution into a major commercial port by the end of the century.

Most of Alexandria's first shops were located along King Street. Merchandise was also sold directly from the wharves or auctioned by the merchant.

A farmers market, established in 1753, supplied fresh produce. Modern-day Alexandria residents shop at malls and supermarkets, yet throngs are still drawn by the ambiance of the Saturday morning farmers market held on the block-wide brick courtyard in front of city hall. Homemade jams and jellies sparkle in the morning light, fresh herbs in pots are ready for the home gardener to plant, and foods of all kinds—including produce, baked goods, and grilled meats—are offered by farmers and purveyors. The square is centered around a beautiful fountain. Visit the farmer's market any Saturday between 5 and 10 a.m. at the corner of King and Royal Streets.

—Office of Historic Alexandria; Alexandria Archeology Museum

THE TAYLOR FAMILY
Produce Farmers

Left to right: Ken Taylor, Clifton Plue Walker, Robert Taylor, and Burnell Taylor

"Being a produce farmer is hard. You can't raise it if you can't sell it," says Burnell Taylor, owner of Taylor Produce in Petersburg, established in 1985. The family sells picked-daily vegetables and fruits. Taylor says selling directly to the customer at his produce stand and store is considerably more lucrative than selling produce wholesale.

Taylor, along with his brother Robert II, his son, and Clifton Plue Walker (an employee for 36 years), farm the 300 acres in Dinwiddie County that have been part of the half-English, half-Irish Taylor family since the 1700s. The farm is located about six miles south of Pamplin Historical Park, which preserves the battlefield where the Siege of Petersburg occurred on April 2, 1865. The Taylor land was also the site of Civil War combat; the Battles of Reams Station, fought over the Weldon Railroad that connected Virginia to the Carolinas, were fought there.

Back in 1960, Burnell's father and grandfather were still using their mules "Nell and Belle" to plow and harvest grain, soybeans, and about 100 acres of feed corn.

The Taylors also raised hogs until 1996—around the same time that they opened the produce stand—when hog prices dropped to 27 cents a pound. In fact, feeding the 250 hogs was one of Ken's first farm jobs. "When other school kids went out for sports after school, I came home to work on the farm," says Ken in his heart-of-Virginia accent. At the ripe old age of ten, Ken says, he was driving a tractor and wrestling irrigation pipe that was larger than him. And now, as an adult, he's taken on a second job, working at another produce stand after mornings working on the Taylor farm.

Ken and his parents work 14 to 18 hours a day, and by midsummer have already been working for 200 days straight. Besides planting and harvesting, there's irrigating, cultivating, and spraying to complete on some part of the farm every day. "Work starts early on the farm. We pick produce from 6:30 to 10 a.m., before it gets too hot," the sandy-haired, blue-eyed farmer explains. "Then, from 10 to 11 a.m., there's running the tomatoes. They come out of the fields in buckets and we have to separate them into three grades: red, pink, and green. We have so many; we have to pick the full-sized green ones at the same time as the ripest ones to keep up with the crop. The green ones ripen in the shed. From one crop of 7000 plants, there will be truckloads of tomatoes."

That produce is trucked daily seven miles away to the stand on South Crater Road, which is visited by hundreds of customers each day. Some are restaurant proprietors who will buy whole cases of particular items. Others come daily or a few times a week just to buy a couple of vine-ripe tomatoes—Taylor Produce's top money maker—right off the truck. "We don't know all the customers' names, but we recognize their faces and know when they come back," says Barbara Taylor, Burnell's wife and Ken's mother. Barbara works at the stand most days from 8 a.m. to 7 p.m. Burnell farms during the week but works the stand on weekends. "People want to see the farmer," he says. "They expect me to be there."

To keep the produce stand supplied, vegetables will be planted at several intervals from March through August.

"We'll grow 20,000 tomato plants each year, planting about 7000 three times: in April, June, and July," explains Burnell. "We plant Silver Queen corn in April and June. In fact, April is a big month for planting. Tobacco, peanuts, squash, cucumbers, peppers, eggplant, snap beans, butter beans, cantaloupes, and watermelons are also planted then. We can plow 25 to 30 acres in one day and put in the seeds by hand. Unfortunately, we're only allowed to plant eight acres of tobacco. The state wants to keep prices high, so it puts limits on how much we can grow. That's also true for peanuts.

"In June, it's time to plant cucumbers, squash, and cabbage again. In between plantings, we have to spray the fields with fungicide and insecticide every few weeks—every week for tomatoes." They must also irrigate either daily or weekly. And in May and June, when the strawberries planted in October are ripening, they will have people coming out to the farm "to pick and pay." The Taylors participate in both the Pick-Your-Own and Virginia's Finest programs operated by the Virginia Department of Agriculture and Consumer Services.

August calls for tobacco picking in the fields closest to the house. "It will take six weeks to pick all the tobacco," according to Burnell. "It has to be picked by hand, and you begin with the largest, bottom leaves that are ready. It's flue-cured tobacco that gives the aroma to cigarettes, and we cure it in our tobacco barn. We'll have 30,000 pounds—about five truckloads—to take to the auction in Oxford, North Carolina. A lot of the tobacco growers are going to contract sales, but I think you get more money from auctions. You take a chance, though."

Fall is peanut-harvest time. "I remember when we had to chop the peanuts by hand and hang them on poles to dry. Then we'd put them in a machine that separated the peanuts from the plant," recalls Clifton Plue Walker, whose mother also worked with the Taylors. "Now we harvest peanuts with machinery pulled by a tractor, so it's a lot easier."

The Taylors will continue to pick produce to sell at their stand until November and December, when they sell Christmas trees. The stand is closed during January and February. And then another year of farming begins.

Virginia Crafts: Truly One of a Kind

In 1608, eight German and Polish glassmakers brought to Jamestown by the London Company began America's first industry—a glassmaking factory. Since then, Virginia has continued its strong tradition of crafts. Travelers can spend several vacations going from one Virginia region to another, browsing and buying wildlife decoys and bronze wildlife sculptures on the Eastern Shore and handmade brooms, rugs, and dolls in the Heart of Appalachia at the opposite corner of the state, in southwestern Virginia. The arts venues themselves are works of art, with Old Town Alexandria's Torpedo Factory Art Center being a prime example of working studios and galleries on three floors of a sprawling building that once housed naval weapons. The state's fine arts museums—ranging from The Chrysler Museum in Norfolk and the Virginia Museum of Fine Arts in Richmond to smaller art museums sprinkled throughout the Commonwealth—have done much to encourage the development of artists and galleries.

A member of the lily-of-the-valley family, asparagus was cultivated 2000 years ago and brought to this country by our early settlers. Thomas Jefferson grew it in his Monticello greenhouses. Today's Virginia asparagus is grown commercially mainly in Northampton County.

Asparagus stalks are either white or green. Formerly, it was available fresh only in the spring months; now, thanks to imports from other countries, it can be purchased almost year-round. Julia Child says the best way to eat asparagus is to pick it up in your fingers. Select asparagus that is firm and not shriveled. Look for tips that are tightly closed. Store unwashed asparagus up to one week in a plastic bag in the refrigerator with the bottom of the stalks wrapped in dampened paper towels. Asparagus has only 21 calories per 3½-ounce serving.

To Cook Asparagus

"Wash well, scrape, cut off the tough end, tie up in bunches and put in boiling water with a spoonful of salt. Boil 30 minutes or till tender. Lay it on slices of toast in a dish, pour melted butter over it, and serve hot."

—Mrs. Philip Withers, Lynchburg, *Housekeeping in Old Virginia,* 1879

FRESH ASPARAGUS WITH BROWNED BUTTER-PECAN SAUCE OR ORANGE BEURRE BLANC

Use the winning sauces in this recipe to liven up other vegetables, too, such as green beans, broccoli, or carrots.

FOR ASPARAGUS:

2 pounds fresh asparagus   salt to taste

Decide which sauce to make and prepare it first. Cook asparagus over medium-low heat, covered, in ½ inch water in medium saucepan until crisp-tender, about 5 minutes; drain. Season with salt. Arrange asparagus in serving dish; drizzle with sauce, and serve remaining sauce in gravy boat. Makes 8 servings.

FOR BROWNED BUTTER-PECAN SAUCE:

8 tablespoons butter (1 stick)   1 teaspoon dried marjoram leaves
1 cup chopped pecans

Heat butter and pecans in small skillet over medium-high heat until butter and pecans are browned, stirring frequently; stir in marjoram just before the end of cooking time. Pour butter and pecans over asparagus; season with salt to taste, and serve hot.

FOR ORANGE BEURRE BLANC:

¾ cup orange juice   16 tablespoons (2 sticks) butter, cut
3 tablespoons white wine vinegar   into 16 pieces, softened
3 tablespoons minced shallots   salt and white pepper to taste
2 teaspoons finely grated orange rind

Heat orange juice, vinegar, shallots, and orange rind to boiling in small saucepan; boil rapidly until mixture is reduced to about 2 tablespoons, about 3 to 5 minutes. Reduce heat to very low; whisk in butter a tablespoon at a time, whisking until each tablespoon butter is melted before adding the next. Season with salt and white pepper to taste; serve immediately. Makes generous 1 cup sauce.

Recipe courtesy of Southeast United Dairy Industry Association.

THE INN AT MONTROSS'S CREAM OF ASPARAGUS SOUP

This recipe makes the most of the Northern Neck's "impressive" asparagus.

4 tablespoons salted butter   ⅓ cup coarsely chopped celery
1 pound Northern Neck asparagus,   1 clove garlic, crushed
  chopped (remove tips for garnish   1 sprig fresh thyme or
  if desired)   ¼ teaspoon dried thyme
1 (4-ounce) potato, coarsely chopped   1 bay leaf
¼ cup coarsely chopped yellow
  onion

2 tablespoons flour
2 tablespoons sherry
4 cups chicken broth (if not homemade, use low-sodium product)

½ cup heavy cream
salt, pepper, and cayenne to taste
   (optional)

Melt butter in a large stock pan and add asparagus, potato, onion, celery, garlic, thyme, and bay leaf. Sauté, stirring occasionally, for 10 to 15 minutes to release flavors. Add flour and stir constantly until incorporated; particles will stick to the bottom of the pan, just be careful not to burn it. Add sherry and deglaze (scrape ingredients from the bottom of the pan using the liquid). Add chicken stock and simmer 45 minutes.

Remove from heat and purée until smooth, using an immersion blender, or cool slightly and purée in batches, using a food processor. Return soup to low heat and add cream. Add additional cream as desired. Season with salt, pepper, and cayenne to taste. Serve hot immediately with a garnish of asparagus tips. Soup can also be refrigerated 4 to 5 days. Makes 6 servings.

Chef Scott Massidda, of The Inn at Montross, is known locally as the "soup master." Originally established in 1684 as John Minor's Ordinary (tavern), this colonial home located in the historic Northern Neck of Virginia—the birthplace of George Washington, James Madison, James Monroe, and General Robert E. Lee—has hosted many residents. The original ordinary, damaged by fire, was rebuilt in the 1790s. It is currently a five-guestroom inn and comfortable, 50-seat fine-dining restaurant. The cuisine is French inspired, and all soups, breads, pasta, and desserts are house made. The Inn is owned by Chefs Scott Massidda and Cindy Brigman (phone (804) 493-0573).

GOAT HILL FARM'S
GRILLED ASPARAGUS WITH VINAIGRETTE

The crisp, nutty flavor of newly harvested asparagus makes this the perfect dish for spring.

1 pound fresh asparagus spears
2 tablespoons olive oil

vinaigrette dressing

When the coals on the grill are all evenly burning, put the asparagus on. Grilling time for freshly harvested asparagus should be short. Turn the spears a few times so they have an even grill pattern on them. Remove from the grill and lightly drizzle with vinaigrette dressing; garnish with loose chive blossoms (see sidebar). Makes 4 servings.

Terri Lehman and John O'Malley Burns tend Goat Hill Farm in Rappahannock County, where, in the shadow of the rolling hills of the Blue Ridge Mountains, asparagus is one of the early crops that "makes spring so enjoyable," says Terri, adding: "We compete with our two Labs to see who gets to harvest it first!" To gain a better understanding of how, when, and where their food comes from, customers can come directly to Goat Hill Farm to help harvest the products they want to buy, which include seasonal vegetables and apples. Terri also runs a specialty food market in Washington, Virginia, called The Epicurious Cow. For information call (540) 675-2269 or visit www.epicuriouscow.com.

A Vivacious Vinaigrette

To liven up your favorite vinaigrette-dressing recipe, make it with opal basil–enhanced vinegar, as Goat Hill Farm's Terri Lehman suggests. Here's how, in Terri's words: "When herb beds are overflowing with basil during the months of August and September, I like to snip the tops of opal basil, put them in glass jars filled with Champagne vinegar, and let them brew over the winter in our root cellar until springtime. Then strain off the vinegar into a wonderful decanter, and you have this gorgeous magenta vinegar with hints of basil and spicy pepper."

Garnish It with Chive Blossoms

Chive blossoms, the pink, round blossoms of the chive plant, are one of the special treats of springtime on Goat Hill Farm, in Washington, Virginia. To enhance the farm's grilled-asparagus recipe (adjacent), gently pull a handful of blossoms from the plant's base and sprinkle them over the asparagus. They have a sweet flavor that is addictive, and they are excellent over just about any food.

BROCCOLI

ROTELLE WITH BROCCOLI AND SPICY PEANUT SAUCE

*This easy vegetarian main dish, with a sauce
reminiscent of Indonesian satay, is cooked with one pot.*

4½ tablespoons peanut butter
4 tablespoons hot water
1½ to 2 tablespoons soy sauce
1½ teaspoons Worcestershire sauce
1 teaspoon minced garlic
¾ teaspoon sugar
¼ teaspoon cayenne

salt to taste
½ pound rotelle or fusilli
½ pound broccoli, the flowerets cut into ¾-inch pieces and the stems peeled and cut crosswise into ¼-inch-thick slices
1 red bell pepper, chopped

In a large bowl whisk together flavorings. Boil the pasta until almost *al dente*, add the broccoli and the bell pepper, and boil the mixture for 2 to 3 minutes, or until the vegetables are *al dente*; drain. Combine pasta and sauce and toss thoroughly. Makes 2 servings.

BROCCOLI AND SAUSAGE QUICHE

*Double your pleasure! This recipe makes two.
Use for a large group or freeze the second one after baking.*

1 pound bulk sausage, browned and drained
2 cups fresh broccoli, chopped and blanched, or 1 (10-ounce) box frozen chopped broccoli, thawed
1 small onion, peeled and diced

2 cups shredded cheddar cheese
2 (9-inch) pie crusts
8 eggs
2 cups milk
salt and pepper to taste

Preheat oven to 350° F. In a skillet, brown sausage with onions. Blot grease. Layer sausage-onion mixture, broccoli, and cheddar cheese equally in pie crusts. Blend together eggs, milk, salt, and pepper. Pour over sausage mixture. Bake 30 to 35 minutes, or until firmly set. Let stand at least 15 minutes. Cut each into 6 or 8 slices and serve hot. Makes 2 quiches or 12 to 16 servings.

Recipe courtesy of Suzie Blanchard, chef/owner of The Inn at Meander Plantation in Locust Dale, which dates to 1766 (phone (800) 385-4936 or visit www.meander.net).

Surprisingly, until early in the twentieth century, almost no one outside the Italian-American community ate broccoli. Then, some enterprising Italian market gardeners in California sent samples of broccoli packed in ice to East Coast markets to generate interest in the crop. The marketing ploy worked, and now broccoli is one of the staples of the greengrocer. Broccoli is at its best when purchased fresh. Look for closely bunched blue-green flowerets and firm stalks. Any woody stalks with noticeable open cores at the base will be tough and hollow. Limp, tired looking heads have lost texture that can't be regained. Old broccoli will have yellow flower buds or buds that will fall off when stroked with a finger. Broccoli should be stored, unwashed, in a plastic bag in the refrigerator. It should last several days. One-pound bunch makes about six cups when trimmed and cut into pieces, or about four servings after cooking. Broccoli can be eaten raw or cooked; cook briefly so the vegetable stays crisp and green. Because broccoli is a member of the cabbage family, lengthy cooking will result in an odiferous, olive-green mush. Cooked broccoli can be safely refrigerated for four days.

HELEN'S BROCCOLI SALAD

*Always a favorite at potluck dinners and buffets, this make-ahead salad is flavored
with two of Virginia's popular farm products: peanuts and pork.*

8 cups broccoli florets (cut from
  2 bunches)
1 red onion, chopped
½ cup raisins
1 cup mayonnaise

6 slices bacon, crisp-cooked, drained,
  and crumbled
2 tablespoons balsamic vinegar or
  red wine vinegar
½ cup chopped peanuts

Toss broccoli, onion, raisins, and bacon in a large bowl. Combine mayonnaise and
vinegar in a small bowl; mix well. Add to broccoli mixture and mix gently until coated. Chill if desired. Before serving, sprinkle with peanuts. Makes 8 servings.

---

*∽ A native of Amelia County, Helen W. Smith was an extension agent with the Virginia Cooperative Extension for
25 years. "I guess you can call me a veteran," she says. ∽*

LEMON BROCCOLI SPEARS

*Healthful but rather bland—and even stinky when overcooked—
broccoli benefits from a lightly flavored lemon butter and a whiff of tarragon.*

1 pound frozen broccoli spears
1 small onion, sliced into rings
2 tablespoons butter, melted
1 tablespoon lemon juice

¼ teaspoon dried tarragon or 1 teaspoon fresh chopped tarragon
salt and pepper, if desired

Place broccoli in a large saucepan with ½ cup water. Place onion on top of broccoli.
Cover and bring water to a boil. Reduce the heat and cook until broccoli is tender,
about 10 to 12 minutes. Combine margarine, lemon juice, and tarragon. Drain broccoli, arrange on plates topped with onion, and drizzle with butter mixture. Add salt
and pepper, if desired. Makes 6 servings.

Microwave directions: Place broccoli spears in a 2-quart rectangular dish. Cover
with vented plastic wrap. Microwave on high 10 to 12 minutes, or until tender. Drain
and let stand. Combine onion, margarine, and tarragon in a 1-cup glass measure.
Cover with vented plastic wrap and microwave on high 3 minutes, or until onion is
tender. Add lemon juice and pour over broccoli. Add salt and pepper if desired.
Makes 6 servings.

Most people know of the
Cooperative Extension service through their local contact, the county agricultural
extension agent, better
known as the county agent.
Nearly every county in the
United States has at least one
agent, and these public officials fulfill a variety of job
responsibilities. First and foremost, county agents help
farmers. They stay informed
about the latest advances in
seed varieties, fertilizers, tilling methods, and mechanized
equipment from the agricultural experiment stations,
then share that information
with farmers through radio
shows, seminars, newspaper
columns, and house calls to
farms.

The county agent serves the
general public as well, providing information on every-
thing from canning and
preserving foods to pruning
shrubs, communicating with
children, cleaning drapes.
Many agents advise 4-H
organizations and work with
local civic leaders to improve
community living. To find an
agent near you, look in the
county-government pages of
your local phone book, or
visit www.ext.vt.edu/offices.

CARROTS

SHIELDS TAVERN CARROT PUDDING
SPICED WITH CARDAMOM

Pan-roast whole cardamom pods, cool, and reduce to a powder in a spice grinder to heighten the flavor of this exotic spice and improve the taste of this exotic pudding.

3 large eggs, separated
2 tablespoons sugar
1½ tablespoons cornstarch
1 cup milk
2 pounds medium carrots, peeled, cooked, and mashed (about 3 cups)

3 tablespoons unsalted butter
1 teaspoon salt
1 cup fresh bread crumbs
1 cup half-and-half
½ teaspoon ground cardamom

Preheat oven to 300° F and butter a 2-quart casserole. Beat the egg yolks with the sugar until light and fluffy. Mix cornstarch with a small amount of milk. Heat remaining milk over low heat. Add the cornstarch-milk blend to the heated milk and stir until smooth and slightly thickened.

Take a small amount of this thickened mixture and stir it thoroughly into the egg yolks and sugar. Pour the resulting combination into the leftover thickened mixture. Cook over medium-low heat, stirring constantly until smooth and thick, about 5 minutes. Stir in the carrots, butter, salt, and bread crumbs. Add the cream and cardamom.

Beat the egg whites until they hold firm peaks; fold into carrot mixture. Pour into prepared casserole. Place the casserole in a larger pan of hot water and bake for 30 minutes. Increase the heat to 350° F and bake for an additional 45 minutes, or until a knife inserted in the center comes out clean. Makes 10 to 12 servings.

⌘ The recipe for this pudding appears in The Colonial Williamsburg Tavern Cookbook. *Shields Tavern specializes in low-country cuisine made with fresh products from local farms, rivers, and the Bay, and is situated next door to King's Arms Tavern on Duke of Gloucester Street (phone (800)* TAVERNS, *(800) 828-3767, or (757) 229-2141, or visit www.colonialwilliamsburg.org).* ⌘

MORNING-GLORY MUFFINS

If you like carrot cake, you'll like these rich muffins,
which are full of fiber but better-tasting than bran muffins.

1⅓ cups all-purpose flour
¾ cup sugar
1½ teaspoons each baking soda and
   ground cinnamon
⅓ teaspoon salt
⅔ cup oil
2 eggs

1¼ teaspoons vanilla extract
1⅓ cups grated, peeled apple (about
   1 large apple)
⅓ cup raisins
⅓ cup flaked coconut
⅓ cup shredded carrots
⅓ cup chopped walnuts (optional)

Preheat oven to 350° F. In a large bowl combine the flour, sugar, baking soda, cinnamon, and salt. In a separate bowl mix the oil, eggs, and vanilla. Stir the wet into the dry ingredients just until moistened. Fold in the apples, raisins, coconut, carrots, and nuts. Fill greased or paper-lined muffin cups two-thirds full. Bake for 25 to 30 minutes, or until a toothpick inserted in center of muffin comes out clean. Makes 12.

These muffins are a specialty of La Vista Plantation Bed & Breakfast, owned by Michele and Edward Schiesser and located in the lush Spotsylvania County countryside, just outside the historic city of Fredericksburg. The 1838 Greek Revival is situated on ten acres that include mature trees, flowering shrubs, pastures, woods, gardens, and a pond stocked with bass and sunfish (phone (800) 529-2823 or (540) 898-8444; or visit www.lavistaplantation.com).

SOUTHERN-STYLE CARROTS

A easy, make-ahead side dish, this carrot casserole may be prepared
early in the day and refrigerated to bake before serving.

8 medium carrots, peeled and thinly
   sliced (3 cups)
½ cup finely chopped onion
½ cup mayonnaise
1 to 2 tablespoons grated horseradish
½ teaspoon salt

¼ teaspoon freshly ground black
   pepper
1 slice bread
1 tablespoon butter, softened
¼ teaspoon paprika

Preheat oven to 375° F. Butter a 1½-quart casserole; set aside. Bring 2 cups of water to a boil in a medium saucepan. Add carrots and cook 5 to 6 minutes. Drain, reserving ¼ cup cooking water. Place carrots in prepared casserole. Combine reserved cooking water with onion, mayonnaise, horseradish, salt, and pepper. Spoon over carrots.

Butter bread and sprinkle with paprika. Tear into chunks and place in a food processor or blender. Pulse until crumbly. Sprinkle breadcrumbs over carrot mixture. Bake uncovered 20 to 25 minutes. Makes 4 to 6 servings.

Recipe adapted from Specialties of the House, A Culinary Collection from the Friends and Regents of the Kenmore Museum, Fredericksburg, Virginia. Kenmore was the home of George Washington's sister Betty Lewis and is open to visitors (phone (540) 373-3381 or visit www.kenmore.org).

The Vegetable Garden

"Comp adopted as his personal contribution to the family welfare the responsibility of the vegetable garden. The rows were laid out with geometric precision and plowed free of crab grass before it could become more than a green fuzz on the surface of the earth. The yearly yield was a deluge of agrarian wealth, and the family rarely bought food at the grocery store. There were beans, butter beans, peas, tomatoes, okra, corn, squash, onions, potatoes, turnip greens, mustard, peppers, beets, radishes, carrots, and eggplant. They grew prolifically and they poured into the large back porch and kitchen in an overwhelming volume in season. They were eaten and they were canned and they were dried for the winter. The boy's mother had a tendency toward excessive generosity with the produce and would lade city kin with enough vegetables for a week when they came visiting. This infuriated Comp, who thought two tomatoes comprised a handsome enough gift for a thank-you note."

—Ferrol Sams,
Run with the Horsemen

EGGPLANT

Eggplant Pudding

"Quarter the eggplant and lay it in salt and water the overnight, to extract the bitterness. The next day, parboil, peel, and chop fine, and add bread crumbs (one teacup to a pint of eggplant), eggs (two to a pint of eggplant), salt, pepper, and butter to taste; enough milk to make a good batter. Bake in an earthen dish 20 minutes."

—Mrs. Robert L. Owen, Lynchburg, *Housekeeping in Old Virginia*, 1879

LOBLOLLY FARMS' EGGPLANT SALAD

Cold, thick, and aromatic, this salad is called melitzanosalata *in Greece. It's usually served as an appetizer with wine and olives, but is an excellent accompaniment to fish or roasted meat.*

3 medium eggplants (about 1 pound each), rinsed
1 small onion, minced
2 cloves garlic, minced
1 large tomato, chopped into small pieces

¼ cup olive oil
3 tablespoon red wine vinegar
1 teaspoon crumbled dried oregano
salt and pepper to taste
Greek black olives (such as kalamata)
green bell-pepper rings

Preheat oven to 375° F. Place eggplants on a baking sheet and bake 45 to 60 minutes, or until skin turns black (this will lend a smoky flavor to the salad). Peel off the skin while still warm; chop flesh into small pieces. Add onion, garlic, tomato, oil, vinegar, oregano, salt, and pepper. If needed to make salad thick and smooth, add additional oil and vinegar. Place in a salad bowl, cover, and chill well. Garnish with olives and pepper rings. Makes 6 servings.

Rick Hall owns and operates both Loblolly Farms and Seaside Produce in Accomac. Over the years, says his daughter Erin Hall, "we've grown pretty much every major crop (and some less major ones) that will grow on the Eastern Shore. This year we're growing cucumbers, peppers, jalapeños, eggplant, sweet potatoes, and Hayman potatoes, a white sweet potato. This is my mother Cynthia's recipe." Loblolly Farms sells produce to the general public. Call ahead to check availability (phone (757) 787-8955).

A SIMPLE RATATOUILLE FOR THE MICROWAVE

Make this version of the garden dish in the microwave in a matter of minutes.

1 (1-pound) eggplant, stemmed and cubed
1 cup chopped onion
2 cloves garlic, minced
1 teaspoon dried basil leaves or 1 tablespoon chopped fresh basil
2 medium zucchini, sliced ¼-inch thick

2 green bell peppers, cut into strips
2 medium tomatoes, coarsely chopped
¼ cup sliced black olives (optional)
2 tablespoons olive oil
¼ teaspoon each salt and pepper (or to taste)

Put eggplant, onion, garlic, and basil into a 3-quart casserole. Cover and microwave on high 6 minutes. Add zucchini and bell peppers; re-cover and microwave on high 4 minutes. Add tomatoes; re-cover and microwave on high 4 minutes. Drain vegetables; add olives and olive oil. Sprinkle with salt and pepper; toss gently. Serve warm or cold. Makes 4 servings.

FETTUCINE WITH EGGPLANT

Roasting eggplant at high heat evaporates the moisture and concentrates the flavor. The result is a textured, Mediterranean-inspired vegetarian main dish.

1 medium eggplant, about 1 pound
⅓ cup olive oil, divided
1 small green bell pepper, cut into strips
1 medium onion, coarsely chopped
2 cloves garlic, minced
3 medium tomatoes, about 1 pound (substitute canned diced tomatoes, if desired)
⅓ cup each halved, pitted green olives and raisins
¼ cup balsamic or red wine vinegar
2 tablespoons capers
¼ teaspoon each ground cinnamon, salt, and pepper
10 ounces fresh spinach fettucine, cooked and drained

Preheat oven to 450° F. Brush a baking sheet with 1 tablespoon oil. Trim off stem and cap of eggplant. Do not peel. Slice crosswise into ¼-inch slices. Place about one-third to half the slices on prepared baking sheet in one layer. Bake 10 minutes. Using a spatula, turn slices over and bake 5 minutes more; set aside and keep warm. Repeat until all eggplant slices are cooked.

Heat remaining oil in a skillet over medium-high heat. Sauté bell peppers until they turn soft and bright green. Add peppers to eggplant. Add onion and garlic to same skillet. Sauté 5 minutes, or until onion is soft. Add tomatoes, olives, raisins, vinegar, capers, cinnamon, salt, and pepper. Simmer until most of the liquid has evaporated. Cut eggplant slices into quarters; add to tomato mixture along with bell peppers. Heat and serve over fettucine. Makes 4 servings.

EGGPLANT

Eggplant

A member of the nightshade family that includes the potato, tomato, and sweet pepper, the eggplant was cultivated as far back as the fifth century A.D. by the Chinese. Ladies once made black dye from eggplant to stain their teeth before polishing. In contrast to the small eggplants of China, large-fruited varieties were cultivated in India, a major center of distribution for eggplant in the sixteenth century; eggplants continue to grow wild there.

Europeans had differing opinions about the purple vegetable. The Spanish, who introduced eggplant to America, called it the "apple of love." Northern Europeans, however, called it the "apple of madness." Before 1900, many ornamental varieties of eggplant grew in the United States.

GREENS

BRAISED SWISS CHARD, BABY BEETS, AND WHITE BEANS

*Bruce MacLeod uses fresh local ingredients
grown by Manakintowne Farms to create this and other regional dishes.*

½ cup dried cannellini beans
salt and pepper
12 baby striped beets or red beets
6 teaspoons unsalted butter, divided
1 medium-sized white onion, diced

2 cloves garlic, thinly sliced
1 bunch red Swiss chard, washed
  several times
1 cup chicken broth

Soak beans 6 hours or overnight. Drain beans; cover with fresh water by 1 inch. Bring to a boil, reduce heat to simmer, and cook until beans are tender, about 1 to 1½ hours. If necessary, add more water during cooking. Add ½ teaspoon salt and let sit 10 minutes; drain and set aside.

Preheat oven to 400° F. Discard all but ½-inch of beet stems; scrub well to remove dirt. Make a pouch of aluminum foil and place the beets inside. Add 1 teaspoon butter, ¼ teaspoon salt, a pinch of pepper, and an ice cube. Seal the pouch and roast about 30 minutes, or until tender; let cool. To avoid staining your hands, wear plastic gloves to rub the beet skin off; set beets aside.

In a medium saucepan over medium heat, melt remaining 5 teaspoons butter. Add onion and garlic; sauté until soft without browning. Remove stems of chard and cut on a bias into ¼-inch pieces. Add stems to saucepan and sauté briefly. Roughly chop the leafy portion of the chard. Add to saucepan along with reserved beans, beets, broth, and salt and pepper to taste. Cook 10 minutes, or until chard is tender. Makes 4 servings. Serve with game birds, rabbit, or chicken.

✒ The award-winning chef Bruce MacLeod has worked in restaurants nationwide and was the executive chef of Keswick Hall at Monticello, an elegant 48-room resort operated by Orient-Express Hotels, located minutes from the famous home of Thomas Jefferson. Part of Keswick Hall is the Ashley Room, a fine-dining restaurant (phone (800) 274-5391 or (434) 979-3440, or visit www.keswick.com). ✒

SAUTÉED LAMB'S QUARTERS

This dish features rich, earthy, nutty flavors of the green known as lamb's quarters and makes an excellent bed for grilled shrimp or scallops.

1 tablespoon olive oil
2 cloves garlic, minced
1 pound lamb's quarter tops

1 teaspoon lemon or lime juice
salt and pepper to taste

Heat oil in a large skillet. Sauté the garlic in the olive oil but do not brown. Toss in the lamb's quarters. The stems and leaves wilt but do not cook down as much as spinach. Season with juice, salt, and pepper. Makes 4 servings.

✒ This recipe was contributed by Terri Lehman of Goat Hill Farm, who advises that lamb's quarters, also known as wild spinach, is best if the top half of the plant, where the stems are still very tender, is the part that's harvested and cooked. Goat Hill Farm, a small property in the foothills of the Blue Ridge Mountains, is best known for its selection of heirloom tomatoes and specialty greens. ✒

When selecting greens, look for leaves that are fresh, young, tender, and free of blemishes. Select greens with healthy, green leaves; avoid those with coarse, fibrous, or yellow-green leaves. Most greens can be stored for up to two weeks. To maintain quality, refrigerate greens in a plastic bag. The young, tender leaves of most greens can be used for salads, while the older, but still tender, leaves are good for cooking.

For best results, cook turnip greens only until crisp tender, in as little water as will keep them from sticking, for about 20 to 25 minutes. To preserve their green color, cover them as they boil for about one minute, just long enough for them to wilt and compact. Then remove the cover for a minute to let the vapors escape. Repeat several times while cooking.

Cook mustard greens in a covered pan with a little water 15 to 20 minutes. To prepare kale, cut off and discard root ends, tough stems, mid-ribs, and discolored leaves.

COLLARDS WITH VIRGINIA HAM

Serve this vegetable in a bowl with its "potlikker."

1 meaty bone from a Virginia ham or
    1 pound smoked ham hocks
1 cup chopped onion
½ teaspoon Tabasco or hot pepper
    sauce

2 large cloves garlic, minced
2 pounds collard greens
2 cups dry white wine
2 tablespoons soy sauce

In a very large soup or pasta pot, place ham bone, onion, garlic, and Tabasco. Add enough water to barely cover bone. Cover and bring to a boil. Uncover pot and boil 5 minutes.

Cut tough stems from center of each collard leaf. Rinse leaves very well in cold water; then chop very coarsely. Add collards to pot along with wine and soy sauce. Bring liquid to a simmer; then cover and lower heat. If necessary during cooking, add more water so greens don't stick to the pot. Stirring occasionally, cook 1½ to 2 hours, or until collards are very tender. Remove ham bones and meat from pot; cool, chop meat, and return to pot. Makes 6 servings.

VIRGINIA SPICY-SAUSAGE-AND-KALE SOUP

Hearty enough for a main dish at lunch or dinner,
this recipe freezes well for a future fast meal.

1 cup chopped onion
2 cloves garlic, minced
2 tablespoons olive oil
1 pound potatoes, peeled and cubed
1 cup thinly sliced carrots
8 cups chicken broth, divided
1 pound fully cooked spicy sausage,
    cut into ¼-inch slices

6 medium tomatoes or 2 (16-ounce)
    cans tomatoes, chopped
1½ cups cooked kidney beans or
    1 (15-ounce) can
1 pound kale, washed, trimmed, and
    coarsely chopped
salt and pepper to taste

Heat oil in a large pot. Stir in onion and garlic and sauté about 2 minutes. Add potatoes, carrots, and 2 cups chicken broth. Simmer 10 minutes, or until potatoes are tender. Mash potatoes and carrots with a potato masher or purée some of mixture in blender. Add remaining broth, sausage, tomatoes, kidney beans, kale, salt, and pepper; cover. Stirring occasionally, simmer gently until kale is tender, about 20 minutes. Makes 8 (1½-cup) servings.

Greens

Descendants of wild cabbage, greens, such as kale, mustard, and collards, are among the oldest cultivated plants in the world. The Bible mentions the life cycle of mustard greens. Europeans have records from the first century A.D. of growing collards, which later turned up in the gardens of colonial Americans. Since antebellum times, greens have been a common part of the fare of Southerners. One popular tradition that has survived to this day is eating boiled greens, black-eyed peas, and hog jowls on New Year's Day to bring good luck for the coming years.

A variety of different plants are grown for greens, all of which offer excellent nutrition and taste. Most leafy greens are good sources of antioxidant vitamins like A, C, and E, which might reduce the risk of heart disease. They also contain calcium, iron, folic acid, fiber, and other important nutrients.

HERBS

If you purchase herbs in plastic packages, refrigerate them in the package. When buying fresh bunches of herbs, do not wash them before refrigerating. Place them in a plastic bag, squeeze the air out, and close securely. Wash just before using. You can freeze a bunch of fresh herbs to keep them longer; however, do not defrost them before using. Simply snip off the frozen leaves with scissors. If you can't find a fresh herb, use about one third the amount of dried herb.

PRESIDENT TYLER'S MINT JULEP

Sip a mint julep in the afternoon while reading the paper, as President John Tyler did on the south porch of his plantation home, Sherwood Forest.

12 fresh mint leaves on stem plus
  6 fresh mint leaves on stem
1 teaspoon sugar
2 teaspoons water

2½ ounces 86- to 100-proof good
  bourbon
1 thirsty gentleman

Tear the 12 mint leaves partially while leaving them on the stem. Place in a tall (12-ounce) glass or silver julep mug with sugar and water. Muddle or stir until sugar is completely dissolved. Fill glass with finely cracked ice. Add bourbon; stir. Ice will dissolve partially. Add more ice to fill glass to rim, again stirring. Tear the 6 mint leaves partially to release aroma and insert into ice with leaves on top. Serve with or without straw. Makes 1 serving.

This recipe was adapted from The James River Plantations Cookbook *by Payne Bournight Tyler, a member of President John Tyler's family. President Tyler was twice governor of Virginia; he also served as a U.S. president, a U.S. senator, a U.S. representative, and as chancellor of the College of William and Mary.*

BUFFALO HERB FARM'S SORREL SOUP

Sorrel is an herb that looks like spinach but with a stronger flavor; it is perfect in cream soups. In springtime, sorrel is mildest and best.

2 medium onions
4 tablespoons butter
4 large potatoes, scrubbed and diced
½ cup sorrel leaves, packed
½ cup spinach leaves, packed

½ cup parsley, packed
2 cups stock (vegetable or chicken)
½ cup white wine
1 teaspoon salt
2 cups half-and-half

Sauté onions in butter in large saucepan over medium heat for 5 minutes. Add potatoes, lower heat, and cook until tender. Add sorrel, spinach, and parsley. Add hot stock and simmer for 10 to 15 minutes.

Remove from heat and add wine and salt. Purée in blender until smooth. Add half-and-half and reheat to serve. If serving soup chilled, add half-and-half just before serving. Makes 4 servings.

Buffalo Springs Herb Farm is an eighteenth-century farmstead located in the northern end of Rockbridge County in the town of Raphine. Farm visitors can tour the gardens, visit the plant house stocked with herb plants and garden accessories, and purchase herbal products, dried flowers, and garden books at the Big Red Barn. A variety of herbal programs and workshops are scheduled throughout the season, and luncheons are offered on selected days and by reservation (phone (540) 348-1083 or visit www.buffaloherbs.com).

PURPLE BASIL PESTO

This lovely garnish adds a splash of color to any dish in which you might use basil.

3 cups chopped fresh purple basil   ½ cup pine nuts or walnuts
3 cloves garlic, minced   ⅓ cup olive oil

Combine all ingredients in food processor. Blend throughly. Toss with pasta, serve on minestrone, or use as a ravioli filling. Makes 1 cup.

Since 1989 Shenandoah Growers in Harrisonburg has offered a full line of fresh culinary herbs grown in the Shenandoah Valley and packaged year-round. Their certified-organic, hand-cut fresh herbs have been included in Virginia's Finest program for several years (phone (540) 896-6939 or visit www.freshherbs.com).

COLORFUL GRILLED VEGETABLES WITH PASTA

Like meats, vegetables derive a crispy texture and smoky flavor from grilling.

1 (1-pound) eggplant, cut into   4 cups (3-inch) sliced green onions
   ½-inch-thick slices   (about 2 bunches)
1 teaspoon salt, divided   2 tablespoons extra-virgin olive oil
¾ pound zucchini, quartered length-   1 tablespoon grated lemon zest
   wise and cut into 1-inch-thick   ½ cup thinly sliced fresh basil
   slices   12 ounces penne pasta, cooked
1 red bell pepper, seeded and   ¼ cup grated fresh Parmesan cheese
   quartered   (about 1 ounce)
4 plum tomatoes, halved

Place eggplant in a colander, sprinkle with ¾ teaspoon salt. Toss gently to coat. Cover and let stand 30 minutes. Rinse eggplant with cold water and drain well. Prepare grill. Place eggplant, zucchini, and bell pepper on grill rack coated with cooking spray. Grill 10 minutes, turning once. Add tomatoes and onions, cook 5 minutes, turning often. Remove the vegetables from grill, cut all into 1-inch pieces except tomato. Cut tomato halves in half lengthwise. Combine ¼ teaspoon salt, oil, lemon zest, and basil in large bowl. Add vegetable mixture, pasta, and cheese; toss well. Makes 6 main-dish servings or 12 side-dish servings.

This recipe was provided courtesy of Sharkawi Herb Farm in Broad Run (phone (540) 347-4747 or visit www.sharkawifarm.com).

Fresh Herbs

According to Pete Napolitano, author of *Produce Pete's Farmacopeia*, there's a powerful difference between fresh herbs and dried ones. He explains: "With the exception of oregano, which may be more flavorful dried, fresh green herbs have an aroma and flavor that make their dried counterparts seem bland by comparison. Just brushing your hand across a bunch of fresh thyme or pinching a leaf of basil or rosemary will release their rich fragrances—one whiff and you'll be in the mood to cook. Many home cooks grow a pot or two of herbs even if all they have is a sunny windowsill for a garden, but there are a number of fresh herbs that are widely available in good produce markets. Most are quite perishable and should be used as quickly as possible after purchase."

LIMA BEANS

LIMA BEAN HUMMUS

Traditional hummus made from chickpeas is tan. This interesting variation is a delightful pale green and makes a delicious appetizer served with pita bread wedges or crackers.

2 cups fresh lima beans or 1 (10-ounce) package frozen lima beans
1 large clove garlic, peeled and sliced
½ cup well-stirred tahini (Middle Eastern sesame paste)
5 tablespoons fresh lemon juice

½ teaspoon salt or to taste
dash cayenne pepper
ground black pepper to taste
chopped fresh parsley, chives, or green onions for garnish

Cook lima beans as package directs. Drain; save cooking water. In a food processor, combine cooled beans, garlic, tahini, lemon juice, salt, cayenne, and black pepper to taste. Purée. Add 1 to 4 tablespoons reserved cooking liquid to make an easily spreadable mixture. Refrigerate. Hummus will thicken upon refrigeration. Bring to room temperature before serving. Makes about 2 cups.

This unique recipe was created by Jane Olmsted, an avid herb gardener and longtime resident of Arlington.

THREE SISTERS SUCCOTASH

Corn, beans, and squash, known as the "three sisters," were planted together by Native Americans.

3 bacon slices, cut crosswise into ¼-inch strips
½ cup chopped onion
1 (15-ounce) can whole kernel corn, including liquid, or 1½ cups fresh kernels
1 (10-ounce) package frozen baby lima beans or 2 cups shelled fresh limas

2 small yellow squash, sliced (2 cups)
1 teaspoon low-sodium chicken bouillon granules
½ teaspoon ground cumin
¼ teaspoon pepper
1 medium-sized green bell pepper, cut into strips
½ cup cherry tomato halves

Cook bacon in large saucepan over medium heat until crisp and brown; drain and crumble. Sauté onion in bacon drippings until soft. Drain liquid from canned corn into saucepan. Add lima beans, squash, bouillon granules, cumin, and pepper; cover. Stirring occasionally, cook over low heat until limas test done, about 10 minutes. Stir in corn and bell pepper. Cook uncovered until vegetables are tender and most of liquid evaporates, about 5 minutes. Add tomatoes and reserved bacon; cover and let stand 5 minutes. Makes 6 servings.

Lima beans are quick and easy to prepare. Loaded with protein, thiamine, riboflavin, folate, iron, potassium, and fiber, they provide great nutritional value.

Lima beans can be purchased fresh in the pods, frozen, canned, or dried as seeds. Lima-bean pods should be well filled and dark green in color. When buying shelled lima beans, look for dry, plump limas with tender skin that are green or greenish-white in color. Shelled lima beans will stay fresh for about one week.

Lima Beans

Believed to be at least 4000 years old, beans, members of the legume family, are among the oldest foods known to man. Ancient Peruvians placed large lima beans of various colors in the tombs of their dead. On his first voyage to the New World, Columbus found lima beans cultivated by Indians in Cuba.

The lima is also known as the Sieva bean, butter bean, Civet bean, Sewee bean, Carolina bean, and sugar bean. When mottled with purple, lima beans are called calico or speckled butter beans. Small-seed baby-bush limas and large-seed Fordhook-bush limas are the main varieties sold commercially.

MUSHROOMS

THE BAILIWICK INN'S
WILD MUSHROOM AND BRIE SOUP

Rich mushroom flavor permeates this silky soup.

1½ tablespoons butter or margarine
¼ cup finely chopped onion
1 clove garlic, minced
½ pound shiitake mushrooms, stems discarded
½ pound cremini (brown) mushrooms or white button mushrooms

½ cup dry sherry
1¾ cups chicken broth
½ cup heavy cream
½ teaspoon dried thyme
3 ounces Brie cheese, rind removed
salt and pepper to taste

In a large heavy pot, melt butter over medium-high heat. Add onion and garlic; sauté until light brown. Coarsely chop shiitake and cremini mushrooms. Add to pot and sauté until mushrooms begin to give up some liquid. Add sherry and incorporate any brown bits that may be scraped from the bottom of pan. Simmer about 5 minutes to reduce slightly and evaporate alcohol.

Add broth, cream, and thyme. Bring to a gentle simmer. Remove ½ cup soup liquid and blend it with cheese in a small bowl. Return to soup and simmer briefly. Makes 4 servings. Recipe may be doubled or tripled.

This dish is a specialty of The Bailiwick Inn's Chef Jeffrey Prather. The first Confederate officer of the Civil War was killed on what is now the lawn of the inn, a Federal-style house in Fairfax that was built in the early 1800s and used as a hospital during the war. Today the 14-guestroom luxury inn includes a fine-dining restaurant where Chef Prather's eclectic American cuisine is served for lunch on Wednesday and Friday, and dinner daily, except on Monday (phone (703) 691-2266 or visit www.bailiwickinn.com).

LIMA BEANS

The Three Sisters

Although Native American tribes had plenty of land, they used it wisely for efficient food production. One ancient tradition was planting three vegetables together. Corn, beans, and squash were sown together on the same bit of land. This combination replenished soil nutrients and aided growth. Corn demands a lot of nitrogen, and beans replace it. The beans used the corn stalks as poles to climb. The squash shaded the land below, retaining moisture and blocking weeds. Gardeners today can still use this inventive way to grow highly nutritious fresh vegetables (see recipe on page 192).

Mushrooms

Unless you're an expert at recognizing poisonous mushrooms when foraging for wild fungi, it's best to purchase mushrooms in stores. The most common and least expensive is *Agaricus bispora* or "white button." The more exotic farmed mushrooms—such as shiitake, oyster, and portobella—have a more pronounced flavor. Their meaty texture belies the fact that mushrooms are extremely low in calories (only 20 calories for 5 medium white buttons). They're free of sodium and fat.

When selecting fresh mushrooms, look for tightly closed caps that are smooth, firm, and free of bruises and spots. Refrigerate packaged mushrooms in their own perforated carton. After opening or if purchased in bulk, store loose mushrooms in a paper bag or perforated bag. Use within three days.

Clean mushrooms just before using. Use a damp paper towel or mushroom brush to remove particles of growing soil. Or place the fungi in a colander and quickly rinse with cold water, patting dry with paper towels. Never soak mushrooms; they're porous and absorb water. If the stem end is dry, cut off a thin slice. Other than the tough stems of shiitakes, the entire mushroom is edible. There are about 20 to 24 medium mushrooms in one pound of fresh mushrooms, or six cups when sliced. Cooking mushrooms halves the yield.

L'AUBERGE PROVENÇALE'S EXOTIC MUSHROOM TIMBALE

Different varieties of mushrooms lend this dish its special appeal.

8 ounces mushrooms (shiitake, oyster, porcini, and/or others)
3 tablespoons unsalted butter
2 teaspoons chopped shallots
½ teaspoon chopped garlic
1 tablespoon chopped tarragon
1 cup milk
3 whole eggs plus 1 egg yolk
½ cup heavy cream
freshly grated nutmeg

Preheat oven to 325° F. If using shiitakes, discard stems. Slice mushrooms. In heated skillet add mushrooms and butter. Cook about 3 minutes. Add shallots, garlic, and tarragon and cook until tender. Add salt and pepper to taste. Strain, reserve liquid, and set aside. In a bowl, lightly beat eggs and yolk. Stir in cream. Add milk and reserved mushroom liquid. Add mushrooms, salt and pepper, and nutmeg. Stir gently to combine.

Butter lightly 4-ounce metal molds or ramekins and place in a deep baking dish. Ladle equal amounts of the mushroom mixture into molds. Carefully add hot water to deep baking dish about half way up the molds. Bake 25 minutes or until timbales feel firm. Remove from oven. Makes 4 servings.

This dish, created by Chef Alain Borel, is one of many that features the local ingredients of the Virginia hunt country and is served in the 1753 manor house of L'Auberge Provençale, a romantic country inn located about one hour west of Arlington, in Mt. Airy. Borel and his wife Celeste are fourth-generation innkeepers (phone (540) 837-1375 or (800) 638-1702, or visit www.laubergeprovencale.com).

REDNECK "RISOTTO"

Chef Jimmy Sneed served this popular mushroom grits recipe at his acclaimed restaurant in Richmond, The Frog and the Redneck.

2 pounds fresh shiitake mushrooms
extra-virgin olive oil
sea salt and ground black pepper
2 cloves garlic, peeled and chopped
2 shallots, peeled and chopped
4¼ cups chicken broth, divided
1 cup stone-ground grits
1 tablespoon butter
12 ounces high-quality sausage patties, cooked and cubed
6 ounces grated Parmesan cheese, divided

Shiitakes are generally very clean and may need only a slight brushing off. Remove stems from mushrooms; discard. Slice caps into ⅛-inch slices. Heat a cast-iron or other heavy pan until very hot. Pour in oil to a depth of ¼ inch. Add mushrooms and cook for 30 seconds. Add salt and pepper to taste. Add the garlic and shallots; cook and stir for 1 minute. Add ¼ cup broth to stop the cooking.

Heat the grits and 4 cups broth while stirring. Simmer 30 to 35 minutes. Stir in butter and 1 teaspoon salt. Mix the grits, sausage, shiitake mixture, and half of the cheese. Spoon the "risotto" into heated soup plates and sprinkle with the rest of the cheese. Makes 6 servings.

This was adapted from a recipe of Chef Jimmy Sneed, who with his partner Adam Steely operated The Frog and the Redneck restaurant in Richmond during the past ten years. Acclaimed by Esquire, Gourmet, and Bon Appetit magazines, Sneed has appeared on many TV programs and was nominated for a 1995 James Beard Award for Best American Chef in the mid-Atlantic region.

OKRA

MARY RANDOLPH'S "OCHRA" SOUP

An adaptation of an early nineteenth-century recipe, this flavorful vegetable soup included instructions such as, "At 12 o'clock, put in a handful of lima beans" and "At half past 1 o'clock add three young cimlins [yellow squash] cleaned and cut in small pieces."

4 cups chicken broth
3 cups sliced fresh okra or 1 (16-ounce) bag frozen cut okra
1½ cups shelled fresh or frozen baby lima beans
1 cup chopped onion
1 teaspoon salt

½ teaspoon pepper
½ teaspoon each dried thyme and basil
4 cups sliced yellow squash
4 cups chopped fresh tomatoes or 2 (16-ounce) cans diced tomatoes, including liquid

In a large saucepan over high heat, bring broth to a boil. Add okra, lima beans, onion, salt and pepper; cover pot, reduce heat, and simmer for 30 minutes. Add squash and tomatoes, including liquid. Simmer for 1 hour, stirring occasionally, until beans are very tender. Serve hot. Makes 3 quarts (12 servings). Mrs. Randolph suggests to "have rice boiled to eat with it."

The recipe for this dish appeared in the 1824 version of The Virginia Housewife, *written by Mary Randolph and reprinted by The University of South Carolina Press in 1985. She married David Meade Randolph in 1782. In the years that followed, Moldavia, their imposing home in Richmond, was celebrated for its lavish hospitality. A change in fortune forced Mrs. Randolph to open a boarding house in Richmond in 1808 where, by all accounts, the food and accommodations were splendid.*

FRIED OKRA

The recipe eliminates okra's slimy tendencies, rendering it crisp on the outside and moist inside.

1½ pounds fresh okra
2 eggs
⅓ cup buttermilk
vegetable oil for frying

1 cup flour
1 cup cornmeal
½ teaspoon salt

Rinse okra and pat dry with paper towels. Cut crosswise into ¾-inch slices. In a large bowl, beat eggs lightly. Stir in buttermilk; fold okra in gently, and allow to soak for 10 minutes. Combine flour, cornmeal, and salt in another bowl; set aside.

Heat at least an inch of oil in a heavy saucepan or deep fryer. Oil should be maintained at 375° F. Coat about 15 pieces of okra (or as many as will fit in one layer in the cooking vessel) in flour mixture and fry until golden brown. Remove with a slotted spoon and let drain on paper towels. Repeat with additional batches until all okra is fried. Makes 6 servings.

Okra

A staple in Southern diets for generations, okra originated in Ethiopia, spread across the Eastern Mediterranean and North Africa, and came to New Orleans with slaves. Gumbo z'herbs (with herbs) was once a traditional dish thought to bring good luck on Good Friday. It included okra and at least seven kinds of greens.

Okra is a member of the hibiscus family and its relatives include many ornamental flowering plants and cotton. Okra is a podded vegetable that has natural thickening properties when cooked, a quality used to enrich Creole gumbos. Whether mixed in gumbo, served with tomatoes, or fried, okra is a great-tasting Southern specialty that provides fiber, vitamin C, calcium, and potassium.

ONIONS

Onions

The Allium family isn't a singing group, but it does make recipes sing. It's difficult to make a savory recipe without some kind of onion. Fall harvest brings onions that are dry stored to last year-round. Their papery skins in brown, purple, and white are thicker than those enrobing spring's sweet and green onions or scallions, available fresh year-round. Dry onions need air and shouldn't be stored in plastic bags. Chilling onions cuts down on the sulfuric compounds that bring tears to your eyes when cutting them. For refrigerator storage, place onions in a paper bag. Chopped raw onions can be frozen; use them only for cooking.

Botanically, green and dried onions differ only in the stage of harvest. Left firmly rooted, scallions would grow into full-size onions. Scallions are sold with their roots on. Cut the roots off and pull off the outer, tough layer of skin. Use the white bulb and the light-green tender tops.

Shallots are mild and delicate pink, with just a hint of the odor of their cousin, garlic. Cut off both ends and remove the thin outer skin. Chives are valued for their green tops and can be grown in a windowsill pot year-round. Snip with scissors or slice cross-wise. Add them toward the end of cooking so they will stay bright green.

CARAMELIZED ONION TART

Raw onions transform into a rich sweetness when caramelized.

1 tablespoon butter	¼ teaspoon pepper
2 tablespoons olive oil	¼ teaspoon nutmeg
2 pounds large onions (about 4), peeled and chopped or thinly sliced	2 eggs
	¾ cup milk
	1 cup grated Swiss cheese, divided
1½ tablespoons flour	1 (9-inch) pie crust, not baked
½ teaspoon dried thyme	2 tablespoons grated Parmesan cheese
½ teaspoon salt	

To caramelize the onions: Melt butter with oil in a large skillet over medium heat. Add onions; when steaming, reduce heat to low. Stirring often, cook 40 to 50 minutes, or until golden brown.

Preheat oven to 400° F. Stir flour, thyme, salt, pepper, and nutmeg into onions. In a bowl, beat together the eggs and milk; add ½ cup Swiss cheese and the caramelized onions. Sprinkle remaining ½ cup Swiss cheese in bottom of pie crust and pour onion mixture on top. Sprinkle tart with Parmesan cheese and bake 30 to 35 minutes, or until center reaches 160° F. Let cool 15 minutes before serving. Makes 6 servings.

SILKY CREAMED ONIONS

This easy, luscious side dish pairs well with roasted meats and can be readily adapted for use with various kinds of peas.

2 (15-ounce) jars small whole onions	1 cup milk
4 tablespoons butter	½ teaspoon salt
6 tablespoons flour	¼ teaspoon white pepper
2 cups half-and-half cream	⅛ teaspoon ground nutmeg

Drain onions; set aside. Melt butter in a saucepan. Stir in flour. Gradually stir in cream and milk. Add salt, white pepper, and nutmeg. Stirring constantly over medium heat, cook until sauce thickens, about 5 minutes. Stir in onions and cook until onions are hot. Makes 6 servings.

ONIONS ROASTED IN SKINS

4 medium-sized yellow onions	½ teaspoon salt
¼ cup butter or margarine	dash of crushed red pepper flakes
1½ teaspoons mixed Italian seasoning	½ cup fresh bread crumbs
1 teaspoon sugar	

Preheat oven to 400° F. Line an 8-inch square baking dish with foil. Slice off stem and root ends of onions. Using a paring knife, cut a cone-shaped hollow 1 inch deep in the top of each onion. Place onion in dish with hollowed side up. Melt butter and stir in seasoning, sugar, salt, and pepper flakes. Add bread crumbs; mix. Spoon crumb mixture into hollowed onions. Bake about 1 hour, or until fork tender. Makes 4 servings.

PEAS

FRENCH-STYLE PEAS

2 green onions, thinly sliced
1 tablespoon butter
2 cups shelled fresh peas or 1 (10-ounce) package frozen peas

½ teaspoon sugar
⅛ teaspoon white pepper
1 cup shredded iceberg lettuce

Place onions and butter in a 1-quart casserole. Microwave on high 1 minute. Add peas, sugar, and pepper. Cover and microwave on high 4 to 5 minutes, or until peas are crisp tender. Stir in lettuce. Re-cover and let stand 2 minutes. Makes 4 servings.

SUGAR SNAP PEAS WITH PEPPER TRIANGLES

*The brilliant colors of the peppers and pea pods
make this a beautiful side dish to enliven the plate.*

1 orange, red, or yellow bell pepper
1 pound sugar snap peas, rinsed
2 tablespoons water*
4 teaspoons snipped fresh chives or
   2 teaspoons dried

½ teaspoon grated fresh lemon peel
1 tablespoon butter
2 teaspoons fresh lemon juice
⅛ teaspoon each salt and black
   pepper

Slice off stem end of bell pepper. Discard seeds and membranes. Cut pepper into 1-inch chunks; then cut each chunk diagonally to form triangles. Stem and de-string peas, if necessary.

Microwave directions: Place peppers and peas in a 1-quart casserole. Add water, chives, and lemon peel to casserole; toss to distribute ingredients. Cover with lid or vented plastic wrap. Stirring midway through cooking, microwave on high 4 to 6 minutes, or until peas turn bright green and are crisp tender. Drain liquid from peas. Add butter; stir to melt. Add lemon juice, salt, and pepper. Serve immediately.

Skillet directions: *Substitute oil for water in recipe. Heat 2 tablespoons oil in a skillet. Add peppers and peas. Sauté about 8 minutes, or until vegetables are crisp tender. Add chives, lemon peel, butter, lemon juice, salt, and pepper. Cook 1 minute longer and serve immediately. Makes 5 servings.

Green Peas

It's probably no accident that the sweet pea is the flower for April, the month when green peas begin to ripen. Fresh green peas are available fleetingly or not at all. When choosing fresh green peas from the garden or market, select those that are young, tender, and sweet, with crisp-looking well-filled pods and a velvety touch. Avoid flat pods and those noticeably pale green in color with a swollen appearance, which indicates they are overmature and tough. To shell peas, push on the seam until it cracks open; then slide the peas out.

Choose edible pod peas such as sugar snaps, snow, or Chinese pea pods that are firm and crisp, not wrinkled or wilted looking. Edible pods can have a tough string along the side. Nip the end away from the stem and pull the string that guards the pea's side. Seal fresh green peas as well as edible pod peas in plastic bags, refrigerate, and use as quickly as possible. Green peas can also be blanched, chilled, and frozen.

For optimal quality peas, commercial packers have four hours from picking in the fields to processing when the sugar and starch content is just right. Frozen peas cook especially fast and shouldn't be overcooked lest they turn olive green and shrivel. They can also be thawed and used in salads without cooking.

"Peas Come to Table"

The English pea was Thomas Jefferson's favorite vegetable. He grew 15 types of the English pea and wrote frequently about peas in his Garden Book, particularly noting when "peas come to table." By planting peas at various times, Jefferson could eat fresh peas from his garden from about May 15 to July 15.

True, the president liked peas, but his motive for carefully tracking the peas' progress stemmed from his competitive nature. He sought to win an annual neighborhood contest to see which farmer could harvest the first peas of spring. The winner of the contest had the honor of hosting the other contestants in a dinner that, of course, included the peas. Unfortunately, though Jefferson's mountaintop garden had a southern exposure with warmth and light ideal for growing peas, he often lost the contest to a neighbor named George Divers.

As Jefferson's grandson recalled: "A wealthy neighbor (Divers), without children and fond of horticulture, generally triumphed. Mr. Jefferson on one occasion had them first, and when his family reminded him that it was his right to invite the company, he replied, 'No, say nothing about it, it will be more agreeable to our friend to think that he never fails.'"

—Thomas Jefferson Foundation

JEFFERSON'S FRESH PEA SOUP

This recipe was one of our third president's favorite ways to eat peas. The soup is quite different from split-pea soup, which is made from dried peas. This fresh green soup is puréed.

1 cup fresh peas
2½ cups boiling water
½ teaspoon sugar
½ tablespoon chopped sorrel
   or parsley

1 tablespoon flour
1 tablespoon butter, melted
2 egg yolks

Drop peas into boiling water; cook until tender. Remove peas using a slotted spoon. Add sugar and sorrel to the pot liquid. Make a paste of flour and butter; whisk into liquid along with egg yolks. Stirring constantly over medium heat, cook until thickened. Purée peas and return to mixture. Makes 3 servings.

This recipe was adapted from Thomas Jefferson's Cookbook, *edited by Marie Kimball and published by the University Press of Virginia in 1976.*

SENATOR HANGER'S FRESH GREEN-PEA SALAD

Made the day before needed, this salad is especially easy to serve for a party.

2 cups fresh green peas or 1
   (10-ounce) box frozen peas
1 cup sliced celery
1 cup chopped green bell pepper
1 small onion, thinly sliced

2 hard cooked eggs, chopped
½ cup grated cheddar cheese
½ cup mayonnaise
3 tablespoons white wine vinegar
salt and pepper to taste

If using fresh peas, cook in ½ cup water until crisp tender. Freeze to make firm. If using frozen peas, do not defrost. Put frozen peas in a large serving bowl. Add celery, bell pepper and onion. Add eggs and cheese. In a separate bowl, mix mayonnaise with vinegar. Add to pea mixture with salt and pepper. Cover and chill overnight. If desired, serve on lettuce leaves. Makes 5 servings.

According to State Senator Emmett W. Hanger, Jr., member of the Agricultural, Conservation, and Natural Resources Committee, Virginia without a solid agricultural industry is like substituting salt for sugar in your favorite recipe. "Agriculture is key to Virginia's homespun lifestyle," says the senator. "Open space and land conservation has been an issue of great importance to me because the 24th Senatorial district includes part of Rockingham and all of Augusta county, the number-one and number-two agricultural districts in Virginia. I am sharply aware of the financial and environmental benefits of the agricultural industry and quite concerned about the future of family farms. I serve several agriculture commissions and introduced laws creating the Office of Farmland Protection, tax breaks for land donations that preserve open space, incentives for best management practices for farmers and industries, and aquacultural issues such as the sale of farm-raised trout."

PUMPKINS
AND SQUASH

PUMPKIN BREAD

Serve this bread cold or toast it for a breakfast treat.

3¾ cups sugar
3¾ cups self-rising flour
5 eggs
3 cups pumpkin

1½ cups oil
2 cups chopped nuts
1½ teaspoons ground cinnamon
1¼ teaspoons nutmeg

Preheat oven to 300° F. Grease liberally three loaf pans. In a large mixing bowl, combine all ingredients. Divide batter among the three pans and bake for about 1 hour, or until a toothpick inserted in the center comes out clean. Makes 3 loaves.

Shelvia Harrell lives in farming community Capron, where pumpkins are a popular crop.

DOMINIC'S PUMPKIN-BREAD PUDDING

No, it's not made with pumpkin bread—just day-old bread and puréed pumpkin, but it's rich, fragrant, and addictive.

FOR BREAD:

3 eggs
1 cup packed dark-brown sugar
16 ounces puréed (or 1 can) pumpkin
1 tablespoon each pumpkin-pie spice
    and cinnamon

1 tablespoon vanilla extract
2 cups half-and-half
4 cups cubed day-old white bread

FOR SAUCE:

½ cup butter (1 stick)
1 cup packed dark brown sugar

1 cup heavy cream

Preheat oven to 350° F. Butter a 2-quart rectangular glass baking dish; set aside. In a large mixing bowl, beat eggs lightly with a whisk. Blend in sugar, making sure all lumps are dissolved. Whisk in pumpkin, then pie spice, cinnamon, and vanilla. Blend in half-and-half and bread. Pour into prepared dish and bake 30 to 40 minutes, or until pudding reaches 160° to 165° F as measured in the center with a food thermometer. When it is close to time for the pudding to finish baking, combine butter and brown sugar for the sauce in a heavy-bottomed saucepan over medium heat. Stir until butter melts. Add cream and heat until sugar dissolves and sauce thickens slightly. Serve both pudding and sauce warm. Makes 8 servings.

Dominic Mobley owned Dominic's Waterside Grill. The casual restaurant was known for its baked-spinach-and-artichoke dip, prime rib, signature chicken, and devilishly good desserts, including this pudding.

Pumpkins

Both pumpkins and other squash were cultivated by Native Americans. As American settlers and Europeans became familiar with it in the eighteenth century, the pumpkin became part of legends and fairy tales, from Cinderella's pumpkin coach to Peter the Pumpkin Eater to the jack-o'-lantern in the Legend of Sleepy Hollow.

Today, Halloween celebrations are not complete without a carved pumpkin face! Pumpkins are a great source of vitamin A, calcium, potassium, phosphorous, vitamin C, and fiber. Many also enjoy the bright orange winter squash for its excellent taste and nutrition.

When buying, select a firm, heavy pumpkin without blemishes or spots. Look for pumpkins with a rich orange color and an attached, dry stem. A well-formed, heavy pumpkin will have more meat, less waste, and sweeter flavor than a lighter one. Avoid pumpkins with scars or cracks. If stored in a cool, dry, well-ventilated place, pumpkins will last up to three months. Pumpkin purée can be refrigerated for three to five days or frozen for later use.

CREAM OF SQUASH SOUP

This silky soup contains a significant amount of vitamin A.

2 tablespoons butter
½ leek, rinsed well and diced
2 medium potatoes, peeled and diced
6 small butternut squash, peeled and cubed

1 medium onion, diced
8 mint leaves
3 quarts chicken broth
1 cup heavy cream
salt and pepper to taste

Melt butter in a large saucepan; add leek, potatoes, onion, squash, and mint. Stir for 5 minutes. Add broth and bring mixture to a boil; then reduce heat to simmer until vegetables are cooked. Purée and gradually add cream. Add salt and pepper to taste. Lace in food processor. Makes 12 servings.

⁓ This recipe was provided courtesy of La Petite France, a fine-dining restaurant on Maywill Street in Richmond. Specialties include Dover sole, chateaubriand for two, and lobsters (phone (804) 353-8729 or visit www.lapetite france.net). ⁓

ACORN SQUASH WITH APPLESAUCE

To save 33 minutes, microwave the squash.

2 medium-sized acorn squash
1 teaspoon oil
2 cups unsweetened chunky apple-sauce

½ teaspoon cinnamon
2 tablespoons apple juice concentrate
¼ cup raisins

Preheat oven to 350° F. Cut squash in half. Using a spoon, scoop the seeds and fiber from the squash. Rub cut side of squash with oil and place squash on a large, oiled cookie sheet. Bake 45 minutes.

Note: To microwave squash, place cut-side down in a glass baking dish. Cover with vented plastic wrap and microwave on high 12 minutes.

In a small bowl, combine applesauce with cinnamon; add juice concentrate and raisins. Spoon mixture into hollowed squash. Bake an additional 20 minutes, or until piping hot. Makes 4 servings.

⁓ Recipe adapted from Specialties of the House, Kenmore Museum, Fredericksburg, Virginia. ⁓

BATTLETOWN INN'S BAKED SQUASH

This easy, flavorful side dish has graced the menu for decades to the delight of patrons.

7 small yellow squash, sliced (about 1¼ pounds
1 small onion, diced
2 tablespoons butter

½ cup light cream
¼ cup crushed saltine crackers
salt and pepper to taste
2 tablespoons bread crumbs

Preheat oven to 400° F. Butter a 1½-quart rectangular casserole; set aside. Boil squash in salted water until tender, about 10 minutes. Drain and mash. Sauté onion in butter. Add cream, crackers, squash, and salt and pepper to taste. Pour into a prepared casserole; dot with crumbs and additional butter. Bake 30 minutes, or until top is lightly browned. Makes 6 servings.

∽ *The Battletown Inn, located in Berryville, was built in 1809 as the family home of the town's founder. Its reputation for fine Virginia cuisine and hospitality still exists today. The restaurant features Southern cooking and New American cuisine. Lodging at the inn offers twelve rooms and mini-suites with private baths (phone (800) 282-4106 or (540) 955-3697).* ∽

MARK EARLEY'S SQUASH SAUTÉ

Mark Earley created this simple recipe to take full advantage of the abundance of squash that spills forth from his father's half-acre garden each summer.

1 tablespoon butter
2 tablespoons extra-virgin olive oil
1 large onion, thinly sliced
¼ cup white wine
2 yellow squash, thinly sliced
2 zucchini, thinly sliced

1 (4-ounce) can chopped mild green chilies
2 cloves garlic, minced
1 cup diced fresh or canned tomatoes
salt and pepper to taste
freshly grated Parmesan cheese

Heat butter and olive oil in a large skillet. Add onion; cook until tender, stirring often. Add wine and deglaze the pan. Add squash and zucchini; sauté until almost tender. Add chilies, garlic, and tomatoes; cook another minute. Add salt and pepper to taste; garnish with cheese. Makes 4 servings.

∽ *Republican candidate for governor in 2001 and the state's former attorney general, Mark Earley is a longtime supporter of the Right to Farm Act. He believes Virginia should add an agriculture secretary to its government. "Virginia's farming communities are the heartland of Virginia, the original stewards of our environment and open spaces," said Earley. The Norfolk native lives in Midlothian with his wife, Cynthia. They have six children.* ∽

Buyer's Guide to
SUMMER SQUASH

Summer squashes, such as yellow crookneck and zucchini, have soft shells, edible skins, and seeds, and are harvested before maturity. Look for squash that are well formed, with no cuts or bruises in the flesh. Squash should be tender, with skin that is glossy, not dull, hard, or tough. Avoid stale or over-mature squash, which will have a dull appearance and a hard, tough surface. Such squash usually have enlarged seeds and dry, stringy flesh. If refrigerated, summer squash will keep up to two weeks.

Zucchini

One of the most prolific vegetables, zucchini is a member of the squash family, which is native to the Americas and was first cultivated by Indians. The vegetable is a flavorful, nutritious one that can be enjoyed raw, steamed, boiled, fried, or baked. Zucchini seeds house most of the vegetable's flavor; the smaller the seed, the better the flavor.

Blending well with most vegetables and meats, zucchini is a regular part of the diet of millions of Americans. Zucchini, especially raw, is a good source of vitamin C and contains some vitamin A. It is low in sodium and has only about 12 calories per serving.

Zucchini should be firm and crisp, with a glossy color. Look for zucchini with small stems and no wrinkles near the ends. Avoid those with cuts or bruises in the flesh.

Zucchini is usually a deep green color with faint stripes or specks of gray or gold. The best-tasting zucchini is relatively small, up to seven inches long. It will keep in the refrigerator for one to two weeks.

OAK GROVE ZUCCHINI BREAD

Squares of this sweet, rich bread are easier to handle than slices from the typical loaf of zucchini bread, and the batter bakes faster in a shallow pan.

2 cups sifted unbleached flour
2 teaspoons baking soda
1 teaspoon salt
¼ teaspoon baking powder
3 teaspoons cinnamon
3 large eggs or 2 extra-large eggs

1 cup canola oil
1 cup brown sugar
2 medium zucchini, grated (2 cups)
2 teaspoons vanilla
1 cup raisins
1 cup chopped walnuts

Preheat the oven to 350° F. Grease 1 (13 × 9 × 2-inch) pan or 2 (8-inch square) pans; set aside. Sift together the flour, baking soda, salt, baking powder, and cinnamon. Combine the eggs, oil, sugar, zucchini, and vanilla in a separate bowl. Mix well. Stir in the flour mixture. Stir in the raisins and nuts and pour into prepared pan(s). Bake for 40 minutes for large pan or 25 minutes for 2 square pans, or until bread tests done. Cool on a wire rack. Makes 18 squares.

The healthy air revives you on the approach to Oak Grove Plantation Bed & Breakfast, a sienna-colored lane lined with loblolly pines. The air is alive with the sound of country—crickets, frogs, cicadas, and birds. Visitors enjoy sipping cool lemonade and iced tea on the front porch on lazy summer days. Today the inn, located in Cluster Springs, is operated by members of the same family that occupied the antebellum home in the 1820s (phone (434) 575-7137 or visit www.oakgroveplantation.com).

LYNNE'S ZUCCHINI FRITTERS

These easy, delicious vegetable pancakes can accompany a meal as side dish or preface one as an appetizer.

⅓ cup buttermilk baking mix such as Bisquick
¼ cup Parmesan cheese
¼ teaspoon each salt and pepper

2 eggs, slightly beaten
2 cups grated zucchini squash
2 tablespoons margarine, divided

Combine baking mix, cheese, salt, pepper, and eggs. Fold in zucchini. In a large skillet over high heat, melt 1½ teaspoons margarine. Drop 4 spoonfuls of batter into skillet and brown; turn once to brown the other side. Repeat making three more batches. Makes 16 (3-inch) fritters and about twice as many appetizers.

Lynne Kea was the vice mayor of Ivor.

SPINACH

SAUTÉED STRIPED BASS ON SHALLOT-INFUSED SPINACH

This recipe showcases two of Senator John Chichester's favorite Virginia foods.

1 pound fresh spinach
3 slices high quality white or Italian bread
4 striped-bass (rockfish) fillets, about 1½ pounds

6 tablespoons olive oil, divided
1 shallot, minced
salt and pepper to taste
1 fresh lemon, cut into 4 wedges

Remove stems from spinach. Wash several times in warm water; drain, leaving water remaining on leaves. Chop spinach very coarsely and set aside.

Remove crusts from bread. Tear bread into large chunks and place in a food processor fitted with a steel blade. Pulse 30 seconds to make crumbs. Transfer breadcrumbs to a piece of wax paper. Rinse bass and pat dry with paper towels. Sprinkle with salt and pepper and dredge in breadcrumbs. Heat 2 tablespoons oil in a large nonstick skillet over medium-high heat for several minutes. Cook fish about 4 minutes on each side, or until crumbs are brown. Transfer fish to a plate and keep warm.

Wipe pan clean with a paper towel. Heat remaining 4 tablespoons oil in same skillet. Add shallots and sauté 30 seconds. Immediately add spinach, cover, and steam just until spinach wilts, about 5 minutes. Distribute spinach on four dinner plates and center fish on top of spinach. Serve with lemon wedges. Makes 4 servings.

The Honorable John H. Chichester was a State Senator for 29 years. He was first elected in 1978. Senator Chichester was chairman of the Senate Finance Committee, chairman of the Senate Agriculture, Conservaion and Natural Resources Committee, chairman of the Council of State Governments, and serves on the Board of Trustees for the Jamestown-Yorktown Foundation. He retired in 2007. He and his wife, Karen, live in Fredericksburg.

EASY SPINACH SOUFFLÉ

Time this dish to emerge from the oven while diners are being seated, so it will stay high and fluffy. Separating the eggs is the most difficult step of this easy side dish.

1 (10-ounce) package frozen chopped spinach
⅓ cup cooking liquid from spinach
½ cup butter
¼ cup flour

⅓ cup milk
2 eggs, separated
¼ teaspoon each salt and pepper
½ cup grated Swiss or cheddar cheese

Preheat oven to 350° F. Grease a 1½-cup soufflé dish; set aside. Cook spinach according to package directions, reserving ⅓ cup liquid. Drain spinach well; set aside. Place butter in a large saucepan over medium heat. When melted, whisk in flour and cook, stirring constantly, 2 to 3 minutes. Stir in milk and reserved spinach liquid. Cook until thick. Remove from heat; add spinach, egg yolks, salt, and pepper.

Beat egg whites until stiff enough to hold peaks. Fold into spinach mixture. Pour mixture into prepared dish and top with cheese. Set dish in a shallow pan of water and bake 35 to 40 minutes, or until knife inserted in center comes out clean. Makes 4 servings.

Spinach

Spinach is a rather late arrival to the world's farmers market. It originated in southeast Asia and traveled to Spain with the Moors in the eighth century. Spinach is one of the first vegetables that can be planted in spring; it can also be planted in August for fall harvest.

Choose large, fresh, crisp, dark-green leaves, whether the flat or crinkled variety. Avoid decayed, crushed, wilted, or bruised leaves. Don't wash spinach before storing it in the refrigerator. However, before using, rinse judiciously several times in warm water. Fresh spinach keeps three to five days in the refrigerator. It is high in vitamins A and C and iron and is extremely low in calories.

Truck Farming

Irrigation, the railroads, and gas-powered vehicles changed agriculture forever. Farmers could grow more crops on less desirable, distant land and get their produce to market easier. After 1887, when refrigerated trains were introduced, intensive fruit and vegetable growing for distant urban centers quickly began to replace the local garden. Farmers were quick to use motorized transportation to carry perishable produce to nearby urban centers or rail shipment points. Thus the term "truck farming" was coined.

VIRGINIA'S EXPLORE PARK

The park is set amid 1,100 acres of rolling hills and tall stands of trees. Hiking trails, fishing, canoeing, kayaking, and mountain biking are available.

DAYS/HOURS: The outdoor living-history museum is open from April to November. Recreation areas are open all year on a limited basis.

FEES: Admission is charged.

DIRECTIONS: Travel south on US 220 from Roanoke and turn north onto the Blue Ridge Parkway. At the park's sign at milepost 115, turn right onto the Roanoke River Parkway and drive 1.5 miles.

MORE INFORMATION: Phone (800) 842-9163 or visit www.explorepark.org.

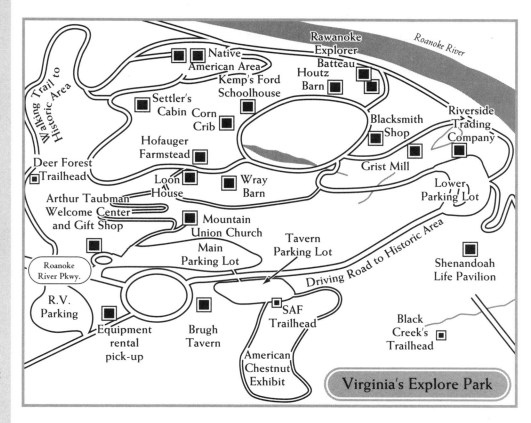

The settlement of the Appalachian region in western Virginia began with wild game—buffalo, elk, and deer—creating a pathway through the valleys in search of food. This route became known as the Great Warrior Path once Iroquois from the north began to move south. When Europeans began to arrive in the area, the path became known as the Great Wagon Road.

Horse-and-wagon teams gave way to massive Conestogas. By 1775, the road stretched 700 miles, from the Great Lakes through the Shenandoah Valley. Historians say that the road was one of the most heavily traveled in America toward the end of the colonial era. Virginia's Explore Park depicts the history of the land and the people who traveled this road to settle western Virginia.

Begin your tour at the Hospitality Plaza. Tickets and information are available in the Arthur Taubman Welcome Center. Also within the Hospitality Plaza are two historic buildings and the modern Blue Ridge Parkway Visitor Center, which features a 100-seat theater, the Rawanoke Trading Company (a gift shop), and two exhibit galleries.

The Brugh Tavern, built as a private residence between 1780 and 1800, serves lunch and dinner daily except Monday. You might even see a private wedding taking place at the nearby Mountain Union Church (circa 1880). A beautiful example of Greek Revival architecture, the church was originally located in Botetourt County and was reconstructed here from 1995 to 1998.

TOURING THE HISTORIC AREA

The park's biggest feature is the outdoor living-history museum, which depicts life in the area as it might have been at three distinct times—in 1671, 1740, and 1850. Three re-created settlements, separated by walking trails, are set off in shady, picturesque areas and are staffed by historically-garbed interpreters who reenact what it was like to live and work at the place and time featured.

The 1671 Native American Village replicates eastern woodland culture and lifestyles. Interpreters demonstrate the skills of the Siouan-speaking people who lived along the broad floodplains, mountains, and ridges of the Great Valley at the time of their first contact with European people.

The 1740 Settler's Cabin is typical of the temporary cabins that had to be erected for shelter by early settlers. Also shown are the gardens that had to be planted for food. This rough "replica" cabin and its interpreters help visitors visualize a settler family's first cabin and experience their struggle to "wrest their existence from a strange new world."

The nineteenth-century settlement is the most extensive and includes the 1880 to 1890 Esom Slone's Gristmill, which once stood on the south prong of Pigg River, about four-and-a-half miles northwest of Ferrum. The skills of a blacksmith were among the services most needed by early settlers, whose wagons were in constant need of repair, and are demonstrated in the 1850 Blacksmith Shop.

Also featured are a cargo boat and school typical of the period, as well as the impressive Hofauger Farmstead (circa 1837), where Samual and Elizabeth Hays Hofauger raised four children. The German-style farmhouse was originally located on Colonial Avenue in Roanoke County. According to one of the park's interpreters, "The bricks would have been purchased, but Mr. Hofauger would have had to cut down the logs for the home's walls. The framed logs would first have to be chinked with wood scraps to close the gaps with a lime-and-mud mixture applied to insulate and waterproof the walls."

Visitors to the park can also take advantage of six miles of nature trails, a fishing area, and canoeing and kayaking on the Roanoke River, as well as twelve miles of mountain-bike trails.

African American Farmers

❖ In 1920, one in every seven farmers was African American and they owned 14% of the nation's farms.

❖ In 1982, one in every 67 farmers was African American.

❖ In 1910, African American farmers owned 15.6 million acres of farm land nationally; by 1969 they held only 6 million acres.

❖ In 1982, African American farmers owned 3.1 million acres of farmland nationally.

❖ Between 1920 and 1992, the number of African American farmers in the United States declined from 925,710 to 18,816, or by 98%.

❖ In 1984 and 1985, the U.S. Department of Agriculture lent $1.3 billion to farmers nationwide to buy land. Of the 16,000 farmers who received those funds, only 209 were African American.

❖ Almost half of all African American–operated farms are smaller than 50 acres.

❖ In the late 1980s, there were less than 2000 African American farmers in the United States under the age of 25.

❖ Today, there are only 18,000 black farmers, representing less than 1% of all farms.

—Black Farmers and Agriculturists Association (phone (252) 826-2800)

part seven
GRAINS

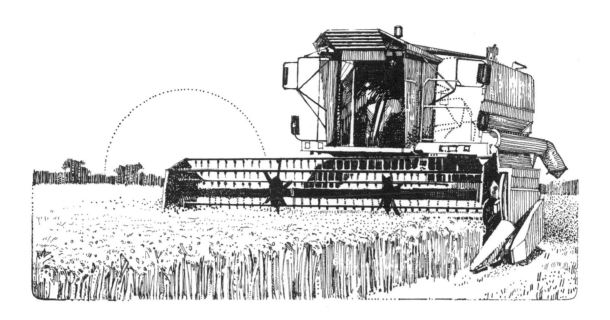

Whereas western Virginia's ridges and valleys are best-suited for raising livestock, dairy cows, and poultry, the state's flat coastal plain—the Eastern Shore peninsula, bounded by the Chesapeake Bay and the Atlantic Ocean—is ideal for growing wheat.

Unless you take the long road around the Bay or cross the Tunnel-Bridge to Norfolk and drive north, you'd need a boat to reach Virginia's other wheat fields. The next major wheat-producing counties, after Accomac and Northampton, are on the Northern Neck (Northumberland and Westmoreland in the Potomac River area), and Essex County along the Rappahannock River. While waiting for the wheat to grow, you might want to go crabbing or fishing in the nearby Bay or rivers. Crab cakes make great whole-wheat sandwiches.

Essex is also the top barley-producing county, followed closely by Westmoreland. Rye is grown in the same areas as barley.

Of the three grains, wheat production grown on 170,000 acres contributes by far the most money to Virginia's economy, earning cash receipts of about $35 million annually, while barley and rye together contribute nearly $10 million. Yet the opposite holds in terms of Virginia's grain contributions to the country as a whole. The Old Dominion ranks 8th among all U.S. states in barley production, 15th in rye production, and 20th in wheat.

When Virginia's grain production was at its highest, during the 1930s, five times more acreage was harvested than is today. But today, grain fields on the mainland are adjacent to the busy I-95 corridor, where housing and population have mushroomed. Additionally, some of the prime wheat-growing Northern Neck and Eastern Shore real estate has been gobbled up by affluent city dwellers for vacation homes.

Nevertheless, for a state barely half the size of North Dakota (America's leading wheat-producer) but with five times the population, Virginia's grain harvest is impressive.

Wheat

Grain, whole or ground into meal or flour, is the principal food of man and of domestic animals. Its cultivation began in the Neolithic period. Wheat was one of the first grains domesticated by humans. Bread wheat is known to have been grown in the Nile valley by 5000 B.C., and its cultivation spread from the Mediterranean eastward and northward, reaching England by 2000 B.C. Since agriculture began, wheat has been the chief source of bread for Europe and the Middle East, while rice has been more important in eastern Asia.

Wheat, which is the dry fruit of a cereal grass, is usually planted by sowing machines of the drill or broadcast type. Little cultivation is necessary beyond preparation of the land by plowing, harrowing, and, sometimes, dusting to control pests. Like the seeds of most grains, wheat seeds grow in concentrated clusters that are gathered efficiently by modern mechanical harvesting machines. The food content of the seeds (as they are commonly called) is mostly carbohydrate, but some protein, oil, and vitamins are also present. Wheat and other grains are easy to handle, and because of their low water content can be stockpiled for long periods.

chapter one

WINTER WHEAT

∽ *Virginia was the first colony to grow wheat, beginning in the early 1600s. Today, wheat is the eighth most lucrative agricultural crop; almost 14 million bushels are harvested each year. Growers choose what type of wheat to grow based upon adaptability, climate, and yield. The wheat suitable for growing in Virginia is winter wheat, which is planted in the fall for spring harvest. Winter wheat is a white cereal grass used mainly to make flour for bread and pastries. Wheat crops are generally rotated with corn, hay, and pasture in Virginia.*

MELT-IN-YOUR-MOUTH DINNER ROLLS

Make pan rolls or Parker House rolls with this recipe.

1 (1¼-ounce) packet active dry yeast
2 cups warm water (about 105° F), divided
½ cup shortening
3 tablespoons sugar

1½ teaspoons salt
1 egg
5 to 6 cups flour, sifted
melted butter for tops of rolls

Dissolve yeast in ¼ cup warm water. In a large mixing bowl, cream shortening with sugar and salt. Stir in egg and dissolved yeast. Stir in flour alternately with the remaining 1¾ cups warm water. Knead until smooth. Oil a large mixing bowl and place dough in it, turning to coat. Cover with a tea towel and let rise in a warm place until double in size, about 1 hour. Punch down dough.

To make Parker House rolls: Remove ⅓ of dough. On a lightly floured surface, roll out ⅜-of-an-inch thick. Cut with a floured 2½-inch biscuit cutter. Brush top lightly with melted butter and fold each piece of dough almost in half so that larger part overlaps; press folded edge. Place, 1 inch apart, on a lightly buttered cookie sheet. Brush tops with melted butter. Cover with towel and let rise in a warm place. Repeat with remaining 2 batches of dough.

To make pan rolls: Remove ⅓ of dough and roll with hands into a 12-inch rope. Cut crosswise into 12 pieces. Roll into balls and place in a buttered 9-inch layer-cake pan. Brush tops with melted butter. Cover with towel and let rise in a warm place. Repeat with remaining 2 batches of dough.

Preheat oven to 400° F. Bake Parker House rolls 12 to 15 minutes; bake pan rolls 15 to 20 minutes. Makes 36 rolls.

Recipe provided courtesy of Woodbourne, originally a part of the Poplar Forest tract of approximately 4,000 acres inherited by Thomas Jefferson from his wife Martha Wayles Skelton. The historic home was built in three stages—a central portion and two wings—from 1780 to 1820. The home and more than 900 acres of land were purchased from Thomas Jefferson in 1810 by attorney William Radford whose descendants still occupy the residence. It is not open to the public.

AUNT SILENCE'S JUMBLES

Before circles of dough became common, the dough for these crisp, thin lemon cookies, derived from the sixteenth-century English recipe for "jumbals," was cut into thin strips and twisted into various shapes like pretzels.

1⅔ cups sugar	zest from 1 lemon (grated yellow
1 cup butter (2 sticks), at room	color from peel)
temperature	1 teaspoon lemon extract
4 eggs	2¾ cups flour (not sifted)
2 tablespoons lemon juice	

Preheat oven to 350° F. Butter cookie sheets; set aside. In a large mixing bowl, cream sugar with butter. Beat in eggs, zest, juice, and extract. Stir in flour. Make only 12 cookies at a time. Drop 1 teaspoon of batter onto cookie sheet; spread thin. Repeat to fill cookie sheet. Bake until light brown around the edges, about 12 minutes. Transfer from cookie sheet to cooling racks; let cool completely. Store in an airtight container. Makes 96.

This recipe was provided courtesy of Scotchtown, one of Virginia's oldest plantation houses and home to Patrick Henry during the Revolutionary War. This National Historic Landmark is located ten miles west of Ashland in upper Hanover County (phone (804) 227-3500 or visit www.apva.org/scotchtown).

Patrick Henry's Home

"Give me liberty or give me death!" intoned Patrick Henry, Virginia's first governor, at St. John's Episcopal Church in Richmond. The date was March 3, 1775, and Henry was living at Scotchtown, a tobacco plantation and home, which he purchased in 1771 for 600 pounds. It was here, in the home's basement, where his first wife Sarah Shelton Henry reputedly was kept when she "lost her reason" after the birth of their sixth child, Edward, around 1771. Today her condition might be attributed to post-partum depression. Sarah, or "Sallie," ran the plantation while her husband galloped about appearing in courthouses and political assemblies. After Sallie died in 1775, Henry married Dorthea Dandridge in 1777. She was the granddaughter of Governor Alexander. Henry had 17 children in all. Docent Harriet Campbell Little used to play in the deserted 16-room manor house as a girl and got the Association for Preservation of Virginia Antiquities interested in buying Scotchtown, which they renovated and opened to the public in 1964. The home is furnished with antiques and showcases an original portrait of George Washington painted by Charles Peale Polk. Outbuildings include a kitchen, Henry's law office, and a 29-foot-deep dry well that kept food at 42° F year-round. Scotchtown is open April through October (call (804) 227-3500).

DEVELOPMENT OF THE REAPER
BY VIRGINIAN CYRUS MCCORMICK

The fact that most Americans work in cities and not on farms is due in great part to Cyrus McCormick's 1831 invention of the mechanical reaper, a horse-pulled mechanism that cut as much grain in one day as 12 to 16 men with reaping hooks could cut in the same period. McCormick was a native Virginian, and his "Virginia Reaper," as it was known, cut wheat stalks and laid them on the ground to be raked, bundled, and carried out of the field.

The back-breaking work of harvesting grain by hand, portrayed in Egyptian tomb paintings, was accomplished essentially the same way for 7000 years until the 22-year-old McCormick came along. In 1831, 90% of the population was engaged in farming to feed the nation; today fewer than 2% of the U.S. population is directly involved in farming. For this invention, McCormick was inducted into the National Inventors Hall of Fame.

McCormick's father, Robert, Jr., was born at Walnut Grove, the family farm in Rockbridge County, near Steeles Tavern and Lexington. Robert grew up, married Mary Ann Hall, and settled in a log cabin on the McCormick land. After inheriting Walnut Grove, he purchased three adjoining farms, which increased the size to 1800 acres. Here he operated sawmills and flour mills; he also was fond of astronomy and other sciences.

Cyrus's father was a dreamer who invented and patented a clover sheller, hempbreak, blacksmith bellows, and hydraulic machine and had been trying to build a reaping machine. All his inventing invoked his son's talent. Born in 1809, Cyrus grew up experimenting with various tools in the hope of designing equipment that would simplify farmers' work. He tinkered in his father's blacksmith shop, made a light cradle to ease the work at harvest, and built a world globe on which he placed the seas and continents. He also liked to play the fiddle.

Cyrus had observed his father's unsuccessful efforts to make a mechanical reaper, but the invention was not a simple one; working out the cutting process was its most challenging aspect. In 1831, Cyrus built his first reaper. He demonstrated it on John Steele's field on wheat and oats and continued to make improvements before patenting it in 1834. McCormick finally offered his reaper for sale in Virginia in 1840. It enabled farmers to harvest more than ten acres of grain per day. Before his invention, farmers harvested with cradle scythes, and a skilled worker could harvest at most two or three acres per day.

Sales of McCormick's reaper at first spread slowly, but then so fast he couldn't produce enough in the Walnut Grove blacksmith shop. In 1847, McCormick moved his manufacturing operation to Chicago, due to the city's central location in the Midwest. He could ship the reapers to eastern states via the Great Lakes and to the South via the Mississippi River. McCormick became internationally famous in 1851, when he demonstrated his reaper in London. By late 1851, Chicago newspapers reported that the McCormick Harvesting Machine Company was the largest implement factory in the world. When Chicago became a major railroad center that decade, sales and distribution grew further.

McCormick remained president of his company until his death in 1884. In 1902, the company merged with four other implement companies to form the International Harvester Company (now Navistar International Corporation). McCormick's sons, Cyrus, Jr. and Harold Fowler McCormick, presided over the new company during its first 40 years.

In addition to McCormick's success as an inventor, he was also a pioneer in business techniques. He offered easy credit, so farmers could pay for machines from their increased harvests. He gave written performance guarantees, and he advertised his product.

TRADITIONAL HARVESTING METHODS

"Reaping Hook" or Sickle
With the sickle or reaping hook one man could cut from one-half to one acre in a hard day's work. The cut grain was later bound by hand.

Cradle
The cradle was the most efficient means of cutting grain before McCormick's invention of the reaper. The cradle consisted of a broad scythe with a light frame of four wood fingers attached to it. The advantage of the cradle was that by a turn to the left the operator could throw the grain into a swath, ready to be raked and bound into sheaves. This improvement was introduced in America about 1776, according to Professor Brewer of Yale, and was the common instrument of grain harvesting as late as 1840. For cradling grain, two acres was considered a day's work.

Scythe
The scythe was the companion tool to the reaping hook or sickle. It was always used for mowing grass but sometimes oats and barley were cut with it. It was not generally used for cutting wheat. With the scythe a man could cut up to three acres a day.

Silos

Tall cylinders that rise high above the farm, silos are as much a part of the rural landscape as the red barn. Silos store silage, the chopped-up wheat, oats, or hay that farmers feed their livestock over the winter months. Before silos were invented, cows gave less milk during the winter because they had no green grass to eat. Silos enable farmers to store a winter's supply of feed without it becoming spoiled.

Silos convert the grain or fodder through anaerobic acid fermentation into succulent feed similar to sauerkraut. Usually made of concrete, ringed with steel reinforcements, and capped with a metal dome, silos often are kept sealed airtight to allow microbial bacteria that don't use oxygen to begin the process of fermenting.

At the bottom of the silo, a compressed air blower sends the grain or fodder through a chute or pipe attached to the exterior up to the top, where it goes into the silo through a sealable door. Inside the silo, a machine that usually rests on top of the silage evenly scatters the silage and unloads it when needed. A winch on the outside pulls a cable that raises or lowers the unloader/distributor inside the silo as needed.

McCORMICK'S—AND THE WORLD'S—FIRST REAPER

This first machine required only two people for operation: a person to ride the horse and a man to rake the cut grain from the platform. The world's first reaper incorporated seven basic elements that have ever since been found essential in virtually all grain-cutting machines: (1) straight reciprocating knife; (2) fingers or guards; (3) revolving reel; (4) platform; (5) master wheel; (6) side moving cutter; (7) divider at the outer edge of the cutter bar.

McCormick's reaper of 1831 shows the wide master wheel which carried most of the weight of the machine and, through ground transaction, supplied power to operate the reel and the reciprocal knife. While this first machine required only 2 people for operation, it cut as much grain in one day as 4 to 5 men with cradles or 12 to 16 men with reaping hooks.

McCORMICK'S PATENT REAPING MACHINE

The McCormick Patent Reaping Machine of 1857 combined machinery for reaping and mowing. Its chief improvements over the 1831 reaper were seats for driver and raker, a cutting knife fabricated in sections rather than one piece, and an all-metal main wheel. This machine also cut a wider swath than the first reaper and was pulled by two horses. The McCormick Patent Reaping and Mowing Machine was manufactured from 1852 to 1865, with various improvements being incorporated from time to time.

McCORMICK'S AUTOMATIC SELF-RAKE REAPER

The McCormick Automatic Self-Rake Reaper was originally patented in 1858 and was manufactured and sold in large numbers from 1862 until about 1875, when it was replaced by a more efficient machine bought out by McCormick. The harvester, known as McCormick's "Old Reliable," was a one-man machine that released yet another person to aid in other harvest jobs. Its automatic rake swept cut grain off the platform, depositing the grain in neat gavels on the ground, ready to be bound into bundles by the hand binders.

McCORMICK'S COMBINATION REAPER AND MOWER

This machine was manufactured and sold by McCormick from 1869 to 1879. The "Advance," a combined mower and reaper, had an automatic rake as part of the reel. Platform and reel were removable so that the machine could be used as a straight hay mower.

McCORMICK MARSH TYPE HARVESTER

The McCormick Marsh Type Harvester, built from 1875 to 1883, consisted of the same cutting mechanism as McCormick's earlier reapers, with an elevator and binding platform added. Two men rode on the platform, binding grain by hand as it was delivered by the elevator. This machine was patented as early as 1858 but was not put into general use until 1875. With the Marsh type harvester, two men bound the grain while earlier harvesters had required four to five men for binding.

McCORMICK'S HARVESTER AND BINDER

McCormick Harvester and Binder of 1876 was the first practical self-binder ever built. People traveled miles to see the first machine controlled by one man, which cut and bound grain in a single operation. McCormick built and sold 50,000 of these binders between 1877 and 1885.

McCormick Harvester and Twine Binder manufactured in 1881 was McCormick's first binder, which tied the bundles with twine. After the development of this machine, only minor improvements tending to give greater durability and lighter draft were added, such as an adjustable canvas grain shield on the rear of the platform.

McCORMICK-DEERING TRACTOR BINDER

The McCormick-Deering Tractor Binder is operated from the Farmall tractor through the shaft running out of the rear, thus making the binder independent of ground conditions. This power take-off, as it is called, is regularly supplied with all Farmall tractors. The binder, being independent of ground conditions, can operate when a horse-drawn binder would find it difficult, if not impossible, to cut grain.

McCORMICK-DEERING HARVESTER-THRESHER

McCormick-Deering Harvester-Thresher is the most modern type of grain-harvesting machine. It cuts 40 to 50 acres per day and threshes the grain, delivering it after a thorough cleaning, into a grain tank. From the tank, the grain can be drawn off into a motor truck or wagon and hauled to the granary.

The Windrow-Harvester cuts grain and leaves it in a windrow on top of the stubble. After the grain cures on the stubble it is picked up by an attachment on the platform and threshed. The windrow-harvester makes it possible to cut grain earlier (avoiding natural hazards such as winds and hails) and to better harvest woody grain (because the weeds dry out with the crops before threshing).

—Source: *McCormick Reaper Centennial Source Material,*
International Harvester Company: Chicago, 1931

Byrd Mill

Virginia grain gourmands and fine chefs such as Walter Bundy of the Jefferson Hotel and Jimmy Sneed of The Frog and the Redneck use the authentic stone-ground products of Byrd Mill. The original mill was built in 1740, and young Patrick Henry visited it often, bringing corn, wheat, and buckwheat from his father's nearby plantation. Byrd Mill operated at its original site until 1968, when fire ended production in the original building. Byrd Mill relocated to Ashland, Virginia, and still manufactures many of those "old tyme" products such as buckwheat, whole wheat, and unbleached flour, stoneground cornmeal and grits, and gourmet mixes from $3.

Buckwheat, a popular crop of Virginia colonists, is known for its great nutritional value. *Pioneer's Porridge*, made from stoneground white and yellow grits, cracked wheat, and whole rice, is reminiscent of the days when porridge was boiled in a large kettle over an open fire. *Stoneground grits*, made from white corn, have a rich corn flavor and hearty texture. Boil these grits in chicken, beef, pork, or wild game broth as do chefs Bundy (page 49) and Sneed (page 194), to serve as a delicious dinner side dish. Phone (800) 247-8357 or visit www.byrd mill.com.

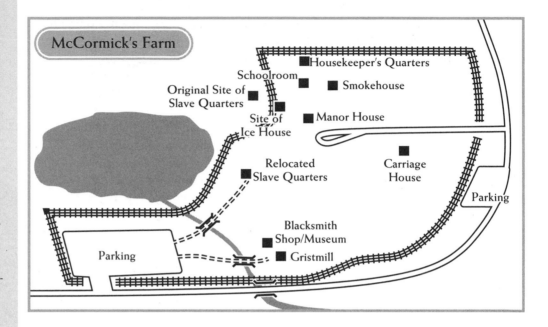

School-aged children learn that Cyrus McCormick invented the reaper, but many may not have visited the idyllic setting where the young man dreamed up his revolutionary invention. Walnut Grove Farm, where Cyrus Hall McCormick lived for 38 years, is located near Lexington. The property remained in the McCormick family until 1954, when McCormick heirs gave the historic property to Virginia Tech University. Five acres of the original 1,800-acre Walnut Grove Farm are preserved as a tribute to Cyrus McCormick and the ingenuity of the McCormick family. The area is designated as both a National Historic Landmark and a Virginia Wayside site.

If you drive to the farm via Interstate 81, take Exit 205 east. First you'll pass two gas stations, but in less than a mile, traffic will be a mere memory and you'll find yourself in the pastoral countryside of the Shenandoah Valley McCormick so loved. On the left side of the road will be a working farm, the Virginia Agricultural Experiment Station, where, in true McCormick fashion, ongoing research is done to provide information and improve agriculture.

On the right side of the road, McCormick's birthplace, the Manor House, is being used as the facility's office. You can park in the lot and walk from there to see the outbuildings or continue driving around the bend and park near the mill pond. At the pond is the Gristmill, built before 1800 and operated for grinding wheat until 1931. Its overshot-type water wheel generates about 17 horsepower as water from the pond across the road turns it.

Next to the Gristmill is the Blacksmith Shop, still equipped with the original forge on which Cyrus first planned reaper designs with his father and where the

Tour in a Nutshell

• CYRUS McCORMICK'S FARM •

Walnut Grove Farm, birthplace and home of Cyrus McCormick, inventor of the mechanical reaper, houses a gristmill, a blacksmith shop/museum, a relocated slave quarters, a smokehouse and schoolroom, and early versions of the machine.

DAYS/HOURS: Walnut Grove Farm is open daily from 8:30 a.m. to 5 p.m.

FEES: There is no charge for admission.

DIRECTIONS: From Lexington, take US 11 north to SR 606 or I-81 to Exit 205 east and follow the signs to the farm.

MORE INFORMATION: The farm is currently a part of the Shenandoah Valley Agricultural Research and Extension Center of Virginia Tech University. Call (703) 377-2255 or visit www.vaes. vt.edu/steeles/mccormick/mccormick.html.

two made and repaired farm implements. Upstairs is the reaper museum. The main thing to see, of course, is the Virginia reaper. The original reaper is long gone, but a life-size replica of the first reaper is here as well as scale models of various later versions and some early farm implements.

The property also has a carriage house that is not open to the public at this time. The original smokehouse is behind the manor house, and the housekeeper's quarters depict those of the slave housekeeper of the 1830s. Mrs. McCormick (Polly) is said to have taught many of the area children in the schoolroom on site. Like most farm boys of his generation, Cyrus got his "book learning" from *Webster's Speller, Adams' Geography*, and *The Bible*, on display here along with textbook pages and woodcuts from books of the period. There are also reproductions of 1800-era children's toys.

Gluten Lends Chewiness

Gluten is the mixture of proteins present in cereal grains such as wheat. The long molecules of gluten, insoluble in water, are strong and flexible and form many cross linkages. This gives flour its characteristic chewiness and permits breads and cakes to rise during baking as the gases within expand and are trapped in the gluten superstructure. Various flours have different ratios of gluten to starch (called hardness) and are appropriate for different types of foodstuffs. Thus soft flour is used for cakes, harder flour for pastry, harder flour for bread, and the hardest, or durum, for pasta.

DID YOU KNOW . . . that the brunch isn't as modern as we think? The meal can be traced back to the late 1880s, when it was called a "company breakfast" and served at gatherings of literary and artistic individuals.

No major crop fell in quantity
so dramatically over the Civil
War's decade as tobacco, but
wheat also declined substan-
tially, by about one-third,
according to G. Terry Sharrer,
author of the book *A Kind of
Fate: Agricultural Change in Virginia*. Much of the war's fighting had taken place in the
Piedmont, north of the James
River, and in the lower
Shenandoah Valley, the principal wheat-growing areas.
And the damage was not simply collateral. Union General
Philip Sheridan was intent
upon destroying the Confederacy's "breadbasket"—the
South's ability to feed itself.

"I have destroyed over 2000
barns filled with wheat, hay,
and farming implements, over
70 mills filled with flour and
wheat; have driven in front of
the army over 4000 head of
stock, and have killed and
issued to the troops not less
than 3000 sheep," Sheridan
reported to General Ulysses
S. Grant.

After the war, the rising tide
of immigrants began to shape
a new wheat belt beyond the
Mississippi, Sharrer explains.
Whereas Virginia wheat farmers were left with almost no
machinery and devastated
soil, the westerners had higher yields from "new" land and
more and better equipment. It
took many decades for Virginia farmers to recover.

KENMORE GINGERBREAD

Highly spiced foods were very popular in colonial cookery.

½ cup butter
½ cup brown sugar
1 cup molasses
½ cup warm milk
2 tablespoons ground ginger
1 heaping teaspoon cinnamon
1 heaping teaspoon mace
1 heaping teaspoon nutmeg

2 to 3 ounces brandy
3 eggs
3 cups flour
1 teaspoon each cream of tartar and
    soda
1 large orange
1 cup raisins (optional)

Preheat oven to 350° F. Grease either a (9 × 5 × 3-inch) loaf pan or a (9 × 13-inch)
sheet pan; set aside. Cream butter with sugar in a large mixing bowl. Add molasses
and milk, ginger, cinnamon, mace, and nutmeg; add brandy. Beat eggs until light and
thick. Add flour and cream of tartar to butter mixture alternately with milk. Grate
colored peel from orange. Add to batter along with juice from the orange (about ½
cup). Add raisins, if using.

Pour batter into prepared pan and bake until a toothpick inserted in center comes
out clean, about 30 minutes for sheet or 40 minutes for loaf. Cool slightly before
serving.

---

*This recipe was provided courtesy of Kenmore, the Fredericksburg home of George Washington's sister and her
husband, where the president's mother also spent her final years. Sister Betty Washington Lewis ran a military commissary to support the cause for independence, while Fielding Lewis manufactured weapons for the colonists. Kenmore treats
guests today to a glimpse of one of the eighteenth century's most lavishly ornamented homes (phone (540) 373-3381
or visit www.kenmore.org).*

JOHN'S CRACKED-WHEAT BREAD

Make this fiber-filled bread either in a bread machine or by hand.

½ cup cracked wheat
1⅔ cups water, divided
2½ teaspoons dry yeast
2 cups bread flour
1⅓ cups whole-wheat flour

¼ cup plus 1 tablespoon oats, divided
1⅓ teaspoons salt
2½ tablespoons oil
1⅓ tablespoons honey

Soak cracked wheat in 1 cup water for at least 1 hour. If using a bread machine, place
ingredients in the container in this order: yeast, flour, whole-wheat flour, ¼ cup oats,
salt, oil, and honey. Add cracked wheat, including all soaking water, plus the remaining ⅔ cup water. Turn on bread machine and let it run through the mixing and first
rising. If not using bread machine, combine ingredients and knead by hand for about
10 minutes. Let rise in a warm place until double in bulk.

Punch down the dough and place it in a well-greased (9 × 5 × 3-inch) loaf pan
(greasing not necessary if using a Teflon-coated pan). Wet top of loaf and sprinkle
with remaining tablespoon oats. Spread oats uniformly using a wet knife. Let rise in a
warm place until double in bulk.

Preheat oven to 375° F. Bake 35 to 40 minutes, or until medium brown. Turn loaf
out onto cooling rack immediately. Makes 1 large loaf.

Note: John likes to knead and let the dough rise once in a bread machine. Then he transfers the punched-down dough to a loaf pan for its second rising and bakes it in the oven.

Tomato connoisseur John A. Kelly toured 200 houses in one year before choosing his home in McLean with just the right southern exposure and space to plant his large home-grown tomato garden. He makes all the family's bread and likes this recipe for making fresh tomato sandwiches. ✒

GADSBY'S TAVERN SALLY LUNN BREAD

This slightly sweet, pale yellow bread is delicious cold or toasted.

4 cups flour, divided	1 cup milk
⅓ cup sugar	½ cup shortening
½ teaspoon salt	¼ cup water
2 packages active dry yeast	3 eggs

Using solid shortening, grease a 10-inch fluted Bundt pan or tube-cake pan; set aside. In a large bowl of electric mixer, combine 1⅓ cups flour, sugar, salt, and yeast. Place milk, shortening, and water in a small saucepan. Heat until mixture reaches 110° to 120° F as measured with a food thermometer. If hotter, it will kill the yeast. The shortening does not need to melt.

Blend warm liquids into the flour mixture. Beat at medium speed for 2 minutes, scraping the sides of the bowl occasionally. Gradually add ⅔ cup of the remaining flour plus the eggs; beat at medium speed for 2 minutes, scraping sides of bowl. Add the remaining 2 cups flour. The batter will be thick but not stiff.

Cover bowl with plastic wrap and let the dough rise in a warm, draft-free place until it doubles in bulk (about an hour). Beat the dough down using a spatula and turn it into the prepared pan. Cover pan with same plastic wrap and let rise about 30 minutes, or until dough increases by ⅓ to ½ in height.

Place oven shelf in lower middle position. Preheat oven to 350° F 10 minutes before baking. Remove plastic wrap and bake 40 to 50 minutes. Turn bread out onto a rack to cool. Makes 1 loaf, about 20 slices.

Gadsby's Tavern in Alexandria was frequented by George Washington, the Marquis de Lafayette, John Paul Jones, John Adams, Thomas Jefferson, and James Madison. Built in 1792, the four-story Georgian building was constructed as the City Hotel and was considered a veritable skyscraper. Today, colonial-attired waiters and entertainers take diners back to the eighteenth century (phone (703) 548-1288; museum (703) 838-4242; or visit www.gadsbys tavern.org). ✒

Who Was Sally Lunn?

There are so many legends about the origin of this bread, an English fiction writer Pamela Oldfield wrote a novel titled *Sweet Sally Lunn*. There are several old accounts of the origin of the name "Sally Lunn." She allegedly was an English girl who sold bread on the streets of the fashionable spa town of Bath, crying "Soleil Lune!" to advertise the buns. In French, the words mean "sun" and "moon"—the images evoked to describe the golden tops and white bottoms of the buns, which were then baked in various types of pans including round, loaf, and muffin. Because the bun is similar to French brioche, others say she must have been a French woman. However, her name is not French. By the time the dish reached America, the bread had become "Sally Lunn" and was baked in a Turk's head mold, which is similar to a Bundt pan. Sally Lunn bread was well known in the southern colonies.

General George Washington's typical breakfast was recorded by numerous family members and friends. In consisted of "three small mush cakes (Indian meal) swimming in butter and honey" and "three cups of tea without cream," according to his step-granddaughter, Nelly Custis Lewis.

Lewis included the recipe for the mush cakes in a letter she wrote: "The bread business is as follows if you wish to make two-and-a-half quarts of flour [white cornmeal] up: Take at night one quart of flour, five tablespoonfuls of yeast, and as much lukewarm water as will make it the consistency of pancake batter; mix it in a large stone pot and set it near a warm hearth (or a moderate fire); make it at candlelight and let it remain until the next morning, then add the remaining quart and a half [of cornmeal] by degrees with a spoon; when well mixed let it stand 15 or 20 minutes and then bake it. Of this dough in the morning, beat up a white and half of the yolk of an egg—add as much lukewarm water as will make it like pancake batter; drop a spoonful at a time on a hoe or griddle (as we say in the South). When done on one side, turn the other—the griddle must be rubbed in the first instance with a piece of beef suet or the fat of cold corned beef..."

—*Mount Vernon*
Ladies' Association

OLD VIRGINNY SPOONBREAD

Soothing spoonbread puffs like a soufflé when it emerges from the oven and is delectable when served hot—with plenty of butter, of course.

1 cup water-ground cornmeal	5 tablespoons butter or margarine
1 teaspoon salt	1 cup milk
2 cups boiling water	4 eggs

Preheat oven to 425° F. Combine cornmeal and salt in a mixing bowl; stir in boiling water until mixture is smooth. Let stand for a few minutes. Meanwhile, put butter into a 1½-quart soufflé dish. Place in oven to melt.

Stir milk into cornmeal mixture. Add eggs one at a time, beating well after each addition. Stir in melted butter from dish. Pour batter into the hot baking dish. Bake 25 to 30 minutes, or until top is puffed and brown. Makes 6 servings.

MOUNT VERNON INN'S BREAD PUDDING

Serve this traditional pudding warm, with a garnish of sweetened whipped cream.

8 slices day-old white or French bread, crusts removed	1½ teaspoons vanilla extract
½ cup seedless raisins	1 teaspoon ground cinnamon
3 tablespoons melted butter	½ teaspoon each salt and ground nutmeg
3 cups half-and-half	4 eggs
⅔ cup sugar	

Preheat oven to 350° F. Butter a 2-quart rectangular glass baking dish. Cut bread in cubes to make 4 cups (add more bread, if necessary). Scatter in dish along with raisins and drizzle with butter.

In a large mixing bowl, combine half-and-half and sugar. Stir with a wire whisk. Stir in vanilla, cinnamon, salt, and nutmeg. One at a time, add eggs, whisking well after each addition. Pour over bread cubes and bake 55 to 60 minutes, or until top is brown and a silver knife inserted in center comes out clean. Serve slightly warm or chilled. Garnish with sweetened whipped cream, if desired. Makes 6 generous servings.

⤳ The charming Mount Vernon Inn Restaurant is at the entrance to the mansion grounds on Mount Vernon Circle at the southern end of the George Washington Parkway. A period-attired staff serves both modern and colonial dishes at lunch and dinner. Wedding parties and other large functions may be held in the Sunken Garden outdoor courtyard or in the new Octagonal Dining Pavilion (phone (703) 780-0011 or visit www.mountvernon.org). ⤳

STRATFORD HALL GINGER COOKIES

These delightfully crisp cookies are not as hard on the teeth as ginger snaps.

3 sticks melted margarine	4 teaspoons baking soda
½ cup molasses	2 teaspoons ground cinnamon
2 cups sugar	1 teaspoon ground cloves
2 eggs	1 teaspoon ground ginger
4 cups flour	additional sugar for coating

In a large bowl, beat together margarine, molasses, sugar, and eggs. Sift together flour baking soda, cinnamon, ginger, and cloves. Stir into margarine mixture. Refrigerate dough for several hours until firm.

Preheat oven to 350° F. Roll dough into small balls, each about half a tablespoon. Roll balls in sugar and place on greased cookie sheets about 2 inches apart. Bake 8 to 10 minutes, or until firm. Makes about 72 cookies.

This Robert E. Lee family recipe is served in the kitchen to those touring the manor house of Lee's homeplace, Stratford Plantation, a 1544-acre working farm in Stratford, on the Potomac River in Westmoreland County. The manor house, Stratford Hall, has not changed since colonial times. Four generations of Lees lived in the home (phone (804) 493-8038 or visit www.stratfordhall.org).

MARTHA WASHINGTON'S GREAT CAKE

This dense cake is similar to fruit cake.

1½ cups golden raisins	1 cup sugar, divided
1 cup currants	1 cup butter (2 sticks), softened
1 cup water	1 teaspoon lemon juice
4 ounces candied orange peel	2¼ cups sifted all-purpose flour
4 ounces candied lemon peel	½ teaspoon mace
4 ounces candied citron	¼ teaspoon ground nutmeg
3½ ounces candied red or green cherries	2 tablespoons sherry
¼ cup brandy	additional brandy or sherry for soaking
5 large eggs, separated, left at room temperature 1 hour	candied cherries for decoration (optional)

The afternoon before cake baking, prepare raisins and currants by soaking in water overnight. Prepare orange peel, lemon peel, citron, and cherries by soaking in brandy and letting stand overnight. On cake-baking day, preheat oven to 350° F. Grease 2 (9 × 5 × 3-inch) loaf pans; set aside. Beat egg whites with ½ cup sugar until stiff peaks form; set aside.

In the largest mixer bowl, beat butter, the remaining ½ cup sugar, egg yolks, and lemon juice at high speed until light and fluffy, about 5 minutes. Combine sifted flour, mace, and nutmeg. Stir into egg mixture alternately with sherry. Drain raisins and currants; combine with fruit and mix well into batter. Gently fold in reserved egg whites and divide batter into the prepared pans.

On the lowest oven rack, place a roasting pan partly filled with 1-inch of boiling water. Place cakes on middle rack. Bake 20 minutes. Then lower the heat to 325° F and bake 55 minutes longer, or until center springs back when pressed with a finger. Cool cakes on a wire rack 15 minutes before removing from pans. Let cool completely and wrap in cheesecloth soaked with additional brandy or sherry and store in a tightly covered tin for 1 month or more. Remoisten cheesecloth when necessary. Cut into thin slices. Makes 2 loaves.

This version of Martha's famous recipe came from Evans Farm Inn, a popular McLean restaurant for 50 years until it was torn down by developers in 2001 to make way for a large housing development. The farm had a millpond and a mill set on about 50 acres of what became prime real estate ten miles from downtown Washington.

"Martha Washington's Famous Great Cake"

The day after Christmas 1776, General George Washington and his troops won the Battle of Trenton after crossing the icy Delaware River. That same day he received from Mount Vernon a "Great Cake" from his wife. Loaded with spices and "currans and raisins of ye sun," fruit cake was immensely popular all year round for any festive occasion, from state dinners to family gatherings. A Great Cake recipe from an old Mount Vernon manuscript dated 1781 begins, "Take 40 eggs . . ." and calls for four pounds of butter and eight cups of sugar. If your household isn't quite accustomed to the volume of guests who visited Mount Vernon, you can make the two-loaf version here.

—*Mount Vernon Ladies' Association*

IN THE FOOTSTEPS
OF WHEAT FARMER WASHINGTON

I hope, some day or another, we shall become a storehouse and granary for the world.

—George Washington,
Letter to Marquis de Lafayette, June 19, 1788

George Washington is best known as America's first president, but if you asked him what he did for a living, he would proudly tell you he was a farmer. Although his first career was as a surveyor and he was Commander in Chief of the Revolutionary Army, the General was also a leader in the development of American agriculture.

George Washington reluctantly served his new nation as president. His passion was his land, and Mount Vernon was where he really wanted to be. He enjoyed growing crops and experimented with various techniques and tools to discover what worked best.

Modern-day farmers who support methods called "sustainable agriculture" mirror Washington's concern for the long-term productivity of his land. By constant experimentation—bolstered by studying agricultural books and correspondence with leading farmers in America and Europe, he was able to improve the quality of his soil through crop rotation, fertilizers, and other land-conservation techniques.

Tobacco, although the most valuable crop for colonists, severely depleted the soil. Many tobacco farmers would just move farther west when the soil wore out. Recognizing the need to replenish soil rather than move, Washington used a seven-year crop-rotation system to preserve his fields.

Washington used manure from his livestock to fertilize fields and used fencing to keep animals both on and off the fields. Testing over 60 different crops and many different planting techniques, he diversified his 8,000-acre Mount Vernon "plantation"—a farm growing primarily one crop—into a farm where he grew wheat, corn, potatoes, buckwheat, oats, and rye. He also planted grasses in hopes that his soil would remain fertile year after year.

Washington advocated the production of wheat and other grains rather than tobacco, and resolved to make America a "granary for the world." Perhaps his most dramatic invention was America's first 16-sided treading barn for processing wheat and other grains. He built it on Dogue Run, one of his five farms.

THE 16-SIDED TREADING BARN

After switching from tobacco to wheat as his main cash crop, Washington believed there was a more efficient way to process his wheat and other grain crops. Traditionally, wheat was threshed by hand. The wheat plant was beat with a flail until the grain was broken out of the straw. Some farmers used horses to trample wheat on open ground to get the grain out, but a lot of wheat was lost when using this method. Bad weather could also cause grain to be ruined.

Washington decided to move this activity indoors to reduce loss, improve the quality of his grain, and reduce any losses due to theft. Work on the barn began in 1792. It took two years for Washington's carpentry crew to finish the unique building.

Although he was in Philadelphia serving as President, Washington carefully supervised the construction of his new barn. He even calculated that the number of bricks needed to complete the first floor would be 30,820!

The original barn survived until the 1870s and is among the nation's best-documented agricultural buildings of any period. The president's plans for the barn survived as well as a photograph taken during its last years of existence and made from a glass-plate negative. Various plantation records, the building specifications, and bills for materials prepared by Washington were preserved as well.

In 1992, work began on a reconstruction of Washington's 16-sided treading barn. After more than five years of dedicated effort by Mount Vernon staff, consultants, interns, and volunteers, the barn opened to visitors in 1997 as part of an exhibit, "George Washington: Pioneer Farmer."

The barn has 10,000 three-foot cypress shingles and more than 4000 linear feet of two-and-a-half-inch-square oak treading floorboards nailed into place with 2600 six-inch wrought-iron spikes. The wood came from the existing 300 acres of the Mount Vernon estate, and all finishing work was done using tools and techniques used in the eighteenth century. The bricks were made according to methods used in the 1700s.

The reason for being circular is so the horses can jog around treading the grain. The barn isn't perfectly round because in colonial times it was easier constructing straight sides instead of curved walls.

WASHINGTON'S OTHER FARMS

No estate in United America is more pleasantly situated than this. It lyes in a high, dry, and healthy Country. . . on one of the finest Rivers in the world.

—George Washington to Arthur Young,
British agriculturist, December 12, 1793

Dogue "Run" (meaning "a small, swift stream") was only one of Washington's five farms. More than 3,000 acres were planted in a variety of crops on it and Union Farm, Muddy Hole Farm, and River Farm. Each of these four outlying farms was equipped with support buildings, such as overseers' houses, barns, and slave quarters.

The mansion people know today as Mount Vernon was the fifth, called Mansion House Farm, which has been restored to its appearance in 1799, the last year of his life. George Washington lived here for more than 45 years. The estate, first known as Little Hunting Creek Plantation, was originally granted to Washington's great-grandfather John Washington in 1674 and covered 2000 acres. It eventually passed to Washington's older half-brother, Lawrence, who renamed the property Mount Vernon, after his commanding officer, Admiral Edward Vernon of the British navy.

George Washington inherited the property upon the death of his brother's widow in 1761, when he was 29. Over the years, he enlarged the mansion and built up the property to the nearly 8000 acres that comprised his five working farms. The estate was, as much as possible, a self-sufficient community; it was cheaper to produce everything needed on the estate rather than buying it.

Fabrics were made of wool and flax grown on the estate. In the greenhouse, Washington experimented with unusual plants and trees to learn which could be cultivated for the benefit of his plantation. A slave tended the fire to keep the Greenhouse warm and lived in the stove room.

Vegetables, fruit, berries, and herbs were grown for the family's food in the kitchen garden, first laid out in 1760. It was the colonial "supermarket." The garden—walled to protect the plants from wild animals—was terraced to give the gardener two levels for planting. As "mistress of the plantation," Martha Washington oversaw this garden carefully to ensure that the evening meal was elegant and abundant.

She also supervised the preserving of hams and bacon that would be eaten by the Washingtons and their guests. Hogs were generally slaughtered and butchered by slaves in December or January. The meat was then smoked to preserve it for the rest of the year. Martha was very proud of the quality meats preserved on the estate and sometimes sent gifts of ham to their friends.

The Potomac River was also "farmed" by Washington. Every spring the catch, mostly shad and herring, were salted and stored in large barrels in the salt house for use on the plantation and for sale along the east coast of America and in the West Indies. In one year, the Mount Vernon slaves caught more than one million fish in a six-week period. Salt fish was also an important part of the diet of Mount Vernon's slaves.

When Washington was home, his daily routine was unchanging. Each day, Washington rose early, ate breakfast, and then rode out to his farms to oversee their operation. He modified tools and methods to suit his needs and believed in the conservation of trees for wood. As a leader in new agricultural practices, he was one of the first farmers to develop a system of selective breeding to raise stronger livestock and promoted the use of the mules, which were stronger and easier to care for than horses. His interest in farming and his determination to make Mount Vernon a profitable venture never waned.

GEORGE WASHINGTON SLEPT HERE—AND HERE, AND HERE

"It will not be doubted that with reference either to individual or National Welfare, Agriculture is of primary importance. In proportions as Nations advance in population and other circumstances of maturity, this truth becomes more apparent and renders the cultivation of the soil more and more an object of public patronage."
—George Washington,
Eighth Annual Address to Congress, December 7, 1796

Along a gentle crescent of waterfront following the western bend in the Potomac, the father of our country was born, matured, and laid to rest.

GEORGE WASHINGTON BIRTHPLACE NATIONAL MONUMENT

George Washington was born in 1732 at Popes Creek Plantation in Westmoreland County on what is now known as the Northern Neck. The 550-acre George Washington Birthplace National Monument site, maintained by the National Park Service, features pristine beaches along the five-mile-wide Potomac River, as well as upland forest with stands of historic trees and wildlife, open farmlands, and marshlands with unique plant and animal species.

The house where George was born and first slept burned in 1779, but visitors can tour the Memorial House, a reconstruction set upon the original foundations. This house is Georgian in style and set upon a re-created mid-1700s plantation that includes a kitchen, garden, cemetery, and the Colonial Living Farm, which is worked by methods employed in colonial days. George lived at this plantation for the first few years of his life as well as intermittently after his father Augustine's death in 1743, when he spent extended times with his half-brother Augustine, Jr. ("Austin").

GEORGE WASHINGTON'S FERRY FARM

From the ages of 6 to 19, George lived on a farm in Fredericksburg on another river—the Rappahannock. It was named Ferry Farm because a ferry landing was

GEORGE WASHINGTON'S BIRTHPLACE NATIONAL MONUMENT

This first home of our first president is open daily from 9 a.m. to 5 p.m., except Christmas Day and New Year's Day. Admission is charged and includes exhibits showing parts of the site's 100,000-artifact collection, a guided or self-guided tour of the historic area, and, for those age 17 and older, a 14-minute film. The 550-acre site is located at 1732 Popes Creek Road in the town of Washington's Birthplace, just east of the little Northern Neck town of Oak Grove on Route 3. Call (804) 224-1732 or visit www.nps.gov/gewa.

GEORGE WASHINGTON'S FERRY FARM

Washington's second home, now an archaeological site with some exhibits, is open February 21 through December 30 from 10 a.m. to 5 p.m., Monday through Saturday, and noon to 5 p.m. on Sunday. From January 2 to February 20, hours are 10 a.m. to 4 p.m. on Saturday and noon to 4 p.m. on Sunday. Admission is charged. Ferry Farm is just across the Rappahannock River from downtown Fredericksburg on Route 3 (phone (540) 370-0732 or visit www.kenmore.org).

there for crossing the river. For the outcries of historians and citizens, a Wal-Mart store would have been built on this site of our first president's boyhood home. The land was saved by the Historic Kenmore Foundation, and the discount store found a location farther out on the same road. On Ferry Farm, Washington received his formal education and taught himself surveying while not chopping down a cherry tree or throwing a dollar across the Potomac (it was a piece of slate that he threw across the Rappahannock, not the silver dollar that lives on in legend; no silver dollars were minted at the time). The mainly archaeological site, now with exhibits and ongoing excavations, was a major artillery base and river-crossing site for Union forces during the Battle of Fredericksburg.

MOUNT VERNON

The third farm Washington called home is the most visited home in America aside from the White House. Mount Vernon and the surrounding lands had been in the Washington family for nearly 90 years by the time George inherited it all in 1761, at the age of 29. Washington was a yeoman farmer managing the 8,000-acre plantation. He also oversaw the transformation of the main house from an ordinary farm dwelling into what was, for the time, a grand mansion.

The red-roofed house is made of yellow pine painted and coated with layers of sand to resemble white-stone blocks. The first-floor rooms are quite ornate, especially the formal large dining room, with its molded ceiling decorated with agricultural motifs. Throughout the house are other, smaller symbols of the owner's eminence, such as a key to the main portal of the Bastille—presented to Washington by the Marquis de Lafayette—and Washington's presidential chair. Guides stationed throughout the house describe the furnishings and answer questions. The real treasure of Mount Vernon is the view afforded from a 90-foot portico that overlooks an expanse of lawn sloping down to the Potomac. In springtime the view of the river (a mile wide where it passes the plantation) is framed by the blossoms of redbud and dogwood.

You can stroll around the estate's 500 acres and three gardens, visiting the workshops, the kitchen, the carriage house, the greenhouse, the slave quarters, and—down the hill toward the boat landing—the tomb of George and Martha Washington. There's also a four-acre, hands-on exhibit focusing on Washington's role as a pioneer farmer; a reconstruction of his 16-sided treading barn is the exhibit's centerpiece. Among the souvenirs sold at the plantation are stripling boxwoods that began life as clippings from bushes planted in 1798, the year before Washington died. A tour of house and grounds takes about two hours. Private, evening candlelight tours of the mansion can be arranged.

In 2006, the Donald W. Reynolds Museum and Education Center and the Ford Orientation Center opened. A decade in the planning and building and part of a $110 million program to illuminate our first president, the center includes 25 new theaters and galleries that tell the detailed story of George Washington's life. More than 500 original artifacts, 11 History Channel videos, and immersive theater experiences illuminate the remarkable story of the first American hero.

Three miles south of the estate, visit George Washington's Distillery and Gristmill, located on Route 235. The water-powered mill is operated by millers in colonial attire who explain how the structure works and the role it played in Washington's entrepreneurial farming operation. The distillery demonstrates eighteenth-century liquor-making techniques and includes five copper stills.

Tour in a Nutshell
· GEORGE ·
WASHINGTON
SLEPT HERE
(*continued*)

MOUNT VERNON
George Washington's family plantation is open daily year-round, including holidays. During March, September, and October, hours are 9 a.m. to 5 p.m.; from April through August, hours are 8 a.m. to 5 p.m., and between November and February, hours are 9 a.m. to 4 p.m. Admission is charged. Mount Vernon is 16 miles southeast of Washington, D.C. or eight miles south of Alexandria, at the southern end of the George Washington Parkway (phone (703) 780-2000 or (703) 799-8606, or visit www.mountvernon.org.

Barley

Barley, an annual grass, was known to the ancient Greeks, Romans, Chinese, and Egyptians and was the chief bread material in Europe as late as the sixteenth century. It has a wide range of cultivation and matures even at high altitudes, because its growing period is short; however, it cannot withstand hot, humid climates. Today barley is typically a special-purpose grain with many varieties rather than a general-market crop. It is a valuable stock feed, and high-quality barley is used for malting beer and whiskey. It is a minor source for making flour and breakfast foods. Pearl barley is often used in soups. In the Middle East a limited amount of barley is eaten like rice. In the United States most spring barley comes from the western states and most winter barley is grown in the southeastern states for autumn and spring pasture and as a cover crop.

chapter two

BARLEY AND RYE

These two cereal grains are planted on about 70,000 acres of Virginia farmland; about five million bushels of barley and more than a quarter of a million bushes of rye are produced in the Old Dominion. Rye and barley are classified in the same division, order, and family, and grow in the same regions of the state: the northern Piedmont and Coastal Plain. Barley, a nutty-tasting chewy grain, is often used in soups, salads, and side dishes. Rye, made into flour, is generally limited to making bread and baked goods, although rye berries—available in some health-food stores—add a nutty crunch to rice pilafs.

BARLEY SOUP WITH DILL AND CARAWAY

Make this hearty winter soup with a ham bone or leftover cooked chicken.

3 cups chicken broth
1 cup water
3 large fresh tomatoes or 1 (14½-ounce) can stewed tomatoes, including liquid
1¼ cups sliced fresh mushrooms (about 4 ounces)
½ cup pearl barley

½ cup chopped onion
1½ teaspoons crushed dillweed
½ teaspoon caraway seeds
¼ teaspoon each sugar and pepper
1 ham bone or 1 cup chopped, cooked ham or chicken
sour cream (optional)

Combine broth, water, and tomatoes in a large saucepan. Cover and bring to a boil. Stir in remaining ingredients and ham bone, if using. If using chopped meat, add during the last 10 minutes of cooking. Re-cover and simmer until barley is tender, about 45 minutes. Top each bowl with a dollop of sour cream. Makes 4 servings.

BARLEY LENTIL SALAD

The combination of barley and lentils packs this salad with more than 7 milligrams of dietary fiber.

5 cups water
1 cup raw medium barley
1 vegetarian bouillon cube
½ cup green lentils
¼ teaspoon pepper
2 cups chopped fennel or celery
1 cup chopped red bell pepper

4 green onions with tops, thinly sliced
½ cup Italian dressing
8 ounces Jarlsberg cheese, cut into matchsticks
8 leaves red-leaf or green-leaf lettuce

Bring water to boil in a 2-quart saucepan. Add barley and bouillon cube and simmer, covered, 10 minutes. Add lentils and pepper; re-cover. Simmer 15 minutes, or until crisp tender. Drain any liquid; cool mixture.

Add fennel, bell pepper, onion, and dressing; toss. Stir in cheese. Refrigerate and use within 4 days. Serve on lettuce leaves. Makes 8 servings.

Buyer's Guide to BARLEY

You've probably eaten barley in a bowl of soup, but it can be used in many other dishes. This grain is available in several different forms. "Hulled," or whole-grain barley has only the outer husk removed and is the most nutritious. "Scotch" barley is husked and coarsely ground. "Pearl" barley, the most prevalent type, is hulled and also has the bran removed. It has been steamed and polished and comes in three sizes—coarse, medium, and fine. "Quick" barley is pearled and steamed and rolled. Pearl barley is especially good for making soups and stews.

This chewy, nutty grain is a great source of fiber. It takes about an hour to cook on the stove and about half that time in the microwave. If using the quick-cooking variety, it only takes ten minutes to cook and requires less liquid. Depending upon the store, barley may be found with the dry beans and rice, in the dry-soups section, or in the health-foods aisle. Keep barley at room temperature in the pantry. As long as it's kept dry, it is safe to use.

ESSEX COUNTY BARLEY PRIMAVERA

Quick-cooking barley gets this side dish on the table in 20 minutes.

1½ cups low-sodium chicken broth
1 cup quick-cooking barley
¼ cup chopped onion
1 clove garlic, minced
½ cup each thinly sliced carrots and
  mushrooms

½ cup broccoli florets
¼ cup each red and yellow
  bell peppers, chopped
1 tablespoon each olive oil and wine
  vinegar
¼ cup walnuts, toasted*

Combine broth and barley in a 2-quart casserole. Cover with lid or vented plastic wrap. Microwave on high 5 minutes. Then microwave on medium (50%) 10 minutes. Let stand covered.

Place onion, garlic, carrots, and mushrooms in a 4-cup glass measure. Cover with vented plastic wrap. Microwave on high 3 minutes. Add broccoli and bell peppers; re-cover. Microwave on high 2 minutes.

Blend oil and vinegar together; drizzle over barley. Add vegetables; toss together. Sprinkle walnuts over top. Makes 4 servings.

*To toast walnuts, place in a 1-cup glass measure. Stirring midway through cooking, microwave on high 2 minutes or lightly brown in a toaster oven.

BARLEY MUSHROOM PILAF

If you're tired of rice and potatoes, use barley to make this fluffy, rice-like side dish.

1 tablespoon olive oil
½ cup each chopped onion and
  celery
1 cup sliced mushrooms
1 clove garlic, minced

3 cups low-sodium chicken broth
1 cup medium pearl barley
2 green onions, thinly sliced
salt and pepper to taste, if desired

Heat oil in a large saucepan. Add onion, celery, mushrooms, and garlic. Sauté about 4 minutes, stirring constantly.

Stir in broth and barley. Cover and bring to a boil. Reduce heat and simmer until all liquid is absorbed, about 45 minutes. Fluff with a fork and stir in green onions. Season with salt and pepper, if desired. Makes 4 servings.

SAUERKRAUT-RYE BREAD

Grilled Eastern European sausages and Virginia ham spread with mustard taste especially good in sandwiches made from this hearty bread.

½ cup lukewarm water (about 105° F)
2 tablespoons light molasses
1 (¼-ounce) package active dry yeast
  (or 2½ teaspoons)
1¼ cups white bread flour
1 cup whole wheat flour
1¼ cups rye flour
2 tablespoons cocoa

2 tablespoons caraway seeds
1¼ teaspoons salt
¾ cup chopped sauerkraut, reserve
  ½ cup liquid
½ cup buttermilk
3 tablespoons oil
2 tablespoons Dijon mustard

Place water in a small bowl; stir in molasses. Sprinkle yeast on top but do not stir; set aside 5 minutes until a foamy consistency.

In a large bowl of electric mixer, place white, whole wheat, and rye flours, cocoa, seeds, and salt. Using mixer on low speed, stir in sauerkraut, sauerkraut liquid, buttermilk, oil, and mustard. Add yeast mixture and mix well to form a stiff dough, adding more bread flour if necessary. Turn out dough onto a floured board and knead 5 minutes, or until the dough becomes soft and elastic.

Lightly oil a large bowl and place dough in it. Cover with a tea towel and let rise in a warm place until double in bulk, about 1 hour. Punch dough down and place in a greased (9 × 5 × 3-inch) loaf pan. Let rise until double in bulk, about 45 minutes.

Preheat oven to 350° F. Bake 30 to 35 minutes, or until loaf sounds hollow when thumped. Transfer to a cooling rack. Makes 1 (1½-pound) loaf.

Rye breads are especially popular in the Roanoke area of Virginia, where large numbers of Germans settled along the Great Wagon Road (see sidebar). This recipe was adapted from an old recipe of pioneers who emigrated west.

WAGON ROAD PUMPERNICKEL

If possible, make this solid, flavorful loaf a day before needed so the crust will soften and become chewy.

2 cups warm water
2 (¼-ounce) packages active dry
   yeast (about 1½ tablespoons)
2 tablespoons molasses
2 teaspoons caraway seeds
2 teaspoons salt

1 cup lukewarm mashed potatoes
2 cups dark rye flour plus additional
   if needed
1 cup bran
3½ to 4 cups flour, divided

Place water in a very large mixing bowl. Test with a food thermometer to be sure the water is between 105° and 115° F; hotter water will kill the yeast. Stir yeast into water. Stir in molasses, caraway seeds, and salt, then potatoes. Stir in rye flour, bran, and 1 cup flour. Beat dough with a wooden spoon or electric mixer dough hook about 2 minutes.

Add remaining flour ½ cup at a time until dough can be handled. Turn dough onto a floured board or other surface and knead about 10 minutes, adding as little flour as possible so dough stays soft and elastic. Turn dough in an oiled bowl to coat all sides. Cover bowl with plastic wrap or a tea towel. Let rise in a warm place until double in size, about 2 hours.

Divide dough in half and roll in additional rye flour. Place each ball on a greased baking sheet. Re-cover and let rise until almost doubled in bulk, about 1 hour. Preheat oven to 375° F. Spray dough liberally with water and cut an "X" in the top of each ball, using a sharp knife. Bake the round loaves until brown, about 30 minutes. Loaves should sound hollow when tapped. Cool on a rack. The recipe makes 2 loaves but is easily divided to make one.

German immigrants who traveled to the Roanoke Valley along the Great Wagon Road brought with them their love for this dark bread.

The Great Wagon Road

The Great Wagon Road from Pennsylvania through Virginia was the path many Germans, Scotch-Irish, and other settlers took in their migration to the valley region to search for new farmlands. In 1750 it was the western frontier of America. To the west were the Appalachians; to the east, the Blue Ridge Mountains. At first it was not a road at all but the natural course run by buffalo herds. Later it became "The Great Warrior's Path" used by Native Americans for raids. During the first years, settlers walked leading pack animals. In places the path was only three or four feet wide, with the wilderness encroaching. Although it was called a wagon road, most people walked the path, with small wagons carrying their few possessions. A good day's journey covered ten miles with a wagon. As more settlers left the east seeking new lives, the "road" became a pair of tracks worn by the many wagons that had crossed its lengths.

When settlers stopped to care for their animals and prepare food, perils awaited. Indians attacked, especially during the French-and-Indian War; later, thieves robbed the settlers. It was hard to get a good nights rest, no matter how tiring the day had been. The tough and determined people who made this journey were the ancestors of today's Shenandoah and Roanoke Valley residents.

HISTORIC GRISTMILLS OF VIRGINIA

When it comes to bread, we have it easy. It was not until ancient Egyptian times, when grain was broken into coarse fragments by a mortar and pestle, did man figure out he could use something hard other than his teeth to make grains edible. The earliest device for producing flour consisted of two roughened grinding surfaces, called millstones.

Improvements continued in the form of the grist mill. But turning the millstones between which grain was reduced to a powder required power, and the foremost achievement of colonial Virginia's early settlers was to harness nature's water power for this purpose.

Flour milling was one of the most important services needed in the colony and remained so through the end of the eighteenth century. The local custom mill, which ground grain to the customer's order, and, later, the larger merchant mill, which ground flour for the market by the sack or the shipload, were treated as public utilities. To obtain flour and meal, one would supply his own wheat and corn and then wait his turn. For one bushel of wheat (60 pounds) one would receive 37 pounds of flour and 12 pounds of bran.

As early as 1645, the Virginia House of Burgesses considered flour milling essential to the common welfare and enacted regulations to protect the public interest. These laws reflect the dual image of the miller. On the one hand, millers in general were strictly regulated to safeguard their customers against mis-branding, short-weighing, and poor quality-inspection procedures. On the other hand, individual millers were respected by their neighbors as men of means who generally were the most highly skilled mechanics and engineers in their communities, because at that time, the mill was probably the most sophisticated piece of food-processing machinery that existed.

The location of these mills determined the routes on which many turnpikes were constructed, just as the location of the tobacco-rolling roads determined the routes of the first roads to the Tidewater ports. The wheat of the Piedmont and the Valley was hauled to the mills in great Conestoga wagons, drawn by six-horse teams gay with bells and bunting. Converting their cargo into flour en route, the teams then went on to a primary market at Tidewater, and so constituted those caravans of "flour wagons" which in 1777 were already the life of the Tidewater trade.

Today, because of the development of wheat varieties that do not require the heavy friction provided by millstones, most grinding is now done in roller mills. Corrugated rollers gradually reduce wheat kernels to powder, effecting separation of kernel and husk. Initial rolling takes place in three to six stages, the last stage of which yields bran, middlings, and flour. Finished flour consists almost entirely of endosperm, or nutritive tissue. Middlings are composed of fragments of endosperm, fragments of husk, and husk fragments with adhering particles. Bran, the broken husk of the grain, is used as feed for livestock and to provide roughage in some types of breakfast cereals.

However, the old way of Virginia life can still be glimpsed at its many historic grist mills. Some of them grind into life for tourists to view. For example, Colvin Run Mill, one of the few all-brick mills in Virginia, is a model of the many mills that served the state in the seventeenth to early twentieth centuries. As rebuilt, Colvin Run Mill recreates the atmosphere of its early times. A tour of the Mill offers twenty-first-century visitors the chance to share in the excitement of watching and listening to its massive machinery and to admire the skill of craftsmen who—with wood and iron—fashioned this efficient, self-contained system.

—Some information
provided by Colvin Run Mill

Virginia's Historic Gristmills

HISTORIC GRISTMILL is at 112 River Road in Cedar Bluff (phone (276) 964-9691).

JESSE'S MILL is a roller-process mill turned into a restaurant in Lebanon (phone (276) 889-8041).

MILL HOUSE MUSEUM-HISTORIC OCCOQUAN. This eighteenth-century grist-mill in Occoquan houses a museum of local history (413 Mill Street; phone (703) 491-7525).

STRATFORD MILL, at Robert E. Lee's birthplace, was reconstructed in 1939 on the foundations of the 1740s original. Corn, wheat, oats, and barley are ground as they were in Lee's time and are sold at the Plantation Store (Route 3 in Stratford; phone (804) 493-8038 or visit www.stratfordhall.org).

WADE'S MILL is a working flour mill circa 1750, built by Captain Joseph Kennedy, one of the early settlers in the Shenandoah Valley. In 1882, James F. Wade bought the mill and four generations operated it. The mill is powered by a 21-foot water wheel and is on the National Register of Historic Places. Visitors welcome. (55 Kennedy Wades Mill Road, Raphine (540) 346-1400 or (800) 290-1400; or visit www.wadesmill.com).

part eight
WINE

Sitting on the deck of a Virginia winery, looking over the orderly rows of grapevines while sipping a Chardonnay or Cabernet, is a serendipitous way to spend a weekend afternoon. The lushness of the fruit on its ordered trellises nourishes the eyes but belies the capricious nature of winemaking. As Charles Raney, one of Virginia's twentieth-century pioneer winegrowers, says, "I named my winery Farfelu, which comes from a French word that means screwy, a little nuts, or unpredictable." The term aptly describes Virginia's 400-year-old attempts to make palatable wine.

Virginia's wineries are picturesque and beautifully located. Most are situated within sight of mountains or along rivers and streams. The main winegrowing areas are in the Shenandoah Valley, the counties surrounding Monticello, Northern Virginia, the Northern Neck, the Eastern Shore, and the Roanoke area. Three counties in the Monticello area—Orange, Madison, and Albemarle

Counties—produce 49% of the state's wine grapes. Wines contribute about $38 million to the state's economy—more than cash receipts from tomatoes and almost as much as from apples—and this figure doesn't include the dollars generated by wine-related tourism or the more than 500 wine events and festivals held throughout the year.

Virginia has more than 125 wineries. In 1982 there were 17 wineries in the state, so the number of wineries has increased by more than 700%. Virginia's wine-grape growers' production is headed for 500,000 cases of wine annually from nearly 3,000 acres of grapes. About half of wine produced in 2008 is from three vinifera—Chardonnay, Cabernet Franc, and Merlot—plus one hybrid, Vidal Blanc. Some 50 kinds of grapes are grown, and production nears 10,000 tons per year. Undoubtedly more wineries will open in the years to come.

A SHORT HISTORY OF WINEMAKING IN VIRGINIA

Your sailing ship is gliding up the James River in the early 1600s. The fragrance of ripening grapes is in the breeze, and you see large white scuppernongs floating in the water. You might be tempted to assume that if native grapes could grow with such profusion here, Virginia would be a perfect place to make wine.

In fact, winemaking was an important objective of the English settlers at Jamestown, for the English had long considered wine a staple. The Virginia Company, chartered by King James I to exploit the economic opportunities of the New World, had planned to develop a wine industry to help make the colony self-sufficient and financially successful, according to Hilde Gabriel Lee and Allan E. Lee in their book, *Virginia Wine Country Revisited.*

The settlers at Jamestown performed their first crush and made their first wine in 1609 from wild native scuppernong grapes, but their recorded comments about its palatability were less than complimentary. The large green grapes, sometimes called "muscadine," have a musky flavor and an odor similar to a wet dog. The colonists also fermented berries, apples, and peaches into "mobby" (brandy) and cider, made beer or ale, and distilled spirits. They then tried importing rootstock from Europe in order to grow European types and styles of wine, but none would grow.

"Failure with the European varietals lies with the delicate nature of these exotic vines," say the authors of *Virginia Wine Country Revisited.* "The cold winters and hot, humid summers of the mid-Atlantic region of North America were simply not suitable for this species of grape at that time in history. Then, few vinifera vines survived more than one or two winters. Those roots and stems that escaped ruin by winter's cold could have their buds and leaves destroyed by late spring frosts. Other factors that prevented success with European wine grapes early on were drought, black rot and mildew from the humid summers, phylloxera (root aphids), and caterpillars."

As the nineteenth century began, hopes of a domestic wine industry at last began to bear fruit. After 200 years of attempting and failing to grow Vitis Vinifera grapes—the vine species native to Europe that produces 99% of the world's wines today—Virginians concluded that they would need to develop hybrids between native American and European varieties. The native varieties supplied the hardiness needed for native climate conditions, and the European varieties contributed finesse and complexity. Some of these new hybrid grapevines still grown today are the Alexander, Catawba, Concord, Delaware, Isabella, Niagara, and Norton. The latter was named for Dr. D. N. Norton of Richmond, who domesticated one of the best hybrids. The wine from the Norton grape became famous as Virginia Claret and wins awards at home and in Europe. The Catawba and Delaware are still used today for the many sparkling wines made in the eastern United States.

THE CIVIL WAR

Just as the Virginia wine industry was reaching peak production from American hybrids, along came the Civil War. Many of the battles of the war were fought in and around Virginia's best wine-growing regions. Vineyards were destroyed, stocks and supplies were stolen, field hands became Confederate soldiers, and transporting wine to market became impossible.

After the war, California, a state untouched by the conflict, began a runaway domination of the wine market. Between 1860 and 1880, California's market share rose from 15% to more than 60%. Then, just as Virginia was beginning to recover from Reconstruction, along came Prohibition, effectively drying up the state's wine industry. In 1914, Virginia voted to become a "dry state," so that even when Prohibition was repealed, the state remained dry. By 1960, Virginia's wine industry was practically nonexistent.

VIRGINIA'S FINE WINES

Finally, in the 1970s, a number of factors began to coincide that would eventually make producing fine wines in Virginia a possibility again. Falling prices for livestock, tobacco, and some other farm products caused farmers to look for a more valuable product. An influx of population, higher salaries, and increased appreciation for wine created a ready market. And improvements in the science of growing wine grapes made it possible to grow them in Virginia's variable conditions, which can include late-spring frosts and heat and humidity.

Two pioneers, Charles Raney of Farfelu Vineyard and Archie Smith, Jr., of Meredyth Vineyards, successfully grew French hybrids. This encouraged others to try. Winegrowers learned how to protect the rootstock in the winter and prune as late as possible in spring to avoid danger from frosts. They also began to use "canopy management" (a technique to control the amount of shade from grape leaves) to eliminate fungus caused by high humidity.

Legislative action also aided the industry's comeback. In 1980, the state legislature passed a progressive Farm Winery Law that dictated that wineries could sell wine both wholesale and retail without additional licenses. The legislature also

"We could, in the United States, make as great a variety of wines as are made in Europe, not exactly of the same kinds, but doubtless as good."

—Thomas Jefferson

DID YOU KNOW . . . that Thomas Jefferson, like the Jamestown colonists, tried his hand at growing European varieties, but like so many others before and after him, he, too, failed? Though Jefferson always believed that the Charlottesville area—today one of the state's biggest wine regions—would be suitable for wine growing, his success with wine was limited to fostering the young nation's appreciation for the beverage. Jefferson served as wine advisor to four other presidents and proffered the concept that wine was a healthier drink than hard spirits. "In countries which use ardent spirits," he is famous for saying, "drunkenness is the mortal vice; but in those which make wine for common use, you never see a drunkard."

Major Wine Varieties Grown in Virginia

1. CHARDONNAY   The most popular varietal grown in Virginia, this white usually comes as a medium to full-bodied dry wine. It may be fruity, with a hint of apples.

2. CABERNET FRANC   Not quite as full-bodied as its cousin Sauvignon, this red has fewer tannins and less acid but is more herbaceous and aromatic. Its grapes grow in cooler climates and ripen early.

3. MERLOT   Cherry-like in aroma, the merlot has hints of the Cabernet's herbaceousness but with a softer flavor. It is medium-to-full bodied, dry, and less tannic than Cabernet.

4. CABERNET SAUVIGNON   Some call this medium-to-full-bodied red "the king of wine." It is tannic, dry, and complex. Its flavors can emerge as those of currants, green olives, herbs, bell peppers, with hints of mint and leather.

5. VIDAL BLANC   A crisp and very dry white, with aromas that compare to green apples or nectarines; light to medium in body.

6. VIOGNIER   Dry, esteemed white derived from a very rare wine grape. Its floral qualities are vibrant and its intriguing bouquet is reminiscent of apricots, peaches, and pears.

7. WHITE RIESLING   This white-to-medium-bodied varietal has a spicy, fruity bouquet and is usually off dry or semi-sweet. It sometimes evokes flavors that suggest the smells of honey and apricot nectar.

created a wine-marketing program via the establishment of the Virginia Winegrowers Advisory Board, as well as positions for a state enologist and vitaculturist.

Today Virginia is home to 80 wineries that, together, produce more than 4,000 tons of grapes annually. Some 50 kinds of grapes are grown, most notably the varietals Chardonnay, Cabernet Sauvignon, White Riesling, Cabernet Franc, and Merlot and the hybrids Vidal Blanc and Seyval.

Virginia's Wine-Growing Regions

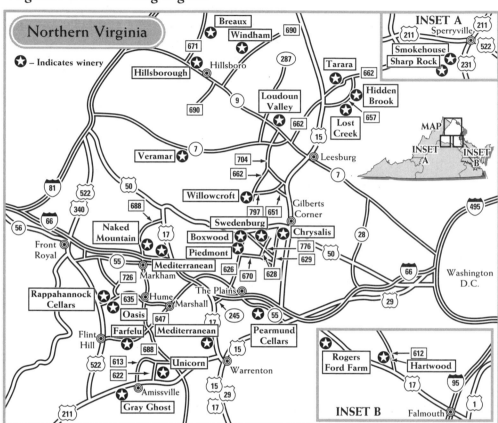

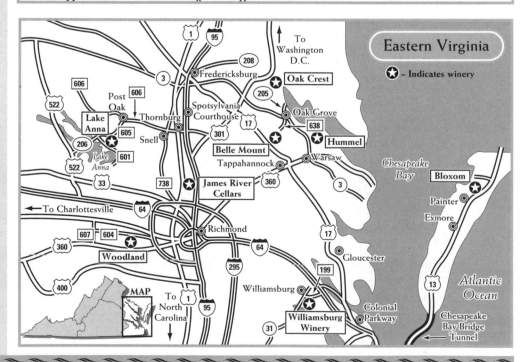

Central Virginia (Map)

Sperryville · Washington, D.C. · 211 · 229 · 522 · 522
Rose River · 643 · Syria · 670 · Prince Michel · 522
Skyline Dr. · 648 · 651 · 231 · 609 · Leon · Culpepper · Old House
Christensen Ridge · 652 · Madison · 33
Stone Mountain · 627 · 810 · 612 · 230 · 230 · 614 · 15 · 615 · Orange · 20 · 522
White Hall · 632 · 633 · Autumn Hill · 678 · 777 · Horton · 33
White Hall · 603 · 663 · Burnley · Gordonsville
Crozet · Earlysville · 810 · 743 · 606 · Barboursville · 743 · 619 · Keswick
King Family · Oakencroft · 240 · 654 · Charlottesville · 64 · Cooper
Rockbridge · 250 · 6 · Veritas · Blenheim · Jefferson · 64 · Grayhaven · 522
Afton Mountain · 606 · Wintergreen Resort · First Colony · 720 · 795 · Kluge · 15 · Gum Spring · 250
Blue Ridge Pkwy. · 664 · Cardinal Point · 20 · 6 · 6
Hill Top · 151 · 29
Wintergreen · Mountain Cove · 626
651 · Lovingston · 723
60 · 718 · 20 · 15
Rebec · 56
151 · 610
Amherst · 60
Stonewall · 721 · 15
Lynchburg · 29 · 608 · 26 · 727 · 60
To Bedford · Concord · 460 · Farmville · 460 · To Petersburg
24 · 727 · 658 · Worsham
501 · 615 · 665 · 604 · 665
501 · 686
To Chatham · 47 · 15

MAP

★ – Indicates winery

Central Virginia

Southwest Virginia (Map)

Highlands Harvest · 614 · 620 · 19 · Davis Valley · 617 · 52
71 · Dye's · Lebanon · 71 · 683 · Fincastle · Peaks of Otter · 43
Abingdon · 19 · 58 · Wytheville · 21 · Valhalla · 220 · Roanoke · 682
722 · 58 · Abingdon · 81 · 680 · Bedford · 29
221 · AmRheins · 812 · 460 · Lynchburg
122 · 655 · Hickory Hill · Gretna
Blue Ridge Pkwy. · 919 · 654 · 608
Boundary Rock Farm · Floyd · Rocky Mt. · 799
To INSET · Abingdon · 722 · 40 · 626 · Chatham
Château Morrisette · 221 · Tomahawk Mill · 969 · 649
81 · 720 · Callands
Meadows of Dan · Villa Appalaccia · 57 · 57
710 · 758 · 58
Martinsville · MAP
★ – Indicates winery · 58 · INSET
Southwest Virginia · 8 · To Danville · 58

Who Was Filippo Mazzei?

In 1976, during the American Bicentennial celebration, Charlottesville and Albemarle County established a "sister city" relationship with Poggio a Caiano, Italy. Here's why. Filippo Mazzei was born there in 1730. After moving to London, he began an enterprise that specialized in importing Italian and French wines and oils as well as other products. There he met American statesman Benjamin Franklin, who was in London as a commercial "ambassador" for his home state, Pennsylvania, and some Virginia businessmen. Encouraged by Franklin and the Virginians, Mazzei sailed from England to Virginia in 1773, and made plans to start an agricultural enterprise in the Shenandoah Valley.

But Mazzei made the fortunate mistake of visiting Monticello. It took Jefferson less than a day to convince Mazzei of the exceptional viticultural suitability of the area. The Italian began work on establishing vineyards but soon gave up his agricultural pursuits to participate in the American fight for independence. Governor Patrick Henry sent Mazzei on a delicate and risky mission to obtain loans for purchasing weapons and equipment. While living in Paris, at Jefferson's request Mazzei recruited Italian craftsmen to work on building the U.S. Capitol. He also wrote a four-volume historical research about the United States.

—*Virginia* magazine, Spring 2001

Sulfites? Or Merely a Hangover?

Used for centuries for their antioxidant and antimicrobial action, sulfites are small amounts of sulfur compounds that are used to keep millions of bottles of wine each year from turning into vinegar. The Food and Drug Administration estimates that 1 in 100 people is sensitive to sulfites to some degree. Asthmatics are most at risk for dangerous reactions.

According to the Society of Physicians for Wine and Health, most reactions that people attribute to sulfites are actually caused by other compounds in the wine, including phenols and histamines. Those symptoms are grouped under the "red-wine headache syndrome." (It's interesting to note that red wines contain less sulfites than white wines do—but more of many of the other compounds.) Of course, too much wine can cause dehydration, vasodilation, and a drop in blood sugar. That's a hangover.

—Steve Werblow

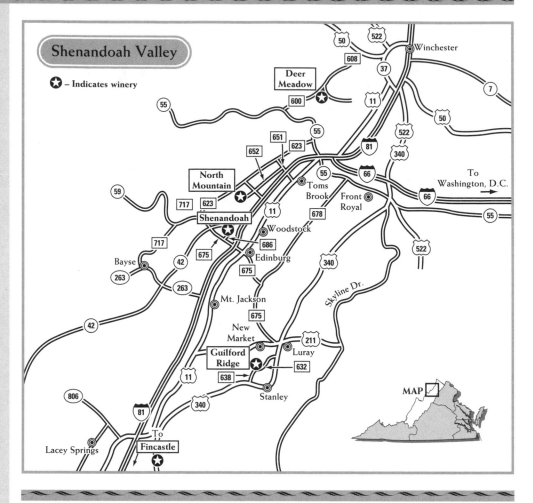

SPAGHETTI BOLOGNESE À LA COLLIS-WARNER

The First Lady of Virginia, Lisa Collis-Warner, likes to make this fragrant main-dish recipe for Governor Mark Warner and their three daughters Madison, Gillian, and Eliza.

1 small onion, chopped
2 cloves of garlic, minced
1 tablespoon olive oil
½ pound lean ground beef
½ pound mild Italian sausage, crumbled
1 (28-ounce) can crushed tomatoes
¾ cup dry white wine

4 fresh basil leaves, chopped, or
　1 teaspoon dried basil
⅛ teaspoon red pepper flakes
salt and pepper to taste
water (optional)
1 pound of uncooked spaghetti
grated Parmesan cheese (optional)

In a large saucepan over medium heat, cook garlic and onions in olive oil about 4 minutes, or until tender. Add ground beef and sausage; cook 8 minutes, or until all redness is gone. Add tomatoes, wine, basil, and red pepper flakes. Cook 45 to 60 minutes, stirring occasionally. (Should sauce become too thick, add water in ¼-cup increments.) Add salt and pepper to taste.

Cook spaghetti according to package directions, drain, toss with ¾ of the sauce. Put into six bowls, top with remaining sauce and cheese, if desired. Makes 6 servings.

PRINCE MICHEL'S CHICKEN RIESLING WITH SPINACH SPAETZLE

In this dish, the herbal acidity of the dry
Riesling provides the perfect balance of flavors for the sauce.

FOR SPAETZLE:

1 pound spinach leaves, stems removed	⅓ teaspoon baking powder
2½ cups flour, sifted	2 eggs
1 teaspoon salt	4 tablespoons unsalted butter, softened

FOR CHICKEN:

2 tablespoons olive oil	4 mushrooms, cleaned and sliced
4 chicken breasts with first wing joint attached, rib bones removed	1½ cups Rapidan River Dry Riesling
salt and white pepper	½ cup tomatos concassé
1 onion, peeled and sliced	1 sprig fresh thyme
	¾ cup heavy cream

Wash the spinach 3 times in cold water baths to remove any sand. Place the wet spinach in a large pot. Heat just until wilted, then refresh under cold running water. Drain, squeezing out and reserving the liquid. Add enough water to the reserved liquid to make ½ cup. Purée the spinach, liquid, and eggs in a food processor. Transfer to a mixer. Add flour, salt, and baking powder. Beat with the paddle attachment until you have a soft dough, almost a batter.

Bring a large saucepan of salted water to a boil. Reduce the heat to a simmer. Using a spaetzle press (or a colander with large holes), press the dough into the simmering water. The spaetzle dumplings will rise to the surface. Let them cook a few minutes longer, or until they appear light and fluffy. Remove from the water using a slotted spoon or skimmer and refresh in a bowl of ice water. Drain, then set aside. Repeat procedure with any remaining batter. (You can cook the dumplings up to 2 days ahead.)

Sprinkle chicken with salt and pepper. In a large heavy-bottomed skillet, heat oil. Lightly brown chicken on all sides. Add onions and mushrooms to the pan and lightly brown. Add the tomatos concassé, thyme, and wine. Simmer until the chicken is firm and cooked through. Remove chicken; discard the skin. Keep warm. Continue cooking the pan juices until reduced to 1 cup. Add cream and reduce the liquid by half, or until the sauce is thick enough to coat the back of a wooden spoon. Strain the sauce through a fine sieve and season to taste.

When ready to serve, add chicken to sauce and heat, if necessary, to desired serving temperature. In a small pan, cook butter over low heat until it begins to turn light brown and smells nutty. Pour off and set aside the butterfat, discarding the browned bits stuck to the bottom of the pan. Toss the spaetzle with the browned butter. Makes 4 servings.

∽ *Frenchman Jean Leducq established Prince Michel Vineyards in 1983, and now has more than 100 acres planted in grapes. The vineyard's Prince Michel and Rapidan River wines have won more than 700 awards. Leducq created Prince Michel Restaurant to offer visitors the classic French cuisine that would complement his wines. The same menu is served in both the restaurant's formal Jefferson Room and its more casual Lafayette Room. In addition, the winery has luxury hotel suites. Prince Michel is open daily. It is located midway between Culpeper and Madison on Route 29 South (phone (540) 547-3707 or (800) 800-9463).* ∽

Spaetzle

Spaetzle are an ancient Alsatian dumpling made by forcing the pasta through a specially made form and dropping it directly into the boiling water, notes French Master Chef Alain Leconte, owner of Prince Michel Vineyards and Prince Michel Restaurant. Leconte suggests serving the same type of wine to accompany the dish as used in making the dish.

It's All about Flow

Ever wonder why so many vineyards are planted on hillsides? It's not just the pretty view (though that doesn't hurt). Rather, it's about flow. Cold air flows downhill, because it's heavier than warm air. As a result, vines on a valley floor are more likely to be damaged by frost than vines on a hillside. Also, most grapevines hate "wet feet"— they're much healthier in soils that drain quickly. Hillsides often feature relatively droughty soils, and gravity helps drain water away. Last, having the vines stacked up a hillside, especially a south-facing one, maximizes their exposure to sunlight.

—Steve Werblow

There is plenty to enjoy about wine, but there's also plenty of wine lingo that can be a bit intimidating. Here are some of the words and phrases that are commonly punted about in the local wine shop:

APPELLATION—a place name indicating where most or all of the grapes that comprise the wine were grown. A winemaker can't just slap on the name of his hometown; appellations must be recognized as American Viticultural Areas (AVAs)—distinct and unique from other grape-growing regions—by the U.S. Bureau of Alcohol, Tobacco, and Firearms. The concept is similar to systems elsewhere, such as France's Appellation d'Origine Controlee (AOC), which identifies the grape varieties that may be grown in a geographic area, the production limits per acre, and the alcohol content. Virginia has six AVAs: Shenandoah Valley, Monticello, Northern Neck George Washington's Birthplace, Virginia's Eastern Shore, Rocky Knob, and North Fork of Roanoke. The largest is Shenandoah Valley, which covers 2,400,000 acres. Rocky Knob is Virginia's smallest at 9000 acres.

CLIMATE—As meteorologists say, "climate is what you expect; weather is what you get." Despite the curveballs Mother Nature likes to throw,

CHATEAU MORRISETTE'S BRAISED LAMB SHANKS WITH PANCETTA, PEARL ONIONS, TOMATO, AND CABERNET SAUVIGNON

Chef Natasha Shishkevish uses the winery's Cabernet Sauvignon to infuse flavor into this classic lamb-shanks preparation.

4 large lamb shanks
flour, salt, and pepper
2 tablespoons olive oil
1 cup peeled pearl onions
½ cup diced pancetta (Italian bacon)
3 cloves garlic, coarsely chopped
7 Roma tomatoes, peeled, seeded, and roughly chopped

1½ cups Chateau Morrisette Cabernet Sauvignon
2 cups beef broth
2 sprigs fresh thyme
1 sprig fresh marjoram
2 tablespoons finely chopped Italian parsley

Preheat oven to 350° F. Heat olive oil and season lamb shanks with salt and pepper. Dredge in flour and brown on all sides in oil. Place lamb in a baking pan and set aside. In same skillet over medium heat, brown pearl onions lightly. Add pancetta and garlic. Cook for several minutes until pancetta begins to brown on the edges. Add tomatoes and stir for 1 to 2 minutes more. Add wine and stock. Scraping the bottom and sides of skillet, bring mixture up to a boil. Pour over lamb shanks and place herb sprigs on top. Seal tightly with aluminum foil.

Bake for 1½ to 2 hours, or until meat is falling off the bone. Remove foil and let cool to lukewarm. Remove shanks from sauce and remove pearl onions, herbs, and pancetta. Discard herbs only and degrease sauce. Purée the sauce with a hand blender or in a food processor until tomatoes and garlic are incorporated, then return pearl onions and pancetta to puréed sauce. Bring back to a boil and reduce until slightly thickened. Add chopped parsley and season with salt and pepper to taste. Reheat the lamb shanks gently in the sauce. Makes 4 servings. Polenta or mashed potatoes complement this dish nicely.

Natasha Shishkevish earned a degree in theatre arts and couldn't find work, so she began catering. She then graduated from the Culinary Institute of America and worked at several other well-regarded restaurants before becoming chef at Chateau Morrisette's restaurant. Chateau Morrisette is located along the Blue Ridge Parkway in Meadows of Dan (phone (540) 593-2865; www.thedogs.com).

PAN-ROASTED DUCK BREAST WITH BLACK MISSION FIG SAUCE

Palladio Restaurant Chef Melissa Close designed this recipe to impart the flavor of the Barboursville Vineyards Merlot to the duck.

2 tablespoons olive oil
1 shallot, minced
2 cups black mission figs, stems removed, quartered
1 cup Barboursville Vineyards Merlot
salt and pepper to taste

¼ cup demi-glace (a rich brown sauce found in specialty grocery stores)
4 duck breast halves
soft polenta
1 cup baby spinach leaves, wilted

For sauce, heat olive oil in a heavy bottom saucepan over medium heat. Add shallot and sauté until soft. Add figs and wine. Reduce heat to medium-low. Reduce liquid by ¾. Add demi-glace and reduce by ¼. Season with salt and pepper; keep warm.

Trim skin on duck-breast halves, leaving ¾ of skin still attached. Score skin with three diagonal cuts. Season both sides with salt and pepper. Heat a sauté pan over medium-high heat. Place duck skin-side down. Cook until skin is very brown and crispy, about 5 minutes. Flip duck and cook for another 3 to 5 minutes, depending upon desired doneness. Drain on paper towel. Let rest 3 to 4 minutes.

Slice duck into 6 to 8 pieces. Place polenta in middle of plate. Fan duck around bottom half of polenta. Place small amount of spinach at top of duck. Drizzle sauce all around plate, spooning a good bit over duck. Garnish with figs. Serve with a bottle of Barboursville Vineyards Merlot. Makes 4 servings.

Named for Andrea Palladio, the sixteenth-century architect who inspired Thomas Jefferson's architectural style, Palladio Restaurant presents an elegantly balanced menu of classic Northern Italian cuisine along with the wines of Barboursville Vineyards, which the restaurant overlooks. The restaurant closes every January while the senior staff visits the leading kitchens of Tuscany, Piedmont, Lombardy, and Venice.

VIRGINIA FARM PIE

*Similar to a shepherd's pie, this main dish's flavor
is enhanced by cooking the meat in Oakencroft Winery's Countryside Red.*

1 pound ground beef
1 medium onion, chopped
3 carrots, peeled, quartered lengthwise, and sliced
1 clove garlic, minced
⅔ cup Oakencroft Countryside
   Red wine
2 tablespoons tomato paste

1 tablespoon chopped fresh parsley
½ teaspoon each dried thyme and
   rubbed sage
1 bay leaf, crumbled
salt and pepper to taste
3 cups mashed potatoes
½ cup grated sharp cheddar cheese,
   divided

Preheat a large skillet over high heat. Crumble beef into skillet and brown, stirring after 2 minutes. Add onion, carrots, and garlic. Continue to cook, stirring occasionally, until onion is soft. Drain fat; deglaze the pan with wine (add wine to loosen and scrape any browned bits from bottom of skillet). Add tomato paste, parsley, thyme, sage, bay leaf, salt, and pepper. Reduce heat, cover, and simmer 10 to 15 minutes, adding up to ⅓ cup water if mixture becomes dry.

Preheat oven to 375° F. Transfer meat mixture to a 10-inch pie plate. Stir ¼ cup cheese into potatoes and make a wreath of potatoes around outside edges of meat. Sprinkle remaining ¼ cup cheese on top. Bake 20 minutes, or until cheese melts and browns slightly. Makes 4 servings.

This recipe is courtesy of Oakencroft Vineyard and Winery, which is in an idyllic farm setting with Blue Ridge Mountain views. Oakencroft's wines include Countryside White, Countryside Red, Chardonnay, Cabernet, and Merlot. It is located in Charlottesville and is the oldest winery in Albemarle County (call (434) 296-4188 or visit www.oakencroft.com).

Wine Basics A–Z
(continued)

it's vitally important that wine-grape growers match their plantings to the climate of a particular region. Understanding the climate of a growing region helps you determine whether it would be a good place for a particular varietal. Chances are, a cool region won't make a very good Cabernet Sauvignon (because Cab needs lots of heat to ripen).

ENOLOGY—the study of the exciting alchemy that makes grapes into wine.

HYBRID—the product of breeding two species. In the wine-grape world, this usually refers to cross-breeds of European and native American grapes. Hybrids are most commonly found on the East Coast or in the Midwest.

ROOTSTOCK—Many grapevines are grafted onto roots that have been specially bred to resist certain diseases or pests, including the dreaded root louse, phylloxera, which has destroyed thousands of acres of vineyards in the United States and Europe over the past two centuries. Vineyardists spend a great deal of time learning which rootstocks, grafted to which varietal clones, perform best in various soils and conditions.

TANNIN—a natural component of wood, fruit, and seeds that gives wine its structure and "pucker factor"—that dry feeling on your tongue and in your mouth that marks certain wines, particularly Cabernet Sauvignon. Tannins help cleanse the mouth of fat, which is why tannic wines work best with rich meals (even if they can be a bit tough to take by themselves). Winemakers can influence the tannin levels of their wines through various handling and crushing techniques, the length of time they leave stems and seeds in contact with the juice, and the characteristics of oak barrels that may be used in aging certain wines.

TERROIR—the mysterious influence of the soil and climate on the grape. Terroir can be cut pretty fine—particular soils in specific vineyards can yield grapes with very special characteristics. Because most wines represent blends of grapes from various vineyards, terroir can be hard for most of us to observe first-hand.

TRELLIS—the structure of stakes and wires that vineyardists use to train grapevines. Rather than letting the vines sprawl, most grape growers tie canes to wires or at least use the wires to support the mass of vegetation. The result is better airflow through the vines (which reduces disease) and more sunlight exposure for the grapes and the leaves that feed them. It's also easier to harvest the grapes when workers don't have to crawl into a tangled mass.

interview

TO YOUR HEALTH!
A TOAST TO VIRGINIA WINES

An Interview with State Viticulturist Tony K. Wolf

"Making wine requires a carefully orchestrated recipe, beginning with the quality of the fruit, and a knowledgeable, hard-working viticulturist and winemaker who understands the peculiarities and limitations of Virginia-grown grapes. You need well-adapted varieties, an excellent site, including good elevation, soil, and available water, and you need a dash of good luck thrown in," says State Viticulturist Tony K. Wolf, Ph.D.

After almost 400 years of trying, Virginia seems to have found that recipe, and Dr. Wolf is its resident "chef." He is the state's Viticulture Extension Specialist at the Alson H. Smith, Jr. Agricultural Research and Extension Center in Winchester. Dr. Wolf was brought on board by Virginia Tech in 1986 to serve the Virginia grape industry and—as evidenced by numerous awards—he has done an outstanding job. He was awarded the Wine Industry Productivity Award (1998), presented by the Vinifera Wine Growers Association, and he was co-winner of the Virginia Wine Industry Person of the Year Award (1997), presented by the Virginia Department of Agriculture and Consumer Services.

Dr. Wolf plays an important part in the continuing success of wine production in the state, directing grape research and extension programs and recommending methods for improving grape quality and vineyard productivity for Virginia's growing conditions. He also provides educational resources to assist Virginia and regional grape producers, conducts research, and teaches. He earned his M.S. from Penn State University and a Ph.D. from Cornell. Here he answers the author's questions.

What was the profile of Virginia's wine industry when you arrived on the scene?

"In 1986, the industry was barely ten years old. There were 40 wineries and about 1300 acres of grapes. At that point, only seven wine-grape varieties were being touted for Virginia commercial vineyardists, and some writers made disparaging comments about the state's wines. We began a ten-year wine-grape-variety evaluation at the Winchester facility in 1989 to help recommend new varieties and guide the Old Dominion's young wine industry toward future accolades. Writing in *Wine Spectator* magazine in 1992, Thomas Matthews proclaimed Virginia was 'the most accomplished of America's emerging wine regions.' Today the state's 80 farm wineries produce in excess of 300,000 cases of wine from around 2200 acres of grapes. Nationally, Virginia ranks tenth in commercial wine-grape production."

Beyond Chardonnay and Virginia's number-two vinefera, Cabernet Sauvignon, is there an effort by Virginia wineries to plant more "trendy" wine-grape varieties?

"Yes, there's movement by some wineries to plant varieties more adapted to the state's growing conditions, or those that define a unique market niche. Norton, Viognier, Petite Verdot, Tannat (Uruguay), Sangiovese, and Syrah are some of the contenders. Further, much more attention is now given to clones of specific varieties rather than simply choosing a variety."

What does it take for a relatively new winery to produce top-quality wines?

"In some cases, it can happen rapidly with the right components. Jim Vascik and his winemaker wife Debra, of Valhalla Vineyard near Roanoke, won the 2000 Governor's Cup for their Syrah, plus 31 international medals only five years after their first planting. They had good land—an old peach orchard, good elevation, and are good students of the science."

Does the size of the winery matter?

"The success of a Virginia winery can depend upon quantity as well as quality. Before Patrick Dueffler of The Williamsburg Winery began his business, he did his homework and found that, based on efficiency of scale, it takes producing 50,000 cases of wine per year to make it a viable enterprise. Businesses that produce 25,000 to 50,000 are not as efficient."

What technologies and resources are routinely used today that were not available—or were not widely used—in the 1980s?

"A few of the obvious ones are personal computers and the Internet, canopy management, new classes of chemical pest control, more adapted varieties, irrigation, and a host of educational materials specific for Virginia vineyardists. Many of today's aspiring winemakers have their first contact with the Agricultural Research and Extension Center electronically and continue to obtain information through Listserv mailings and web-based newsletters."

How does your program at Virginia Tech help Virginia winegrowers?

"Canopy management—controlling the spacing and arrangement of vines and the degree of shading from the grape leaves—is both a research and educational focus of my program. We knew grapes that developed in shaded canopy interiors were more subject to rots, and even in the absence of disease, quality was inferior to that of well-exposed fruit. The program has helped vineyardists adopt one or more forms of canopy management, such as altered training systems, shoot positioning, selective leaf thinning, and shoot topping, all to improve grape and wine quality."

What pests attack Virginia's grapevines?

"Virginia's top wine variety (about 25% of acreage) is Chardonnay. It's adaptable to a wide range of growing conditions; however, it is susceptible to powder mildew, bunch rot, and Pierce's Disease. Bunch rot and powdery mildew are caused by fungi and thrive on tightly clustered and damp grapes.

"Winegrowers in the eastern Piedmont are at risk of Pierce's Disease, even though they have higher winter temperatures and freedom from winter-injury concerns. Pierce's Disease is caused by a bacterium that blocks the water- and nutrient-conducting vessels of plants so the grape leaves begin to dry or to scorch. Infected vines can die in as little as one to two years. The disease agent, carried by insects,

Wine Basics A–Z (continued)

VARIETAL (OR VARIETY)—wine made from a wine grape that exhibits specific, recognizable characteristics and has a unique heredity—for instance, Pinot Noir or Chardonnay. Varietal wines are made entirely, or mostly, from a particular variety. Federal varietal laws allow winemakers to designate a bottle as a varietal if it contains just 75% of that variety. Some states have stricter guidelines.

VINEFERA—a species of winegrape native to Europe (*Vitis vinifera*). Many East Coast wines, including Niagara, Concord, and Catawba, are made from native American grapes, the species *Vitis labrusca*.

VINTAGE—the year grapes were harvested to yield a particular wine. Weather conditions during that year help make it "a good year" or "a bad year" for that wine. Though varietal wines are generally bottled and recognized by vintage, some wines, including sparkling wines and Ports, are blends of various vintages. That's not necessarily a bad thing; it helps the winemaker craft a desired level of complexity or uniformity from year to year.

VITICULTURE—the art and science of raising grapes. Good wine starts in the vineyard, which makes viticulture the basis for fine wine.

Beer and Bourbon in Virginia

Distilling isn't new to Virginia. George Washington operated a very profitable distillery in the eighteenth century, and the Distilled Spirits Council, in partnership with Mount Vernon, is currently rebuilding our first president's distillery to full working order at a cost of $1.2 million. Today, only A. Smith Bowman Distillery in historic Fredericksburg operates commercially in Virginia, but its heritage is considerable. The distillery's "Virginia Gentleman" and "Bowman's" bourbons have been Virginia staples for almost 70 years.

In addition, Virginia has almost 40 breweries making lagers, ales, and stouts. Most are microbreweries and brewpubs, but two huge, national-brand breweries produce most of the beer in Virginia. In the Shenandoah Valley, Coors Brewing in Elkton brews more than five million barrels, while Anheuser-Busch in Williamsburg makes more than nine million barrels annually.

Microbreweries and brewpubs make a smaller contribution. Some of the larger ones are Old Dominion Brewing in Ashburn, the Virginia Beverage Company in Alexandria, and Richbrau, Williamsville, and Legend Breweries in Richmond. At brewpubs, you can order a "flight" of beer—a rack of small glasses holding an assortment of the establishment's beers and ales.

decimated 40,000 acres of grapes in the Anaheim, California, area in the late nineteenth century and is again the highest disease priority in much of California due to the recent (unintended) introduction there of a very efficient insect vector."

How much will Virginia's wine industry grow during the next decade?

"The steadily improving quality of Virginia wines, the regional and national attention they garner, and the slow but positive penetration of market share that Virginia wines are capturing all translate to increased demand. So, I'll go out on a limb and make some conservative growth projections: barring catastrophic events on Wall Street, substantial increases in energy prices, war, or other factors that rattle investor and consumer confidence, Virginia grape acreage will expand to 3500 acres by 2010.

Will the number of wineries increase?

"Most of that new acreage will be developed commensurate with new wineries, as opposed to independent grape producers. The number of wineries will increase during this period from the current 80 to 95—a conservative figure that acknowledges that 5 to 10 existing wineries will go out of business. The growth will occur principally in the counties that flank the eastern side of the Blue Ridge Mountains, extending into Bedford, Franklin, and Patrick Counties—those southern counties still relatively underexploited."

What innovations will be made in vine management?

"Blended wines, with proprietary names, will continue to make inroads on the more traditional, varietally-named wines. Vine training and trellising will probably see minor changes, the focus instead being on ease of vine management, vigor accommodation, and acceptable but not excessive yields. A philosophy of grape- and wine-quality improvement will continue to gain converts over the simple notion of yield maximization."

Dr. Wolf, aside from a research vineyard, you have no vineyard of your own. But if someone gave you 100 acres of your choice plus startup costs, where and what would you plant?

"I would locate my vineyard in Bedford County and plant five varieties: the reds Cabernet Franc, Cabernet Sauvignon, and Merlot; and the whites Viognier and Petit Verdot. Keep in mind that exclusive of land price, it's an average cost per acre of $7000 to 12,000 to start a new vineyard."

tour

A WEEKEND TOUR OF CENTRAL VIRGINIA WINERIES

For wine connoisseurs and nature lovers alike, an excursion to Virginia's handsome wineries, tucked into the lush farm landscape and often housed in historic structures, is truly an escape. Visiting one winery per weekend, it would take more than a year-and-a-half to see all 80.

Information about Virginia wineries is available by mail and on the Internet. To receive a free copy of the Virginia Wineries Festival and Tour Guide or to obtain other information on Virginia wines and wineries, contact the Virginia Wine Marketing Office at (800) 828-4637 (VA-VINES) or visit www.virginiawines.org.

This weekend tour is to three picturesque wineries near each other in the central region, which includes Orange County, the state's top wine-producing municipality. They all make excellent wines as evidenced by having accumulated hundreds of medals. Two have outstanding restaurants; one has historic ruins; and one offers lodging in luxury suites. You can try recipes from these vineyards included in this chapter.

Enjoy the scenery, sip wine, and dine and sleep in elegant style. Elsewhere in the central region are about 25 more wineries for your exploration. Combine this tour with the Monticello tour (page 150) for a longer vacation in the Charlottesville area. To begin this tour, drive toward the intersection of Interstate 64 and Highway 29 in Charlottesville and follow the directions below, beginning at Oakencroft.

Tour in a Nutshell

• WHEN, WHERE, HOW, HOW MUCH? •

Information about the location and offerings of all of Virginia's wineries can be found online at www.virginia wines.org. The site also features details about wine history, pairing food and wine, events and festivals relating to wine, and much more. Or call (800) 828-4637 to receive a free copy of the Virginia Wineries Festival and Tour Guide or to contact the Virginia Wine Marketing Office.

OAKENCROFT VINEYARD AND WINERY
The winery is open daily from 11 a.m. to 5 p.m. between April and December, by appointment in January and February, and on weekends in March. At the intersection of I-64 and Highway 29 in Charlottesville, turn north on Route 29 and west on Barracks Road (Route 654) 3.5 miles. Call (434) 296-4188 or visit www.oakencroft .com. Tasting fees charged. Food is not available on the premises.

BARBOURSVILLE VINEYARD AND HISTORIC RUINS
Open daily (except on major holidays) from 10 a.m. to 5 p.m. Monday through Saturday and from 11 a.m. to 5 p.m. on Sunday. Palladio Restaurant hours are noon to 3 p.m. Wednesday through Saturday and / to 9:30 p.m. Friday and Saturday. To reach

the winery, which is located about 20 miles northeast of Charlottesville, turn east on Route 33 from Route 29 and drive 6 miles. Turn right on Route 20 and take the first left onto Route 678. Proceed 0.5 mile and turn right on Route 777 (Vineyard Road), then right at the first driveway and follow the signs. Call the vineyard at (540) 832-3824 or visit www. barboursvillewine.com. Call Palladio Restaurant at (540) 832-7848; reservations are suggested for lunch and required for dinner (book by phone or at www.palladio restaurant.com). The menus change monthly. Tasting fees for the winery are $3 per person and include the glass.

PRINCE MICHEL WINERY AND RAPIDAN RIVER VINEYARDS

The winery is open daily year-round (except on major holidays) from 10 a.m. to 5 p.m. The restaurant is open only for catered events. Prince Michel Winery is located on Route 29 South midway between Culpeper and Madison, in Leon. For more information, call (540) 547-3707 or (800) 800-9463 or visit www.princemichel.com. Wine tastings are free.

OAKENCROFT VINEYARD AND WINERY

Begin your tour in the morning, at the intersection of Interstate 64 and Highway 29 in Charlottesville. Go north on Route 29 and turn west on Barracks Road (Route 654). About three-and-a-half miles later, you'll arrive at Oakencroft Vineyard and Winery, one of the state's most picturesque. As many as five species of waterfowl may be spotted on the lake in front of the winery courtyard. The Blue Ridge Mountains form a backdrop for the winery and vineyards. The winery was built from an old smokehouse on the family's 250-acre farm.

It's appropriate to begin your tour at Oakencroft because it was founded by Felicia Warburg Rogan, known as the matriarch of the Virginia wine industry; she planted her vineyard in 1978. Its first vintage was fermented in stainless-steel milk tanks purchased from a Shenandoah Valley dairy. Most of the whites these days are aged in old French oak barrels. Oakencroft currently produces Countryside Red, Countryside White, Blush, Chardonnay, Cabernet Sauvignon, and Merlot.

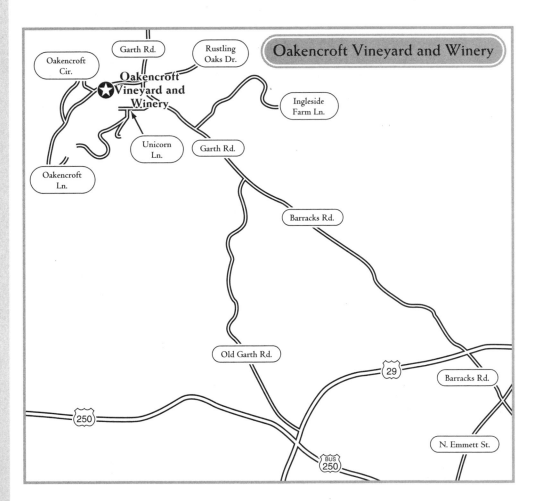

BARBOURSVILLE VINEYARDS AND HISTORIC RUINS

Drive to Barboursville Vineyards in time for a special lunch at Palladio, a fine Northern Italian–style restaurant. In addition, while exploring the vineyard's 830 acres of lovely rolling hills, you can tour the historic ruins of one of the largest and finest residences in the region—that of Governor James Barbour, designed by his friend Thomas Jefferson to be the grandest residence in Orange County. Virginia governor from 1812 to 1814, Barbour was also a U.S. senator, secretary of war, and ambassador to Great Britain. The mansion burned in 1884.

The estate winery, vineyards, and gift shop are close to the Blue Ridge Mountains and are owned by the winegrowing Zonin family of Italy. Presently, more than 100 acres are planted and the vineyards continue to expand. Under the direction of general manager and winemaker Luca Paschina since 1990, Barboursville consistently produces quality wines in the Italian and French styles that have won international recognition. Included in the 21 wines produced—the state's largest selection of estate produced and bottled vinifera wines—are Chardonnay, Sparkling Brut, Chardonnay Reserve, Sauvignon Blanc, Pinot Grigio, Riesling, Traminer Aromatico, Cabernet Blanc, Rosato, Pinot Noir, Merlot, Cabernet Franc, Cabernet Sauvignon, Cabernet Sauvignon Reserve, Barbera Reserve, Octagon, Malvaxia Reserve, Viognier, Sangiovese, and Phileo.

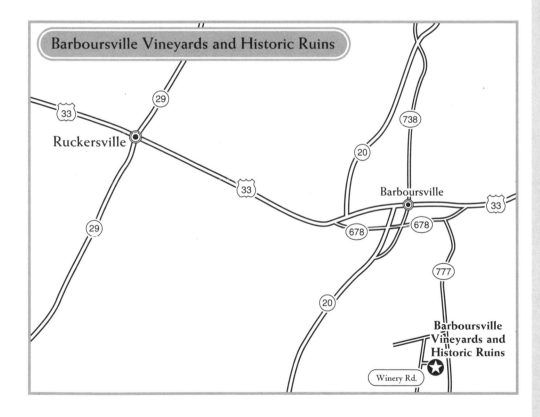

Cooking with Wine

In addition to its merits as a beverage, wine shares its attributes as a recipe ingredient. Both red and white wine are used as a marinade, because their slight acidity tenderizes meat and poultry and helps these dense foods absorb flavors from herbs, spices, and vegetables. Fruits can be "macerated" in still or sparkling wines.

As a cooking liquid, wine adds flavor and moisture to long-cooking stews and sauces. Examples are the classic Coq au Vin (chicken cooked in red wine) and Bordelaise sauce. Short cooking times also benefit from using wine as a cooking liquid, as in fish poached in white wine. Sometimes wine is used to finish a dish—to add a spoonful to cream soup, to deglaze a pan, or to make a salad dressing.

The alcohol in wine will evaporate in a stew cooked for at least 15 minutes or when wine is rapidly reduced for a minute or two. This rids it of any unpleasant alcohol taste and frees the flavor of the vintage. This is why experts admonish to cook with wines you deem drinkable. It's not necessary to cook with expensive wines, however avoid supermarket varieties labeled "cooking wines." These wines frequently contain salt, can be of inferior quality, and are definitely not drinkable.

Virginia Spring Water

In addition to the water used to make beer and distilled spirits, Virginia pure spring water is also bottled in several parts of the state. Some of the companies are Amelia Springs Water in Amelia; Endless Caverns Premium Mountain Spring Water in New Market; Grayson Mountain Water Company, Inc.; Miller's Spring Water in Chesapeake; Misty Mountain Spring Co. in Abingdon; and Mount Carmel Water, Alton.

Unique local soft drinks made in Virginia include the Northern Neck Bottling Co. Carver's Original ginger ale made in Montross (www.realginger ale.com); Root 66 root beer made by Roadside Beverage Co. in Charlottesville; and Shenandoah Honey-Sweetened root beer made by Shenandoah Brewing Co. in Alexandria (www.shenandoah brewing.com).

PRINCE MICHEL WINERY AND RAPIDAN RIVER VINEYARDS

End your day at Prince Michel Winery, overlooking the immaculately ordered vineyard. Consider peeking in on the museum where antique winemaking equipment from France is displayed.

The lovely French-style winery reflects its ownership by French businessman Jean Leducq. He purchased the property and that of nearby Rapidan River Vineyards from a German surgeon. The white wines of Rapidan, such as Riesling and Gewurtztraminer, continue to be produced in a Germanic style, while the Prince Michel wines, including Cabernet Sauvignon, Merlot-Cabernet, and Chardonnay, have a French character.

Prince Michel Vineyard and Winery was founded in 1982, and has since grown to become one of the largest wineries in the state and along the east coast. It is home to both Prince Michel and Rapidan River wines. The friendly and knowledgeable staff offer complimentary wine tastings in the wine shop atop the barrel caves and tank room. You can take a self-guided tour of the wine-making facility—no reservations necessary. Enjoy a glass of wine in the atrium or picnic with friends and family on the grounds.

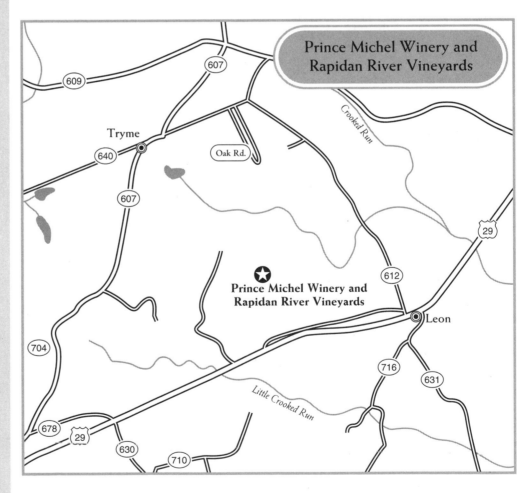

part nine
OTHER FARM PRODUCTS

Although most people associate farming with food crops, sales of crops that are not edible comprise more than 25% of the estimated $3 billion generated by Virginia agriculture. Such crops include tobacco, hay, corn for silage, soybeans, cotton, horses, Christmas trees, flowers, and other nursery products.

Tobacco contributed significantly to the prosperity of the Virginia Colony. Although, it is still one of the most valuable crops grown in Virginia, revenue and the number of acres dedicated to its cultivation have steadily fallen. The crop reached its high in 1930, when 193,000 acres were planted. Fewer than 20,000 acres of tobacco are planted today.

"Sixe mares and a [male] horse" arrived with the settlers at Jamestown in August 1610, but the horses were, unfortunately, eaten during "the starving time." More horses arrived once the colonists began to cultivate tobacco and required horses for plowing; and then, during the prosperous middle third of the 1700s, wealthy planters imported "blooded" horses that gave rise to the American thoroughbred. Racing and fox hunting became popular, along with gentile riders decked out in hunting regalia. Today, equine industry's annual sales total $160 million.

Hay grown to feed livestock is Virginia's most valuable crop, at least in terms of the acreage planted (more than 1.3 million acres valued at more than $300 million if all were sold). Most hay, however, is used on the farm where it is grown, so actual cash receipts are nearly $50 million. Cotton, which bottomed out at only 100 acres planted in 1978, has rebounded to more than 100,000 acres planted today, netting nearly $50 million.

Sales of floriculture products, which include cut flowers, cultivated greens, potted flowering plants, foliage plants, and bedding and garden plants, have been on the rise. Virginia now ranks sixteenth among the states in the amount of floriculture products sold, with wholesale revenues of more than $80 million.

Virginia's forests still cover nearly two-thirds of the state—15.4 million acres, an astounding figure considering the overwhelming population growth. Though forest timber is not considered a farm crop, Christmas trees are. Christmas-tree farms have expanded rapidly during the past decade. There are about 1,600 farms where about two million Virginians will buy or cut their own trees each year, which results in annual revenue of more than $20 million.

Virginia Horses Today

❖ There are over 170,000 horses in Virginia and about 2% of all Virginia households own horses. The average number owned is three.

❖ Almost 20,000 Virginians are employed in horse-related occupations.

❖ The Virginia equine industry contributes over $1 billion in sales annually to Virginia businesses and individuals.

❖ Among the most popular of Virginia horses are thoroughbreds, including quarter horses, Arabians, and ponies.

❖ The most common uses of horses are, in order: recreational/trail riding, show/competition, breeding, and racing/training.

❖ Virginians spend $2,800 per horse per year. Taken collectively among the many different trades, services and professions, this translates into $680.5 million in direct expenditures in support of horses.

❖ Agriculture and agriculture service sector business sales from the equine industry total $230.9 million.

❖ More than 800,000 people participate in or attend equine events in Virginia annually. These visitors account for more than $160 million in direct expenditures in the state.

❖ Virginians spend an estimated $125 million annually for horses (purchase or lease) and use more than 4 million acres of land for these horses, which has an assessed value of more than $6 billion.

—Virginia Equine Education Foundation of Warrenton

chapter one
HORSES

∽ *Horses today contribute to the visual beauty of Virginia and are a major attraction for visitors. The annual state calendar is filled with polo matches, driving competitions, steeplechase races, pony-club rallies, farm and stable tours, jumping competitions, endurance rides, rodeos, and dressage competitions. Our genteel state brings to mind a picture of horses and their distinguished riders (such as Jackie Kennedy Onassis) and horse farmers (such as Senator John Warner and his former wife, Elizabeth Taylor, who lived on his elegant Atoka horse farm).*

Virginia horses have earned more Olympic equestrian medals than those from any other state, and Virginia is home to more than twice the number of horse-related hunt clubs than any other state. In addition, the equine industry is a profitable one. Sales related to horses total $60 million annually, ranking the state fourth nationally.

VIRGINIA HUNTS

A sleek, black thoroughbred streaks over a fence, a red-coated rider glued to his back. The duo is hot on the hounds, who are, in turn, tracking a wily, wild red fox. You can see such a sight between September and March, hunt season (as opposed to hunt*ing* season) in the Old Dominion.

The aim of the hunt is not to kill but to chase. A successful hunt ends when the fox is accounted for by entering a hole in the ground, called an "earth." Once there, hounds are rewarded with praise from their huntsman. The fox gets away and is chased another day.

The breed of hounds mainly used today is Penn-Marydel, which stands for Pennsylvania, Maryland, and Delaware, areas in which these hounds of many colors were originally bred. However, a pack of hounds seems to have been kept in Northampton County as early as 1691, and in 1730, eight prosperous tobacco planters imported red English foxes because grey American foxes would "go to ground" (hide underground and not run).

The region known as Virginia's hunt country lies east of the Blue Ridge and stretches from Loudoun to Albemarle Counties. The firmer footing (and fewer waterways) of the Piedmont make this area more hospitable to fox hunting. The hunt lifestyle—which is dependent upon the undisturbed expanses of land over which the hunts take place—has contributed to the preservation of large estates and horse farms in the area.

"Hunts are conducted over farms of all kinds," according to Wea Ohrstrom Nichols, a member of the Orange County Hunt. "The hunts ask permission from farmers to ride across their fields, and most give it. The hunters are careful not to trample or destroy planted crops, and they close any gates behind themselves so livestock can't escape. The farm owners are invited to become members of the hunt, and many join," Nichols explains. In order to hunt, one must be an invited member of one of the 28 hunts in Virginia. Then you need a horse, usually a thoroughbred or quarterhorse. Formal hunts require hunting attire; jeans are suitable for casual hunts. The hunt clubs provide the hounds, which are trained and maintained by the Master of Foxhounds.

Those Pleasant "Golden" Years

Pleasant Colony, one of the world's leading sires, enjoyed a retirement at Blue Ridge Farm equal to the finest senior living facilities for humans. In 1981, the almost 17-hand-high dark bay stallion won the Kentucky Derby and the Preakness, missing the Triple Crown by a length-and-a-half in the Belmont. After almost two decades as a world-class sire, the gentle 23-year-old enjoyed his retirement with a private paddock adjacent to his stall which allowed him to be in or out day and night, as he wished.

∽ DID YOU KNOW . . . that the Piedmont Foxhounds were the first organized hunt club in the United States, in 1840? A year later came the Albemarle County Hunt, followed by the Rappahannock Hunt in 1926 and the Glenmore Hunt in 1930. Rappahannock has access to the largest hunting territory in Virginia—384,000 acres—one of the largest in the United States. By the 1930s, 14 of the most famous pack hounds in the United States were concentrated in northern Virginia, and the official state dog was named the American foxhound. Today, 37 states have hunt clubs that are listed as members of the Masters of Foxhounds of America. Virginia has by far the most—28. Pennsylvania is second in the number of clubs, with 12.

JACKIE BURKE'S PIMM'S CUP

This is the perfect beverage for hot June afternoons tailgating at the Upperville Horse Show, where Virginia's fine young horses have been showcased since 1853.

assorted fresh fruits such as blue-
    berries, strawberries, chopped
    peaches, or apples
ice cubes

Pimm's No. 1 Cup (a British liqueur)
ginger ale, tonic water, or lemon-lime
    soda
fresh mint leaves

Scatter some fruit in the bottom of an 8- to 10-ounce beverage cup or glass. Fill with ice cubes and pour in enough Pimm's to come halfway up the cup. Top off the cup with ginger ale and add a sprig or two of mint. Allow 1 or 2 servings per person.

Jackie Burke lives in the Virginia hunt country, writes about horses, and is herself a fine rider, fox hunter, horse-show judge, and steeplechase trainer. Burke also organizes riding tours through her company Visites Hippiques.

HUNTER'S REST
ROASTED PEPPER-AND-BASIL PASTA SALAD

6 large bell peppers (2 green, 2 red,
    and 2 yellow, or any assortment)
1 tablespoon olive oil
2 cups chopped Vidalia onion, white
    or yellow
½ teaspoon fennel seeds, crushed
2 cloves garlic, minced
3 large, peeled tomatoes, chopped
    but not drained

½ teaspoon salt
¼ teaspoon pepper
1 (16-ounce) box penne pasta or
    other short tubular shape, cooked
½ cup chopped fresh basil or other
    fresh herb (do not substitute dried
    herbs)
½ cup grated Parmesan cheese

Preheat oven to 450° F. Place peppers on a baking sheet and roast 10 minutes, or until black and charred. When cool enough to handle, pull off skin and cut into julienne strips; set aside.

Heat oil in skillet over medium-low heat. Cook onion, fennel seeds, and garlic, covered, for about 10 minutes, stirring occasionally. Add tomatoes and bring to a boil. Reduce heat to simmer and cook uncovered for 30 minutes, stirring occasionally. Add pepper strips and cook 3 minutes more. Combine tomato mixture, pasta, and basil in a large serving bowl. Sprinkle with cheese. Chill well.

If transporting the salad to a hunt or other outdoor event, keep it in an insulated cooler with ice. Remove from cooler about 30 minutes before serving. Makes 8 servings.

Betsy Burke Parker was the horse and field-sports editor for the Fauquier Times-Democrat *in Warrenton. Parker is a licensed steeplechase trainer and was formerly a champion amateur steeplechase jockey. She now runs Hunter's Rest in Rappahannock County, a boarding and training operation. Parker hunts regularly with the Old Dominion Hounds.*

Foxes and Feasts

The most festive day of the hunt year is opening day of the formal hunt season, according to Jackie Burke in her book *Capital Horse Country*. "A big feed is always part of the day," Burke continues. "Big spreads of grits, Virginia ham, and other delicacies served on polished hunt boards (hence the name) anytime up into early afternoon are tagged 'hunt breakfasts.'" Burke explains that while fancy hunt breakfasts can be held after riders go home to change into fresh clothes, most are tailgate picnics where tired, sweaty riders gather with their horses in the countryside. For polo, steeplechasing, and other competitions, a tailgate break-fast is also in order.

DID YOU KNOW . . .
that The National Sporting Library houses more than 12,000 volumes, dating from 1528, on horse rac-ing, dressage, eventing, show jumping, breeding, equitation, veterinary care, foxhunting, polo, racing, sporting art, and much more? The nonprofit research center for horse and field sports was found-ed in 1954 by George L. Ohrstrom, Sr. and Alexan-der Mackay-Smith. The library is in the historic town of Middleburg, about an hour west of Washington, D.C., at the corner of Route 50 (Washington Street) and the Plains Road. The library, open weekdays, is housed in a new 15,000-square-foot facility (call (540) 687-6542).

THE HOMESTEAD'S BEEF STROGANOFF

The Homestead's longtime executive chef Albert Schnarwyler—now retired—says this recipe, one of his favorites, is an excellent dish for an elegant hunt breakfast when doubled or quadrupled.

1 large onion, diced	2 tablespoons flour
½ cup butter	3 cups chicken or veal broth, boiling
2 ounces tomato paste	1 cup sour cream
⅛ teaspoon oregano	½ cup mushrooms, sliced and sautéed
1 small bay leaf	1½ pounds beef tenderloin, cut into
pinch of thyme	thin strips
salt and pepper to taste	cooked noodles or rice

Sauté onion in butter until golden and tender. Add tomato paste, oregano, bay leaf, thyme, salt, and pepper. Sauté on low heat for a few minutes. Add flour and mix well. Add broth and cook 30 minutes. Remove bay leaf; blend in sour cream and mushrooms.

In a hot skillet, sauté beef until done, about 3 to 4 minutes. Add sauce to beef and reheat gently. Serve over hot noodles or rice. Makes 5 servings.

The Homestead, tucked within Virginia's Allegheny Mountains in Hot Springs, was founded as a small inn in 1766 by Commodore Thomas Bullitt, who received unsolicited room-and-board requests at his own home from travelers seeking the rejuvenation and cure of area hot springs. Today, the premier resort features numerous amenities and access to skiing, skating, shooting sports, horseback/carriage rides, and three golf courses, one of which is the famed Cascades (phone (540) 839-1766).

MEADOW CREEK DAIRY CHEESE GRITS

An excellent side dish for any meal of the day.

3¾ cups water	½ cup milk
1 cup quick grits	1¼ cups grated Appalachian Jack
1 teaspoon salt	cheese or cheddar cheese
¼ teaspoon pepper	4 cloves garlic
1 large egg	

Boil the water in a heavy saucepan. Slowly pour in the grits, stirring constantly to avoid lumps. Add the salt and the black pepper. Cook, stirring often, on low heat until thick and smooth, about 7 minutes. Remove the pan from the heat.

In a bowl, beat the egg and milk together. Fold the egg mixture into the grits. Add half the cheese and the garlic and mix well. Pour the grits mixture into an oiled 2-quart baking dish. Top the casserole with the remaining cheese.

Bake, uncovered, at 375° F for 20 to 30 minutes, or until the top is golden. Remove from oven and let sit for 5 minutes before serving. Makes 6 servings.

Meadow Creek Dairy is a family farm in the mountains of southwest Virginia. Helen and Jim Feete opened the dairy in 1980, and they raise a Jersey herd via ecologically-friendly methods. The dairy produces handcrafted cheeses, including Appalachian Jack a "dry Jack," which is made with whole milk and is lower in moisture and aged longer than Monterey Jack. Call (888) 236-0622 or visit www.meadowcreekdairy.com.

TURKEY AND OYSTERS IN CHAMPAGNE SAUCE

This splendid main dish, perfect for large groups,
has graced the tables of countless hunt breakfasts.

FOR TURKEY:

1 (20-pound) turkey	1 onion, cut into wedges
3 cups water plus more if needed	1 bay leaf
1 carrot, cut into chunks	

FOR OYSTERS AND SAUCE:

2 quarts oysters	stock from turkey
1 pound butter	1 bottle of good champagne
1 cup minced onion	½ cup cognac
2 cups flour	1 bunch fresh parsley, rinsed, stems
1 teaspoon nutmeg	removed, and chopped
salt and pepper to taste	hot, cooked white rice

Preheat oven to 350° F. Place turkey in a roasting pan with a lid. Add water along with carrot, onion, and bay leaf. (Note: Maintain about ½-inch of water in the bottom of pan during cooking.) Cover and roast 4 hours, or until thermometer inserted in thigh reads 180° F. Turkey should be fork tender but not stringy. Do not overcook. Transfer turkey to a platter; cut legs and wings off turkey to help it cool faster. Strain broth in pan and save to make sauce. When turkey is cool enough to handle, debone and cut meat into bite-size chunks; set aside.

Strain liquid off oysters; reserve oyster liquor for sauce. Pick over oysters in case any shells remain. Cook oysters in a buttered skillet only until edges begin to curl.

To make sauce, melt 1 stick of butter in a large pot. Sauté onions until tender. Add remaining 3 sticks of butter; melt and blend in flour. Add nutmeg, salt, and pepper. Using a whisk, gradually blend in reserved turkey broth and oyster liquor. Blend in champagne and cognac. Cook over medium-high heat, stirring often, until sauce thickens. If sauce is too thick, add additional broth in moderate amounts. The sauce should be thick enough to coat a spoon.

Stir in cooked turkey and oysters. Reheat gently and keep warm in a chafing dish. Sprinkle with parsley and serve over rice. Makes 45 to 60 servings. Recipe can be halved.

⁓ This recipe is one of Catherine Doores's, who, during her 22-year career as a cook at Whitewood Farm (located between Middleburg and Upperville), sometimes prepared hunt breakfasts for as many as 500 people. She grew up on her grandfather's farm in Warrenton, where she helped tend the family's huge vegetable garden for their own use. "When I was a child," she says, "I thoroughly enjoyed helping in the garden." Doores has two sons, four grandsons, and two great-granddaughters. ⁓

OVERNIGHT BRUNCH PUFF

Assemble this dish with bacon or sausage or, if you prefer,
with crab meat, shrimp, chopped spinach, or chopped broccoli.

1 pound bacon or bulk sausage
2 onions, sliced
12 slices good-quality white bread
8 ounces shredded cheddar cheese,
   divided

8 eggs
4 cups milk
1½ teaspoons salt
½ teaspoon dry mustard
¼ teaspoon pepper

Cook bacon or sausage; place on a paper towel. Pour off all but 2 tablespoons drippings. Sauté onion until soft. Butter a (9 × 13-inch) rectangular baking dish and place 6 slices bread in one layer on the bottom. Sprinkle half of bacon or sausage, half of onions, and half of cheese. Repeat these layers.

In a mixing bowl, beat together eggs, milk, salt, dry mustard, and pepper. Pour over top layer of casserole. Cover and refrigerate at least 24 hours.

Preheat oven to 350° F and bake casserole 45 to 50 minutes, or until puffed and brown. Serves 6 hungry hunters or 8 spectators.

SENATOR JOHN WARNER'S FAVORITE COOKIES

These treats are chock full of chewy delight.

1 cup butter (2 sticks)
1 cup packed brown sugar
¾ cup sugar
2 eggs
1 teaspoon vanilla
1½ cups flour

1 teaspoon baking soda
1½ cups semisweet chocolate chips
1 cup flaked coconut
½ cup sunflower seeds
¼ cup chopped dates
¼ cup chopped almonds

Preheat oven to 325° F. Cream butter with brown sugar and sugar. Stir in eggs and vanilla. Stir in flour and baking soda; then stir in remaining ingredients. Drop dough by teaspoons onto baking sheets, leaving about 2 inches between each for cookies to spread. Bake for 12 minutes or until light brown. Remove immediately to a cooling rack. Makes about 6 dozen cookies.

Republican Senator John William Warner was first elected to the U.S. Senate in 1978. He was reelected to serve his fifth six-year term in November 2002 and is the chairman of the Senate Armed Forces Committee. Until the early 1990s, Senator Warner owned a 500-acre horse farm called Atoka, midway between Upperville and Middleburg. He is now residing in Alexandria.

Making Hay While the Sun Shines

Hay is wild or cultivated plants, mainly grasses and legumes, mown and dried for use as livestock feed. Typically, grasses such as timothy, or legumes such as alfalfa or clover are used to make hay, which is one of the leading crops of the United States. In Virginia, 1,310,000 acres are devoted to hay.

Farmers "make hay while the sun shines" to dry and preserve it so it won't spoil. After mowing first thing in the morning—as soon as the dew has evaporated, the hay is spread in the field or raked into rows called "windrows." It must dry quickly and uniformly because its nutritive value and palatability are reduced by overexposure to sunlight or rain. Unequal drying often results in loss of the leaves, which form two thirds of hay's feed value. Windrows are turned with pitchforks the following day to allow the hay to dry uniformly. Curing (reducing the moisture to about 20%) may be done in the field, by barn finishing, or by artificial dehydration. Field-cured hay should be ready for storage the following afternoon. The hay is stored indoors in a hayloft or piled in a haystack. Barn-finished hay is partially dried in the field and then placed in a hayloft, where drying is finished by forcing natural or heated air through the hay.

SOFT SPICE BISCOTTI

"Biscotti" means twice baked. You can bake these cookies once for a soft sweet or bake them twice for crispness.

1 cup sugar	2 teaspoons water
1 cup packed dark brown sugar	2 teaspoons cinnamon
½ cup sliced almonds	1 teaspoon ground cloves
⅓ cup oil	2½ cups all-purpose flour
2 egg whites	2 teaspoons baking powder
l egg	

Preheat oven to 375° F. Coat a baking sheet with cooking spray; set aside. In the large bowl of an electric mixer, combine sugar, brown sugar, almonds, oil, egg whites, egg, water, cinnamon, and cloves. Mix at low speed for 1 minute. Then add flour and baking powder. Gradually mix until well blended. Dough will be soft.

Turn dough out onto a lightly floured surface; shape dough into 2 rectangles. Place on baking sheet and flatten dough to ¾-inch thickness. Bake 25 minutes. Remove rectangles from baking sheet and cool 10 minutes on a wire rack. Cut each rectangle diagonally into ¾-inch slices. Biscotti will be soft. If twice-baked type are preferred, stand slices on their edges so hot air reaches both cut sides and bake an additional 10 minutes. Makes 24 biscotti.

This recipe was provided by Holly McPeak, a nutritionist with the U.S. Department of Agriculture and a member of the advisory board of the culinary school of Stratford University. McPeak is a 20-year resident of Loudoun County, most recently Lucketts.

CONGRESSMAN TOM DAVIS'S CHOCOLATE CHIP OATMEAL COOKIES

These cookies are a special favorite of the Davises and their three children, and can be taken on the trail for a delicious snack.

1 cup Crisco shortening	½ teaspoon salt
¾ cup sugar	1 teaspoon baking soda
¾ cup light brown sugar	⅔ cup oatmeal (quick cooking)
2 beaten eggs	1 cup nuts (optional)
1 teaspoon vanilla flavoring	1 package chocolate chips (6 ounces)
1¾ cups flour	

Cream together shortening and sugars. Add eggs and vanilla and mix. In a separate bowl, sift together flour, salt, and baking soda, then add to sugar mixture. Add oatmeal, nuts, and chocolate chips. Drop by teaspoon onto baking sheet. Bake at 350° F for 12 to 15 minutes. Enjoy!

The Honorable Thomas M. Davis represents Virginia's 11th District and was first elected in 1994. He has a law degree from the University of Virginia. Davis also attended Officer Candidate School, served on active duty in the U.S. Army, and spent eight years with the Virginia National Guard and the U.S. Army Reserve. In January 2001, Tom was named chairman of the newly formed Government Reform Subcommittee on Technology and Procurement Policy. He also has reclaimed his seat on the Energy and Commerce Committee, with a spot on the Subcommittee on Telecommunications and the Internet. Both posts are critical to Northern Virginia's high-tech community. His wife, Peggy, is a gynecologist in Fairfax.

VIRGINIA RACES AND SHOWS

Today there are more than a dozen major horse-breeding farms in Virginia and hundreds of small ones. Many are multipurpose: they breed and break in horses, and they rehabilitate, train, and sell horses to race or show. Racehorses are bred for two types of racing: steeplechasing and racing on an oval track, which is known as flat-track racing. The Kentucky Derby is a flat-track race, and Virginia's new $60 million racing facility Colonial Downs, which opened in September 1997 in New Kent County near Williamsburg, hosts flat-track races too. In steeplechasing, horses jump over obstacles such as fences, water hazards, and natural "brush," or hedges, made of packed pine or cedar on a planned course.

Virginia has more than twice the steeplechases (35) of any other state, and they are often run for the benefit of local charities. Spring and autumn usher in steeplechase and point-to-point racing with equestrian competition. The Virginia Gold Cup (spring), held the same day as the Kentucky Derby, and the International Gold Cup (fall) held in The Plains, Virginia, provide the setting for the largest steeplechase events in the state.

Point-to-point is a type of steeplechase race. Peter Winants, former director of The Sporting Library explains: "While both styles of competition feature races over fences, steeplechases generally offer big-money prizes and are sanctioned by the National Steeplechase Association. Point-to-points are sponsored by local hunts and winners might win trophies but not money. Many top-notch riders make a living competing in steeplechases; point-to-points usually are attended by folks in casual attire. The fancy clothes and hats are saved for steeplechases."

The Hunt Country Stable Tour, held each Memorial Day weekend, offers an educational tour of various equine show, training, and breeding facilities in the Middleburg/Upperville area. A dozen farms open their stables, and it's a rare opportunity to see places where horses live better than people.

SHOWING OFF

Horse shows began as fairs to sell horses. They developed into programs of exhibitions, demonstrations, and competitions. The Upperville Colt and Horse Show, begun in 1853, is the oldest in the United States, and the Warrenton Pony Show, established in 1920, is the oldest of its kind. Many shows include dressage, jumper courses, saddle-horse competitions, and simulated fox-hunting courses.

Dressage is the classic art of riding, where the rider uses subtle shifting of his weight, a squeeze of a leg or a pull on the reigns to lead his horse through a series of serpentine figures, sideways movements, and smooth transitions, from a trot to a halt. But despite the formal top hat, white gloves, and tails, dressage is also a very competitive sport. Dressage shows, competitions, and workshops are hosted at Morven Park in Leesburg and the Virginia Horse Center in Lexington. To find out about upcoming events, See the Virginia Dressage Association Web site at www.virginiadressage.org.

Many other horse-related events are held today in Virginia. Horse lovers and equestrians from across the country travel to the Shenandoah Valley town of Lexington for the Virginia Horse Center's full schedule of shows, clinics, and festivals. On Virginia's Eastern Shore, there's the famous Chincoteague Pony Roundup held each July and made famous by the equestrian childrens' writer Marguerite Henry, in her book *Misty of Chincoteague*. Other attractions in the Commonwealth feature beautiful horses such as Busch Gardens Williamsburg's Clydesdales. The Marriott Ranch in Hume offers an Old West experience for families, with trail rides and chuck-wagon dinners. The Willow Run Polo School teaches the basics of polo, while the Virginia Regional Therapeutic Riding Center at MadCap Farm emphasizes equestrian skills for physically- or emotionally-challenged riders.

Watch an action-packed polo match or a careful jumping round, drive past mountains and green rolling pastures where mares and foals frolic, or find a mount and head off into the sunset over the Blue Ridge Mountains. You'll quickly see why "Virginia Is for Horse Lovers."

❖ The oldest horse show in
the country, The Upperville
Colt and Horse Show, began
in 1853 and takes place today
at its original site in
Upperville.

❖ Two of the Civil War's
most renowned horses, Traveler (owned by Robert E. Lee)
and Little Sorrel (owned by
"Stonewall" Jackson), are both
buried in Lexington.

❖ Virginia was the birthplace
of one of the country's greatest
athletes. Triple Crown–winner
Secretariat was born at The
Meadow Farm in Doswell.
Secretariat was the only ath-
lete to grace the covers of *Time*,
Newsweek, and *Sports Illustrated*
within the same week, and still
holds track records.

❖ "Sea Hero," of Upperville,
was the fourth Virginia horse
to win the Kentucky Derby,
following Secretariat, Pleasant
Colony, and Reigh Court. His
owner, Paul Mellon, is the
only man to have won the
premier races in the United
States (Kentucky Derby),
England (Derby at Epsom),
and France (Arc de Triomphe
at Longchamps).

❖ Virginia members of the
U.S. Equestrian Team took
home five medals in the 2000
Sydney Olympics. David
O'Connor of The Plains won
the gold medal in the equestrian decathlon, riding Custom
Made, a 15-year-old Irish
sport horse. O'Connor and his
wife Karen, along with Middleburg's Nina Fout and Bluemont resident Linden
Weisman, won bronze medals
in the team event.

SENATOR CHARLES HAWKINS' CORNBREAD

The senator says he enjoys this cornbread with fresh, ripe tomatoes.

2½ cups self-rising cornmeal	1 egg
1½ cups buttermilk	1 teaspoon sugar
½ cup melted butter	

Preheat oven to 325° F. Generously grease an 8 x 8-inch baking pan. In a mixing bowl, combine all ingredients. Pour batter into prepared pan and bake 25 to 30 minutes, or until cornbread tests done. Makes 9 squares.

☞ *Republican Senator Charles R. Hawkins is Chair of the Virginia Senate Agriculture, Conservation, and Natural Resources Committee. A resident of Chatham, he states: "My history is steeped in rural Southside Virginia. I consider myself fortunate to have had that background, when so many have not had this rural heritage to form their viewpoints on agriculture."* ☜

BANANA BOURBON CAKE

*Tasting like a rich banana bread, this cake is delicious with or without
the bourbon icing and can be made ahead for a hunt breakfast or other occasions.*

FOR CAKE:

1½ cups chopped pecans	1 cup (2 sticks) unsalted butter,
1½ cups golden raisins	room temperature
3 cups flour, divided	2 cups sugar
1 tablespoon baking powder	3 ripe bananas, mashed
1 teaspoon each ground cinnamon	4 eggs
and ginger	¾ cup Virginia Gentleman bourbon
½ teaspoon nutmeg	whiskey

FOR BOURBON ICING:

½ cup butter	1 pound powdered sugar
1 (8-ounce) package cream cheese	3 tablespoons bourbon whiskey

Preheat oven to 350° F. Toss pecans and raisins with ½ cup flour; set aside. Sift remaining 2½ cups flour with baking powder, cinnamon, ginger, and nutmeg; set aside. Beat together butter and sugar until light and fluffy. Add bananas and eggs, one at a time, stirring after each. Fold in flour mixture alternately with bourbon, beginning and ending with dry ingredients. Fold in pecans and raisins.

Pour batter into ungreased 10-inch tube pan or Bundt pan. Bake 50 to 60 minutes, or until cake tests done. Cool and remove from pan. If desired, frost with bourbon icing. Makes 16 servings.

To make the frosting, cream softened butter and softened cream cheese, then stir in powdered sugar and bourbon.

☞ *This recipe was contributed by Terri and Henry Walters of the Sugar Tree Inn, a rustic log cabin with rocking chairs, a swing on the front porch, and a restaurant. The structure was built by local craftsmen over six years, using pioneer techniques and no nails. The fireplace in the living room contains 55 tons of quarried limestone set by hand. Some of the nine rooms and two suites have fireplaces, and all have country quilts. The inn is atop a 3000-foot peak in the Blue Ridge Mountains (phone (800) 377- 2197 or (540) 377-2197 or visit www.sugartreeinn.com).* ☜

PAUL MAXWELL, BLUE RIDGE FARM

Secretariat, Race Horse of the Century

Virginia native Secretariat was one of the greatest athletes of all time. Secretariat was born at Meadow Farms Stables in Caroline County, Virginia, on March 30, 1970. The big chestnut horse won the Triple Crown in 1973 while setting records in the Kentucky Derby, the Preakness, and the Belmont stakes, which he won by an amazing 31 lengths, setting a new world record that still stands. When he outran the field, Secretariat wasn't racing against other horses, but against the clock; there wasn't another horse in the same zip code. Secretariat was the first horse to win the Triple Crown in 25 years. He graced the covers of _Time, Newsweek,_ and _Sports Illustrated_ all in the same week.

Secretariat retired to stud at Claiborne Farm, Kentucky. He sired 41 stakes winners and became a noted broodmare sire, but at age 19 he came down with laminitis and could not be saved. A necropsy showed that all the horse's vital organs were normal in size, except for his heart, which was twice the nine-pound size of the average horse's. Secretariat had a heart worth its weight in gold!

The Caroline County Government is raising funds to create the Secretariat Museum of Thoroughbred Racing and an equine facility at the 340-acre Meadow Farm, which is now privately owned.

Route 623 in Upperville is one of the most breathtaking roads in the state. The county artery parallels hand-constructed stone walls and post-and-rail fences that line the green pastures of the soft Blue Ridge Mountain foothills. Magnificent, glossy thoroughbreds and their delicate foals gracefully bend to nibble the grass, swishing their thick, flowing tails. Blue Ridge Farm, one of the oldest active thoroughbred horse-breeding farms in the country, is located here along Rokeby Road, just before Route 623 meets Rectortown Road.

The 516-acre Blue Ridge Farm is an unspoiled property with gravel-packed roads that undulate beneath overhanging old-growth hardwood trees. Tenant and manor houses dot the property, the oldest being Fountain Hill, a fieldstone house built in 1790. The white barns are made of wood; some could use some sanding and repainting. There are three stallion barns and three broodmare barns, and a yearling barn. The grassy paddocks where the thoroughbreds are "turned out " (given their freedom out of doors) are very large, three to four acres each. It's a very peaceful, quiet, comfortable place for raising horses.

It is here that Paul Maxwell arrived in 1990 from Cool Moore Stud Farm in Ireland, where he was working and learning about the horse industry. Maxwell, a native of Ireland, is experienced in riding, raising, training, and selling horses. He worked at Blue Ridge Farm for a number of years, handling the stallions until he decided to go out on his own. He leased one of Blue Ridge's three broodmare barns and opened his own stable at the farm. In 2001, Maxwell and George Grayson, a member of the family who owns Blue Ridge Farm, formed a partnership to run the entire farm's horse business.

The farm offers a variety of services, including breeding, foaling, boarding, and sales preparation for horses belonging to a wide range of clients. Each year, most of the yearlings raised here will be sent to auction sales while others are condi-

Wild Island Ponies

Virginia's "wild" Chincoteague ponies would be hard pressed to drag anyone away. The horses of the distinctive Chincoteague Pony breed are small and congenial. The horses reside on the islands of Chincoteague and Assateague, off the coasts of Virginia and Maryland, as they have since their legendary Arabian descendants first swam ashore from a wrecked Spanish boat in the 1700s. And though they roam free, grazing on the natural food sources provided by the Chincoteague National Wildlife Refuge, the Virginia Chincoteagues are owned and their numbers managed by the local volunteer fire department, which auctions foals to afficionados of the coveted breed every summer, following the annual pony round-up and swim. A recent high bidder pledged more than $10,000 for a Chincoteague baby. These ponies, first made famous by the factual book *Misty of Chincoteague*, written in 1927 by Marguerite Henry, evolved into a size considerably smaller than the average horse, due to the lower-protein diet provided by their island environment.

To contact the National Chincoteague Pony Association (www.pony-chincoteague .com) and the National Park Service, Assateague Island National Seashore, call (410) 641-1441 or visit www.nps.gov/asis.

tioned and sent to trainers to start or further their racing careers. The work is demanding and lasts 24 hours a day every day of the week. "Breeding and foaling seasons are the most hectic times for me," says Maxwell. Explaining the process, he says, "During breeding season, there may be 100 mares at the farm, most belonging to other owners."

Breeding is timed for the foals to be born before the end of April so the horses will be at the most advantageous age when old enough to race. At 48 hours after breeding, the mares are given a sonogram to see if the egg ovulated; if not, the stallion will try again. Mares will return home after 40 days or when the foal's heartbeat is heard. It takes 11 months for gestation, and the mares generally return to Blue Ridge one month before giving birth. The mares usually don't need help foaling. But Buddy Martin, the farms' night watchman, has helped deliver quite a few.

Blue Ridge Farm stands five thoroughbred stallions and a Connemara, one of the oldest horse breeds in the United States. Among the five stallions currently standing at the farm is champion sprinter Housebuster, who won more than $1.2 million and has sired 24 stakes winners to date.

Also at the farm are Supremo and Prenup, ranked the number-one and number-three sires of two-year-olds in Virginia in 2000; and Rock Point, who won $362,604 during his racing career. Another stallion, Hay Halo, has sired 19 stakes winners. Their stud fees range from about $2000 to $7500. Pleasant Colony, one of the world's leading sires, who came within 1½ lengths of winning the Triple Crown, is in retirement here.

The horses under Maxwell's care seem very content and extremely well cared for. That means doling out a lot of food and water. Horses at Blue Ridge Farm gulp down as many as 12 gallons of water each day. They may consume as much hay per day as they like but are limited to 16 pounds of grain each.

Amid high-pressure stakes to produce excellent quality stock, the relaxed atmosphere at Blue Ridge Farm is conducive to providing just what the horses need. And the transplanted Irishman couldn't have landed in a better place to use his skills than Virginia's hunt country.

This Year, Cut Your Own

Christmas-tree farming is a major agricultural industry in Virginia, with about two million trees harvested and sold annually from 1600 farms throughout the state. Virginia Christmas-tree growers offer a wide selection of trees in a wide range of sizes. Consumers may choose and cut their own tree or purchase a freshly cut or live tree. Choose-and-cut farms have revived the tradition of the entire family selecting and cutting the family Christmas tree.

Call (804) 786-3951 to receive the Virginia Christmas Tree Guide for information about the Virginia Department of Agriculture and Consumer Services (VDACS), or visit www.virginia christmastrees.org, the Web site of the Virginia Christmas Tree Growers Association, to locate a choose-and-cut farm.

chapter two

CHRISTMAS TREES

∽ *Christmas-tree farming is a major agricultural industry in Virginia, with about two million trees harvested and sold annually from 1600 farms throughout the state. From highways and byways, look across the landscape to the battalions of little evergreens like camouflaged soldiers marching across fields. The number of Christmas-tree farms has grown rapidly during the past decade, and annual revenues from Christmas greenery has passed $50 million. This is more income than from most of Virginia's crops, when compared individually; for example, winter wheat garners cash receipts of about $35 million. More than a million Virginians will buy or cut their own trees each year from tree farms, which are scattered statewide in about half the counties.*

CHRISTMAS THE COLONIAL WAY

Christmas is come, hang on the pot,
Let spits turn round and ovens be hot.
Beef, pork, and poultry now provide
To feast thy neighbours at this tide.
Then wash all down in good wine and beer
And so with Mirth conclude the year.

—Christmas verse from an
eighteenth-century Virginia "almanack"

All year in Colonial Williamsburg, men in knee-length britches tip their hats and women in mobcaps curtsy to passersby, their long skirts sweeping down brick sidewalks. This restored former capital of the vast Virginia Colony appears much as it did after its founding in 1699 by English settlers. But it is at Christmas time that the effects of Williamsburg's commitment to period authenticity is perhaps most enjoyable.

The Christmas season in the 1700s was a time of lavish hospitality and hearty appetites. The eighteenth century was noted for its "groaning boards"—sideboards laden with roast beef and venison, Virginia ham, and other local delicacies. Wild fowl, seafood, mincemeat pies, plum puddings, fruitcakes and sweetmeats, fruits, nuts, jellies, Sally Lunn, and spoonbread—the hearty farmers of the period enjoyed them all, especially at Christmas, just as today's visitors can.

Repasts are held at the Williamsburg Lodge's banquet room and the Colonial Taverns. You can toast the season at the Baron's Feast, Yuletide Suppers, Virginia Country Christmas Dinner, or Groaning Board dinner (so named because the tables are said to "groan under the weight of the food"). Often such feasts are delightfully supplemented by costumed hosts and hostesses and wandering minstrels. Sometimes an entire table of desserts would be served late at night to colonial celebrants during a holiday dance or "Collation." As Sally Fairfax wrote in 1771, "Mama made 6 mince pies and 7 custards, 12 tarts, 1 chicking pye, and 4 puddings for the ball."

In addition to experiencing the culinary joys of the colonial Christmas, those who delight in decorations will not be disappointed. Although Christmas trees did not appear in Williamsburg until 1842, and, of course, electric lights didn't exist, natural decorations abound. Decorations center on those plant materials that were available to eighteenth-century Virginia housewives:

fruits, greenery, pine cones, seeds, and nuts. Natural materials like the dried pods of okra, magnolia, and milkweed, sweet gum balls, bayberry and chinaberry, nuts, cotton bolls, mistletoe, and various pine cones are used in abundance. Holly, nandina, and pyracantha add the red color. Greens such as ivy, cedar, balsam, pine, and boxwood are combined with the leaves of magnolia, aucuba, or camellia to create wreaths, swags, and table decorations. However, the lavish fruit decorations of today's Williamsburg are an embellishment. Citrus fruits—oranges, limes, and lemons—and pineapples were precious commodities in the eighteenth century and would not have been wasted on decorations.

Kicking off the Christmas season is the traditional Grand Illumination, which is usually held the first Sunday in December. For the "illumination," all the windows throughout the 173-acre historic district—500 shops, taverns, and homes—are lit with hundreds of candles. Throughout the Christmas season, the candles are lit every night. The beating of the holiday drums commemorates the southern tradition of transmitting greetings from plantation to plantation. Other highlights include a military rifle drill performed by soldiers —fireworks, the firing of cannons, a Fife and Drum Corps parade, and twilight entertainment including holiday concerts, period music, madrigal singers, colonial dancers, and eighteenth-century plays.

In colonial times, December 25 was observed primarily as a holy day and a time for family. Servants and laborers had a day or two of rest. But it was not a day that concentrated on children. In fact, children were not invited to the balls, the fox hunts, or fine entertainment, and they did not give gifts to their elders. However, money, books, clothing, and candies were given by parents or masters to children, slaves, servants, and apprentices. Children's main participation for Christmas consisted of helping decorate or prepare dinner, visiting friends, and attending church.

Families in Williamsburg worshiped in Bruton Parish Church and took the sacrament. The church, too, was decorated. One communicant in the early 1700s reported, "The Church looks more like a Greenhouse than a Place of Worship. The pulpit itself has such Clusters of Ivy, Holly, and Rosemary about it, that a light Fellow said we heard the Word out of a bush, like Moses."

At Christmas as well as all year round, visitors can attend Bruton Parish Church, an Episcopal denomination in continuous use since 1715. The walls and windows are original as is the west gallery, where students of the College of William and Mary sat. Although the church is located in the Historic Area, it is privately owned and operated, so it has regular services and musical performances. Colonial Williamsburg organizes caroling through the Historic Area.

Christmas in Williamsburg of yesteryear lasted more than a day. Preceded by the four-week Advent season, it began on Christmas Eve and lasted through Twelfth Night on January 6. Today, visitors can experience a colonial Christmas the entire month of December.

Christmas is a popular time to visit Colonial Williamsburg, so investigate the possibilities early in the year to leave plenty of time for making reservations. Call (800) 404-3389 or visit www.history.org.

—*A Williamsburg Christmas*,
The Colonial Williamsburg Foundation

STANDING RIB ROAST WITH INDIVIDUAL YORKSHIRE PUDDINGS

Many Virginians defer to their English heritage and serve
"the king" of beef roasts for Christmas dinner.

FOR ROAST:

1 standing rib roast, small end preferred (allow at least ½ pound per person)

3 cloves garlic, peeled and cut in half

seasonings: lemon pepper, garlic powder, dried oregano, salt, and pepper

flour

FOR PUDDINGS:

beef drippings from roast

1 cup milk

2 large eggs

1 cup flour

½ teaspoon salt

Move oven rack to lowest position. Preheat oven to 475° F. Be sure you have a food thermometer to measure for doneness. Make 6 small slits in fat pockets of roast or near rib bones and insert garlic. Shake seasonings over all surfaces of roast, then dust with flour, which helps form a crisp, brown surface. Place roast bone-side down on a 2-piece broiler pan or on a rack set in a shallow baking pan. Roast 25 minutes. Reduce the oven temperature to 325° F and roast for about 15 minutes per pound.

To test for doneness, insert food thermometer in the center of roast. Remove the roast from the oven when the temperature has reached 140° F and let stand. Transfer roast to a carving platter and cover loosely with foil.

While roast rests, move shelf in oven to middle position. Raise oven temperature to 450° F. Spoon ½ teaspoon of drippings from roast into each of the 12 compartments of a metal muffin pan, and place pan in oven.

While pan is heating, pour milk into bowl and beat in eggs. Stir flour and salt into milk mixture; beat until well blended. Ladle the batter into each compartment of heated muffin pan. Bake 10 minutes. Do not open the oven door. Reduce temperature to 350° F and continue to bake about 15 minutes, or until puddings are puffed and medium brown. Makes 12 servings.

Christmas on Virginia's Historic Farms and Plantations

The vast majority of Virginians several hundred years ago lived on small farms or plantations (large farms growing primarily one crop). Their sincere, down-home observances of the Christmas season are replicated today on many of the state's historic farm properties. Staunton's Holiday Lantern Tour at the Frontier Culture Museum allows visitors to experience holidays of old, complete with warm fires, candlelight, and holiday cheer. Family vignettes about the holiday heritage of Christmas in 1720s Germany, 1730s Northern Ireland, 1690s England, and the 1850s Shenandoah Valley are exhibited.

The apple trees at the Claude Moore Colonial Farm need encouragement to bear well in the coming year, so guests at Christmas gather in the orchard to "wassail" the trees with singing, dancing, and chants. Hot cider, sugar cakes, colonial games, and a roaring bonfire round out the celebration. The Historic Crab Orchard Museum and Pioneer Park exhibits "Christmas on the Frontier," and the Hardy Plantation, where famous educator Booker T. Washington was born, hosts an old Virginia Christmas candlelight tour.

Virginia is in Christmas glory at her large plantations. The

Christmas on Virginia's Historic Farms and Plantations
(*continued*)

Mansion at Mount Vernon is adorned simply with fresh greenery. There, while touring the third floor, which is only open to the public at Christmas, visitors will hear stories about how George and Martha Washington celebrated the holidays. More activities await on the grounds, including complimentary hot cider and cookies and holiday caroling around a roaring bonfire.

Gunston Hall, the home of George Mason, offers steaming hot cider warmed over a bonfire, delicious demonstrations of open-hearth cooking, and horse-drawn carriage rides while nestled under the blankets as you are whisked down the lane in the brisk night air.

You can take candlelight tours of private historic homes in towns throughout the state in mansions open to the public, such as Mount Vernon, Gunston Hall, Sully, Shirley, Berkeley, Evelynton, Sherwood Forest, Piney Grove, North Bend, Tudor Hall at Pamplin Historical Park, Poplar Forest, Chippokes, Lee Hall, Woodlawn, Popes Creek (George Washington's birthplace), Stratford Hall, Belle Grove, and Point of Honor. Teas, progressive dinners, banquets, and buffets, as well as foods made with historic "receipts" are also offered at many plantations.

THE CHRISTMAS WELCOMING BREAD

On Michie Tavern's first Christmas in the 1700s, the doors were left open to greet friends and weary travelers. The Michies prepared these special biscuits as gifts for all to enjoy.

FOR BISCUITS:

2 cups flour	1 cup milk
1 teaspoon salt	3 tablespoons butter or margarine,
1 teaspoon baking powder	melted
1 teaspoon baking soda	

FOR ICING:

½ cup milk	¾ cup chopped walnuts
½ teaspoon lemon extract	½ cup candied red cherries, chopped
½ cup powdered sugar	¼ cup raisins

Preheat oven to 500° F. Combine flour, salt, baking powder, and baking soda in a mixing bowl. Stir in milk and butter. Roll dough ½-inch thick on a floured board and cut with a biscuit cutter and place on a baking sheet. Bake 7 minutes. Remove from oven and transfer to a cooling rack.

For icing, combine milk and lemon extract. Stir in sugar until smooth. Add walnuts, candied cherries, and raisins. Frost cooled biscuits. Makes 12 biscuits.

Historic Michie Tavern in Charlottesville was a meeting place for such patriots as Thomas Jefferson, James Madison, and Patrick Henry. The old inn still prepares this bread and serves it to guests during Yuletide. The tavern's fare consists of dishes dating to the 1700s, including colonial fried chicken, black-eye peas, stewed tomatoes, biscuits, and cornbread (phone (434) 977-1234 or visit www.michietavern.org).

PARTY POTATOES

With these potatoes on the Christmas Day menu, your family will look forward to dinner almost as much as to the visit from Santa.

8 to 9 medium-sized Russet potatoes	⅔ cup warm milk
½ cup butter, cut up	1½ cups grated cheddar cheese
1½ teaspoon salt	1 cup heavy cream, whipped
½ teaspoon black pepper	

Peel and boil potatoes until tender; drain, cut up, and place in a large bowl of electric mixer. Beat, adding the butter, salt, pepper, and warm milk. Continue beating until mixture is quite fluffy. Correct seasoning, adding a little onion or garlic powder, if desired. Spread warm mixture in a buttered (9 × 13-inch) casserole. Note: Casserole may be partially made ahead and refrigerated. Just before baking, bring to room temperature.

Preheat oven to 350° F. Whip heavy cream and fold in grated cheese. Spread over top of potato mixture. Bake 25 to 30 minutes, or until top is golden brown. Serve immediately. Makes 8 to 10 servings.

This recipe was provided by Jane Mengenhauser, who served for many years as the food editor of The Journal Newspapers. *The Alexandria resident enjoys using recipes that evoke memories of happy holiday meals. Potato dishes are high on her list of favorites—especially this one.*

BLEU SPRUCE CHEESE APPETIZER

You'll have almost as much fun decorating this tree as you will the real one.

1 (8-ounce) package cream cheese
4 ounces bleu cheese, crumbled
2 tablespoons brandy or pineapple
  juice
1 teaspoon instant minced onion or
  1 tablespoon minced fresh onion

1 teaspoon Worcestershire sauce
1 (8-ounce) can crushed pineapple,
  drained
8 ounces shredded sharp cheddar
  cheese (2 cups)

GARNISHES FOR CHRISTMAS TREE:
  fresh parsley, sliced pimientos, pecan halves, and fresh lemon

Mix softened cream cheese with bleu cheese and blend in brandy, Worcestershire, onion, and pineapple. Fold in cheddar cheese. Place mixture on a serving platter and, using your fingers, shape into a Christmas tree silhouette. Cover with plastic wrap and refrigerate.

To serve, decorate tree with parsley leaves and cut small squares of pimientos to resemble ornaments. Arrange pecan halves on trunk and cut a star for the top of tree from a lengthwise slice of lemon rind. Makes 12 to 16 appetizer servings. (Note: Cheese mixture may be molded into any shape and decorated appropriately for any occasion. Serve with assorted crackers.)

OLD-FASHIONED TART CHERRY PIE

Bright red as holly berries, a cherry pie makes an attractive appearance for holiday desserts.

2 (14.5-ounce) cans tart red cherries
  packed in water
1 cup sugar
½ cup flour
⅛ teaspoon salt

2 tablespoons butter
¼ teaspoon almond extract
1 (15-ounce) package refrigerated pie
  crusts, room temperature
cinnamon sugar

Preheat oven to 425° F. Reserve 1 cup cherry liquid. Drain cherries in a sieve or colander; set aside. Combine sugar, flour, and salt in a heavy saucepan. Whisk to stir in reserved liquid. Cook over medium-high heat, stirring constantly until quite thick, about 4 minutes. Stir in butter and extract; then gently fold in cherries.

Following package directions for a 2-crust pie, place 1 pie crust in a 9-inch pie pan. Pour cherry filling into crust. Place second pie crust on top of pie; seal and crimp. Make several slits in top crust for steam to vent; sprinkle top crust with cinnamon sugar. Bake 30 to 35 minutes, or until pastry is nicely browned. Cool partially on a wire rack. Serve slightly warm. Makes 8 servings.

Cherries in Virginia aren't a big industry, but they are in plenty of people's backyards. Wear plastic gloves when picking cherries to avoid staining your hands.

Christmas on Virginia's Historic Farms and Plantations (continued)

A Colonial Christmas at Jamestown Settlement contrasts seventeenth-century English Christmas customs with the holiday season in the difficult early years of the Jamestown colony. Fort interpreters adorn the enclosure with greenery and demonstrate cooking and stitchery.

At Yorktown Victory Center, "soldiers" give accounts of Christmas during the American Revolution in a re-created Continental Army military encampment. Visitors learn how to prepare cartridges, load a cart with supplies, and cook in the camp kitchen. At Yorktown's 1780 Virginia farm, where hardships of a small farmer worsened during the winter, interpreters demonstrate recipes from Mary Randolph's *The Virginia Housewife* and visitors dip a candle to take home.

For Civil War buffs, Fort Ward in Alexandria, Pamplin Historical Park in Petersburg, and the Fredericksburg Battlefield portray a Civil War "Christmas in Camp" that shows how Christmas was observed during the Civil War, with living-history interpreters and period music. There's also a free open house at Richmond's Museum of the Confederacy. A Civil War Santa Claus appears at each of these sites.

Forests still cover two thirds of Virginia, an extraordinary fact considering the overwhelming population growth in some areas. (To be considered "forest," land must have a certain number of trees per acre.) "Actually there is more forest land today than either in the 1600s or during World War II," says David Coffman, Forest Conservation Educator for the Virginia Depatment of Forestry in Charlottesville. "That's because Indians burned forests to clear land, and forest fires went unchecked. Now land is reforested at a high rate."

Private, non-industrial entities own 77% of the 15.4 million acres of forest land. That doesn't include National Parks. The forest industry owns 10%; and federal, state, and local governments own the remaining 13%. An additional 579,000 acres of parks, wilderness, scenic, and historic areas provide recreational activities, most in National Parks. Hardwood timber makes up 78% of timberland, and pine (principally loblolly pine) makes up the remainder. Common tree types include ash, beech, birch, black tupelo, hemlock, hickory, locust, maple, red cedar, spruce, sweet gum, and tulip trees, and, of course, dogwood trees that bloom with the state flower.

Forest timber is not considered a farm crop, but the importance of forests—to the economy and the environment—

A Christmas-tree farmer doesn't work in December only to retire for the remainder of the year. Steve Satterfield will tell you that Elysium Tree Farm, which he and his wife Jo have owned for 20 years, keeps him plenty busy. And Satterfield knows what he's doing. Not only did he grow up on a farm, but he also worked as a forester and is a former director of the Cooperative Forestry Program for the U.S. Forest Service.

The Satterfields raise 10,000 trees on Elysium Tree Farm, which is located on 63 acres of Orange County, between Fredericksburg and Charlottesville in Virginia's scenic Piedmont region. It takes about 30 minutes to drive there, either from Spotsylvania Mall in Fredericksburg or from Charlottesville. If coming from Culpeper, it's 18 miles south on a series of hills that go southwest.

Situated on a high hill near Clark's Mountain, the farm faces the Shenandoah National Park section of the Blue Ridge Mountains. It overlooks scenic farms and forests on all sides, but Satterfield says, "Look east and there's nothing higher until you get to Europe." That's because from there, Virginia slopes toward Tidewater and the mighty Chesapeake Bay.

In the winter, he cuts down the stumps left from Christmas tree customers, and removes any dead trees. Cut with a chain saw, the stumps will rot over time, but it's a good idea to treat the stumps so weevils won't find a home and then dine on the nearby green trees. In March, it's time to start a new crop of trees—1500 to 1700 every year. His wife, Jo, helps too. They dig the furrows in the fall before the ground hardens, then run the tractor over them to tamp the earth back down. This makes an easier job of planting the new seedlings that will be delivered by UPS. Scotch and white pine will arrive from the Virginia Agricultural Experiment Station, and from Pennsylvania and Michigan nurseries will come the Douglas and concolor firs and the Colorado blue spruce.

The bare-root seedlings with the dirt knocked off arrive tied in bundles of 50 in boxes of shredded wet paper wrapped in plastic. The two-year-old seedlings—costing between 25 and 50 cents each—are four to eight inches in size.

Steve says, "Usually we have them planted within a few days after arrival," adding that in years with insufficient rainfall, sometimes almost an entire seedling crop may be lost. But, he says, they plant far more than they sell. "It will take the seedlings between eight and ten years—sometimes twelve years—to grow six feet."

During the second half of May, the underbrush and high grass between the tree rows must be mowed. This is done so Satterfield can see the shape of the tree in time for the worst task of the year: shearing. It's a daylight-to-dark job, three weeks in a row during June—optimum time to begin shearing before the branches "harden up." If they are sheared too early, the trees may get confused and put out new growth.

"Growth for the pines in our area will usually be complete by early July," explains Steve. "With pines, the rule of thumb for shearing is to do it when the new needles reach 50% of their full length. Experience has shown that this will produce a strong bud set for the next year's growth and will avoid the tree breaking dormancy and sending out new growth late in the summer or fall. Firs and spruces produce buds along the entire branch, so shearing time is not as critical as with pines, which predominate in Virginia except for the mountain areas. While pruning, I also remove the lower branches to make room for tree stands," Steve concludes.

In mid-September, it's time to mow again for the last time before winter. And before they know it, the time for cutting has arrived. The closest grocery is eight miles away, and it's there Jo will stock up on baking supplies. She serves home-made cookies and spiced cider to all who come to cut their own trees. The Satter-fields emphasize warm hospitality, high-quality trees, and modest prices.

A Christmas-tree flag signals the way up the road to the farm, and parking is by the shed where saws are shared. Steve says, "You'd be surprised how many people will come over the hill after dark, in the rain or fog to pick out a Christmas tree!" Between Thanksgiving and Christmas, the farm is open on Fridays from 1 p.m. to dark, on weekends from 8 a.m. to dark, and at other times by appointment. Trees cost $10 to $25.

Many customers come back year after year, and many saw their own trees. Some wander around for hours looking for the perfect tree, enjoying being in the country. And some do a double take when they see Steve. Since his retirement from the Forest Service, he's grown a long beard. Dressed in his red-plaid flannel shirts and suspenders, he looks like . . . you know who.

ELYSIUM'S CHRISTMAS TREE SUGAR COOKIES

Bake the Satterfield's cookies to munch while the family settles down to trim the tree, but set aside a few for Santa.

⅔ cup shortening
¾ cup sugar
½ teaspoon vanilla
1 egg
4 teaspoons milk

2 cups sifted all-purpose flour
1½ teaspoons baking powder
¼ teaspoon salt
green sugar sprinkles

Preheat oven to 375° F. Thoroughly cream shortening, sugar, and vanilla. Add egg; beat until light and fluffy. Stir in milk. Sift together dry ingredients; blend into sugar mixture. Divide dough in half. Chill 1 hour. On lightly floured surface, roll to ⅛ inch. Cut in desired shapes with cutter. Place on greased cookie sheet; lightly brush with milk and sprinkle with green crystals. Bake about 6 to 8 minutes. Cool slightly; remove from pan. Cool on rack. Makes 2 dozens.

Recipe courtesy of Jo and Steve Satterfield, owners of Elysium Tree Farm, phone (540) 672-4512.

ELYSIUM'S HOT SPICED CIDER

1 jar pasteurized apple cider
   (64 ounces)

1 tablespoon whole cloves
2 cinnamon sticks

Heat all ingredients and serve warm.

Recipe courtesy of Jo and Steve Satterfield, owners of Elysium Tree Farm.

cannot be overestimated. Virginia continues to be one of the nation's largest producers of wood furniture in the United States. The harvesting, processing, and marketing of wood products contributes $11.5 billion annually to the state's economy and accounts for more than 220,000 jobs.

Plan an Orange Getaway

Elysium Tree Farm is located in Orange County, site of many historic sites, including Civil War battles, James Madison's Montpelier, and many antebellum structures as well as beautiful countryside. Orange County also is home to several wineries and the most extensive plantings of wine grapes in Virginia, several acclaimed bed-and-breakfasts, and numerous modestly priced eateries.

The Homecoming

The fictitious family in the book was modeled after my own family," says Earl Hamner, author of *The Homecoming*, which was the basis for the TV series *The Waltons*. "We lived in the backwoods of the Blue Ridge Mountains during the Depression of the 1930s. A more factual description of the family and our growing up is recorded in my new book, *Goodnight, John-Boy*."

Olivia had already started her applesauce cake when the children trooped in with the walnuts. The kitchen steamed with the aroma of cloves, cinnamon, and nutmeg. At the old, wood-burning cooking range Olivia was stirring the applesauce and singing "O Little Town of Bethlehem."

CAROLYN CHENEY'S PECAN PIE

Be watchful so you don't overcook this pie. It's best a tad gooey in the center.

2 tablespoons margarine, melted	⅓ cup light corn syrup
2 tablespoons flour	½ teaspoon vanilla
3 eggs	⅛ teaspoon salt
½ cup sugar	1¼ cups pecans, halves or pieces
⅔ cup dark corn syrup	1 (9-inch) unbaked pie crust

Place oven rack in center position. Preheat oven to 425° F. Blend margarine and flour. Beat in eggs, then sugar. Stir in dark and light corn syrups, vanilla, and salt. Stir in pecans and pour into unbaked pie crust. Bake 10 minutes. Reduce heat to 325° F and continue to bake 25 to 30 minutes, or until center barely jiggles. Do not cook so long that pecan layer "cracks." Let stand at least 1 hour before serving. Makes 8 servings.

The family of McLean resident Carolyn Cheney anticipates her favorite pecan pie for dessert at Christmas time and whenever else they can get it.

OLIVIA'S APPLESAUCE CAKE

This recipe featured in Earl Hamner's novella The Homecoming *is based on a recipe of his mother, and the whiskey frosting is one invented by his wife Jane.*

FOR CAKE:

1 cup butter	2 cups light raisins
3½ cups flour	2 teaspoons cloves
1 cup sugar	1 cup chopped walnuts
2 eggs	2 teaspoons nutmeg
2 cups applesauce (about 20 ounces)	1 teaspoon baking soda
1 teaspoon cinnamon	pinch of salt

FOR FROSTING:

¼ cup butter	2 tablespoons bourbon whiskey
2 cups powdered sugar	pinch of salt
1 tablespoon cream	

Sift together flour, baking soda, salt, cinnamon, cloves, and nutmeg. Take ½ cup flour mixture and stir into the nuts and raisins. Set both aside. Cream butter until whipped soft. Add sugar a little at a time until mixture is smooth. Beat in eggs vigorously. Stir in applesauce. Alternately stir in flour and raisins and mix well. Pour batter into a well-greased tube cake pan. Bake in preheated oven at 350° F for 1 hour, or until done when tested with a toothpick. Cool 10 minutes, then turn out on cake rack. Let cake cool completely.

To make frosting, cream butter; add sugar and salt. Stir in cream and whiskey. Whip until smooth. Frost cake and decorate with a sprig of holly or flowers in season. Makes 16 servings.

chapter three
FLORICULTURE

∽ *Greenhouse and nursery plants are the top "crop" in cash receipts earned. Sales of flowers and decorative plants have risen every year. Wholesale receipts for cut flowers, potted flowering plants, foliage plants, and bedding/garden plants are more than $90 million. "There seems to be a likely correlation between the state's population increase and floriculture sales," according to Commissioner of Agriculture Carlton Courter. This is also true in the state's turf grass (grass for lawns and pastures) industry, where maintained turf jumped 66% from 1982 to 1998. There are now more turf grass acres maintained in the Old Dominion than acres cut for hay.*

GARDENS AND ARBORETUMS OF VIRGINIA

Tour in a Nutshell

GARDENS AND ARBORETUMS OF VIRGINIA

ORLAND E. WHITE ARBORETUM is open daily from dawn until dusk. The arboretum is located at 400 Blandy Farm Lane in Boyce and can be reached by calling (540) 837-1758 or visiting www.virginia.edu/blandy. From Washington (about 70 miles), take I-66 West to Route 17 North (Exit 23 for Delaplane/Paris). Follow Route 17 North to its junction with Route 50 West at a traffic light. Turn left onto Route 50/17; the Arboretum is approximately 7 miles on the left, about 3 miles past the point where the road crosses the Shenandoah River. Admission is free.

THE EDITH J. CARRIER ARBORETUM of James Madison University in Harrisonburg is open daily from dawn until dusk. For more information, call (540) 568-3194 or visit www.jmu.edu/arboretum/index.htm. Take Exit 245 from I-81 and go east on Port Republic Road, turn left onto Forest Hills Drive, and proceed to University Boulevard. Admission is free.

LEWIS GINTER BOTANICAL GARDEN is open daily from 9 a.m. to 5 p.m. Information about the garden, located at 180 Lakeside Avenue in Richmond, can be obtained by calling (804) 262-9887 or visiting www. lewisginter.org. From downtown Richmond, take I-95

It should be no surprise that Virginia, with its hospitable mid-Atlantic climate, three planting seasons, and British roots, would be a land of flowers and formal gardens. More than 20 arboretums, botanical gardens, and historic English bowers are open to the public. Here is a rundown on four of them:

ORLAND E. WHITE ARBORETUM

"I think one of the Commonwealth's best-kept secrets is the State Arboretum of Virginia at Blandy Experimental Farm," said Delegate Vincent F. Callahan, co-chair of the House Ways and Means Committee. The 170-acre arboretum is part of the 700-acre Blandy Experimental Farm, a research facility for the University of Virginia, where students learn about environmental science. The arboretum was named for the farm's first director.

The collections feature more than 1,000 varieties and species representing 100 genera and 50 families. The collection of more than 5,000 woody plants includes the largest variety of boxwood in North America and more than half the world's pine species. The collection emphasizes native plants and their exotic relatives.

The Virginia Native Plant Trail includes woodlands, a meadow, and a wetland. The arboretum also includes perennial gardens, a garden of culinary and medicinal herbs, an amphitheater for concerts and performances, Dogwood Lane, and a one-room schoolhouse. Visitors can explore free of charge from dawn to dusk year-round.

EDITH J. CARRIER ARBORETUM

Also free and open daily is the 125-acre Edith J. Carrier Arboretum at James Madison University. The trails wind through the native oak-hickory forest. In spring, visitors can wander through the sea of daffodil blooms in the April Walk garden. The arboretum is an outdoor living classroom. Its forested slopes, lowland swale, pond, and forested savanna provide a unique habitat for a wide diversity of flora and fauna.

The arboretum's environment serves as a haven for many species of trees, shrubs, wildflowers, and many rare and endangered species native to the mid-Appalachian area. Whether seeking serenity or a thirst for knowledge about plants, one of America's most precious natural resources, this arboretum is the place.

LEWIS GINTER BOTANICAL GARDEN

In Richmond is the Lewis Ginter Botanical Garden, formerly an Indian hunting ground. The garden is named for a prominent Richmond businessman, who owned the property during the late 1800s. Opened in 1984, it strives to display the best in horticulture for each season.

The more than 25 acres of gardens includes one of the largest and most diverse perennial gardens on the East Coast. Other areas include an elegant Victorian-style garden restored by The Garden Club of Virginia; an exotic Asian garden; a study garden with an extensive collection of daffodils and daylilies; and a garden featuring dwarf conifers.

A children's garden is planted to attract butterflies and birds, and there's also an island garden—a wetland environment with a stunning display of pitcher plants, water irises, and lotuses. The property has two delightful cafes: a moderately priced self-service eatery with attractive indoor and outdoor seating, and the slightly more expensive Tea House with large windows that offer panoramic views of the lake and gardens. The food is freshly prepared.

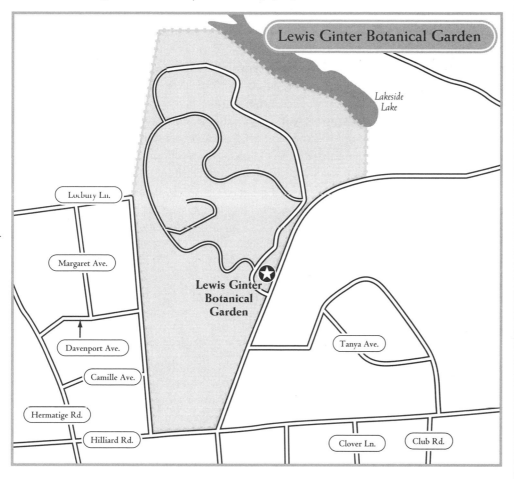

Tour in a Nutshell
· GARDENS AND ·
ARBORETUMS
OF VIRGINIA
(*continued*)

North to Exit 80, Lakeside Avenue. Keep to the right and turn right at the first light onto Lakeside Avenue. Follow Lakeside to the entrance just beyond the intersection of Lakeside Avenue and Hilliard Road. Admission is charged for adults and free for children under age 2.

NORFOLK BOTANICAL GARDEN

Next to the Norfolk International Airport is a 155-acre oasis known as Norfolk's Garden by the Sea. Surrounded by the cool waters of Lake Whitehurst, Norfolk Botanical Garden dates to 1938, when 250 African American women, sponsored by a Works Progress Administration grant, pushed wheelbarrows of fill—150 truck loads—to erect a levee across the lake. They cleared the dense native vegetation and planted 4000 azaleas. Today, Norfolk Botanical Garden features one of the largest and most diverse collections of azaleas, camellias, roses, and rhododendrons on the East Coast. Norfolk Botanical Garden is the nation's only botanical garden that can be toured by both tram and boat, including a new train model that is wheelchair accessible.

Individual garden themes include colonial herb, medicinal, Japanese, desert, sunken, rose, rhododendron, holly, fragrance, and Virginia native plants. The Woodland was set aside as an area that emphasizes conservation and wildlife. The climate-controlled Tropical Pavilion houses more than 100 varieties of plants from tropical regions around the world. A full-service restaurant, The Azalea Room, is open from mid-March until mid-November. The back patio overlooks the tranquil Japanese Garden.

NORFOLK BOTANICAL GARDEN is open from 9 a.m. to 7 p.m. between April 14 and October 15, and from 9 a.m. to 5 p.m. for the remainder of the year. The garden is at 6700 Azalea Garden Road in Norfolk. Call (757) 441-5830 or visit www.norfolk botanicalgarden.org for more information. From Route I-64 East, take Exit 279 for Norview Avenue. Follow Norview for a mile, then turn left on Azalea Garden Road. Admission is $6 for adults, $5 for seniors, $4 for youth between the ages of 6 and 16, and free for children under age 5.

Cloning George Washington's Trees

Only 13 of the original trees planted at Mount Vernon by George Washington are still living—two tulip poplars, two white ashes, a white mulberry, a hemlock, and seven American holly trees. These trees, planted some 215 years ago, bear silent witness to the life and times of our first president. Experts cloned these last trees and produced 50 duplicates of each tree for delivery to Mount Vernon. The project is a gift from a Michigan family of nursery owners, David Milarch and his son Jared. They founded the Champion Tree Project to produce genetic duplicates of the largest specimens of 826 U.S. tree species. A thousand of those trees were used to help restore Mount Vernon's forests. "Tree-grafting has been done for thousands of years, but harvesting buds from trees as old as Mount Vernon's originals is an art," chief horticulturist J. Dean Norton told Jeff Baron of *The Washington Post* in August 2001. Francis Gouin, a retired University of Maryland horticulture professor who has developed techniques for propagating older trees, chose the buds that will become landmark Mount Vernon trees in the next century and the century after that—all genetically identical to the originals. Buds taken from a tulip poplar, just an eighth-of-an-inch long, are the youngest part of that original tree.

LANDSCAPING AND LAWNS

The industry that produces cut flowers and plants used for landscaping and decorating is burgeoning. Greenhouses the size of football fields are sprouting up, and inside them, machines inject flower seeds into thousands of thumb-sized cartons. Endless rows of potted flowers grow on metal trays.

Ironically, the nursery business feeds off factors that are typically responsible for the depletion of farm acreage—urbanization and development. With every new apartment complex, housing development, and strip mall comes the need for decorative plants like pre-grown oaks and potted petunias. Increasing numbers of nursery owners—including many traditional farmers—are scrambling to fill the demand. Floriculture sales tripled since 1996 in Virginia. Nurseries rake in $90 million, more than most of the state's crops.

Turfgrass—grass raised for lawns and pastures—is also a valuable farm crop in Virginia. There are now more turf grass acres maintained in the Old Dominion than acres cut for hay. Sod farms in the state grow 4,800 acres of turf to be harvested for newly landscaped sites and maintenance of older turf. Sales of new sod and sprigs total about $20 million, but maintenance of existing turf generates close to $3 billion for the economy.

Home lawns account for more than a million acres of turf grass in Virginia. There are also about 30,000 acres of turf in the state's regional and city park systems, and more than 300,000 acres are maintained in state roadsides. Golf courses maintain nearly 40,000 acres of turf grass. Counting golf courses, home lawns, schools, parks, churches, cemeteries, airports, and government property, a total of 1.7 million acres of turf is being maintained.

chapter four
TOBACCO

∽ *The ability of the Virginia colonists to grow tobacco and sell it to the English ensured the colony's ultimate survival, but after being Virginia's top cash crop for 400 years, it's now being eclipsed by soybeans, corn, and greenhouse products. Virginia remains the fourth-largest producer of tobacco, but today fewer than 20,000 acres are planted. But land devoted to flue-cured tobacco—which is the kind used to produce cigarettes—has declined from a high of 140,000 acres in 1930, to just more 10,000 acres today. There's a corresponding decline in the number of farmers growing the leaf, the number of warehouses, and the number of tobacco auctions so long associated with the Dan River area. The majority of the state's tobacco is grown in counties in this area near the North Carolina border. The county with the most acreage planted in tobacco—6910 acres—is Pittsylvania, home of Danville and its longtime tobacco auctions.*

Tobacco for Your Health?

The need for finding new uses for Virginia-grown tobacco is obvious, but what those new uses may be is not so apparent. Believe it or not, researchers are attempting to use tobacco leaves to grow human proteins. Why? It could lead to the production of life-saving drugs and other commercial products. Finding a cure for cancer and other life-threatening diseases would be a wonderful use for Virginia-grown tobacco. The Virginia Farm Bureau Federation nurtured a new biotechnology partnership between ToBio LLC, a farmer-owned tobacco production business, and CropTech Corporation. Because of tobacco's genetic adaptability, CropTech determined that it is the best plant resource for the building-block proteins used in pharmaceuticals. The project would require thousands of acres of tobacco per year to meet the demand. Eventually, more than 800 pharmaceuticals could be produced from tobacco plants.

Others are exploring the idea of growing cut flowers in tobacco-transplant greenhouses—typically 35 feet wide and 200 feet long—that are used only 3 to 4 months of the year. The young tobacco plants are moved outdoors in the spring for planting, leaving the greenhouses unused for the remainder of the year.

Booker T. Washington National Monument

In Franklin County, 25 miles from Roanoke, this national monument maintained by the National Park Service preserves the 207-acre tobacco farm where Booker T. Washington was born into slavery on April 5, 1856. Since it was illegal to educate slaves, his only experience with school before the end of the Civil War was carrying books to and from school for his slaveholder's daughter. After the war, he went to great lengths to obtain an education himself and for other African Americans. The now renowned educator went on to found Tuskegee Institute in Alabama in 1881 and became an important, and controversial, African American leader in post–Civil War U.S. society. The Booker T. Washington National Monument staff interprets the realities of slave life in Piedmont Virginia, the quest by African Americans for education and equality, and the postwar struggle over political participation in the U.S. government. Visitors are invited to step back in time and experience firsthand the life and landscape of people who lived in an era when slavery was part of the fabric of American life.

The free visitor center houses exhibits, an audiovisual program, and bookstore, and is a good place to collect information about the site. Visitors

TOBACCO'S BEGINNINGS IN THE NEW WORLD

Experts believe that the tobacco plant, as we know it today, is native to the Americas. Native Indians smoked tobacco in pipes long before Christopher Columbus sailed to the New World in 1492. Within a week of his landfall, Columbus noticed the natives' fondness for chewing the aromatic dried leaves or inhaling their smoke through a Y-shaped pipe called the "toboca" or "tobaga." Columbus scolded his men for sinking to the level of the savages, only to discover, as he reportedly said, "it was not within their power to refrain from indulging in the habit."

Columbus brought some tobacco seeds back to Europe, where farmers began to grow the plant for use as a medicine that helped people relax. In 1560, a French diplomat named Jean Nicot—from whom tobacco receives its botanical name, Nicotiana—introduced the use of tobacco in France. The tobacco plant belongs to the nightshade family, Solanaceae. The major kind is genus Nicotiana, species *N. tabacum.*

Commercial production of tobacco began in North America in 1612, after an English colonist named John Rolfe—who later married Pocahontas (see page 159)—successfully cultivated a new type of tobacco from the West Indies that would grow well in Virginia and sell profitably in England. This was wonderful news, considering that many of the Jamestown colonists had died, were starving, or suffered miserably when their farming efforts had been unsuccessful.

Throughout Virginia and the greater Chesapeake, the potential cash value of tobacco soon captivated the imaginations of the colonists. They began to plant tobacco in every available clearing, from fields to the forts and streets of Jamestown, and eventually in much of Tidewater Virginia. By 1699, England was importing more than 20 million pounds of colonial tobacco per year.

"Early on, planters stripped the leaves from the stalks, packed them in hogsheads (large wooden barrels holding 800 to 1000 pounds of tobacco), and conveyed them via river to Norfolk for shipment to the mother country. Less fortunate farmers not near rivers were forced to use the laborious manner of rolling the hogsheads down the muddy and crude roads to the seacoast," according to the article "A History of Tobacco in Danville, Virginia" by James I. Robertson, Jr. for the Danville Chamber of Commerce, 1955.

Soon, slaves became the backbone of the tobacco economy, tilling the ground, planting the seeds, raising the plants, and harvesting and curing the tobacco. Due to the use of slaves in tobacco farming, slave populations grew to comprise as much as 35% of the Chesapeake region's population between 1690 and 1750. Despite some opposition to slavery, by the time of the Revolution slavery was both politically and socially accepted in order to grow this plant of gold.

—World Book Online Americas Edition and Tobacco Coast

GOING, GOING, GONE

Imagine the fate of a whole year's work being decided in less than a minute. For more than 100 years, that was just part of life for Virginia's Dan River–area tobacco growers. Sometime between the middle of August and November, the season during which the well-known Danville tobacco auctions were conducted, a farmer's entire crop was piled up alongside other farmers' piles, row after row upon the warehouse floors, and sold by an auctioneer chanting at a rate of about 400 words per minute. A good auctioneer could sell a 200-pound pile of tobacco in as little as ten seconds.

The warehouse operator would oversee the sale, beginning the day's transactions by starting each pile of tobacco at a certain price. The tobacco auctioneer, leading the way beside him, would then begin the bidding with his melodic and sonorous chant. The buyers, lined up on the other side of the row of tobacco, indicating their bids by raising a finger, nodding their heads, winking, rolling their eyes, or giving a yell—distinctive signals, which a good auctioneer can recognize quickly. A ticket marker would indicate the name of the purchaser and the price of each pile as it was sold. Despite the swiftness with which the decision was made, auctions have long been considered the best way for a farmer to sell his tobacco at the highest possible price.

Danville's foothold in the trading of tobacco dates all the way back to 1793. It was then—only a year after the little town was established on the bluffs overlooking the Dan River—that the first tobacco warehouse was constructed.

"In 1858 the idea to use the competitive-pricing system for tobacco was born in Danville, which became the birthplace of the loose-leaf auction," according to the article "A History of Tobacco in Danville, Virginia" by James Robertson, written for the Danville Chamber of Commerce. Thomas Neal, the owner of the Danville's largest warehouse at the time—which was the length and width of a city block— reasoned that auctions would raise tobacco prices, and they did. Neal originated the practice of laying the tobacco in neat and aligned piles on the warehouse floor and of using government inspectors to ensure that quality standards were met. Piles were quality-graded before each sale.

By 1860, there were 8 warehouses and 13 factories in Danville, with the finished products valued at $610 million. Then the Civil War broke out. The factories closed, six of the warehouses became prisons for captured Union troops, and the remaining two were used as hospitals for Confederate wounded. The city assumed the role of a major supply depot for the Confederacy. The Richmond and Danville Railroad, completed in 1856, which had been a boon to the tobacco industry, became a strategic rail link for the Confederacy. For the last week of the Confederacy, Danville was its capital.

Danville eventually reassumed its prominent role in the tobacco industry, home to as many as 200 warehouses in the 1980s; and it held multiple auctions every year. But the staccato of the auctioneers' chants today is almost gone. In the year 2000, due to decreasing demand for U.S.-grown tobacco, the majority was sold directly to product manufacturers via contract. The Associated Press reported that the number of auctions held in Virginia alone fell from 17 to 9 between 2000 and 2001. Under contract sales, there's no warehouse middleman. But some farmers still believe they can get higher prices for their crop at auction, even when paying the 10% auction-house commission.

to Booker T. Washington National Monument can tour a living history farm, as well as picnic on the grounds. Hiking facilities include the Plantation Trail, a quarter-mile walking trail through the historic area of the park, and a one-and-a-half-mile Branch Trail through natural areas. The monument is open daily, year-round, from 9 a.m. to 5 p.m. Phone (540) 721-2094 or visit www.nps.gov/bowa/.

✎ DID YOU KNOW . . . By 1830, the city of Danville was the nation's leading tobacco center. It became the practice to pile the loose leaves in baskets along the curbs where the crop could be seen by all. The blaring of a bugle announced the beginning of the day's sale, and the buyers walked up and down the street, making offers to farmers for their piles. By 1850, about 90% of all the tobacco sold in the city was by this method. The city contained seven factories, and production was valued at $331 million annually.

—James Robertson, Jr., Danville Chamber of Commerce

AMERICAN INDIANS AND VIRGINIA CROPS

Cigarette-Manufacturing Machine Invented in Virginia

In 1882 the cigarette was still a specialty item—made by hand, sold for a penny apiece, and very much the stepchild of other tobacco products. But change was in the wind. An automated cigarette-rolling machine, developed by James Bonsack, an 18-year-old Virginia mechanic from a small town near Roanoke, was put into use in 1883. Bonsack's machine revolutionized production. The "Automated Cigarette Rolling Machine" turned out 200 cigarettes a minute—the equivalent work of 50 male workers. Soon the retail price of cigarettes was cut in half, and by 1910 the number of cigarettes produced had leaped from 500 million to 10 billion.

Long before English settlers landed in Virginia, the Indians cultivated tobacco and native food crops. If it hadn't been for Indians teaching the colonists to grow crops, the Jamestown settlers would have starved—and it would have taken much longer to colonize Virginia and the New World. The valuable tobacco crop supported the colony and was eventually used as money. Unfortunately, by helping a handful of colonists survive those first critical years in Jamestown, the Indians unwittingly hastened their own demise.

At the time of the founding of Jamestown in 1607, the original natives of what would become Virginia numbered perhaps 50,000. The largest group in the area was the Powhatan Confederacy—more than 32 Algonquian-speaking tribes in coastal Virginia controlled by Chief Powhatan, father of Pocahontas.

Among these Indians, both men and women were responsible for securing food. The Powhatan hunted for meat, fished, and gathered roots, fruits, nuts, and berries. But they gained more than half their food by farming. Corn, squash, and beans were the most important crops, and they were planted together (see Three Sisters Succotash on pages 192–193). This was practical for several reasons. Clearing patches of woods was not a simple task for a society with just stone points, bone tools, and fire, and planting the three crops together saved space. Squash covers the ground, shading out weeds; cornstalks make a "pole" for the beans to climb; and beans enrich the soil with nitrogen.

The European colonists wanted ownership and control of land and resources, whereas the Powhatan did not view land as something that could be owned. Unfortunately for the Indians, they were not able to remain in their ancestral territories due to the sheer number of colonists flooding the region. As a result, most Indians moved away from the growing settlements and took their cultures with them. Possibly the most enduring American Indian influence on contempoary Virginia is the crops we grow and eat.

VIRGINIA'S RECOGNIZED AMERICAN INDIAN TRIBES

The following tribes were recognized by the Virginia House of Delegates and Senate between 1983 and 1989, and are members of the Virginia Council on Indians: Chickahominy and Eastern Chickahominy, "Coarse Ground Corn People" (Providence Forge); Mattaponi (West Point); Monacan Nation (Madison Heights); Nansemond (Chesapeake), Pamunkey (Indian Neck) Upper Mattaponi (Mechanicsville).

chapter five
COTTON

Does cotton look like marshmallows? If so, there's a good reason. Cotton is a member of the mallow family, which also includes hibiscus, okra, and the swamp mallow.

Marshmallow is the common name for a tall, leafy, perennial plant (mallow), native to Eastern Europe. It has toothed, heart-shaped, or three-lobed leaves and clusters of showy, pinkish flowers about one-inch wide. It reaches a height of up to four feet. In the United States, the marshmallow grows wild in marshy areas as far west as Michigan and Arkansas. The roots of the mallow were once used to make a creamy confection, a puffy imitation of which is a necessary ingredient in S'mores.

The immature flower bud of cotton, called a "square," blossoms and develops into an oval boll that splits open at maturity, revealing a mass of long, white seed hairs, called lint, that cover a large number of brown or black seeds

∽ *Cotton was one of the earliest crops grown by European settlers, planted at the Jamestown colony in 1607. It was also one of the state's most significant crops for almost three centuries. The boll weevil migrated from Mexico to the United States, beginning in 1892, and began chewing its way through America's cotton crop. With their formidable snouts, boll weevils can destroy 40 to 160 miles in twelve months. Every year, more acres were devastated in Virginia, and the state's cotton crop bottomed out in 1978, when only 100 acres were planted statewide. But help was on the way. In the late 1970s, the National Boll Weevil Eradication Program was launched by USDA's Animal and Plant Health Inspection Service (APHIS) along the Virginia–North Carolina border. By 1987, the weevil had been eradicated in Virginia. Today, cotton has bounced back, and more than 100,000 acres are now planted. Virginia is number 13 in upland cotton, producing more than 180,000 bales, and the value of the state's cotton (lint and seed) is nearly $50 million. The Old Dominion is the northernmost cotton-growing state in the South. The six adjoining counties of Southampton, Greenville, Sussex, Surry, Isle of Wight, and Suffolk, in southeastern Virginia, produce 80% of the state's crop.*

essay

COTTON:
History and Harvesting

Cotton production in Virginia is fluffing up. Cotton is Virginia's sixth most-valued crop, and the industry is growing and at the same time improving the quality of its product.

One reason cotton is widely used around the world is because the cotton fiber is easily spun into yarns. It is also strong, absorbs dyes readily, is easy to wash, and can be made into many textile products.

Cotton is a natural vegetable fiber that's of greatest value for making into cloth. American Upland cotton is a low, multibranched shrub that must be planted every year. Scientists have placed cotton fiber and boll fragments from the Tehuacán Valley of Mexico at about 7000 years old. The plant has been grown and used in India for at least 5000 years, and perhaps much longer. Cotton was used also by the ancient Chinese, Egyptians, and North and South Americans, and it is the main fiber used today in those areas.

Virginia is the northernmost state that can grow cotton. To grow cotton successfully, you need a long growing season, lots of sunshine and water while it's growing, and dry weather for harvest. After the crop is harvested, cotton farmers chop or shred the stalks with machines and plow them under. Planting time in Virginia for cotton is in the spring.

"Three mechanical systems are used to harvest cotton," according to the National Cotton Council of America. "Cotton-picking machines use rotating spindles to pick (twist) the seed cotton from the burr. Doffers then remove the seed cotton from the spindles and drop the seed cotton into the conveying system. Cotton-stripping machines use rollers equipped with bats and brushes to knock the open bolls from the plants into a conveyor. A third kind of harvester uses a broadcast attachment similar to a grain header on a combine. All harvesting systems use air to elevate the seed cotton into a basket where it is stored until it can be dumped into a boll buggy, trailer, or module builder."

When cotton arrives at the cotton gin, it is vacuumed into the building through pipes placed in the trailers or trucks. In many plants, it first enters dryers that reduce the moisture content for easier processing. Next the cotton travels to equipment that removes burrs, sticks, dirt, leaf trash, and other foreign matter. It then moves to the gin stand, where lint is separated from the seeds. After separation from the seeds, the lint is packed tightly into bales, which weigh about 500 pounds each. The National Cotton Council says the Chinese produced about 20 million bales of cotton in 2000, but the United States is second, with 17.2 million bales in that year.

About two thirds of the harvested crop is composed of the seed, which is crushed to separate its three products—oil, meal, and hulls. Cottonseed oil is a common component of many food items, used primarily as a cooking oil, shortening, and salad dressing. The oil is used extensively to make such snack foods as crackers, cookies, and chips. The meal and hulls are used as livestock, poultry, and fish feed and as fertilizer.

—Virginia Tech Extension, National Cotton Council of America, and Microsoft Encarta Online Encyclopedia, 2001

THE JAMES RIVER PLANTATIONS

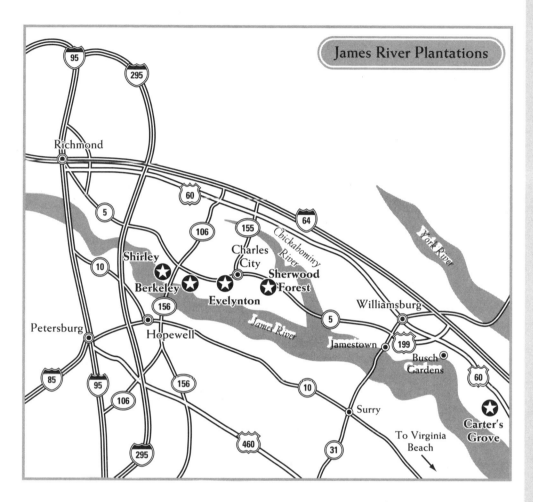

James River Plantations

Possibly the most impressive assemblage of eighteenth-century plantations in the United States is located along the James River. To the first English settlers, the James was a great highway that facilitated communications and commerce, most of which owe their existence to the tobacco crop that was exported to England and made the planters wealthy. Some are open to the public and some are not.

To tour the major plantations on the north side of the James, take Route 5 east from Richmond or west from Williamsburg. Route 5 is a two-lane highway that meanders between tall stands of fruitwood trees—pecan, hickory, cherry—and feathery cedar trees. In some places, the trees meet over the road, creating a cool, green canopy. Sometimes the road splits wheat and corn fields where twentieth-century silos stand sentinel.

When approaching the plantations, visitors are amazed that, while urban sprawl has overrun so many other once-pristine places, this peninsula of Virginia still boasts huge tracts of land that have withstood development of any kind. In fact, other than an old-fashioned gas station or restaurant here and there, Charles City County is almost devoid of businesses. Many of these tracts still belong to the same families that received the original land grants from the British throne. Agriculturist Lott Cary, the first black American missionary to Africa and founding

THE JAMES RIVER PLANTATIONS

The outstanding manor homes and grounds of these five plantations on the river are not only breathtaking to behold but offer lessons in American history—lessons of founding settlers, patriots, presidents, and Civil War conflicts.

DAYS/HOURS: All plantations covered here are open from 9 a.m. to 5 p.m. daily year-round except on Thanksgiving and Christmas Days. (Berkeley opens at 8 a.m.)

FEES: Admission to all but Carter's Grove is $9.50 for adults, $6 for students, and free for children under age five. Admission to Carter's Grove is $18 for adults and is included in the price of some Colonial Williamsburg passes.

MORE INFORMATION: Call **Berkeley Plantation** at (804) 829-6018, or visit www.berkeleyplantation.com. **Evelynton Plantation** is now closed to the public. The phone number of **Sherwood Forest Plantation** is (804) 829-5377, or visit www.sherwoodforest.org. Call **Shirley Plantation** at (804) 829-5121 or (800) 232-1613, or visit www.shirleyplantation.com. **Carter's Grove** is currently closed to the public; visit www.colonialwilliamsburg.org.

father of Liberia, was born here, in Charles City. Thomas Jefferson married Martha Skelton at "The Forest" here, and General Robert E. Lee spent much of his boyhood here.

The formal fronts of the great plantation homes faced the river. Most guests would have arrived by boat, a safer, more comfortable way to travel. But there were also entrances from the back, where carriages and horsemen could pull up. Drivers headed east on Route 5 from Richmond will encounter the following plantations in the order they are discussed. All of these can be toured (see hours in tour information below) and all have period furnishings, many original to the mansions.

Shirley Plantation, Virginia's oldest, is also the oldest continuously-owned family business in the United States. Land claim here dates to 1613 and once included 18,000 acres. The plantation has been home to the Carter family for ten generations. Robert E. Lee's mother was born here, and his parents were married in the parlor. A stunning 350-year-old willow-oak tree shades the magnificent lawn that faces the river. The mansion, finished in 1723, has a unique three-story staircase built without support, and a separate two-story brick kitchen.

Berkeley Plantation was home to generations of Harrisons, including president William Henry and Benjamin, signer of the Declaration of Independence. The manor house was built in 1726. Englishmen celebrated Thanksgiving at Berkeley in 1619, before the Pilgrims of Massachusetts. Civil War history is rich here, dating from 1862, when George McClellan brought his Union army to the James River (Harrison's Landing) after fighting in the Seven Days battles. The bugle call Taps was first played here during that period.

Evelynton Plantation is a traditional home, built in the 1930s to replace the one burned by Union forces during the Civil War Battle of Evelynton Heights because of the plantation's association with ardent secessionist Edmund Ruffin, who fired the first shot of the war. The beautifully-decorated Georgian Revival manor house sits on the original foundation. The property—named for William Byrd's daughter—was once part of nearby Westover Plantation that is rarely open to the public. Evelynton is now closed to the public.

Sherwood Forest was the home of John Tyler and his young wife after he retired as president. The house, dating from 1730, is the longest wood-frame house in the country, at 300 feet. It has beautiful grounds with more than 80 varieties of trees and is furnished with period antiques. It's still owned by the Tyler family and is occupied by John Tyler's grandson. The grounds are open to the public.

Not along Route 5 but barely 20 miles away is **Carter's Grove.** Run by Colonial Williamsburg and located eight miles east of Williamsburg on US 60, the home has been called one of the most beautiful in America. The wealthiest and most powerful of the tobacco planters was Robert "King" Carter, whose grandson Carter Burwell began building the mansion you see today. Of special interest there are The Archaeology Museum and Wolstenholm Towne, an archaeological excavation of one of the earliest English settlements, which was wiped out in an attack in 1622; the slave quarter; and several fields planted in historic crops. In 2003, Carter's Grove was closed for an assessment of the property, grounds, and programs, and will reopen in the future.

part ten
HONORABLE MENTIONS

HONEY BEE

Coaxing sweet stuff from bees and trees is the business of Virginia's apiarists and sap collectors. Before it can be collected, honey is "manufactured" in one of the world's most efficient factories, the beehive. Bees may travel as far as 55,000 miles and visit more than two million flowers to gather enough nectar to make just a pound of honey.

The color and flavor of honey differ depending on the bees' nectar source (the blossoms). Several types of unique honey are collected by hobbyists and commercial beekeepers, but according to Keith Tignor, Virginia State Apiarist, four types are most common. Honey produced when bees visit the clusters of small white flowers of the sourwood tree (also known as Lily of the Valley tree) is unique to the Appalachian area. Black locust, from the tree of the same name that grows in the mountains of the eastern United States, is a premium honey that becomes darker and acquires a mild licorice taste the longer it's stored. Tulip-poplar honey, also known as a baker's honey, is dark amber and can be almost bitter. Clover honey, the most popular and plentiful in the United

States, is mined primarily from the flowers of the white clover, alsike clover, and the white and yellow sweet-clover plants. Depending on location and source, clover honey varies in color from water-white to extra light amber and has a mild, delicate flavor.

Maple syrup is one of the oldest agricultural commodities produced in the United States and is unique in the world to the northeast corner of our continent. Native Americans are credited with discovering how to convert maple-tree sap into maple syrup; they traded syrup long before any European settlers arrived.

Along about Washington's birthday, farmers begin tapping maple trees. Then they settle into the arduous procedure of boiling nature's product into the liquid sugar that *The Old Farmer's Almanac* in 1798 predicted "will have the preference of every true American." Although there's not enough real maple syrup to top all of America's pancakes, a pass down the syrup aisle is a clue that indeed Americans love their maple syrup—flavored, reduced sugar, or sugarless—and Virginians are no exception.

Beekeeping

When people look to return to the land, they might consider another hobby besides gardening. A vocation that dates back to antiquity, beekeeping serves as an enjoyable, productive hobby as well as a nice income booster. A small colony of bees can supply a neighborhood with all the honey it can eat, plus more to sell on the side.

The basic beekeeper needs a hive, smoker, veil, hive tool, a pair of gloves, and some bees. The cost might not exceed $140 when ordered from a hardware store or mail-order supply house. Used hives, with or without bees, from an experienced beekeeper, are often a good buy. Package or starter bees, which literally come in a package, can be obtained from a number of suppliers in the state.

The best time of year to start a hive is early in the spring, when fruit trees bloom. After the beekeeper assembles a hive, complete with the foundation for the combs, and paints the exterior, he places the package bees inside. After "hiving a swarm" of bees, as it is called, he feeds the bees for a short time with damp granulated sugar spooned into the beehive. As the colony expands, the bees then require new "supers," or sections to be added onto the hive. During the spring and summer, the bees collect flower nectar and pollen,

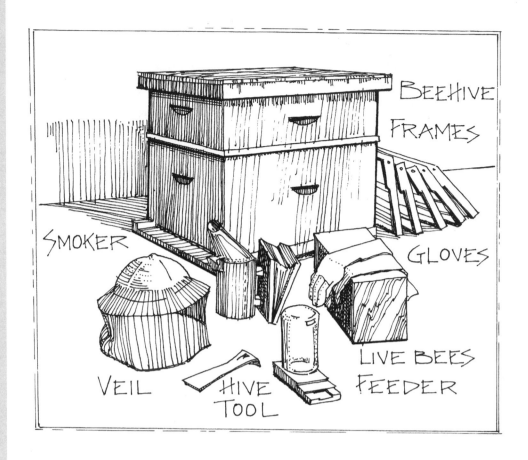

BEEHIVE FRAMES

SMOKER

GLOVES

VEIL

HIVE TOOL

LIVE BEES FEEDER

chapter one
HONEY

∽ *Virginia buzzes with honey production; its 2.4 million commercial bee colonies produce close to 200,000 pounds of honey each year, valued at almost $700,000. Although bees are kept in many parts of the state, the importance of bees in the Shenandoah Valley is two-fold. In addition to manufacturing honey, bees perform a vital second function—pollination for the valley's huge tree-fruit business. About one third of the human diet is derived from insect-pollinated plants such as fruits, vegetables, and legumes; honey bees are responsible for 80% of this pollination.*

FRUIT SMOOTHIE

1 pint fresh strawberries, stemmed
   and sliced, or 2 cups frozen strawberries, slightly thawed
1 cup low-fat milk
½ cup honey

1 cup (8 ounces) plain or vanilla
   low-fat yogurt
1 teaspoon vanilla extract
1 cup crushed ice (5 to 6 cubes)

In a blender or food-processor container, combine all ingredients; process until smooth. Serve immediately. For variety, use 2 cups of any fresh or frozen fruit or combination of fruits such as sliced strawberries and bananas or sliced peaches and whole raspberries. Makes 4 servings.

This recipe was provided by the Virginia State Beekeepers Association.

SAM SNEAD'S TAVERN HOUSE DRESSING

Spinach, mixed greens, and fruit salads taste especially good with this dressing.

¾ cup cider vinegar
6 tablespoons honey
¼ small onion
1½ cups oil
1 tablespoon chopped fresh parsley

1 tablespoon celery seeds
1 tablespoon poppy seeds
1½ teaspoons ground mustard
½ teaspoon paprika

In a blender or food processor fitted with a steel blade, place vinegar, honey, and onion. Pulse until onion is minced. Add oil, parsley, celery seeds, poppy seeds, mustard, and paprika. Blend on high speed until creamy. Makes about 3 cups.

Professional golfer Sam Snead was born in Hot Springs. He took an old 1920s bank building and turned it into a sporty tavern. The bank's vault holds the tavern's wine. The vault door, considered an engineering marvel, weighs 2000 pounds but is balanced so well that it can be closed with one hand. The tavern is part of The Homestead, a luxurious historic hotel in Virginia's Allegheny Mountains. Sam Snead's Tavern is in a separate building and the most casual of The Homestead's dining venues. Phone (800) 838-1766 or (540) 839-1766.

SOUTHERN-STYLE
HONEY-BARBECUED CHICKEN

Here's a barbecue for your oven.

1 (2½-to-3 pound) chicken, cut-up
salt and pepper to taste
1 cup thinly sliced onions
¾ cup tomato sauce
¼ cup honey

¼ cup vinegar
2 tablespoons Worcestershire sauce
1 teaspoon paprika
¼ teaspoon bottled hot-pepper sauce

Place chicken, skin-side down, in a large baking dish. Sprinkle with salt and pepper. Combine remaining ingredients; mix well. Pour mixture over chicken. Bake, uncovered, at 375° F for 30 minutes. Turn pieces and bake 20 minutes longer, or until chicken is glazed and no longer pink. Makes 4 servings.

This recipe was provided by the Virginia State Beekeepers Association.

Beekeeping
(continued)

which they store in their hive as honey, sealing it in wax in honeycombs. A beekeeper then brushes the bees off the honeycomb, cuts the comb from the frame, chops it up, and strains the pieces through a colander into jars. Preparations must be made to feed the bees over the winter. Usually, late-fall flowers provide enough raw materials for them to make their own food.

Select mild honeys to use with foods that have a delicate flavor. Use stronger honeys in spreads or other recipes where a distinct honey flavor is desired. Honey has more sweetening power than sugar due to its high fructose content and it helps prevent baked goods from drying out and becoming stale due to its ability to absorb and retain moisture. Honey can be used as a binding or coloring agent as well as a sweetener.

Store honey at room temperature, as refrigeration accelerates crystallization (the natural process in which liquid in honey becomes solid). If the honey does crystallize, simply place the honey jar in warm water and stir until the crystals dissolve. Or microwave it without a lid, stirring every 30 seconds. Be careful not to boil or scorch the honey. A 12-ounce jar of honey equals a standard measuring cup.

HONEY-BAKED RED ONIONS

Try these colorful onions for an interesting side dish.

3 large red onions (about 3 pounds)
¼ cup water
⅓ cup honey
3 tablespoons butter or margarine, melted

1 teaspoon paprika, preferably sweet Hungarian
1 teaspoon ground coriander
½ teaspoon salt
⅛ teaspoon cayenne pepper

Peel and cut onions in half crosswise. Place cut side down in shallow baking dish just large enough to hold all onions in one layer. Sprinkle with water; cover with aluminum foil. Bake at 350° F for 30 minutes. Turn onions cut side up. Combine remaining ingredients. Spoon half of mixture over onions. Return to oven and bake, uncovered, 15 minutes. Baste with remaining honey mixture; continue baking 15 minutes or until tender. Serve with poultry or pork. Makes 6 servings.

This recipe was provided by the Virginia State Beekeepers Association.

FINGER-LICKING HONEY SPARERIBS

3 pounds pork spareribs
salt and pepper to taste
1 cup chili sauce
½ cup honey, or more

¼ cup minced onion
2 tablespoons dry red wine, optional
1 tablespoon Worcestershire sauce
1 teaspoon Dijon mustard

Sprinkle spareribs with salt and pepper. Place on a rack over a roasting pan; cover with foil and bake at 375° F. Combine remaining ingredients in a small saucepan and bring to a boil over medium heat, stirring constantly. Reduce heat and simmer, uncovered, 5 minutes. When ribs have cooked 35 to 45 minutes, remove cover and brush generously with sauce. Bake 45 additional minutes, brushing with sauce every 15 minutes, until spareribs are fully cooked and tender. Cut spareribs into serving portions and serve with remaining sauce. Serves 4.

This recipe was provided by the Virginia State Beekeepers Association.

He who figures to get more than one gallon of syrup from less than 35 gallons of sap is not good at figuring nor at making maple syrup.
—Anonymous

It's a lot of work to turn sap into syrup. To make one gallon of maple syrup takes about 40 gallons of sap—all the sap from two maple trees in an entire sugaring season.

The first step is to tap the trees. Use a drill with a half-inch bit and drill a tap hole about two inches deep, two to four feet above the ground. Insert a metal or plastic collection spout and a bucket or plastic bag or tubing line for each tap hole. After collecting sap, you'll have to boil it down. Boiling sap is best done outdoors lest you're left with a layer of sugary residue on your walls.

Boil the sap until it reaches exactly 219° F, according to the state extension service. Heat concentrates the sugar, which then develops the characteristic color and flavor of maple syrup. The hot syrup must be filtered through wool, orlon, or other filtering materials to remove sugar sand and other impurities. Then it is ready to bottle.

chapter two

MAPLE SYRUP

∽ *Outside the United States and Canada, cooks have developed few recipes using maple syrup, for only in Germany and Japan have the trees been planted in appreciable numbers, and it takes 40 years before a sugar maple can be tapped.*

In Virginia, the southernmost producer of maple syrup in the country, recipes abound. The majority of the state's syrup is produced in Highland County near the West Virginia border, where the two varieties of trees whose sugar-water sap can be turned into maple syrup—the sugar maple and the black maple—live in their perfect higher-altitude climate. Some of the county's trees have yielded their special sap for 300 years.

Maple syrup has been strictly a "sideline" farm crop; however, the production of maple syrup and other maple products is often a full-time operation while the sap is running (during the transition weeks between winter and spring).

To ensure you are getting
real maple syrup and not an
imitation breakfast syrup,
check the label for the
phrase "Pure Maple Syrup"
and the name of the producer. Opened maple-syrup
containers should be refrigerated. If you see mold appearing, discard. You can freeze
maple syrup for up to one
year, but be sure to leave half
inch of room for expansion,
and seal it tightly. It will take
about one hour at room temperature for the maple syrup
to thaw. Maple sugar (from
grated maple-sugar leaves) is
a good substitute for brown
sugar and honey in recipes.

⌘ DID YOU KNOW . . .
that one tablespoon of
maple syrup has only 40
calories and contains
manganese, magnesium,
potassium, vitamins B_1,
B_2, B_6, niacin, iron, and
calcium?

HIGHLAND INN MAPLE MUFFINS WITH MAPLE BUTTER GLAZE

If you want to prepare these muffins ahead, just cool completely after baking, wrap tightly in foil, and freeze. When ready to eat them, reheat in a 325° F oven for about 10 minutes.

FOR MUFFINS:

2 eggs	1 cup bran flakes
1 cup sour cream	1 teaspoon baking soda
1 cup Highland County maple syrup	¾ cup chopped hazelnuts
1 cup flour	

FOR GLAZE:

¼ cup Highland County maple syrup	2 tablespoons butter, softened

Preheat oven to 400° F. In a large bowl, beat eggs to blend. Stir in sour cream and maple syrup. Add flour, bran flakes, and baking soda. Stir until batter is moist. Mix in nuts. Generously grease a 12-cup muffin tin and fill cups ¾ full. Bake 15 to 20 min-utes. To make glaze, combine syrup with butter. Dip warm muffins into glaze. Serve warm. Makes 12 muffins.

⌘ *The Highland Inn in Monterey was built in 1904 to lodge tourists escaping from the summer heat of nearby cities. The grand Victorian structure has 17 guest rooms and a dining room and has been restored to preserve its charm (phone (540) 468-2143; or visit www.highland-inn.com).* ⌘

FERRY FARM MAPLE-HONEY SAUCE

George Washington's mother, Mary, frequently made this sauce, which tastes especially good over buckwheat pancakes, waffles, and root vegetables such as carrots, parsnips, and rutabagas.

¾ cup maple syrup	2 teaspoons ground cinnamon
½ cup honey	½ teaspoon caraway seeds

Combine maple syrup and honey in a small saucepan and heat slowly. Add cinnamon and caraway seeds. Bring to a hard boil and serve hot. Makes 1¼ cups.

⌘ *This is a historic recipe attributed to the mother of our first president.* ⌘

MAPLE-GLAZED SWEET POTATOES

*So sweet they could almost be dessert, these potatoes
make an excellent accompaniment to Virginia ham, chicken, and turkey.*

6 large sweet potatoes
¾ cup firmly packed brown sugar
½ cup water
4 tablespoons butter (½ stick)
¼ cup maple syrup

juice of 1 orange
grated zest of 1 orange (orange color
   from rind)
½ cup black walnuts or other nuts,
   chopped

Preheat the oven to 375° F. Generously butter a (13 × 9 × 2-inch) baking dish; set aside. Bring a large pot of salted water to a boil. Add the sweet potatoes and boil until just tender, about 30 to 35 minutes. Drain and peel the potatoes. Cut into quarters and spread in prepared baking dish.

Combine brown sugar, water, butter, syrup, zest, and orange juice in a heavy-bottomed saucepan. Stir to dissolve sugar, bring to a boil, and cook until the mixture forms a syrup, about 5 minutes. Pour syrup over potatoes and sprinkle with nuts. Cover dish tightly with foil.

Bake 30 minutes. Remove foil and continue to bake about 10 minutes more. Remove from oven and let stand 5 minutes before serving. Makes 6 servings.

This recipe was adapted from Chesapeake Bay Cooking *with John Shields, the companion cookbook to the PBS television series of the same name.*

MAPLE CRUNCH COOKIES

*Innkeeper Pat Adams won a blue ribbon at the 1999 Highland County Fair
for these thin, crispy cookies flavored with pure maple syrup.*

¼ cup maple syrup
¾ cup soft shortening
1 cup granulated sugar
1 egg
2 cups all-purpose flour

1 teaspoon baking soda
1 teaspoon cinnamon
½ teaspoon salt
½ teaspoon ginger
¼ teaspoon cloves

Cream maple syrup, shortening, and sugar. Add egg and beat until fluffy. Measure dry ingredients and sift together twice to blend and then sift into creamed mixture. Stir until thoroughly blended. Drop by teaspoonsful onto ungreased baking sheet. (Note that they spread out quite a bit, so don't crowd.) Bake at 375° F for 10 to 12 minutes, or just until golden brown. Makes 6 dozen cookies.

Pat Adams's Mountain Laurel Inn in Monterey is housed in an elegant Victorian home that was totally renovated in 1996. In addition to overseeing the bed-and-breakfast, Adams caters local events and raises lamb, beef, and turkeys (phone (800) 510-0180 or visit www.va-bedandbreakfast.com).

Drive a Virginia Scenic Byway

William Least Heat Moon's best-seller, *Blue Highways*, described America from the backroads and offered homespun views of travel off the beaten path. Virginia's version of blue highways are Scenic Byways, officially designated and marked en route by blue signs. The oldest Virginia Byway is Route 5 between Richmond and Williamsburg, the first sanctioned Byway and one of Virginia's oldest roads. The 50-mile drive still traverses scenes unchanged since the seventeenth and eighteenth centuries, when the road was laid down along Indian trails following the James River. The Mount Vernon Memorial Highway opened in 1932 and was later linked to the George Washington Memorial Highway; the drive stretches for 17 glorious miles, winding along the Potomac River, past lovely stands of maples, oaks, sycamores, and elms and including historical sites such as George Washington's Mount Vernon estate and gardens along the way.

Contact the Highland County Chamber of Commerce in Monterey to find out more about maple-related activities in the area. Phone (540) 468-2550 or visit www.highland county.org. To reach Monterey from I-81, near Staunton, take Exit 222 (U.S. Route 250) west 45 miles.

⌘ DID YOU KNOW . . .
that the Highland County Fair is one of the oldest continuously operating county fairs in the state and celebrated its 50th anniversary in 2000?

tour

CALLING ALL MAPLE LOVERS

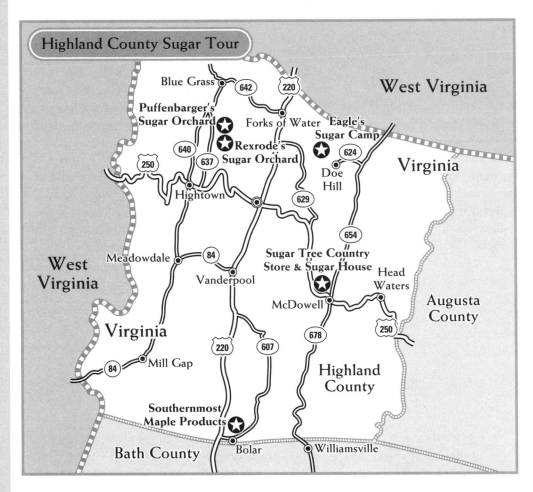

Highland County, the heart of maple-syrup country, calls itself "Virginia's Switzerland," but, unlike the densly-populated Alpine commonwealth, it is the most sparsely populated of Virginia's 95 counties. Pastoral fields, farmlands, and the area's national forests are natural bird and wildlife habitats. Scenic mountain roads lead to a unique, rural setting in the Allegheny Mountains of Virginia's Western Highlands.

And it is here that maple syrup has been in the making since American Indians inhabited the area. Attractions and events celebrating the nectar abound. Here are a few to consider:

Exhibits that trace the history of the syrup-making process are displayed at the small **Maple Museum** situated on U.S. Route 220 just south of Monterey, the Highland County seat, population 200 or so. The museum is a replica of an old-time "sugar house." Admission is free.

During the second and third weekends of March, the **Highland Maple Festival** features sugar tours, arts and crafts, antiques, baby farm animals, clowns and toys, dances, shows, the Maple Queen pageant and ball, and food, food, food.

Before departing Highland County, stock up on the maple products sold at two picturesque country stores where maple syrup is also made. **Southernmost Maple Products** is located 15 miles south of Monterey on Route 607 (off US 220 at Bolar). Sugar water is funneled into the only piggyback evaporator to be found in the southern states. The rustic country store shelves a variety of maple-imbibed products, plus flour, honey, jellies, baked goods, maple pit-cooked barbecue, and pork skins. **Sugar Tree Country Store and Sugar House** is just off Route 250 behind the Obaugh Funeral Home near the center of McDowell. This original 1840s country store employs a modern reverse-osmosis concentrator and oil-fired evaporator. Traditional iron-kettle cooking is demonstrated, and antique maple-producing tools are on display. Country-store merchandise, maple products, and food are for sale (phone (800) 396-2445 to have products shipped).

Maple-sugar "camps" throughout Highland County welcome visitors to view the process of syrup making. Try taking a tour of the camps. Be sure to don warm clothing and boots and to fetch a map of the tour at your first stop; all turns will be plainly marked.

Eagle's Sugar Camp is eight miles north of McDowell. Take Route 654 to Doe Hill, turn left on Route 624, and proceed two miles to the camp. Showing the use of open pans and a wood-fired evaporator, this camp has been producing syrup for more than 200 years, with some trees nearing the age of 300 years.

Puffenbarger's Sugar Orchard is on Route 637 north of Monterey near Blue Grass. The most modern equipment is used here: a vacuum pump to increase the flow of sugar water and miles of plastic tubing to gather it. Processing is accomplished through reverse osmosis and finished with the use of oil-fired evaporators. Food and maple donuts can be purchased here.

Rexrode's Sugar Orchard is north of Hightown on Route 637 and features some large maple trees more than 200 years old. The Rexrodes use the old-fashioned open-pan system of evaporation as well as the newer wood-fired method. Food is available.

Sugar Maple Tree

The maple is one of North America's most versatile and best-loved deciduous trees. In addition to maple syrup, the sugar maple tree (*Acer saccharum*) is one of the most valuable hardwoods, used for flooring, bowling pins, and furniture. Most maple syrup is made from sugar maple sap because it has an average sugar content of 2%. Because sap from other maple species is usually lower in sugar content, approximately twice as much would be needed to yield the same amount of finished syrup. Ornamental maples, such as the Norway and Schwedler maple, have a milky sap and cannot be used for syrup production.

Sugar maple is a native North American tree with unparalleled fall color. The fire-red-to-yellow color of the maple's fall foliage makes a splashing contribution to the beauty of Virginia's autumnal countryside. One way to remember what its leaf looks like is that the sugar maple leaf has five big points and there are five letters in the word "maple." You can also look at the Canadian flag with its single red maple leaf in the center. Most maple trees are planted by nature. Maple-tree seeds (samara) travel on the wind and are known as "helicopters" for their propeller shape and whirling flight.

RESOURCES

Restaurants and Inns

ALEXANDER'S
4536 Oceanview Avenue; Virginia Beach, VA 23455
(804) 464-4999; www.alexandersonthebay.com
This elegant restaurant is a standout for its terrific view of the Bay. Main dishes range from seafood to steak and veal. Be sure to ask for directions—Alexander's is off the beaten path.

APPLE TREE BED & BREAKFAST
115 East Laurel Avenue or P. O. Box 878
Damascus, VA 24236; (540) 475-5261
Located in the heart of the Virginia Highlands close to Mount Rogers, the highest mountain in Virginia, this 1904 transitional Victorian house is on the Appalachian Trail and within a block of the Virginia Creeper Trail.

THE ASHBY INN
Paris, VA; (540) 592-3900
The inn was built as a home in 1829 near the foothills of the Blue Ridge Mountains and the site of the Ashby Tavern, frequented by George Washington when he was a young surveyor. Most of the inn's furnishings date to the early 1800s.

ASHTON COUNTRY HOUSE BED & BREAKFAST
1205 Middlebrook Avenue (SR 252); Staunton, VA 24401; (540) 885-3001 or (877) 885-3001;
www.ashtonhousebnb.com
A Victorian mansion built in 1860, this house has lofty ceilings, a 40-foot center hall, solid brick interior walls, and magnificent heart pine and maple floors. There are swings on the large porch, scenic mountain vistas and flowered grounds.

THE BAILIWICK INN
4023 Chain Bridge Road; Fairfax, VA 22030;
(703) 691-2266; www.bailiwickinn.com
This Federal-style house in Fairfax that was built in the early 1800s and used as a hospital during the Civil War. Today the 14-guestroom luxury inn includes a fine-dining restaurant overseen by Chef Jeffrey Prather.

THE BATTLETOWN INN
102 W. Main Street; Berryville, VA 22611;
(540) 955-3697; www.battletown.com
The house was built in 1809 for Sara Stribling, the daughter of Benjamin Berry, the founder and namesake of Berryville. In 1946, the Battletown Inn opened in the house. For the next 35 years Mrs. Mary Murray operated the restaurant and created a reputation for fine Virginia cuisine and hospitality.

CHESAPEAKE CHARM BED & BREAKFAST
202 Madison Avenue; Cape Charles, VA 23310;
(757) 331-2676; www.chesapeakecharmbnb.com
The B & B is located in the small town of Cape Charles, one of Virginia's largest historic districts and formerly the southernmost terminus for the New York, Philadelphia, and Norfolk Railroad.

CHRISTIANA CAMPBELL'S
Waller Street; Colonial Williamsburg, VA 23187;
(800) 447-8679 or (757) 229-2741;
www.history.org/visit/dining/index.cfm
George Washington's favorite tavern in Williamsburg, today specializes in seafood dishes just as it did in his time. Situated across the grounds from the capitol, the tavern was run by Campbell to support herself and her two small children after her husband's untimely death.

COLONIAL GARDENS BED & BREAKFAST
1109 Jamestown Road; Williamsburg, VA 23185;
(757) 220-8087 or (800) 886-9715
This Colonial style modern home is located in the City of Williamsburg's historic corridor. The quiet woodland setting

with seasonal gardens invites you to relax and enjoy warmth and hospitality.

CUZ'S UPTOWN BARBECUE
Route 460; Pounding Mill, VA; (540) 964-9014
This restaurant serves delectable ostrich fillets, with meat from ostriches raised at Sandy Head Ostrich. In addition to their restaurant, Mike and Yvonne offer guest lodging in log cabins nestled at the base of the mountains, complete with Jacuzzis and fireplaces, a secluded outdoor pool, and clay tennis courts.

FEDERAL CREST INN BED & BREAKFAST
1101 Federal Street; Lynchburg, VA 24504; (804) 845-6155 or (800) 818-6155; www.federalcrest.com
This stately 8,000-square-foot Georgian Revival mansion was built on almost an acre of land at the crest of Federal and Eleventh Streets in 1909 by a wealthy Lynchburg lawyer.

FIREHOOK BAKERY & COFFEEHOUSE
Main Bakery: 214 N. Fayette Street; (703) 519-8020
Old Town: 105 S. Union Street; (703) 519-8021
www.firehook.com
The goal of this neighborhood bakery is to make quality breads and pastries. The original main bakery had a wood-burning oven, which was brought from Spain by ship and built brick by brick by Emanuel de la Rosa, from Barcelona.

FOUR & TWENTY BLACKBIRDS RESTAURANT
650 Zachary Taylor Highway; Flint Hill, VA 22627;
(540) 675-1111
Housed in a former general store, this fine-dining restaurant in the Virginia countryside is charming with its antiques and assorted blackbird salt shakers. Chef Heidi Morf changes her menu every three weeks, and chooses only the best ingredients.

GADSBY'S TAVERN
138 North Royal Street; Alexandria, VA 22314;
(703) 548-1288; www.gadsbystavern.org
This Alexandria tavern was frequented by George Washington, the Marquis de Lafayette, John Paul Jones, John Adams, Thomas Jefferson and James Madison. Built in 1792, the four-story Georgian building was then considered a veritable skyscraper. Today, Colonial attired waiters and entertainers take you back to the eighteenth century.

HARMONY FARM BED & BREAKFAST
3510 Black Ridge Road Southwest; Floyd, VA 24091;
www.harmony-farm.com; (540) 593-2185
Located in beautiful Floyd County on the eastern flank of the Blue Ridge Mountains, this B & B is 0.6 mile from the scenic parkway and 1 mile from Chateau Morrisette Winery. The farm consists of 90 acres of forests, open fields, wildflower beds, and a pond that provide habitat for wildlife.

HIGHLAND INN
P. O. Box 40; Monterey, VA 24465; (540) 468-2143;
www.highland-inn.com
Located in Monterey, the Highland Inn was built in 1904 to lodge tourists escaping from the summer heat of nearby cities. The grand Victorian structure has been restored, and has 17 guest rooms and a dining room.

HILDA CROCKETT'S CHESAPEAKE HOUSE
Tangier Island, VA; (757) 891-2331;
http://tangierisland-va.com/cheshouse
Located on Main Street in Tangier Island, this restaurant is open from April 15 to October 15.

THE HOMESTEAD
Hot Springs, VA 24445; (540) 839-1766 or
(866) 354-4653; www.thehomestead.com
The Homestead, tucked within Virginia's Allegheny Mountains in Hot Springs, was founded as a small inn in 1766 by Com-

modore Thomas Bullitt, who received unsolicited room-and-board requests at his own home from travelers seeking the rejuvenation and cure of area hot springs. Today, the premier resort features numerous amenities and access to skiing, skating, shooting sports, horseback/carriage rides, and three golf courses.

HOPE AND GLORY INN
634 King Carter Drive; Irvington, VA 22480;
(804) 438-6053 or (800) 497-8228;
www.hopeandglory.com
Built in 1890 as a schoolhouse, this whimsically decorated inn and four guest cottages offer a charming getaway near the Rappahannock River. The grounds are landscaped in English cottage garden style and feature old fashioned flower varieties.

THE HOTEL ROANOKE & CONFERENCE CENTER
110 Shenandoah Avenue, Roanoke, VA 24016;
(540) 985-5900 or (800) 222-TREE;
www.hotelroanoke.com
The Hotel Roanoke & Conference Center surrounds you with the warmest of traditional southern hospitality. From the Florentine marble floors to the vaulted ceilings, the 1882 hotel has been lovingly restored to its rich, nineteenth-century elegance and is listed in the National Register of Historic Places.

INDIAN FIELDS TAVERN
9220 John Tyler Highway; Charles City, VA 23030;
(804) 829-6003
This tavern opened in 1987, in what was formerly the falling-down farmhouse of an old 1880s Mennonite dairy farm. The eatery uses herbs from its garden in the fine Southern cuisine.

THE INN AT LITTLE WASHINGTON
Middle and Main Streets; Washington, VA 22747;
(540) 675-3800; www.theinnatlittlewashington.com
Patrick O'Connell was voted America's best chef of 2001 by the James Beard Foundation, The inn previously won four Beard Awards including: Restaurant of the Year; Best Service; Best Chef in the Mid-Atlantic Region; and Best Wine Service.

THE INN AT MEANDER PLANTATION
US Route 15 (HCR 5, Box 460A); Locust Dale, VA 22948; (800) 385-4936; www.meander.net
Patented in 1727, the owner of this first plantation in Madison County was Col. Joshua Fry, the partner of Peter Jefferson. The duo drew the first official map of the State of Virginia. Peter's son Thomas as well as General Lafayette visited here often. The Inn is located in pastoral countryside north of Orange.

THE INN AT MONTROSS
21 Polk Street or PO Box 908; Montross, VA 22520; (804) 493-0573; www.innatmontross.com
Originally established in 1684 as John Minor's Ordinary (tavern) this Colonial home located in the historic Northern Neck of Virginia is currently a five-guestroom inn and 50-seat fine-dining restaurant. Chef Scott Massidda is known locally as the "Soup Master."

THE IVY INN RESTAURANT
2244 Old Ivy Road; Charlottesville, VA 22903;
(804) 977-1222; www.ivyinnrestaurant.com
One mile from the University of Virginia in Charlottesville, Ivy Inn was once part of a larger estate owned by William Faulkner, distinguished University "writer in residence." The restaurant has several dining rooms decorated in handsome Colonial furnishings, and there's outdoor dining seasonally on a large patio.

JASMINE PLANTATION BED & BREAKFAST
4500 N. Courthouse Road; Providence Forge, VA 23140; (804) 966-9836
This eighteenth-century restored farmhouse between Richmond and Williamsburg is situated on 47 acres in Virginia's historic

plantation country. Visitors are invited to walk the grounds, relax in one of the many common areas, or enjoy the wildlife. The Inn serves a full country breakfast.

THE JEFFERSON HOTEL
101 West Franklin Street; Richmond, VA 23220; (804) 788-8000 or (800) 424-8014; www.jeffersonhotel.com
Built in 1895 and recognized as one of the grandest hotels in America, this hotel is a National Historic Landmark and a charter member of Historic Hotels of America. Lemaire, the Five-Diamond restaurant, features a menu of distinctive southern dishes and is named for Etienne Lemaire, who served as Maitre d'Hotel to Thomas Jefferson.

KESWICK HALL/KESWICK CLUB
701 Club Drive; Charlottesville, VA 22947; (434) 979 3440 or (800) 274-5391; www.keswick.com
Keswick Hall at Monticello is an elegant 48-room resort, operated alongside Keswick Club restaurant.

KING'S ARMS TAVERN
Duke of Gloucester Street; Colonial Williamsburg, VA 23187; (800) 828-3767 or (757) 229-2141; www.history.org/visit/diningexperience
Known in colonial times as the restaurant where the elite meet and eat, the atmosphere at Colonial Williamsburg's premier tavern is one of simple elegance, one that befits the statesmen and gentry who often dined here. The menus feature Peanut Soup, Game Pye, and Prime Rib of Beef.

L'AUBERGE CHEZ FRANÇOIS
332 Springvale Road; Great Falls, VA; (703) 759-3800; www.laubergechezfrancois.com
The Haeringer family's popular Alsatian-style restaurant, open since 1954, is one of Virginia's finest restaurants. The cooking is hearty and the portions, generous. Open Sunday for lunch and dinner, Tuesday through Saturday for dinner.

L'AUBERGE PROVENÇALE
P. O. Box 119; White Post, VA 22663; (540) 837-1375; www.laubergeprovencale.com
The antique-filled 1753 manor house of L'Auberge Provençale, is about one hour west of Arlington in Mt. Airy. Chef Alain Borel and his wife Celeste are fourth-generation innkeepers.

LA PETITE AUBERGE
311 William Street; Fredericksburg, VA 22401; (540) 371-2727
Owner/chef Christian Renault has been turning out local foods with a French accent in Fredericksburg for over two decades. The historic 1880 building that houses the multi-room dining venue was originally a liquor store with a questionable reputation, and then became a hardware store.

LA PETITE FRANCE
2108 Maywill Street; Richmond VA 23230; (804) 353-8729; www.lapetitefrance.net
At this fine-dining restaurant in Richmond, the emerald-green walls are hung with reproductions of eighteenth-century English landscapes and portraits.

LA VISTA PLANTATION BED & BREAKFAST
4420 Guinea Station Road; Fredericksburg, VA 22408; (540) 898-8444 or (800) 529-2823; www.lavistaplantation.com
This 1838 Greek Revival is situated on ten acres that include mature trees, flowering shrubs, pastures, woods, gardens, and a pond stocked with bass and sunfish.

MAHI MAH'S SEAFOOD RESTAURANT AND SUSHI SALOON
615 Atlantic Avenue; Virginia Beach, VA 23451; (757) 437-8030; www.mahimahs.com
At Mahi Mah's, you can sit by the fireplace and have a view of the ocean or dine outdoors in warmer weather.

MARTHA WASHINGTON INN
150 West Main Street; Abingdon, VA 24210; (540) 628-3161 or (888) 999-8078; www.marthawashingtoninn.com
This hostelry and fine dining restaurant is located in the historic

district of Abingdon, Virginia, in the far west of Virginia. Built in 1832, the mansion later served as a women's college and a Civil War hospital. It opened in 1935 as a hotel and has 51 rooms and 10 suites appointed with fine antiques and reproductions.

MICHIE TAVERN
683 Thomas Jefferson Parkway; Charlottesville, VA 22902; (804) 977-1234; www.michietavern.com
Historic Michie (pronounced MIKE'-ee) Tavern was a meeting place for such patriots as Thomas Jefferson, James Madison and Patrick Henry. The old inn still prepares this bread and serves it to guests during Yuletide. The Tavern serves midday fare of recipes dating to the 1700s.

THE MOUNTAIN LAUREL INN
Box 27 Main Street; Monterey, VA 24465; (540) 468-3401 or (800) 510-0180; www.va-bedandbreakfast.com
This B&B is a turn-of-the-century elegant Victorian home that was totally renovated in 1996. Innkeeper Pat Adams caters for local events including tea parties, lunches, and dinners. She also raises lamb, beef, dairy, and turkeys.

MOUNT VERNON INN RESTAURANT
P. O. Box 110; Mount Vernon, VA 22121-0110; (703) 780-0011.; www.mountvernon.org
Located at the entrance to the mansion grounds on Mount Vernon Circle, this restaurant has period-attired staff to serve modern and Colonial dishes at lunch and dinner. Wedding parties and other large functions may be held in the Sunken Garden outdoor courtyard or in the new Octagonal Dining Pavilion.

OAK GROVE PLANTATION BED & BREAKFAST
P. O. Box 45; Cluster Springs, VA 24535; (804) 575-7137 or (877) 343-7871; www.bbonline.com/va/oakgrove
At this antebellum home, The air is alive with the sound of country—crickets, frogs, cicadas and birds. Today, nearly 180 years after its construction, the same family welcomes you with Southern hospitality.

PICKETT'S HARBOR BED AND BREAKFAST
28288 Nottingham Ridge Lane; Cape Charles, VA 23310; (757) 331-2212; www.pickettsharbor.com
This working vegetable farm has remained in innkeeper Sara Goffigon family for three centuries. It even has a private Chesapeake beach.

PORCHES ON THE JAMES B & B
Old Stage Highway; Smithfield, VA 23430; (757) 356-0602 or toll-free (866) 356-0602
Porches on the James is a modern country home on a bluff 60 feet above the historic James River near Smithfield. True to its name, guests can relax on the expansive porch. A beach and boat dock are available to guests arriving by land or sea.

THE RED FOX INN AND TAVERN
2 East Washington Street; Middleburg, VA 20118; (540) 687-6301 or (800) 223-1728; www.redfox.com
The inn stands at the center crossroads of Middleburg, a historic village in horse-farm country. Built in 1728, the original fieldstone structure is on the national Register of Historic Places.

SAM SNEAD'S TAVERN/THE HOMESTEAD HOTEL
1 US Route 220; Hot Springs, VA 24445; (866) 354-4653 or 540-839-1766; www.thehomestead.com
Located in a separate building, the tavern is the most casual dining venue at The Homestead in Virginia's Allegheny Mountains.

SHIELDS TAVERN
Duke of Gloucester Street; Colonial Williamsburg, VA 23187; (800) 447-8679; www.history.org/visit/diningexperience
The tavern offers coffeehouse fare in the tradition of James Shields in the 1740s, and is situated next door to King's Arms Tavern on Duke of Gloucester Street.

THE SMITHFIELD INN, BED & BREAKFAST, RESTAURANT AND WILLIAM RAND TAVERN
112 Main Street; Smithfield, VA 23430;

(757) 357-1752; www.smithfieldinn.com
George Washington DID sleep here. This 1752 house built by Henry Woodley served as an inn when the main stage coach route passed through Smithfield from Norfolk to Richmond. A second owner, William Rand, applied for a license to operate a tavern on the premises in 1759.

SOUTHERN INN RESTAURANT
37 South Main Street; Lexington, VA 24450; (540) 463-3612; www.southerninn.com
This Lexington landmark offers casual, upscale dining. Owner/chef George Huger offers a contemporary, seasonal menu utilizing local produce, meats and other products, as well as fresh seafood and in-house baked goods. The Southern Inn's cellar boasts a wide selection of Virginia wines.

STEELES TAVERN MANOR COUNTRY INN AND ALPINE HIDEAWAY COTTAGE
Route 11, Box 39; Steeles Tavern, VA 24476; (540) 377-9261
Located near the Cyrus McCormick Farm, an owner of this property hosted McCormick's first public exhibition of the reaper in a field of oats in front of the tavern. The current inn, built is 1916, has elegant rooms and first class cuisine, indulging guests with candlelight dinners and delectable homemade breakfast.

STONE MANOR BED & BREAKFAST
1135 Stone Manor Place; Goodview, VA 24095; (540) 297-1414
Located on Virginia's largest lake, Smith Mountain Lake, this inn offers recreational opportunities like boating, swimming, fishing, and golf right outside their door. The B&B even has a private beach and dock.

SUGAR TREE INN
Steeles Tavern; (800) 377-2197 or (540) 377-2197; www.sugartreeinn.com
Located near Lexington and McCormick Farm, the Sugar Tree Inn is at Exit 205 of I-81, on Highway 56. The large log cabin with nine rooms and two suites is located in Vesuvius, in the Blue Ridge Mountains.

THE SUMMERFIELD INN
101 W. Valley Street; Abingdon, VA 24210; (540) 628-5905 or (800) 668-5905; www.naxs.com/abingdon/suminn
Nestled in the foothills of the Appalachians in southwestern Virginia, this spacious 1920s-era Colonial Revival home offers guests luxurious comfort and hospitality. There are four bedrooms in the Parsonage or Main House and three in the Carriage House.

THE SURREY HOUSE
11865 Rolfe Highway; Surry, VA; (757) 294-3389; www.surreyhouserestaurant.com
Just across the river from Williamsburg via the Jamestown-Scotland free ferry run by the Virginia Department of Transportation, this restaurant lies in a pretty little town and offers some fine Southern cookin' for breakfast, lunch and dinner daily brought by servers in long country dresses.

THE TOBACCO COMPANY RESTAURANT
1201 East Cary Street; Richmond, VA; (804) 782-9555; www.thetobaccocompany.com
Housed in an 1878 tobacco warehouse, this popular Richmond restaurant serves more than 5,000 diners weekly and is open from 11:30 a.m.–2 a.m. daily.

THE TRELLIS RESTAURANT
Duke of Gloucester Street; Williamsburg, VA 23185; (757) 229-8610; www.thetrellis.com
One of Virginia's best restaurants is co-owned by chef Marcel Delsaulnier, award-winning cookbook author. Dine indoors or out for lunch and dinner. The menu is designed seasonally to incorporate the best of Virginia's farms.

VICTORIAN INN
138 East Main Street; Luray, VA 22835; (540) 743-1494 or (866) 937-3466; www.woodruffinns.com
The Victorian Inn is one of four properties of The Woodruff Collection of Bed & Breakfast Inns in Luray, three Victorian

homes plus river-front cottages on the Shenandoah. Chef Lucas Woodruff prepares the lavish breakfasts and wedding receptions held on the properties.

WAYSIDE INN
7783 Main Street; Middletown, VA 22645;
(540) 869-1797 or (877) 869-1797;
www.alongthewayside.com
Since 1797 the Wayside Inn has been lodging guests. Nestled in the Shenandoah Valley at the foot of the Massanutten Mountains, this distinctive inn has 24 guest rooms and suites, each decorated with its own theme of a bygone era. Fresh regional American cuisine is served in seven delightful dining rooms by servers in authentic Colonial costumes.

WHITE FENCE BED & BREAKFAST
(formerly The Ruby Rose Inns)
275 Chapel Road; Stanley, VA 22851; (540) 778-4680 or (800) 211-9885; www.whitefencebnb.com
This lovely Victorian home is surrounded by mountains, tall oaks and colorful flowerbeds. Just minutes from Shenandoah National Park and a national forest, guests can hike, walk nature trails, ski, canoe, go tubing, ride horseback, golf or fish. Nearby are antique shops, flea markets and auctions.

Historic Sites

BELLE GROVE PLANTATION
336 Belle Grove Road; Middletown, VA 22645;
(540) 869-2028; www.bellegrove.org
Planted in the Shenandoah Valley near Middletown, Belle Grove is an 18th-century grain and livestock farm once on 7500 acres. The unique limestone house was completed in 1797 for President James Madison's sister Nelly. Today, the plantation includes the main house and gardens, original outbuildings, a classic 1918 barn, an overseer's house, the slave cemetery, a heritage apple orchard, fields and meadows, and mountain views.

BOOKER T. WASHINGTON NATIONAL
MONUMENT
12130 Booker T. Washington Highway; Hardy, VA, 24101; (540) 721-2094; www.nps.gov/bowa
Open daily, all year, 9 a.m.–5 p.m. Visitors to Booker T. Washington National Monument can tour a living history farm, as well as picnic on the grounds. Hiking facilities include a quarter-mile walking trail through the historic area and 1.5-mile trail through natural areas.

BUSHONG FARM
New Market Battlefield State Park; 8895 George Collins Parkway; New Market, VA 22844;
(540) 740-3101 or (866) 515-1864;
www4.vmi.edu/museum/nm/index.html
The Civil War Battle of New Market was fought partially on the Bushong Farm, established in 1818. Today, visitors can explore nine structures interpreting mid-19th century Shenandoah Valley farm life. Open daily, 9 a.m.–5 p.m., year-round. Admission is $5 for adults and $2 for ages children 6–15 (includes New Market Battlefield and The Hall of Valor).

CLAUDE MOORE COLONIAL FARM
6310 Georgetown Pike; McLean, VA 22101;
(703) 442-7557; www.1771.org
A few miles from Washington, D.C. this pastoral site portrays family life on a small, low-income farm just prior to the Revolutionary War. Open April to mid-December, Wednesday through Sunday, from 10 a.m.–4:30. Adults $2; children $1.

COLONIAL WILLIAMSBURG
P. O. Box 1776; Williamsburg, VA 23187-1776;
(800) 404-3389; www.history.org
This living-history village is a perennial family vacation spot. Christmas is a popular time to visit Colonial Williamsburg, so leave plenty of time for making reservations.

GEORGE WASHINGTON BIRTHPLACE
NATIONAL MONUMENT
1732 Popes Creek Road; Washington's Birthplace, VA 22443-5115; (804) 224-1732 or (804) 224-1732

ext. 227; www.nps.gov/gewa
The farm and a reproduction first home of our first president are open daily, 9 a.m.–5 p.m. Admission is $2 per person and includes museum exhibits from the site's 100,000-artifacts, a guided or self-guided tour of the historic area.

GEORGE WASHINGTON'S FERRY FARM
268 Kings Highway at Ferry Road; Fredericksburg, VA 22405; (540) 370-0732; www.kenmore.org
Washington's second home, now an archeological site with some exhibits, is open daily from February 21 through December 30. Admission is $3. Ferry Farm is just across the Rappahannock River from downtown Fredericksburg on Route 3.

GUNSTON HALL
Mason Neck, VA; (703) 550-9220;
www.gunstonhall.org
George Mason's home, kitchen, farm and outbuildings plus a nice museum are open year round 9:30-5. Gunston Hall's famous boxwoods are thought to be the oldest in the country and were planted around 1755. Adults $5.

HAMPTON MANOR
(Private residence; not open to the public.)
This lovely home in Caroline County was built from Jeffersonian plans during the area's golden age between the War of 1812 and the Civil War. In the late 1930s, the surrealist painter Salvador Dali lived in the house. It is not open to the public.

HISTORIC CRAB ORCHARD MUSEUM &
PIONEER PARK
US Rts. 19 and 460 at Crab Orchard Road.
3663 Crab Orchard Road, Tazewell VA 24651;
(540) 988-6755; www.craborchardmuseum.com
On an archeological dig just west of the town is this 110-acre farm that exhibits Indian artifacts and farming methods in southwest Virginia. Farm buildings and craft shops are open year-round, Monday–Saturday, 9 a.m.–5 p.m. and Sunday, 1–5 p.m.

James River Plantations

BERKELEY PLANTATION
12602 Harrison Landing Road, Charles City
(804) 829-6018; www.berkeleyplantation.com
Built in 1726, Berkeley was home for generations of Harrisons, including President William Henry Harrison.

CARTER'S GROVE
Not currently open to the public. One of the most beautiful homes in America was built by tobacco planter Robert "King" Carter's grandson Carter Burwell. Of special interest there are the Archaeology Museum and Wolstenholm Towne.

EVELYNTON PLANTATION
No longer open to the public. Built in the 1930s to replace the one burned by Union forces during the Civil War Battle of Evelynton Heights, the Georgian Revival manor house sits on the original foundation and is named for William Byrd's daughter.

SHERWOOD FOREST PLANTATION
5416 Tuckahoe Avenue, Charles City
(804) 829-5377; www.sherwoodforest.org
Grounds open to the public. Mansion open only to pre-arranged group tours. The home of President John Tyler dates from 1730, and at 300-feet is the longest wood frame house in the country

SHIRLEY PLANTATION
501 Shirley Plantation Road, Charles City;
(804) 829-5121 or (800) 232-1613;
www.shirleyplantation.com
Virginia's oldest plantation dates to 1613, and it once included 18,000 acres. The beautiful home has been the Carter family residence for 10 generations. Robert E. Lee's mother was born here.

JAMESTOWN SETTLEMENT AND YORKTOWN
VICTORY CENTER
Jamestown-Yorktown Foundation
P. O. Box 1607; Williamsburg, VA 23187-1607

(757) 253-4838 or (888) 593-4682;
www.historyisfun.org

KENMORE
1201 Washington Avenue; Fredericksburg, VA 22401; (540) 373-3381; www.kenmore.org
Kenmore, the Fredericksburg home of George Washington's sister Betty and her husband Fielding Lewis, is now open daily March through December. Admission is $6. The plaster ceiling moldings in the eighteenth-century home are outstanding—even more ornate that those at Mount Vernon.

MEADOW FARM
3400 Mountain Road; Glen Allen, VA 23060;
(804) 501-5520; www.co.henrico.va.us/rec
The living-history museum tells stories of a middle-class farm during the mid-1800s. Open March through early December, Tuesday–Sunday, noon–4 p.m. and on weekends only from mid-January through early March.

MCCORMICK FARM
Shenandoah Valley AREC
128 McCormick Farm Circle; Steeles Tavern, VA 24476; (540) 377-2255; www.vaes.vt.edu/steeles/mccormick/mccormick.html
This Walnut Grove farm was birthplace and home of Cyrus McCormick, inventor of the first successful mechanical reaper. Today the homestead is a National Historic Landmark and Virginia Wayside site. Tour a grist mill, blacksmith shop/museum, relocated slave quarters, smokehouse, and schoolroom.

MONTICELLO/
THE THOMAS JEFFERSON FOUNDATION
P. O. Box 316; Charlottesville, VA 22902;
(804) 984-9822; www.monticello.org
The Monticello facilities include the mansion, 2,000 of Jefferson's original 5,000 acres, the International Center for Jefferson Studies, a museum shop, and the Thomas Jefferson Center for Historic Plants, which propagates heirloom varieties and makes them available to institutions and individuals.

MONTPELIER
P.O. Box 911 (11407 Constitution Highway)
Orange VA 22960; (540)-672-2728 ext. 100;
www.montpelier.org
This elegant plantation was home to President James Madison's family for three generations from 1723 to 1844 when President Madison's grandfather was first deeded the land. Today, the estate includes 2,700 acres, more than 130 buildings, extensive gardens and forests, and a steeplechase course. Open year-round; adults $7.50.

MOUNT VERNON/MOUNT VERNON LADIES'
ASSOCIATION
George Washington Parkway; (703) 780-2000 or (703) 799-8606; www.mountvernon.org
The most visited home in America aside from the White House, George Washington's mansion on the Potomac has an excellent Pioneer Farmer exhibit. Open daily all year including holidays, Mount Vernon is 16 miles southeast of Washington, D.C. or eight miles south of Alexandria. Admission is $9 for adults.

SCOTCHTOWN
Route 2, Box 168; Beaverdam, VA 23015;
(804) 227-3500; www.apva.org/scotchtown
One of Virginia's oldest plantation houses and home to Patrick Henry during the Revolutionary War, this National Historic Landmark is open to the public from April through November. It is located ten miles west of Ashland in upper Hanover County.

STRATFORD HALL PLANTATION
483 Great House Road off Route 3; Stratford, VA 22558; (804) 493-8038; www.stratfordhall.org
This 1,544-acre working farm in Stratford, on the Potomac River in Westmoreland County, is home to Stratford Hall. Four generations of Lees lived in the home, which has not changed since colonial times, beginning with Thomas Lee, who built it, and ending with Robert Edward Lee.

WOODBOURNE
(Private home; not open to the public.)
Originally built on part of the Poplar Forest tract of approxi-

mately 4,000 acres inherited by Thomas Jefferson from his wife Martha Wayles Skelton, this historic home was built in three stages—a central portion and two wings—from 1780 to 1820.

WOODLAWN PLANTATION
9000 Richmond Highway; Alexandria, VA 22309; (703) 780-4000; www.woodlawnplantation.org
Woodlawn Plantation was originally part of the Mount Vernon estate. The house was built for Washington's step-granddaughter, Nelly Custis, who married his favorite nephew, Lawrence Lewis. Throughout the month of March is Wood-lawn's annual needlework exhibit of 700 items. Open daily March through December, 10 a.m.–5 p.m.

WOODROW WILSON'S BIRTHPLACE AND MUSEUM
18-24 Coalter Street; Staunton, VA 24402; (540) 885-0897 or (888) 496-6376; www.woodrowwilson.org
This home was restored to depict Wilson's family life in the Shenandoah Valley before the Civil War, and features period furniture. Open daily all year.

Food & Winery Festivals

For a complete and up-to-date listing of Virginia's food festivals, visit http://www.vdacs.virginia.gov/news/festival.shtml. For a complete listing of Virginia's wine events, visit www.virginiawines.org/events/index.html

APPLE FESTIVALS
www.virginiaapples.org/events/

Other Attractions, Events Programs and Enterprises

APPALACHIAN COPPERSMITH
Porter Caldwell; (540) 473-2167; www.caldwellmtncopper.com

CHESAPEAKE BAY FOUNDATION
Virginia State Office; 1108 East Main Street, Suite 1600; Richmond, VA 23219; (804) 780-1392; www.cbf.org

CHESAPEAKE BAY PROGRAM OFFICE
Annapolis, Maryland; (800) 968-7229; www.chesapeakebay.net/virginia.htm

CHIPPOKES PLANTATION STATE PARK
695 Chippokes Park Rd.; Surry, VA 23883; (757) 294-3625; www.chippokes.state.va.us
For reservations or information on availability of cabins, camping accommodations, or particular park amenities, call (800) 933-7275 (in Richmond, (804) 225-3867). You can also reserve accommodations online.

CHRIST CHURCH
118 North Washington Street; Alexandria, VA 22314; (703) 549-1450; www.historicchristchurch.org/index.html
Both George Washington and Robert E. Lee were pewholders in this 1773 church that remains in nearly original condition and is still used for services.

DANVILLE TOBACCO AUCTIONS
www.visitdanville.com
The tobacco auctions are silent since most farmers went to con-tract growing. Tobacco warehouses are now a historic district.

HIGHLAND MAPLE FESTIVAL/MAPLE MUSEUM
The Highland County Chamber of Commerce
P. O. Box 223; Monterey VA 24465; (540) 468-2550; www.highlandcounty.org.
For additional information during the Maple Festival, stop by the information booths located in the schools and the Highland County Courthouse. Festival maps are available at locations throughout the county. During the festival, tune to the local radio station 89.7 FM for up-to-date information.

HILL CITY MASTER GARDENER ASSOCIATION
P.O. Box 2275; Lynchburg VA 24501; (434) 847-1585 or (804) 847-1585 (gardening hotline)
You can find the Virginia Cooperative Extension Service vol-unteer educators at Lynchburg City Market each Saturday during the growing season. Compost Education Center Chair, Roger K. Shoemaker can be reached at (434) 239-6041.

THE HUNT COUNTRY STABLE TOUR
(540) 592-3711;
www.middleburgonline.com/horses.html
The tour, held each Memorial Day weekend, offers an educa-tional tour of various equine show, training, and breeding facilities in the Middleburg/Upperville area. A dozen farms open their stables; see places where horses live better than people.

MAIZE QUEST AT BRIDGEMONT FARMS
P.O. Box 465; Mt. Jackson, VA 22842; (540) 477-4200; www.cornmaze.com
Maize Quest is a group of progressive farmers who provide guests with unique form of family entertainment. Your family and friends will delight at the challenge and adventure within the unique maze carved into a cornfield at a family farm. Open from August to early November.

MANNING'S HOMINY
Lake Packing Co., Inc; Box 200, Lottsburg, VA; (800) 324-3759; www.manningshominy.com
Manning's Hominy is produced using a unique process. Unlike whole kernel hominy that is lye peeled and whitened with sodium bisulfite, Manning's Hominy is steam peeled and depends on no additives for whitening. This product is avail-able in the canned food section of most local grocery stores.

MARION DUPONT SCOTT EQUINE MEDICAL CENTER
Morven Park; Leesburg, VA; (703) 771-6843; http://emc.vetmed.vt.edu
Ever see a horse on a treadmill? At the Equine Medical Center a horse can have an EKG and upper-airway evaluation on one of the few horse treadmills in the world. The hospital contains 29 stalls plus eight infectious-disease wards, operating rooms with horse-sized gurneys, and state-of-the-art diagnostic machinery.

MONTPELIER HUNT RACES
11407 Constitution Highway; Montpelier Station, VA 22957; (540) 672-2728 (mansion tours) or (540) 672-0027 (race information)
www.montpelierraces.com
On the first Saturday of November, one of the nation's oldest and most respected steeplechase events is run on the estate of our fourth President James Madison.. The course encircles a 100-acre field and consists of seven jumps over timber or brush.

MORVEN PARK MANSION
17263 Southern Planter Lane; Leesburg, VA 20176; (703) 777-2414; Equestrian Center: 41793 Tutt Lane; Leesburg, VA 20176; (703) 777-2890; www.morvenpark.org
Morven Park's Mansion, Winmill Carriage Collection, and Museum of Hounds and Hunting are located just west of downtown Leesburg off of Route 7 (Market Street). Morven Park's Equestrian Center is located one mile North of Leesburg off Route 15 on Route 740 (Tutt Lane).

NATIONAL SPORTING LIBRARY
102 The Plains Road or P.O. Box 1335; Middleburg, VA 20118-1335; (540) 687-6542; www.nsl.org
The library houses over 12,000 volumes, dating from 1528, on horse racing, dressage, eventing, show jumping, breeding, equitation, veterinary care, foxhunting, angling, polo, racing, shooting, sporting art and much more. Library hours are Mon-day, 1–4 p.m., Tuesday–Friday, 10 a.m.–4 p.m., and Satur-day by appointment only.

PICK-YOUR-OWN FARMS
(804) 786-5867
www.vdacs.virginia.gov/vagrown/index.shtml
Pick-your-own farms are listed in the VDACS "Virginia Grown" program guide. Call for a copy.

ROUTE 11 CHIPS
7815 Main Street; Middletown, VA 22645; (800) 294-SPUD (7783) or (540) 869-0104; www.rt11.com
From its 6,000-square-foot factory on Route 11, the main drag of Middletown, the company pumps out about 1,000 pounds of potato chips per day. They are open to the public on Friday, 10 a.m.–6 p.m., and Saturday, 9 a.m.–5 p.m.

SHENANDOAH GROWERS
3453 Koehn Drive; Harrisonburg, VA 22802; (888) 390-6466 or (540) 896-6939; www.freshherbs.com
Since 1989, Shenandoah Growers has a full line of year-round fresh packaged culinary herbs grown in the Shenandoah Valley. Their certified organic fresh herbs have been included in Virginia's Finest program for several years.

UPPERVILLE COLT AND HORSE SHOW
P. O. Box 1288; Warrenton, VA 22186; (703) 347-2612; www.upperville.com
The Upperville Colt and Horse Show, grand-pere and a grand peer of the nation's horse shows, dates back to 1853. The show covers six days the first week of June, and includes jumping and other events in addition to sales.

VIRGINIA'S EXPLORE PARK
P.O. Box 8508; Roanoke, VA 24014-0508; (540) 427-1800 or 9800) 842-9163; www.explorepark.org
This park offers a glimpse into the life of the Native Americans in this region in the 17th century as well as life for those who settled in this part of Virginia in the 18th and 19th centuries.

Contemporary Vineyards and Working Farms

BARANCA ACRES LTD. EMU FARM
134 Baranca Acres Drive; P. O. Box 38; Fork Union, VA 23055; (434) 842-1111; www.emuofvirginia.com
This small emu farm produces pure emu oil, emu meat and emu meat products. Besides selling to some stores and restaurants they sell directly on the farm, and arranged farm visits are welcome.

BARBOURSVILLE VINEYARDS AND HISTORIC RUINS
17655 Winery Road (P. O. Box 136) Barboursville, VA 22923; (540) 832-3824 or (540) 832-7848 (restaurant); www.barboursvillewine.com
This Blue Ridge vineyard is home to award-winning wines and Palladio restaurant, which hosts a guest-chef series. Barboursville Vineyards preserves the ruins of Governor James Barbour's mansion designed by his friend Thomas Jefferson to be the grandest residence in Orange County.

BENT-TREE FARM
7995 Wood Drive; Disputanta, VA 23842; (804) 991-2121
Bent Tree Farm produces Briar-Patch Cheese, which has won various competitions at the Virginia State Fair.

BUFFALO SPRINGS HERB FARM
West Raphine Road; Raphine, VA 24472; (540) 348-1083; www.buffaloherbs.com
Visitors to this eighteenth-century farmstead in the northern Rockbridge County can tour the gardens, visit the plant house stocked with herbs and garden accessories, and purchase herbal products, dried flowers, and garden books. Workshops and luncheons are scheduled throughout the season.

BYRD MILL CO.
Ashland; (888) 897-3336; www.byrdmill.com
This mill has been producing quality flour and meals since 1740. They offer stone-ground buckwheat, whole wheat and unbleached flour; cornmeal and grits; and gourmet mixes. Of special note are the stone-ground yellow grits.

CHATEAU MORRISETTE WINERY
Milepost 171.5 Blue Ridge Parkway; P. O. Box 766; Meadows of Dan, VA 24120; (540) 593-2865; www.chateaumorrisette.com

Wines are produced in this "French Country" winery with spectacular views and a fine-dining restaurant. Chateau Morrisette produces Chardonnay, Merlot, Black Dog, Our Dog Blue and Sweet Mountain Laurel labels.

CONICVILLE OSTRICH FARM
14144 Senedo Road; Mount Jackson, VA 22842;
(540) 477-3574; www.conicvilleostrich.com
This small farm in Shenandoah County, owned by Willard and Lorna Lutz, raises ostrich, cattle, chickens, and organically grown berries. All the animals graze free and are naturally raised on alfalfa and corn. No commercial fertilizers, pesticides, or herbicides are used.

DEAUVILLE FALLOW DEER FARM
7648 Crooked Run Road; Basye, VA 22810;
(540) 856-2130
Not far from Bryce Resort is a herd of about 150 Fallow deer, an unusual breed; most are spotted but some are white or brown. Owner Gail Rose says many of the deer will eat out of hand. She provides visitors a bucket of corn to hand-feed the deer.

DICKIE BROTHERS ORCHARD
2552 Dickie Road; Roseland, VA 22967;
(434) 277-5516; www.dickiebros.com
Dickie Brothers offers "pick-your-own" apples, on-site retail sales, and mail orders. The orchard is located near Massies Mill, about 40 miles south of Charlottesville and 32 miles north of Lynchburg.

DRINKING SWAMP FARM
430-436 Blues Lane, Haynesville, VA; (804) 394-3508;
Makers of homemade goat cheese.

EASTFIELDS FARMS
Peter and Diane Perina
P.O. Box 275 (Route 622); Mathews, VA 23109;
(804) 725-3948
At this quaint, early 1800s waterfront farm, pick-your-own or buy-spray-free blueberries, asparagus, and other vegetables. Picnic area by the water. Farm-raised clams and oysters grown and available on premises. Local distributor offering discounts on oyster and clam cages and floats. Also aquaculture netting for fish cages, and oyster and clam seeds are available.

ELYSIUM TREE FARM
21041 Clarks Mountain Rd., Rapidan, VA;
(540) 672-4512
Trees include White, scotch and Austrian pines, Douglas firs.

S. WALLACE EDWARDS & SONS, INC.
P.O. Box 25; Surry, VA 23883; (800) 222-4267 or
(800) 290-9213; www.vatraditions.com
Over the last 80 years, Edwards & Sons have been making quality Virginia ham, sausage and other food products.

ELYSIUM TREE FARM
21041 Clarks Mountain Road; Rapidan, VA 22733;
(540) 672-4512
Open Thanksgiving through Christmas on Fridays 1 p.m. until dark and Saturdays and Sundays, 8 a.m. until dark. Also open by appointment. Trees include White, scotch and Austrian pines and Douglas firs.

GEORGETOWN BUFFALO FARM
This largest buffalo farm east of the Mississippi River was founded in 1978 but closed in 2004. The farm was located at the foot of the Blue Ridge Mountains.

GOAT HILL FARM/THE EPICURIOUS COW
13830 Lee Highway; Amissville, VA 20106;
(540) 675-2269; www.epicuriouscow.com
Terri Lehman and John O'Malley Burns tend Goat Hill Farm in Rappahannock County. Customers can come directly to Goat Hill Farm to help harvest the products they want to buy. Terri also runs a specialty food market near "Little" Washington, called The Epicurious Cow.

L'ESPRIT DE CAMPAGNE
1247 Wrights Mill Road (Route 645); Berryville, VA 22611; (800) 692-8008 or (540) 955-1014;
www.lespritdecampagne.com
In 1984, Joy and Carey Lokey began L'Esprit de Campagne,

which plants, grows, processes, packages, and distributes more than 50,000 pounds yearly of Virginia sun-ripened, dried Roma tomatoes and fruits.

LOBLOLLY FARMS AND SEASIDE PRODUCE
P.O. Box 680; Accomac, VA 23301; (757) 787-8955
Loblolly Farms sells Hayman potatoes and other produce to the general public. Call ahead to check availability.

MANAKINTOWNE SPECIALTY GROWERS
2570 Federal Hills Farm Road; Powhatan, VA 23139; (804) 379-8253
Rob and Joe Pendergraph grow specialty vegetables, herbs, and edible flowers.

MEADOW CREEK DAIRY, LLC
6380 Meadow Creek Road; Galax, VA 24333;
(276) 236-2776 or (888) 236-0622;
www.meadowcreekdairy.com
Makers of Appalachian Jack and Meadow Creek Feta, this dairy practices sustainable agriculture by allowing its cows to graze on fresh pasture grass every day.

OAKENCROFT VINEYARD & WINERY
1486 Oakencroft Lane; Charlottesville, VA 22901;
(804) 296-4188; www.oakencroft.com
Oakencroft, the oldest winery in Albemarle County and the closest to Charlottesville, has a tasting room and picnic area.

PRINCE MICHEL & RAPIDAN RIVER VINEYARDS
HCR 4, Box 77; Leon, VA 22725; (540) 547-3707
or (800) 800-9463); www.princemichel.com
Located midway between Culpeper and Madison on Route 29 South, Prince Michel offers lodging and dining. Call for reservations.

RUCKER FARM
13357 Crest Hill Road; Flint Hill, VA 22627;
(540) 675-3444
This boutique creamery in Flint Hill is nestled in the foothills of the Blue Ridge Mountains. Owners Heidi and Lindsay Eastham keep only 30 goats, let them range free, and use only the morning milk.

SANDY HEAD OSTRICH FARM
Route 3, Box 520A; Tazewell, VA 24651;
(540) 988-9090
Located at the base of Buckhorn Mountain in Tazewell County, this 30-acre farm primarily raises ostriches for their meat, hides, feathers, and eggs.

SHARKAWI HERB FARM
6068 Old Bust Head Road; Broad Run, VA 20137;
(540) 347-4747; www.sharkawifarm.com
Founded in 1985 by Sabry and Salwa Alsharkawi, this family-run farm produces all natural dried herbs and spices, flavored green and black teas, naturally caffeine-free fruit and herbal tisanes. It is a member of Virginia's Finest program.

SMITHFIELD FARM/SMITHFRESH ORGANIC MEATS
568 Smithfield Lane; Berryville, VA 22611;
(877) 955-4389; www.smithfieldfarm.com
A family farm since 1816, Smithfresh Meats has been home to farm animals of all types. All of our animals are handled humanely and are never fed animal by-products or given growth hormones, antibiotics, or commercial dewormers. Their pastures have not been chemically fertilized or treated with pesticides and herbicides.

STRIBLING ORCHARD
11587 Poverty Hollow Lane or P. O. Box 116;
Markham, VA 22643; (540) 364-3040;
www.striblingorchard.com
For information about Stribling's seasonal selections as well as details about other pick-your-own orchards, call or visit online.

THISTLE COVE FARM
Route 1 Box 351; Tazewell, VA 24651;
(540) 988-4121; www.thistlecovefarm.com
The Bennetts breed American Curly Horses and Romney and Shetland sheep and conduct educational tours for school children and other guests to acquaint visitors with a homestead farm and the work needed to keep it running. Thistle Cove

Farm holds the Appalachian Heritage Festival the fourth Saturday in September.

TOMAHAWK MILL WINERY
9221 Anderson Mill Road; Chatham, VA 24531;
(804) 432-1063; www.tomahawkmill.com
In Chatham, 30 minutes north of Danville, this winery is housed in an 1860 water-powered grist mill on Tomahawk Creek. Members of the Anderson family operated it continuously as a water-powered flour and saw mill from 1888 to 1988.

THUNDER RIDGE EMU FARM
9217 Center Street; Manassas, VA 20110;
(703) 631-9074; www.thunderridgeemu.com.
This farm is located a few minutes from Manassas on 30 acres in the foothills of the Shenandoah mountains. Anne Geller's emu roam freely in large fenced pastures. She began raising her birds in 1993.

VIRGINIA GOLD ORCHARD
100 Asian Pear Way; US 11 Fancy Hill;
Natural Bridge, VA 24578; (540) 291-1481;
www.virginiagold.com
Students at nearby Washington & Lee University in Lexington are fortunate to enjoy Virginia Gold Orchard's Asian pears in their dining halls. But most of the orchard's harvest is sold by mail order from September through February.

VIRGINIA TROUT COMPANY
Route 220, 5 miles north of Monterey;
(540) 468-2280
The Company has thousands of rainbow trout on view. Fish for your own dinner or purchase frozen trout to go. Open daily.

WESTMORELAND BERRY FARM AND ORCHARD
1235 Berry Farm Lane; Oak Grove, VA 22443;
(800) 997-BERRY or (804) 224-9171;
www.westmorelandberryfarm.com
Pick your own or pick up a package of wonderful berries, fruit, other produce, and homemade jams at Westmoreland Berry Farm located on the Northern Neck in a unique setting of woods water, and wide-open spaces. The farm is open from mid-April to mid-December.

YODER DAIRY
5102 Princess Anne Road; Virginia Beach, VA 23462; (757) 497-3518; www.yoderdairies.com
Yoder Dairies has been serving Norfolk, Virginia Beach, and Chesapeake areas since 1929, when Eli and Elmer Yoder, two Amish farmers from Kempsville, Virginia, began what would eventually grow into the present dairy. Their milkmen make home deliveries between 12:30 a.m. and 7 a.m., and they also have a retail store at the address listed above.

Museums

AMERICAN WORK HORSE MUSEUM
P. O. Box 1051; Lexington, VA 24450;
(540) 464-2950; www.horsecenter.org
Open whenever the Coliseum is open, which is generally 9 a.m.–5 p.m. on the weekdays and every weekend, depending on which of the Virginia Horse Center's more than 70 shows yearly is on the grounds.

BLUE RIDGE INSTITUTE & MUSEUM
Ferrum College; Ferrum, VA 24088;
(540) 365-4416; www.blueridgeinstitute.org
The Blue Ridge Institute consists of a modern brick building that houses exhibits and a farm museum complex of historic houses, barns and outbuildings moved piece by piece from their original locations. The buildings were reconstructed in an agricultural setting on the Ferrum College campus.

CHIPPOKES FARM AND FORESTRY MUSEUM
AT CHIPPOKES PLANTATION
Route 634 just off Route 10 at Chippokes Plantation State Park; Surry; (757)) 294-3439;
www.dcr.virginia.gov/state_parks/chf.shtml
The Chippokes Farm and Forestry Museum is located in one of

the oldest continually farmed plantations in the country. Thousands of artifacts are on display in a series of farm buildings.

FIRST PEANUT MUSEUM
201 Hunter Street; Waverly, VA 23890;
(804) 834-3327 or (804) 834-2151
This small building is decorated with various peanut artifacts such as black-and-white photographs showing the peanut cultivation and production process of yesteryear and even curtains made of burlap peanut sack. Hours are Thursday through Monday, 2–5 p.m. Admission is free; donations appreciated.

FRONTIER CULTURE MUSEUM
P.O. Box 810; Staunton, VA 24402-0810;
(540) 332-7850; ext. 124 for information, 159 for reservations; www.frontiermuseum.org
This unique museum offers 17th-, 18th-, and 19th-century European and American history as an experience, featuring appropriate furnishings, crops, animals, foods, and a knowledgeable staff of costumed interpreters that help create a living illustration of life in Europe before immigration to America and the culture they built on one of America's first frontiers

THE MARINERS' MUSEUM
100 Museum Drive; Newport News, VA 23606;
(757) 596-2222
The museum is open daily, except Thanksgiving and Christmas, 10 a.m.–5 p.m. Admission is $6 adults, $4 students (any age), free for children ages 5 and under, and $14 for families of three or four. Discounts are available for AAA, active-duty military, and persons ages 65 and above.

REEDVILLE FISHERMAN'S MUSEUM
504 and 512 Main Street; Reedville, VA 22539
Open from January to March by appointment only; in March and April on Saturday and Sunday, 10:30 a.m.–4:30 p.m.; May through October, daily, 10:30 a.m.–4:30 p.m.; and November through December 20, Friday–Monday, 10:30 a.m.–4:30 p.m.

SOUTHAMPTON AGRICULTURAL &
FORESTRY MUSEUM
26135 Heritage Lane; Courtland, VA 23837;
(757) 653-9554; www.rootsweb.com~vaschs
In Southside Virginia on the flat, sandy soil of peanut-growing land, this community-built museum contains more than 4,000 historic items and several structures related to agriculture, forestry, and farm life.

VIRGINIA QUILT MUSEUM
301 South Main Street; Harrisonburg, VA 22801;
(540) 433-3818; www.vaquilt.org
In a historic house, hundreds of quilts are on display from antique classic designs to modern whimsical throws.

THE WATERMAN'S MUSEUM
309 Water Street; Yorktown, VA; (757) 887-2641;
www.watermans.org
The five galleries inside house ship models, dioramas, and artifacts themed on Chesapeake watermen, bay boats, harvesting fish, aquaculture, tools, and treasures. Outdoor exhibits include an original three-log canoe, dredges, engines, and other equipment used by working watermen past and present.

Virginia's Farmers Markets

For more information, contact the Agricultural Commodity Program Manager, VDACS, (840) 786-2112. (*All are open-air/seasonal, unless otherwise noted.*)

ABINGDON FARMERS MARKET
Latture Field parking lot, Appalachian Sustainable Development Abingdon, VA 24212; (276) 623-1121; www.abingdonfarmersmarket.com (Saturday)

ALEXANDRIA FARMERS' MARKET
Market Square, 301 King Street, Alexandria 22314
(703) 838-500; alexandriava.gov/market/farmers-market.html (Saturday, 5–10:30 a.m. year-round)

ALTAVISTA FARMERS' MARKET, ALTAVISTA
Trade lot, Altavista 24517; (434) 369-5037
(Wednesday and Saturday, April–October)

ANNANDALE FARMERS' MARKET
Mason District Park; 6621 Columbia Pike; Annandale, VA 22003; (703) 642-0128; www.fairfaxcounty.gov/parks/farm-mkt.htm (Thursday)

ANNANDALE (WAKEFIELD) FARMERS' MARKET
Wakefield Park; Braddock Road West at the Beltway; Annandale, VA 22312; (703) 642-0128; www.fairfaxcounty.gov/parks/farm-mkt.htm (Wed.)

ARCHWOOD GREEN BARNS FARMERS' & GARDENERS' MARKET
4557 Old Tavern Road; The Plains, VA 20198; (540) 253-5289 (Sunday)

ARLINGTON COUNTY FARMERS' MARKET
North 14th Street & North Courthouse; Arlington, VA 22210; (703) 228-6423 or (703) 228-6407; www.arlingtonfarmersmarket.com; (Sat. year-round)

ASHLAND/HANOVER FARMERS MARKET
Duncan St., Ashland 23005; (804) 798-9219; www.town.ashland.va.us (Saturday)

BEDFORD FARMERS' MARKET
Washington & Center Streets; Bedford, VA; (540) 586-2148; www.centertownbedfordcom (Tuesday, Friday, Saturday)

BLACKSBURG FARMERS' MARKET (DOWNTOWN)
Roanoke Street & Draper Road; Blacksburg, VA 24063; (540) 239-8290; bfarmersmarket@gmail.com (Wednesday, May–November; Saturday, year-round)

BROADWAY FARMERS' MARKET
Central Avenue & Mason Street; Broadway, VA 22815; (540) 896-4992; www.bhp-va.org (Saturday)

BUCKINGHAM COUNTY FARMERS MARKET
Route 20 & 15 (Dillwyn); Arvonia, VA 23004 (434) 983-5366 (Friday, 4–7 p.m.)

BUENA VISTA COMMUNITY MARKET
Magnolia Parking Lot; Buena Vista 24416; (540) 261-6436; www.bvmarket.com (Wednesday and Saturday)

BURKE CENTRE FARMERS' MARKET
VRE Parking Lot, 5671 Roberts Parkway; 6000 Burke Commons Road; Burke, VA 22015; (703) 642-5173; (Saturday)

BYRD HOUSE MARKET
William Byrd Community House; 224 S. Cherry Street; Richmond, VA 23220; (804) 643-2717; www.wbch.org (May–October, Tues., 3:30–7 p.m.)

CAPE CHARLES FARMERS MARKET
Cape Charles, VA 23310; 757-331-4884 (Saturday, 1–5 p.m.)

CASCADES FARMERS' MARKET
Cascades Park & Ride; Leesburg, VA 22075; (540) 777-0534; www.loudounfarms.org (Sunday)

CHARLOTTESVILLE CITY FARMERS' MARKET
Water & South Streets; Charlottesville, VA 22902; (434) 970-3371; www.charlottesville.org (Saturday)

CHERITON FARMERS MARKET
Main Street, Cheriton, VA 23316; (757) 331-1126 (Saturday, 9 a.m.–1 p.m.)

CHESAPEAKE FARMERS' MARKET
Chesapeake City Park; 500 Greenbrier Parkway; Chesapeake, VA 23322; (757) 382-6348 (Wednesday and Saturday)

CHINCOTEAGUE FARMERS MARKET
4103 Main Street; Chincoteague, VA 23336; (757) 336-2610 (Thursday, 9 a.m.–noon; Holiday Saturdays, 9 a.m.–noon)

CLARENDON FARMER'S MARKET
Clarendon Metro Park; Arlington, VA 22201; (703) 276-0228; www.clarendon.org/farmers.html (May–October, Wednesday)

CLARKE COUNTY FARMERS MARKET
Town Parking Lot, S. Church Street; Berryville, VA 22611; (540) 955-4463; www.clarkecountyfarmersmarket.com (Saturday)

CLINTWOOD FARMERS' MARKET
Main Street; Clintwood, VA; (540) 926-4605

COLUMBIA PIKE HOME GROWN FARMERS MARKET
Columbia Pike & S. Walter Reed Drive; Arlington, VA 22204; (703) 892-2776 (Sunday)

CROZET FARMERS MARKET
Corner of Jarmans Gap Road & Crozet Avenue; Crozet, VA 22932; (434) 823-7878 or (434) 982-3521 (Saturday)

CULPEPER FARMER'S MARKET
E. Main Street & Commerce (adjacent to train depot); Bealeton, VA 22712; (540) 439-8326 SEASONAL (Saturday, 7:30 a.m.–noon)

DALE CITY FARMERS MARKET
Center Plaza, Dale Boulevard; Dale City, VA 22193; (703) 670-7112; www.pwcparks.org/dcrc (Sunday, April–November)

DANVILLE COMMUNITY MARKET
629 Craghead Street; Danville, VA 24541; (804) 797-8961; www.visitdanville.com

DAYTON FARMERS' MARKET
3105 John Wayland Highway; Dayton, VA 22803; (540) 879-3801; www.daytonfarmersmarket.com (Thursday–Saturday, 9 a.m.–6 p.m., year-round)

DEL RAY FARMERS' MARKET
Oxford & Mt. Vernon; Alexandria, VA 22301; (703) 683-2570 (Saturday)

EASTERN ORANGE COUNTY FARMERS' MARKET
Locust Grove Town Center at the intersection of Routes 20 and 611; Spotsylvania, VA 22553; (540) 785-8769 (Sunday and Wednesday)

FAIRFAX FARMERS' MARKET
Van Dyck Park, Old Lee Highway; Fairfax, VA; (703) 642-0128; www.fairfaxcounty.gov/parks/farm-mkt.htm (Tuesday)

FALLS CHURCH FARMERS' MARKET
300 Park Avenue; Falls Church, VA; (703) 248-5027; www.fallschurchva.gov (Saturday)

FARMVILLE AREA FARMERS MARKET
Farmville Train Station on W. Third Street; Farmville, VA; (434) 983-5383 (Saturday, Tuesday, and Wednesday)

FLUVANNA FARMERS' MARKET
Pleasant Grove (US 53, 1 mile west of Route 15); Palmyra, VA 22963; (434) 591-1950 (Tuesday, 3–7 p.m.)

FREDERICKSBURG CITY FARMERS' MARKET
900 block Prince Edward Street; Fredericksburg, VA; (540) 372-1010; www.fredericksburgva.gov (Monday–Saturday)

FRYING PAN PARK
Frying Pan Farm Park in front of Frying Pan Country Store; Herndon, VA 22090; (703) 642-0128; www.fairfaxcounty.gov/parks/farm-mkt.htm (Wednesday)

GALAX DOWNTOWN FARMERS MARKET
Galax, VA 24333; (540) 238-8130

GLADE SPRING FARMERS' MARKET
Glade Spring, VA 24340; (276) 356-6865 (Sat.)

GOOCHLAND FARMERS MARKET
Grace Episcopal Church across from Goochland
Courthouse; 2955 River Road West; Goochland, VA
23063; (804) 332-3144; www.centerforrural
culture.org (Saturday)

HARRISONBURG FARMERS' MARKET
Municipal Parking Lot, South Liberty Street;
Harrisonburg, VA 22803; (540) 867-0546
(Saturday and Tuesday)

HAYMARKET FARMERS' MARKET
Haymarket Town Hall; 15025 Washington Street;
Haymarket, VA; (703) 753-2600 (Saturday)

HERNDON FARMERS' MARKET
Old Town Herndon next to Town Hall; Herndon,
VA; (703) 642-0128; www.fairfaxcounty.gov/parks/
farm-mkt.htm (Thursday)

HEATHSVILLE FARMERS MARKET
Off Route 360 behind old courthouse;
Heathsville, VA 22473; (804) 580-3377
(third Saturday of April–October)

HIGHLAND COUNTRY MARKET
Spruce Street; Monterey, VA 24465; (540) 468-
1922; www.thehighlandcenter.org (Friday)

HISTORIC MANASSAS FARMERS' MARKET
Church & Quarry Streets; Manassas, VA 20110;
(703) 361-6599; www.historicmanassasinc.org
(Saturday and Thursday)

IRVINGTON FARMERS MARKET
Irvington, VA 22480; (804) 438-9324;
kdraffetto@kaballero.com (Saturday)

KINGSTOWNE FARMERS' MARKET
Kingstowne Town Center, Kingtowne Boulevard;
Alexandria, VA22312; (703) 642-0128; www.fairfax
county.gov/parks/farm-mkt.htm (Friday)

LEESBURG FARMERS' MARKET
Parking lot of Virginia Village Shopping Center,
Catoctin Circle; Leesburg, VA 20175; (703) 777-
0534; www.loudounfarms.org (Saturday)

LEXINGTON DOWNTOWN FARMERS' MARKET
McCrum's Parking Lot, Jefferson Street; Lexington,
VA 24450; (540) 463-7191; www.downtown
lexington.com (Wednesday, May–October)

LOVETTSVILLE FARMERS' MARKET
Game Protective Association, Route 287;
Lovettsville, VA 20175; (703) 777-0534;
www.loudounfarms.org (Tuesday)

LURAY/PAGE COUNTY FARMERS MARKET
Luray-Norfolk Western Train Depot; Luray, VA
22835; (540) 652-3201 (Saturday)

LYNCHBURG COMMUNITY FARMERS' MARKET
Main at 12th Street; Lynchburg, VA 24504;
(434) 455-4487; www.lynchburgva.gov
(Monday–Saturday year-round)

MADISON COUNTY FARMERS' MARKET
Hoover Ridge Park; Madison, VA 22727;
(540) 948-6881 (Saturday)

MARTINSVILLE UPTOWN FARMERS' MARKET
100 Church & Moss Streets; Martinsville, VA
22727; (276) 638-4221; www.martinsville
uptown.net (Wednesday, Friday, Saturday)

MATHEWS FARMERS' MARKET
Old Courthouse Green, Court Street; Mathews, VA
23109; (804) 725-7196 (Saturday)

MCLEAN FARMERS' MARKET
1659 Chain Bridge Road, Lewinsville Park; McLean,
VA 22101; (703) 642-0128; www.fairfaxcounty.gov/
parks/farm-mkt.htm (Friday)

MIDDLEBURG FARMERS' MARKET
Federal Street in parking lot; behind Middleburg

Bank; Middleburg, VA 20175; (703) 777-0534;
www.loudounfarms.org (Saturday)

MOUNT VERNON FARMERS' MARKET
2501 Sherwood Hall Lane (Sherwood Library);
Mount Vernon, VA; (703) 642-0128; www.fairfax
county.gov/parks/farm-mkt.htm (Tuesday)

NELSON FARMERS MARKET
Route 151; Nellysford, VA; (434) 361-9147 (Sat.)

NEWPORT NEWS FARMERS MARKET
2801 Jefferson Avenue; Newport News, VA 23607;
(757) 247-2351; www.nnparks.com/parks_farmers-
market2.php (Wednesday and Saturday year-round)

NORFOLK, FIVE POINTS COMMUNITY
FARM MARKET
1132 Norview Avenue; Norfolk, VA 23513; (757)
237-2555 or (757) 853-0300; http://groups.
hamptonroads.com/5pointsfarmmarket (Saturday,
year-round; Thursday and Friday, June–October)

OLDE TOWNE CURB MARKET
Historic Smithfield; Smithfield, VA 23430; (757)
357-3502; www.shopsmithfield.com (Saturday)

ORANGE COUNTY FARMERS' MARKET
Summer Market–Main Street (Wednesday,
May–October); Winter Market–Orange Train
Station (Saturday, November–April); Orange, VA
22960; (540) 672-2540

PATRICK COUNTY FARMERS' MARKET
Courthouse Parking Lot; Stuart, VA;
(540) 694-6094

PEOPLE'S MARKET OF LEBANON
Lebanon Elementary & Middle Schools
Lebanon, VA; (276) 889-8056

PETERSBURG FARMERS' MARKET
Sycamore Street across from visitors center
Old Town Petersburg 23803; (804) 733-2352
(Saturday, seasonal)

PURCELLVILLE FARMERS' MARKET
Purcellville, VA; (703) 777-0534;
www.loudounfarms.org (Thursday)

PULASKI FARMERS MARKET
Historic Train Station; 20 S. Washington;
Pulaski, VA 24301; (540) 994-4200
(Saturday, May–October)

RADFORD FARMERS' MARKET
Norwood Square parking lot; Radford, VA 24141;
(540) 633-0081; www.mainstreetradford.org (Sat.)

RESTON FARMERS' MARKET
Lake Anne Plaza (N. Shore Drive & Village Road)
Reston, VA; (703) 642-0128; http://restonfarmers
market.com/index.htm (Saturday)

RICHLANDS FARMERS MARKET
200 Washington Square; Richlands, VA 24641;
(276) 964-4886

RICHMOND 17TH STREET FARMERS' MARKET
100 North 17th Street; Richmond, VA; (804) 646-
0477; www.17thstreetfarmersmarket.com
(Thursday, Saturday, & Sunday, April–December)

ROCKY MOUNT FARMERS MARKET
435 Franklin Street; Rocky Mount, VA; (540) 483-
0907; www.rockymountva.org (Monday–Saturday)

ROANOKE HISTORIC CITY FARMERS' MARKET
Campbell Street Market Square; Roanoke, VA
24011; (540) 342-2028; www.downtownroanoke
.org (Monday–Saturday year-round)

SALEM FARMERS' MARKET
Main & Broad Streets; Salem, VA 24153;
(540) 375-3028 (Monday–Saturday)

SALUDA OUTDOOR FARMERS' MARKET
Courthouse Square; Saluda, VA; (804) 758-4120

SCOTTSVILLE TRI-COUNTY FARMERS' MARKET
Dorrier Park; Scottsville, VA 24590; (434) 295-8361;
www.scottsville.org (Thursday)

SOUTH BOSTON FARMERS' MRKT. (DOWNTOWN)
Broad Street; South Boston, VA 24592;
(434) 572-2369 (Monday–Saturday)

SOUTH HILL FARMERS MARKET
Market Square Parking Lot–Intersection of
Mecklenberg Avenue & Danville Street; South Hill,
VA 23970; (434) 447-3191; www.southhillva.org
(Saturday)

SOUTH RIDING FARMERS' MARKET
Town Green, South Riding, VA; (703) 777-0534;
www.loudounfarms.org (Saturday)

SOUTHWEST VIRGINIA DIRECT SALES MARKET
Farmers Market Drive; Hillsville, VA 24343;
(276) 728-5540

SPOTSYLVANIA COURTHOUSE FARMERS' MRKT.
Route 208 across from court house; Spotsylvania,
VA 22553; (540) 785-8769; haredom@juno.com;
(Wednesday & Saturday)

SPOTSYLVANIA FIVE MILE FORK FARMERS MARKET
Route 3 and Gordon Road; Spotsylvania, VA 22553;
(540) 785-8769 (Saturday)

STAUNTON-AUGUSTA FARMERS' MARKET
Wharf Parking Lot; Staunton, VA; (540) 885-8523;
www.safarmersmarket.com (Saturday)

STERLING FARMERS' MARKET
Briar Patch Park; Sterling, VA 24459;
(703) 777-0400; www.loudounfarms.org

SUFFOLK FARMERS MARKET
Historic Downtown, Main & Prentis Streets;
Suffolk, VA 23434; (757) 923-3880;
www.Suffolk-Fun.com (Saturday)

SURRY FARMERS' MARKET
Courthouse Square; Surry, VA 23883;
(804) 294-5215

TAZEWELL FARMERS MARKET
Farm Bureau Parking Lot; Tazewell, VA 24651;
(276) 988-7322 (Saturday)

VERONA FARMERS' MARKET
Augusta Co. Government Center; Verona, VA;
(540) 363-5152 (Wednesday)

VIENNA FARMERS' MARKET
Nottoway Park, 9601 Courthouse Road; Vienna, VA
22312; (703) 642-5173; www.fairfaxcounty.gov/
parks/farm-mkt.htm (Wednesday)

VIENNA SATURDAY FARMERS' MARKET
Caboose Parking Lot, Corner of Church Streeet &
Dominion Road, NE; Vienna, VA 22183; (703) 281-
1255; www.viennafarmersmarket.com (Saturday)

VINTON FARMERS' MARKET
204 Lee Avenue; Vinton, VA 24179;
(540) 983-0613; www.town.vinton.va.us (daily)

VIRGINIA BEACH FARMERS' MARKET
3640 Dam Neck Road; Virginia Beach, VA 23453;
(757) 385-4395; www.vbgov.com/farmersmarket
(year-round)

WARRENTON FARMERS' MARKET
Fifth & Lee Streets (Saturday); Main & Court Streets
(Wednesday) Warrenton, VA; (540) 347-2405;
www.townofwarrenton.com

WAYNESBORO RIVERFRONT MARKE
Pavilion at Constitution Park; Waynesboro, VA;
(540) 932-7685; www.waynesbororiverfrontmarket.
com (Saturday)

WEST END FARMERS' MARKET
Ben Brenman Park, 4600 Duke Street; Alexandria,
VA 22304; (703) 461-6900; www.cameronperks.com

WESTLAKE FARMERS' MARKET
Intersection of Booker T. Washington Highway and
Enterprise Lane, Moneta, VA; Rocky Mount, VA
24151; (540) 482-0577 (Saturdays)

WILLIAMSBURG FARMERS MARKET
Merchants Square, Duke of Gloucester Street;
Williamsburg, VA 23187; (757) 259-3768;
www.williamsburgfarmersmarket.com
(Saturday and Tuesday)

WINCHESTER FREIGHT STATION
FARMERS MARKET
315 W. Boscawen Street; Winchester, VA 22601;
(304) 229-3457 (Tuesday, Friday, Saturday all year)

WINDSOR FARMERS' MARKET
Route 460 in Windsor (11267 Windsor Boulevard);
Isle of Wight, VA 23397; (757) 357-6126;
www.iwus.net/agriculture (Friday and Saturday)

WYTHEVILLE FARMERS' MARKET
Main Street, Wytheville, VA 24382; (540) 228-6280

YORKTOWN FARMERS' MARKET
Riverwalk Landing; Yorktown, VA 23692; 757-877-
2933; www.riverwalklanding.com (weekends)

Governmental Agencies and Agricultural Industry Boards / Associations

THE NATIONAL CHICOTEAGUE PONY
ASSOCIATION
National Park Service, Assateague Island National
Seashore; (410) 641-1441; www.nps.gov/asis

NATIONAL FISHERIES INSTITUTE, ARLINGTON
1901 N. Fort Myer Drive; Arlington VA 22209;
(703) 524-8880; www.aboutseafood.com

NATIONAL BLACK FARMERS ASSOCIATION
OUTREACH PROGRAM
P.O. Box 508; Heathsville, VA 22473;
(804) 580-9089; www.blackfarmers.org

PESTICIDE CONTROL BOARD
Dr. Marvin Lawson, Program Manager; Office of
Pesticide Services at (840) 371-6558 or (800) 552-
9963; www.vdacs.virginia.gov/pesticides

SOUTHEAST UNITED DAIRY INDUSTRY
ASSOCIATION, VIRGINIA DIVISION
Janet Grubbs, SFNS; Program Coordinator; 521
Saber Drive; Chesapeake, VA 23322; (757) 312-
9324 or (800) 845-6112; www.southeastdairy.org

STATE FAIR OF VIRGINIA
Mailing Address: P. O. Box 26805; Richmond, VA
23261; (804) 569-3232 or (800) 588-3247
www.statefairva.com
Contact the State Fair for information on location and
agriculture-related events.

USDA MEAT AND POULTRY HOTLINE
(888) MPHotline (888) 674-6854
Food-safety specialists will answer your questions Monday
through Friday year round, 10 a.m.–4 p.m. Eastern time.

VIRGINIA STATE APPLE BOARD
900 Natural Resource Drive; Charlottesville, VA
22903; (434) 984-0573, www.virginiaapples.org

VIRGINIA BRIGHT FLUE-CURED TOBACCO BOARD
Virginia Dark-Fired Tobacco Board
D. Stanley Duffer; P. O. Box 129;
Halifax, VA 24558; (840) 572-4568
www.vdacs.virginia.gov/orgdirectory/tobacco.shtml

VIRGINIA CATTLE INDUSTRY BOARD
Reginald B. Reynolds; P. O. Box 9; Daleville, VA
24083; (540) 992-1992; www.vabeef.org

VIRGINIA CHRISTMAS TREE GROWERS ASSOC.
Thomas A O'Halloran
5537 Glengary Lane; Viewtown, VA 22746-1907
(540) 937-3021 or (804) 786-5867
www.virginiachristmastrees.org
Call or visit the Web site for a copy of "The Virginia Christmas Tree Guide" to help you locate a choose-and-cut farm.

VIRGINIA COOPERATIVE EXTENSION
Hutcheson Hall; Virginia Tech; Blacksburg, VA
24061; (540) 231-5299; www.ext.vt.edu
Contact your local office for assistance:
www.ext.vt.edu/offices
Virginia Cooperative Extension is an educational outreach
program of Virginia's land grant universities: Virginia Tech
and Virginia State University, and a part of the national
Cooperative State Research, Education, and Extension Service,
an agency of the United States Department of Agriculture.

VIRGINIA CORN BOARD
Virginia Small Grains Board; Virginia Soybean
Board; P. O. Box 1163; Richmond, VA 23218;
(840) 371-6157; www.vdacs.virginia.gov/about/
boards.shtml

VIRGINIA COTTON BOARD
1100 Armory Drive, Suite 120; Franklin, VA 23851;
(757) 569-1100; www.vdacs.virginia.gov/about/
boards.shtml

VIRGINIA DEPARTMENT OF AGRICULTURE &
CONSUMER SERVICES (VDACS)
102 Governor Street; Richmond, VA 23219;
(840) 786.2373; www.vdacs.virginia.gov

VIRGINIA DRESSAGE ASSOCIATION
Nancy Lowey, President; 10062 Barnetts Ford Road;
Orange, VA 22960; (540) 672-3454

THE VIRGINIA HORSE JOURNAL
7025 Owl Lane; Marshall, VA 20115-2233;
(540) 364-6200; www.virginiahorse.com

VIRGINIA EGG BOARD
Cecilia Glembocki; 911 Saddleback Court; McLean,
VA 22102; (703) 790-1984
virginiaeggcouncil@erols.com

VIRGINIA GOLD CUP ASSOCIATION
P.O. Box 840 or 90 Main Street; Warrenton, VA
20188; (540) 347-1215 or (800) 69-RACES
www.vagoldcup.com

VIRGINIA HORSE INDUSTRY BOARD
P. O. Box 1163; Richmond, VA 23218;
(840) 786-5842; www.vhib.org

VIRGINIA IRISH POTATO, VIRGINIA SWEET
POTATO BOARD
P. O. Box 26; Onley, VA 23418; (757) 787-5867
onleyva@shore.intercom.net

VIRGINIA MARINE PRODUCTS BOARD
Shirley Estes; 554 Denbigh Boulevard, Suite B;
Newport News, VA 23602; (757) 874-3474
saevasfd@pilot.infi.net

VIRGINIA PEANUT BOARD
P. O. Box 59; Franklin, VA 23851; (840) 658-4573

VIRGINIA PORK INDUSTRY BOARD AND
VIRGINIA PORK PRODUCERS BOARD
John H. Parker; P. O. Box 1163; Richmond, VA
23218; (840) 786-7092

VIRGINIA SHEEP INDUSTRY BOARD
Michael B. Carpenter; 116 Reservoir Street;
Harrisonburg, VA 22801; (540) 434-2521

VIRGINIA SOYBEAN BOARD
Phil Hickman; 102 Governor Street, Room 319;
Richmond, VA 23219; (804) 371-6157
www.vdacs.virginia.gov/orgdirectory/soybeans.shtml

VIRGINIA STATE APPLE BOARD
Dave Robishaw; 900 Natural Resources Dr., Ste. 300;

Charlottesville, VA 22903; (434) 984-0573;
www.virginiaapples.org

VIRGINIA STATE BEEKEEPERS ASSOCIATION
Dr. Rick Fell, Department of Entomology, Price Hall;
Virginia Tech; Blacksburg, VA 24061;
(540) 231-7207; www.virginiabeekeepers.org

VIRGINIA STEEPLECHASE ASSOCIATION
Post Office Box 1158; Middleburg, VA 20118;
(703) 777-2414; www.vasteeplechase.com
Virginia has more steeplechases (about two dozen) than any
other state and has as many point-to-point races. If you're visiting the Blue Ridge between March and November, you can
catch a race almost any Saturday.

VIRGINIA WINEGROWERS ADVISORY BOARD
Virginia Wine Marketing Program; P. O. Box 1163;
Richmond, VA 23218; (800) 828-4637
www.virginiawines.org
The advisory board assists vintners and promotes the states
vineyards. Contact the board to receive the "Virginia Wineries
Festival and Tour Guide," published yearly.

Virginia Visitors Bureaus

(The following offices are generally open from 9 a.m.–5 p.m.
They have free Virginia travel brochures, maps and other literature. Toll-free numbers begin with 800, 866, 877, and 888.)

VIRGINIA TOURISM CORPORATION
901 E. Byrd Street; Richmond, VA 23219; (800)
847-4882) or (804) 545-5500; www.virginia.org

ABINGDON VISITORS CENTER
335 Cummings Street; Abingdon, VA 24210;
(800) 435-3440; www.abingdon.com

ALEXANDRIA VISITORS CENTER
221 King Street; Alexandria, VA 22314;
(800) 388-9119; www.funside.com

ALLEGHANY HIGHLANDS CHAMBER OF COMM
241 W. Main Street; Covington, VA 24426;
(540) 962-2178; www.ahchamber.com

AMHERST VISITORS CENTER
153 Washington Street; Amherst, VA 24521;
(434) 946-9314; www.countyofamherst.com

ARLINGTON COUNTY VISITORS CENTER
1301 S. Joyce Street; Suite D-11; Arlington, VA
22202; (800) 677-6267 or (703) 228-0874
www.stayarlington.com

ASHLAND/HANOVER VISITOR
INFORMATION CENTER
112 N. Railroad Avenue; Ashland, VA 23005;
(800) 897-1479 or (804) 752-6766
www.town.ashland.va.us

BATH COUNTY CHAMBER OF COMMERCE
Main Street; Hot Springs, VA 24445; (800) 628-
8092 or (540) 839-5409; www.DiscoverBath.com

BEDFORD CITY & COUNTY DEPT. OF TOURISM
816 Burks Hill Road; Bedford, VA 24523; (877)
447-3257 or (540) 587-5681; www.visitbedford.com

BLACKSBURG/CHRISTIANSBURG
VISITORS CENTER
103 Professional Park Drive; Blacksburg, VA 24060
(877) 367-4843 or (540) 552-2636 or
www.virginianaturally.com

BLUE RIDGE HOST, INC. VISITORS CENTER –
FANCY GAP
7648 Fancy Gap Highway; Fancy Gap, VA 24328;
(276) 398-3207; www.BlueRidgeHost.com

BLUE RIDGE PLATEAU REGIONAL VISITOR CTR.
235 Farmers Market Road (I-77 Exit 14);
Hillsville, VA 24343; (276) 730-3100;
www.VisitTheBlueRidge.com

BLUE RIDGE VISITOR CENTER IN
PATRICK COUNTY
2577 JEB Stuart Highway; Meadows of Dan, VA
24120; (276) 694-6012; www.patrickchamber.com

BOTETOURT OFFICE OF TOURISM
5 West Back Street; Fincastle, VA 24090;
(540) 473-1167; www.botetourt.org/visiting

BRUNSWICK CHAMBER OF COMMERCE
400 North Main Street; Lawrenceville, VA 23868;
(434) 848-3154; www.brunswickchamber.com

BRUNSWICK COUNTY/LAKE GASTON
TOURISM ASSOCIATION
228 North Main Street; Suite B-100; Lawrenceville,
VA 23868; (434) 848-6773; www.tourbrunswick.org

BUENA VISTA REGIONAL VISITOR CENTER
595 East 29th Street; Buena Vista, VA 24416;
(540) 261-8004; www.lexingtonvirginia.com

CARROLL COUNTY CHAMBER OF COMMERCE
515 North Main Street; Hillsville, VA 24343;
(276) 728-5397; www.carrollchamber.com

CEDAR CREEK BATTLEFIELD VISITORS CENTER
8437 Valley Pike; Middletown, VA 22645;
(540) 869-2064; www.cedarcreekbattlefield.org

CHARLOTTESVILLE/ALBEMARLE COUNTY
VISITOR CENTER
Highway 20 Visitor Center; 600 College Drive;
Charlottesville, VA 22902; (877) 386-1102 or
(434) 293-6789; www.pursueCharlottesville.com

CHARLOTTESVILLE DOWNTOWN VISITOR CTR.
610 E. Main Street; Charlottesville, VA 22902;
(877) 386-1102 or (434) 293-6789
www.pursueCharlottesville.com

CHESAPEAKE BAY CENTER
2500 Shore Drive; Virginia Beach, VA 23451
Chesapeake Bay Center: (757) 412-2316
First Landing State Park: (757) 412-2300
www.dcr.virginia.gov/state_parks/fir.shtml

CHESAPEAKE BAY/POTOMAC GATEWAY
VISITOR CENTER
3540 James Madison Parkway; King George, VA
22485; (540) 663-3205; www.northernneck.org

CHESAPEAKE CONVENTIONS & TOURISM
3815 Bainbridge Boulevard; Chesapeake, VA 23324;
(888) 889-5551 or (757) 502-4898
www.visitchesapeake.com

CHINCOTEAGUE CHAMBER OF COMMERCE
AND VISITORS CENTER
6733 Maddox Boulevard; Chincoteague, VA 23336;
(757) 336-6161; www.chincoteaguechamber.com

CITY OF GALAX TOURISM
111 E. Grayson Street; Galax, VA 24333
(276) 238-8130; www.visitgalax.com

COLONIAL BEACH VISITOR CENTER
Chamber of Commerce
1 Hawthorne Street (at the pier); Colonial Beach,
VA 22443; (804) 224-8145; www.colonialbeach.org

COLONIAL WILLIAMSBURG REGIONAL
WELCOME CENTER
Colonial Williamsburg Foundation
101A Visitor Center Drive; Williamsburg, VA
23187; (800) HISTORY or (757) 220-7612
www.history.org

CROSSROAD STORE
4916 Plank Road; North Garden, VA 22959;
(434) 296-3626

CULPEPER REGIONAL VISITORS CENTER
109 S. Commerce Street; Culpeper, VA 22701;
(540) 825-8628; www.visitculpeperva.com

CUMBERLAND GAP NATIONAL HISTORICAL PARK
VISITOR CENTER
US 25E South; Middlesboro, VA 40965;
(606) 248-2817; www.nps.gov/cuga

DANVILLE WELCOME CENTER
645 River Park Drive; Danville, VA 24540;
(434) 793-4636; www.visitdanville.com

ROCKY MOUNT DEPOT WELCOME CENTER
55 Franklin Street; Rocky Mount, VA 24151;
(540) 489-0948 or (540) 483-7660

EASTERN SHORE VA TOURISM COMMISSION
24393 Lankford Highway; Tasley, VA 23441;
(757) 787-8268; www.esvatourism.org

FAIRFAX MUSEUM AND VISITOR CENTER
10209 Main Street; Fairfax, VA 22030; (800) 545-
7950 or (703) 385-8414; www.fairfaxva.gov

FAIRFAX COUNTY VISITORS CENTER
8180-A Silverbrook Road (off I-95);
Lorton, VA 22079; (703) 790-0643; www.fxva.com

FARMVILLE AREA CHAMBER OF COMMERCE
116 North Main Street; Farmville, VA 23901;
(434) 392-3939; www.farmvilleareachamber.org

FREDERICKSBURG VISITOR CENTER
706 Caroline Street; Fredericksburg, VA 22401;
(800) 678-4748 or (540) 373-1776;
www.visitfred.com

FRONT ROYAL-WARREN COUNTY VISITOR CTR.
414 E. Main Street; Front Royal, VA 22630;
(800) 338-2576; www.frontroyalva.com

GILES COUNTY CHAMBER OF COMMERCE
101 South Main Street; Pearisburg, VA 24134;
(540) 921-5000

GLOUCESTER VISITOR CENTER
6467 Main Street; Gloucester, VA 23061;
(804) 693-3215 or (804) 693-0014;
www.gloucesterva.info/pr/tourism.htm

GRAYSON COUNTY TOURISM
INFORMATION CENTER
107 East Main Street; Independence, VA 24348;
(276) 773-2000; www.graysoncountyva.com

GREATER WILLIAMSBURG CHAMBER &
TOURISM ALLIANCE
421 North Boundary Street;
Williamsburg, VA 23187; (800) 368-6511 or
(757) 229-6511; www.VisitWilliamsburg.com

GREENE COUNTY VISITOR'S CENTER
9661 Spotswood Trail; Stanardsville, VA 22973;
(434) 985-9756;
www.greeneva.com/tourism/index.htm

H.L. BONHAM REGIONAL DEVELOPMENT AND
TOURISM CENTER
408 Whitetop Road; Chilhowie, VA 24319;
(276) 646-3306; www.VisitVirginiaMountains.com

HALIFAX COUNTY/SOUTH BOSTON TOURISM
OFFICE AND VISITOR INFORMATION
700 Bruce Street; South Boston, VA 24592;
(434) 572-2543; www.gohalifaxva.com

HAMPTON VISITOR CENTER
120 Old Hampton Lane; Hampton, VA 23669;
(800) 800-2202 or (757) 727-1102
www.hamptoncvb.com

HAMPTON CVB
1919 Commerce Drive, Suite 290; Hampton, VA
23666; (800) 487-8778 or (757) 722-1222;
www.hamptoncvb.com

HARRISONBURG-TOURISM AND
VISITOR SERVICES
212 South Main Street; Harrisonburg, VA 22801;
(540) 432-8935; www.harrisonburgtourism.com

HEART OF APPALACHIA TOURISM AUTHORITY
112 Shawnee Avenue E.; Big Stone Gap, VA 24219;
(888) 798-2386; (276) 523-2005 or 2335;
www.heartofappalachia.com

HERNDON DULLES VISITOR'S CENTER
Old Train Depot
717 Lynn Street; Herndon, VA 20170; (703) 437-
6366; www.visitherndon.com

HIGHLAND COUNTY VISITOR'S CENTER
The Highland Inn
Main Street; Monterey, VA 24465;
(540) 468-2550; www.highlandcounty.org

HILLSVILLE VISITOR'S CENTER
410 North Main Street; Hillsville, VA 24343;
(276) 730-3100; www.TownofHillsville.com

HOPEWELL VISITOR CENTER
4100 Oaklawn Boulevard; Colonial Corner
Shopping Center; Hopewell, VA 23860;
(800) 863-8687; www.ci.hopewell.va.us

LAKE ANNA ECONOMIC DEVELOPMENT &
TOURISM PARTNERSHIP
13721 Anna Point Lane; Mineral, VA 23117;
(800) 398-3977; www.lakeanna.org

LEXINGTON & THE ROCKBRIDGE AREA
VISITOR CENTER
106 East Washington Street; Lexington, VA 24450;
(877) 453-9822; www.lexingtonvirginia.com

LOUDOUN COUNTY VISITORS CENTER
222 Catoctin Circle, Suite 100;
Leesburg, VA 20175; (800) 752-6118 or
(703) 771-2170; www.visitloudoun.org

LURAY-PAGE COUNTY VISITOR CENTER
46 East Main Street; Luray, VA 22835; (888) 743-
3915 or (540) 743-3915; www.luraypage.com

LYNCHBURG VISITORS CENTER
216 12th Street at Church; Lynchburg, VA 24504;
(800) 732-5821 or (434) 732-5821
www.discoverlynchburg.org

MANASSAS VISITORS CENTER
9431 West Street; Manassas, VA 22110; (877) 848-
3018 or (703) 361-6599; www.visitmanassas.org

MARTINSVILLE-HENRY COUNTY VISITOR CTR.
54 West Church Street; Martinsville, VA 24112;
(888) 722-3498 or (276) 632-8006;
www.VisitMartinsville.com

MATHEWS COUNTY VISITOR &
INFORMATION CENTER
Sibley's General Store; 239 Main Street; Mathews,
VA 23109; (804) 725-4229; www.visitmathews.com

MOUNT JACKSON
410 North Main Street; Hillsville, VA 24343;
(540) 477-2121; www.mountjackson.com

NELSON COUNTY VISITOR CENTER
8519 Thomas Nelson Highway (US 29)
Lovingston, VA 22949; (800) 282-8223 or
(434) 263-7015; www.nelsoncounty.com

NEWPORT NEWS VISITOR CENTER
13560 Jefferson Avenue; Newport News, VA 23603;
(888) 493-7386 or (757) 886-7777

FOUNTAIN PLAZA TWO
700 Town Center Drive, Suite 320;
Newport News, VA 23606; (888) 493-7386 or
(757) 926-1400; www.newport-news.org

NORFOLK VISITOR INFORMATION CENTER
9401 Fourth View Street; Norfolk, VA 23503;
(800) 368-3097; www.norfolkcvb.com

NORTHAMPTON COUNTY CHAMBER
109 Mason Avenue; Cape Charles, VA 23310;
(757) 331-2304; www.ccncchamber.com

NORTHERN NECK TOURISM COUNCIL
479 Main Street; Warsaw, VA 22572; (800) 393-6180 or (804) 333-1919; www.northernneck.org

ORANGE COUNTY VISITORS CENTER
122 E. Main Street; Orange, VA 22960; (877) 222-8072 or (540) 672-1653; www.VisitOrangeVirginia.com

PATRICK COUNTY TOURISM OFFICE
106 Rucker Street, Room 218; Stuart, VA 24171; (276) 694-8367; www.visitpatrickcounty.org

PETERSBURG VISITORS CENTER
425 Cockade Alley; Petersburg, VA 23803; (800) 368-3595 or (804) 733-2400; www.petersburg-va.org

PORTSMOUTH (STARBOARDS)
101 High Street; High Street Landing; Portsmouth, VA 23704; (757) 966-5357; www.starboards.biz

PORTSMOUTH VISITOR INFORMATION CENTER
6 Crawford Parkway; Portsmouth, VA 23704; (800) 767-8782 or (757) 393-5111; www.portsva.com

PRINCE WILLIAM COUNTY/MANASSAS TOURIST INFORMATION CENTER
200 Mill Street; Occoquan, VA 22125; (703) 491-4045; www.visitpwc.com

PRINCE WILLIAM COUNTY/MANASSAS CVB
8609 Sudley Rd., Suite 105; Manassas, VA 20110; (800) 432-1792 or (703) 396-7130; www.visitpwc.com

PULASKI COUNTY VISITOR CENTER
4440 Cleburne Blvd; Dublin, VA 24084; (540) 674-1991; www.pulaskicounty.org

REMINGTON
203 East Main Street; Remington, VA 22734; townofremington@verizon.net

RICHMOND REGION VISITORS CENTER
405 N. Third Street; Richmond, VA 23219; (804) 783-7450; www.visit.richmond.com

RICHMOND BELL TOWER
On Capitol Grounds; 101 N. Ninth Street; Richmond, VA 23219; (804) 545-5586

ROANOKE VALLEY VISITOR INFORMATION CNTR.
101 Shenandoah Avenue NE; Roanoke, VA 24016; (800) 635-5535 or (540) 345-8622; www.visitroanokeva.com

ROCKFISH GAP TOURIST INFORMATION CENTER
20 Afton Circle; (atop Afton Mountain); Afton, VA 22920; (540) 943-5187 or (540) 942-6644; www.waynesborova-online.com

SALEM VISITORS CENTER
Salem Civic Center; 1001 Boulevard; Salem, VA 24153; (888) 827-2536; www.visitsalemva.com

SHENANDOAH VALLEY TRAVEL ASSOCIATION
277 W. Old Cross Road; P.O. Box 1040; New Market, VA 22844-1040; (800) 847-4878 or (540) 740-3132; www.visitshenandoah.org

SMITH MOUNTAIN LAKE VISITOR CENTER
16430 Booker T. Washington Highway, Unit 2 Moneta, VA 24121; (800) 676-8203 or (540) 721-1203 or; www.visitsmithmountainlake.com

SMITHFIELD/ISLE OF WIGHT VISITOR CENTER
335 Main Street; Smithfield, VA 23431; (757) 357-5182 or (800) 365-9339; www.smithfield-virginia.com

SOUTH HILL TOURIST INFORMATION CENTER
201 S. Mecklenburg Avenue; South Hill, VA 23970; (800) 524-4347 or (434) 447-4547 www.southhillchamber.com

SPOTSYLVANIA COUNTY VISITORS CENTER
4704 Southpoint Parkway; Fredericksburg, VA 22407; (877) 515-6197; www.spotsylvania.va.us

STAFFORD VISITORS CENTER
224 Washington Street, Route 1001; Falmouth, VA 22405; (540) 654-1844; www.garimelchers.org

STAUNTON CVB
116 W. Beverley Street, second Floor; Staunton, VA 24401; (540) 332-3865 or (800) 342-7982 www.staunton.va.us/visitor

STAUNTON TRAVEL INFORMATION CENTER
1290 Richmond Road; Staunton, VA 24401; (800) 332-5219 or (540) 332-3972; www.staunton.va.us

STAUNTON VISITORS CENTER
35 South New Street; Staunton, VA 24401; (800) 342-7982 or (540) 332-3971; www.staunton.va.us

SUFFOLK (PRENTIS HOUSE) VISITOR CENTER
321 North Main Street; Suffolk, VA 23434; (866) 733-7835 or (757) 923-3880; www.Suffolk-Fun.com

TAZEWELL COUNTY VISITORS CENTER
200 Sanders Lane; Bluefield, VA 24605; (276) 322-1345

VIRGINIA BEACH VISITOR INFORMATION CENTER
2100 Parks Avenue; Virginia Beach, VA 23451; (800) 822-3224 or (757) 437-4919; www.vbfun.com

VIRGINIA'S HEARTLAND REGIONAL VISITOR CTR.
121 E. Third Street; Farmville, VA 23901; (434) 392-1482; www.co.prince-edward.va.us

WARRENTON-FAUQUIER VISITOR CENTER
33 N. Calhoun Street; Warrenton, VA 20186; (800) 820-1021 or (540) 341-0988; www.visitfauquier.com

WASHINGTON HOSPITALITY & VISITORS ASSOC.
P.O. Box 103; Washington, VA 22747; (540) 675-2040; www.thefirstwashington.com

WAYNESBORO TOURISM
301 West Main Street; Waynesboro, VA 22980; (866) 253-1957 or (540) 942-6644 www.waynesboro.va.us/tourism.html

WILLIAMSBURG AREA CVB
421 North Boundary Street; Williamsburg, VA 23185; Mail: Post Office Box 3585; Williamsburg, VA 23187-3585; (757) 253-0192 www.visitwilliamsburg.com

WINCHESTER-FREDERICK COUNTY VISITOR CTR.
1360 S. Pleasant Valley Road; Winchester, VA 22601; (877) 871-1326 or (540) 542-1326; www.visitwinchesterva.com

WYTHEVILLE (E. LEE TRINKLE) REGIONAL VISITORS CENTER
975 Tazewell Street; Wytheville, VA 24382 (800) 446-9670 or (276) 223-3441; www.virginiablueridge.org

WYTHEVILLE CVB
7108 Stoney Fork Road; Highway 52 North; Wytheville, VA 24382; (276) 223-1873; www.vacity.com

VIRGINIA WELCOME CENTERS
(These major-highway visitor centers are generally open from 8:30 a.m.–5 p.m.)

BRACEY   I-85 north at Virginia/North Carolina state line; Bracey, VA 23919; (434) 689-2295

BRISTOL   I-81 north at Virginia/Tennessee state line; Bristol, VA; (276) 466-2932

CLEARBROOK   16 South Loudoun Street; Winchester, VA 22624; (540) 722-3448

COVINGTON   I-64 east at the Virginia/West Virginia state line; Covington, VA; (540) 559-3010

FREDERICKSBURG   I-95S, Mile Marker 131; Fredericksburg, VA 22404; (540) 786-8344

LAMBSBURG   Mile Marker 0, I-77 Northbound Lambsburg, VA 24351; (276) 755-3931

MANASSAS   I-66; 9915 Vandor Lane; Manassas, VA 20109; (703) 361-2134

NEW CHURCH   US 13; New Church, VA 23415; (757) 824-5000

ROCKY GAP   I-77; Rocky Gap, VA 24366; (276) 928-1873

SKIPPERS   I-95; Skippers, VA 23879; (434) 634-4113

BIBLIOGRAPHY

Arthur, T. S. and W. H. Carpenter. *The History of Virginia, from Its Earliest Settlement to the Present Time.* Philadelphia: Lippincott, Grambo and Co., 1852.

Artifacts, Advertisements, and Archaeology. Alexandria Archaeology Museum, 1983.

Barbour, Philip L., ed. *The Complete Works of Captain John Smith (1580–1631),* in three volumes. Chapel Hill: The University of North Carolina Press, 1986.

Barrow, Mary Reid. *The Great Taste of Virginia Seafood: A Cookbook and Guide to Virginia Waters,* Hampton: GB Publishing, 1984.

Barrow, Mary Reid. *The Virginia Beach Harvest Cookbook.* Norfolk: The Donning Company, 1985.

Beatty, Richmond. *William Byrd of Westover.* Shoe String Press, 1970.

Betts, Edwin M., ed. *Thomas Jefferson's Garden Book 1766–1824.* Philadelphia: The American Philosophical Society, 1944.

Betts, Edwin M. *Thomas Jefferson's Farm Book.* Charlottesville: University Press of Virginia, 1987.

Betts, Edwin M. and Hazlehurst Bolton Perkins. *Thomas Jefferson's Flower Garden at Monticello,* 3rd ed. revised and enlarged by P. J. Hatch. Charlottesville: University Press of Virginia, 1986.

Bruce, Philip A. *The Plantation Negro as a Freeman. Observations on His Character, Condition, and Prospects in Virginia.* New York: G. P. Putnam, 1889.

Bullock, Helen. *The Williamsburg Art of Cookery or Accomplish'd Gentlewoman's Companion: Being a Collection of Upwards of Five Hundred.* Williamsburg: The Colonial Williamsburg Foundation, 1966.

Burke, Jackie. *Capital Horse Country: A Rider's and Spectator's Guide.* Charlottesville: Howell Press, 1994.

Cannon, Poppy. *The President's Cookbook: Practical Recipes from George Washington to the Present.* New York: Funk & Wagnalls, 1968.

Cardinal Cuisine, A Cookbook. Alexandria: Mount Vernon Hospital Auxiliary, 1988.

Carlton, Jan. *Richmond Receipts: Past and Present.* Norfolk: The Donning Company, 1987.

Davis, Julia. *The Shenandoah.* New York: Rinehart & Co., 1945.

DeForest, Elizabeth Kellam. *The Gardens and Grounds at Mount Vernon.* The Mount Vernon Ladies' Association, 1982.

Desaulniers, Marcel. *The Trellis Cookbook: Contemporary American Cooking in Williamsburg.* New York: Simon & Schuster, 1992.

Dowdey, Clifford. *Great Plantation: A Profile of Berkeley Hundred and Plantation Virginia from Jamestown to Appomatox.* Berkeley Plantation, 1976.

Dutton, Joan Parry. *Plants of Colonial Williamsburg.* Williamsburg: The Colonial Williamsburg Foundation, 1979.

Episcopal Chicken: A Cookbook Containing a Variety of Chicken Recipes. Norfolk: The Episcopal Church Women, Diocese of Southern Virginia, 1985.

Favorite Virginia Recipes from Bath County. Hot Springs: Hot Springs Presbyterian Church, 1958.

Ferguson, Leland. *Uncommon Ground: Archaeology and Early African America, 1650–1800.* Washington, D.C.: Smithsonian Institution Press, 1992.

The First Ladies Cook Book. New York: Parents Magazine Enterprises, 1982.

Fisher, Ron. *Blue Ridge Range, the Gentle Mountains.* Washington, D.C.: National Geographic, 1998.

Friddell, Guy. *We Began at Jamestown.* Richmond: Dietz Press, 1968.

Friends and Regents of the Kenmore Museum. *Specialties of the House.* Memphis: Wimmer Brothers, 1992.

From Truro Tables. Fairfax: Truro Episcopal Church, 1967.

From Williamsburg Kitchens. Williamsburg: Tory Hill Press, 1968.

Garrison, Webb. *A Treasury of Virginia Tales.* Nashville: Rutledge Hill Press, 1991.

Goodwin, Rutherford. *A Brief and True Report Concerning Williamsburg in Virginia, being an account of the most important occurences.* Richmond: Colonial Williamsburg, Inc., 1959.

Gourmet by the Bay: The Virginia Beach Cookbook. Virginia Beach: Dolphin Circle of the International Order of the King's Daughters and Sons, 1989.

Gray, Lewis Cecil. *History of Agriculture in the Southern United States to 1860,* vol. 1 and 2. Gloucester, MA: Peter Smith, 1958.

Greely, Alexander. *Asian Grills.* New York: Doubleday, 1993.

Haeringer, Jacques E. *The Chez Francois Cookbook.* Reston: Reston Publishing Co., Inc., a Prentice-Hall Company, 1985.

Hariot, Thomas. *A Brief and True Report of the New Found Land of Virginia: A Facsimile Edition of the 1588 Quarto, with an Introduction by the Late Randolph G. Adams.* New York: The History Book Club,1951.

Hatch, Peter J. *The Gardens of Monticello.* Charlottesville: Thomas Jefferson Memorial Foundation, Inc., 1992.

Henry, Marguerite. *Misty of Chincoteague.* New York: Scholastic, 1947.

Herbst, Sharon Tyler. *The New Food Lover's Companion: Comprehensive Definitions of Nearly 6000 Food, Drink, and Culinary Terms, 3rd edition.* Hauppauge, NY: Barrons Educational Series, 2001.

A Heritage of Good Tastes: A collection of traditional and contemporary recipes by The Twig, the Junior Auxilliary of the Alexandria Hospital. Alexandria: The Twig, 1985.

Historic Culpeper Virginia. Culpeper Historical Society, 1972.

Historic Michie Tavern, a Famous Tavern of the 1700s: Cooking Treasures of the Past. Charlottesville: Historic Michie Tavern Musuem, 1976.

Horn, Jane. *Cooking A to Z: The Complete Culinary Reference Source.* Santa Rosa, CA: Cole Publishing Co., 1998.

Horton, Tom. *An Island Out of Time: A Memoir of Smith Island in the Chesapeake.* New York: W. W. Norton & Company, Inc., 1996.

Hume, Audrey Noel. *Archaeology and the Colonial Gardener.* Colonial Williamsburg Archaeological Series No. 9. Williamsburg: The Colonial Williamsburg Foundation, 1989.

Hume, Audrey Noel. *Food.* Williamsburg: The Colonial Williamsburg Foundation, 1978.

Hume, Ivor Noel, et al. *The Archaeology of Martin's Hundred.* New York: Knopf, 1982.

Ingalls, Fay. *The Valley Road.* The World Publishing Co., 1949.

John R. Gonzales. *The Colonial Williamsburg Tavern Cookbook.* Williamsburg: Clarkson Potter, in association with The Colonial Williamsburg Foundation, 2001.

Kelly, Emily Wirsing, et al., comp. *From Ham to Jam.* Staunton: Mary Baldwin Alumnae Association, 1977.

Key, Glenda M. and Ralph H. Yarborough. *Sweet Potato Recipes by Homemakers of Virginia's Eastern Shore.* Richmond: Virginia Sweet Potato Commission.

Kimball, Marie. *Thomas Jefferson's Cook Book.* Richmond: University Press of Virginia, 1976.

Lee, Hilde Gabriel and Allan E. Lee. *Virginia Wine Country Revisited.* Charlottesville: Hildesigns Press, 1993.

Lewis, Edna. *The Taste of Country Cooking.* New York: Knopf, 1977.

Mapp, Jr., Alf J. *Thomas Jefferson: Passionate Pilgrim: The Presidency, the Founding of the University, and the Private Battle.* Lanham, MD: Madison Books, Inc., 1991.

Martin, Peter. *The Pleasure Gardens of Virginia: From Jamestown to Jefferson.* Princeton, NJ: Princeton University Press, 1991.

McConnaughey, Gibson Jefferson. *Two Centuries of Virginia Cooking. The Haw Branch Plantation Cookbook, 1762–1828.* Amelia: Mid-South Publishing Co., 1977.

McGee, Harold. *On Food and Cooking: The Science and Lore of the Kitchen.* New York: Fireside, 1997.

McKee, Gwen, and Barbara Moseley, ed. *Best of the Best from Virginia: Selected Recipes from Virginia's Favorite Cookbooks.* Brandon, MS: Quail Ridge Press, 1991.

Miller, Natalie. *The Story of Mount Vernon.* Chicago: Childrens Press, 1965.

Morgan, Edmund S. *American Slavery–American Freedom: The Ordeal of Colonial Virginia.* New York: W. W. Norton & Company, Inc., 1976.

Morgan, Lynda J. *Emancipation in Virginia's Tobacco Belt, 1850–1870.* Athens: University of Georgia Press, 1992.

Napolitano, Peter. *Produce Pete's Farmacopeia: From Apples to Zucchini and Everything in Between.* iUniverse.com, 2001.

O'Brien, Dawn. *Virginia's Historic Restaurants and Their Recipes.* Winston-Salem, NC: John F. Blair, 1984.

Oliver, Libbey Hodges. *Colonial Williamsburg Decorates for Christmas.* Williamsburg: The Colonial Williamsburg Foundation, 1981.

Olmsted, Frederick Law. *A Journey in the Seaboard Slave States, with Remarks on Their Economy.* New York: Dix & Edwards, 1856.

Page, Margaret and Mary Tennant Bryan, ed. *A Taste of Virginia: Its Houses and Its Food from the Eastern Shore to the Valley.* Richmond: The James River Garden Club, 1992.

Randolph, Mary. *The Virginia Housewife.* A facsimile of the first edition, 1824, with additional material from the editions of 1825 and 1828, with historical notes and commentaries by Karen Hess. University of South Carolina Press, 1985. With a new introduction by Janice Bluestein Longone. New York: Dover Publications, 1993.

Robertson, James I., Jr. *A History of Tobacco in Danville, Virginia.* Danville: Danville Chamber of Commerce, 1955.

Robinson, Martha Hollis. *Culinary Secrets of Great Virginia Chefs,* Nashville: Rutledge Hill Press, 1995.

Salmon, Emily J. and Edward D.C. Campbell, Jr., ed. *The Hornbook of Virginia.* Richmond: The Library of Virginia, 1994.

Selections from Writings of Thomas Jefferson, 1774- 1825. Westvaco Corporation, 1975.

Shifflett, Crandall A. *Patronage and Poverty in the Tobacco South: Louisa County, Virginia, 1860–1900.* Knoxville: University of Tennessee Press, 1982.

Schnarwyler, Albert et al. *Dining at the Homestead.* Hot Springs: Virginia Hot Springs, Inc., 1989.

Sharrer, G. Terry. *A Kind of Fate, Agricultural Change in Virginia, 1861–1920.* Ames: Iowa State Press, 2000.

Sheppard, Donna C. *A Williamsburg Christmas.* Williamsburg: The Colonial Williamsburg Foundation, 1980.

Shields, John. *Chesapeake Bay Cooking with John Shields.* New York: Broadway Books, 1998.

Singleton, Theresa A. *Before Freedom Came: African-American Life in the Antebellum South.* Charlottesville: University Press of Virginia, 1991.

Southampton County Historical Society Cookbook. Lawrenceville: Edmonds Printing Co., 1990.

Smith, Joan, ed. *Woodlawn Plantation Cookbook, with recipes from the Pope-Leighey House and Nelly's Needlers.* Mount Vernon: Woodlawn Plantation/Pope-Leighey House Council, 1979.

Stick, David. *Roanoke Island: The Beginnings of English America.* Chapel Hill and London: University of North Carolina Press, 1984.

Tidewater on the Half Shell, Fine Virginia Recipes. Virginia Beach: Junior League of Norfolk, 1985.

Turgeon, Charlotte. *Favorite Meals from Williamsburg: A Menu Cookbook over 200 Special Recipes for Every Occasion.* Williamsburg: The Colonial Williamsburg Foundation, 1982.

Tyler, Payne Bouknight. *The James River Plantations Cookbook.* Williamsburg: Williamsburg Publishing Company, 1980.

Tyree, Marion Cabell. *Housekeeping in Old Virginia.* A reprint of the original 1879 edition. Louisville: Favorite Recipes Press, 1965.

University of Virginia Hospital Circle. *The Monticello Cook Book.* Richmond: Dietz Press, 1960.

Vintage Virginia: A History of Good Taste. The Virginia Dietetic Association Cookbook. Nashville: Favorite Recipes Press, 2000.

Virginia Celebrates: Recipes and Ideas for Entertaining. Charlottesville: Council of the Virginia Museum of Fine Arts, Thomasson-Grant, 1992.

Virginia Cookery Book. Richmond: Virginia League of Women Voters, 1921.

Virginia Cookery Past and Present (Including a Manuscript Cook Book of the Lee and Washington Families). Franconia: Woman's Auxillary of Olivet Episcopal Church, 1960.

Virginia Cooks: From the Mountains to the Sea. Lenexa, KS: Cookbook Publishers, Inc., 1999.

Virginia Federation. *Recipes From Old Virginia.* Richmond: Dietz Press, 1946, 1955.

The Virginia Hostess, Volume I, Collations, Comfits and Drams. Lorton: Mansur, Caroline E. Pohick Episcopal Church, 1960.

Virginia Seasons: New Recipes from the Old Dominion. Junior League of Richmond, Inc., 1984, 1991.

Virginia Tech Faculty Women's Club. *Centennial Cookbook.* Blacksburg: Southern Printing Company, 1972.

Virginia Waterfront Cuisine. Williamsburg: Bicast Publishing Company, 1995.

What Can I Bring? Sharing Good Tastes and Times in Northern Virginia: A Cookbook. McLean: The Junior League of Northern Virginia, Inc., 1999.

Williams, Dorothy Hunt. *Historic Virginia Gardens: Preservations by The Garden Club of Virginia.* Charlottesville: University Press of Virginia, 1975.

The Williamsburg Cookbook. Williamsburg: The Colonial Williamsburg Foundation, 1988.

Wirt, William Thomas. *Sketches of the Life and Character of Patrick Henry.* Cowperthwaith & Co., 1841.

The Wives Club School of Medicine University of Virginia. *Kitchen Operations.* Charlottesville: J.F. Printing Co., 1964.

Woman's Auxiliary of Grace Church, Walker's Parish. *Favorite Recipes from Old Virginia.* Charlottesville: The Wayside Press, 1957.

Wyman, Mrs. Ethel M. and Willard T. Barker. *Festival Foods of Virginia from Jamestown, Yorktown, Williamsburg, and The Lower Peninsula,* Newmarket, NH: Newmarket Press, 1959.

Zearfoss, Jonathan. *The Great Chefs of Virginia Cookbook.* Norfolk:The Donning Company, 1987.

RECICE INDEX

SUBJECT INDEX

ABOUT THE AUTHOR

The author with a hay fork crafted by Kevin Riddle (see interview, page 110).

Photo by Robert E. Cheney.

CiCi Williamson is a continental traveler and a back-roads wanderer. Having explored six continents, more than 80 countries, and every U.S. state, she always comes home to Virginia and thinks there's no more beautiful place than that.

The author of six cookbooks, for 22 years she wrote a syndicated weekly food column in the *Richmond Times-Dispatch, the Virginian-Pilot, The Journal Newspapers of Alexandria, Arlington, Fairfax and Prince William*, and more than 150 newspapers across the country. CiCi is also a food safety specialist for the U.S. Department of Agriculture's Meat and Poultry Hotline.

In 2002, CiCi Williamson was elected president of the prestigious 1000-member Les Dames d'Escoffier International (LDEI), a women's professional culinary association. Other offices she has held include president of Les Dames d'Escoffier Washington, D.C. chapter, president of the National Capital Area Home Economists in Business, and president of the International Microwave Power Institute (IMPI) Consumer Appliance Section. She was also elected to the board of directors of the Association of Food Journalists and IMPI and is a member of the International Association of Cooking Professionals (IACP), Culinary Historians of Washington and Kappa Kappa Gamma Fraternity and serves as newsletter editor for the Greater McLean Republican Women's Club. CiCi is past feature editor and alumnae editor of the quarterly journal *The Key* of Kappa Kappa Gamma and editor of *The Quarterly* journal of LDEI. The home economist has also created almost 2000 original recipes for publication and has written more than 1500 newspaper and magazine articles.

For 15 years a cooking teacher, CiCi has appeared on ABC's "Good Morning, America," CNN, cable, and local TV shows. In addition to *The Best of Virginia Farms*, she has authored or co-authored *Microwave Know-How, Micro Quick! For Men Only: Mastering the Microwave, Cooking Class: Vegetables*, and *Cooking Class: Seafood*. She is also a writer and updater for Fodor's Travel Publications.

"Food is my profession as well as my passion," confides CiCi.

ABOUT THE ILLUSTRATOR

Garry Pound, a native of Columbus, Georgia, grew up in an artistic environment: his mother is a well-known painter and his father is an architect and expert draftsman. With the encouragement of his parents, Garry has turned his love for the arts into a successful career.

Garry attended Sewanee, the University of the South, where he graduated with honors in 1977. He spent a year at Indiana State University working on his Masters in Art, then he went to Ohio University where he was awarded the Siegfrid Scholarship for overall achievement in graduate studies. He taught classes in art appreciation and critical analysis, receiving his doctorate in Comparative Arts, a cultural-history degree, in 1985.

Dr. Pound returned to Columbus, where he now works as a professional artist. He has a strong interest in the human figure and is well known for his protraits. In Dr. Pound's work one sees truly admirable craft and displays of gentle beauty and heart. His paintings have been described as "eloquent," "magnetic," and "with a breathtaking sesitivity to the nuances of the human form."